T0317265

The Measurement of Labor Cost

Studies in Income and Wealth
Volume 48

National Bureau of Economic Research
Conference on Research in Income and Wealth

The Measurement of Labor Cost

Edited by Jack E. Triplett

The University of Chicago Press

Chicago and London

Jack E. Triplett is associate commissioner, Office of Research and Evaluation, U.S. Bureau of Labor Statistics, Washington, D.C.

The University of Chicago Press, Chicago 60637
The University of Chicago Press, Ltd., London

Printed in the United States of America
90 89 88 87 86 85 84 83 5 4 3 2 1

Library of Congress Cataloging in Publication Data

Main entry under title:

The Measurement of labor cost.

(Studies in income and wealth ; v. 48)
"Papers and discussion presented at the Conference on the Measurement of Labor Cost held in Williamsburg, Virginia, on 3 and 4 December 1981"—Preface.
Includes bibliographical references and indexes.
1. Labor costs—United States—Congresses.
2. Employee fringe benefits—United States—Congresses.
I. Triplett, Jack E. II. Conference on the Measurement of Labor Cost (1981 : Williamsburg, Va.) III. Series.
HC106.3.C714 vol. 48 330s [338.5′12] 83-5920
[HD4975]

ISBN 0-226-81256-1

Since this volume is a record of conference proceedings, it has been exempted from the rules governing critical review of manuscripts by the Board of Directors of the National Bureau (resolution adopted 8 June 1948, as revised 21 November 1949 and 20 April 1968).

This volume is dedicated to Wesley S. Mellow, 10 June 1949 to 10 December 1982, friend and colleague of many participants in the Conference on the Measurement of Labor Cost. His wisdom during the planning for the conference influenced both the original conception and the final program. His work on the economics of labor force behavior and earnings differentials produced results fundamental to a number of conference papers. Those of us who knew him rejoiced in the quality of the man, as we respected the quality of his work. We miss his sound judgment, unique sense of humor, professional supportiveness, and personal warmth.

Contents

Prefatory Note

This volume contains the papers and discussion presented at the Conference on the Measurement of Labor Cost held in Williamsburg, Virginia, on 3 and 4 December 1981. Funds for the Conference on Research in Income and Wealth are provided to the National Bureau of Economic Research by the National Science Foundation; we are indebted for its support. We also thank Jack E. Triplett, who served as chairman of the conference and editor of this volume, and the other members of the program committee, Glen Cain, Richard Freeman, Daniel Hamermesh, and Frank Stafford.

1 Introduction: An Essay on Labor Cost

Jack E. Triplett

It will require the concentration of the minds of many . . . to make the most basic economic concept and its statistical equivalent fully meaningful for economic research.

Oskar Morgenstern, *On the Accuracy of Economic Observations*

1.1 Introduction

Prices are at the heart of economic analysis, so much so that the study of the principles governing economic behavior historically has been termed "price theory." Not surprisingly, economists have expended a great amount of resources on refining concepts that underlie the measurement of prices and on evaluating the correspondence of available measures to the conceptual model.[1]

Wages are no less central to the study of labor markets. And the formal analysis of labor markets used to be called "the theory of wages." But one looks in vain for labor market literature comparable to that available on the measurement of prices.

One can look at the matter in another way. Traditionally, inputs to the production process have been identified as labor and capital. When volume 45 of this series addressed the measurement of capital (Usher

Jack E. Triplett is associate commissioner, Office of Research and Evaluation, U.S. Bureau of Labor Statistics, Washington, D.C.

The author is indebted to G. Donald Wood, Wesley S. Mellow, B. K. Atrostic, Milton Moss, Daniel S. Hamermesh, and Ernst R. Berndt for comments on the draft of this paper; to Richard J. McDonald for helpful discussions on several points; to Julie A. Bunn for research assistance; and to Darlene V. King for efficiently converting the tapes and scribbling she received into a form that can be read by others. Views expressed are those of the author and do not represent official positions of the Bureau of Labor Statistics.

1980), it added to an extensive legacy of research that was explicitly concerned with conceptual and empirical measurement problems. It is difficult to cite comparable material on the measurement of labor input and labor cost.

What accounts for this lacuna? Labor economists have often maintained that wage rates and payment mechanisms are too complex to permit generalization. Orley Ashenfelter noted in the discussion at the Williamsburg conference that a steel industry collective bargaining contract contains pages and pages of wage rates for different occupations, grades, skill levels, and so forth. That is, of course, quite true. Yet, Oskar Morgenstern (1963) noted many years ago, in a passage in his classic book on measurement in economics, that the same thing was true of prices in the iron and steel industry. Enormous price heterogeneity exists among different grades and types of steel, different methods of payment, delivery terms, and so forth. (Stigler and Kindahl [1970, p. 5] note some unspecified multiple of 135 million different prices in the price structure for hot rolled carbon steel sheets.) The complexity of the institutional structure of steel pricing has never inhibited economists from generalizing in that area, or from using the basic concepts of economic theory to specify what is wanted of price statistics.

A different set of perceptions may also have suppressed the growth of literature on the measurement of labor market variables. With respect to the measurement of consumption prices and of capital, it has long been recognized that there are formidable and interesting theoretical problems to be attacked. The empirical measurement literature in both of these areas has been stimulated by, and has proceeded in concert with, theoretical work (more or less; one could easily cite empirical price measurement literature that appears oblivious to, and badly in need of, the theoretical side of the subject). Recognition that labor markets pose equally complex measurement issues has lagged among theorists, and one hears in casual conversation quite the opposite assessment—that labor market analysis contains no particular or unique difficulties. This view, assuming it is widely held, has no doubt inhibited the entry into labor market measurement of the kinds of resources that long have been expended on other areas of measurement in economics. Yet, the theorists' assessment seems highly peculiar: Most of the problems that make capital such a challenging conceptual problem in economics have analogs on the labor side. And in a number of respects, labor markets pose more complex and interesting theoretical problems than the ones usually considered in the measurement of, say, consumer prices.

I will elaborate on these matters later in this essay. It is sufficient to note here that neither the labor economists' idea that the subject is too complex nor the theorists' notion that it is too simple justifies the neglect of labor market measurement issues.

I do not, of course, mean to suggest that the contributions of theorists and labor economists are without value in understanding the measurement of wages, compensation, or labor cost. Clearly, much of the work on price indexes is transferable to labor market measurement. And the literature on capital, having (as is must) analogs on the labor side, suggests approaches that are fruitful.

It is also quite true that a vast amount of recent quantitative research by labor economists, and a fair amount of the work of the older institutionalist school as well, does have implications for the kinds of data that are relevant and necessary for economic analysis of labor markets. Research on "earnings functions" clarifies earnings concepts (see Griliches 1977), as does exploration of "compensating differentials" (C. Brown 1980); work on the relation between education and productivity defines the units in which labor input is appropriately measured.

Much of the measurement work in labor economics, however, has reflected a labor supply perspective. When innovations in theoretical labor market measurement concepts have occurred, they have had supply-side orientations: The work of Pencavel (1977) and Cleeton (1982) concerns the concept of real wages—that is, worker income. Most new data sets developed over the last two decades represent responses to the perceived need for data to study worker behavior. (I have in mind not only the establishment of the National Longitudinal Surveys of Labor Market Experience, the Panel Study of Income Dynamics, and the several Income Maintenance Experiments, but also the relatively recent exploitation of the panel properties in the Current Population Survey to produce analytic data which can be used to examine worker behavior.)[2]

Though research can often be milked for implications for economic behavior on both sides of the market, there is a dearth of direct exploration of employers' behavior toward their work forces, and very little data exist for addressing such questions. The demand side of the labor market has been neglected in research, in conceptual work, and in data development.[3]

To claim that existing research lacks implications for measurement in labor markets would be extravagant and untrue. I do maintain that the effort expended on drawing implications for economic measurement from existing knowledge about the operation of labor markets has been sparse relative to other areas of economics, and the balance of that effort has been disproportionately on the supply side.

Thus, not only to hold the subject matter within reasonable bounds, but also to push the measurement literature in the direction of the greatest gaps, the program of this conference was organized to focus on labor cost, rather than on "compensation" or "earnings" as a measure of worker income. Obviously, this distinction is somewhat artificial and is neither strictly nor uniformly maintained in the papers included in this volume. The labor cost focus does, however, define the perimeters of this introductory essay, which has been conceived as an introduction to the subject of the conference, not as a summary of its individual contributions.

This essay has one main and one subsidiary theme. The principal theme concerns the conceptual framework for measuring the cost of employing labor—the measurement of a factor price. Its initial statement in section 1.2 is abstract and simplified, based on a highly stylized model of production cost; it is developed and expanded in subsequent sections to accommodate relevant empirical knowledge of labor markets. The perspective on this research is intended to highlight the distinction in economic measurement between demand-side and supply-side measurement concepts. The subsidiary theme draws parallels and contrasts for labor cost measurement from the theoretical and empirical price measurement literature.

1.2 The Theoretical Concept of Labor Cost

By the term "labor cost" I mean the employer's cost of hiring an incremental unit of labor. The labor cost concept concerns the definition of a factor price: It is the cost of a unit of input (and not a measure of the cost of the labor content of a unit of output). I use "labor cost," rather than "factor price" or "wage," to acknowledge the complexity of labor hiring costs and to emphasize that all costs of employment are included, not just direct wage payments. And I use "labor cost" in preference to "compensation" because the latter connotes a measure of labor income, which differs conceptually and empirically from a measure of factor cost.

Labor cost measures are wanted for diverse purposes, for example, production function estimation, inflation analysis, and forming intertemporal, interarea, or interindustry judgments about the cost levels or cost experiences of different classes of employers. The most flexible data for analytical purposes are microdata—labor cost levels (i.e., dollars per period) for individual employers, with abundant detail on cost components, plus labor force and employer characteristics. For aggregated or tabulated data, analytical needs specify that published data be available at detailed occupational, industrial, and regional disaggregations, again with detail on components of labor cost.

However the data are presented, some aggregation is normally required to conserve resources—either the user's or those of the compiling statistical agency. Microdata on firms (such as the data employed by Smith and Ehrenberg in this volume) are normally aggregated over workers. Moreover, under the hedonic view of labor markets even the wage rate or labor cost measure for a single worker is an aggregation of lower order cost measures when labor is not homogeneous, as shown in section 1.6. To begin with the theory of aggregate measurements is not idle theorizing, but is rather a statement of the necessary starting place for any systematic exploration of measurement issues.[4]

For a measure of input cost, aggregation rules can be extracted from the economic theory of production and of production cost. Aspects of the theory are discussed in the Gollop-Jorgenson and McMenamin-Russell papers in this volume (see also Diewert 1980, and Caves, Christensen, and Diewert 1982). For present purposes, production theory is highly stylized. Yet, most of the empirical and conceptual issues discussed in this volume can be interpreted as attempts to extend and to make more realistic the stylized picture of the labor market depicted in the theory of demand for inputs.

We begin from a production function

$$Q = Q\ (K, L, M), \tag{1}$$

where Q is output, K and L are vectors of the various types of capital and labor services employed, and M is a vector of materials usage. The elements of the L vector may be thought of as different occupations, different skill groupings or human capital levels, and so forth. It is assumed that each element of the L vector groups workers who are homogeneous. A similar interpretation holds for the K and M vectors.

Beginning the analysis with a production function implies that it applies to an establishment or plant, or to a production process within an establishment. Because "industry" can be defined as a group of establishments having closely related production processes, input cost measures can be rationalized for an industry or for industry groups by appeal to the Marshallian notion of the "representative firm," though that rationalization may need elaboration to incorporate heterogeneity in firm size and entrepreneurial inputs, as emphasized by Oi in the present volume. Despite the continued popularity of aggregate, nationwide production functions in a variety of empirical applications, we take it as evident that none exists. Economy-wide measures of factor costs are best interpreted as averages of individual industry measures (the same interpretation applies to aggregate productivity measures or to any other measurement that is derived from a production theoretic point of view).

Associated with equation (1) is a production cost function, which shows total production cost as a function of input prices, given that input quantities are combined in such a way as to minimize production cost for each output level. To keep notation compact, this cost function is denoted by

$$C = C\ (R, W, P; Q), \tag{2}$$

where R, W, and P are understood as vectors of the costs per unit of input for the various productive factors contained in the vectors K, L, and M, respectively. For a casual labor market, the cost of a unit of labor is primarily the wage rate. Similar simplifications are usually made with respect to unit capital service costs (rental rates) and materials prices.

When the level of output is fixed, the cost function of equation (2) gives the minimum cost necessary to reach a particular production isoquant. Further, when relative prices vary, with output held constant, the cost function will yield different cost levels corresponding to varying points on the isoquant. Such points—minimum cost combinations of factor inputs that lie on the same production isoquant—provide a natural basis for comparisons of aggregate input price levels. A ratio of these points is called an index number—in this particular case, an "input cost index."[5]

An index number is thus an aggregation that is grounded on an economic concept. It can be used for making statements about interarea or interfirm differences of levels, as well as for the more familiar intertemporal computations.

Most of the content of the economic theory of index number measurements (see Samuelson and Swamy 1974, or Diewert 1981) concerns the following three topics.

The Form of the Index Number

An index number computation that is consistent with a specified production or cost function is termed an "exact" index for the underlying cost or production function (Diewert 1976). The form or "formula" of an exact index number depends on the mathematical form of the cost function (which, in turn, is derived from the form of the production function). Gollop and Jorgenson, for example, present index numbers that are exact for a translog production function.[6]

Goodness of Approximations

Widely known standard index number formulas, such as Laspeyres or Paasche or Fisher's Ideal, use only price and quantity information, not the full cost function. They can be interpreted as approximations to the theoretically correct, or exact, index numbers. They are approximations because their input quantity weights can only approximately hold output constant over the index comparison. The exact index number, because it is formed from two points on the same production isoquant, holds output exactly constant. With the approximations, an output error of undetermined size is introduced into the index every time the fixed input assumption is violated by changes in relative input prices (the well-known "substitution bias" of fixed-weight indexes). Recent empirical and theoretical work indicates that good approximations to exact indexes can be computed from fixed-weight or related formulas.[7]

Ordinary regressions that include a dummy variable for time, region, or some other variable of interest can also be interpreted as approximations to exact index numbers. The properties of the approximation are usually unclear unless the relation between the regression and the cost function is known.

Subindexes

One frequently wants a measure less aggregative than the index of all input costs. An index of *labor cost* is one of these "midlevel" aggregations—a measure of the aggregate employment cost of all occupations or labor groups in the *W* vector of equation (2). Following Pollak (1975*a*), the labor cost index is termed a "subindex" of the full input cost index. The Bureau of Labor Statistics (BLS) "Employment Cost Index" (described in Antos, this volume) is such a subindex. Lower level subindexes, such as a labor cost index for blue-collar workers, may also be desired.

Three results from the theory of subindexes are important for the present discussion. First, though it is natural to suppose that an index of labor cost would require only data on labor, this is true only for special cases. As McMenamin and Russell note in their paper in this volume, Blackorby, Primont, and Russell (1978) have shown that only when the cost function is separable on its labor component will the labor cost subindex be independent of capital service costs, materials prices, and technology. This separability condition is roughly[8] equivalent to saying that optimal combinations of engineers and laborers do not depend on the proportions of machines and shovels used in the production process, or on the technology and mix of energy and other materials employed—clearly a condition unlikely to be satisfied empirically. Pollak (1975*a*) considers the interpretation of subindexes when the separability conditions do not hold.

Second, the aggregate input cost index will not necessarily be constructed out of subindexes for capital, labor, and materials costs (*R*, *W*, and *P*). In other words, subindexes constructed in the theoretically appropriate way do not necessarily "add up" in the manner of ordinary fixed-weight index number formulas.

Third, if the theoretical conditions for the aggregation of labor inputs hold empirically (or if they are just maintained), the exact subindex of labor cost can be approximated by a conventional index number formula, such as Laspeyres or Paasche, in a way analogous to the case of the full input cost index.

One would like the theory to provide the conceptual underpinnings for aggregate measures of labor cost. Beyond this, the underlying conceptual framework used in the measurement design provides internal consistency in the data and determines its relevance for the intended use; for this reason, even if researchers use micro data, rather than some aggregate index number, the conceptual measurement model is an issue for all data employed for research.

Use of the standard theory of production to guide labor market measurement implies difficulties in two areas—restrictiveness, and realism or relevance. With respect to the restrictiveness problem, production aggregation theory tells us that stringent separability conditions must be met for labor input or labor cost to be a valid aggregation, and knowledge of production suggests that these conditions are unlikely to hold. For example, Berndt and Christensen (1973) rejected the proposition that white-collar and blue-collar labor could be aggregated, no doubt partly because white-collar labor and capital structures were found to be complements. Grant and Hamermesh (1981) examined five labor categories and (aggregate) capital, and likewise found no support for labor aggregation.[9]

Moreover, whatever may be true for capital and labor *inputs*, the line separating capital and labor *costs* frequently becomes blurred, particularly for costs of safety, workplace amenities, and other aspects of employment that contribute to what labor economists call "compensating wage differentials." For these cases, employers (or some third party) can influence labor cost (a price) by use of a larger quantity of capital or some other input.

Even though separability is a required condition for the construction of consistent labor cost measures, the consequences of violation of the separability conditions are empirical, and in some cases may not be all that serious. Berndt and Christensen (1974) find that assuming labor separability when it is untrue has little consequence for using factor quantities to analyze output and productivity movements, but seriously distorts the prediction of factor shares; since the latter use would employ factor prices as data, their finding reinforces our concern.

In any event, there is little in the theory or the empirical knowledge of production that validates the normal disposition of economists to think of "labor" and "capital" as natural aggregations. The conventional practice has mainly custom and supply-side considerations behind it.

With respect to the relevance of the model, it should be emphasized that the stylized production cost model, or close alternatives, is in common use in empirical research. It hardly represents a methodological straw man. The degree of realism in the model underlying empirical research is a compromise that depends on the problem at hand. Yet, it is beyond debate that the stylized model needs more descriptive realism to engage many of the empirical issues of the day.

There are at least four major respects in which the stylized model of production cost is inadequate. Though the Williamsburg conference did not give full attention to all four, it will nevertheless be convenient to discuss relevant research in labor markets and its implications for the measurement of labor cost in terms of these four topic areas.

1. In the stylized model, it is assumed that only wages matter as a measure of factor cost. That assumption need not necessarily be iden-

tified with a view that benefits and job amenity costs do not exist or that they are small enough so that their level can be ignored (a view that would probably be ascribed to by almost no user of the stylized model). Rather, it says (a) that total compensation is a simple addition of the cost of benefits to the cost of direct wage payments, and (b) that benefit levels are so strongly correlated with wages that little additional information on labor cost is imparted by gathering data on benefits. I believe this point of view is quite widespread, as it implicitly underlies a great amount of research on labor markets. These issues are addressed in section 1.3 of this essay.

2. The stylized model ignores time dimensions in employment arrangements, as well as time dimensions inherent in payment mechanisms. In effect, the stylized model depicts a casual labor market in which neither workers nor employers have any interest in each other after the completion of, and payment for, the current period's labor services. Of course, both employers and workers do care about the stream over time of labor services provided and payments received, a fact that has motivated much recent labor market research. The implications for measuring labor cost are discussed in sections 1.4 and 1.5.

3. The stylized model implies that there is some level of aggregation of the labor input below which one can view workers as homogeneous. The model is inchoate on problems of labor quality that cannot be handled adequately by grouping. Methods for allowing for labor quality in a labor cost measure are discussed in section 1.6.

4. Partly because it relates to a single employer's decision making, the stylized model is silent on the heterogeneity of employers and of employment conditions. However, just as employers care about the productive characteristics of workers, workers care about the characteristics of employers. This is a major contrast with the framework usually employed for the analysis of product markets, in which one usually assumes that the seller exchanges a package of commodities (this is the hedonic view of markets) for a money payment, but does not demand a package of commodities in return. Labor market transactions, however, involve exchanges of packages on both sides of the market. This assures additional complexity that is ignored in the stylized model. This topic is addressed in section 1.6. The empirical importance of the heterogeneity of employers is also a major theme of Oi in this volume, and that discussion need not be duplicated here.

1.3 Benefits

Recognition of the importance of employer provided benefits in calculating labor cost goes back many years. Legally mandated benefit costs (principally social security and unemployment compensation) first assumed importance in the 1930s. Negotiated benefits grew faster than wages during World War II because those costs were less tightly controlled than were direct wage payments. (McMenamin and Russell in this volume indicate the same thing was true of "controls" programs in the 1970s.) Both classes of benefits have grown steadily over the intervening years, whether measured in absolute terms or as a percentage of labor cost, a fact well known and tabulated in the Smeeding and Hamermesh papers in this volume.

Employer provided benefits pose a number of issues for the measurement of labor cost. The wage-benefit model sketched in section 1.3.1 serves to organize the discussion of empirical issues in the following sections.

1.3.1 A Wage-Benefit Model

A crucial parameter in analyzing the size and composition of employer provided benefits is the wage that "workers would forgo to obtain the benefit" (Freeman 1981, p. 491). We assume that workers gain utility from benefits (B), from the goods and services they purchase with direct wage payments (G), and from leisure ($T_0 - L$). The worker's full income constraint is

$$T_0(W + \psi B/L) = \psi B + PG + (W + \psi B/L)\,(T_0 - L), \tag{3}$$

where T_0 is total time available, W the hourly wage, B/L the hourly benefit earning rate, P and G the price and quantity of consumption goods, L hours worked, and ψ the shadow price of benefits.[10] Assuming benefits earned per hour are independent of hours worked, when an hour of leisure is consumed a worker gives up the quantity of goods that an hour's labor earns (W/P) and an hour's worth of benefits, B/L. Accordingly, we may write the labor supply of workers of a specified quality to the firm[11] as:

$$L = L(W/P,\ B/L). \tag{4}$$

Setting P equal to unity, one can invert the labor supply condition, giving

$$W = W(B,\ L,\ 1). \tag{5}$$

Equation (5) states that the wage that must be paid by the employer depends on the number of hours of worker input hired and on the level of benefits.

The theory specifies that

$$\partial W/\partial B \leq 0; \tag{6a}$$

$$\partial W/\partial L \geq 0; \tag{6b}$$

That workers will accept lower wages for greater benefits, or demand higher wages if benefits are lower (condition [6a]), is a consequence of assuming that market purchased goods and services and employer provided benefits are both normal goods, though the lower limit of the workers' willingness to substitute is zero. For the conventional competitive firm, the change in wages necessary to expand or contract the firm's labor force while minimizing cost (condition [6b]) is zero; for other cases, the normal presumption is that higher wages must be paid to attract more workers, so condition (6b) will be positive. The analysis at this point abstracts from dynamic considerations, so that the rate of hiring does not enter into equation (5), only the level of employment (see Phelps et al. 1970).

Though there may be scale economies to the provision of benefits (it may be cheaper per worker for the employer to buy a group insurance policy than for each worker to obtain the same coverage in an individual policy), it seems reasonable to assume that the marginal cost of increasing the size of a benefit is positive and either constant (for example, the cost of $\$UV$ life insurance is U times the cost of an $\$V$ policy) or rising. Thus, if E_i is the employer's expenditure on benefit B_i,

(7) $$\partial E_i/\partial B_i > 0;$$
$$\partial^2 E_i/\partial B_i^2 \geq 0.$$

The firm will arrange its package of wages and benefits to minimize the cost of hiring L workers, given the above conditions. The cost-minimizing conditions determining the optimal amounts of benefits to be provided are

(8) $$\partial E_i/\partial B_i = -\partial W/\partial B_i, \text{ for all } i.$$

Equation (8) says that employers offer benefits up to the point where the incremental cost of each benefit just equals the saving in wage cost that can be gained as a result of offering the benefit.[12] The wage rate offered is determined by simultaneously solving equation (5) for the desired level of L.

An implication that will be useful later is that a benefit will be increased only when the quantity on the right-hand side of equation (8) is greater (in absolute value) than that on the left-hand side. Since the left-hand side is always positive, this implies that employers will not offer a benefit unless the workers' wage-benefit trade-off for that benefit is greater than zero. We return to this point in section 1.3.3.

A number of factors may be expected to influence the parameters of this model:

1. Assuming benefits are normal goods, more will be demanded at higher income levels. This will increase the value of B in equation (4) for any given L, regardless of the effect on condition (6a). Moreover, the absolute value of (6a) may itself grow larger with income if benefits are more income-elastic than market purchased goods, thus strengthening the positive relation between benefits and wage rates.

2. When benefits are not taxed, but wage payments are, this increases the wages that workers would forgo to get benefits. From the workers' point of view, what is being surrendered is not consumption goods with a value equivalent to $\partial E_i / \partial B_i$ (the employers' marginal cost of providing the benefit), but rather goods having the value of $(\partial E_i / \partial B_i) \cdot (1 - t)$, where t is the marginal tax rate.[13] Thus, higher marginal tax rates will increase the absolute value of (6a), when that condition is computed on before-tax wage data.[14]

3. Empirically it has been shown (Freeman 1981 and Mellow 1982) that unions increase the share of benefits in total compensation, presumably by increasing the absolute value of (6a). The precise mechanism for this union effect is unclear.[15]

4. Speculation has it that demographic factors may also affect the value of (6a), with older workers, for example, possibly having greater preferences for benefits than younger ones, and married workers greater than single ones. Women may have different preferences for benefits than do men, but the effect on (6a) could go either way. The "working spouse" model would lower values for (6a), on the grounds that a spouse participates in health plans and so forth provided by the spouse's employer (this argument applies as well to married men, as the family's need for health care would be met by whichever worker received the most favorable terms from his or her employer); on the other hand, the "single parent" model of female preferences should produce higher values for (6a), and hence, in this case, women would demand greater levels of benefits, other things equal.[16]

The preceding four factors originate from the workers side. The level of benefits is also responsive to factors that affect the employers' cost of providing benefits.

5. Mellow (1982) and Oi (this volume) present evidence that large firms supply more benefits, partly because their size gives them scale economies in purchasing them. Mitchell and Andrews (1981) present evidence supporting the existence of scale economies in pension plan administration. In the case of scale economies, the level of benefits goes up because the left-hand side of equation (8) falls. Oi, in this volume, suggests other reasons for an association between firm size and benefit levels.

6. Many benefits (pensions and vacations, for example) are interlocked with tenure and therefore with firm-specific human capital. This says that equation (8)—which predicts that wages and benefit costs trade off at equilibrium on a dollar-for-dollar basis—needs to be modified to accommodate cases where there are other important labor cost components (hiring and turnover costs, for example) that are impacted differently by wage and benefit changes.

7. Condition (8) also needs modification where workers and employers have time horizons for the employment decision such that estima-

tion of a single period's labor cost (or worker compensation) must accommodate to a multiperiod optimization plan (these considerations motivate the "implicit contract" literature). The last two extensions of the wage-benefit model are left for section 1.4.

1.3.2 Do Benefits Matter?

For computing trends in labor cost, it is clear that benefits must be included. Were benefits omitted, time series analyses would understate the growth in labor cost.

But for other analytical purposes, labor economists disagree whether the omission of benefits from labor cost measures is necessarily a serious liability. A widely used undergraduate textbook (Fleisher and Kniesner 1980, p. 23) states one position on this issue:

> When measures of the cost of fringe benefits are not available, the question arises, To what extent is the analysis of labor markets affected? . . . [I]n general it is probably true that the amount of fringe benefits is positively related to nominal wage rates. Thus, the principal effect would be to understate real wage costs more or less consistently by a fraction. The effect of this error on most studies is probably relatively unimportant.

In the following, we refer to this point of view as the "consistency" hypothesis.

The consistency hypothesis is not necessarily at odds with the theoretical model of section 1.3.1. Solutions to the labor cost minimization problem could "stack up" along a path of constant benefit-to-wage proportions, so that wage rates would be a consistent fraction of labor cost for all employers and all groups of workers. For the consistency hypothesis to hold in data for workers at the same earnings level, those workers must all have similar utility functions, and employers must incur similar costs for providing benefits. For consistency to hold *across* earnings levels, in the absence of taxes, unitary income elasticities, both for market-purchased goods and for benefits, are required, plus constant marginal cost schedules for benefits. When taxes enter the system, and wages but not benefits are taxed, marginal rax rates must vary with (nonunitary) income elasticities so that the effects just offset each other, or so that the combined effect just balances any change in the employer's marginal cost of providing benefits. Whether the consistency hypothesis is true is therefore an empirical matter, which requires a fortuitous confluence of values of the economic parameters that determine the proportion of benefits in total labor cost.

Several papers in the present volume provide evidence on the consistency hypothesis. Both Smeeding and Leibowitz ask whether the addition of benefit costs (and in Smeeding's case the value of benefits to recipients) to ordinary wage measures changes the results of standard human capital earnings equations. Both authors conclude that one gets the same results from earnings equations that contain only wages as from those where the dependent variable is augmented to include benefit costs.

Neither conclusion, however, is unchallenged. Smeeding himself notes that the microsimulation methods he uses to construct his data base have a tendency to reduce the variance of the benefits data, a point emphasized and elaborated upon by Martin David in his comment. In effect, microsimulation methods have imposed or partly imposed the consistency hypothesis on the data, so it is not too surprising that the empirical results support the hypothesis.

Leibowitz's data are from a new and relatively unexplored survey and would appear to be ideal for testing the consistency hypothesis. However, Atrostic points out in her comment that Leibowitz's benefits data cover only roughly a third of total benefit costs as measured in other surveys, and she presents evidence that the consistency hypothesis holds only for those benefits that were included in Leibowitz's survey; the hypothesis is rejected when other benefits (especially pension cost) are added to the list.

In summary, then, we have two authors who present results supporting the consistency hypothesis, but those commenting on their papers (and one of the authors himself) emphasize deficiencies in the data employed for their tests.

Complete agreement will never be found between any two sets of data, so determining whether the addition of benefits to wages matters *at all* is not a very interesting question. The relevant issue is: How much does it matter? How does one determine whether an alternative concept of labor cost (for example, one inclusive of benefit costs) is really "better"?

Hamermesh deals with the issue in a way that stresses its economic relevance. He asks whether the measurement change affects an economically relevant result (labor demand elasticities),[17] and whether the change in measurement concept moves the estimate in the direction that would be predicted from econometric theory.

He finds that the addition of benefit costs and other aspects of labor cost to the normal average hourly earnings measures increases the estimated elasticity of demand for labor, and he argues that this result is predicted on a priori grounds. That is, if labor cost were mismeasured, an errors-in-variables econometric argument suggests that labor demand elasticity estimates are biased toward zero. Thus, the fact that elasticity estimates increase when benefits are added to wages indicates that the labor cost measure inclusive of benefits is the better one, even though the change in the elasticity estimates is not statistically significant. Lazear is not fully convinced by this argument, emphasizing instead that what appear to be the theoretically preferable labor cost measures do not always perform "best" (though it is not addition of benefits to hourly wages that Lazear most questions but some of the other Hamermesh adjustments).

Freeman's (1981) orientation is similar to that of Hamermesh, for he indirectly tests the consistency hypothesis by comparing alternative estimates of the economic effect of unions. The union effect on compensation (wages plus benefit costs) is roughly 17 percent, compared with a 15 percent union differential measured from wages alone.[18] From this and other results, Freeman concludes that "standard estimates of the union wage effect understate the differential between unionized and otherwise comparable nonunion workers" (Freeman 1981, p. 509). Other research on the consistency question has been done by Duncan (1976), Atrostic (1981), and Mellow (1982).

It seems doubtful that consistency between wage and benefit costs will be great enough to warrant the omission of benefits from labor cost data. The relatively recent expansion of the BLS Employment Cost Index to include benefits seems a justified and necessary improvement that makes it a better measure for analytic purposes.

1.3.3 Is There a Market Trade-Off between Wages and Benefits?

This is an old research chestnut. Few issues in labor economics have provoked more controversy than this one. The controversy reflects the persistence of the theoretic-institutionalist split in this field (see the exchange between Dunlop 1977 and Ehrenberg, Hamermesh, and Johnson 1977).

On the one hand is the theoretical position. If employers are cost minimizers and workers are utility maximizers, then it must be true that, other things equal, a market trade-off between wages and benefits exists.

The labor market institutionalists' response says, more or less, that the theory may predict a negative trade-off, but the labor market does not work that way. The institutionalist school frequently cites evidence that wages and benefits are positively correlated—the highest paying jobs have the highest benefits. This, of course, is predicted by the theory itself, as noted in section 1.3.1. The theory does not state that the president of the company should receive lower benefits than the janitor, but rather that the negative trade-off between wages and benefits will be found at comparable skill levels and at comparable levels of total compensation. The negative trade-off occurs for job comparisons for which other things are held equal.

Smith and Ehrenberg in the present volume attempt to assemble a body of data in which other things can be held constant in order to test the theoretical prediction of a negative trade-off between wages and benefits. Their study fails to produce evidence to confirm the negative trade-off hypothesis, though the authors argue that a more elaborate data set is required to perform an adequate test; their conclusion is endorsed and enlarged upon by Charles Brown in his comment.

It is surprising that the wage-benefit trade-off question should have become a serious research issue. It was pointed out in section 1.3.1 that the theoretical model implies that wherever the wage-benefit trade-off does not exist, employers will offer no benefits (see eq. [8]). Thus, testing for the *existence* of a negative wage-benefit trade-off can be pursued with a much simpler research strategy than the one followed by Smith and Ehrenberg. All one has to do to "test" for the existence of a wage-benefit trade-off is to find out whether employer provided benefits exist!

Of course, such a test will hardly satisfy the critics of a theoretical approach to labor market analysis, for taking an empirical prediction as an implication—and therefore a test—of the theory requires accepting the relevance of the theory, and that is exactly what the critics deny. They argue that firms are not cost minimizers, that workers are not utility maximizers, or that the labor market contains so many deviations from market equilibrium that the exceptions overpower the generalizations. If the critic does not accept the relevance of the theoretical model for labor market research, it is very unlikely that testing the wage-benefit relation for a negative slope will do much to settle the issue, or that any research results based on implications of a theoretical model will convince.

Serious research on relations between wages and benefits has to take the existence of a wage-benefit trade-off as a necessarily true axiom. And if one accepts the theoretical model, it is unnecessary to design a complicated research project to confirm it, for the most elemental fact of the labor market (that benefits do exist) provides sufficient evidence that the wage-benefit trade-off part of the theory is true.

It is quite a different story if one wishes to estimate the size of the wage-benefit trade-off. That is a reasonable research project. However, research on the slope of the wage-benefit trade-off function must consider labor cost components other than wages or benefits. This is easily shown.

Suppose the firm's labor cost is composed of three groups of cost components—direct wage and salary payments (W), benefits expressed as quantities (B), and the hiring and turnover rate (H). Labor cost per unit of labor is

$$LC = W + \alpha B + \gamma H, \tag{9}$$

where α is the cost per unit of benefits ($= \partial E_i/\partial B_i$ in eq. [7]), and γ is the cost of a unit change in the turnover rate. Assuming no scale economies in the provision of benefits and constant cost for each hire/turnover, the usual mathematical manipulation gives expressions for the wage-benefit trade-off, which are:

$$-\partial W/\partial B = \alpha + \gamma(\partial H/\partial B), \tag{10a}$$

or

$$\text{(10b)} \qquad -\partial W/\partial(\alpha B) = 1 + (\gamma/\alpha)\,(\partial H/\partial B).$$

Thus, from the employer's point of view, minimization of the labor cost function implies that the (negative) trade-off between the quantity of benefits and wages equals the marginal cost of benefits (as in eq. [8]) *plus* the cost of any change in turnover induced by changing the level of benefits. Alternatively (eq. [10b]), benefit *costs* and wage costs trade off on a one-for-one basis in the employer's labor cost function only when benefits have no effect on turnover ($\partial H/\partial B = 0$), or when turnover has no cost ($\gamma = 0$).

Neither of the latter two conditions is at all probable. In fact, benefits that are related to tenure—vacations and pensions, for example—are frequently designed to reduce turnover (further implications of turnover costs are discussed in section 1.4). In the presence of turnover costs, reducing benefits by (say) one dollar and raising wages by one dollar may not leave total labor cost unchanged. This implies that data on wages or salaries and benefits in different firms may not be adequate for exploring wage-benefit trade-offs or employer behavior, if the employers have pursued different strategies with respect to turnover.

At the employer's cost-minimizing point, a dollar spent on each labor cost component must have the same effect on labor supply to the firm. The optimal combination of wage, benefit, and turnover costs in the one-period case will be determined by an expanded set of conditions comparable to equation (8), which incorporate information on worker behavior in an analogous manner to equations (3)–(8). These conditions are omitted here in the interest of brevity, since the outline of the solution is suggested by the preceding discussion. It should be noted, however, that because of the information required, determining the optimal combination of labor cost components is not a simple problem for the employer, even in a single period setting (and, as noted in section 1.4, the problem is properly viewed in a multiperiod optimization context).

To summarize, researchers sometimes have data on the cost of benefits and sometimes on the quantity of benefits that are provided to workers. Since it must be true that employers ultimately care only about the size of the total labor payment and not about its distribution among the various components of compensation, it is tempting to conclude that wages trade for benefits on a dollar-for-dollar basis, and some researchers have made use of such an assumption for empirical work. But even ignoring scale economies in the provision of benefits, marginal tax rate advantages to obtaining benefits in nontaxable form, and other reasons frequently mentioned as causal elements in determining the level of employer provided benefits, analysis of benefits requires information on other labor cost components and cannot proceed on the basis of wage and benefit information alone.

1.3.4 How Should Benefits Be Measured?

Researchers sometimes feel that "how" questions are mundane issues that do not pose any particular analytic difficulties. The discussion that took place at the Williamsburg conference suggests otherwise.

It is generally agreed that medical and other insurance benefits should be handled as if the labor cost element were the premium associated with coverage, rather than the actual insurance payout (see Nichols; McMenamin and Russell; Hamermesh; Lazear; Smeeding; and David, all in this volume). For example, if a company were to self-insure medical benefits and its workers were hit by an epidemic, one would treat the cost of the epidemic as a loss on the firm's insurance business and not as an increase in labor cost in the period in which the epidemic occurred. Many other issues can in principle be handled the same way. In practice, of course, one seldom has a good estimate for the premium that a firm would pay if it were not self-insured.

Moreover, it is a delicate art to determine when a particular outlay is to be treated as a consequence of some other activity of the firm and not as part of its labor cost. Nichols proposes that the cost of a wage-escalator agreement (COLA clause) that yields higher than expected payouts be handled as if the firm were engaging in a speculation on the value of the Consumer Price Index (CPI). There is intellectual appeal to this position, but it seems doubtful that a labor cost measure purged of "unusual" payments under an escalator agreement would be considered appropriate by any employer.

The famous Council on Wage and Price Stability (CWPS) decision on the Teamster contract is another case in point. The Teamsters bargained for additional employer contributions to the pension fund to replace investment losses by the union; CWPS exempted this payment from the measure of labor cost used in determining compliance with the pay standard part of the program. Should it have done so? Nichols argues that investment losses by either the employer or the union (whichever one administers the plan) should be counted as a loss under a separate business activity and not as an addition to labor cost. But clearly economists could come down on either side of that issue. Had employers not had to make additional pension fund contributions, one presumes the union might have negotiated increases somewhere else, which surely would have been counted as labor cost.

For other examples of difficult issues in the measurement of benefits, the reader is referred to the discussions of Smeeding's and Hamermesh's papers. Abundant examples have been generated by practical experience in the BLS Employment Cost Index program and in measurement programs in other countries (see International Labor Office 1979). Issues that concern deferred compensation are discussed in section 1.4. Negative benefits, such as the risk of injury or illness, and other nonpecuniary aspects of the job are discussed in sections 1.5 and 1.6.

1.4 The Time Dimension in Labor Cost Measures

The stylized model of labor cost presented in section 1.2 is a model of a casual labor market in which neither employers nor workers have time horizons that extend beyond the current period. As Lazear (1981) points out, the neoclassical theory of wages, the content of which is equivalent to the stylized model, relates the spot market price of labor to the current period's marginal product. The addition (in section 1.3) of benefits to the traditional concept alters the definition of labor costs, but does not change the context of its analysis. The model remains essentially that of a casual labor market.

It is clear, however, that few labor markets correspond to this model. Workers care about the continuity of employment, and employers desire continuity in their work forces, so both view labor market transactions in a multiperiod setting. The employment continuity that characterizes most labor markets (Hall 1982) means that the familiar product market distinction between spot market and contract measures of price carries over to labor market analysis and affects the construction of labor cost measures as surely as it does measures of product prices.

Two interrelated sources introduce multiperiod considerations into the measurement of labor cost: fixed employment costs and long-term implicit contracts. These are discussed in the following two sections.

1.4.1 Fixed Employment Costs

All costs are variable over some sufficiently long period. A cost is "fixed" over some time period only if the alternatives necessary to eliminate the "fixed" cost in that period are more expensive than the "fixed" cost itself.

The distinction between fixed and variable labor costs corresponds roughly—but not exactly—to the distinction between the number of persons employed and the number of hours worked. Some labor costs (hourly wage payments, for example) vary in total with hours worked; up to the point where overtime schedules come into force, the increase in total outlay will be the same whether a given increase in total employment hours is handled through additions of new employees or through expanding the workweek of current employees.

Other labor cost components do not behave as variable costs. Hiring and turnover produce one-time costs that must be amortized over the worker's employment history. Training of new and continuing employees will be undertaken only if the employees are expected to remain with the firm for some period of time; this cost is a function of the number of new employees hired or upgraded and does not vary directly with hours worked. Many employment benefit costs are not fully variable with workweek changes; medical insurance, for example, is usually a per worker lump sum cost which, though it may disappear with layoffs and may vary with full-time or part-time status or other employee characteristics, does not normally fluctuate with hours worked per week. Some taxes are paid partly on a "per worker" basis and this also contributes an element of fixity to labor cost. Hamermesh, in this volume, presents data indicating that fixed hiring, training, and turnover costs amounted to about 16–17 percent of total labor cost in the private business sector in 1978.[19]

Though turnover and hiring costs have been long recognized as an element of labor cost,[20] modern analysis of them stems from Walter Oi's (1962) classic article, "Labor as a Quasi-Fixed Factor." Oi pointed out that different classes of workers carry different turnover costs. For workers who have specific skills needed by the firm, turnover is very costly because new workers will need training, often through the route of extensive experience on the job, before they can do what experienced workers can do. The implications of this observation have been far-reaching and have been used to explain different cyclical employment patterns of groups of workers with varying skills, as well as aspects of employer practices with respect to layoffs and recalls (see Feldstein 1976). Oi, in this volume, discusses some of the literature that was spawned by his earlier contribution.

One misunderstanding of the "quasi-fixed factor" analysis should be corrected: It is not a hypothesis that the labor input is fixed to the production process.[21] Rather, the hypothesis states that some costs of hiring labor are incurred on a once-and-for-all basis when employment is initiated and do not thereafter vary with that employee's rate of utilization. This hypothesis implies that rehiring or recalling an experienced worker will be less costly to the firm than hiring a new one, and that the firm will take account of these "start-up" employment costs in its labor force policy. Okun's (1981) "Toll" model is equivalent to Oi's quasi-fixed factor hypothesis, and the implications Okun derives from the Toll model are restatements of the implications summarized by Oi in this volume.

The treatment of training, or production of firm-specific human capital, in labor cost measures was the subject of discussion between Lazear and Hamermesh in this volume, a discussion which illuminates some of the issues that arise when quasi-fixed costs are incorporated into the labor cost measure. Their positions can be reconciled along the following lines.

Both, I believe, have in mind a model of production in which output is a function of untrained labor (L_1), capital (K), and specific human capital

(T), and the specific human capital required is produced by the firm itself through training labor (L_2):

$$Q = f(L_1, K, T); \tag{11}$$

$$T = g(L_2). \tag{12}$$

The measure of labor cost required is one component of the cost function that is dual to the production function of equation (11), as derived from normal index number theory for input cost indexes (see section 1.2). The issue is: Where does the cost of L_2 enter the labor cost function associated with equation (11)?

What Hamermesh seems to have in mind is a production function in which L_1 and the specific human capital are combined into a "labor aggregate" (the combination of L and T), the cost of which consists of direct payments to L_1 plus the cost of L_2, with the *hours* being those of L_1. He therefore asks: What is an appropriate measure of labor cost for L_1? and builds an estimate of the value of training into his ECNT measure.

Lazear, on the other hand, thinks that in most actual measurements one probably will not have separate accounting of hours for L_1 and L_2, so instead of dividing total labor outlay by L_1 (to get a measure of cost per unit of labor), it will normally be divided by the sum of L_1 and L_2. In this case, one would not want to treat the total outlay on L_2 as an adjustment to the wage payments to L_1, because, as Lazear puts it, "Accounting for the cost of specific human capital and the teacher's earnings counts twice."[22]

Hiring, turnover, and training costs are included in no regularly published data source now available. Fixed or quasi-fixed benefit costs are included, when they are included, at the level of (average) current period outlays, which may be approximately correct or may be "good enough" but also may not be. Of the data sets especially assembled for the present volume, only Hamermesh incorporates fixed employment costs.[23] It is clear from existing research that much more attention needs to be devoted to adding fixed employment costs to measures of labor cost.

1.4.2 Implicit Contracts

The traditional model of factor demand depicts an employer adjusting the quantity of labor to maintain equality between the current period's price of labor and the value of the current period's marginal product of labor. Labor market institutionalists have criticized the traditional model of factor demand as lacking realism, but for the most part they contented themselves with pronouncements that theory was irrelevant rather than attempting to improve the conceptual framework for labor market analysis.

The implicit contract literature provides a theoretical apparatus capable of dealing with important aspects of the labor market behavior of workers and employers that are neglected in the traditional approach.

> It takes a more complex view of the labor market than is customary in conventional short-run analyses: in uncertainty, labor services are not auctioned off in quite the same way fresh fruit is. Rather, they are exchanged for some implicit set of commitments, hereinafter called an implicit labor contract, on the part of the firm to employ the owner of those labor services for a "reasonable" period of time and on terms mutually agreed upon in advance. (Azariadis 1975, p. 1185)

Examination of explicit collective bargaining agreements between workers and employers has a long labor economics tradition. The implicit contract literature emphasizes the less formal understandings that prevail in both union and nonunion settings and that condition the short-run behavior of both employers and employees. That these agreements are not written down affects the way they are implemented, but there is strong evidence that both parties perceive the existence of unwritten understandings, and laid-off workers often behave as if some commitment had been broken by the employer. As a "RIFFED" federal government worker told the *Washington Post*: "I feel the United States government has let me down, because I never broke faith with them. I was encouraged to come in. They asked me" (28 March 1982, p. A3).

The earliest work on implicit contracts (Gordon 1974; Baily 1974) was directed toward explaining the existence of cyclical employment—it sought to explain the "sticky" wages that have long been singled out as the reason why declines in macroeconomic activity result in a greater fall in employment and output than in wages and prices. However, the implicit contract view has great utility for explaining other aspects of the labor market.

Because workers will not choose employers solely on the basis of wages but will consider all aspects of the proposed contract, other things equal, they will accept somewhat lower wages for a promise of less uncertainty. Such a relationship has long been acknowledged. Economists have often speculated that construction workers, for example, receive higher hourly wages because of frequent interruptions in employment, and they have interpreted the level of construction wages as compensation, in part, for uncertainty.[24] One should note that many of the lowest paid workers have the least job security (see Oi, in this volume). That, however is not a serious objection to the implications of the implicit contract literature. Employers are most likely to enter into contracts offering employment or earnings stability with workers who show stability in their work history.

Our concern in this essay is for implications of the implicit contract view for measuring labor cost. Three deserve attention:

1. When employers give long-term implicit contracts to workers, some

current period costs will be incurred for the purpose of reducing the intertemporal stream of labor cost. This observation obviously goes hand in hand with the fixed labor cost idea discussed in section 1.4.1. As Oi in this volume notes, an implicit contract implies the existence of fixed labor cost.

2. An employer lives up to his end of the implicit contract because failure to do so may affect his reputation as a "good" employer, thereby influencing labor cost that must be paid at a later period.

3. Legally, employers cannot enforce the terms of the long-term employment contract. They can, however, structure pay or benefit packages to reward workers who adhere to the contract and to penalize those who abrogate it.

With respect to the third point, that individual earnings rise with age or experience is a familiar statistical fact. Tradition has associated it with "on-the-job" training (Mincer 1974). Because the training component of jobs is seldom observed directly, the on-the-job training (OJT) explanation is an inference derived from the stylized model of factor demand. If employment were always adjusted to maintain equality between current period earnings and marginal productivity, then the experience-earnings profile would reflect rising individual productivity as experience accumulates.

The implicit contract view challenges the OJT explanation for rising age-earnings profiles, because it predicts that wages may not equal the value of marginal product in every single period of the implicit contract. If employers make multiperiod commitments to workers, they must find some way to hold the workers to their side of the implicit bargain. One way is to compensate workers in the present period partly for performance in past periods. Such compensation schemes not only tie workers to employers, but also assure high levels of effort from workers (Lazear 1981). In the implicit contract view, the president of General Motors is compensated in the $1 million per year range in part because of his past productivity, and in part to create incentives among lower level managers who will strive to earn the prize some time in the future; the explanation is not, as the OJT view would have it, that the president's current period marginal product is so high.

Deferred compensation is a particularly effective way to reward continuous service. Burkhauser and Quinn in this volume emphasize that pensions should not be viewed solely as savings plans, for they may also be used as instruments of the employer's work-force policy. Burkhauser and Quinn show that the asset values of pensions are arranged so that workers who postpone retirement past some age are penalized. They view this as an integral part of the implicit long-term contract. Pension provisions are arranged to encourage the employee voluntarily to terminate the agreement at the time desired by the employer, thereby avoiding the perceived arbitrariness of a fixed, mandatory retirement age or of reducing direct earnings.

For measuring labor cost, the most important implication of the implicit contract literature is that current period employment decisions do not depend, or do not depend solely, on current period cost. Since we want an economic measure to be relevant to economic behavior, what should go into labor cost measures when employers make decisions in a multiperiod framework?

Nearly identical problems have been discussed in the price measurement and the capital measurement literatures. Long-term contracts for delivery of coal and other materials specify prices that differ from the spot market price for the same commodity. In this case, the consensus among economists seems to be that both measures are wanted because they represent different things: The spot market price is the cost of a ton of coal. The contract price, on the other hand, is the cost of the combined commodity "ton of coal and assured supply."[25]

In consumption price measurement, the multiperiod problem most frequently emerges with respect to durable goods, for which the consumption of services in the current period reflects past purchase decisions. Moreover, prices on current asset markets for durable goods imply that the measured user cost of services from durable goods can differ in the short term from rental values (see Gillingham 1983). In this case, the consensus holds that the current rental market provides the appropriate consumption cost measure, as it best represents the opportunity cost of consuming the services of the durable good. But even though the current rental value of an owner occupied house may represent the opportunity cost of living in it, the current rental price does not determine the quantity of housing services demanded, since that was determined in a multiperiod decision made when the owner bought the house (see Pollak 1975*b* and also Muth 1974). The multiperiod consumption decision depends on the array of prices and expected prices through all the periods for which the decision was made.

Pollak (1975*b*) deals with the question of constructing a one-period price measure in a multiperiod decision-making setting. The problem he addresses is analogous to the employer's labor-hiring decision under the implicit contract view of the labor market. Pollak's analysis shows that the solution requires information that is difficult to compile. Because the multiperiod decision requires that the economic agent form expectations of all future prices, the current period's measurement is, in general, a function of all those prices.

Equivalent problems have long been recognized in the capital measurement literature. The durability of capital goods would present no particular analytic problems if the services of capital goods were normally obtained through rental markets. Since that is not generally the case, producers must make investment decisions that involve multiperiod decisions on the input of capital services, decisions that must be based on expectations of prices over the investment planning period (Diewert 1980). Again, the measurement requires information on future prices or price expectations.

Workers are also durable. Just as some capital services are rented, some labor services are acquired through casual labor markets. But the proportion of labor services that are traded in casual labor markets is probably smaller than the proportion of capital services that are provided through rental agreements. For the majority of cases (wherever there are fixed employment costs), employment decisions, no less than investment decisions, require multiperiod planning horizons.

Pollak's (1975*b*) conclusions for consumption price measurement and those summarized by Diewert (1980) for capital measurement appear to hold with full force for the problem of measuring labor cost, though the complexity of the latter problem has not generally been recognized.[26] Because a labor cost index requires information on future prices or price expectations, as does a cost-of-living index or a measure of capital, the information necessary to compute a labor cost index cannot readily be assembled.

Lest this seem too nihilistic, one should quote with approval (and slight modification) a dictum of Zvi Griliches:

> It is easy to show that except for unique circumstances and under very stringent assumptions, it is not possible to devise [an economic measurement]. . . . Despite the theoretical proofs to the contrary the [measurement] exists and is even of some use. It is thus of some value to attempt to improve it even if perfection is unattainable. (Ohta and Griliches 1976, p. 326)

Theory tells us that all economic measurement, done right, is hard. It is perhaps the most difficult work in economics. Recognizing what the difficulties are is a major first step toward good measurement.

In summary, the implicit contract view of the labor market has far-reaching implications for measurement. Sherwin Rosen (1977) remarked that the recognition, some twenty-five years ago, of the importance of human capital altered the perspectives of labor economists away from preoccupation with current period wage differentials to concern for lifetime income. The human capital innovation in labor economics, however, applied to decision making by the worker. It left largely intact the traditional analysis of the employer. Though the human capital view emphasized that employers were hiring a labor input that was not homogeneous, employment decisions were still treated as functions of current period prices. The most recent revolution in labor economics completes the circle: The employment of labor (as has long been understood for the capital input) requires a multiperiod optimization model on the demand side, as does the worker-training decision on the supply side. Both supply of and demand for human skills are now seen as problems that have a strong capital theoretic component.

1.5 Payment and Reward Mechanisms and Other Knotty Problems

Researchers do not necessarily tackle problems just because they are important ones—especially if the problems are difficult (nor should they: good allocation would put scarce research resources where they earn the greatest payout at the margin). As a result, many difficult problems in measuring labor cost have received so little attention that a conceptual framework for dealing with them is not fully worked out.

1.5.1 Promotions and Wage "Drift"

Frequently, a promoted worker receives a new job title and higher pay but no clear increase in duties. Examples are academic promotions, some professional promotions in government employment, and many clerical promotions in the private sector. Although many blue-collar promotions entail a trial period, which implies a change in duties, these workers sometimes earn seniority or longevity pay boosts within a grade or job classification (the federal government has a similar system).

The method used for dealing with promotions and seniority premiums in measures of labor cost will depend on our economic understanding of what they represent. Some promotions are simply disguised pay raises. There is anecdotal evidence that promotion speeds in some occupations reflect labor market forces (again, academia provides a good example), which is suggestive. Richard Ruggles has argued (in a personal communication) that promotion disguised pay raises are so pervasive in the private sector that the change in earnings for a panel of individual workers provides a better measure of labor cost than does taking a sample of jobs (as in the BLS Employment Cost Index). This reinforces a view shared by many labor economists that the concept of a "job" is too fuzzy to use in measurement.

One can think of models for the promotion process other than describing them as disguised pay increases. Discrete adjustment to individual productivity growth with job experience is one example. In this case, promotion pay raises are premiums for labor quality and should not increase the labor cost measure. Presumably some seniority or longevity increases have the same interpretation.

Alternatively, the long-term implicit contract may take the form of a specified progression up the rungs of a formal job ladder (Lazear 1981). As noted in section 1.4, it is much less clear how these wage changes should be treated in a one-period labor cost measure, particularly if the probability of promotion is related to the strength of the external labor market.

Existing data series handle promotions in different ways. Most sensitive to promotions are earnings data obtained by following samples of workers (CPS panel data, NLS, and PSID);[27] these measures fully reflect promotions and longevity increases as workers move up the rungs of the job ladder, without any offsets. Intermediate in sensitivity are average hourly or weekly earnings series (AHE or AWE), the most pervasive government "wage" statistic. Although promotions are fully incorporated into AHE or AWE measures, their influence is offset by new hires or new entrants and by retirement; the level of the series thus reflects the net change in the average occupied rung of the job ladder. Less sensitive to promotions are fixed-weight indexes of employer labor cost (such as the BLS Employment Cost Index), where occupations and other control variables are held constant in the weights, though they may be affected by longevity increases if those are not explicitly controlled for. Most insensitive of all are averages of union negotiated wage scales or other wage schedules that include both promotion and longevity classes.

It is probably true that treating different job titles as the observations in a fixed-weight index misses some wage increases and perhaps some job downgrading in recessionary periods. Average hourly or weekly earnings would pick up these changes. Yet, it is difficult to be very enthusiastic about AHE or AWE measures. McMenamin and Russell, in this volume, cite wage and salary administrators for an estimated 1–3 percent "slippage" inherent in average earnings methods, presumably relative to the correct measure of labor cost.

Promotions are undoubtedly one cause of "wage drift," a loosely defined concept associated with the difference between AHE and measures of labor cost derived from union or other wage schedules. However, neither AHE nor wage schedules may move with the theoretical measure of labor cost or with a fixed-weight index, so it is difficult to know whether the wage drift notion reflects any economic reality.

The correct treatment of promotions in labor cost measures remains a knotty problem. In principle, we know what we want to do: Promotions that reflect labor quality upgrading should be linked or adjusted out of labor cost measures; those that represent disguised pay increases should be handled so that they do move the measurement. But there are formidable data problems in determining which promotions are which, and economists disagree about which kind predominates. The ultimate solution will depend on research which enables us to understand the operation of the promotion process, the economic role of the rungs of the job ladder, and the determinants of career paths.

1.5.2 Payment Periods

Both researchers and statistical agencies express labor cost data in standardized units. Hourly pay is perhaps the most common measurement unit; CPS data are usually published in the form of "usual" weekly earnings.

However, pay rates are quoted to employees in a variety of terms. Why should units of labor always be defined in terms of an hourly rate? Should all consumer products be measured in pounds?

In part, conversion of pay to common time units reflects the habit of viewing labor as homogeneous, or convertible to homogeneous units; were homogeneity the case, differing payment periods would be a mere nuisance to be eliminated by conversion before the data are used for analytic purposes. Since neither workers nor employers nor terms of labor contracts are homogeneous, it is appropriate to ask: What information is lost in the process of converting pay into common units?

There must be reasons why some workers are quoted an hourly pay rate and others a weekly, monthly, or annual rate. A number of plausible explanations exist. Blocks of work time are not necessarily perfectly divisible, and labor types may enter the production function in different ways. In this case, the payment period may reflect the appropriate quantity unit to use in defining an input into the productive process. Michael McKee has suggested (in a personal conversation) that the payment period may be determined by the closeness of the relation between the worker's individual effort and current output. It may also be correlated with the need for, or the difficulty of, close supervision (Lazear 1981) and whether a worker's hours are checked carefully by management. Many workers on weekly salaries are not actually docked for limited hours away from the job, so converting their earnings into hourly pay rates is in some sense distorting the data. The time period for which pay is quoted also may be related to the rigidity of the production process in which the worker works (see Duncan and Stafford 1980).

In all these cases, the method of payment reflects aspects of the employment contract that differ among labor types. Too much effort is probably expended on trying to reduce all pay data to some common denominator, and too little attention is paid to the information which may be lost in the conversion process.

1.5.3 Piece Rates, Commissions, and Bonuses

Piece-rate workers and workers paid on commission are not paid by any time period. How are they to be included in a measure of labor cost?

Two alternatives compete. One method is to compute per period earnings for commission sales workers, either hourly or weekly. For example, the occupational sample for the BLS Employment Cost Index includes stockbrokers, and the index moves with changes in brokers' weekly earnings. A second alternative uses the commission rate schedule; McMenamin and Russell note that the CWPS rule for commission sales workers measured earnings on such a constant output basis. There are problems with either alternative.

First, in noninflationary situations, piece rates or commission schedules tend to fall over time in response to productivity improvement. Using the piece rate or commission schedule under these conditions will record a falling factor price, even though hourly paid workers in the same circumstance exhibit rising earnings. Trends in the piece-rate schedule record movements in "labor cost per unit of output" (labor payments divided by productivity), rather than in the cost of a unit of labor.

On the other hand, coverting commission earnings to an hourly or weekly basis produces short-term fluctuations that are debatable measures of labor cost. Commission compensation schemes are often utilized where output changes are unpredictable, which means that the firm shifts part of the cost of holding idle productive capacity to the workers.[28] Because the number of stockbrokers fluctuates less than the level of stock market transactions, brokers' weekly earnings change with output fluctuations in the firm, and accordingly the constant output rule underlying the measure of labor cost (see section 1.2) is broken.

Alternatively, piece-rate or commission sales workers could be viewed as independent contractors.[29] The "price" for a factor of production must be quoted in units of that factor. If the firm compensates labor by means of a payment per unit of output, this is equivalent to the firm's purchasing output from a subcontractor. The firm is not buying labor inputs at all, even though the firm may own or supply the other factors of production with which the subcontractor works. Because this amounts to defining the piece-rate problem out of the labor cost measure, it is doubtful that such a strategy will prove acceptable either for controls programs or for economic measurement, no matter how attractive the option may seem conceptually.

Bonuses present similar problems. Lazear, in this volume, points to problems with Hamermesh's inclusion of year-end and related bonuses in his labor cost measure, arguing that if what is wanted is a measure of labor cost in efficiency units, then including bonuses that are productivity related will move the labor cost measure in the wrong direction. Suppose we observe a group of workers who receive bonuses depending on their output. One would certainly not conclude that the worker who received the highest bonus represented the highest labor cost to the firm. On the contrary, his earnings reflect some quality premium compared with other workers, as Lazear notes.

On the other hand, suppose one worker were paid $300 a week with no bonus, and the other $250 a week with a sales bonus. Ignoring the bonus would lead one to conclude that labor cost is higher for the worker who receives no bonus, when in fact we do not know whether that is the case or not. If a firm gives a large Christmas bonus in one year and a lower one in the subsequent year, it is not at all clear that such actions reflect changes in the quality of its work force between the two years, and it is even less clear that one should ignore the bonus payment in computing labor cost.

Direct bonuses and commissions that serve as incentive pay are now included in the wage calculation for the BLS Employment Cost Index, and year-end bonuses and the like are put into the benefits section. Lazear does not advocate the exclusion of bonuses, but he is quite right that their treatment poses problems in a labor cost measure.

1.5.4 Taxes

Until we determine what is to be measured conceptually, it is sometimes difficult to know what should be included in labor cost.

Hamermesh, in this volume, treats a decline in the corporate income tax as equivalent to an increase in the "net cost of labor to the firm," and adds this into his "COSTTAX" measure of labor cost. David Hartman pointed out, in the discussion on the paper at the Williamsburg conference, that the corporate income tax is usually thought of as a tax on capital, not a cost of employing labor.

Hartman's observation suggests that Hamermesh's COSTTAX measure applies to situations where a relative factor price is wanted. Lowering the corporate income tax means lowering the tax on capital, which raises the *relative* price of the labor input. The real logic of including a corporate profit tax adjustment in COSTTAX pertains to the labor/capital relative price ratio.

Although it is true that adjusting either price can move the ratio in the proper direction, it is not so clear that one should do this by adjusting the labor cost figure. Suppose a researcher were to use Hamermesh's COSTTAX data along with a user cost-of-capital series that adjusts for corporate taxation (such as Gollop and Jorgenson 1980) in an input substitution study. That would clearly overadjust for the tax effect and distort the measure of relative input prices. Theory suggests that the corporate profit tax adjustment belongs on the capital price, rather than on that of labor.

There is little question that labor cost measures should include employment taxes (such as those that support the unemployment insurance system), but the main measurement issues for present purposes seem to be incidence and distributional ones that are not well worked out. It would take too much space to explore these matters here (see various papers in Katz and Hight 1977).

1.6 Hedonic Methods, Labor Quality, and Compensating Differentials

Hedonic techniques have been circulating in economics for over forty years. Applications have included: valuing quality differences in products to improve measures of prices, real output, and productivity (Griliches 1971); analyzing labor quality (the empirical human capital literature can be regarded as an application of hedonic methods); assessing intangibles, such as risk, to compute compensating wage differentials (Thaler and Rosen 1976; Smith 1979); and valuing air quality and other neighborhood amenities in the housing and urban economics literature (see the bibliography of the paper by James Brown in this volume).

Though hedonic methods have been extensively employed in empirical work, progress in understanding the economics that lies behind them—and which guides our interpretation of the results—lagged well behind. Noteworthy milestones along the path to greater understanding are Rosen (1974) and the discussion that took place at the 1973 meeting of the Conference on Research in Income and Wealth.[30]

1.6.1 Interpretation of Hedonic Results

A hedonic function[31] is a relationship between the market price of some commodity and elements or attributes of that thing itself that, following Lancaster (1971), have come to be called "characteristics," that is,

$$\Pi = h(X_1, \ldots, X_k). \tag{13}$$

If the commodity is labor services, and labor is viewed as an input into some productive process, then the variable Π on the left-hand side of equation (13) is the measure of labor cost that is computed according to the conceptual design outlined in earlier sections of this essay and in the papers included in this volume. The variables $X_1, \ldots, X_k$ on the right-hand side are, of course, the characteristics. Giving an economic interpretation to the characteristics is the first major task.

Recall that in section 1.2 the input "labor services" in the production function of equation (1) represented a vector of different types, skills, or grades of labor:

$$L = (L_1, \ldots, L_n). \tag{14}$$

Each L_i might represent an occupation or an occupational grouping (clerical workers, for example).

Under the hedonic view of the world, each jth observation in L_i is itself regarded as an aggregation, constructed from the quantities of characteristics embodied in that particular worker, that is,

$$L_{ij} = \lambda_i(X_{1j}, \ldots, X_{kj}). \tag{15}$$

Moreover, the characteristics are the true inputs to the production process. Taking the human capital literature as an example, if years of education and years of experience are productive characteristics of labor type L_i, then the quantity (years) of education and experience embodied in L_i are the inputs entered in the production function, rather than the quantity of L_i. A similar interpretation can be given for a hedonic function on consumer goods (where the characteristics of goods are treated as the true arguments of the utility function, not the consumer goods themselves).[32] An alternative rationale exists for the characteristics of hedonic functions when the object is to analyze outputs or supplies.[33]

It *might* be true that the productive contribution of each characteristic is independent of the particular L_i in which it is embodied, in which case it is not necessary to distinguish between labor types once their characteristics have been enumerated. An experienced accountant is simply "more" labor than a beginning machine tender. Much of the labor quality and human capital literature is built on this assumption. More probable, however, are situations in which (say) a year's experience or education has different productive implications in various occupations, or where characteristics that are important in some occupations are of little or no value in others. In both these cases, occupations matter in the structure of production, and there will be one aggregation rule (λ_i in eq. [15]) for each occupation.[34]

In any event, in the "hedonic hypothesis" the *arguments* of a hedonic function are, at least in principle, the arguments of either a utility function or a production function, as the case may be, when the hedonic function is viewed from the buyer's side of the market. This does not, however, imply that the hedonic *function* is derivable from or directly related to the functions that economic units optimize. The function h in equation (13) is not λ_i in equation (15), and the one is not a function solely of the other.

Instead, the hedonic function provides an estimate of the constraint on the behavioral unit's optimization problem. Or, to put it more precisely, those constraints can be derived from hedonic functions, since empirically the forms used to estimate hedonic functions have never explicitly taken on the form of the behavioral constraint.

For simplicity in both the exposition and the economics, assume that the production function of equation (1) contains only one labor type, L_i, or that a suitable partitioning exists so that one can consider input L_i in isolation from all other inputs. Labor input L_i is, however, not homogeneous, as it contains productive characteristics X_1 and X_2 in amounts varying with different individuals (an example might be a service industry in which the output of service depends on the years of training and experience of individual workers).

Cost minimization for a producer requires combining productive inputs in proportions such that ratios of their unit costs equal ratios of their marginal productivities. In the present case, the productive inputs are characteristics X_1 and X_2; a production isoquant for these two inputs can be derived in the regular manner (examples are A and H in fig. 1.1). If X_1 and X_2 are education and experience, the firm's production problem involves finding an optimal composition of these productive labor-force attributes.

Information on unit factor (characteristic) costs can be obtained from the hedonic function. Still assuming for simplicity only two characteristics, the hedonic function of equation (13) can be used to compute

$$\beta = \beta(\partial X_2/\partial X_1, \Pi \text{ constant}). \tag{16}$$

The value of the β function of equation (16) gives the relative price of X_1 in terms of X_2 and is computed from the coefficients of the hedonic function of equation (13). Since an isocost curve shows combinations of inputs that can be obtained for the same outlay (and in this case the inputs are characteristics X_1 and X_2), the β function can be viewed as tracing out an isocost curve, or a portion of one, in characteristics space. One of these is designated as β in figure 1.1. There is one such locus for every value of labor cost for which workers can be hired.

Rosen (1974) emphasizes that the *location* of the hedonic function (or, inter alia, of the β function) is determined by all suppliers and demanders in the market, and that it is an envelope of the behavioral functions on both sides of the market. The present section emphasizes a different aspect of that model—the hedonic function as a carrier to the employer of economic information on factor costs. Notation for more than two characteristics is obvious, but the extension to cases where capital and materials costs or other labor types are incorporated into the cost minimization problem is tedious, though not fundamentally different (see Triplett 1982).

1.6.2 Hedonic Methods as Adjustments for Labor Quality

Hedonic functions provide information about the prices or unit costs of characteristics, and therefore about the costs of productive inputs in cases where the characteristics are the inputs to the productive function. This rationale for hedonic functions can be used to motivate their use for adjusting labor cost measures for labor quality. This subject deserves a whole paper on its own. The following is accordingly only an outline of a more comprehensive treatment. Parts of it are adapted from Triplett (1982) and Pollak (1983).

We first develop the notion of labor quality in the context of measuring labor cost. The basic input cost theory outlined in section 1.2 of this essay applies to any definition of a productive input. Accordingly, index number theory can readily be modified to apply to "characteristics space"—

the case where productive inputs are the characteristics of workers—rather than the normal case in which inputs are taken to be quantities of undifferentiated labor hours (sometimes referred to as "goods space").

Assuming for simplicity that capital and materials are homogeneous goods, and, for the moment, a casual labor market (to avoid the complexities of section 1.4), the production function of equation (1) is rewritten as

$$(17) \qquad Q = Q^*(K, M, X_1, \ldots, X_k).$$

The cost function of equation (2) becomes

$$(18) \qquad C = C^* \, (R, P, \partial\Pi/\partial X_1, \ldots, \partial\Pi/\partial X_k; Q),$$

where C^*, the "characteristics production cost function," is interpreted (as before) as the minimum cost of acquiring a set of inputs sufficient to produce some specified level of Q. Computing equation (18) requires, in addition to the prices of capital and materials, implicit prices for each of the labor characteristics $(X_1, \ldots, X_k)$. Hedonic methods are a means for determining those implicit prices, $\partial\Pi/\partial X_i$.

Just as the input cost index of section 1.2 was computed from the cost function of equation (2), the "characteristics input cost index" is the ratio of values of C^* under alternative price regimes (including alternative implicit prices in eq. [13]). A more extensive treatment of the input cost index in characteristics space is given by Triplett (1982).

A change in labor quality is identified with increases or decreases in the quantities of labor characteristics used as inputs in the production process. In the characteristics input cost index, it is natural to take the notion of labor "quality" as nothing more than a shorthand expression for the quantities of characteristics in the vector $X_1, \ldots, X_k$. Contrary to presumptions often encountered in the literature, analysis of labor quality does not require any explicit scalar measure of "quality" (such as a "labor quality index," which in fact provides no additional information).

Shifts in labor characteristics may reflect simple substitution among characteristics in response to changes in relative input prices. The inputs of characteristics included in C^* in one period are therefore not exactly the same as in some other period; this, of course, is normal in any input cost index. Thus, when labor quality is identified with the productive labor characteristics, $X_1, \ldots, X_k$, a "constant quality" input cost index is nothing more than the normal specification of a theoretical input cost index defined on input characteristics—an index in which the inputs (characteristics) included in both periods are the minimum cost set that are sufficient to produce the specified output level, Q. A "constant quality" index is not necessarily one in which there are no changes in labor characteristics.

Of course, when making comparisons of labor cost, the level of output must be held constant. Frequently, one observes changes in labor characteristics that are inconsistent with the constant output measurement rule, and, for these cases only, a "labor quality adjustment" must be made. Such an adjustment is interpreted as responding to a change in the characteristics set $(X_1, \ldots, X_k)$ by altering the inputs in Q^* in such a way that C^* (eq. [18]) refers to the same level of output (a specified value for Q) in both index comparisons.

In the theoretical, or exact, input cost index, the "quality adjustment" may be quite complicated, involving all of the inputs and not just the one whose characteristics actually changed. One also has to consider rather carefully the source of the changes that have been observed, which is equivalent to specifying precisely the question that is being addressed. We leave these complications aside (see Triplett 1982).

Note that in general the "hedonic" or quality adjusted price index cannot be computed from the hedonic function alone. Like any exact index, the characteristics input cost index requires information from the cost function C^*, and hence from Q^*, whereas the hedonic function only provides information about a portion of the firm's isocost line for productive inputs (eq. [16]). The "hedonic price indexes" that exist in the literature (see Griliches 1971 and Triplett 1975) are not based on cost functions and are best interpreted as approximations to the true characteristics cost indexes, somewhat in the fashion that ordinary fixed-weight price index formulas are thought of as approximations to the true indexes in conventional index number theory.[35]

In summary, the "constant quality" input cost index is simply the theoretical input cost index defined in characteristics space. I use the term "simply" advisedly. Though simple in concept, such an index requires an enormous amount of information, including not only the characteristics costs, but also the full production or cost function defined on characteristics. Its computation involves a host of difficulties (Pollak 1983).

If the production and cost functions are known, then one can possibly use implicit prices obtained from hedonic functions to compute characteristics input cost indexes. However, as will be spelled out in section 1.6.3, if production and cost functions on characteristics are not known (the usual case), serious difficulties surround using hedonic prices to estimate them. This implies that estimating the exact input cost index from price and quantity information is not straightforward in a characteristics world (see also Pollak and Wachter 1975).

To this point, the discussion has concerned the cost index for the full set of inputs in equation (17). As noted in section 1.2, a labor cost index is a subindex of the full input cost index. Its construction requires separability conditions on production and/or cost functions. For the characteristics input cost index, the analogous condition specifies that labor characteristics (or their unit costs) be separable from capital and materials inputs (or their costs).[36] If the labor cost subindex exists, it simplifies the quality problem somewhat because the labor cost index becomes a function only of the $\partial\Pi/\partial X_i$ terms of equation (18) and the level of a "labor aggregator function," the value of which is held constant over the index comparison. The previous discussion of the meaning and interpretation of quality change and the use of hedonic methods to evaluate it carries over to the labor cost subindex in the form of an extension. However, the required separability conditions for constructing subindexes seem less plausible, if anything, for the labor cost index defined in characteristics space, for they imply that the substitution of (say) education and "raw" labor is independent of the mix of capital inputs.

In empirical work one seldom has the luxury of working with the theoretical or exact index, for the information requirements of exact indexes are prohibitive. The best one normally has available are indexes constructed as close approximations to the theoretical concept. One criterion of adequacy in an approximation is the extent that the measures take account of, or control for, quality variation.

A curious anomaly of the literature on economic measurement is the disparity that exists between concerns for "quality error" in price and labor cost measures. In the case of price indexes, quality error has long been judged a serious limitation on the validity of empirical measures (Price Statistics Review Committee 1961). On the other hand, taking average hourly earnings (total payrolls divided by hours paid for) or the related hourly compensation series (both are described in Antos, this volume) as a labor cost measure is a common practice that normally raises the most modest of demurrers.

One would judge from the extent of the literature and of professional discussion that the labor market measures were the better of the two. Yet that is clearly not the case. Whatever the quality error remaining in available price indexes (the Consumer Price Index, for example, or the various forms of the Producer Price Index), a great amount of attention is paid to limiting quality variation in price quotes accepted for those indexes, and price indexes have been designed in other ways as well to be far closer than are AHE measures to the concepts needed for economic analysis (Gillingham 1974 describes the use of the cost-of-living index theory as a framework for constructing the Consumer Price Index). By the normal standards applied to price indexes, AHE measures are woefully deficient, essentially because only total establishment payrolls and hours are collected, rather than an earnings or a labor cost concept.

Gollop and Jorgenson, in this volume, are among the few economists to pay serious attention to the labor quality problem. Remarking that AHE or hourly compensation measures "conceal an enormous heterogeneity," they set out to purge them, to the extent possible, of error attributable to their near total lack of control for labor quality shifts. The size of the task Gollop and Jorgenson set for themselves is indicative of the magnitude of the quality problem in normal earnings measures—their data are factored into some 81,000 cells to control for labor quality, roughly 1600 cells per industry.

Gollop and Jorgenson assume an industry labor aggregator function that is translog in form. The traditional rationale for aggregation of this type is to interpret each of the 1600 cells to be a separate factor of production—that is, the vector of labor services in the production function of equation (1) has 1600 elements. Though it is also traditional to assume that labor services are a natural aggregate, the theoretical justification for doing so requires that the cost function (eq. [2]) be separable on these 1600 cells. Evaluating the plausibility of this separability assumption is nearly impossible owing to the sheer mass of data.

The material in this section supplies an alternative rationale. Gollop and Jorgenson's ten occupational cells are taken as corresponding to the L_i categories in equation (14). Age and education (age being a proxy for work experience) within industry-occupation groupings represent labor characteristics—the X's of equations (13), (15), and (17), and the characteristics are the true productive inputs (or are proxies for the true inputs). Further division of these cells by workers' sex follows precedent in the literature and presumably reflects a correction for omitted characteristics or occupational detail. Under this rationale, the heterogeneity of worker productivity is accounted for by the characteristics, and a labor cost subindex that controls for labor quality can be constructed from the characteristics using the appropriate separability assumptions on equation (18).

Though Gollop and Jorgenson do not formally adopt the rationale presented here, their work is not inconsistent with it. Their procedure amounts to grouping individuals within occupations by the quantities of characteristics embodied in them. This kind of grouping is an alternative to an explicit computation of a characteristics labor cost index. It also corresponds to the way quality change is typically handled in price indexes.

An explicit characteristics-space rationale for work of the Gollop-Jorgenson type has several advantages over the traditional (or "goods-space") rationale. (1) Testing for functional separability involves only the inputs, age (experience), and education in each L_i category, not a set of 1600 inputs. (2) The characteristics variables have an explicit economic justification rather than appearing as ad hoc adjustments, which is the case in traditional treatments. (3) Grouping the characteristics by occupation is supported by the Hicksian aggregation rule outlined in note 34, and those occupational groupings can be tested empirically by straightforward tests on earnings functions; the traditional approach leaves occupational groupings arbitrary, and provides no natural method for testing groupings for realism. (4) Under the characteristics-space rationale, "quality adjustment" can be incorporated into the theory of production and index numbers in a natural way that permits the analysis of alternatives; the traditional conceptual mode leaves quality change as a mathematical parameter imposed from outside economics whose character is obscure, properties ambiguous, and identification improbable.[37]

The Gollop-Jorgenson data base provides researchers for the first time with labor cost measures by industry that are controlled for labor quality variation. It is a particularly valuable contribution in view of the fact that the only government provided labor cost measure that does control for occupational and other shifts (the BLS Employment Cost Index) has little industry detail, which greatly limits its analytical usefulness.

Gollop and Jorgenson follow most studies of labor quality in using some variant of the human capital approach, so the characteristics that are included in the analysis are education and experience measures. This approach has the weight of literature and precedent behind it, yet three reservations should be expressed about the human capital treatment of labor quality.

First, education and experience are not characteristics in the sense that this term was defined and used in equations (13) and (17). Education and experience are not in themselves productive characteristics, but they are proxies, or are associated in some way with skills that are productive or with the acquisition of productive skills. We can think of the true measures as the outputs of processes in which years of education and of experience are the inputs. Of course, the true measures of skills are really wanted in equations (13) and (17), and they would be used there if they were available.[38]

Second, economists have taken both education and experience as good proxies for productive inputs because both are associated with increases in earnings, and standard theory predicts a relation between variance in wages and a measure of marginal product. However, Lazear (1979) has shown that rising experience-earnings profiles may result when firms and workers make implicit, multiperiod contracts, even if there is no association between productivity and experience. Lazear and Moore (1981) estimate that only 11 percent of the association between experience and earnings originates from the higher productivity of more experienced workers; the remainder of the rising experience-earnings profile consists of deferred payment incentives under long-term implicit contracts. Experience is undoubtedly more nearly a productive attribute for the younger groups of workers, as Lazear (1976) himself and many other economists have shown. For older workers, use of experience as a labor quality indicator would appear to overadjust labor cost measures for labor quality.

Of course, the implicit contract argument does not invalidate consideration of experience variables in measuring labor cost, because one would presumably still want to "standardize" labor cost measures for differing points on the time profile of the implicit contract (see section 1.4). But there is reason to question the traditional view of the economic role of experience, and there is room for a great deal of additional research that will specify the appropriate way of treating experience in the measurement of labor cost, and that will define the variables that do measure productive labor characteristics and can be used for studies of labor quality.

Third, and most important, the human capital view of labor quality has often led to the notion that labor quality is a unique scalar measure and that rankings of workers or groups of workers by some "labor quality index" are useful for comparisons over long time periods or across regions (see Johnson in this volume).

Consideration of equations (17) and (18) suggests that any labor quality measure is some aggregation of labor characteristics, and, as in any aggregation, weights matter. Weights in this case could be marginal products of labor characteristics or the implicit prices of equation (18), in which case the labor quality measure amounts to a *quantity* index of characteristics. The labor quality measure, in other words, is not a unique scalar measure, but is instead a construction that resembles Gross National Product or any other aggregate quantity measure in which disparate quantity units are combined into some value measure in order to make meaningful economic statements. It has long been understood (see Samuelson and Swamy 1974, and the references cited there) that such quantity measures produce rankings that are not invariant to relative prices; for example, real consumption in Norway may be above that of Costa Rica when valued by one country's prices, but below when valued by the other's.

It has not been generally understood that the same principle holds for quality measures. The frontiersman of the last century lacks the skills for success in a modern labor market to the same degree that a computer systems analyst is ill-equipped for the world of Natty Bumppo. Nichols remarks in this volume that today's unskilled worker would have been regarded as semiskilled at the turn of the century because today's worker has more education; perhaps so, but many skills that were important then have become obsolete, and we generally lack the information to rank workers of both periods by weighting systems that apply to each period. The habit of taking years of schooling as an invariant measure of labor quality imposes today's weights on intertemporal comparisons of labor skills and obscures the fact that a comparison from yesterday's perspective may well reveal the classical "index number problem."

Even in contemporary comparisons, uncritical application of scalar human capital measures produces potential errors. Layard (1979, p. 52) notes that "college-trained people, if they had not gone to college, would have earned less than those who did not go to college but had the same *measured* abilities" (emphasis supplied). If the implicit prices for labor characteristics produced by college were to fall sufficiently (or were lower in some parts of the country than in others), those other, nonmeasured skills possessed by workers who specialize in nonintellectual occupations would be more highly valued by the market, leading to changes in the rank ordering of worker quality.

This analytic problem deserves more attention in the construction of labor quality measures.

1.6.3 Hedonic Methods and the Estimation of Labor Market Differentials

A hedonic function yields an opportunity locus that can be interpreted as a producer's isocost curve. Having estimated such a thing, it is natural to want to use it for something else. For example, one might wish implicit prices for characteristics for use in explaining demands for those characteristics.

In the labor cost context, we might suppose (despite the caveats of the last section) that characteristics are human capital components, such as education and experience. They might also be strength and dexterity, or any other elements that are associated with the productive contribution of the labor input. Equation (13) is estimated as one form of the ordinary "earnings" function. Alternatively and analogously, one may wish to use hedonic prices to estimate consumers' demands for air quality or other nonmarket goods, starting from a hedonic relation similar to equation (13), but involving (say) real estate prices and housing and environmental characteristics. A third example, from the labor economics literature, involves use of hedonic functions to determine wage differentials that compensate workers for risky or unpleasant occupations.

The question we wish to address takes the following form: Under what conditions, if any, can we use the coefficients of the earnings function to explain the firm's employment of productive characteristics?

One proposal is to estimate the hedonic function (eq. [13]) in the first stage. Next, one estimates the production function of equation (17) or the input demand equations derived from it, in which the labor input is defined by quantities of labor characteristics, and the characteristics implicit prices ($\partial\Pi/\partial X_1, \ldots, \partial\Pi/\partial X_k$) are employed as unit input costs. This is often referred to as the "two-stage" proposal and was originally outlined in Rosen (1974).

Figure 1.1 suggests the problems this proposal poses. The β function in figure 1.1 comes from equation (16) and is drawn for a particular value of labor cost. Its slope shows relative implicit prices for labor characteristics X_1 and X_2. Isoquants A and H are portions of production functions of

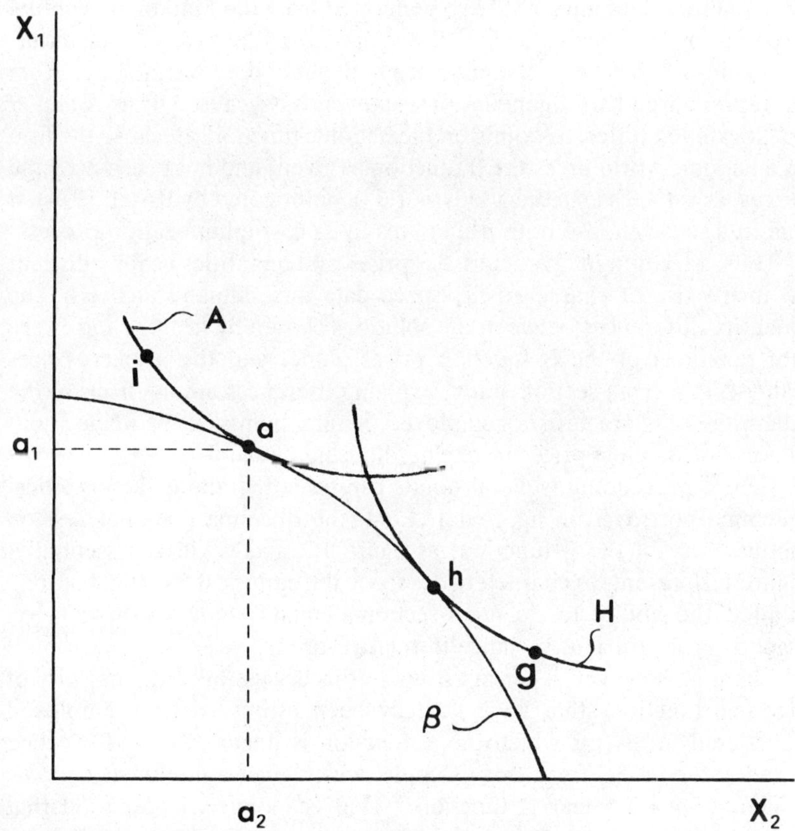

Fig. 1.1

employers A and H. Cost minimization by each results in employment of factor proportions indicated by a and h, respectively.

Suppose initially that nothing was known about the production functions, that we merely observe the implicit prices from the β function and the input quantities corresponding to the points a and h. There is in this example variance in relative characteristics prices (slopes of the β function at a and at h), a necessity for an empirical demand study. Moreover, there is also variance in the quantities of characteristics X_1 and X_2. In the absence of information about the shape and position of the production functions, superficial examination of the prices and quantities suggests a situation which, when encountered in "goods space," signals to the researcher that "all's well."

But knowing the production functions in this case reveals that the price and quantity data have not been generated from the kind of conceptual experiment on which demand theory rests. Differences in the firms' production functions, stemming from the inherent technology, from entrepreneurial heterogeneity, or whatever, have caused firms *A* and *H* to "locate" at different points on the hedonic function. Because the firm in a hedonic world takes the β function as given, and not necessarily the prices, as is the case in the goods world (a point noted by Rosen 1974), it can in a sense choose both *p*'s and *q*'s in its cost minimization process.

Thus, variation in characteristics prices and quantities is not sufficient to justify use of characteristics-space data in a demand analysis. The quantity differences between the solutions chosen by firms *A* and *H* are not functions of the β function prices alone, and the implicit prices cannot, in a cross-section study, explain differences among firms in the quantities of characteristics employed. Similar points can be made about the use of hedonic prices to explain housing demand.

Before proceeding, several points can be noted about the empirical dilemma portrayed in figure 1.1. First, the dilemma does not rest on nonlinearity of the β function, as figure 1.2 makes clear. Essentially, figure 1.2 presents in characteristics space the empirical fact that has long limited the ability to do cross-section demand studies with data on "goods"—insufficient variance in relative prices.

There is, however, a certain irony to this discussion. The majority of hedonic functions that have actually been estimated have employed functional forms for which the β function is linear. The well-worked semilog functional form, for example, which gives a nonlinear hedonic function, has a linear β function.[39] Had economists understood that relative characteristics prices were in fact constant for the hedonic functions most of them were working with, they might never have set off to try to use hedonic prices in a cross-section demand study in the first place. It is ironic that it took a double misunderstanding about the hedonic framework to generate this research. Nonlinearity in the β function, not nonlinearity of the hedonic function, is the necessary condition for generating variance in relative characteristics prices; however, nonlinearity of the β function is not a sufficient condition to justify the use of hedonic prices in a characteristics demand study.

Second, the research dilemma of figure 1.1 is inherent in the concept of a heterogeneous product. If all demanders were like firm *A* in figure 1.1, heterogeneous products would either disappear from the market—leaving only one outcome (a_1, a_2)—or, in the case in which the inputs are supplied in heterogeneous form by act of nature (the labor input), the hedonic function would coincide with firm *A*'s production isoquant, as noted by Rosen (1974). But in the latter case, no buyer would care which variety was purchased, so no *relevant* heterogeneity exists, and the goods might as well be treated as homogeneous within price classes.

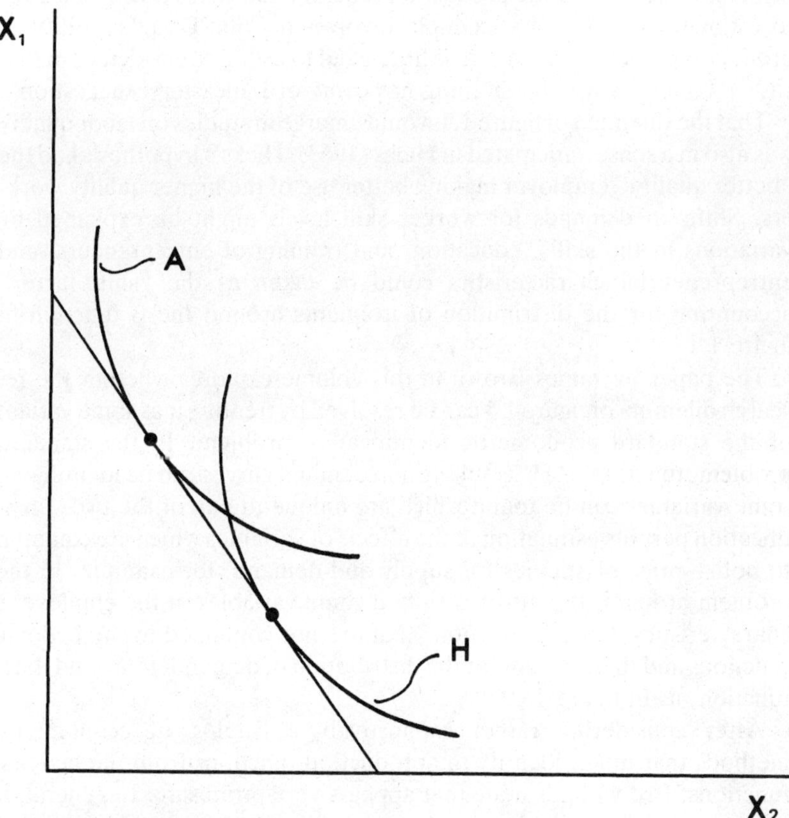

Fig. 1.2

Third, the research dilemma portrayed in figure 1.1 has been well anticipated in theoretical work on consumer demand and, in a sense, on labor quality. Lancaster (1971), noting that buyers undoubtedly have different tastes, proposes something like the following: First, estimate the β function (Lancaster uses programming methods to determine the β function directly, without estimation of the hedonic function). Then assume that consumers (firms buying inputs) all have the same utility (production) functions, save for a shift factor. One can then estimate a distribution function to account for the locations of consumers (firms) around the β function. This procedure would yield the following information. Starting from the slope of the β function at point *a*, firm *H*, faced with the same set of characteristics prices would choose point *g*, giving two points on its isoquant; the same procedure gives point *i* on firm *A*'s isoquant. The procedure is not very practical, because it needs so much a priori specification of the production function that there is little left over to estimate. (Lancaster's example involves a Cobb-Douglas utility or production function, and there is little need to estimate elasticities in that case.) To my knowledge nothing has come of Lancaster's suggestion.

That the dilemma of figure 1.1 would emerge in studies on labor quality was also in a sense anticipated in Hicks (1963). Hicks's hypothesis had the "better quality" employer making better use of the higher quality workers. Shifts in demands for worker skill levels might be explained by variations in the skills, education, and training of entrepreneurs, and entrepreneurial characteristics could be taken as the "shift factor" accounting for the distribution of isoquants around the β function in figure 1.1.

The paper by James Brown in this volume explores whether the research dilemma of figure 1.1 can be resolved by treating it as some variant of the standard econometric identification problem. In the standard problem, functions such as supply and demand curves can be identified if some variables can be found which are unique to one of the two. Identification permits estimation of the effects of variables which are common to both—price elasticities for supply and demand, for example. In the problem at hand, the effort is to find some variables in the employer's characteristics demand functions that are not contained in the hedonic functions and that account for the distribution of demanders around the β function, as in figure 1.1.

After considering rather exhaustively a catalog of econometric methods that might identify the production functions from the hedonic functions, Brown finds none that appears very promising. In general, it seems difficult to conceive of a situation in which one can be sure that differences in quantities of characteristics demanded are not attributable to location decisions of demanders around the β function, as well as cost-minimizing reactions to the relative prices themselves. Brown's conclusion parallels Pollak and Wachter's (1975) finding that implicit prices have limited usefulness for explaining outcomes of household production models.

Thus, econometric solutions seem unattainable; the essence of the solution, if the problem is solvable at all, involves generation of an appropriate data set, not elaboration of econometric methods. The way to look at the problem is to ask whether one could plausibly interpret data sets in a way that is consistent with the conceptual experiment that underlies normal demand analysis—that is, can one envision a particular price-quantity data set on characteristics as having been generated by a process of both varying the characteristics prices faced by an individual economic behavioral unit and observing the changed characteristics quantities as responses?

To show how hard it is to come up with the required data set, it is worth noting a recent example in which a plausible case was constructed. G. Brown and Mendelsohn (1981) estimated demand for "fishing holes" by characteristics. First, they estimated hedonic functions across various fishing sites to obtain implicit prices for the attributes of each site. Then, on the assumption that fishermen did not choose their place of residence on the basis of proximity to a fishing site, and using transportation expenses from home to site as an element of the cost of the fishing expedition, they constructed, essentially, figure 1.3. In this case, because the distance to the site was a unique element in the hedonic function for each fisherman, they were able to estimate fishermen's demands for different characteristics of fishing spots, an accomplishment of considerable ingenuity which will undoubtedly be a substantial service to planning outdoor recreation facilities. However, the fact that the Brown-Mendelssohn data set relates to a problem that is of considerably less than universal interest among economists is probably no coincidence. It is an ingenious solution to a very special problem, and although it may suggest equally ingenious solutions to others, prospects are not high for generating appropriate data sets with more widespread applications.

One should, however, put all this in proper perspective. First, the research dilemma protrayed in figure 1.1 greatly limits the usefulness for behavioral studies of hedonic estimates of implicit prices, but it does not imply that they are useless. Thaler and Rosen (1976), fully recognizing the locational choice problem of figure 1.1, use it to specify that their estimates of the compensating wage differential for risk were a limit (a lower one in their case) on the true estimates: in figure 1.1 terms, the price of X_1 necessary to induce H to employ a_1 units of X_1 is far lower than what is required to induce A to locate at that point, and accordingly, A requires less than H to "compensate" for locating in the vicinity of a_1. Fully understanding the nature of hedonic prices facilitates using them in appropriate ways.

Second, the conceptual problems we have been discussing are merely characteristics-space forms of problems that are ancient in normal goods-space demand analysis. For example, it has long been known that there are regional differences in food prices and consumption. Taking regional variations as appropriate data for demand analysis requires the assumption of common utility functions—that regional consumption differences do not reflect regional differences in tastes. Thus, strong assumptions are always necessary to justify using cross-section data in demand analysis. These problems are so timeworn that they are frequently ignored in empirical applications in goods space. Only because working in characteristics space is new do the problems discussed in this section seem novel.

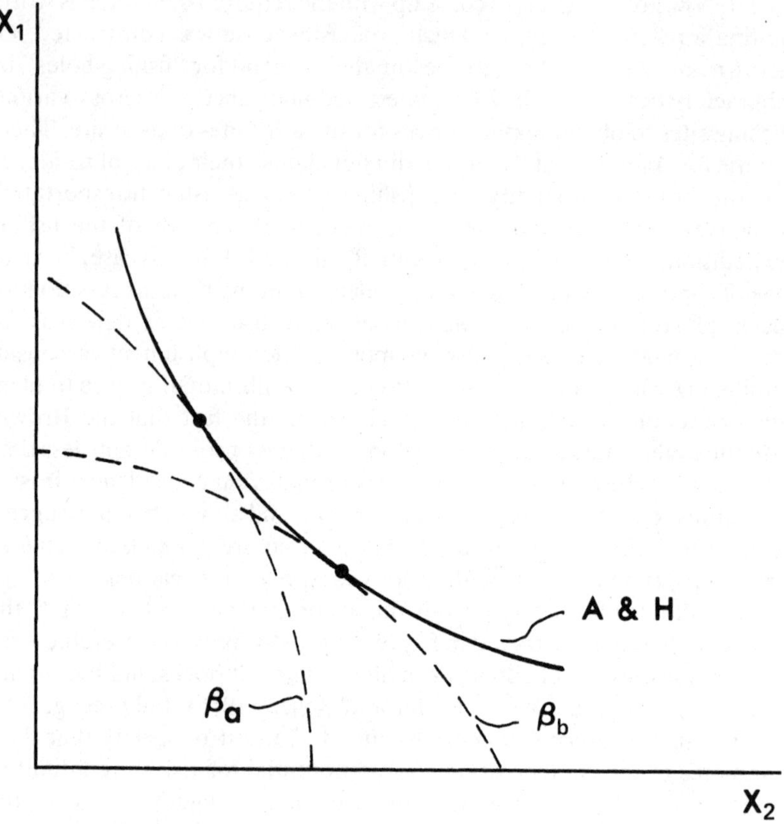

Fig. 1.3

1.6.4 Compensating Differentials in Labor Cost Measures

What makes labor markets unique is the exchange of packages by participants on both sides of the market. Workers sell bundles of productive characteristics to employers. They receive bundles of wages and benefits that include not only the traditional "fringes," but also greater or lesser amounts of job characteristics such as desirable working conditions (freedom from regimentation and arbitrary supervisory practices, for example), workplace safety and health, job amenities such as attractive office furniture and surroundings, employer subsidized consumption on the job, training and advancement opportunities, and so forth. The wage payment is but a single element in a complex exchange of commodities, services, and financial claims.

Because both workers and employers are heterogeneous, the range of bundles from which both make choices is enormous. Other things equal, variation in one element of either bundle will be offset by equivalent variations in other elements.[40] If the wage is the element of the compensation package that offsets variation in some other element, or the net effect of a group of elements, then labor markets will exhibit a set of "compensating wage differentials" that reflect worker valuations on everything from a favorable climate to employer subsidized lunches to the aversion many workers have to working for very large employers (Oi, this volume). Considerable research on compensating differentials has been undertaken in recent years (see the bibliographies in Smith 1979 and C. Brown 1980).

The model underlying compensating wage differentials is basically the wage-benefit model of equations (3)–(8). As an example, consider job safety which can be viewed as a benefit (Thaler and Rosen 1976; Sider 1981). Workers will choose less safe jobs only when employers pay a higher wage to compensate them for the risk of injury (eq. [6a]). Alternatively, the employer can invest in safety equipment; this will reduce the wage premium that must be paid, and the "amount" of safety that will be provided by market mechanisms will be determined by equation (8).[41]

Notice, however, an anomaly: If the employer "pays" for workplace hazards in the form of higher wages, it will be recorded in his labor cost data. Dealing with work hazards through purchase of safety equipment will, in most accounting systems, show up as an increase in the quantity of capital equipment. Since both compensating wage payments and expenditures for safety equipment are necessary because risk creates disutility for workers, both costs need to be considered in labor cost measures on a comparable basis.

The same point can be made about many other nonpecuniary job attributes. Increases or decreases in them may imply changes in the level of wages that must be paid, but there will be concomitant increases in expenditures on other factors, so that considering only those expenditures that are explicit to labor misses labor cost that shows up in the form of employer expenditure on some other input.

Positive or negative nonpecuniary elements may be provided by a third party, such as government or an act of nature. Employers who gain (or lose) by receiving (or not receiving) these "free" job characteristics will adjust wages accordingly. For example, the interarea labor cost comparisons conducted by Johnson (in this volume) control for differences in worker quality among areas; but that, though vital, is only one side of the story. Perhaps both union and nonunion wages are high in Detroit not because of the direct and indirect effects of union power but because of Detroit's amenity levels relative to competitive areas. Comparisons of labor payments among employers who receive differential benefits by act of government or nature may yield misleading information about the true levels of labor cost.

To make things more difficult for measurement, it may not be possible to separate out of the employer's total cost structure those aspects which are uniquely associated with the benefit that workers get from an amenity provided by a third party. Roback (1982) shows that when an amenity (for example, a favorable climate) is both desired by workers and independently productive to firms, then the effect on land rents can be determined, but one cannot tell the direction of the effect on wages. In seeking to allow for the effects of amenities in the labor cost measurement, we lack even the clue of sign that will tell us whether estimated values of regional amenities are reasonable or not.

The existence of compensating wage differentials thus means that a unique measure of labor cost may not be extractable from the employer's total input cost, because the level of labor cost is not independent of the quantity of capital or of some other input. Compensating differentials may also imply that the cost function is not separable on its labor component (see section 1.2), because safety hazards, for example, are likely to differ among occupations, and adding safety equipment will change the occupational wage structure. But the separability property relates to aggregation; the dependence of labor cost on the quantity of capital in the presence of compensating differentials would be true even if the production function contained only one type of homogeneous labor. Thus, the challenge raised to labor cost measures by compensating wage differentials encompasses, but goes beyond, the classical separability issue.

This problem is unique to labor input to production and occurs because each party to a labor market transaction cares about the characteristics of the other party. There are some other markets for which this is also a fact—rental housing is one clear example. But the problem seems far more pervasive and far more important in measuring the cost of the labor input than for any other productive input, and it is considerably more important than is the case for most consumer goods markets. Measuring labor cost is hardly a simple economic task.

1.7 Conclusions

This essay has addressed the problem of producing a conceptual framework for measuring labor cost that reflects a modern view of the operation of labor markets. The theory of labor cost that is derived from the stylized model of production on which the theory of economic measurement is based (section 1.2) has the following properties that are inconsistent with empirical knowledge of labor markets:

1. Unit factor cost consists exclusively of money wage payments.
2. The labor unit is homogeneous.
3. A casual labor market prevails.

4. Production costs can be separated uniquely into labor cost components and costs of other inputs.

Relaxing the first two restrictive properties of the stylized model involves difficult empirical and data development tasks, but does not challenge the fundamental validity of the labor cost measure. Adding costs of benefits clearly is required to reach an adequate measure of labor cost for nearly any purpose (section 1.3). And though there are more conceptual difficulties in measuring some of these benefits than first meets the eye, for the majority of them the measurement can be done within the traditional production theoretic context.

Similarly, dealing with worker heterogeneity can be handled theoretically by modeling the productive characteristics of workers and by extending the basic theory of index number measurements into characteristics space (section 1.6). The formidable conceptual and theoretical problems that remain cannot be denied. But those pale beside the empirical and data base requirements that have inhibited progress on the analysis of heterogeneity in both goods and labor markets.

Far deeper conceptual problems surround the other two major points discussed in this essay, for they call into question whether a one-period measure of labor cost, or indeed a measure of labor cost at all, is either appropriate or achievable.

Because casual labor markets seldom obtain in the modern economy, employment decisions are not based on a single period's labor cost (section 1.4), and for the cost concept that is relevant to employers' decisions, the single period labor cost is not well defined. The identical problem has been discussed in the literature on the measurement of capital and of consumer prices, so it is known to require information about future prices or expected prices. The problem is no more and no less difficult when the objective is measuring labor cost, but the important point is that this serious difficulty be recognized.

Whether a single period measure is relevant or not, perhaps the most basic question to the entire inquiry is whether a labor cost measure can be distinguished uniquely from a measure of all input costs. In the stylized model, this issue takes the form of an empirical question about cost function separability (section 1.2), but in this there is nothing unique to labor input; the technical issue of separability can be raised about any class of inputs, from lubricants to office supplies. What makes the labor input uniquely difficult is that the seller of labor cares not just about the wage but also about employment conditions and other characteristics of the buyer. Because there is so much employer heterogeneity, the variety in compensation packages will be great. And variation in elements of the compensation package leads to variation in the quantities of other inputs, especially capital. This dependence between quantities of one input and "prices" paid for another poses special and very difficult problems for the measurement of labor cost.

This essay began with the observation that labor economists tended to view the subject as too difficult because of the institutional detail, while theorists thought it conceptually too simple to be worth much attention. It concludes with the observation that—whatever the jungle of institutional detail that must be considered—the greatest difficulties are conceptual ones. That, of course, is why economists should find the subject interesting.

Notes

1. The theory of consumption price measurement stretches back to Wicksell, but see Fisher and Shell (1972), Pollak (1971), Samuelson and Swamy (1974), Diewert (1976), Blackorby, Primont, and Russell (1978), and Deaton and Muellbauer (1980). A survey of empirical studies in price measurement is Triplett (1975). See also Griliches (1971).

2. Information sources for the surveys cited include: Center for Human Resource Research (1975) for NLS; Duncan and Morgan (1975) for PSID; Rees (1974), Kehrer (1979), and Spiegleman and Yeager (1980) for the Income Maintenance Experiments; Mellow (1981) and U.S. Department of Labor (1980) for CPS data.

3. Though I believe there is no question that the demand side of labor economics has been neglected, the habit of thinking only in supply-side terms is so ingrained that experience shows I should present an example to support the statements in the text. The regional wage differential literature in labor economics will serve.

Johnson, in this volume, notes a "current consensus" that a North-South differential exists in nominal wages, but not in real wages; the literature he cites and the model of his paper take these putative facts as consistent with labor market equilibrium: ". . . other things equal, a 1 percent increase in the cost of living in an area will increase the equilibrium wage in that area by 1 percent" (Johnson, this volume, p. 311). But a nominal wage differential implies a production cost differential, and, if employer mobility exists, will provoke interregional movement of employers, unless somehow the wage differential is offset by cost differentials for other factors (highly unlikely if there are opportunities for employer specialization). Equivalence between nominal wage and cost-of-living differentials is consistent only with predictions from the theory of worker behavior and is not consistent with general equilibrium at all. In fact, an empirical finding so extraordinarily inconsistent with theoretical prediction is suspect; if it were true, it ought to suggest a vigorous research effort to determine why. Instead, it seems to be an article of faith that nominal wage differentials, when found, can be "explained" by living cost differentials. For a more balanced view of regional differentials, see Hanushek (1981); the regional economics literature has also treated economic differentials from an alternative perspective (see the items cited by Muth, this volume).

4. It is astonishing, but nevertheless true, that at this date one still has to defend the use of measurement theory in formulating economic measurements, even among researchers who comfortably use labor market theory for other purposes. One can only guess about the reasons for such an anachronism, but one possibility is the relative lack of understanding, even among sophisticated data users, of the conceptual complexity of some of the issues that arise in the construction of economic data combined with impatience with theoretical work that does not produce immediately usable "answers." The main use of theory in economic

measurement is to sharpen measurement concepts and to provide an integrated framework against which *consistent* resolution of practical measurement problems can be assured. To be useful, the theory need not—and seldom does—provide ready "cookbook" guidance for measurement decisions. Its role is comparable to John Maynard Keynes's description of the relation between economic analysis and economic policy:

> The Theory of Economics does not furnish a body of settled conclusions immediately applicable to policy. It is a method rather than a doctrine, an apparatus of the mind, a technique of thinking, which helps its possessor to draw correct conclusions. (as quoted in Reder 1982, p. 16)

The use of theory in measurement does not assure that the measurements will always be correct, but experience has shown that the alternative produces ad hoc, inconsistent, and ultimately indefensible decisions.

5. Terminology is not uniform in the literature in part because the explicit literature on the theory of input price measurement is sparse. Caves, Christensen, and Diewert (1982) employ the term "Malmquist index" of input prices. Also, an "input cost index" sometimes refers to a computation intended as a proxy for an output price index (a weighted average of wage rates and materials prices, for example, in lieu of a measure of the price of construction), but that is not the purpose of the measurement discussed in this essay.

6. Actually only their factor quantity index numbers are explicitly based on the translog model; their factor price indexes are defined implicitly with respect to this model and are not derived (as exact input cost indexes would be) from the cost function that is associated with their production model. There is little reason for supposing this makes much difference in their labor cost measures. Deriving the labor cost indexes from the cost function that is dual to the translog production model would be prohibitively expensive, owing to properties of the translog model that, in general, assure that factor quantity and factor price indexes have different functional forms. For the theoretical statement of these issues, see Samuelson and Swamy (1974) and Diewert (1980).

7. Braithwait (1980) found that the Laspeyres index differed from exact indexes of consumption prices by only about one-tenth of an index point per year, a result compatible with estimates in Christensen and Manser (1976) and Goldberger and Gameletsos (1970). Diewert (1976) and Caves, Christensen, and Diewert (1982) show theoretically that certain types of conventional index number formulas will give close approximations to exact indexes.

8. "Roughly" because separability of the cost function is equivalent to comparable separability of the production function only for certain production function forms, not all of them. See Blackorby, Primont, and Russell (1978).

9. The appropriateness of the Grant and Hamermesh approach requires interpreting their demographic groupings as proxies for distinct inputs to the production process—that is, if occupations, skill levels, or other characteristics actually define categories of labor input (the L_i's of eq. [14]), one must assume that these characteristics vary by age, sex, and race in such a way that the latter identify, at least partly, the former. See the discussion of this point in section 1.6.2.

10. The parameter ψ indicates the rate of exchange between benefits and wages on the boundary of the worker's choice set. It can be identified as a locational parameter selected from a hedonic frontier (see section 1.6.3, and also Atrostic 1982, who implements a similar approach empirically). Competition will tend to bring ψ into equality both with the price at which workers could buy benefits on the market and with the employer's marginal cost of providing them (see eq. [8]), and for this reason the price of benefits has often been assumed to be one or the other. Taking the market price of benefits as the value of ψ, however, introduces the implicit assumption that the worker can sell them, which is generally untrue. Setting ψ identically equal to the employer's marginal cost of providing benefits is likewise inappropriate, because benefits are presumably provided when the worker places a higher

value on inframarginal units of them than it costs the employer to provide them. Assuming in the worker's full income constraint that ψ is measured by either the market price of benefits or the employer's cost of providing them improperly introduces elements of the solution to a maximization problem into the constraint that bounds the problem. Put another way, this assumption amounts to specifying that equation (8) is identically true for all levels of benefits, when in fact equation (8) holds only for the benefit level that corresponds to the cost minimizing and utility maximizing employer-employee contract point.

11. Labor supply to a firm is composed of an hours of work decision and a choice of employer. Equation (4) does not necessarily require that workers have different labor supply responses to wages than to benefits, though the results of Atrostic (1982) suggest this to be the case. It does imply that, once in the labor market, workers will choose among alternative employers according to their preferences among employer provided benefits and market purchased consumption goods. Moreover, the choice of employer (and therefore the employer's task of selecting an appropriate package of wages and benefits) is not trivial, since alternative compensation packages are available in the market either because employers have different relative costs of providing various benefits, or because workers have different preferences for benefits, or both. See Antos and Rosen (1974).

12. Freeman (1981) discusses the case in which there are start-up costs for offering a benefit to employees, which introduces another term on the right-hand side of equation (8). This has no effect on the results and is ignored here for simplicity.

13. Some researchers (including Smeeding in this volume and Woodbury 1981), reasoning that because benefits are not taxed they are worth more to workers, have used the marginal tax rate to inflate the value of benefits, rather than reducing the quantity of goods that can be purchased out of wage income (as suggested in the text and as incorporated into the work of Leibowitz in this volume). This practice seems to reflect the habit of writing wages as an argument of the utility function instead of (or as a proxy for) the market purchased goods that belong there, and of omitting either one equation (typically the demand for leisure) or one price (usually consumption goods) from the system being analyzed. In some cases the only objection to the alternative treatment is that it lacks elegance; in others, however, errors result, as David points out in his comment in this volume, because the lack of clarity obscures mistakes in logic.

14. David, in this volume, makes the excellent point that the marginal tax rate will in the long run itself be a function of the proportion of income taken in the form of benefits (because tax rates will be adjusted upward to recoup the revenue loss). This means that taxes will only affect the consumption of benefits of the average worker if there is some sort of money illusion; but because the growth of nontaxable benefits shifts tax burdens toward lower income workers, the main effect of nontaxable benefits may be on income distribution and not on the average consumption of benefits and market purchased goods.

15. Freeman (1981) presents five possible reasons, but the only one I find logically supportable is the possibility that workers can have more faith that benefit plans are sound when a union acts as their agent to oversee them and would, accordingly, be more willing to trade wages for benefits in unionized firms. This motivation seems inadequate to account for the size of the union-nonunion differential in benefits.

16. Atrostic (1981) presents findings that suggest the "single parent" model predominates: Other things equal, female dominated workplaces have higher levels of benefits.

17. For the policy relevance of the elasticity of demand for labor, see Solow's (1980) presidential address.

18. See the table on p. 504 of Freeman (1981). The difference between the two estimates reported in the text is statistically significant at the .01 level.

19. I form this estimate from comparing the ECNT (which includes an estimate of hiring, training, and turnover costs) and COSTWK measures of table C.2 in Appendix C of this volume. The comparable figure for manufacturing in 1978 was 13–14 percent.

20. Oi cites J. M. Clark. Morgenstern (1963, p. 186) includes the "value of tenure" as an element of labor cost.

21. This error is implied by Okun's discussion of Oi's work (Okun 1981, pp. 17, 24).

22. On the other hand, I do not understand Lazear's words, "without counting the output of the human capital," that follow the passage quoted. Because firm-specific human capital is by definition useful only to the firm itself, its production can only be regarded as an intermediate input for the firm in question; thus, it is not failing to account for its *output* in equation (12) that leads to the error, but inappropriately accounting for its *input* in equation (11).

23. Hamermesh's data series are reproduced in Appendix C.

24. This explanation has an ancient history. However, my own observation, from a relatively short tenure as a construction worker quite a number of years ago, is that the trade attracts individuals who have strong preferences for consuming leisure in concentrated and uninterrupted blocks of time. Thus, construction workers tend to be those for whom employment interruptions require the smallest premiums (Thaler and Rosen 1976 make the same point in a different context). The compensating wage differential explanation may be only part of the reason why construction wages have traditionally been higher than in alternative employments.

25. Some contracts make it clear that the incentive for entering into the contract came from the other side of the market and that what was wanted was assured demand.

26. Diewert (1980, p. 475) writes: "In the previous section I may have left the impression that from a theoretical point of view constructing a capital aggregate is no more difficult than constructing a labor aggregate." He then proceeds to list and discuss complexities that make capital measurement a particularly difficult problem, including price expectations, interest and depreciation rates, treatment of taxes, definition of the capital input, time period for measurement, choice of index numbers, and so forth. Since most of this catalog of the "special problems" of capital measurement appear in some form in this essay as problems of labor cost measurement, I would modify Diewert's statement to read: "From a modern understanding of the labor market, constructing a labor aggregate is little, if any, less difficult than constructing a capital aggregate."

27. See references in note 2.

28. Seiler (1982) reports that a compensating differential for earnings uncertainty accounts for up to 50 percent of the higher earnings of incentive pay workers in some occupations in the industries he studied, though the average appears to be substantially lower.

29. Lazear (1981) notes that piece-rate compensation is the extreme case of a short-run labor contract, in which workers are compensated only for current period output. In normal cases, a worker's current period compensation is at least in part a reward for performance in past periods. Piece-rate payment systems will evolve when the costs of supervision are high.

30. Terleckyj (1976), particularly the articles by Ohta-Griliches, King, and Triplett, with the discussion by Barzel and Ingram.

31. This section is based in part on Triplett (1976), modified to apply to labor markets.

32. In Triplett (1976) I introduced the device of characterizing hedonic transactions in consumer goods as if consumers purchased groceries in preloaded carts, with prices attached to the carts. The preloaded carts play the role of conventional goods, variations in the assortments of groceries they contain amount to quality differences as we usually think of them, and the quantities of the various groceries are the characteristics. The characteristics (groceries) are, of course, the true arguments of the utility function, not the goods (the preloaded carts). Estimating hedonic functions on the preloaded grocery carts is equivalent to determining the prices charged for the individual grocery items. The price attached to the *cart* is simply total expenditures on the groceries contained in it. The grocery cart simile carries over by analogy to the case of labor input.

33. In the supplier case, the characteristics are viewed as joint outputs of a productive

process. Implications of this approach in the context of measuring output and productivity are discussed in Triplett (1982).

34. Both cases imply that hedonic functions will differ by occupation, either in the coefficients (implicit prices) on the characteristics they have in common, or in differing lists of characteristics included in them. In the consumption case, I have suggested (Triplett 1971) that testing for equivalence of hedonic functions across commodity groupings is one way of resolving the old empirical problem: "What is a product?" The extension of that idea to the labor market implies that hedonic functions can in principle be used to distinguish between groups of workers who are appropriately classified as separate factors of production, as distinct from other groupings that may represent differing qualities of what is essentially the same productive factor. Clerical workers or blue-collar workers are appropriate empirical groupings if a single hedonic function describes all the workers in the group; if not, one tests lower level aggregations, such as secretaries or machinists. This empirical rule using hedonic functions amounts to an extension of Hicksian aggregation theorems into characteristics space, since in effect the "rule" permits aggregation over characteristics so long as characteristics prices (the hedonic coefficients) move together in the cross section. This proposal is quite different from that of Cain, Hansen, and Weisbrod (1967) and offers substantial empirical advantages for testing existing occupational classifications for economic relevance.

35. The literature contains an enormous amount of confusion about the relation between empirical "hedonic price indexes" and the exact or theoretical price index. The usual source of confusion is the failure to distinguish between the hedonic function itself (eq. [13]) or its derivative, the β function of equation (16), and the characteristics input cost index based on equation (18). This confusion has led to the misguided attempt to derive the former from the latter, or to use the functional form of the production or cost function to derive permissible functional forms for the hedonic function—as, for example, in Lucas (1975) and Muellbauer (1974). Since articles of this genre seem always to conclude (incorrectly) that the well-worked semilog form is impermissible for hedonic functions, it is worth emphasizing that the functional form of the β function, and hence of the hedonic function itself, is independent of the form of production, cost, or utility functions and is wholly an empirical matter. Assertions to the contrary by Lucas and Muellbauer are really statements that the cost function of equation (18) cannot adequately be represented by a semilog function, a fact that is well known; the form of equation (18) says nothing about the form of the hedonic function.

36. The parentheses make explicit reference to the distinction between direct and indirect separability. See note 8.

37. Fisher and Shell (1972) present an insightful analysis of quality change from the traditional view that probably extracts as much from that approach as can be obtained. Nevertheless, their discussion of "parametrizable" quality change has limited applicability to empirical work and leaves the nature of quality change so obscure that its parameter cannot be distinguished from technical change that shifts the production function.

38. The empirical use of proxy variables and proxy relations is not restricted to labor market hedonic functions; it is an integral part of the empirical tradition of hedonic functions in product markets, where the problems created by the use of proxies are well known (Triplett 1969).

39. If

$$\ln \Pi = \beta_0 + \beta_1 X_1 + \beta_2 X_2 + e, \text{ then}$$
$$\partial X_1/\partial X_2 \ (\ln \Pi = \text{const.}) = \beta_2/\beta_1,$$

which is clearly a constant for all X_1 and X_2. Thus, the semilog function yields a linear β function, which means it is linear in what might be called the relative price dimension, which is the one that matters most for doing demand analysis. That all $\partial \ln \Pi/\partial X_i$ are increasing within the semilog form means that increasing outlays on characteristics imply increasing unit characteristics costs, when the characteristics are purchased in a single "package." See Triplett (1976) for further discussion.

40. The uniqueness of both worker and employer does present the possibility that workers will be assigned among employers in such a manner that each will be located in a uniquely "best" job match. If so, none of the available alternative job opportunities for a particular worker will offer an exactly equivalent bundle of job characteristics, and no other worker will be quite so satisfactory for the employer. But given a large enough number of employers and workers, unique assignments will create only small deviations and the statement in the text will be approximately true.

41. Because this example is intended only to be illustrative, and then only for labor cost measurement, there is no need to discuss the numerous caveats that would be necessary for a serious analysis of safety. In particular, there is nothing in equation (8) that shows that the amount of safety provided by the market is the "right" amount by some criterion, or that shows that workers can always correctly judge differences in safety between similar jobs, or that pertains to any of the issues surrounding the regulation of workplace health and safety. See Thaler and Rosen (1976).

References

Antos, Joseph R., and Sherwin Rosen. 1974. Discrimination in the market for public school teachers. *Journal of Econometrics* 3: 123–50.

Atrostic, B. K. 1981. Alternative pay measures and labor market differentials. BLS Working Paper 127. Washington, D.C.: U.S. Bureau of Labor Statistics.

———. 1982. The demand for leisure and nonpecuniary job characteristics. *American Economic Review* 72: 428–40.

Azariadis, Costas. 1975. Implicit contracts and underemployment equilibria. *Journal of Political Economy* 83: 1183–1202.

Baily, Martin N. 1974. Wages and employment under uncertain demand. *Review of Economic Studies* 41: 37–50.

Barzel, Yoram. 1976. Comment on "Automobile prices revisited: Extensions of the hedonic hypothesis." In Terleckyj 1976.

Berndt, Ernst R., and Laurits R. Christensen. 1973. The specification of technology in U.S. manufacturing. BLS Working Paper 18. Washington, D.C.: U.S. Bureau of Labor Statistics.

———. 1974 Testing for the existence of a consistent aggregate index of labor inputs. *American Economic Review* 64: 391–404.

Blackorby, Charles, Daniel Primont, and R. Robert Russell. 1978. *Duality, separability, and functional structure: Theory and economic applications*. New York: North-Holland.

Braithwait, Steven D. 1980. The substitution bias of the Laspeyres price index: An analysis using estimated cost-of-living indexes. *American Economic Review* 70: 64–77.

Brown, Charles. 1980. Equalizing differences in the labor market. *Quarterly Journal of Economics* 94: 113–33.

Brown, Gardner, and Robert Mendelsohn. 1981. Hedonic demand functions with linear and nonlinear budget constraints. University of Washington Discussion Paper 81–12. Seattle, Wash.: University of Washington.

Cain, Glen, W. Lee Hansen, and Burton A. Weisbrod. 1967. Occupational classification: An economic approach. *Monthly Labor Review* 90: 48–52.

Caves, Douglas W., Laurits R. Christensen, and W. Erwin Diewert. 1982. The economic theory of index numbers and the measurement of input, output, and productivity. *Econometrica* 50: 1393–1414.

Center for Human Resource Research. 1975. *The national longitudinal surveys handbook*. College of Administrative Science, The Ohio State University.

Christensen, Laurits R., and Marilyn E. Manser. 1976. Cost-of-living indexes and price indexes for U.S. meat and produce, 1947–1971. In Terleckyj 1976.

Cleeton, David L. 1982. The theory of real wage indices. *American Economic Review* 72: 214–25.

Deaton, Angus, and John Muellbauer. 1980. *Economics and consumer behavior*. New York: Cambridge University Press.

Diewert, W. E. 1976. Exact and superlative index numbers. *Journal of Econometrics* 4: 115–45.

———. 1980. Aggregation problems in the measurement of capital. In Usher 1980.

———. 1981. The economic theory of index numbers: A survey. In *Essays in the theory and measurement of consumer behavior in honour of Sir Richard Stone*, ed. Angus Deaton, 163–208. Cambridge University Press.

Duncan, Greg J. 1976. Earnings functions and nonpecuniary benefits. *Journal of Human Resources* 11: 462–83.

Duncan, Greg J., and James N. Morgan, eds. 1975. *Five thousand American families—putterns of economic progress*, vol. 3. Ann Arbor, Mich.: The Institute for Social Research, The University of Michigan.

Duncan, Greg J., and Frank Stafford. 1980. Do union members receive compensating wage differentials? *American Economic Review* 70: 353–71.

Dunlop, John T. 1977. Policy decisions and research in economics and industrial relations. *Industrial and Labor Relations Review* 30: 275–82.

Ehrenberg, Ronald G., Daniel S. Hamermesh, and George E. Johnson. 1977. Comment. *Industrial and Labor Relations Review* 31: 10–13.

Feldstein, Martin. 1976. Temporary layoffs in the theory of unemployment. *Journal of Political Economy* 84: 937–58.

Fisher, Franklin, and Karl Shell. 1972. *The economic theory of price indices: Two essays on the effects of taste, quality, and technological change*. New York: Academic Press.

Fleisher, Belton M., and Thomas J. Kniesner. 1980. *Labor economics*. 2d ed. Englewood Cliffs, N.J.: Prentice-Hall, Inc.
Freeman, Richard B. 1981. The effect of unionism on fringe benefits. *Industrial and Labor Relations Review* 34: 489–509.
Gillingham, Robert F. 1974. A conceptual framework for the consumer price index. In *Proceedings of the business and economic statistics section*, 246–52. Washington, D.C.: American Statistical Association.
———. 1983. Measuring the cost of shelter for homeowners: Theoretical and empirical considerations. *Review of Economics and Statistics*, forthcoming.
Goldberger, Arthur S., and Theodore Gameletsos. 1970. A cross-country comparison of consumer expenditure patterns. *European Economic Review* 1: 357–400.
Gollop, Frank M., and Dale W. Jorgenson. 1980. U.S. productivity growth by industry. In *New developments in productivity measurement and analysis*, ed. J. W. Kendrick and B. Vaccara. Conference on Research in Income and Wealth: Studies in Income and Wealth, vol. 44. Chicago, Ill.: University of Chicago Press for the National Bureau of Economic Research.
Gordon, Donald F. 1974. A neo-classical theory of Keynesian unemployment. *Economic Inquiry* 12: 431–59.
Grant, James, and Daniel S. Hamermesh. 1981. Labor market competition among youths, white women, and others. *Review of Economics and Statistics* 63: 354–60.
Griliches, Zvi, ed. 1971. *Price indexes and quality change: Studies in new methods of measurement*. Cambridge, Mass.: Harvard University Press.
———. 1977. Estimating the returns to schooling: Some econometric problems. *Econometrica* 45: 1–22.
Hall, Robert E. 1982. The importance of lifetime jobs in the U.S. economy. *American Economic Review* 72: 716–24.
Hanushek, Eric A. 1981. Alternative models of earnings determination and labor market structures. *Journal of Human Resources* 16: 238–59.
Hicks, John R. 1963. *The theory of wages*. 2d ed. London: Macmillan.
Ingram, Gregory. 1976. Comments on "The demand for housing: Integrating the roles of journey-to-work, neighborhood quality, and prices." In Terleckyj 1976.
International Labor Office. 1979. *An integrated system of wages statistics: A manual on methods*. Geneva: International Labor Office.
Katz, Arnold, and Joseph E. Hight, eds. 1977. The economics of unemployment insurance: A symposium. *Industrial and Labor Relations Review* 30: 431–526.
Kehrer, Kenneth C. 1979. The Gary income maintenance experiment: Introduction. *Journal of Human Resources* 14: 431–33.

King, A. Thomas. 1976. The demand for housing: Integrating the roles of journey-to-work, neighborhood quality, and prices. In Terleckyj 1976.

Lancaster, Kelvin. 1971. *Consumer demand: A new approach*. New York: Columbia University Press.

Layard, Richard. 1979. Introduction. *Journal of Political Economy* 87: S1–S5.

Lazear, Edward P. 1976. Age, experience, and wage growth. *American Economic Review* 66: 548–58.

———. 1979. Why is there mandatory retirement? *Journal of Political Economy* 87: 1261–84.

———. 1981. Agency, earnings profiles, productivity, and hours restrictions. *American Economic Review* 71: 606–20.

Lazear, Edward P., and Robert L. Moore. 1981. Incentives, productivity, and long-term labor contracts. Paper read at the annual meeting of the Western Economic Association.

Lucas, R. E. B. 1975. Hedonic price functions. *Economic Inquiry* 13: 157–78.

Mellow, Wesley. 1981. Unionism and wages: A longitudinal analysis. *Review of Economics and Statistics* 63: 43–52.

———. 1982. Employer size and wages. *Review of Economics and Statistics* 64: 495–501.

Mincer, Jacob. 1974. *Schooling, experience, and earnings*. New York: National Bureau of Economic Research.

Mitchell, Olivia S., and Emily S. Andrews. 1981. Scale economies in private multi-employer pension systems. *Industrial and Labor Relations Review* 34: 522–30.

Morgenstern, Oskar. 1963. *On the accuracy of economic observations*. 2d ed. Princeton, N.J.: Princeton University Press.

Muellbauer, John. 1974. Household production theory, quality, and the "hedonic technique." *American Economic Review* 64: 977–94.

Muth, Richard F. 1974. Moving costs and housing expenditure. *Journal of Urban Economics* 1: 108–25.

Ohta, Makoto, and Zvi Griliches. 1976. Automobile prices revisited: Extensions of the hedonic hypothesis. In Terleckyj 1976.

Oi, Walter Y. 1962. Labor as a quasi-fixed factor. *Journal of Political Economy* 70: 538–55.

Okun, Arthur M. 1981. *Prices and quantities: A macroeconomic analysis*. Washington, D.C.: The Brookings Institution.

Pencavel, John H. 1977. Constant-utility index numbers of real wages. *American Economic Review* 67: 91–100.

Phelps, Edmund S. et al. 1970. *Microeconomic foundations of employment and inflation theory*. New York: W. W. Norton.

Pollak, Robert A. 1971. The theory of the cost of living index. BLS Working Paper 11. Washington, D.C.: U.S. Bureau of Labor Statistics.

———. 1975*a*. Subindexes of the cost of living. *International Economic Review* 16: 135–50.

———. 1975*b*. The intertemporal cost of living index. *Annals of Economic and Social Measurement* 4: 179–95.

———. 1983. The treatment of "quality" in the cost of living index. *Journal of Public Economics*, forthcoming.

Pollak, Robert A., and Michael L. Wachter. 1975. The relevance of the household production function and its implications for the allocation of time. *Journal of Political Economy* 83: 255–77.

Price Statistics Review Committee. 1961. The price statistics of the federal government. In U.S. Congress, Joint Economic Committee. *Government Price Statistics, Hearings*, pt. 1. 87th Cong. 1st sess. (also published as National Bureau of Economic Research, General Series, no. 73).

Reder, Melvin W. 1982. Chicago economics: Permanence and change. *Journal of Economic Literature* 20: 1–38.

Rees, Albert. 1974. An overview of the labor-supply results. *Journal of Human Resources* 9: 97–100.

Roback, Jennifer. 1982. Wages, rents, and the quality of life. Unpublished paper. New Haven, Conn.: Yale University.

Rosen, Sherwin. 1974. Hedonic prices and implicit markets: Product differentiation in pure competition. *Journal of Political Economy* 92: 34–55.

———. 1977. Human capital: A survey of empirical research. In *Research in labor economics*, ed. R. G. Ehrenberg. Greenwich, Conn.: JAI Press.

Samuelson, Paul A., and S. Swamy. 1974. Invariant economic index numbers and canonical duality: Survey and synthesis. *American Economic Review* 64: 566–93.

Seiler, Eric. 1982. Piece rate vs. time rate: The effect of incentives on earnings. NBER Working Paper no. 879. Cambridge, Mass.: National Bureau of Economic Research.

Sider, Hal. 1981. Work-related accidents and the production process. BLS Working Paper 117. Washington, D.C.: U.S. Bureau of Labor Statistics.

Smith, Robert. 1979. Compensating wage differentials and public policy: A review. *Industrial and Labor Relations Review* 32: 339–52.

Solow, Robert M. 1980. On theories of unemployment. *American Economic Review* 70: 1–11.

Spiegleman, Robert G., and K. E. Yeager. 1980. The Seattle and Denver income maintenance experiments: Overview. *Journal of Human Resources* 15: 463–79.

Stigler, George J., and James K. Kindahl. 1970. *The behavior of industrial prices*. New York: National Bureau of Economic Research.

Terleckyj, Nestor E., ed. 1976. *Household production and consumption*.

Conference on Research in Income and Wealth: Studies in Income and Wealth, vol. 40. New York: National Bureau of Economic Research.

Thaler, Richard, and Sherwin Rosen. 1976. The value of saving a life: Evidence from the labor market. In Terleckyj 1976.

Triplett, Jack E. 1969. Automobiles and hedonic quality measurement. *Journal of Political Economy* 77: 408–17.

———. 1971. The theory of hedonic quality measurement and its use in price indexes. BLS Staff Paper 6. Washington, D.C.: U.S. Bureau of Labor Statistics.

———. 1975. The measurement of inflation: A survey of research on the accuracy of price indexes. In *Analysis of inflation*, ed. Paul H. Earl. Lexington, Mass.: Lexington Books.

———. 1976. Consumer demand and characteristics of consumption goods. In Terleckyj 1976.

———. 1983. Concepts of quality in input and output price measures: A resolution of the user value-resource cost debate. In *The U.S. national income and product accounts: Selected topics*, ed. Murray Foss. Conference on Research in Income and Wealth: Studies in Income and Wealth, vol. 47. Chicago, Ill.: University of Chicago Press for the National Bureau of Economic Research.

United States Department of Labor. 1980. Using the current population survey as a longitudinal data base. BLS Report 608. Washington, D.C.: U.S. Bureau of Labor Statistics.

Usher, Dan, ed. 1980. *The measurement of capital*. Conference on Research in Income and Wealth: Studies in Income and Wealth, vol. 45. Chicago, Ill.: University of Chicago Press for the National Bureau of Economic Research.

Woodbury, Stephen A. 1981. Estimating preferences for wage and nonwage benefits. NBER Conference Paper Series, Conference Paper no. 102. Cambridge, Mass.: National Bureau of Economic Research.

PART

I Overview: Concepts, Methodology, and Data

2 The Fixed Employment Costs of Specialized Labor

Walter Y. Oi

The discipline of labor economics has now accepted the proposition that labor is a quasi-fixed factor of production. The basic idea can be traced to J. M. Clark (1923) in *Studies in the Economics of Overhead Costs*. The fixed cost hypothesis was developed to explain the occupational differences in employment and wage rate responses to cyclical fluctuations in the aggregate level of output and employment. The early models did not provide satisfactory explanations for the macroeconomic behavior of unemployment and money wages. Search and contract theories were constructed to fill this void. Hall emphasized the importance of long-term "permanent" jobs which provide the support for contract theories of the labor market. But contract and search theories must ultimately rest on a foundation of fixed costs of one sort or another. Prudent research strategy calls for us to inquire about the factors that can explain why firms and individuals choose to invest in specialized resources which generate these fixed costs.

I shall advance the hypothesis that specialized labor and fixed employment costs are derivatives of an organization of production that reflects the heterogeneity of firms. A comparatively small number of firms grow to extraordinarily large sizes because they are controlled by exceptionally talented and able entrepreneurs. They assemble large production teams by adopting rigid, batch assembly line production processes that are most efficient for the volume production of standardized goods. Each giant

Walter Y. Oi is professor of economics at the University of Rochester, New York, and the Hoover Institution.

The author wishes to thank Jack Triplett, whose encouragement persuaded him to undertake this project. Conversations with Barbara Mann and Stanley Engerman helped to clarify his thoughts. The tabulations from the May CPS were carried out by Barbara Mann. The author alone is responsible for remaining flaws.

firm is characterized by a sufficiently unique organization that can justify and sustain the substantial investments in recruiting and firm-specific training which are optimal only for the largest firms. Employee compensation packages are designed to attract and retain specifically trained workers. Those employees who join and remain with the giant firms are rewarded by implicit contracts that guarantee stable wages and tenured employment. Other individuals who prefer the flexibility and adaptability of small establishments must accept the risks of employment instability due to the shorter life expectancy of small firms. Rigid production techniques and intertemporal substitutions of maintenance activities provide an explanation for Okun's law which deals with the procyclical movements of labor productivity. The empirical evidence and theory developed in this paper support the conclusion that the concept of firm-specific human capital is only applicable to one sector of the economy, namely, the large firms with one thousand or more employees.

2.1 The Quasi-Fixity of Labor

> Once the holding of unused productive capacity was conceived as "idle overhead," it was inevitable that the idea should be extended to human powers as well as to the powers of physical plant and machinery. . . . Wherever a laborer has invested time and money in specialized training, the result is in a sense *fixed capital* which is useful in one occupation and in no other and which must earn whatever return it can because the investment cannot be withdrawn and moved into some other line of business. In such a case, it seems fairly clear that labor involves an overhead cost. (J. M. Clark, 1923, p. 15)

This excerpt contains the ideas of labor as a quasi-fixed factor and of firm-specific human capital.

The cyclical behavior of labor markets exhibits an uneven incidence of unemployment, a compression of occupational wage differentials in the upswing, persistent differences in labor turnover rates, and hiring/firing practices that smack of discrimination. If the partial elasticity of substitution of skilled labor A for the fixed factor capital K is less than that of unskilled labor B for K ($\sigma_{AK} < \sigma_{BK}$), the larger cyclical shifts in demand for unskilled labor can be explained by a neoclassical theory of factor demands. However, that theory cannot explain lags in turning points or differences in labor turnover. These phenomena can better be understood by introducing the concept of labor as a quasi-fixed factor.

Labor cost contains two components—a variable wage that must be paid to obtain a worker's services and a fixed employment cost that a firm incurs to acquire and train a specific stock of employees. In equilibrium, labor's marginal value product (MVP) is equated to the sum of the expected wage plus the amortization of the fixed employment cost, $q = F/\Sigma(1+r)^{-t}$; MVP $= W + q$. Since q is a sunk cost, workers in a particular skill will be retained as long as MVP exceeds the variable wage. Workers with high degrees of fixity, meaning high ratios $[q/(W+q)]$, thus experience smaller relative fluctuations in factor demands. Further, the returns to an investment in fixed employment costs can be increased by adopting policies that reduce labor turnover. One should therefore find a negative correlation between an occupation's degree of fixity and its labor turnover rate. The empirical tests generally confirmed the implications of a theory of labor as a quasi-fixed factor.[1]

2.2 Unemployment and Rigid Wages

Quasi-fixity cannot explain the persistence of involuntary unemployment and the sluggish response of wages to changes in aggregate demand. I shall not try to survey the substantial literature that has been motivated by these phenomena. I shall instead provide a brief review of the salient facts and summarize my assessment of search and contract theories. The value of search and contracts obviously depends on the duration of employment relations, which is discussed in section 2.2.4.

2.2.1 The Macrobehavior of the Private Business Sector

In the postwar period, 1947–79, output of the private business sector almost trebled from an index of 48.7 to 144.0 (table 2.1). Fluctuations in output and labor input (measured by man-hours or unemployment rates) were only weakly correlated. Procyclical movements in labor productivity and hours per employee accounted for much of the year-to-year changes in output. Hall (1980) emphasized the absence of market clearing adjustments in money wages; the simple correlation between annual rates of changes in man-hours and wages was −.123 for the decade of the 1970s. Data for the longer time series, 1947–79, suggest that the economy may have undergone a structural change, but the two key puzzles which were emphasized by Hall still remain. We must still explain why wages fail to clear the labor market and why labor productivity follows a strong procyclical pattern.

2.2.2 Search and the Pseudoidleness of Prospectors

Idleness can be efficient. Stigler (1962) and Alchian (1969) recognized that search was costly, but unemployed workers willingly incurred these costs to find and secure better paying jobs. In Hutt's (1977) terminology, an unemployed worker is in *pseudoidleness* while he is searching for work or serving the productive function of *availability*—awaiting a call to fill a specialized job.[2]

Table 2.1 Productivity and Related Variables[a]

Year	Output X	Total Hours H	Hourly Compen-sation W	Price Deflator P	Adult Pop. (20–64) N	Labor Force LF	Employed Persons E
1947	48.7	90.9	36.0	65.1	84,969	59,350	57,038
1948	50.9	91.5	39.0	70.6	86,013	60,621	58,343
1949	50.0	88.5	39.7	69.8	87,021	61,286	57,651
1950	54.6	89.5	42.4	70.8	88,201	62,208	58,918
1951	57.8	92.1	46.6	76.0	89,017	62,017	59,961
1952	59.5	92.2	49.6	77.1	89,729	62,138	60,250
1953	62.0	93.2	52.8	77.9	90,242	63,015	61,179
1954	60.9	90.1	54.5	78.6	90,775	63,643	60,109
1955	65.7	93.5	55.8	79.8	91,414	65,023	62,170
1956	67.6	94.9	59.5	82.2	92,052	66,552	63,799
1957	68.5	93.5	63.4	84.8	92,634	66,929	64,071
1958	67.0	89.3	66.2	86.4	93,202	67,639	63,036
1959	71.9	92.8	69.0	88.1	93,824	68,369	64,630
1960	73.2	92.9	71.9	89.3	94,477	69,628	65,778

1961	74.2	91.5	74.6	89.8	95,289	70,459	65,746
1962	78.8	92.9	78.1	90.6	96,227	70,614	66,702
1963	82.3	93.4	81.0	91.4	97,490	71,833	67,762
1964	86.9	94.9	85.3	92.7	98,565	73,091	69,305
1965	92.9	97.8	88.7	94.2	99,574	74,455	71,088
1966	98.1	100.0	94.9	97.2	100,585	75,770	72,895
1967	100.0	100.0	100.0	100.0	102,635	77,347	74,372
1968	105.1	101.8	107.6	103.9	104,353	78,737	75,920
1969	108.3	104.6	114.9	108.8	105,981	80,734	77,902
1970	107.3	103.0	123.1	113.9	107,594	82,715	78,627
1971	110.3	102.4	131.4	118.9	109,313	84,113	79,120
1972	117.5	105.5	139.7	123.2	111,071	86,542	81,720
1973	124.4	109.6	151.2	130.3	112,833	88,714	84,409
1974	121.4	110.3	164.9	143.1	114,653	91,011	85,934
1975	118.7	105.6	181.3	157.5	116,510	92,613	84,783
1976	126.4	108.6	197.2	165.5	118,466	94,773	87,485
1977	133.8	112.8	213.0	174.8	120,578	97,401	90,546
1978	140.7	118.1	231.2	187.2	122,717	100,420	94,373
1979	144.0	122.0	252.8	203.8	124,797	102,908	96,945

Source: Economic Report of the President, 1980, table B-37, p. 246.

[a]The first four columns are indexes with 1967 as the base. The last three columns are in thousands.

> When actively searching for work, the situation is that he is really investing in himself by working on his own account without immediate remuneration. He is *prospecting*. He is doing what he would pay an efficient employment agency to do if the course of politics had allowed this sort of institution to emerge in modern society. He judges that the search for a better opening was worth the risk of immediately forgone income. If his relatives or his friends or the state is keeping him, then in a sense they also may sometimes be regarded as investing in him, and it may still be wrong to think of him as idle. But this condition is very difficult to distinguish *in practice* from the various types of "preferred idleness." Thus, unemployment insurance may lessen his incentive to find work, and an apparent or supposed search for the best employment opportunity may be a mask for what is known as loafing. (Hutt 1977, pp. 83–84)

Search and turnover models have been severely criticized by K. Clark and Summers (1979). These models imply large flows into and out of unemployment with only a thin tail of long unemployment spells. Hall (1972) figured that 3.3 points of the unemployment rate could be attributed to normal turnover and search. Estimates for completed spells of unemployment by Clark and Summers sharply reduce this figure to only 0.25 percent. Further, 64 percent of job changes were made with no intervening spell of unemployment. According to Rosenfeld (1977), an individual who was unemployed for four weeks or more devoted only seventeen hours a month to search. Only 35 percent of successful job seekers found their jobs through direct applications to employers. Finally, most workers take the first job offer they receive, and the jobs which they take are held for only short periods lasting less than two years. In the light of these facts, Clark and Summers conclude that it is irrational for an unemployed worker to remain idle while he is searching for a better job.[3]

I see at least three problems that may limit the applicability of traditional search models. First, these models posit an underlying distribution of wage offers and assume that workers search for better paying jobs. The wage rate is, however, simply a proxy for the total utility of employment at different firms. Wage information can be cheaply communicated, but prospectors must visit heterogeneous firms to ascertain the quality of employment. Second, most models assume, for analytic ease, that individuals are alike. Search costs and the returns of search will obviously vary across individuals. Third, the models neglect firm heterogeneity. Search is surely a reciprocal process in which the unemployed seek jobs, and firms search for qualified applicants for vacant jobs.

2.2.3 Risk Sharing and Implicit Contracts

I can identify at least four reasons that can explain the existence of long-term employment agreements: (1) sharing the risks of uncertain product demands, (2) sharing the risks of uncertain labor productivity, (3) agency costs, and (4) transaction costs of which the most important are the fixed costs of recruiting and training. If workers are risk averse and firms have a comparative advantage in risk bearing, a mutually advantageous agreement can be struck wherein part of the risk of employment instability is shifted to the firm. Gordon (1974) and Baily (1974) appealed to this principle to rationalize implicit long-term contracts. But what is to prevent postcontractual opportunistic behavior? Compliance is hopefully assured by reputation. In short, contract theories must presume that each firm is sufficiently long-lived to have a reputation that is worth protecting.

If productivity is uncertain, payments by results and spot contracts result in uncertain labor incomes. Given risk aversion, F. Smith (1977) has shown that a long-term contract with rigid wages and tenured employment will dominate a contract with fluctuating wages. An implication of this model is that, in competitive equilibrium, junior workers are underpaid, while senior (unsuccessful) workers receive a wage that exceeds their marginal value product.[4]

The delegation of authority is unavoidably accompanied by agency costs of the type analyzed by Jensen and Meckling (1976). The costs of monitoring and malfeasance in a principal-agent relation can be reduced by negotiating long-term contracts that contain substantial elements of deferred compensation.[5] The presence of long-term contracts and deferred pay confound the econometric task of estimating the empirical relation between pay and marginal value products.

A common thread running through these contract theories is that there is more than one dimension to "work." Risk sharing involves a package in which the worker accepts a lower stable wage in return for an implicit insurance policy that yields income smoothing in an uncertain world. In the Becker-Stigler (1974) model, one can imagine that the firm demands a tied bundle consisting of an agent's work effort plus the tied risks of potential losses due to malfeasance or shirking. Specific human capital also involves a tie linking a trained worker to his unique work setting. The forging of these ties in implicit or explicit long-term employment arrangements is presumably advantageous to both parties. The firm's reputation is allegedly the support which persuades workers to believe that the promises will be kept, while deferred benefits induce workers into keeping their part of the bargain. These implications suggest contract theories should only apply to those firms with credible reputations.

2.2.4 Job Tenure and Turnover

A search model examines the behavior of an individual seeking a permanent job, while contract theory describes the behavior of a firm that tries to design pay and employment policies that will attract and retain "permanent" workers. Employment relations are established and broken, and these labor flows determine a distribution of job tenures. If risk sharing and mobility costs are important to workers, and if fixed employment costs are significant, we should observe long, mean durations of job tenure. The gross flow statistics reveal high labor turnover rates which seem to contradict the underpinnings of search and contract theories.

Labor turnover is costly, and many economists have argued that much can be learned by studying the organization of Japanese firms which purportedly promise their employees guaranteed "lifetime" employment contracts. The myth of the protected and coddled Japanese worker was so pervasive that I never questioned its validity. A very different picture is painted by Koike (1978):[6]

> Those who deserve to be regarded as having "lifetime employment" are *not* Japanese workers, but those in the organized sector of the United States with five or more years of continuous service. (p. 46)

The data assembled by Koike (pp. 64–65) reveal that the percentage of employed persons with fifteen or more years of continuous service is larger in the United States. The percentage with ten or more years was around 34 percent in both countries, while the percentage with less than one year was larger in the United States. I suspect that the wider dispersion of job tenures in the United States can partially be explained by differences in the size distribution of firms.

Using estimated marginal retention rates, Hall (1982) constructed distributions of "eventual" job tenures. A representative worker can be expected to hold ten jobs over a lifetime. Most jobs are of short duration, but by the age of thirty, 40 percent of employed persons will be at a job that they will hold for twenty or more years. There are obvious sex differences; 50 percent of thirty-year-old men will find permanent job attachments compared to only 25 percent of thirty-year-old women. Director and Doctors (1976) found that among blue-collar workers at three large factories, blacks had slightly longer job tenures than whites. Hall's distributions, which pertain to random samples of employed persons, confirm this finding: namely, race is unrelated to job tenure. The picture of the labor market implicit in these job tenure distributions is one of turbulence during the first five to ten years in the labor force. Young persons move from job to job as they look for a "permanent" job. With increasing age, larger fractions eventually settle into a job that will last for twenty or more years. Data from the May 1979 Current Population Survey (CPS) reveal some interesting interactions between job tenure and firm size which are explored in section 2.3.

Our concerns over unemployment and rigid wages have promoted the development of search and contract theories that rest on the presence of fixed costs. The magnitude of these fixed costs obviously varies across individuals and firms. A marginal firm, whose survival probabilities are slim, is unlikely to make large investments in recruiting and training. An individual with few assets and general talents will not incur high search costs. Search and contract theories are only applicable to a sector of the economy for which these fixed costs are significant. Attention is directed in the next section to the characteristics of firms and workers that put them into this sector.

2.3 The Production and Compensation of Specialized Employees

Training and goods are joint products. Firms "produce" specifically trained employees whose internal value to the firm exceeds their external value in an outside labor market. Firm-specific human capital and the discrepancy between internal and external values can only be sustained when the host firms are sufficiently differentiated from one another. Variations in entrepreneurial ability can generate a distribution of firms that differ in size and organization. The very large firms achieve the economies of volume production by installing rigid, specialized production plants. The resulting organizations yield short-run factor demands that produce procyclical patterns in labor productivity. Less able entrepreneurs, who control smaller production teams, occupy a different segment of the "product line." They survive by assembling adaptable production teams that utilize general-purpose equipment and employ workers with general human capital. Firm-specific human capital is a phenomenon that is only observed in that sector of the economy consisting of very large firms. The labor market in this part of the economy does *not* conform to the neoclassical theory of factor markets.

2.3.1 Fixed Employment Costs and the Joint Production of Training and Goods

The full costs of quasi-fixed labor inputs are the sum of variable and fixed components. Wages and fringe benefits that make up total employee compensation are usually included in the first component.[7] The fixed employment costs, which represent outlays for recruiting and training, are likely to be higher, the greater the specificity of the firm's labor force.

If a resource is *specialized* and *specific* to a firm, it earns an equilibrium return that contains an element of economic rent. Its internal value will exceed its external value. Firms may purchase specialized resources from outside vendors, but the usual arrangement involves vertical integration wherein specific factors are "internally produced."[8] The firm that demands specially trained labor input will ordinarily find that specific training can be most economically provided through internal or in-house production. It thus becomes a multiproduct firm that jointly produces goods and specific human capital.

The costs of producing specific human capital will depend on the technology of production and the input prices which include the wages paid to apprentice-trainees and instructors, materials costs, and the opportunity costs of forgone output. If S units of specific human capital are produced and supplied to each new hire, the gross return realized by the firm will be equal to the present value of increments to labor productivity (in value terms) attributable to S. The gross returns will be larger, the lower the interest rate, and the greater the durability of S.[9] The optimum investment in firm-specific human capital is attained by equating marginal costs to marginal returns. This investment is likely to vary across individuals and firms. More specific human capital will be invested in those individuals who have longer expected employment tenures and larger increments in productivity. If apprentice-trainees agree to share the costs by accepting a lower wage during the training period (which translates into a fall in the price of an input entering the production function), the marginal cost of specific training falls thereby increasing the equilibrium investment in S. Other implications could be derived by placing more structure on the model.[10]

A firm hires individuals of varying abilities to perform different tasks, and the nature of the tasks will surely affect the returns to specific training. Orientation costs are, for example, small when the job involves simple tasks that are performed in more or less the same way in many firms. Other jobs that require the use of specialized equipment or close cooperation with team members may demand extensive orientation and training. We have read about the highly valued clerk who through formal training and informal on-the-job experience has learned how to deal with the firm's best customers. Substantially more training must be supplied to those managers and supervisors who are asked to monitor performance, to train new employees, and to handle unanticipated departures from normal work routines. These examples suggest that specific human capital is largely concentrated among highly paid, skilled workers.

Individuals who have a greater capacity to learn are likely to acquire larger stocks of both types of human capital. The marginal returns to specific human capital S are likely to be greater, the larger the supply of the cooperating input of general human capital G. Equalization of marginal returns across individuals will thus yield a positive correlation between S and G. Further, general human capital G determines an individual's external market wage W.[11] The usual principles of production can thus generate a positive association between the wage rate and the degree of fixity. Moreover, the returns to a given investment in specific human capital are likely to vary across firms. Those firms that enjoy higher returns will realize greater gains by demanding more able workers whose general human capital will have a complementary effect on the productivity of specific human capital. This heterogeneity of firms thus reinforces the tendency for wages to be positively correlated with investments in firm-specific human capital.

2.3.2 The Planning of Production by Heterogeneous Firms

The analysis of labor markets has explicitly recognized the presence of individual worker differences in both observable variables (education, job experience, race, sex, etc.) and unobservable traits (intelligence, honesty, perseverence, etc.) These differences operating through the supply side play important roles in explaining the dispersion in earnings, the differential incidence of unemployment, job mobility, and so on. On the demand side, there are obvious differences among firms. Industrial differences are usually explained by arguing that there are different technical substitution opportunities embedded in the production functions applicable to different industries. However, firms in a given industry also differ in behavior and in the organization of production. These firm differences cannot be adequately explained by our received theory of value.

Economic theory only provides a loose definition for the concept of the *firm*. Coase (1937) persuasively argued that the firm is a viable organization because some resource allocations are more economically made by command rather than by market transactions. Alchian and Demsetz (1972, p. 778) emphasized the role of coordinating team production when they wrote, "It [the firm] is the centralized contractual agent in a team productive process, not some superior authoritarian directive or disciplinary power." Following Kaldor (1934), I shall assume that the "centralized contractual agent" can be equated to a *single*, firm-specific entrepreneurial input.[12] The quality and quantity of this input will surely vary, and it is this variation which can explain the size distribution of firms.

The Entrepreneurial Input in a Neoclassical Model

Before turning to those aspects of production which deal with adaptability, specific training, and recruiting, attention is directed to a neoclassical model in which output Q is produced by combining three inputs:

$$(1) \qquad Q = f(N, K, T); \qquad \frac{dQ}{dK} = f_K, \ \frac{dQ}{dN} = f_N, \ \frac{dQ}{dT} = f_T.$$

Capital K is purchased at a price R. A firm that hires M workers of type μ obtains a labor input measured in efficiency units of $N = \mu M$. All entrepreneurs are endowed with the same fixed supply of calendar time $\bar{H}$ which can be allocated to coordinating production or monitoring worker performance. Monitoring is an essential joint input that must be supplied by the entrepreneur to assure that each of the M workers contributes μ efficiency units of labor services.[13] Entrepreneurs are assumed to be alike as monitors, and they must devote h hours to monitor each worker. They do, however, differ in their capacity to coordinate production. These differences will be described by an entrepreneurial ability parameter λ which transforms the time allocated to coordinating and decision making into efficiency units of managerial effort T. The supply of managerial effort which cooperates with the hired input is thus determined by entrepreneurial ability λ and the *number* of employees M:

$$T = \lambda H = \lambda(\bar{H} - hM). \tag{2}$$

More productive workers can command higher wages along a market wage structure $W(\mu)$ with $W'(\mu) > 0$. The profits of a competitive firm are thus given by

$$\pi = PQ - RK - W(\mu)M. \tag{3}$$

Inputs of capital K and employees M, as well as worker quality μ, are chosen to maximize profits. The first-order conditions are

$$Pf_K = R, \tag{3a}$$

$$P(\mu f_N - \lambda h f_T) = W(\mu) \text{ or } P\mu f_N = W(\mu) + \delta \qquad (\delta = P\lambda h f_T), \tag{3b}$$

$$Pf_N = W'(\mu). \tag{3c}$$

This system of three equations determines the profit-maximizing values of (K, M, μ). The properties of this model can be more easily understood by temporarily assuming that worker quality μ is held constant.

In equilibrium, the MVP of capital is equated to its price R. However, the MVP of workers exceeds their wages by an amount equal to the implicit monitoring cost δ which represents the opportunity cost of diverting h hours of entrepreneurial time away from coordination to the supervision of worker performance. The marginal rate of substitution of capital for workers is equated to relative factor prices where the pertinent "price" of labor is its full cost, defined as the sum of the wage needed to obtain a worker's services plus the opportunity cost of the time required to guarantee that the worker will contribute μ efficiency units of work effort:[14]

$$-\frac{dK}{dM} = \frac{\mu f_N}{f_K} = \frac{W(\mu) + \delta}{R}. \tag{4}$$

Firms that incur higher monitoring costs face a higher full price of labor. Consequently, they adopt more capital-intensive production techniques.

Profits, in this model, are the returns to the quasi-fixed entrepreneurial input. If the production function, equation (1), is homogeneous of the first degree, profits in a competitive industry will be directly proportional to the shadow price of entrepreneurial time:[15]

$$\pi = P\lambda f_T \bar{H}. \tag{5}$$

Profits are positively related to λ and P, and inversely related to h, R, and $W(\mu)$. A marginal entrepreneur is one whose ability level λ_0 is such that he realizes the same income from either pursuit, entrepreneur or worker; i.e., $\pi_0 = W$. Those whose entrepreneurial ability exceeds this threshold level ($\lambda > \lambda_0$) will make up the supply of entrepreneurs, while the remaining individuals constitute the supply of hired workers. The production function and the right tail of the frequency distribution of entrepreneurial abilities, $\phi(\lambda)$ to the right of λ_0, jointly determine an equilibrium size distribution of firms. The output supplied by each firm is thus a function of real input prices, entrepreneurial ability, and the monitoring loss parameter, $Q = Q[(R/P), (W/P), \lambda, h]$. In competitive market equilibrium, the product price equates the industry supply, Q^s, to the market demand, $Q^d = D(P)$:

$$Q^s = \int_{\lambda_0}^{\infty} Q\left(\frac{R}{P}, \frac{W}{P}, \lambda, h\right)\phi(\lambda)d\lambda = D(P). \tag{6}$$

Inframarginal entrepreneurs with high values of λ earn economic rents $(\pi - W)$ that are *not* eliminated by competitive market forces. Although higher entrepreneurial abilities entail higher monitoring costs, output, employment, and profits are positively related to ability λ. As a consequence, more able entrepreneurs control larger firms.

For a given worker type, say μ_1, inputs of K and M are demanded so that the constrained marginal cost $\bar{\gamma}$ is equated to the product price:

$$\bar{\gamma} = \frac{R}{f_K} = \frac{W_1}{\mu_1 f_N - \lambda h f_T} = P \qquad [W_1 = W(\mu_1)].$$

The opportunities to vary worker quality introduces a new degree of freedom. The input mix for $\bar{\gamma}$ need not correspond to a global minimum of costs. If the quality margin is equated to the other two margins, the firm attains a global maximum of profits described by the equality of the unconstrained marginal cost to price:

$$\gamma = \frac{R}{f_K} = \frac{W(\mu)}{\mu f_N - \lambda h f_T} = \frac{W'(\mu)}{f_N} = P.$$

The nature of the full equilibrium is clarified by examining the way in which the choice of worker quality affects the costs of the labor input. A given input of labor services measured in efficiency units can be produced by various combinations of numbers M and qualities μ. The full cost of labor is the sum of wages and implicit monitoring costs:

$$C = [W(\mu) + \delta]M = [W(\mu) + \delta]\left(\frac{N}{\mu}\right).$$

We can derive the marginal cost of a move to higher quality accompanied by a decrease in numbers, holding N constant:

$$\frac{dC}{d\mu} = \frac{N}{\mu^2}[\mu W'(\mu) - W(\mu) - \delta].$$

The sign of $(dC/d\mu)$ will depend on μ and the implicit monitoring cost δ which is higher for larger firms. There is an ability level λ_1 for which μ_1 would have been that firm's optimal choice of worker quality. A firm with a higher ability entrepreneur $(\lambda_A > \lambda_1)$ incurs a higher monitoring cost so that $\mu_1 W'(\mu_1) < W(\mu_1) + \delta_A$. The λ_A firm can reduce the full costs of labor by substituting quality for quantity. In equilibrium, the worker productivity which minimizes full labor cost satisfies the condition that the marginal cost of quality equals the full cost of an additional worker:

$$\mu W'(\mu) = W(\mu) + \delta. \tag{7}$$

Entrepreneurs will locate along the wage structure $W(\mu)$ in a manner analogous to the hedonic price model of Rosen (1974). Large firms that incur higher monitoring costs will demand more productive workers who command higher wages, requiring less monitoring per efficiency unit of labor services. The equilibrium market wage structure must equilibrate the relative demands and supplies for workers of varying productivities. Moreover, it must exhibit increasing returns to quality, meaning that if individual A is twice as productive as B, A must receive a wage that is more than twice B's wage.[16] More productive workers are matched with more able entrepreneurs, thereby generating a positive relation between wages and firm size. This assignment of workers to firms is socially optimal in the sense that it minimizes the full social cost of producing monitored labor services.

A displacement of equilibrium results in distributional effects among the firms in a given industry as well as allocative effects across industries. The nature of these adjustments can be described with the aid of an illustration. Suppose that a wage tax is placed on workers in a particular industry. In a Marshallian analysis, the "representative firm" will contract output, profits will fall, and capital will be substituted for labor. The industry demand for capital will decline if the elasticity of substitution is less than the price elasticity of demand. In the presence of heterogeneous firms, these conclusions have to be qualified. Marginal entrepreneurs, whose abilities are only slightly above the threshold level λ_0, are driven out of the market as profits fall below the alternative wage that they could have earned as workers. The tax imposes a greater burden on the smaller surviving firms whose higher labor/capital ratios cause larger upward shifts in their marginal cost curves. For the industry as a whole, the adjustment in product price due to the tax, will depend on four factors: (a) production technology, (b) the price elasticity of the product demand curve, (c) the increase in the threshold ability level λ_0 due to the tax, and (d) the frequency distribution of abilities $\phi(\lambda)$. A dispersion of entrepreneurial abilities could thus result in a situation where the smaller firms cease or contract production, while the larger firms actually expand their output, employment, and profits.[17]

Differences in entrepreneurial ability can generate an equilibrium size distribution of firms even though all entrepreneurs have access to the same production technology and to common, perfectly competitive factor markets. Ability in my model is not "Hicks neutral." Specifically, talented entrepreneurs have a comparative disadvantage at monitoring. As a consequence, they try to economize on monitoring by adopting capital-intensive production techniques and hiring more productive workers. These are implications that can be empirically tested.

Monitoring, Training, and Productivity

Monitoring costs could be reduced if production could be organized so that workers are paid by "results." The production methods that allow for piece-rate compensation may exclude techniques that can realize the economies of specialization and team production.[18] Team production requires the joint input of monitoring to prevent shirking. The costs of monitoring teams cannot be easily allocated to individual team members. The determination of an optimal level of monitoring thus involves elements of the problem of public goods.

The production of specialized teams ordinarily requires specific training that raises a worker's productivity in only one particular firm. If some minimal amount of firm-specific human capital is required to become a team member, what determines the manner and timing of its production? With respect to general human capital, Ben-Porath (1967) showed that if an individual maximizes utility, a rising marginal cost curve will generate a time path of investments in human capital that are spread out over time. The stock of capital will increase at a decreasing rate, resulting in the familiar concave age-earnings profile. A firm's investments in specific human capital ought to follow a similar path, increasing at a diminishing rate as a function of length of service. Further, if the returns to specific human capital are shared, productivity and wages should both increase with job tenure. Medoff and Abraham (1981) have challenged the validity of this model. They reported that wages within a job grade increase with tenure, but productivity measured by supervisory ratings or physical output rates is unrelated to job experience. Wages are evidently *not* determined by the equilibrium returns to human capital and, by implication, they have to be explained in some other way, such as risk sharing or paternalism.

The Medoff-Abraham conclusion rests on the tacit assumption that workers are like single product firms; i.e., secretaries type, roofers lay shingles, and scientists publish articles. In reality, most workers resemble multiproduct firms that jointly supply several products. In addition to typing, a secretary may be responsible for organizing the office, training new employees, and being available for service as a temporary replacement for an absentee. Firm-specific training is not intended to increase typing speed. It is designed to improve performance in those aspects of the job that are unique to the firm. The option value of this backup capability (which is similar to Hutt's example of an idle worker performing the productive function of "availability") should be included in measuring a worker's total productivity. Additionally, a worker who is reliable and requires less monitoring has a higher *net product* which cannot be measured by simply observing his *gross product*. These related, firm-specific dimensions of workers' value to their employers are largely neglected in conventional measures of labor productivity. Reliance on conventional measures thus tends to understate the impact of firm-specific training on total labor productivity.[19]

Specialization and Team Production

A firm can realize the gains from specialization by organizing production around units and teams. The output of the entire team can be observed, but the marginal contribution of a particular worker is not easily ascertained because of (a) interdependence in the production function and (b) variations in the supply of work effort. If effort and performance are to be properly compensated, someone has to monitor and meter worker performance. In the Alchian-Demsetz model, the entrepreneur is the specialist who detects shirking and metes out rewards. The delegation of authority in a principal-agent relation is unavoidably accompanied by shirking and incompatible incentives that produce "agency costs." Jensen and Meckling (1976) point out that agency costs (monitoring, bonding, and the residual loss) constitute an efficient allocation of resources. Without them, a firm could not obtain and retain the services of agents and employees who have comparative advantages in performing certain tasks. In short, agency costs have to be incurred if a firm is to achieve the requisite size and organizational structure that are needed to exploit the economies of specialization and volume production.

In the neoclassical model discussed earlier, all firms used the *same* production function to produce a homogeneous good Q. However, the firms in a given industry appear to produce slightly differentiated products. Large firms specialize in the production of standardized goods, while small firms supply customized goods that are produced in small batches.

Standardized goods are most efficiently produced by combining specialized capital with a disciplined labor force that will conform to prescribed work schedules. Production is characterized by a putty clay technology in which capital can be substituted for labor in the ex ante planning stage, but once in place, machines and men are employed in virtually fixed proportions which simplifies the monitoring task. The rigidity of this organization seems well suited to exploit the volume economies emphasized by Alchian (1959).[20]

If a firm expects to sell only fifty units of a good, it will choose an adaptable production technique. If, however, the planned volume is one hundred thousand units, production will be organized around an assembly line.[21] Specialized, durable machines will be designed for batch production, and these machines will be operated by fixed complements of workers. Monitoring costs can be reduced when workers are compelled to adhere to the same inflexible work schedules and when the opportunities for discretionary behavior are limited by a fixed-proportions technology. To the extent that worker preferences vary, the lower monitoring costs are not a windfall. Large firms must pay a compensating wage difference to attract marginal team members.[22]

The coordination of very large production teams is facilitated by developing detailed job descriptions. Job applicants are tested and interviewed, and prior work histories are carefully reviewed to determine if the applicant's qualifications meet the prescribed job specifications. Applicants are passed over and job vacancies are kept open until a suitable match is found. Small firms which have lower monitoring costs and more adaptable production teams are able to fill job vacancies more quickly because the requirements of the job can be more easily modified to fit the applicant's qualifications. The relative rigidities of production plans thus predict that the ratio of applicants to job vacancies will be higher at larger firms and for those positions that have tighter, inflexible job specifications.[23]

The new employees at very large firms are likely to receive more firm-specific training. But training here must be broadly defined to include the acquisition of new skills (e.g., learning how to operate a word processor or a forklift truck) as well as the adaptation to a particular production process (meaning compliance with prescribed working practices or learning preferred ways to perform certain jobs). When all of a team's members are more or less alike and follow standardized work routines, monitoring costs are reduced, and some monitoring could even be delegated to subordinates.[24] The fixed costs of assembling and training a homogeneous labor force may not be warranted for small firms that have shorter, uncertain lives.

Small firms are drawn to a segment of the industry product line containing what can be called customized goods. Products are supplied in small batches and are often differentiated to meet idiosyncratic demands. A firm in this market should assemble an adaptable production team which can easily adjust to changing demands. I have argued earlier that the capital to labor ratio will be smaller because the lower monitoring cost reduces the full cost of labor. The lower capital intensity of smaller firms is further reinforced if substitutions across differentiated products are more easily made by moving men rather than machines. Part-time workers can be more efficiently employed by small firms which are continually adjusting to changes in the level and composition of productive activities. The virtual absence of firm-specific training at small firms can be explained by the adaptability and generality of production and by the shorter expected lives of these firms.

Every industry contains firms of varying sizes and types. At one end of the spectrum, little companies produce goods in small batches by using labor-intensive adaptable techniques and by hiring low-wage workers with general human capital. At the other extreme, very large firms specialize in the volume production of standardized goods. Production is organized around assembly lines (or fixed plants designed for large batches) that are characterized by (a) ex post fixed factor proportions, (b) rigid work schedules, (c) detailed job descriptions, (d) homogeneous inputs, (e) high capital utilization rates achieved through multiple shifts, and (f) quantum adjustments to changing demand conditions. The composition of a firm's product line and the organization of production are thus determined in a manner that maximizes the returns to the scarce entrepreneurial input.

2.3.3 Short-Run Cyclical Adjustments and Okun's Law

The fixed cost hypothesis was originally advanced to explain different employment and wage responses to cyclical changes in aggregate demand. The literature in the last two decades has examined a broader range of issues including search and contract theories, labor turnover, equilibrium unemployment rates, the duration of job tenures, and, last but not least, Okun's law which dealt with the cyclical behavior of labor productivity. Specifically, Arthur Okun found that a 1 percent decrease in the unemployment rate (which is approximately equal to a 1 percent increase in the aggregate labor input) was accompanied by a 3 percent increase in aggregate output. This empirical regularity is contrary to a naive production function model in which capital is fixed in the short run, resulting in diminishing returns to the variable labor input. Hall (1980) offered a conjectural explanation wherein labor markets are dominated by workers on long-term contracts who felicitously vary their work efforts in a procyclical fashion. The background model is one where the effective labor input is a function of work effort which, in turn, responds positively to changes in product demand.[25] A durable labor input may play an important role in Okun's law, but the elusive concept of "work effort" can, I believe, be replaced by a more plausible argument that appeals to an efficient intertemporal allocation of specifically trained workers.

Short-run adjustments to demand shifts will be determined by the production technology, factor supply conditions, and opportunities for product substitutions. I shall direct attention to two themes that have not been adequately developed in the literature and that go a long way in explaining Okun's law. The first is concerned with the organization of volume production in which zero ex post factor substitutions (fixed factor proportions) are a consequence of volume production. The second theme extends the idea of joint production to the intertemporal allocation of quasi-fixed factors to market and nonmarket activities.

The essence of the first theme can be found in the peak load pricing model and is implicit in the regenerative growth model of Gordon and Walton (1982).[26] In the Steiner (1957) model, outputs in peak and slack periods are produced by combining capital and labor in fixed (one-to-one) proportions; $X_j = K_j = L_j$ for $j = 1, 2$. Capital is specialized with no alternative use, while the variable labor input is general. If demands produce a firm peak ($X_1 = K$ and $X_2 < K$), the output/capital ratio is less than unity in the slack period. As the firm moves from slack to peak periods, the output/capital ratio rises, but no one would point to this as an example of increasing returns.

The application of the peak load model to Okun's law is clarified by assuming that there are three inputs: specific labor A, variable general labor B, and specific capital K. If one unit of A is required for the maintenance of one unit of K whether it is or is not in use, the labor input in the peak period is $L_1 = (A + B_1)$ where $B_1 = X_1$. In the slack period, the labor input falls to $L_2 = (A + B_2)$ where $B_2 = X_2 < X_1$. The A labor is specialized and is retained during slack periods. As the firm moves from slack to peak periods, the output/labor ratio climbs because the A labor is, in a sense, more efficiently utilized during peak periods.

The peak load model has been extended by Turvey (1968), Wenders (1976), and others to allow for a portfolio of diverse technologies. Capital-intensive plants that yield the lowest full-cycle costs are fully utilized in all periods, while standby plants with lower capital/labor ratios are idle in slack periods but activated to meet peak demands. Large manufacturing firms seem to embrace a similar strategy. Those plants (or parts of a plant) that are operated on multiple shifts tend to be highly capital intensive. Standby plants and shifts that are added to meet peak demands have lower ratios of capital to variable labor inputs. In a cyclical downturn, entire plants and shifts are closed down, thereby producing a countercyclical movement in the ratio of output to *variable* labor inputs. However, the diminishing returns to variable labor have to be combined with increasing returns to the quasi-fixed labor inputs in determining the cyclical behavior of *total* labor productivity.[27] If production entails fixed proportions in which quasi-fixed and variable labor inputs are combined with capital, short-run adjustments to demand shifts could generate time paths for output and employment that conform to Okun's law. Further, since large firms are more likely to adopt putty clay technologies, the procyclical movements in labor productivity should be stronger for larger firms.

The second theme acknowledges that all large firms are vertically integrated, multiproduct enterprises. Resources at the command of a firm can be allocated in at least three directions, namely, to the production of (1) final goods Q, (2) firm-specific human capital, or (3) increments to the value of existing physical plant and equipment. The joint production of training and goods has already been discussed, and the same idea can be extended to the joint internal production of capital values.

Machines do not run like the "one-hoss shays" of some economic models. Depreciation is *not* exogenous, and investments (additions to the capital stock) do not always take the form of new capital goods purchased from outside vendors. Further, machines are not homogeneous, and one of the important quality features is the probability of breakdown. Resources are allocated to maintenance and repairs to sustain the service flows from capital and to raise the market value of the existing capital stock. Each firm will choose a quality of capital (I shall emphasize age as a proxy for quality) and a level of maintenance inputs that maximize total profits.

A firm can control the age distribution of its capital stock through its choice of age of additions (new vs. used, and if used, the age of used equipment) and the age at which equipment is scrapped or sold in the used market. These decisions are made by comparing three components of capital costs—amortization, maintenance, and disruption. Since depreciation and obsolescence rates decline with age, newer machines entail higher amortization charges. These may be offset, in part or in whole, by lower maintenance and disruption costs, where the latter include the opportunity costs of forgone output and the costs of any tied inputs that must be retained during any downtime. Small firms are more likely to purchase used machines and to discard them at older ages for two reasons: First, maintenance is a labor-intensive activity that must be closely supervised. The lower "price" of maintenance due to lower monitoring costs leads to a substitution of more maintenance for lower amortization charges. Although the probability of a breakdown rises with increasing machine age, each disruption entails lower costs when the firm uses an adaptable production technique that allows for variable factor proportions. Thus, small firms that have a comparative advantage in maintenance and in coping with disruptions, tend to own older machines. The giant firms that have large, inflexible production lines face higher maintenance prices. They willingly accept the higher amortization costs of new equipment in order to economize on monitoring and disruption costs. The optimal trade-offs of amortization versus maintenance/disruption costs are determined by relative "prices" which happen to be related to firm size. The age structure of a firm's capital assets can thus be explained by the minimization of the sum of amortization, maintenance, and disruption costs.[28]

The principle that maintenance can be substituted for investment is well known.[29] Durable capital is scrapped at older ages in those countries where the wage rate is low in relation to the price of new equipment. This same principle applies to the intertemporal substitutions that a firm can make in response to cyclical fluctuations in relative factor prices and product demands. In a recession, the shadow prices of quasi-fixed specialized resources fall, but firms continue to retain them. Product prices decline in relation to the implicit value of internal investments. As a consequence, quasi-fixed inputs are shifted away from the production of goods toward internal investments in specific human capital and in maintenance of physical capital.[30] The market value of capital assets increases (or falls by less than it otherwise would in the absence of increased maintenance), thereby reducing the effective depreciation rate. These increments to capital values are all implicit and never appear on the company's books.

The process is reversed when the firm experiences an upturn in product demand. The demand for variable inputs increases, and specialized workers are reassigned from maintenance to the production of goods. Physical capital is more intensively utilized, and with less maintenance, it depreciates at a faster rate. To the extent that Okun's law only deals with cyclical movements in the value of final goods Q (and ignores the countercyclical movements of increments to implicit capital values), we get a biased picture of the cyclical behavior of "total" labor productivity. The magnitude of the output response is muted if we followed the correct procedure and related changes in the value of "total product" (including internally produced increments to capital values) to changes in labor inputs.[31]

The force of these two themes—fixed factor proportions in producing goods and intertemporal product substitutions—obviously varies across firms and industries. The high shadow price of entrepreneurial time in large manufacturing firms raises the costs of monitoring workers as well as the costs of enforcing compliance with frequent changes in prices and wages. Hence, large firms should exhibit greater rigidities in prices and wages accompanied by discrete quantum adjustments in output and employment. The firm adjusts to a downturn by closing down entire plants and shifts, releasing variable labor inputs, and placing some trained workers on temporary layoffs. The specialized workers who are retained are diverted to the nonmarket activities of rebuilding human and nonhuman capital. At the other end of the size distribution, small entrepreneurs confront a lower opportunity cost of time. They are better suited to monitor workers in adaptable production teams, and more importantly, they can negotiate frequent changes in prices and wages. Although a recession may drive many small firms into bankruptcy, the surviving small firms may, as a result of their flexibility, experience less volatility in output and employment. King (1923) found, for cxamplc, that the reductions in employment in the recession of 1920–22 were relatively greater in large firms, as revealed by the data of table 2.2.

Employment in the volatile manufacturing sector is heavily concentrated in large firms. In this sector, fixed factor proportions and intertemporal substitutions in the production of goods versus internal investments are likely to produce strong procyclical movements in labor productivity. In other sectors, small firms with flexible prices and adaptable production teams should exhibit weak procyclical or even countercyclical patterns in the ratio of output to employment.

2.3.4 Impact of Firm Size on Compensation and the Composition of Employment

Fixed employment costs are incurred to recruit and train a *firm-specific* labor force. The amount invested in and the returns to specific human capital will be larger, the greater the durability of the asset measured by the worker's expected job tenure. The retention rate is a function of the level and structure of compensation, the quality of working conditions, and the composition of the firm's labor force. The design of a compensation package and the selection of new employees are clearly more important to those firms that make large investments in specific human capital.

Total employee compensation (TEC) is the sum of gross wages plus employer contributions for fringe benefits; TEC $= WH + BH$, where W is the hourly wage rate, H denotes total paid hours (the sum of hours actually worked H_W plus paid leisure hours H_L for vacations, holidays, sick leave, etc.), and B is the employer outlay for fringes converted to an hourly rate. The total hourly compensation of employees which appears in government publications[32] is given by $C = (\text{TEC}/H) = W + B$. But C is not the right measure for the compensation component of full labor costs.[33] A better measure is provided by compensation per hour actually worked, which I shall call *pay*, $C^* = (TEC/H_W) = C/(1 - \phi)$, where

Table 2.2 Employment, Hours, and Earnings for Selected Quarters, 1920–1922

	All Industries			Factories		
Firm Size	1920:3	1921:3	1922:1	1920:3	1921:3	1922:1
			Number of Employees			
1–21	10,110	9,843	8,739	1,360	1,251	1,121
22–99	4,630	4,084	3,956	1,950	1,541	1,573
100+	14,440	11,151	11,452	8,060	5,668	5,927
Total	29,180	25,078	24,147	11,370	8,460	8,621
			Scheduled Full-Time Weekly Hours			
1–21	54.1	53.9	53.0	52.1	51.9	51.0
22–99	52.0	51.4	51.3	51.8	50.4	49.9
100+	49.1	48.3	47.8	50.1	49.1	49.3
Total	51.3	51.0	50.3	50.7	49.7	49.6
			Actual Weekly Hours			
1–21	52.9	52.7	51.7	51.0	50.8	49.7
22–99	48.6	48.8	49.0	46.2	47.2	46.3
100+	48.9	45.5	45.6	49.0	44.4	45.7
Total	50.3	48.8	48.1	48.7	45.9	46.3
			Average Hourly Earnings			
1–21	0.44	0.43	0.44	0.50	0.52	0.54
22–99	0.56	0.54	0.52	0.58	0.56	0.54
100+	0.63	0.57	0.56	0.64	0.56	0.53
Total	0.55	0.51	0.51	0.61	0.56	0.53

Source: W. I. King, *Employment, Hours, and Earnings in Prosperity and Depression* (New York: National Bureau of Economic Research, 1923), pp. 30, 82, 87, 113.

$\phi = H_L/H$ is the paid leisure ratio describing the fraction of total paid hours that the worker can take in leisure. The components of employee compensation from two surveys are summarized in table 2.3. In the BLS survey of all establishments in the private business sector, the hourly wage W was only 78.1 percent of pay per workhour C^*; it was only 70.3 percent in the Chamber of Commerce survey of large firms. Establishments in the BLS survey reported giving an average of four weeks of paid leisure, while the large firms in the CC survey gave nearly seven weeks.[34] Fringe benefits B accounted for 15.5 and 19.1 percent of total compensation in the two surveys. Roughly 40 percent of these fringes were legally required for social security, worker compensation, and unemployment

Table 2.3 Components of Total Employee Compensation

Item	Bureau of Labor Statistics 1977	Ratio[a]	Chamber of Commerce 1979	Ratio[b]
Gross hourly wage, W	6.28	2.18	7.311	2.37
Compensation per paid hour, C	7.43	2.32	9.037	2.52
Compensation per workhour, C^*	8.04	2.37	10.387	2.59
Paid leisure percentage, ϕ	7.59	1.29	13.00	1.23
Legally required benefits, B_{LR}	0.51	3.00	0.658	3.60
Employer benefits, B	1.15	3.59	1.730	3.49
Total benefits, $(B + \phi W)$	1.63	3.33	2.680	3.26

Sources: U.S. Bureau of Labor Statistics. 1980. "Employee Compensation in the Private Nonfarm Sector, 1977." Washington, D.C.: Government Printing Office. U.S. Chamber of Commerce. 1981. "Employee Benefits: Historical Data, 1951–79." Washington, D.C.

NOTE: All figures except for C^* and ϕ are in current dollars per paid hour.

[a]Ratio of the 1977 value to the 1967 value.

[b]Ratio of the 1979 value to the 1969 value.

insurance. Differences by occupation and industry from the BLS survey are shown in table 2.4, and the CC data for some twenty industries appear in table 2.5.

The relation of wage to pay can be described by the ratio W/C^*. Recall that $C = W + B$, and $C^* = C/(1 - \phi)$, so that

$$\frac{W}{C^*} = \frac{1 - \phi}{1 + \dfrac{B}{W}}.$$

Reference to table 2.6 reveals that the wage to pay ratio, W/C^*, fell from 83.1 percent in 1951 to 70.4 percent in 1979. This secular trend resulted from increases in both the benefits rate B/W and the paid leisure ratio ϕ. Legally required supplements B_{LR} accounted for 18.4 percent of total benefits $(B + \phi W)$ in 1951 and 24.6 percent in 1979. I conjectured that as B_{LR} rose, private fringes would fall so that the sum (as a percentage of total compensation) would remain roughly stable. Although private pension contributions grew more slowly than social security, it increased in relation to total compensation.

The cross-sectional industrial dispersion in the W/C^* ratio is substantial (table 2.5), ranging from 83.5 percent in textile mills to 65.4 percent in petroleum. The relative importance of fringe benefits is greater in the regulated public utilities, banking, and the public sector. The variance in W/C^* is largely attributable to variations in the paid leisure ratio. Employees in chemicals and public utilities get more than eight weeks of paid leisure, while workers in retail trade got only four weeks. The data of table 2.7, showing the percentage of workers receiving three selected

Table 2.4 **Employee Compensation in the Private Nonfarm Sector, 1966 and 1977**

	All Employees		Office Workers		Nonoffice Workers	
	1966	1977	1966	1977	1966	1977
C^* = Compensation per work hour						
All industries	3.40	8.04	4.51	9.96	2.92	6.96
Manufacturing	3.67	8.82	5.28	11.80	3.17	7.77
Nonmanufacturing	3.23	7.68	4.15	9.42	2.75	6.49
W = Wage (average hourly earnings per paid hour)						
All industries	2.88	6.28	3.79	7.74	2.48	5.44
Manufacturing	3.05	6.64	4.36	8.80	2.64	5.86
Nonmanufacturing	2.77	6.11	3.52	7.42	2.36	5.18
ϕ = Paid leisure percentage (paid nonworkhours/paid hours)						
All industries	5.9	7.3	7.5	8.2	5.1	6.7
Manufacturing	6.8	8.9	8.3	9.6	6.3	8.4
Nonmanufacturing	5.3	6.5	7.2	7.7	4.4	5.4
W/C^* = Wage as percentage of compensation per workhour						
All industries	84.7	78.1	84.0	77.7	84.9	78.2
Manufacturing	83.1	75.3	82.6	74.6	83.3	75.4
Nonmanufacturing	85.4	79.6	84.8	78.8	85.8	79.8
B_{LR}/C = Legally required benefits to compensation per paid hour						
All industries	5.31	6.86	3.84	5.42	6.14	8.01
Manufacturing	4.97	6.61	3.51	5.11	5.72	7.31
Nonmanufacturing	5.23	6.99	3.90	5.59	6.46	9.80

Source: U.S. Bureau of Labor Statistics, 1980. "Employee Compensation in the Private Nonfarm Economy, 1977." Summary 80-5.

Table 2.5 **Employee Benefits in Large Companies by Industry**

Industry	Compensation per Workhour, C^*			Wage to Compensation Ratio, (W/C^*)			Paid Leisure Ratio ϕ		
	1967	1973	1979	1967	1973	1979	1967	1973	1979
Total, all industries	4.009	6.479	10.386	77.1	72.7	70.4	10.6	12.7	13.0
Total manufacturing	4.013	6.231	10.231	76.2	73.3	70.2	10.3	12.0	12.4
Food	3.803	6.017	9.520	75.9	72.7	70.5	11.9	13.2	11.7
Textiles/apparel	2.502	3.989	6.172	88.3	85.8	83.5	6.9	8.7	9.2
Paper/lumber	3.662	5.668	9.494	80.1	75.5	70.8	8.9	10.2	12.3
Printing	4.466	6.470	10.264	78.2	75.8	71.6	10.4	11.3	11.8
Chemicals	4.337	6.869	11.951	73.7	69.4	66.0	13.6	15.9	16.2
Petroleum	5.231	7.692	14.867	73.4	68.3	65.4	15.1	17.3	15.9
Rubber/leather/plastic	3.740	6.112	8.906	77.2	72.9	71.6	10.8	12.4	11.9
Stone/clay/glass	3.611	5.960	9.592	78.2	72.0	70.7	10.3	13.2	12.1
Primary metals	4.344	6.617	10.931	75.8	72.5	66.9	10.3	10.9	13.1
Fabricated metals	3.913	6.341	9.637	78.9	73.1	70.8	9.3	11.6	11.8
Machinery	4.028	6.471	10.619	77.9	73.4	70.4	10.2	11.9	12.1
Electrical machinery	3.746	6.112	10.454	78.2	74.2	70.2	10.9	12.1	13.6
Transportation equip.	4.247	6.676	11.751	77.5	71.8	68.9	10.9	13.3	13.6
Instruments	3.694	6.103	9.738	77.9	73.1	70.8	10.9	12.6	11.9
Total nonmanufacturing	4.141	6.796	10.619	75.9	71.8	70.8	11.3	13.7	13.6
Public utilities	4.650	7.530	13.012	65.3	70.9	67.5	12.4	15.0	15.8
Department stores	2.703	4.547	6.679	80.0	76.2	73.7	8.6	10.3	11.2
Trade (wholesale/retail)	3.253	5.202	8.460	79.7	75.7	75.8	8.6	10.3	9.8
Banks/finance	3.899	6.447	9.553	73.1	69.8	68.5	11.8	14.0	14.2
Insurance	4.136	6.494	10.078	75.2	71.0	69.2	12.1	14.0	14.1
Hospitals	x	x	7.622	x	x	75.6	x	x	12.4
Miscellaneous industries	4.473	7.208	11.628	79.3	76.2	71.4	9.6	11.8	13.9
Mean (20 industries)				77.19	73.52	70.32	10.68	12.50	17.81
Std. dev.				4.29	3.69	2.76	1.86	2.08	23.15

Source: U.S. Chamber of Commerce. 1981. "Employee Benefits: Historical Data, 1951–79." Washington, D.C.

Table 2.6 Employee Benefits in Large Companies, 1951–1979 (in current dollars)

Year	Comp. per Workhour C^*	Wages to Comp. (percent) W/C^*	Paid Leisure (percent) ϕ	Legal Req. Benefits (percent) B_{LR}/B	Wage Index W_{LC}/W_{PS}
1951	2.024	83.1	8.0	18.4	115.9
1953	2.179	82.7	8.2	16.8	111.9
1955	2.359	81.9	8.5	17.6	112.9
1957	2.696	80.6	9.0	17.7	115.0
1959	3.010	79.9	9.6	18.2	119.0
1961	3.159	78.3	10.2	20.1	115.6
1963	3.456	77.8	10.5	22.1	117.9
1965	3.691	78.4	10.2	19.9	117.7
1967	4.010	77.1	10.6	22.3	115.3
1969	4.630	76.1	11.2	22.7	115.9
1971	5.369	74.0	12.5	20.6	119.6
1973	6.479	72.7	12.7	23.1	119.6
1975	7.697	71.0	13.7	22.7	120.5
1977	8.779	70.3	13.2	23.1	117.5
1978	9.550	70.1	13.4	24.3	117.7
1979	10.387	70.4	13.0	24.6	118.7

Source: U.S. Chamber of Commerce. 1981. "Employee Benefits: Historical Data, 1951–79." Washington, D.C.

fringe benefits, reveal that males in large firms are more likely to get these fringes, implying lower W/C^* ratios.

Several explanations can be offered for the secular growth in fringe benefits: (a) Leisure is a normal good, and as real incomes grew, individuals demanded more leisure in the form of paid vacations rather than in shorter workdays. (b) The higher marginal tax rates which accompany higher wages reduce the net "after-tax" prices of certain fringes. (c) Pensions and deferred pay account for a larger share of the compensation of salaried employees and of workers in large firms who are likely to be more firm specific. More generous but less portable fringe benefits reduce labor turnover, thereby increasing the returns to specific human capital. In addition, deferred pay discourages malfeasance and shirking, thereby reducing monitoring costs.[35] The cross-sectional differences in the wage to pay ratio are broadly consistent with the fixed cost hypothesis. Specifically trained workers in large firms and high-wage industries are provided with compensation packages that put more pay in the form of pensions.

The W/C^* ratio has clearly declined over time and varies across firms and industries. Empirical studies that fail to recognize the changing relation of W to C^* could contain serious biases.[36] The increasing impor-

Table 2.7 **Percentage of Employees Receiving Selected Benefits (all industries by firm size, May 1979)**

Firm Size	Hourly Wage	Group Health	Pension Plan	Disability Insurance
		All Employees		
1–24	4.90	34.1	21.1	8.2
25–99	5.61	64.8	48.1	20.2
100–499	6.26	76.4	70.8	33.0
500–999	6.36	80.0	80.1	40.8
1,000+	7.33	85.6	88.5	55.1
Total	6.23	67.4	61.9	33.7
		Male Workers		
1–24	5.63	41.9	23.2	11.0
25–99	6.58	73.4	52.8	26.0
100–499	7.43	83.7	73.3	41.1
500–999	7.73	87.9	82.0	50.5
1,000+	8.49	91.7	91.4	63.7
Total	7.34	75.7	66.4	41.8

Source: Current Population Survey, May 1979, unpublished data.

tance of deferred pay suggests that the labor input is becoming more firm specific. Long-term contracts and quasi-permanent jobs are evidently assuming greater importance in the labor market.

The organization of production and the composition of employment are obviously influenced by industrial affiliation. Within an industry, the Census of Manufactures data show that the ratio of production to non-production workers is inversely related to establishment size. Additional empirical regularities are revealed by data from the May 1979 *Current Population Survey* (CPS). Selected characteristics of all employed persons by firm size and sex are shown in table 2.8, and similar data for male employees in manufacturing appear in table 2.9. The attributes identified in these tables are familiar, and I shall remark on only some of them.

Education. Larger firms demand more highly educated persons who have already demonstrated their capacity to absorb training. The relation is stronger for males and for salaried workers. In fact, there is almost no relation between firm size and years of schooling for hourly male workers in manufacturing.[37] The patterns conform to the monitoring cost hypothesis in which more productive workers are matched with more able entrepreneurs.

Race, sex, and city size. Nonwhites accounted for 9.5 percent of employed persons. The percentage varies across industries, but there is no systematic relation to firm size. Females, who make up 44 percent of employment, are more heavily represented in smaller firms because of their propensity to hold part-time jobs. The percentage of workers in cities with a population of a million or more is unrelated to firm size.

Part-time employment. Some part-time jobs are permanent, but many are staffed by temporary workers who require more supervision. In all industries, 34.0 percent of employees in small firms held part-time jobs, and this falls to 11.7 percent in the largest firms. Differences in monitoring costs could have been responsible for this inverse relation which is observed within an industry.

Age and job tenure. Larger firms have older workers, and the relation is stronger for males. Table 2.9 reveals, however, that the mean age of male production (hourly) workers varies little across size categories. The striking relation is that between years of job tenure and firm size. The mean duration rises from 4.04 years in small firms to 8.68 years in large firms. Longer job tenure generally corresponds to lower labor turnover rates which squares with the hypothesis that workers in large firms have more firm-specific human capital.[38] Males and salaried workers who receive more training have longer job tenures.

Hourly wage rates. Several economists have observed that wages are positively related to firm size.[39] As one moves from small to large firms (<25 vs. 1,000 + employees), the average hourly wage in 1979 climbed from $4.897 to $7.327 for an unadjusted differential of 49.6 percent.[40] Workers at small firms are more likely to be females, hold part-time jobs, and have less job tenure and education. When Mellow (1981) included personal characteristics in a log-linear wage equation, the estimated firm size differential fell to 24.7 percent. The inclusion of union membership further reduced the differential to 14.3 percent.[41]

Capacity utilization and shift work. When continuous production is dictated by technology, workers must be hired for around-the-clock operations. However, in the vast majority of industries, firms can choose the length of the workweek of fixed capital by varying the number and length of shifts. The equilibrium capital utilization rate will be higher the larger the share of costs attributable to capital, and the smaller the wage differential for shift work. According to Foss (1981), the workweek of fixed capital varied from a high of 140 hours in petroleum refining to a low of 42 hours in apparel. Instead of the usual division into durables and nondurables, I separated manufacturing into two sectors by using Foss's estimates of capital utilization rates.[42] Some 81.5 percent of manufacturing employees worked on the day shift, and the percentage was higher for females and salaried workers. Nearly a fourth of employees in high-use

Table 2.8 **Characteristics of Employees in All Industries by Firm Size: May 1979**

Characteristic	Total	1–24	25–99	100–499	500–999	1,000+
	In Firms with an Employment of					
			All Employees			
No. of workers	17,301	4,548	2,521	2,479	951	6,802
Age	36.44	35.33	36.57	36.59	36.29	37.09
Job tenure	6.51	4.04	5.18	6.30	6.80	8.68
Hourly wage	6.231	4.897	5.606	6.258	6.358	7.327
Education	12.66	11.94	12.30	12.91	13.25	13.10
Percentage of workers:						
Female	43.8	48.2	44.0	47.2	50.5	38.5
Nonwhite	9.5	9.5	8.7	9.2	9.2	10.1
Part-time	19.4	34.0	20.0	14.2	17.4	11.7
Union	22.7	5.9	17.3	25.5	28.3	34.2
Pension plan	61.9	21.1	48.2	70.8	80.1	88.5
Large cities	35.0	28.7	33.2	34.3	34.0	40.3
Hourly workers	55.4	57.7	58.3	58.3	53.8	53.7
			Male Workers			
No. of workers	9,731	2,357	1,411	1,310	471	4,182
Age	36.80	34.26	36.41	37.01	36.91	38.28
Job tenure	7.62	4.34	5.80	7.26	7.85	10.18
Hourly wage	7.340	5.628	6.583	7.426	7.729	8.490

Education	12.7	11.8	12.1	12.9	13.5	13.2
Percentage of workers:						
Nonwhite	8.3	8.7	8.2	8.3	7.9	8.2
Part-time	9.2	17.8	9.4	7.0	7.2	5.3
Union	28.2	9.1	21.8	30.2	33.8	39.9
Pension plan	66.4	23.3	52.8	73.3	81.9	91.4
Large cities	34.9	28.1	32.7	36.4	35.7	39.0
Hourly workers	53.0	57.1	56.3	50.0	45.4	51.4
			Female Workers			
No. of workers	7,570	2,191	1,110	1,169	480	2,620
Age	36.0	36.5	36.8	36.0	35.7	35.2
Job tenure	5.11	3.72	4.39	5.22	5.76	6.30
Hourly wage	4.805	4.111	4.364	4.949	5.013	5.471
Education	12.6	12.1	12.5	12.9	13.0	12.8
Percentage of workers:						
Nonwhite	11.1	10.4	9.2	10.1	10.4	13.1
Part-time	32.5	51.4	33.3	22.2	27.3	21.8
Union	15.6	2.4	11.5	20.3	39.6	25.1
Pension plan	56.1	18.8	42.3	67.9	78.3	83.9
Large cities	35.1	29.3	33.9	31.8	32.3	42.4
Hourly workers	58.4	58.3	60.8	57.1	62.1	57.3

Source: *Current Population Survey*, May 1979, unpublished data.

Table 2.9 **Male Employees in Manufacturing: May 1979**

Characteristic	Total	In Firms with an Employment of 1–24	25–99	100–499	500–999	1,000+
			Salaried Workers			
No. of workers	1,012	69	103	130	58	652
Age	40.21	36.06	40.15	41.12	42.76	40.26
	(11.87)	(13.98)	(13.10)	(12.80)	(11.74)	(11.16)
Job tenure	10.58	4.84	8.17	9.10	9.47	11.97
	(10.02)	(7.07)	(8.72)	(8.83)	(11.31)	(10.25)
Hourly wage	9.864	7.713	8.500	8.849	9.905	10.506
Education	13.99	12.41	12.90	13.62	13.97	14.41
Percentage of workers:						
Nonwhite	7.1	10.1	8.7	4.6	10.7	7.4
Part-time	3.0	20.2	5.8	3.0	5.1	0.6
Union	9.1	10.1	8.7	13.1	6.9	8.6
Pension plan	84.6	21.7	48.5	78.5	93.1	97.5
Large cities	43.3	46.3	37.9	42.3	32.8	45.1

Hourly Workers

No. of workers	1,781	154	233	251	93	1,050
Age	36.74	32.81	36.93	36.65	34.70	37.48
	(13.21)	(14.61)	(15.45)	(13.51)	(11.19)	(12.43)
Job tenure	8.75	3.92	5.89	7.54	8.13	10.44
	(9.32)	(6.09)	(8.11)	(8.76)	(7.89)	(9.75)
Hourly Wage	6.757	5.316	5.727	6.104	6.407	7.385
Education	11.27	10.69	10.79	10.79	11.31	11.57
Percentage of workers:						
Nonwhite	9.0	9.7	9.4	7.6	7.5	9.2
Part-time	2.8	9.7	7.7	2.0	2.2	1.0
Union	53.6	15.6	25.8	43.0	55.9	67.7
Pension plan	77.9	26.6	45.9	70.9	87.1	93.4
Large cities	33.5	46.1	33.0	38.2	27.9	31.1

Source: Current Population Survey, May 1979, unpublished data.

NOTE: Numbers in parentheses are standard deviations.

manufacturing worked on late/night shifts, and 14.2 percent in low-use manufacturing. There is a strong positive association between the percentage on late/night shifts (the complement of the percentage on day shifts) and firm size as evidenced by the data in table 2.10. It rises from 6.3 to 27.9 percent in high-use manufacturing and from 5.7 to 18.5 percent in low-use. The higher incidence of shift work in large firms is a consequence of the decision to engage in the volume production of standardized goods.

Firm size is systematically related to differences in wages, the organization of production, and the composition of employment. The received theory of labor markets acknowledges the presence of heterogeneous workers, but we still cling to Marshall's concept of a "representative firm." The latter convention must be abandoned to explain the empirical regularities exhibited in tables 2.8, 2.9, and 2.10.

2.3.5 Monitoring and Fixed Employment Costs in a World of Heterogeneous Firms

The uniqueness of a *firm* is essential for the existence of specific human capital. It is meaningless otherwise to speak about training that raises a worker's productivity in *one firm*, while leaving his productivity unchanged in other firms. If that is a true result, that *one firm* must have been different from all others. Fortunately, firms are heterogeneous, and profits can be increased by incurring those fixed employment costs that are needed to recruit, train, and retain a firm-specific labor force. Firms can differ in many ways, and the dimension which I have emphasized is that of entrepreneurial ability. Able entrepreneurs have the capacity to convert calendar time into larger supplies of managerial effort which allow them, through the usual law of variable proportions, to assemble large production teams. Following Lucas (1978), I assumed a background distribution of entrepreneurial abilities, $\psi(\lambda)$, which yields a critical ability level λ_0 such that if $\lambda < \lambda_0$, the individual does *not* become an entrepreneur. The relative frequencies of entrepreneurs of moderate abilities [λ just slightly greater than λ_0 in the truncated distribution of $\psi(\lambda)$] will be large, resulting in numerous small firms bearing a close resemblance to their neighbors. The rare, high-λ entrepreneurs from the extreme right tail of $\psi(\lambda)$ assemble very large corporations that are few in number. These giant firms are almost unique.

Entrepreneurs enter different industries, and in each industry competition produces an equilibrium size distribution of firms.[43] Employment is an imperfect but readily available measure of size. Small firms are defined here as those with less than twenty-five employees, while large firms have one thousand or more workers. Firm size distributions vary across industries. In all industries, 26.3 percent of total employment was located in small firms and 39.3 percent in large. The corresponding figures in manufacturing were 8.3 and 57.8 percent.

Talented entrepreneurs can economize on the time losses to monitoring and supervision in several ways. Production can be organized around teams and units, and authority can be delegated by stacking these teams in a hierarchical structure. The standardization of products and procedures (exemplified by the assembly line) limits the opportunities for discretionary behavior thereby simplifying the monitoring task. Capital is intensively utilized by operating multiple shifts. This mode of operation is profitable because of the high ratios of specialized capital to labor which accompany volume production.[44] Further, the planning of production is extended to recruiting and personnel management. Job descriptions and task assignments are spelled out in great detail. Applicants are screened and tested to determine if they can meet the rigid job specifications. Recruiting costs are higher in large firms which will hold job vacancies open until a suitable candidate is found. More highly educated persons are recruited to staff the salaried, firm-specific positions, as evidenced by data in the top panel of table 2.9. Specific training is provided to new employees to adapt them to the firm's prescribed operating practices. These recruiting and training activities "produce" a labor force of reasonably homogeneous individuals, and such teams are obviously easier to supervise. In a sense, higher fixed employment costs can be substituted for lower subsequent monitoring costs. Those firms that incur high fixed costs have a strong incentive to design selection and compensation practices that reduce the turnover of specifically trained workers. If firms are successful in retaining specifically trained workers, data on job tenures tell us something about the relative importance of firm-specific human capital.[45] Job tenures are longer (suggesting larger investments in firm-specific human capital) for persons who are males, are more highly educated, work at large firms, hold salaried positions, and are employed in industries which exhibit higher capital utilization rates.

Less able entrepreneurs command smaller teams and produce customized goods.[46] They spend less on recruiting because jobs are flexible and work can be redesigned to fit the individual applicant. Small firms have shorter life expectancies and hence have less to gain from firm-specific training and specialized durable machinery. Fixed employment costs are small, and labor costs are almost entirely composed of wages that must be paid to attract general human capital from competing employments.

The behavioral differences among firms are confounded by the presence of unions. Some 22.7 percent of all employed persons were members of trade unions or employee associations, and the membership climbs to 34.2 percent of employees in large firms.[47] On the supply side, there are likely to be scale economies in organizing workers, collecting

Table 2.10 Wages, Age, and Job Tenure in Manufacturing: May 1979 (by firm size)

A. High-Use Manufacturing

Characteristic	In Firms with an Employment of					
	1–24	25–99	100–499	500–999	1,000+	Total
			All Employees			
No. of employees	126	163	237	89	1,223	1,838
Percent day shift	93.7	89.6	79.3	77.5	72.1	76.3
Hourly wage	5.256	6.069	6.482	6.997	8.012	7.405
Age	35.23	37.94	37.46	46.97	38.08	37.74
Job tenure	4.15	6.96	7.67	7.63	10.68	9.37
Percent female	40.5	34.4	30.0	25.8	20.9	24.8
			Salaried Male Workers			
No. of employees	18	29	60	25	338	470
Percent day shift	88.9	100.0	93.3	88.0	87.6	89.1
Hourly wage	7.924	9.774	8.998	10.361	10.855	10.413
Age	37.44	44.93	40.52	42.32	40.55	40.79
Job tenure	4.78	12.90	10.88	9.44	12.50	11.86
			Hourly Male Workers			
No. of employees	57	78	106	41	630	912
Percent day shift	89.5	83.3	72.6	64.4	61.6	66.8
Hourly wage	5.422	5.902	6.084	6.517	7.552	7.061
Age	32.23	35.49	35.31	35.10	37.84	46.87
Job tenure	3.11	6.19	7.54	7.32	11.00	9.52

B. Low-Use Manufacturing

Characteristic	In Firms with an Employment of 1–24	25–99	100–499	500–999	1,000+	Total
All Employees						
No. of employees	212	358	387	145	1,132	2,234
Percent day shift	94.3	90.2	90.4	82.8	81.5	85.8
Hourly wage	5.423	5.449	5.709	6.075	7.185	6.412
Age	35.33	38.16	38.65	34.96	37.65	37.51
Job tenure	4.36	5.41	6.76	7.27	9.21	7.59
Percent females	30.2	35.8	44.4	41.4	35.2	36.8
Salaried Male Workers						
No. of employees	51	74	70	33	314	542
Percent day shift	96.1	90.5	95.7	87.9	92.4	92.6
Hourly wage	7.639	8.001	8.722	9.561	10.131	9.389
Age	35.57	38.28	41.61	43.09	39.95	39.71
Job tenure	4.86	6.31	7.57	9.48	11.40	9.48
Hourly Male Workers						
No. of employees	97	155	145	52	420	869
Percent day shift	90.7	85.8	83.4	75 0	69.8	77.6
Hourly wage	5.254	5.639	6.119	6.320	7.134	6.440
Age	33.15	37.66	37.63	34.38	36.94	36.61
Job tenure	4.40	5.74	7.54	8.77	9.61	7.94

Source: Current Population Survey, May 1979, unpublished data.

NOTE: The two-digit industries included under high use were industries 29, 33, 26, 28, 22, 30, 32, 21, 37, and 27. The remaining industries were put into low use. See note 42 of text.

dues, and enforcing compliance. The demand for unionism is also likely to be greater in larger firms for at least three reasons: First, a union may be the preferred institution to supply certain services of a public goods nature (e.g., grievance procedures, negotiating better working conditions, or resolving conflicts). Second, a union that can restrict membership may be able to raise wages above competitive levels if the host firm is earning economic rents. Third, big firms in small labor markets may have some monopsony power. The data of tables 2.8 and 2.10 indicate that the incidence of unionism is indeed positively correlated with firm size.

Some interesting interactions are observed in table 2.11 which presents data for male production workers in manufacturing classified by firm size, job tenure, and union membership. The incidence of unionism was 58.3 percent for the entire sample, and by firm size groups, the percentages in unions were 21.9 small, 46.5 medium, and 67.7 large. New employees with less than one year of job tenure accounted for 17.1 percent of employment; this measure of the annual accession rate varied from a high of 35.0 percent in small, nonunionized firms to a low of 8.7 percent in large unionized firms. Holding firm size constant, new employees are less likely to be assigned to jobs on the regular day shift. The relative frequency of shift work which reflects the firm's capital utilization rate is considerably higher in the union sector, but the reason for this is unclear. High capital utilization rates may be associated with larger union wage gains, or trade unions may be better able to supply the services and contractual arrangements demanded by employees on late/night shifts.

Wages of the blue-collar workers in table 2.11 are positively related to firm size and job tenure. The percentage wage gains due to size and tenure are larger in the nonunion sector, but in each size/tenure cell, unionized workers were uniformly better paid.[48] However, wage differences understate the differentials in total employee compensation because union workers receive proportionally more in fringe benefits. Although collinearity makes it difficult to disentangle firm size and union effects, the data of table 2.11 and the results reported by Mellow (1981) support the conclusion that other things equal, workers in large firms are paid higher wages and receive more fringes. These higher wages may contain elements of economic rents or compensating differences for working conditions, or they may simply represent the equilibrium payments to superior employees whose higher productivity cannot be linked to observable traits. The latter interpretation is in line with the monitoring cost hypothesis in which able entrepreneurs are matched with more productive workers.

Based on data from two longitudinal surveys, Mincer (1981) reported that the wage-experience profile was flatter for unionized workers. Union members claimed that they got less "training" at their jobs which could account for the flatter profile. However, an employee's response to a survey question is not a reliable basis for estimating the amount of specific training that he has received. Further, the wage rate is an imperfect measure of pecuniary returns. A regression equation in which wages of employed persons are related to job tenures will yield a smaller slope coefficient relative to a second regression in which expected wages are related to job tenures.[49] Both regressions will understate the pecuniary returns to job experience. Unionized workers are covered by collective bargaining agreements and implicit long-term contracts whose compensation packages exhibit the property that the wage to pay ratio (W/C^*) falls with increasing job tenure; i.e., the value of a union member's claims to pensions and other fringe benefits rises with seniority. Expected pay per workhour is a better measure of pecuniary returns. We have to estimate regressions using an expected pay variable to determine if the experience profile of pecuniary returns is really flatter for union members.

Finally, it has been observed that unionized workers receive a larger fraction of *pay* in the form of pensions and fringes. Mincer (1981) attributed this magnification of the demand for fringes to the fact that union members are more highly paid and hence face higher marginal tax rates. If true, the ratio of fringe benefits to wages should be larger in states that have higher state income tax rates. Alternatively, it can be argued that fringe benefits and deferred pay are incorporated into compensation packages of those firms (union and nonunion) that are trying to retain their specifically trained workers. Reference to the left panel of table 2.11 reveals that in the nonunionized sector, the percentage of employees who are eligible for pension plans is positively related to firm size. The phenomenon is not unique to the unionized sector.

The data on job tenures are consistent with a model in which specific training assumes greater importance in larger and unionized firms. A tenured worker is defined here as one who has been with his current employer for five or more years. Table 2.11 reveals that 55.4 percent of male production workers in manufacturing were tenured, while 71.7 percent of employees in large unionized firms were tenured. For nonunion workers, the mean duration of job tenure was 2.7 years longer in large versus small firms, and the difference is due to higher retention rates during the first five years. Once workers pass beyond the five-year point, the conditional mean duration of job tenure is unrelated to firm size.[50] The job tenure differential between small and large unionized firms is 5.9 years, and marginal retention rates appear to be higher in large firms at each year of service point. If years of job tenure are subtracted from the mean age, we can derive the mean age of workers at entry. This exercise reveals that in large firms, tenured workers were recruited at younger ages.[51] Those individuals who obtain tenure at small firms evidently hold

Table 2.11 Characteristics of Hourly Male Workers in All Manufacturing: May 1979 (by union status, job tenure, and firm size)

Characteristic/ Firm Size	Nonunion with Job Tenure of				Union with Job Tenure of			
	<1	1–5	≧5	Total	<1	1–5	≧5	Total
No. of employees								
1–99	106	107	90	303	19	27	39	85
100–999	36	77	71	184	21	34	105	160
1,000+	65	102	172	339	62	139	510	711
Percentage on day shift								
1–99	80.2	86.9	95.6	87.1	73.7	85.2	94.9	87.1
100–999	66.7	81.8	88.7	81.5	52.4	55.9	81.0	71.9
1,000+	69.2	68.6	75.6	72.3	41.9	51.1	66.5	61.3
Hourly wage								
1–99	4.571	4.964	5.691	5.042	5.099	6.717	7.813	6.858
100–999	4.809	5.481	6.504	5.744	6.029	6.353	6.701	6.539
1,000+	5.106	6.226	7.077	6.443	6.908	6.982	7.795	7.559

Percentage on pension plans								
1–99	25.4	25.2	38.9	29.4	36.8	70.4	84.6	69.4
100–999	41.7	57.1	74.6	60.9	81.0	91.2	94.3	91.9
1,000+	80.0	84.3	96.5	89.7	90.3	92.1	96.7	95.2
Age in years (mean and standard deviation)								
1–99	29.06	30.07	46.14	34.49	25.84	32.00	48.05	37.99
	(13.42)	(12.58)	(14.02)	(15.29)	(9.17)	(12.19)	(11.79)	(14.77)
100–999	24.97	31.95	42.73	34.74	27.76	28.09	42.82	37.71
	(8.69)	(11.81)	(12.36)	(13.33)	(8.34)	(8.25)	(11.00)	(12.33)
1,000+	26.88	31.27	39.79	34.75	29.11	29.39	42.52	38.78
	(10.31)	(10.65)	(11.36)	(12.16)	(10.73)	(9.27)	(11.23)	(12.35)
Job tenure in years (mean and standard deviation)								
1–99	—	2.36	12.92	4.67	—	2.30	12.77	6.59
		(0.98)	(8.52)	(7.18)		(1.17)	(8.27)	(8.10)
100–999	—	2.31	12.62	5.84	—	2.71	14.12	9.84
		(1.05)	(7.63)	(7.24)		(1.06)	(8.90)	(9.37)
1,000+	—	2.25	13.22	7.38	—	2.35	15.95	11.90
		(1.01)	(8.78)	(8.67)		(1.06)	(8.83)	(9.91)

Source: Current Population Survey, May 1979, unpublished data.

several jobs before they find a suitable match with a viable firm that will remain in business for fifteen or more years. It would be interesting to discover whether the older tenured workers at viable small firms had received more or less firm-specific training in relation to tenured workers at large manufacturing firms.

2.4 Concluding Remarks

The labor market for the economy as a whole is populated by a wide diversity of workers and firms. The entrepreneurs who control small firms confront a lower shadow price of time which gives them a comparative advantage in monitoring worker performance, coping with disruptions and high labor turnover rates, providing maintenance for used equipment, and haggling over frequent changes in prices and wages. Their production teams include less experienced workers and more part-time employees. They apparently lack the organizational ability to operate multiple shifts. They choose to supply products where technology discourages standardization and volume production. Specialization and specific training might be profitable if the firm could be assured of its survival and its ability to retain specialized resources. But such assurances cannot be supplied, even by government regulation. Some workers obviously dislike the discipline and rigidity of employment at large firms and choose to work for small employers. They receive little or no specific training, are paid lower wages, and get relatively few fringe benefits. A relatively small number of individuals form permanent attachments with viable small employers.[52] However, most workers in this part of the labor market possess general human capital that can readily be shifted to numerous small firms that are only slightly differentiated from one another. The uncertain and possibly short lives of these firms reduce the returns to specific investments, but this uncertainty is apparently not the source of employment instability.[53] The important fact is that variable wage payments comprise almost all of the full costs of the labor input. A neoclassical model in which labor's marginal value product is equated in each period to the market wage rate describes the behavior of firms and workers in the portion of the labor market populated by "small firms."

The neoclassical model has been replaced by a loosely knit theory in which the labor market is characterized by implicit long-term contracts, rigid wages, formal layoff policies, lifetime tenured employment, deferred pay, and mandatory retirement. Fixed employment costs are, according to Hall (1980), the glue that binds workers and firms together. The authors of the new labor economics recognize that firm-specific investments in recruiting and training are endogenous, but they largely ignore this endogeneity. The existence of these fixed costs is simply assumed to focus attention on the implications of a quasi-fixed labor input.

The thesis advanced in this paper is that recruiting and training only make sense in a world of heterogeneous, differentiated firms. The heterogeneity in my model is generated by a distribution of entrepreneurial abilities. The outliers succeed in building very large corporations that are few in number and are spread across industries. Each very large firm is nearly unique. Managerial efforts are directed to the development of standardized products and the organization of integrated but inflexible production lines. Companies make large investments in recruiting and training firm-specific labor forces. Workers in large firms are paid higher wages as well as compensation in the form of pensions and fringes that are designed in part to reduce the turnover of specifically trained employees. The full cost of the labor input is thus the sum of total employee compensation, the amortization of fixed employment costs, and the implicit costs of monitoring worker performance. Since wages represent only a part of full labor costs, they are unlikely to be frequently adjusted in response to short-run changes in demand. The prices quoted by large firms also tend to be rigid because every price change has to be closely supervised to prevent chiseling and cheating by numerous subordinates who staff a complex distribution network. Price and wage rigidities may have been responsible for more employment instability and may also have contributed to an increased demand for outside representation of workers by organized labor unions.[54] The specificity of the labor input, personnel management, and the organization of production along rigid assembly-line techniques have surely been influenced by the shadow price of the entrepreneurial input. The structure of each firm is rationally determined to maximize profits in a world where there are trade-offs between monitoring costs and the fixed costs of specialized resources. The portion of the labor market in which we find large firms is described by the perceptive picture painted by Hall (1982). However, it is a picture that applies to only a part of the economy, albeit an important part containing at least 40 percent of total employment.

Specific human capital has proven to be an important concept in the theory of labor economics. However, firm-specific capital can only be produced and employed in a segment of the economy occupied by very large firms. The predictions of a theory that embraces this concept can be borne out by the empirical evidence if these large firms account for a dominant share of the aggregate labor market. The empirical studies of the last two decades suggest that this is indeed the case. But there is another important sector of the labor market where there is little room for specialized labor. The caricatures of the large and small firms in these two sectors are like Marshall's "representative firm." They are simply analytic prototypes picked from a continuum of firm sizes, production adaptability, and labor specificity. Firms and workers are indeed heterogeneous. A theory of labor economics that explicitly acknowledges this heterogeneity and incorporates it into its analytic models can, I believe, add considerably to our understanding of the behavior of labor markets.

Notes

1. Details of the theory can be found in Oi (1962) and Becker (1964). Reder (1955) offered an alternative theory in which the cyclical changes in occupation wage differentials were explained by countercyclical variations in hiring standards that result in the upgrading and downgrading of employees. The Reder model must be tied to a theory of factor demand shifts in order to explain employment responses.

2. Hutt (1977) identified six categories of idleness: (1) valueless resources, (2) pseudoidleness which is defined as a state in which the capital value of an asset exceeds its scrap value even though its net hire value is nil, (3) preferred idleness exemplified by the labor-leisure choice, (4) participatory idleness in arrangements to share monopoly rents, (5) enforced idleness due, for example, to legal limits on workhours, and (6) withheld capacity to obtain monopoly rents. Idleness of the first three types constitutes an efficient allocation of resources.

3. Additional evidence and citations to the literature can be found in Clark and Summers (1979), pp. 53–54.

4. This model helps to explain academic tenure; see Oi (1979). It also provides an explanation for mandatory retirement which is more fully analyzed by Lazear (1979).

5. The rationale for this argument was developed by Becker and Stigler (1974). Deferred pay can be viewed as an alternative to bonding, which puts the Becker-Stigler model in the spirit of the principal-agent literature.

6. I was introduced to the Koike article by Hall (1982). In addition to his discussion on job tenures, Koike points out an important difference in trade union behavior. The employment agreements negotiated by Japanese unions contain *no* seniority rules for layoffs and recalls.

7. Total compensation does not vary in direct proportion to man-hours because some components (e.g., disability and health insurance) are linked to the number of employees rather than man-hours. The nonlinearities in the relation of compensation to man-hours can be put into the fixed employment costs.

8. A specially designed machine or plant can be purchased on a "made-to-order" basis. However, when such inputs are demanded on a regular basis, the firm is likely to engage in vertical integration to control the source of supply. Klein, Crawford, and Alchian (1978) point to the concept of "postcontractual opportunistic behavior" to justify vertical integration in cases where the situation could result in a bilateral bargaining game. The principle is illustrated by the acquisition of Fisher Bodies by General Motors.

9. The durability of firm-specific human capital is jointly determined by the expected job tenure of a trained worker and the rate of technical obsolescence/depreciation applicable to such capital. Rapid changes in technology and in product demands increase the obsolescence rate, thereby reducing the durability of specific human capital.

10. Rosen (1972*b*) constructed a model in which inputs of labor L and firm-specific knowledge Z produced two joint products in fixed proportions: output Q and an increment to knowledge ΔZ. Knowledge is a permanent, nontransferable asset which produces a volume effect similar to the one examined by Alchian (1959). In a second model, Rosen

(1972*a*) assumed that each multiproduct firm supplied its workers with work plus training that added to the workers' general human capital. Employees recognized the composition of the tied package and were thus willing to accept lower wages which reflected the implicit market value of general human capital. Training and work (the production of goods) are presumably tied because of some unspecified economies of joint production. The economies argument is more plausible when the training is firm specific.

11. Suppose that the productivity of the ith individual, μ_i, depends on inputs of general and specific human capital, $\mu_i = \mu(G_i, S_i)$. If μ is homogeneous of the first degree, $\partial\mu/\partial S$ is a function of the ratio (G/S). The marginal product of S is equalized when $(G_i/S_i) = (G_j/S_j)$ for all i, j. If market wages are proportional to general human capital, an optimal allocation of specific human capital will result in more S allocated to individuals with more G. However, the degree of fixity will be a constant.

A positive relation between the wage rate and the degree of fixity can be derived by relaxing the assumption of first-degree homogeneity or by introducing additional arguments into the μ function.

12. Alfred Marshall and his followers were mainly interested in issues of allocative efficiency across commodities which were equated to industries. The concept of a "representative firm" was sufficient for this purpose, but it left little room for heterogeneity. The theory was mainly concerned with the determinants of an optimum (equilibrium) firm size that could be reconciled with two maintained assumptions: (1) first-degree homogeneity of the production function and (2) perfect competition in factor markets. Kaldor (1934) obtained a determinate firm size by appealing to the fixity in supply of at least one input. The proposition that firm size is ultimately limited by a scarcity of the entrepreneurial input was also advanced by Robinson (1958), Georgescu-Roegen (1967), and Friedman (1976). I shall also invoke this same assumption.

13. Capital is assumed to require *no* monitoring. In the adjustment cost model of Lucas (1967), the installation of new capital entailed an opportunity cost of forgone output. This is not the same as monitoring. In his distinction between man and machine, J. Clark (1923) pointed out the importance of monitoring and metering worker performance:

> Having learned one way of doing a thing, a worker tries variants on it, sometimes with a purpose, sometimes aimlessly, but always following the bent of "monkeying." . . . He is very imperfectly adapted to continuous toil and when he does work, he works now faster and now slower with an irregular rhythm. . . . Especially when working for a purely collective end, his ardors while often strong appear to be characteristically intermittent and unreliable. As a class, he needs personal incentives to work, rewards for good performance, and penalties for bad, more immediate and substantial than his share in the welfare of the whole industry or the whole community. (p. 8)

14. The shadow price of an efficiency unit of managerial effort is Pf_T, but a unit of calendar time yields λ efficiency units so that entrepreneurial time has a shadow price of $P\lambda f_T$. Since h hours are required to monitor each worker, we get the implicit monitoring cost, $\delta = P\lambda h f_T$.

15. Homogeneity implies that $Q = Kf_K + Nf_N + Tf_T$. Substitution into the expression for profits yields $\pi = P(M\lambda h f_T + Tf_T)$. Equation (5) is obtained by recalling that $T = \lambda(\bar{H} - hM)$.

16. If wages are proportional to productivity, $W(\mu)/\mu$ will be a constant. In this event, $[\mu W'(\mu) - W(\mu)] = 0$, and in the presence of positive monitoring costs, all firms will try to substitute higher quality for fewer numbers. The resulting increase in demand for more productive workers will raise their wages. Hence, in equilibrium, $W(\mu)$ must be convex so that $W''(\mu) > 0$.

17. Friedman (1976) explicitly acknowledged the presence of heterogeneous firms in his analysis of the relation of the firm to the industry. He examined a case in which firms with different cost curves had to adjust to an increase in the demand facing the industry. If the increase in product demand raises the price of a factor that is specific to the industry, the

quasi-marginal cost curve for an exceptional firm could bend backward; i.e., the exceptional firm contracts output in response to an increase in product price. Friedman did not try to explain the reasons for different cost curves. In my model, a dispersion of entrepreneurial abilities generated cost differences wherein more able entrepreneurs enjoyed lower marginal cost curves.

18. Tailors, punch press operators, and door-to-door salesmen are often paid by "piece rates." Such compensation methods can be implemented when output is easily observed and directly linked to particular employees. If each worker in Adam Smith's pin factory performed all tasks (sharpening the pin and placing the head on it), they could have been paid by the piece, thereby reducing monitoring costs. The gains from specialization and the division of labor evidently outweighed the monitoring cost savings. Payment by results may provide incentives for greater work effort which can explain its adoption in some firms. An analysis of this method of compensation can be found in Pencavel (1977).

19. Rees and Shultz (1970) found, for example, that a secretary's pay was positively related to typing speed, but the relation was nonlinear. Only a small part of the dispersion in pay could be explained by typing speed. A significant part of pay evidently represented compensation for productive activities other than typing. The relation of total productivity to length of job service cannot be determined by observing only one dimension of productivity.

20. Alchian argued that unit costs will decline as a function of the planned volume of output. Wright (1936) observed the same regularity in his study of progress functions in the production of air frames. Oi (1967) explained the progress function in terms of intertemporal factor substitutions and the economies of joint production. Planned volume (batch size) is obviously important in designing the production organization.

21. The critical volume at which an assembly line constitutes the least-cost production method obviously depends on the product. The requisite volumes are likely to be large for goods like pogo sticks, toasters, and bikes, but a volume of ten to twenty oceangoing oil tankers is sufficient to justify the construction of an assembly line.

22. The compensating wage difference will obviously be larger, the larger the size of the team that is asked to conform to the same common schedule and working conditions, and the greater the dispersion in worker preferences. These results are rigorously derived by Deardorff and Stafford (1976). Union workers are typically employed in large firms which provide them with inferior working conditions. According to Duncan and Stafford (1980), the union wage differential cannot be interpreted as simply a monopoly return. Part of it represents a compensating difference that must be paid to attract workers into accepting employment in less desirable work settings.

23. This implication provides yet another reason for the positive association between wages and firm size. Individuals who seek work at large firms will, on average, incur higher search costs because rigid job specifications will not be modified to meet individual worker differences. In equilibrium, larger firms must pay higher wages to compensate employees for the higher expected search costs. The fixed and flex-wage models of Pissarides (1976) incorporate the idea of search on the part of firms.

24. If input is more cheaply monitored, a master carpenter might teach his apprentices certain standardized ways of performing various tasks. When all apprentices use the same work methods, the quality and quantity of output may be more accurately and cheaply gauged by observing the input of apprentice time rather than measuring the flow of output. Investments in entry-level training and screening could thus reduce subsequent monitoring costs.

25. The argument is put as follows: "In slack weeks, hours of work are set at lower levels and the intensity of work may fall as well. The general flavor of the arrangement is that workers work harder when there is much or more work to do." However, in an earlier passage dealing with employment bargains for salaried workers, Hall writes, "Employers have the right to demand intense effort for a few weeks or months but not permanently.

Periods of extraordinary effort must be counterbalanced by restful periods. For salaried workers, arrangements of this kind develop by custom and are rarely spelled out in formal contracts." But why are implicit arrangements preferable to explicit incentives for extra effort? We could appeal to the difficulties of enforcing contingent contracts. There is another weakness in the argument. If "intense effort" can only be demanded for short bursts, we are still left with the puzzle of explaining Okun's law which sometimes applies to adjustment periods extending over several quarters.

26. Gordon and Walton appeal to Stigler's concept of "adaptability" to explain the rapid postwar recoveries in Europe. Wars do not destroy productive factors in balanced proportions. As a consequence, the surviving stocks of capital are not efficiently utilized. A small investment in a particular type of capital that restores the designed factor proportions can lead to a sharp increase in output. The installation of a conveyor belt might, for example, enable a company to make efficient use of its specialized but idle mining equipment. This investment will increase output and the output/capital ratio, but this does not contradict the law of variable proportions as a principle applicable to the ex ante planning of production.

27. With only one technology and two types of labor, the latter effect dominates, and the cyclical adjustments generate a positive correlation between output changes and changes in the output/labor ratio. The pattern is, however, attenuated by the presence of diverse technologies because the standby capacity usually has a lower output/labor ratio. The strong procyclical behavior of labor productivity suggests that the effect of fixed proportions outweighs the influence of diverse technologies.

28. Shinohara (1962) reported that 40 percent of the capital assets of small Japanese firms were purchased as used equipment, compared to only 6 percent for large firms. The flow is evidently one in which new machines tend to be purchased by large firms and, as they age, some are sold to small firms. A similar pattern is observed in international trade. The high-wage, industrialized nations regularly export used durable machinery to less-developed countries. Smith (1974) appeals to differences in relative factor prices to explain the trade in used assets.

29. The present value of the net quasi-rents that can be earned by a durable asset declines with age because of rising maintenance costs. A machine is scrapped when its present value falls below its scrap value. Parks (1979) analyzed the interactions of maintenance, scrapping, and the replacement demand. Grunfeld (1960) provided an early empirical study which emphasized the substitution of maintenance for investment.

30. The tacit assumption here is that capital can be more cheaply transported over time; i.e., increments to capital values depreciate more slowly than increments to inventories of final goods. Internal investments will be biased toward physical capital because the firm is contracting employment in a recession.

31. "Total product" is the sum of the value of final goods plus the implicit value of increments to capital assets. More maintenance during a recession reflects a firm's rational responses to changing relative factor and product prices. When the prices of goods fall in relation to the shadow prices of internally produced investments, the "output mix" understandably shifts away from the production of goods.

32. See, for example, *The Economic Report of the President, 1980*, table B-37, p. 246.

33. In addition to employee compensation, full labor costs must include the amortization of fixed employment costs. If complementary inputs of protective clothing, noise suppressors, and so forth are supplied by the firm, their costs are properly included in full labor costs.

34. I am unaware of any studies that analyze the factors which determine paid leisure time across firms and industries and over time. Paid leisure hours H_L are like the "income in kind" in the British truck system analyzed by Hilton (1957). Paid holidays and vacations place a lower bound on an individual's leisure time consumption. Additional leisure via absenteeism entails a loss of earnings. Rest and recuperation may increase productivity, but these gains redound to the individual. Why do firms impose a lower bound on rest and

recuperation time? I am forced to appeal to an argument like Hilton's in which workers are myopic, and merciful employers nudge them toward the "right" mix of work and leisure.

Banks allegedly insist on vacations so that an employee's books can be audited while he is away. The Rand Corporation gives their employees higher rates of pay when they are on vacation because they *need* more money for travel and lodging. Finally, we have to explain why employees in the public sector and in social service agencies get considerably more paid leisure than workers in the private business sector.

35. Postponing compensation may be an efficient means of controlling executives and public servants. It discourages them from engaging in theft, larceny, and dysfunctional acts. The deterrent effects of deferred pay must, however, be balanced against higher wages that can elicit greater work effort.

The growing demand for private pensions may partially be traced to lower after-tax prices. Discontinuities in the structure of social security benefits may also help to explain the growth. Failure to take early retirement at age 62 is accompanied by a loss in social security wealth. The defined social security benefits may not be enough to warrant full retirement as a utility maximizing choice. If private pensions or savings were available to supplement social security, a worker could avoid the implicit taxation of social security wealth by retiring at age 62. Legislation that raised the defined social security benefits may have prompted the growth in employer contributions to private pensions.

36. The supply of labor is not a function of the wage rate but is, instead, a function of pay per workhour C^*, working conditions, and anticipated future rates of pay. In a demand study, the appropriate "price" should be the full labor cost. The data of tables 2.4, 2.5, and 2.6 indicate that the wage rate is an imperfect measure of pay and probably an even poorer proxy for the full labor cost.

37. Although the CPS asked for the individual's occupation, I classified respondents according to whether they were or were not "paid by the hour." I shall refer to the hourly paid employees as production workers, even though this differs from the census definition of a production worker.

38. In a steady state, the annual turnover rate is equal to the proportion of workers with less than one year of job tenure, but the mean duration is determined by the entire frequency distribution. The correlation between turnover and mean job tenure is thus imperfect, except in the special case where the functional form of the frequency distribution is the same across firms and industries.

39. See, for example, Lester (1967), Masters (1969), and Mellow (1981). Several arguments have been proposed to explain the firm size profile. Lester (1967) and Duncan and Stafford (1980) argued that large firms must pay higher wages which contain a compensating difference for less desirable working conditions. Employees must accept the greater discipline and rigidities of working in large teams. A slightly different argument was proposed by Stigler (1962):

> It is well known that wage rates are less in small plants than in large, and the difference reflects at least in part (and perhaps in whole) the lower cost of the small-scale employer of judging quality. . . . Men should in general enter smaller companies, the greater their ability. (p. 102)

This argument is contrary to a model in which small employers are "small" because they lack the ability to judge and to organize large production teams.

40. The sample means shown in table 2.8 differ from those in Mellow (1981) because I excluded individuals who did not report the timing of work. The timing question was used to determine the frequency of shift work.

41. Mellow estimated two separate regressions. The coefficient of the largest firm size dummy variable fell to .056 in the union regression and to .119 in the nonunion regression. The treatment of unionism as exogenous (either as a dummy variable or as a classificatory variable) can be questioned.

42. The Foss estimates are based on the 1976 Census of Manufactures. The two-digit manufacturing industries wre divided into two groups as follows:

Workweek of Fixed Capital in Manufacturing Industries, 1976

High-Use Manufacturing		Low-Use Manufacturing	
Industry	Hours	Industry	Hours
29. Petroleum	140	35. Machinery	80
33. Primary metals	119	20. Food	75
26. Paper	115	34. Fabr. metals	75
28. Chemicals	112	36. Elec. machinery	73
22. Textiles	110	38. Instruments	69
30. Rubber	108	24. Lumber	58
32. Stone, glass	98	39. Misc. mfg.	57
21. Tobacco	91	25. Furniture	51
37. Transport. equip.	87	31. Leather	44
27. Printing	82	23. Apparel	42

Source: Foss 1981, table 2, p. 9.

Over the period 1929–76, the capital utilization rate in manufacturing rose by 24.5 percent.

43. Although λ was assumed to be an exogenous parameter, it can surely be influenced by economic forces. The process by which a chief executive officer is selected and retained varies across firms. In some cases, an owner-operator begins with a small firm and, through on-the-job experience, he gains the skills to expand the size of his team. In other instances, a candidate may be picked and groomed for the position, which is another way of saying that the firm is investing in specific human capital to raise the value of λ for this candidate. For my purposes, it is sufficient to assume that entrepreneurial ability λ corresponds to firm size.

44. The sparse use of part-time employees by large firms reflects their higher monitoring costs. Disruptions are also costlier when firms adopt inflexible production plans. Large firms enter into vertical integration to avoid unanticipated breaks in the supplies of raw materials. They purchase new as opposed to used equipment. They also invest more in safety to reduce the frequency of industrial accidents. The data on work injury rates examined by Oi (1974) clearly show that work injury risks are substantially lower in the largest establishments.

45. Job tenure is obviously an imperfect proxy for firm-specific human capital. Specifically trained workers ought to remain with their employers for longer periods, but a host of other factors affects the mean duration of job tenure. These include things like the worker's age, the cyclical volatility of demand, the survival probabilities of firms, wage levels, mobility costs, and so forth.

46. The customization may be evident in the product (the tailor-made suit), or it may be incorporated in other, not directly observable, attributes such as credit terms, delivery service, or implicit warranties.

47. Unions and employee associations were combined in the CPS. I shall refer to the combined group as "unions."

48. The impact of unionism on wages has been extensively studied by Lewis (1963), Mellow (1981), Mincer (1981), and in numerous studies cited by Freeman and Medoff (1981). The union wage differential has increased in the 1970s. Over the course of the last thirty years, the data reveal an upward trend in the ratio of nonproduction to production workers in manufacturing. If salaried nonproduction workers can be substituted for blue-collar workers, the rising union wage differential in the 1970s should have accelerated this trend.

49. The expected wage is equal to the wage times the proportion of the period that the individual is employed. Mincer (1981) found that the probability of a temporary layoff was

inversely related to seniority and that union members experienced higher layoff rates. Most unions establish seniority rules that place the burden of temporary layoffs on junior employees.

50. This conclusion is tentative. I have not examined the job tenure distributions by single years which might reveal the source of the difference in mean durations.

51. The age at entry for the *i*th worker, α_i, is the difference between his current age A_i and his years of job tenure T_i. The mean age at entry can thus be calculated from the tables as $\bar{\alpha} = \bar{A} - \bar{T}$.

Constructed Mean Age at Entry of Tenured Workers
(men with five or more years of job tenure)

Firm Size	Nonunion	Union
1–99	33.2	35.3
100–999	30.1	28.7
1,000+	26.6	26.6

Tenured workers at large firms joined their employers at a younger mean age (26.6 years) than the mean age of all new employees in 1979. However, the tenured workers at small firms were drawn from the right side of the age distribution of new employees.

52. Table 2.11 reveals that only 33.2 percent of male workers in small firms had five or more years of job tenure. Employment durations tend to be shorter for at least two reasons: First, these jobs may serve as stepping stones and training grounds for new entrants. The age distributions of employees in different industries show that young persons are more heavily represented in trade, personal services, and the low-wage manufacturing industries. This allocation can be explained by a reciprocal search process in which individuals seek high-paying jobs and firms look for suitable candidates. New entrants who lack job experience and work histories may take jobs at small firms that provide little specific training, but these jobs enable them to establish track records documenting their reliability, honesty, and capacity to work with others. Second, the turnover of small firms due to bankruptcies and takeovers are responsible for some job terminations.

53. The data of table 2.2 collected by King (1923) indicate that in the recession of 1920–22 the variability of employment was less in small firms. A perusal of data in *County Business Patterns* also suggests that employment is less volatile in small establishments. However, both data sets describe the behavior of employment for the aggregate of firms in each size category and could thus conceal considerable churning among firms within each size group. It is unclear how a prior job affects the behavior of a released employee. Individuals who worked at small firms possess only general human capital that can readily be transferred to many jobs. Workers who are separated from large companies may try to find an employer who can utilize his specific human capital. But if training is truly *specific*, it has little or no value to others. This reasoning suggests that specifically trained, unemployed workers (ignorant of the nature of their human capital) are more likely to experience the long spells of unemployment that were reported by K. Clark and Summers (1979).

54. The unionized sector in manufacturing is mainly located in large firms and in industries with high capital utilization rates. The unionized firms that have adopted rigid production techniques tend to experience greater employment variability, and the burden of unemployment is mainly placed on junior employees. The evidence examined by Mincer (1981) and the studies cited by Freeman and Medoff (1981) indicate that the incidence of temporary layoffs is higher in the unionized sector. This finding in combination with the fact that premiums for unemployment insurance are *not* based on actuarially fair experience ratings, led me to the tentative conclusion that the present unemployment insurance program redistributes income from nonunionized workers to union members. This conclusion must await further empirical study.

References

Alchian, A. A. 1959. Costs and outputs. In *The allocation of economic resources*, ed. M. Abramovitz. Stanford: Stanford University Press. (Reprinted in 1977. *Economic forces*. Indianapolis: Liberty Press.)

———. 1969. Information costs, pricing, and resource unemployment. *Journal of Economic Inquiry* 7: 109–28.

Alchian, A. A., and H. Demsetz. 1972. Production, information cost, and economic organization. *American Economic Review* 62: 777–95.

Baily, M. N. 1974. Wages and employment under uncertain demand. *Review of Economic Studies* 41: 37–50.

Becker, G. S. 1964. *Human capital: A theoretical and empirical analysis*. New York: Columbia University Press for the NBER.

Becker, G. S., and G. J. Stigler. 1974. Law enforcement, malfeasance, and compensation of enforcers. *Journal of Legal Studies* 3: 1–18.

Ben-Porath, Y. 1967. The production of human capital and the life cycle of earnings. *Journal of Political Economy* 75: 352–65.

Clark, J. M. 1923. *Studies in the economics of overhead costs*. Chicago: University of Chicago Press.

Clark, K. B., and L. H. Summers. 1979. Labor market dynamics and unemployment: A reconsideration. *Brookings Papers on Economic Activity*, part 1, 13–60.

Coase, R. H. 1937. The nature of the firm. *Economica* 4: 386–405.

Deardorff, A. V., and F. P. Stafford, 1976. Compensation of cooperating factors. *Econometrica* 44: 671–84.

Director, S. M., and S. I. Doctors. 1976. Racial differences in blue-collar turnover rates. *Industrial Relations* 15: 338–42.

Duncan, G. J., and F. P. Stafford. 1980. Do union members receive compensating wage differentials? *American Economic Review* 70: 355–71.

Foss, Murray R. 1981. *Changes in the workweek of fixed capital*. Washington, D.C.: American Enterprise Institute.

Freeman, R. B., and J. L. Medoff. 1981. The impact of collective bargaining: Illusion or reality? NBER Working Paper no. 258. Cambridge, Mass.: National Bureau of Economic Research.

Friedman, Milton. 1976. *Price theory*. Chicago: Aldine Publishing Co.

Georgescu-Roegen, N. 1967. Chamberlin's new economics and the unit of production. In *Monopolistic competition theory: Studies in impact*, ed. R. Kuenne. New York: Wiley.

Gordon, Donald F. 1974. A neoclassical theory of Keynesian unemployment. *Journal of Economic Inquiry* 12: 431–59.

Gordon, D. F., and G. M. Walton. 1982. A theory of regenerative growth and the experience of post–World War II West Germany. In *Explorations in the new economic history*, ed. R. L. Ransom, R. Sutche, and G. M. Walton. New York: Academic Press.

Grunfeld, Yehuda. 1960. The determinants of corporate investment. In *The demand for durable goods*, ed. A. C. Harberger, 211–66. Chicago: University of Chicago Press.

Hall, R. E. 1972. Turnover in the labor force. *Brookings Papers on Economic Activity*, part 3, 709–64.

———. 1980. Employment fluctuations and wage rigidity. *Brookings Papers on Economic Activity*, part 1, 91–123.

———. 1982. The importance of lifetime jobs in the U.S. economy. *American Economic Review* 72: 716–24.

Hilton, G. W. 1957. The British truck system in the nineteenth century. *Journal of Political Economy* 65: 237–56.

Hutt, W. H. [1939] 1977. *The theory of idle resources*. Reprint. Indianapolis: Liberty Press.

Jensen, M., and W. Meckling. 1976. Theory of the firm, managerial behavior, agency costs, and the ownership structure. *Journal of Financial Economics* 4: 305–60.

Kaldor, N. 1934. The equilibrium of the firm. *Economic Journal* 44: 60–76.

King, W. I. 1923. *Employment, hours, and earnings in prosperity and depression, United States 1920–1922*. New York: National Bureau of Economic Research.

Klein, B., R. J. Crawford, and A. A. Alchian. 1978. Vertical integration, appropriable rents, and the competitive contracting process. *Journal of Law and Economics* 21: 297–326.

Koike, Kazuo. 1978. Japan's industrial relations: Characteristics and problems. *Japanese Economic Studies* 7: 42–90.

Lazear, E. P. 1979. Why is there mandatory retirement? *Journal of Political Economy* 87: 1261–84.

Lester, R. 1967. Pay differentials by size of establishment. *Industrial and Labor Relations Review* 7: 57–67.

Lewis, H. Gregg. 1963. *Unionism and relative wages in the United States*. Chicago: University of Chicago Press.

Lucas, Robert E., Jr. 1967. Adjustment costs and the theory of supply. *Journal of Political Economy* 75: 321–34.

———. 1978. On the size distribution of business firms. *Bell Journal of Economics* 9: 508–23.

Masters, S. L. 1969. An interindustry analysis of wages and plant size. *Review of Economic Statistics* 51: 341–45.

Medoff, J. M., and K. G. Abraham. 1981. The role of seniority in U.S. workplaces: A report on some new evidence. NBER Working Paper no. 618. Cambridge, Mass.: National Bureau of Economic Research.

Mellow, Wesley. 1981. Employer size, unionism, and wages. In *New approaches to labor unions*, *Research in labor economics*, supplement 1982, ed. R. G. Ehrenberg. Greenwich, Conn.: JAI Press.

Mincer, Jacob. 1981. Union effects: Wages, turnover, and job training. In *New approaches to labor unions, Research in labor economics*, supplement 1982, ed. R. G. Ehrenberg. Greenwich, Conn.: JAI Press.

Oi, W. Y. 1962. Labor as a quasi-fixed factor. *Journal of Political Economy* 70: 538–55.

———. 1967. The neoclassical foundations of progress functions. *Economic Journal* 77: 579–94.

———. 1974. On the economics of industrial safety. *Law and Contemporary Problems* 38: 669–99.

———. 1979. Academic tenure and mandatory retirement under the new law. *Science* 206: 1373–78.

Parks, Richard W. 1979. Durability, maintenance, and the price of used assets. *Economic Inquiry* 27: 197–217.

Pencavel, J. H. 1977. Work effort, on the job screening, and alternative methods of remuneration. *Research in Labor Economics* 1: 225–58.

Pissarides, C. A. 1976. *Labor market adjustment*. Cambridge: Cambridge University Press.

President's Council of Economic Advisers. 1980. *Economic report of the president*. Washington, D.C.: Government Printing Office.

Reder, M. W. 1955. Theory of occupational wage differentials. *American Economic Review* 45: 833–52.

Rees, Albert, and George P. Shultz. 1970. *Workers and wages in an urban labor market*. Chicago: University of Chicago Press.

Robinson, E. A. G. 1958. *The structure of competitive industry*. Chicago: University of Chicago Press.

Rosen, S. 1972*a*. Learning and experience in the labor market. *Journal of Human Resources* 7: 326–42.

———. 1972*b*. Learning by experience as joint production. *Quarterly Journal of Economics* 86: 366–82.

———. 1974. Hedonic prices and implicit markets. *Journal of Political Economy* 82: 34–55.

Rosenfeld, Carl. 1977. Job search of the unemployed, May 1976. *Monthly Labor Review* 100 (November): 39–43.

Shinohara, M. 1962. *Growth and cycles in the Japanese economy*. Tokyo: Kinokuniya Bookstore Co.

Smith, Freeman. 1977. Wage trends as performance displays productive potential: A model and application for academic early retirement. *Bell Journal of Economics* 8: 419–43.

Smith, M. A. M. 1974. International trade in second-hand machines. *Journal of Development Economics*, pp. 261–78.

Steiner, P. O. 1957. Peak loads and efficient pricing. *Quarterly Journal of Economics* 71: 585–610.

Stigler, George J. 1962. Information in the labor market. *Journal of Political Economy* 70: 94–105.

Turvey, Ralph. 1968. *Optimal pricing and investment in electricity supply*. Cambridge, Mass.: MIT Press.
Wenders, J. T. 1976. Peak load pricing in the electric utility industry. *Bell Journal of Economics* 7: 232–41.
Wright, T. P. 1936. Factors affecting the costs of air frames. *Journal of Aeronautical Sciences* 3: 122–28.

Comment Ernst R. Berndt

For quite some time now, Walter Oi has been working on ideas concerning fixed and variable labor inputs into production processes; the idleness, slack capacity, and utilization of these fixed inputs; and implications for cyclical variations in the employment and wage rates of labor. Professor Oi is very much aware of the complexity of the labor market. This paper represents, I think, Professor Oi's converging ideas on how the labor market really works, and how its complexities can be unraveled and understood most usefully and succinctly. It is most appropriate that we open the NBER conference with Professor Oi's paper, for it deals in an original way with classic research issues that have a long and distinguished tradition within the NBER.

Essentially, the paper consists of three distinct essays, each dealing in a different way with the single theme that it is fixed employment costs which provide the glue that binds together workers and firms. The first essay consists of a review and assessment of the literature dealing with the notion of labor as a quasi-fixed factor of production. In the second essay, Oi summarizes search theory and the implicit contract literature and then analyzes implications for wage flexibility and turnover. In brief, Oi argues that search and implicit contract theories are in fact appropriate only for one portion of the labor market, albeit an important one, namely, large firms employing specialized labor. The third essay builds on the first two and sets out novel insights and hypotheses. Specifically, in this essay Oi puts forth a somewhat different notion of "dual labor markets," based here on the heterogeneity of firms.

I begin with a brief review of the first essay. Total labor cost to a firm consists of variable wages paid to workers in return for a flow of productive services plus the periodic rent on the firm's investment outlay incurred while hiring and training its workers. Hiring costs include the direct costs of recruiting and payroll processing, plus such indirect costs as those incurred in terminating, laying off and recalling workers, and

Ernst R. Berndt is professor of applied economics at the Sloan School of Management, Massachusetts Institute of Technology, Cambridge, and a research associate with the National Bureau of Economic Research.

incremental costs of unemployment insurance resulting from higher labor turnover rates.

Following Gary Becker, Oi notes that training can either be general (when benefits could possibly be realized by several different employers) or specific (when benefits in the form of enhanced marginal productivity of the worker can be extracted by only one employer). In competitive markets, firms will provide general training only if the costs are borne by the recipient. When training is specific, however, competitive firms may willingly undertake investment costs, which will result in a wedge between current marginal revenue product and the current wage, the wedge consisting of the periodic rent earned by the firm on its investment in specific training. The value to the firm of any specific training investment can be increased by extending the expected period of employment through, for example, offering different age-income profiles and more attractive pension plans (as has been argued by Donaldson and Eaton 1976).

Professor Oi notes that, in a production cycle, the timing of demand changes for different labor types depends on the relative size of the periodic rent in total labor costs, so that employment variations—both up and down—are less volatile and less frequent for workers with higher degrees of fixity. Oi neglects to mention here the fact that to some extent alternative hypotheses can produce the same cyclical behavior. For example, more than a decade ago Griliches (1969) put forward an hypothesis concerning technology, namely, capital-skill complementarity. Recently Morrison and Berndt (1981) have shown that when physical capital is the only quasi-fixed input, the elasticity of demand for skilled labor with respect to output will be less than one if and only if skilled labor is a Hicks-Allen complement with physical capital. Given such capital-skilled labor complementarity, short-run increasing returns to aggregate labor can easily occur, even when skilled labor is a fully variable factor. Hence, somewhat different frameworks can "explain" the same procyclical phenomena. However, as Professor Oi notes, while the technological substitutability-complementarity story can explain relative shifts in factor demands, by itself it is unable to explain the exact *timing* of employment turning points, the latter seemingly requiring at least some story on costs of adjustment for physical capital and skilled labor.[1]

The above discussion points out, I believe, that the notion of quasi-fixity of certain inputs is related quite closely to the notions of Lucas (1967*a*, *b*) and Treadway (1971) concerning internal and external increasing marginal costs of adjustment. I would have preferred to have seen Professor Oi provide a more detailed and rigorous comparison of these two conceptual frameworks. I conjecture that the Oi quasi-fixed factor, static equilibrium framework is more likely to yield corner solutions, since in the Lucas-Treadway dynamic framework, adjustment costs are increasing at the margin in a continuous way. Also, in the empirical review, I would have liked to have seen some discussion of the contributions of Brechling (1975) and Nadiri and Rosen (1973) in which the cyclical behavior of employment is broken down into number of employees and average hours at work per employee.

In his second essay, Professor Oi begins by noting that quasi-fixity, a demand notion, cannot by itself explain the sluggish response of wages to changes in aggregate demand or the persistence of involuntary unemployment. For some time now, a number of economists have viewed a great deal of unemployment as frictional, voluntary, and in some sense "optimal," since in this view persons are envisaged as investing time and resources while unemployed into searching for, finding, and securing better paying and more satisfying jobs. As noted by Professor Oi, such search models tend to imply large flows into and out of unemployment, with only a thin tail of individuals experiencing long unemployment spells. Recent empirical studies cited by Oi cast considerable doubt on the quantitative significance of such search behavior. For example, according to Clark and Summers, turnover and search accounted for only about one-fourth of 1 percent of unemployment, and in fact 64 percent of job changes were made with no intervening spell of unemployment at all. Moreover, Clark and Summers observed that most workers take the first job offer received, with this job lasting typically less than two years. In such a world, the assumption that search can be conducted more efficiently when unemployed must be rejected—it is irrational for a person to remain unemployed in order to allocate time to job search. Oi concludes, therefore, that such search theories which rationalize voluntary unemployment are not very useful empirically.

While search theories examine the behavior of an individual seeking a permanent job, contract theories based on different attitudes toward risk by firms and workers attempt to explain the behavior of firms in designing compensation packages and employment policies that attract and retain "permanent" workers. If the benefits of risk sharing and the costs of mobility are important to workers, and if fixed employment costs comprise a substantial portion of a firm's total labor cost, then one would expect to observe job durations with long mean tenure. Arguing both analytically and with the benefit of empirical research, Oi contends that such behavior is to be found only in sectors of the economy consisting of large firms. For example, Oi cites empirical research results recently reported by Hall indicating that a representative worker could be expected to hold ten jobs over a lifetime, and that by age thirty, 40 percent of workers will be at a job they will hold on average for twenty years. Hall also reports that the time profile of employment turnover is most important: job tenure turbulence is high during the first five to ten years in the labor force, when young people experience high turnover rates in search of "permanent" lifetime jobs. As their ages increase, more workers settle into permanent jobs lasting for twenty or more years.

Oi concludes this essay by noting that firms and individuals are heterogeneous and therefore exhibit different patterns of fixed employment costs and job tenure. Specifically, a marginal firm whose survival probabilities are slim is unlikely to make substantial investments in recruiting and specific training; hence, argues Oi, small firms should be expected to be less interested in contracting. Moreover, an individual with few assets and only general training will tend to be less interested in incurring the high fixed costs of job search; hence younger and generally trained workers should be expected to be less interested in searching. By contrast, large stable firms are more interested in contracting, and experienced workers with some specific training have more incentive to search.

This then brings us to the third essay in which Professor Oi displays his considerable skill as an insightful and strategic craftsman. The notion that both employers and employees are heterogeneous has been around for quite some time and has been formalized in a number of stochastic search and contract models. Oi, however, strategically simplifies by suggesting a particular structure to the forms of the underlying distributions. Let there be two groups of firms—call them giants and small firms (the firm is viewed as a team in the sense of Alchian and Demsetz—more on this later). Let there also be two types of workers—those with general human capital training and those with specific training. A firm that "produces" quasi-fixed labor inputs can be thought of as a multiproduct firm whose outputs are the regular products plus laborers embodying additional specific training.[2] More specific capital will be invested in those individuals who have longer expected employment tenures and who can manifest larger productivity increases through training. Oi then suggests that specific training would be concentrated on more highly skilled and malleable/educable workers; this implies a positive relation between the current wage rate and the degree of fixity.

Turning then to the heterogeneity of firms, Oi identifies and highlights several systematic differences in the way heterogeneous firms organize their production. First, firms differ in their ability to exploit internal gains of specialization. The central agent performing this task for the team is the entrepreneur (coach) who both supplies managerial input and monitors worker performance. Hence the full labor costs of a worker to the firm include at least the wage rate and the cost of monitoring performance. Differences in workers and entrepreneurs are described in terms of two parameters: μ, the implicit monitoring costs each worker generates by being employed, and λ, the ability of entrepreneurs to transform hours into effective managerial input. High-λ entrepreneurs are found in large firms, for they supply more effective managerial input, thereby increasing the scale of output produced by capital and labor inputs. However, since these high-λ entrepreneurs have a comparative disadvantage in monitoring performance, they attempt to compensate by adopting capital-intensive production methods and by hiring more productive workers who command higher wages. But how do giant firms with assembly-line and batch production processes reduce monitoring costs of workers? Here Oi evokes the old image of IBM employees. New employees at giant firms receive more firm-specific training which "adapts" them to a particular team production process, encourages compliance with the prescribed job description, and teaches them preferred ways of performing tasks. When all of the team's members are more or less homogeneous and work in the same way, monitoring costs can be sharply reduced. In a sense, then, large firms substitute additional fixed employment costs now for lower monitoring costs later on. For small firms producing more customized outputs, the fixed costs of assembling and training a homogeneous team may not be warranted. Hence, in Oi's view, since it is the entrepreneurial input that is most scarce, differing firms organize production teams and supply those kinds of products in various ways, each so as to yield the largest return to the scarce entrepreneurial input.

Turning to somewhat related issues, Oi notes that capital typically requires maintenance which in turn, he suggests, necessitates use of specific-trained workers.[3] Maintenance, however, is a labor-intensive activity requiring extensive monitoring. Firms facing high wages and high monitoring costs will tend to substitute new machines for lower maintenance. Such substitution between maintenance and investment can occur across time in response to cyclical fluctuations in marginal productivities—more maintenance in recession when the marginal revenue product of production work is lower, and correspondingly less maintenance and more production in the upturn. Assignments of specific workers to maintenance and training from the production of goods is therefore countercyclical and can help explain Okun's observed, short-run, increasing return to labor. I might add here that I have not seen much evidence yet that in the current recession workers are devoting more time to rebuilding human and nonhuman capital, nor that this rebuilding is greater, as Oi would suggest, in large, capital-intensive firms. One industry worth examining in this regard is the electric utility industry, for its variations over time in excess capacity are well known, good data are available, and it does not contain the additional problem of using output inventories as a buffer stock, for electricity is not easily stored.

Turning now to the compensation of fixed factors, Oi notes that perhaps more generous but less portable fringe benefits reduce labor turnover and thereby increase the capitalized value of specific training. Moreover, deferred payment in the form of pensions discourages malfeasance and shirking of tasks by employees, thereby reducing monitoring costs. Oi points to evidence that deferred compensation is becoming increasingly important, and from this he concludes that in the United States labor is becoming more firm specific. In my judgment, such an important conclusion is not yet warranted on the basis of the evidence Oi cites. Some of the recent increasing importance of deferred compensation and pensions may be due simply to the changing age distribution of the labor force, and some may also be due to the U.S. experience of wage and price controls in the 1970s, compliance with which created incentives for firms to increase the fringe and deferred payment items of the compensation package. Moreover, if Oi's hypothesis were true, labor productivity should be more procyclical today than before. I recall recent *Economic Reports of the President* in which it was mourned that in the last decade, during upswings, labor productivity had risen much less than previously. Also, is labor productivity more procyclical in the capital-intensive manufacturing sector today than in the service sector? I know of no careful study on this issue.

In the closing pages of his paper, Professor Oi examines empirical relationships among firm size, wage rates, education, race and sex, age and job tenure, capacity utilization, shift work, and unionization. The remarkable and, I think, most significant feature of Oi's paper is that fixed employment costs and the particular highly structured heterogeneity he envisages among firms and individuals has clear implications for the signs of correlations among these variables. My only criticism is that, by and large, the way in which Oi examines these relationships empirically is just two at a time, using bivariate regressions or simple correlations. The rich set of testable hypotheses generated by Professor Oi deserves a much more careful and detailed examination within a multivariate regression and partial correlation framework.

This paper suggests numerous directions for future research, in addition to those noted by Oi and suggested by me earlier. Specifically, I would hope that, in the future, attempts be made to obtain direct estimates of fixed employment costs over time and space, that dynamic optimization be incorporated more explicitly, that implications of specific training for market structure be examined more carefully in a multi-industry framework, and that the empirical notion of the firm be considered in greater detail. Regarding this last point, I am uncertain what best corresponds in the real world to the firm or team envisaged by Oi, particularly given numerous recent mergers, growth of conglomerates, and heterogeneity of firms across countries such as the United States and Japan.

These further research issues offer each of us great opportunities. If only there were more applied theorists, like Walter Oi, whose insightful analyses generate such well-structured opportunities for important additional empirical research.

Notes

1. See, however, section 4 in Morrison and Berndt (1981) on the issue of whether costs of adjustment are either necessary or sufficient for the existence of short-run increasing returns to aggregate labor.

2. This proposition was developed in the internal costs of adjustment literature about a decade ago by Brechling and Mortenson (1971, p. 5) who stated that:

> The assumption that internal costs of adjusting input levels exist is equivalent to the proposition that the inputs used by the firm at one point in time are at least partially "produced" by the firm at some earlier date. For example, the existence of hiring and training costs imply that the raw material, a newly-employed worker, must be processed and modified in certain ways by the firm before his services are appropriate for use in the production process. . . . In other words, the production rates and the time rates of change in input levels are measures of jointly produced output and inputs, respectively. Hence, more rapid changes in input levels can be obtained only either at the expense of output, if the firm's resources are given, or by increasing resource levels, if output is maintained at some predetermined level.

3. Such a relationship could generate the capital-skill complementarity observed by Griliches (1969).

References

Brechling, Frank P. R. 1975. *Investment and employment decisions*. Manchester: Manchester University Press.

Brechling, Frank P. R., and Dale T. Mortenson. 1971. Interrelated investment and employment decisions. Paper presented at the winter meetings of the Econometric Society in New Orleans.

Donaldson, David, and B. Curtis Eaton. 1976. Firm-specific human capital: A shared investment or optimal entrapment? *Canadian Journal of Economics* 9: 462–72.

Griliches, Zvi. 1969. Capital-skill complementarity. *Review of Economics and Statistics* 51: 465–68.

Lucas, Robert E., Jr. 1967*a*. Optimal investment policy and the flexible accelerator. *International Economic Reveiw* 8: 78–85.

———. 1967*b*. Adjustment costs and the theory of supply. *Journal of Political Economy* 75: 331–44.

Morrison, Catherine J., and Ernst R. Berndt. 1981. Short-run labor productivity in a dynamic model. *Journal of Econometrics* 16: 339–65.

Nadiri, M. Ishaq, and Sherwin Rosen. 1973. *A disequilibrium model of demand for factors of production*. NBER General Series no. 99. New York: Columbia University Press for National Bureau of Economic Research.

Treadway, Arthur B. 1971. On the multivariate flexible accelerator. *Econometrica* 39: 845–55.

3 Structural Estimation in Implicit Markets

James N. Brown

3.1 Introduction

At least since the time of Adam Smith, economists have viewed the employment relation as a transaction in several dimensions, with employers and employees embodying multiple characteristics of interest to each other, and with the allocation of workers and wages across jobs the result of implicit markets for those characteristics.[1] Only recently, however, have economists begun to estimate the structural parameters of these implicit markets for characteristics. Although the labor economics literature contains a long line of empirical work relating differences in wages to differences in worker and job attributes, as yet there have been few attempts to go beyond these "hedonic" descriptions of labor market outcomes and estimate the underlying structural demand and supply functions for characteristics that generate these outcomes.[2]

To some extent, this scarcity of structural analyses may be attributable to lags in the development of the appropriate theory and methodology.[3] Such lags, however, cannot completely explain this scarcity, for several studies that are analogous in nature have now appeared in other fields, particularly in the field of urban economics.[4] It is more likely that the relative scarcity of structural hedonic studies of the labor market stems from the generally inconclusive results obtained by researchers who have estimated compensating wage differentials for various job or worker characteristics. Although these researchers have repeatedly found evidence consistent with the presence of compensating wage differentials for

James N. Brown is assistant professor of economics, Princeton University.

The author is grateful to Sherwin Rosen and Harvey S. Rosen for helpful discussions on the subject matter of this paper. Any remaining errors are entirely his own. He also wishes to thank the Hoover Institution for financial support during the completion of this paper.

jobs requiring additional schooling or postschool training, attempts to estimate compensating differentials related to other characteristics of the job-worker match have generated less clear-cut results.[5] In contrast, researchers in the field of urban economics, for example, have consistently found evidence of negative housing price differentials associated with air pollution, and estimates of these differentials have served as a basis for several "structural" analyses of the demand for clean air.[6]

The estimation of compensating differentials that have appropriate signs is clearly a convenient starting point, if not a necessary condition, for the estimation of a market structure that might have generated those differences. Given the weak and varied nature of the wage differentials estimated so far, it is therefore not surprising that so few structural hedonic analyses of labor market data have been carried out. Nevertheless, with future improvements in the accuracy and completeness with which total compensation and job and worker attributes are measured, one might reasonably hope that more "believable" differentials will yet be found. Consequently, it seems reasonable to expect more structural hedonic analyses of labor market data to appear in the future. This expectation seems especially well justified, moreover, when one considers the many policy issues that require information about market structure for their resolution.[7]

Given the very likely appearance of more structural hedonic analyses of labor market data in the future, the very limited appearance of such analyses in the past, the growing experience with analogous studies in other fields, and the importance of correct methodology in such applications, some assessment of the experience to date with structural estimation in hedonic price models appears worthwhile. This paper is intended to contribute to that assessment.

The general focus of this paper centers on the conditions under which one can estimate the structural equations that generate an observed hedonic price locus, as well as the methods one might use to do so. The more specific focus of this paper centers on the two-stage procedure for estimating structural equations in implicit markets that was first suggested by Rosen (1974).[8] The paper begins with a brief summary of this empirical procedure and notes that, although the procedure has now been applied by several researchers, there appears as yet to be only limited recognition of the restricted set of conditions under which this method actually will yield estimates of structural parameters.

In developing this point, the paper discusses three related subjects that seem to have received insufficient explicit attention in the past. The first of these subjects concerns the use of "constructed" marginal prices in the estimation of structural equations for markets in which no direct observations on marginal prices are available. Contrary to suggestions originally made by Rosen (1974), and also by Freeman (1974), it is argued here that the use of such constructed marginal prices may have fundamental effects on the identification of structural equations and on the statistical methods required for consistent estimation of structural parameters in implicit markets.

The second subject addressed in this paper concerns the behavioral endogeneity of marginal attribute prices at the level of the individual market participant and the special data requirements implied by this endogeneity. Contrary to recent assertions by some authors, it is argued here that structural parameters can be estimated using data from a single implicit market. However, it is also argued that, holding constant the number of observations, data from several markets will generally be preferable to data from a single implicit market.

The third subject addressed in this paper concerns the potential problems and consequences of specification error that are peculiar to structural estimation in implicit markets. The general conclusion of this section and, indeed, of the paper as a whole is that, while the two-stage procedure suggested by Rosen may provide consistent estimates of structural parameters in implicit markets, estimates based on this procedure should be viewed with particular caution.

3.2 The Two-Stage Procedure for Structural Estimation in Implicit Markets

Perhaps the best starting point for a discussion of structural estimation in hedonic price models is Rosen's (1974) article. Although not the earliest discussion of the structural determinants of observed hedonic price loci, this article probably has been the most influential, and it provides a useful context for the discussion to follow.[9]

In his 1974 article, Rosen considered the relation between the "hedonic" price equations that many researchers had estimated for various commodities (see, e.g., Griliches 1971) and the structural demand and supply functions for "characteristics" that in principle had generated those hedonic price loci. The fundamental question addressed by Rosen was the following: Given that one observes an empirical relation between the price of some product, P, and the vector of characteristics embodied by that product, Z, what structural interpretation can one attach to this relation? In particular, how is such a relation generated by and related to the underlying distributions of tastes and technologies among market participants, and can the parameters that characterize those tastes and technologies and their distributions be derived from knowledge of the $P(Z)$ locus itself?

In answering this question, Rosen emphasized two basic points: first, any observed $P(Z)$ locus, being a joint envelope of (compensated) marginal bid and offer functions for buyers and sellers, will not generally convey any direct structural information about the families of bid and offer functions from which it is generated; and second, as a general matter, in the absence of extreme simplifying assumptions regarding tastes, technologies, and the distributions of tastes and technologies, no simple analytic relation exists between the functional form and parameters of the $P(Z)$ relation and the functional forms, parameters, and distributions of consumers' tastes and producers' technologies—thus precluding any analytically based inference about structural equations and parameters simply from observations on a $P(Z)$ locus alone.[10]

For those interested in recovering the structural compensated demand and supply parameters underlying observed hedonic price loci, these two results offered little encouragement. However, as a by-product of his analysis, Rosen was also led to suggest a two-stage empirical procedure for estimating the structural parameters underlying observed hedonic price loci that did not require the derivation of an exact analytical relation between the structural parameters of interest and the observed market locus parameters.

Following Rosen's presentation of this procedure, assume that consumers' marginal willingness to pay for characteristic Z_i is some function $F_i(\cdot)$ of a vector of characteristics, Z, as well as a vector of exogenous shift variables, Y_1. Similarly, assume that the marginal supply price of Z_i is some function $G_i(Z_i, Y_2)$, where Y_2 denotes a vector of exogenous variables shifting supply. Letting $p_i(Z)$ denote the implicit marginal price for attribute Z_i, the tangency of compensated bid and offer functions at each level of characteristic Z_i implies the following model for the data (ignoring random terms):

$$p_i(Z) = F_i(Z, Y_1) \quad \text{(demand)}, \tag{1}$$

$$p_i(Z) = G_i(Z, Y_2) \quad \text{(supply)}, \tag{2}$$

for which Rosen (1974) suggested the following estimating procedure:

> First, estimate $P(Z)$ by the usual hedonic method, without regard to Y_1 and Y_2. That is, regress observed differentiated products' prices, P, on all their characteristics, Z, using the best-fitting functional form. This econometrically duplicates the information acquired by agents in the market, on the basis of which they make their decisions. Denote the resulting estimate of the function $P(Z)$ by $\hat{P}(Z)$. Next, compute a set of implicit marginal prices $\partial P(Z)/\partial Z_i = \hat{p}_i(Z)$ for each buyer and seller, evaluated at the amounts of characteristics (numerical values of Z) actually bought or sold, as the case may be. Finally, use estimated marginal prices $\hat{p}_i(Z)$ as endogenous variables in the second-stage simultaneous estimation of equations (1) and (2). Estimation of marginal prices plays the same role here as do direct observations on prices in standard theory and converts the second-stage estimation into a garden-variety identification problem. (p. 50)

This procedure has since been applied by a steadily growing number of researchers, but although several applications and discussions of the procedure have now appeared, there seems still to be only limited recognition of the conditions under which the method actually will yield estimates of structural parameters. The following discussion elaborates on these conditions and the problems that may arise when these conditions are not met.

3.3 The Role of Constructed Marginal Prices in Structural Estimation

In his original statement of the two-stage procedure, Rosen asserted that estimated marginal prices could play the same role in structural estimation that direct observations on marginal prices would play, if available. He went on to say that, as long as some sample variation in marginal attribute prices could be observed, the identifiability of equations (1) and (2) would be determined by the standard rank and order conditions applicable to any market for which direct observations on prices exist. Each of these statements, however, requires qualification. Without qualification, each statement could lead researchers applying the two-stage technique to misinterpret resulting estimates of structural parameters.

Perhaps the most important thing to notice about equations (1) and (2) is that they are only part of a larger system of equations that also includes the equation used to define marginal prices. Consequently, when determining whether the parameters of equations (1) and (2) are identified, the rank and order conditions that must be considered are those that pertain to the entire three-equation system, and not just those that would pertain to equations (1) and (2) taken in isolation, as would be appropriate if equations (1) and (2) described a series of equilibria in separate, explicit markets for which direct observations on prices were available. The implication of this fact is that structural parameters which might otherwise be identified may not be identified when constructed marginal prices are used in place of direct observations on marginal prices. This fact seems to have gone unnoticed both by Rosen in his original statement of the two-stage procedure and by some researchers who subsequently have applied the technique. Neglect of this fact can lead to potentially serious misinterpretation of empirical estimates and in some cases appears to have done so.[11]

To illustrate the potential for such misinterpretation with an extreme case, suppose that the estimated first-stage equilibrium price locus for some implicit market is given by

$$\hat{P}(Z) = \hat{g}_0 Z_i + \tfrac{1}{2}\hat{g}_1 Z_i^2 , \quad (3)$$

so that the equilibrium marginal price function for Z in that market is estimated by

$$\hat{p}_i(Z) = \hat{g}_0 + \hat{g}_1 Z_i . \tag{4}$$

Suppose further that the structural demand and supply equations to be estimated are given by

$$p_i(Z) = a_0 + a_1 Z_i + a_2 Y_1 + u^d \quad \text{(demand)}, \tag{5}$$

$$p_i(Z) = b_0 + b_1 Z_i + b_2 Y_2 + u^s \quad \text{(supply)}, \tag{6}$$

where u^d and u^s denote random components of demand and supply, respectively.[12]

Looking only at equations (5) and (6) and interpreting them as if they described a series of equilibria in separate, explicit markets for which direct observations on prices were available, the parameters of these supply and demand functions would appear to be identified. Unfortunately, however, when one recognizes the presence of equation (4) as well in the structural model of this market, it becomes clear that the parameters of equations (5) and (6) are not identified. Because the variable $p_i(Z)$ must be replaced by $\hat{p}_i(Z)$ in the estimation of equations (5) and (6), and because $\hat{p}_i(Z)$ is an exact linear function of Z_i, observations on these marginal "prices" will not really provide any extra information beyond that already contained in observed sample values of Z_i. Indeed, it is easily verified that, as a result of this additional, mechanical dependence between marginal prices and observed values of Z_i, estimation of equations (5) and (6) using $\hat{g}_0 + \hat{g}_1 Z_i$ in place of $p_i(Z)$ will result in estimates of a_0 and b_0 that are both equal to $\hat{g}_0$, estimates of a_1 and b_1 that are both equal to $\hat{g}_1$, estimates of a_2 and b_2 that are both equal to zero, and values of R^2 equal to unity for either structural equation.[13]

More generally, in the presence of more than one characteristic, similar results emerge. Again taking an extreme example, if the estimated first-stage market locus were given by

$$\hat{P}(Z) = \hat{g}_1 Z_1 + \tfrac{1}{2}\hat{g}_{11} Z_1^2 + \hat{g}_2 Z_2 + \tfrac{1}{2}\hat{g}_{22} Z_2^2 + \hat{g}_{12} Z_1 Z_2 , \tag{7}$$

so that the implicit marginal price for characteristic Z_i were given by

$$\hat{p}_i(Z) = \hat{g}_i + \hat{g}_{ii} Z_i + \hat{g}_{12} Z_j , \quad (j \neq i), \tag{8}$$

then estimation of the following structural demand and supply equations:

$$p_i(Z) = a_{0i} + a_{1i} Z_i + a_{2i} Z_j + a_{3i} Y_1 + u_i^d , \quad (i = 1, 2), \tag{9}$$

$$p_i(Z) = b_{0i} + b_{1i} Z_i + b_{2i} Z_j + b_{3i} Y_2 + u_i^s , \tag{10}$$

using $\hat{p}_i(Z)$ instead of direct observations on $p_i(Z)$ would lead to the following results:

(i) $\hat{a}_{01} = \hat{b}_{01} = \hat{g}_1$,

(ii) $\hat{a}_{02} = \hat{b}_{02} = \hat{g}_2$,

(iii) $\hat{a}_{11} = \hat{b}_{11} = \hat{g}_{11}$,

(iv) $\hat{a}_{22} = \hat{b}_{22} = \hat{g}_{22}$,

(v) $\hat{a}_{12} = \hat{a}_{21} = \hat{b}_{21} = \hat{b}_{12} = \hat{g}_{12}$,

(vi) $R^2 = 1$ for either structural equation.[14]

In this case, again, due to the presence of a third equation creating an exact link between marginal prices and observed values of Z, second-stage "structural" estimation would only reproduce first-stage estimated parameters.

It is worth emphasizing that results (i)–(v) would be obtained regardless of whether the researcher used ordinary least squares or some instrumental variables technique in attempting to estimate the structural supply and demand curves. Fundamentally, this problem arises from the exact, definitional dependence of the variable $\hat{p}_i$ on the set of regressors included in the structural equation to be estimated. As long as this exact dependence were present, the extreme results listed above would persist.[15]

The previous simple examples illustrate the potential for the use of constructed marginal prices to yield nonsense results in some cases. In extreme cases such as these, however, it is unlikely that the researcher would be unaware of the problem, given the extreme symptoms that are present. Nevertheless, although such extreme cases are unlikely to go unnoticed in practice, they are worth recognizing for two reasons.

First, these extreme examples emphasize the fact that structural estimation in implicit markets requires that marginal prices do more than simply vary—they must vary in a manner that is not collinear with the variables included on the right-hand side of the structural equations to be estimated. This point deserves emphasis, for it implies restrictions on the set of structural equations that can be estimated in conjunction with any given estimated marginal price function. Moreover, because there will generally be no guarantee that variables appearing in the estimated marginal price function for some implicit market should not also appear in the structural equations for that market, these extreme examples also illustrate the fact that it may often be impossible to estimate correctly specified structural equations using constructed marginal prices.[16]

Second, these extreme examples highlight the results toward which structural estimates may tend in less obvious cases, characterized by less than exact collinearity between constructed marginal prices and structural regressors. To explore these less obvious cases in more detail, suppose now that the marginal price function defining $\hat{p}_i(Z)$ includes some variable X not included in either of the structural equations to be estimated, so that the relevant three-equation system becomes

$$\hat{p}_i(Z) = a_0 + a_1 Z_i + a_2 Y_1 + u^d, \tag{11}$$

$$\hat{p}_i(Z) = b_0 + b_1 Z_i + b_2 Y_2 + u^s, \tag{12}$$

$$\hat{p}_i(Z) = \hat{g}_0 + \hat{g}_1 Z_i + \hat{g}_2 X. \tag{13}$$

In this case, the absence of exact collinearity between $\hat{p}_i(Z)$ and the set of structural regressors will allow the extreme results illustrated above to be avoided. Nevertheless, the additional relation between marginal prices and attribute values given by equation (13) must still be accounted for in any structural estimation of equations (11) and (12). Failure to do so could still result in the same sort of problems that arose in the more extreme case of exact collinearity between $\hat{p}_i(Z)$ and the set of structural regressors.

To illustrate this point most simply, suppose that the parameter b_1 in equation (12) is effectively infinite, so that equations (11) and (13) can be treated as a self-contained system of equations, and consider the results of estimating equation (11) by ordinary least squares. In this case, it is easily seen that ordinary least-squares estimation of equation (11) using values of $\hat{p}_i(Z)$ constructed from equation (13) will result in estimates of a_1 and a_2 with the following probability limits:

$$p\lim \hat{a} = a_1 + (\hat{g}_1 - a_1)\left[\frac{\sigma_d^2}{\hat{g}_2^2\sigma_X^2(1-\rho_{XY_1}^2)+\sigma_d^2}\right],$$

$$p\lim \hat{a}_2 = \mathrm{a}_2 + (\hat{g}_2\beta_{XY_1} - a_2)\left[\frac{\sigma_d^2}{\hat{g}_2^2\sigma_X^2(1-\rho_{XY_1}^2)+\sigma_d^2}\right],$$

where ρ_{XY_1} denotes the population correlation coefficient between X and Y_1, β_{XY_1} denotes the population regression coefficient for X as a function of Y_1, and σ_X^2 and σ_d^2 denote the population variances of X and u^d, respectively.[17] As these expressions show, even in this simple case for which ordinary least-squares estimation of equation (11) would normally be appropriate, the manner in which marginal price observations are constructed will cause ordinary least-squares estimates of a_1 and a_2 to be biased toward $\hat{g}_1$ and $\hat{g}_2\beta_{XY_1}$, respectively. This bias will be more extreme as the ratio $\sigma_X^2(1-\rho_{XY_1}^2)/\sigma_d^2$ diminishes, with the extreme results initially discussed applying when that ratio equals zero (i.e., when marginal attribute prices embody no variation that is uncorrelated with the set of structural regressors in the equation estimated). Analogous results apply for ordinary least-squares estimation of b_1 and b_2.

As should be obvious, the existence of a definitional relation linking $\hat{p}_i(Z)$ and Z_i contaminates ordinary least-squares efforts to estimate behavioral relations between $p_i(Z)$ and Z_i. Although this point seems obvious, it seems to have gone unnoticed in several discussions of the two-stage procedure and in some applications of that procedure as well. Freeman (1979), for example, has offered the following elaboration on the two-stage procedure as outlined above:

> There are three possibilities. First, if the supply of (commodities) with given bundles of characteristics is perfectly elastic at the observed prices, then the implicit price function of a characteristic can be taken as exogenous to individuals. A regression of observed levels of the characteristic against the observed implicit prices . . . incomes, and other socioeconomic indicators of individuals should identify the demand function. . . .
>
> Second, if the available quantity of each model is fixed, individuals can be viewed as bidding for fixed quantities of models with given bundles of characteristics. A regression of each individual's price against the quantity of the characteristic actually taken, incomes, and other variables should identify an inverse demand function. . . .
>
> Finally, if both the quantities demanded and quantities supplied of characteristics are functions of prices, a simultaneous equation approach can be used. (pp. 196–97)

Following these suggestions in their empirical study of the demand for clean air, Harrison and Rubinfeld (1978) assumed a completely inelastic supply curve for clean air at various residential sites and applied ordinary least squares in estimating the following inverse demand functions for reductions in air pollution as measured by nitrogen oxide content (table 3.1). Harrison and Rubinfeld defined log (W), the "marginal willingness to pay," as a constant plus the sum of log(NOX) and the logarithm of median housing values. However, if housing values are roughly proportional to income in Harrison and Rubinfeld's sample, as may be suggested by the simple correlation of .82 between median housing values and mean income in their data, the variable log(INC) in Harrison and Rubinfeld's demand equations may simply act as a proxy for the logarithm of median housing values in the definition of log(W). If so, then Harrison and Rubinfeld may simply have reproduced their definition of log(W). The suspicious pattern of Harrison and Rubinfeld's coefficients suggests this possibility.[18]

Given the obvious problems that result from ordinary least-squares estimation of structural equations in implicit markets, regardless of the true underlying market structure, consider now the use of instrumental variables in the estimation of structural supply and demand curves, assuming as before that estimated marginal prices contain some variation that is linearly independent of the regressors included in the structural equations to be estimated (as in equations [11]–[13]). It is easily determined that, due to the presence of X in the marginal price function given

Table 3.1 **Partial Listing of Harrison and Rubinfeld's Estimated Inverse Demand Parameters**

		Independent Variables[b]				
Dependent Variable[a]	Constant	log (NOX)	log (INC)	log (PDU)	Y_1log (NOX)	Y_2log (NOX)
log(W)	1.08	.87	1.00	—	—	—
log(W)	1.05	.78	1.01	−.24	—	—
log(W)	2.20	.97	.80	—	−.03	−.07

Source: Harrison and Rubinfeld (1978), p. 89. Observation units were census tracts. No standard errors were presented for these coefficient estimates, but all coefficients were statistically nonzero at a .01 level of significance.

[a]W = marginal willingness to pay, measured in dollars and calculated as a constant plus the sum of the logarithms of nitrogen oxide concentration and median value of owner-occupied homes for the corresponding census tract.

[b]NOX = nitrogen oxide concentration in pphm; INC = household income in hundreds of dollars; PDU = persons per dwelling unit; $Y_1 = 1$ when $95 \leq \text{INC} < 130$, 0 otherwise; $Y_2 =$ 1 when $\text{INC} \geq 130$, 0 otherwise.

by equation (13), equations (11) and (12) are identified.[19] In this case, therefore, application of some instrumental variables procedure should generate consistent estimates of structural parameters.

To demonstrate this point, consider the two-stage least-squares estimators for the parameters a_1 and a_2 from the structural inverse demand function (11). These estimators can be viewed as deriving from a regression of constructed marginal prices on Y_1 and on fitted values of Z_i taken from an auxiliary regression of Z_i on Y_1 and Y_2, and are given by

$$(14) \qquad \hat{a}_1 = \frac{\text{cov}\,(\hat{p}_i,\, \hat{Z}_i \,|\, Y_1)}{\text{var}\,(\hat{Z}_i \,|\, Y_1)},$$

$$(15) \qquad \hat{a}_2 = \frac{\text{cov}\,(\hat{p}_i,\, Y_1 \,|\, \hat{Z}_i)}{\text{var}\,(Y_1 \,|\, \hat{Z}_i)},$$

where $\text{cov}\,(\hat{p}_i, \hat{Z}_i | Y_1)$ denotes the sample partial covariance of $\hat{p}_i$ with fitted values of Z_i, holding Y_1 constant; $\text{var}\,(\hat{Z}_i | Y_1)$ denotes the sample partial variance of fitted values of Z_i, holding Y_1 constant; and $\text{cov}\,(\hat{p}_i, Y_1 | \hat{Z}_i)$ and $\text{var}\,(Y_1 | \hat{Z}_i)$ are defined analogously. Using the definition of $\hat{p}_i$ from the estimated marginal price function (13), and expressing $\hat{Z}_i$ as $k_0 + k_1 Y_1 + k_2 Y_2$, where $k_1 = \text{cov}\,(Z_i, Y_1 | Y_2)/\text{var}\,(Y_1 | Y_2)$ and $k_2 = \text{cov}\,(Z_i, Y_2 | Y_1)/\text{var}\,(Y_2 | Y_1)$, these estimators can be rewritten as

$$(16) \qquad \hat{a}_1 = \hat{g}_1 + \hat{g}_2 \left[\frac{\text{cov}\,(X,\, Y_2 \,|\, Y_1)}{\text{cov}\,(Z_i,\, Y_2 \,|\, Y_1)}\right] = \hat{g}_1 + \hat{g}_2 \beta_{XZ_i} | Y_1,$$

$$(17) \qquad \hat{a}_2 = \hat{g}_2 \left[\frac{\text{cov}\,(X,\, Y_1 \,|\, \hat{Z}_i)}{\text{var}\,(Y_1 \,|\, \hat{Z}_i)}\right] = \hat{g}_2 \beta_{XY_1} | \hat{Z}_i,$$

where $\beta_{XZ_i|Y_1}$ denotes the estimated partial regression coefficient for X with respect to Z_i, holding Y_1 constant and using Y_2 as an instrument for Z_i; and where $\beta_{XY_1|Z_i}$ denotes the estimated partial regression coefficient for X with respect to Y_1, holding $\hat{Z}_i$ constant.

Given the presence of $\hat{g}_1$ and $\hat{g}_2$ in these expressions, one might expect that instrumental variables estimates of a_1 and a_2 would be biased by the use of constructed marginal prices, as was the case in the extreme examples initially discussed. This expectation would not be correct, however.

In interpreting the above estimators for a_1 and a_2, it is helpful to notice that for the system of equations given by

(18) $$p_i = a_0 + a_1 Z_i + a_2 Y_1,$$

(19) $$p_i = g_0 + g_1 Z_i + g_2 X,$$

variations in Z_i, Y_1, and X must be related according to the following equation:

(20) $$(a_1 - g_1)\Delta Z_i + a_2 \Delta Y_1 - g_2 \Delta X = 0.$$

Thus, given any two values of the vector (Z_i, X, Y_1) that satisfied equations (18) and (19) and for which Y_1 remained constant, a_1 could be derived from the relation

(21) $$a_1 = g_1 + g_2 \left.\frac{\Delta X}{\Delta Z_i}\right|_{\Delta Y_1 = 0}.$$

Similarly, given any two values of the vector (Z_i, X, Y_1) that satisfied equations (18) and (19) and for which Z_i remained constant, a_2 could be derived from the relation

(22) $$a_2 = g_2 \left.\frac{\Delta X}{\Delta Y_1}\right|_{\Delta Z_i = 0}.$$

Holding Y_1 constant, equations (18) and (19) imply that marginal prices will vary (as measured by $g_2 \Delta X$) as Z_i varies only to the extent that a_1 differs from g_1. Thus, a_1 can be measured as differing from g_1 by the extent that marginal prices vary as Z_i varies, holding Y_1 constant. Similarly, holding Z_i constant, equations (18) and (19) imply that marginal prices will vary (as measured by $g_2 \Delta X$) as Y_1 varies only to the extent that a_2 differs from zero. Thus, a_2 can be measured as differing from zero by the extent that marginal prices vary as Y_1 varies, holding Z_i constant.

This reasoning clearly applies regardless of whether one interprets equations (18) and (19) as deterministic or as stochastic. In the latter case, this reasoning provides the conceptual basis for the estimators given by equations (16) and (17). Although these estimators will be influenced by the definitional relation linking marginal prices and attribute levels, this influence has a legitimate theoretical interpretation. As long as $\hat{g}_1$ and

$\hat{g}_2$ are consistent estimates of the true equilibrium relation between marginal prices and values of Z_i and X, consistent estimation of a_1 and a_2 requires only that $\beta_{XZ_i|Y_1}$ and $\beta_{XY_1|Z_i}$ be estimated consistently. Given the structure of equations (11)–(13), moreover, it is clear that the use of Y_2 as an instrument for Z_i in equation (11) would implicitly provide the consistent estimates of $\beta_{XZ_i|Y_1}$ and $\beta_{XY_1|Z_i}$ required. Thus, conditional on the presence in the equilibrium marginal price function of some variable X that is not perfectly collinear with the set of structural regressors, and conditional on consistent estimates of the equilibrium marginal price function, the application of instrumental variables procedures can generate consistent estimates of structural parameters in implicit markets.[20]

To summarize the results of this section, consistent estimation of structural parameters in implicit markets is possible, and constructed marginal prices can play the same role in structural estimation that direct observations on marginal prices would play if they were available, but only if three conditions are met (in addition to the usual requirement that structural equations be correctly specified): First, constructed marginal prices must embody some variation that is orthogonal to the set of structural regressors in the equation estimated. Second, constructed marginal prices must be consistent estimates of true marginal prices. Third, constructed marginal attribute prices and observed attribute levels must be treated econometrically as jointly endogenous variables, regardless of the true underlying market structure.[21] The following sections elaborate on the first two of these conditions.

3.4 The Role of Cross-Market Data in Structural Estimation

The preceding section emphasized the requirement for structural estimation that constructed marginal prices embody some variation orthogonal to the set of structural regressors. Little was said, however, about the possible sources of such variation. This section addresses that subject, focusing in particular on the assertion made by some researchers (see, e.g., G. Brown and Mendelsohn 1980) that this variation must reflect differences across separate implicit markets in the marginal price functions facing market participants. It is argued here that structural identification in implicit markets does not necessarily require the presence of cross-market variation in marginal prices, although such cross-market variation will generally be preferable to an equivalent amount of within-market price variation, given the limited ability to test for specification error with data taken from a single implicit market.

To provide a context for the assertion that cross-market price variation is necessary for structural identification in implicit markets, consider the data requirements for the estimation of a demand function in a standard market model. Because only one price can be observed within a single market, it is clear that data from more than one market will be necessary to estimate any response of quantity demanded to changes in prices. Given such multimarket data, the ideal experiment for identifying the effect of price on quantity demanded might then involve a comparison of quantities demanded across several markets having identical demand curves (identical levels of income, for example) but different supply curves and, consequently, different prices. In the absence of such an ideal data set, essentially the same sort of comparison could be made statistically by comparing the covariation of quantities and prices that is orthogonal to income, for example, with the variation in prices that is orthogonal to income.

Now, consider instead a single implicit market. Price variation can be observed within such a market, so it may appear that the same statistical method can be applied within a single implicit market as is applied in the case of several separate explicit markets. However, the price variation observed within a single implicit market, unlike the price variation observed across separate explicit markets, cannot possibly be exogenous to shifts in the demand curves being estimated, since marginal prices within a single implicit market can vary across consumers only if demand curves vary across consumers. Thus, although one might observe variation in marginal prices and quantities demanded within a single implicit market, such variation does not clearly correspond to the basic conceptual experiment underlying the estimation of demand curves in standard markets. It is therefore not clear that making use of this variation just as one would for a set of ordinary markets will yield coefficients with structural content.

This behavioral endogeneity of marginal prices at the level of the individual market participant has led some researchers to assert that data from a single implicit market cannot be sufficient to estimate structural demand and supply parameters. G. Brown and Mendelsohn (1980), for example, state that

> data from a single market, producing necessarily one set of prices, are inadequate for estimating the demand functions for characteristics. Each consumer faces the same relative prices of characteristics in one market so no demand function can be estimated. . . . To estimate demand, variation in the price at each level is necessary. . . . The way to obtain suitable price variations is clear, if tedious. Each location is regarded as a separate market. Price variations across markets form the essential ingredients for estimating demand functions for characteristics, along with associated quantities of characteristics and other socioeconomic demand determinants. (pp. 3–4)

The analysis of the previous section, however, suggests that this assertion may be incorrect, since there appeared in that analysis no obvious requirement that X embody such cross-market variation.

To investigate this issue, consider a single implicit market for which the underlying structural inverse supply and demand functions are given by equations (11) and (12). Suppose further that for this market the equilibrium sorting of buyers and sellers leads to an equilibrium marginal price function that can be written as

$$p_i(Z) = g_0 + g_1 Z_i + u, \tag{23}$$

where u is a zero-mean disturbance term uncorrelated with all variables except Y_1 and Y_2.[22]

In this case, it is easily seen that structural estimation using the two-stage procedure would not be possible with data from only this market. As discussed earlier, the estimated equilibrium marginal price function must include some variable orthogonal to Z_i, Y_1, and Y_2 in order for structural estimation to be feasible, but given the present assumptions regarding u, no such function could be estimated. Thus, structural estimation would not be possible with data taken from this one market alone.

In contrast, suppose now that data are available from several such markets. In this case structural estimation may be possible if g_0 and g_1 vary across markets.[23] In effect, the availability of cross-market data allows market-specific dummy variables to play the role of X in an augmented equilibrium marginal price function, and these market-specific dummy variables may have nonzero coefficients in that function, even though no variable other than Z_i has a nonzero coefficient within any single market. In cases such as this, multimarket data will be necessary and may be sufficient for structural estimation.

Although necessary in some cases, however, cross-market data will not be necessary in all cases. To illustrate, consider the estimation of equation (11) using data from a single implicit market in which X denotes the square of Z_i. From a conceptual or sample design viewpoint, identification by this nonlinearity can be viewed as consistent with a hypothetical comparison of observed *differences* in quantities demanded and observed *differences* in marginal prices across *pairs* of consumers with identical differences in quantities demanded at given marginal prices (i.e., identical differences in Y_1). In order for this conceptual experiment to be valid, marginal price differences must vary across pairs of consumers, and consumers must respond identically to differences in marginal prices, even though they implicitly choose different levels of marginal prices. But these requirements amount to nothing more than the inclusion of Z_i^2 (or some higher order term) in the equilibrium marginal price function and exclusion of Z_i^2 (or that higher order term) from the structural inverse demand function. Thus, as long as one can assume an equilibrium marginal price function that is quadratic in Z_i, one can in principle estimate an inverse demand function that is linear in Z_i using data from a single implicit market. More generally, as long as one can assume an equilibrium marginal price function that is of order m in Z_i, one can in principle estimate an inverse demand function that is of order $m-1$ in Z_i using data from a single implicit market.[24]

Nevertheless, although one can in principle estimate an inverse demand function of order $m-1$ in Z_i by first estimating an equilibrium marginal price function of order m in Z_i, there is no guarantee that the data taken from any single market actually will support such estimation, either in the sense of generating a sufficiently nonzero coefficient on Z_i^m in the estimated marginal price function, or in the sense of justifying the restriction that Z_i^m be excluded from the inverse demand function. Furthermore, the appropriateness of this latter restriction can never be tested using data from a single market alone, since the inclusion of Z_i^m on both sides of the inverse demand function would then lead to the extreme results discussed earlier.

It is in this regard that cross-market data will generally be preferable to single-market data. By allowing a broader set of structural equations to be estimated than would an equivalent amount of within-market data, cross-market data provide a greater opportunity to test the restrictions on which structural estimation is based. However, although the opportunity for such testing is extended by the availability of cross-market data, and although cross-market data may allow the estimation of structural equations that could not be estimated with single-market data, cross-market data will not always be sufficient for structural estimation, nor will cross-market data allow statistical testing of this sufficiency.

To demonstrate that cross-market data may not be sufficient for structural estimation in implicit markets, one need only note in the context of equations (11), (12), and (23) that if a_0, b_0, a_1, and b_1 also vary across markets as g_0 and g_1 were assumed to vary, structural estimation again would be impossible, even with cross-market data.[25] Moreover, as in the case previously discussed, the researcher could never test the appropriateness of imposing constancy on these coefficients, since allowing them to vary in estimation would once again result in the extreme problems discussed initially. Thus, structural estimation, whether on the basis of single-market or cross-market data, ultimately must rest on a priori restrictions that may not be met by the data and that cannot all be tested. Given this fact, it is worthwhile to consider the potential problems and consequences of specification error that may affect structural estimation in implicit markets. The following section addresses this issue.

3.5 Specification Error in Implicit Markets

In contrast to the case of ordinary markets for which direct observations on prices are available, structural estimation in implicit markets requires not only that structural equations be correctly specified, but also that the first-stage equation used to construct marginal price "observations" itself be correctly specified. Because the estimated first-stage $P(Z)$ function fundamentally determines the "data" on which second-stage structural estimation is based, any error made in the estimation of that function will generally be translated into errors in the estimation of structural equations. This point is surely not surprising, but it is especially important to emphasize in the context of implicit markets, where theory provides little basis for the specification of either the first-stage market locus or the second-stage structural equations, and where the "constructed" nature of the dependent variable creates an inherent risk that second-stage structural estimation may only reproduce parameters of the estimated marginal price function.

To illustrate some of the problems of specification that are peculiar to structural estimation in implicit markets, consider the consequences that arise when some variable is incorrectly excluded from the estimated marginal price function for an implicit market. Suppose, for example, that the true equilibrium marginal price function for this market is given by

$$p_i(Z) = g_0 + g_1 Z_i + g_2 X + g_3 W, \tag{24}$$

but that the researcher instead constructs marginal prices using the relation

$$\hat{p}_i(Z) = \hat{g}_0 + \hat{g}_1 Z_i + \hat{g}_2 X, \tag{25}$$

with the $\hat{g}_i$ derived from a first-stage regression of P on Z_i, Z_i^2, and $Z_i X$. Suppose further that the true structural equations for this market are those given by equations (11) and (12), and that the researcher estimates correctly specified versions of these equations. Finally, suppose that the omitted variable W is orthogonal to all variables in the structural supply and demand functions, so that its omission from the marginal price function does not cause any direct bias in estimated structural parameters.

In this case, one might expect the omission of W from the marginal price function (or, more precisely, the omission of the product of Z_i and W from the first-stage estimated $P(Z)$ locus) not to induce bias in structural estimates, since this "measurement error" would be confined to the dependent variable alone and would not be directly correlated with the variables included in the structural equations estimated. Nevertheless, because the omission of $Z_i W$ from the estimated first-stage $P(Z)$ locus will generally lead to inconsistent estimates of g_1 and g_2, and because errors in the estimation of g_1 and g_2 will lead to "measurement errors" in the estimation of p_i that are correlated with Z_i, structural parameter estimates will be made inconsistent by this omission, even though the structural equations themselves are correctly specified. In general, only if the product of Z_i and W were orthogonal to the variables included in the first-stage estimated $P(Z)$ locus, and W orthogonal to the instrumental variables used in estimating the structural demand and supply equations, would structural parameter estimates not be made inconsistent by such omission.[26]

Alternatively, suppose again that the variable W is incorrectly omitted from the estimated marginal price function, but now suppose also that W is incorrectly included in the structural inverse demand function. In this case again, it is obvious that, because estimated coefficients in the marginal price function will generally be made inconsistent by the exclusion of W from that function (or, more precisely, by the exclusion of Z_iW from the first-stage estimated $P(Z)$ locus), estimates of a_1 and a_2 also will be made inconsistent by this exclusion. Furthermore, it is a straightforward matter to see that the resulting estimated structural coefficient for W in this case will be biased toward the coefficient for W in the true marginal price function.[27] Thus, even though W does not appropriately belong in the structural inverse demand function, it may appear statistically significant in that function, and the researcher may be given no warning that the inclusion of W in the structural demand function is inappropriate, as would generally be provided by a low t-statistic if the marginal price function were correctly specified.

The potentially serious consequences of incorrectly excluding some variable from the estimated marginal price function for an implicit market may appear to warrant the inclusion of possibly extraneous variables in that function. The incorrect inclusion of such variables, however, may also have potentially serious consequences. To illustrate this fact, suppose now that W no longer belongs in the true equilibrium marginal price function for the implicit market discussed above, but that W is incorrectly included in the estimated version of the marginal price function for that market.

In this case, as before, even if estimated structural equations are correctly specified, specification error in the marginal price function can lead to inconsistent estimates of structural parameters by way of measurement error in the dependent variable that is correlated with the arguments of the structural equations estimated. Unlike the case where W is incorrectly excluded from the estimated marginal price function, however, incorrect inclusion of W in the estimated marginal price function will cause inconsistent estimates of correctly specified structural equations only if W is correlated with the arguments of those structural equations. Assuming that W truly is an extraneous variable, such inconsistency would therefore appear to be unlikely. Nevertheless, given the ad hoc manner in which the estimated $P(Z)$ locus is usually specified, the possibility of such bias should not be overlooked.[28]

Moreover, the potential consequences of incorrectly including W in the estimated marginal price function may become more serious when the estimated structural equations themselves are misspecified. Given that W has been incorrectly included in the estimated marginal price function, if W is also incorrectedly included in the estimated structural demand function, it can be seen that the estimated structural coefficient for W will be biased toward the coefficient for W in the estimated marginal price function, with exact quality holding when W is orthogonal to X, given $\hat{Z}_i$ and Y_1.[29] Thus, as before, the incorrect inclusion of an irrelevant variable in an estimated structural equation can result in statistically significant estimated structural coefficients for that variable, and the researcher may be given no warning that such inclusion is inappropriate, as would generally be provided by a low t-statistic if the marginal price function were correctly specified.

As a final example, suppose again that the irrelevant variable W is incorrectly included in the estimated marginal price function, and suppose now that the variable X is incorrectly included in the structural demand equation. In this case, the presence of W in the marginal price function and absence of W from the structural demand function will allow estimates of a_1 and a_2 to be calculated, but given that W is an irrelevant variable, it can easily be shown that the estimated structural coefficients for Z_i, Y_1, and X will be biased toward the coefficients for those variables in the marginal price function, with exact equality holding when W is orthogonal to the variables included in the structural demand and supply functions.[30] Once again, misspecification may result in estimated structural parameters that merely reflect estimated parameters of the marginal price function, and once again there may be no clear statistical evidence of such misspecification.

This last example is relevant not only to cases in which structural equations have been misspecified, but also to cases in which correctly specified structural equations are not identified but nonetheless estimated on the basis of an extraneous variable included in the estimated equilibrium marginal price function. As this example indicates, the presence of such bogus identification will generally result in estimated structural parameters that mimic previously estimated parameters of the marginal price function. In cases where estimated structural parameters and estimated parameters of the marginal price function appear to coincide, therefore, one might be tempted to infer that such bogus identification is present. Unfortunately, this inference would not be without risk, for it is always possible that the two sets of parameters could be similar for legitimate reasons. Nevertheless, given the ex-post, curve-fitting nature of the process by which first-stage specification generally occurs, an extra burden of proof might reasonably be expected to fall on the researcher, especially when structural and marginal price function parameters appear to coincide. In such cases particularly, one should be wary that irrelevant variables or inappropriate variables have been included in both the first and second stages of the estimation procedure.

Considering the potential for structural parameter estimates to mimic first-stage locus parameter estimates when both the marginal price function and structural demand or supply functions are misspecified, it is worth noting that, in many instances, the "structural" parameter estimates implied by such inadvertent reproduction of the equation used to construct marginal prices may be qualitatively similar to those implied by demand theory. For example, if one first estimates the market locus given by equation (7) and then uses equation (8) to construct marginal prices, inadvertent reproduction or near reproduction of equation (8) would lead to estimated demand curves that tended to display symmetry of cross-price effects and that also tended to display negative own-price effects for characteristics in which the estimated version of equation (7) was concave. This tendency suggests that one should interpret with caution studies that present negative estimated own-price effects and symmetry of estimated cross-price effects as evidence that structural demand curves really have been estimated.[31]

In this regard, consider the estimates reported by Witte, Sumka, and Erekson (1979, hereafter Witte et al.) in their application of the two-stage procedure to the housing market.[32] In their study, Witte et al. first estimated, for each of four cities, a quadratic market locus relating housing values to various characteristics, including dwelling quality, dwelling size, and lot size (see table 3.2).

Using these estimates to construct marginal characteristic prices, Witte et al. then estimated a set of linear (inverse) demand and supply functions, imposing constancy of structural coefficients across markets (see table 3.3).

Upon inspection, the following characteristics of Witte et al.'s estimates become apparent. First, there is a general similarity in magnitude between estimated own-price effects on demand and on supply. In only two of the nine cases shown in table 3.3 are the two estimated effects not similar in magnitude. Second, the estimates in table 3.3 display the symmetrical pattern implied by the equations used to construct estimated marginal prices. On the demand side this pattern might be explained by Slutsky symmetry, but on the supply side it seems unlikely that anything other than the method by which marginal prices were constructed can account for this pattern. Third, there is a general similarity in magnitude between the coefficients on squared values of characteristics from the first-stage equation and Witte et al.'s estimated own-price effects on supply and demand from the second-stage estimation. In particular, there is a tendency for δ_{11} to exceed δ_{22}, which exceeds δ_{33} (in absolute value), and there appears to be a corresponding decline in the absolute value of

Table 3.2 **Partial Listing of Witte, Sumka, and Erekson's Estimated Market Locus Parameters**

	Estimated Parameters					
City	δ_{11}	δ_{22}	δ_{33}	δ_{12}	δ_{13}	δ_{23}
Greenville	−7.40	−3.23	[a]	[a]	[a]	0.65
	(3.05)	(1.21)	—	—	—	(0.27)
Kinston	8.53	−0.78	−0.001	−2.00	0.75	−0.17
	(6.75)	(1.25)	(0.02)	(4.95)	(0.83)	(0.31)
Lexington	9.29	−0.40	−0.011	6.13	0.19	−0.05
	(2.77)	(1.41)	(0.01)	(2.29)	(0.24)	(0.10)
Statesville	[a]	−2.47	[a]	14.18	[a]	[a]
	—	(1.02)	—	(3.94)	—	—

Source: J. Brown and H. Rosen (1981), p. 10. Numbers in parentheses are standard errors. These estimates are based on an estimating equation of the form

$$R = a + \sum_{i=1}^{5} \delta_i Z_i + \sum_{i=1}^{5} \sum_{j=1}^{5} \delta_{ij} Z_i Z_j + \sum_{i=1}^{5} \gamma_i D_i + U,$$

where: R denotes annual contract rent; Z_1 denotes dwelling quality; Z_2 denotes dwelling size; Z_3 denotes lot size; Z_4 denotes neighborhood quality; Z_5 denotes accessibility; D_1 denotes a dummy variable = 1 if heat charges included in rent; D_2 denotes a dummy variable = 1 if furnishings included in rent.

[a]Witte et al., excluded these variables because they did not add significantly to the explanatory power of the regression (see Witte et al., 1979, p. 1151, note 13).

the coefficients in table 3.3 as one reads along the main diagonal from northwest to southeast. Similarly, Witte et al.'s estimated values of δ_{13} tend to be small in absolute value, as do the estimated coefficients for Z_3 in the demand and supply equations for Z_1, and for Z_1 in the demand and supply equations for Z_3. Finally, although not reproduced here, in only eight out of twenty-four cases were Witte et al.'s estimated coefficients on demand and supply shift variables statistically nonzero at less than a .10 level of significance.[33] Thus, although one cannot reject the hypothesis that these estimates accurately reflect structural parameters, the patterns they display suggest that these estimates may reflect the construction of marginal prices more than they reflect any true market structure.

The discussion in this section emphasizes the misinterpretation of structural estimates that may result from specification error in implicit markets. Like structural estimation in ordinary markets, structural estimation in implicit markets ultimately rests on a priori restrictions that may not be met by the data and that cannot all be tested. Nevertheless, certain types of misspecification in implicit markets will result in structural estimates that, through their similarity to estimated marginal price function parameters, offer at least circumstantial evidence that such misspecification is present. Given this fact, and given also the limited theoretical basis for identifying restrictions imposed in hedonic structural estimation, it seems especially important that structural studies of im-

Table 3.3 **Partial Listing of Witte, Sumka, and Erekson's Estimated Structural Parameters**

	Independent Variables[a]		
Dependent Variables	Z_1	Z_2	Z_3
Demand price for Z_1	−8.65	5.00	0.41
	(4.78)	(4.63)	(0.36)
Supply price for Z_1	11.08	7.83	−0.74
	(2.87)	(2.76)	(0.49)
Demand price for Z_2	8.12	−6.97	0.41
	(2.49)	(2.41)	(0.19)
Supply price for Z_2	6.41	−0.71	0.28
	(1.16)	(1.12)	(0.20)
Demand price for Z_3	−0.28	0.38	−0.03
	(0.19)	(0.19)	(0.01)
Supply price for Z_3	0.12	−0.02	0.01
	(0.09)	(0.09)	(0.02)

Source: J. Brown and H. Rosen (1981), p. 9. Numbers in parentheses are standard errors.
[a]Z_1 = dwelling quality; Z_2 = dwelling size; Z_3 = lot size.

plicit markets provide sufficient information to assess the likelihood of such misspecification. Of the structural hedonic studies that have been carried out, however, few have provided such information. Considering the questions that have been raised in this section, one would hope that future structural studies of implicit markets will not be similar in this regard.

3.6 Summary and Conclusion

Structural estimation in implicit markets differs from structural estimation in explicit markets in one fundamental respect: the absence of directly observed prices for the good implicitly traded and the consequent presence in implicit markets of a third equation linking prices and quantities, in addition to the usual demand and supply functions. Due to the required use of constructed marginal attribute prices in implicit markets, a complete description of the process by which "observed" data are generated in such markets must include this third equation. Failure to consider this third equation can lead the researcher to use inappropriate data or inappropriate statistical methods in the estimation of structural parameters.

The use of constructed marginal attribute prices in implicit markets imposes additional restrictions on the research methods required for structural estimation in implicit markets. Constructed marginal prices may play the same role in structural estimation that direct observations on marginal prices would play if they were available, but they will not necessarily play that role, and their ability to play that role is less general than many discussions and applications of the two-stage procedure might lead one to expect.

First, constructed marginal prices must embody some variation that is orthogonal to the set of regressors included in the structural equations estimated. This requirement applies to ordinary markets as well as implicit markets, but in ordinary markets with directly observed prices, the required variation can be purely random. In contrast, in implicit markets this variation must be generated by some observable variable not included in the set of structural regressors. Relative to the case of ordinary markets for which direct observations on prices are available, therefore, the requirement that constructed marginal prices not be perfectly collinear with the set of structural regressors limits the set of structural equations that can be estimated in conjunction with any given equilibrium marginal price function, and may require that estimated structural equations omit some variable that would not have to be omitted from those equations if marginal prices were directly observable. Consequently, because there will generally be no guarantee that all variables included in the equilibrium marginal price function for some implicit market should not also appear in the underlying structural demand and supply functions for that market, there will generally be no guarantee that structural estimation using constructed marginal prices will not suffer from potentially serious omitted variables bias that would not be present if marginal attribute prices were directly observable. Moreover, relative to the case of ordinary markets, the researcher may have little opportunity to test statistically for the structural significance of omitted variables, since the inclusion of these variables in the structural equations to be estimated could result in exact duplication of the estimated marginal price function or near duplication of that function, depending on the variables in question and the true underlying structure of the implicit market studied.

Second, constructed marginal prices must be treated as jointly endogenous with observed attribute levels in implicit markets, regardless of the true parameters of the structural equations estimated (except, of course, when one side of the market is characterized by complete homogeneity). In contrast to the case of ordinary markets, therefore, the use of constructed marginal prices prevents the researcher from exploiting, for example, the assumption of vertical or horizontal structural demand or supply curves in order to identify parameters of interest. Consequently, structural parameters that might be identified in the context of ordinary markets with directly observable prices might not be identified in the context of implicit markets with constructed marginal prices.

Third, marginal attribute prices must be constructed without error if potentially serious misinterpretation of estimates is to be avoided. Unlike the case of ordinary markets, measurement error in the dependent variable cannot generally be assumed to be uncorrelated with structural regressors. Consequently, such measurement error can generally be expected to lead to inconsistent parameter estimates. Incorrect exclusion or inclusion of variables from the estimated marginal price function may lead to economically reasonable and statistically significant structural coefficients for structurally irrelevant variables when structural equations have been misspecified. The use of constructed marginal prices therefore creates the inherent risk that structural estimation will be biased by the definitional relation linking marginal prices and observed attribute levels in a manner not statistically discernible to the researcher. Given this fact, structural estimates in implicit markets should be viewed with particular caution.

Notes

1. The standard reference in this area, of course, is Adam Smith's statement that "the whole of the advantages and disadvantages of the different employments of labor and stock must, in the same neighborhood, be either perfectly equal or continually tending toward equality" (Smith 1937, p. 99).

2. There are several studies of labor market data that interpret observed "hedonic" relationships as structural on the basis of an assumed homogeneity of preferences or technologies. There are far fewer studies (see, e.g., R. Smith 1974; Woodbury 1983; Atrostic 1982; and Sider 1981) that estimate structural equations in a manner that allows for heterogeneity on both sides of the market. It is this latter type of analysis to which the statement in the text refers.

3. A selective chronology of theoretical and methodological work relevant to the development of structural analyses in implicit markets would include the following: A. Smith (1937); Court (1941); Roy (1950); Houthakker (1952); Tiebout (1956); Tinbergen (1956); Griliches (1961); Alonso (1964); Becker (1965); Lancaster (1966); Muth (1966); Lewis (1969); Griliches (1971); S. Rosen (1974); Freeman (1974); Sattinger (1975); Lucas (1975); Epple (1980); J. Brown and H. Rosen (1981). Although several theoretical and empirical papers on the subject of implicit markets were written prior to 1974, it was not until S. Rosen's (1974) exposition that an empirical procedure for estimating structural demand and supply functions in implicit markets was clearly spelled out.

4. In the urban economics literature, the technique has been applied by McDougall (1976) in estimating the demand for local school and police services; by Harrison and Rubinfeld (1978) and Nelson (1978) in estimating demand and supply functions for clean air; and by Witte, Sumka, and Erekson (1979), Linneman (1980, 1981), and Blomquist and Worley (1981) in estimating demand and supply functions for various housing and neighborhood attributes.

5. On this subject, see R. Smith (1979), C. Brown (1980), and the papers cited therein.

6. See, for example, Harrison and Rubinfeld (1978) and Nelson (1978).

7. At the macrolevel, any evaluation of the potential effects of policies applied to entire markets would generally require knowledge of structural parameters. Knowledge only of market equilibrium, compensating wage loci would not be sufficient, since any policy applied to entire markets would generally alter those loci in a manner that could be predicted only with knowledge of those markets' underlying structural demand and supply parameters, as well as the distributions of tastes and technologies within those markets.

At the microlevel, any assessment of the potential success of efforts to alter the specific bundles of job characteristics jointly chosen by workers and firms, whether by the monetary inducements of taxes and subsidies or by imposed restrictions on quantities, would also require knowledge of the structural bid and offer functions for the relevant characteristics. In general, only with such knowledge could one predict the likely substitution among various job characteristics induced by those policies.

8. This procedure was discussed and applied also by A. M. Freeman in papers dating approximately from the time of Rosen's original contribution (see, e.g., Freeman 1974, 1979).

9. For an earlier paper on the subject of equilibrium in implicit markets, see Lewis (1969). For an analysis similar to and contemporary with Rosen's, see Freeman (1974).

10. The obvious exception to this statement, as noted by Rosen and Freeman, occurs when one side of the market is characterized by complete homogeneity, so that the observed $P(Z)$ locus is equivalent to the compensated marginal bid or offer function for that side of the market.

11. With the exception of the recent papers by Epple (1980) and J. Brown and H. Rosen (1981), I have found no explicit discussion of this fact in the implicit markets literature. Moreover, at least two empirical applications of the two-stage procedure (Harrison and Rubinfeld 1978; Witte, Sumka, and Erekson 1979) appear to suffer from misinterpretation due to neglect of this fact. Several other studies may suffer from such misinterpretation, but the authors of those studies present insufficient information for the reader to determine whether this is so.

12. This example, along with the accompanying discussion, is taken from J. Brown and H. Rosen (1981). Harvey S. Rosen deserves equal credit for the points made here.

It should be noted that the equilibrium price locus and marginal price function for an hedonic market will not generally be independent of the structural demand and supply functions underlying that market. Indeed, the distributions of shift variables and random elements in the structural functions will, by way of those functions and the condition of market equilibrium, fully determine the equilibrium price locus and marginal price function. Thus, one cannot arbitrarily choose any set of structural functions that might correspond to any given equilibrium price locus and marginal price function (and vice versa). Strictly speaking, therefore, there is no guarantee that structural functions such as (5) and (6) would appropriately correspond to equilibrium functions such as (3) and (4). Nevertheless, for present purposes, this point need not be developed. The present discussion seeks only to explore the consequences of estimating, for whatever reason, equations (5) and (6) using marginal prices constructed according to equation (4). No claim is made here that such estimation would be generally appropriate.

13. These results are easily demonstrated by considering first the ordinary least-squares estimator for the column vector $(a_0 a_1 a_2)'$ from the regression $p_i = Xa + u$, where X denotes the row vector $(1, Z_i Y_1)$. This estimator is given by the familiar expression $\hat{a} = (X'X)^{-1} X'p_i$. Given that marginal price "observations" are constructed according to equation (4), this expression for a can be rewritten as $\hat{a} = (X'X)^{-1}X'X\hat{g}$, where $\hat{g}$ denotes the column vector $(\hat{g}_o, \hat{g}_1, 0)'$. Carrying out the multiplication, the result is that $\hat{a} = \hat{g}$. Furthermore, because such a regression would simply reproduce an identity, the value of R^2 corresponding to such a regression would necessarily be unity. Similar results apply for the estimation of equation (6).

To generalize this result, consider next the estimation of equation (5) using two-stage least squares. In this case, the estimator for the parameter vector a would be given by $\hat{a} = (\hat{X}'\hat{X})^{-1}\hat{X}'p_i$, which can be rewritten as $\hat{a} = (\hat{X}'\hat{X})^{-1}\hat{X}'\hat{X}\hat{g}$, or $\hat{a} = (\hat{X}'X)^{-1}\hat{X}(\hat{X} + e)\hat{g}$, where e denotes the vector of residuals from the first-stage auxiliary regression of X on a set of instrumental variables, and where $\hat{g}$ is defined as before. Noting that e must be orthogonal to the elements of X, the result that $\hat{a} = \hat{g}$ is once again derived. Unlike the case of ordinary least-squares estimation, however, the value of R^2 corresponding to this estimated equation will not equal unity, since $\hat{X}$ will not match X perfectly. Similar results apply for the estimation of equation (6).

14. The proof here is identical to that in note 13, with the obvious redefinition of X, $\hat{a}$, and $\hat{g}$.

15. See note 13 for a discussion of this point.

16. In extreme cases such as those just discussed, it may appear that the researcher can always avoid the extreme results mentioned simply by including some additional variable in the estimated marginal price function. This solution may not always be possible, however, since there is no guarantee that the data will allow the inclusion of that variable to make any effective difference in constructed marginal prices.

Because the use of constructed marginal prices may require estimated structural equations to exclude some variable that would not have to be excluded if marginal prices were directly observable, the use of constructed marginal prices may prevent estimation of structural equations that could be estimated if direct observations on marginal prices were available. To elaborate, consider an implicit market for which the structural demand and supply functions are given by equations (11) and (12) and for which Y_1 and Y_2 are matched in this market such that the following equilibrium marginal price function results: $p_i = g_0 + g_1 Z_i + u$. If p_i were directly observable, and if Y_1 and Y_2 were not collinear, the matrix of reduced form coefficients for the system given by equations (11) and (12) would be nonsingular, and those equations would be identified. But given that p_i (or equivalently, u) is not observable, that matrix will be singular when $\hat{p}_i$ is used in place of p_i, unless some other variable is included in the estimated marginal price function. It is entirely possible, however, that u might be uncorrelated with all other variables. Thus, the lack of observability of p_i may prevent the identification and estimation of equations that would otherwise be identified.

17. These expressions follow from application of the standard expression for ordinary least-squares bias in the presence of simultaneity. See, for example, Dhrymes (1974), p. 168.

18. It is unlikely that Harrison and Rubinfeld are alone in reporting biased estimates of structural parameters in implicit markets. Unfortunately, only one other structural hedonic study (Witte, Sumka, and Erekson 1974) presents sufficient information for the reader to assess the possibility of bias due to the use of constructed marginal prices. This other study is discussed in section 3.5.

19. This statement follows from the fact that equations (11) and (12) each exclude two exogenous variables and include two endogenous variables, thus satisfying the order condition for identification, while the pattern of the exclusion restrictions embodied in equations (11)–(13) allows the rank condition for equations (11) and (12) to be met as well.

20. As will be seen, differences in functional form between the equilibrium marginal price function and the structural equation to be estimated also can allow estimation of structural parameters.

21. This statement assumes that neither side of the market is characterized by complete homogeneity.

22. The comments made in the second paragraph of note 12 apply here also.

23. As will be discussed, variation in g_0 or g_1 across markets will allow identification of structural parameters in this case only if those parameters do not also vary across markets.

In the absence of such cross-market variation in structural parameters, cross-market variation in the parameters of equilibrium marginal price functions may result from differences across markets in the joint distributions of X_1, Y_2, u^d, and u^s.

24. Noting that any function can be approximated arbitrarily closely by a polynomial of a suitably chosen order, it is clear from this discussion that differences in functional form between the equilibrium marginal price function and the structural equation to be estimated also can allow estimation of structural parameters.

25. In this case, the interacted set of market-specific dummy variables implicitly included in $\hat{p}_i$ by way of cross-market variation in g_0 and g_1 would also appear in the set of structural regressors, leading to the extreme results initially discussed. It should be noted, however, that if a_0 and b_0 (or a_1 and b_1) were constant across markets, variation in g_1 (or g_0) would allow identification of structural parameters.

26. If the estimated marginal price function were correctly specified, the two-stage least-squares estimators for a_1 and a_2 in this case would be given by

$$\hat{a}_1 = \hat{g}_1 + \hat{g}_2\left[\frac{\text{cov}(X, Y_2 | Y_1)}{\text{cov}(Z_i, Y_2 | Y_1)}\right] + \hat{g}_3\left[\frac{\text{cov}(W, Y_2 | Y_1)}{\text{cov}(Z_i, Y_2 | Y_1)}\right],$$

$$\hat{a}_2 = \hat{g}_2\left[\frac{\text{cov}(X, Y_1 | \hat{Z}_i)}{\text{var}(Y_1 | \hat{Z}_i)}\right] + \hat{g}_3\left[\frac{\text{cov}(W, Y_1 | \hat{Z}_i)}{\text{var}(Y_1 | \hat{Z}_i)}\right],$$

and $\hat{a}_1$ and $\hat{a}_2$ would provide consistent estimates of a_1 and a_2. With the product of Z_i and W omitted from the first-stage estimated $P(Z)$ locus, however, the resulting estimators for a_1 and a_2 would be given by

$$\hat{\hat{a}}_1 = \hat{\hat{g}}_1 + \hat{\hat{g}}_2\left[\frac{\text{cov}(X, Y_2 | Y_1)}{\text{cov}(Z_i, Y_2 | Y_1)}\right],$$

$$\hat{\hat{a}}_2 = \hat{\hat{g}}_2\left[\frac{\text{cov}(X, Y_1 | \hat{Z}_i)}{\text{var}(Y_1 | \hat{Z}_i)}\right],$$

where $\hat{\hat{g}}_1$ and $\hat{\hat{g}}_2$ are derived from a first-stage regression that omits the product of W and Z_i from the estimated $P(Z)$ locus.

Upon comparison of these expressions with those given above, it is clear that, in general, $\hat{\hat{a}}_1$ and $\hat{\hat{a}}_2$ will be consistent for a_1 and a_2 only if W is orthogonal to Y_1, given Y_2, and to Y_2, given Y_1; and if $\hat{\hat{g}}_1$ and $\hat{\hat{g}}_2$ are consistent for g_1 and g_2. In general, this latter condition will require that Z_iW be orthogonal to the variables included in the $P(Z)$ locus.

27. This result is most easily seen by considering the ordinary least-squares estimator for a_3 in the "true" demand equation

$$p_i(Z) = a_0 + a_1 Z_i + a_2 Y_1 + a_3 W + u^d.$$

Given that the true marginal price function is equal to $g_0 + g_1 Z_i + g_2 X + g_3 W$, but that the researcher has incorrectly specified $\hat{p}_i(Z)$ as $\hat{g}_0 + \hat{g}_1 Z_i + \hat{g}_2 X$, the resulting regression of $\hat{p}_i$ on $\hat{Z}_i$, Y_1, and W can be written as

$$\hat{p}_i(Z) = (a_0 + \hat{g}_0 - g_0) + (a_1 + \hat{g}_1 - g_1)\hat{Z}_i + a_2 Y_1 + (a_3 - g_3)W + [(\hat{g}_2 - g_2)X + u^d].$$

Assuming that a_3 is truly zero, the ordinary least-squares estimate of a_3 will tend toward $-g_3 + (\hat{g}_2 - g_2)\beta_{XW|Y_1, Y_2}$, rather than zero.

28. Given that W has been incorrectly included in the estimated marginal price function, the two-stage least-squares estimators for the parameters a_1 and a_2 will be given by

$$\tilde{a}_1 = \tilde{g}_1 + \tilde{g}_2\left[\frac{\text{cov}(X, Y_2 | Y_1)}{\text{cov}(Z_i, Y_2 | Y_1)}\right] + \tilde{g}_3\left[\frac{\text{cov}(W, Y_2 | Y_1)}{\text{cov}(Z_i, Y_2 | Y_1)}\right],$$

$$\tilde{a}_2 = \tilde{g}_2\left[\frac{\text{cov}(X, Y_1 | \hat{Z}_i)}{\text{var}(Y_1 | \hat{Z}_i)}\right] + \tilde{g}_3\left[\frac{\text{cov}(W, Y_1 | \hat{Z}_i)}{\text{var}(Y_1 | \hat{Z}_i)}\right],$$

where $\tilde{g}_1$ and $\tilde{g}_2$ are derived from a first-stage regression that incorrectly includes the product of W and Z_i in the estimated $P(Z)$ locus. Assuming that Z_iW is truly an extraneous variable in the first-stage estimated $P(Z)$ locus, $\tilde{g}_3$ will have a probability limit of zero, and $\tilde{g}_1$ and $\tilde{g}_2$ will remain consistent estimators for the true marginal price function. Thus $\tilde{a}_1$ and $\tilde{a}_2$ will remain consistent for a_1 and a_2. Given the ad hoc nature in which the $P(Z)$ locus is usually specified, however, with W chosen on the basis of a nonzero estimated value of $\tilde{g}_3$, it is not unlikely that the final terms in these two expressions will be nonzero in any given sample.

29. In this case, the estimated coefficient for W in the structural inverse demand function will be given by

$$\tilde{g}_3 + \tilde{g}_2\left[\frac{\text{cov}(X, W \mid \hat{Z}_i, Y_1)}{\text{var}(W \mid \hat{Z}_i, Y_1)}\right].$$

Thus, although the true structural coefficient for W may be zero, the estimated structural coefficient for W will not generally be zero and will approach the coefficient for W in the marginal price function as the sample "effect" of W on X, holding $\hat{Z}_i$ and Y_1 constant, diminishes.

It is worth noting that when W is incorrectly included in a structural equation as well as in the estimated marginal price function, the incorrect inclusion of W in the marginal price function will no longer affect the coefficient estimates for the other structural regressors.

30. In this case, the estimated structural coefficients for Z_i, Y_1, and X will be given by

$$\tilde{\tilde{a}}_1 = \tilde{g}_1 + \tilde{g}_3\left[\frac{\text{cov}(W, Y_2 \mid Y_1, X)}{\text{cov}(Z_i, Y_2 \mid Y_1, X)}\right],$$

$$\tilde{\tilde{a}}_2 = \tilde{g}_3\left[\frac{\text{cov}(Y_1, W \mid \hat{Z}_i, X)}{\text{var}(Y_1 \mid \hat{Z}_i, X)}\right],$$

$$\tilde{\tilde{a}}_X = \tilde{g}_2 + \tilde{g}_3\left[\frac{\text{cov}(X, W \mid Y_1, \hat{Z}_i)}{\text{var}(X \mid Y_1, \hat{Z}_i)}\right].$$

In the event that the extraneous variable W is uncorrelated with Y_1, Y_2, and X, when Y_1, $\hat{Z}_i$, and X are held constant, these estimators will reduce to

$$\tilde{\tilde{a}}_1 = \tilde{g}_1,$$

$$\tilde{\tilde{a}}_2 = 0,$$

$$\tilde{\tilde{a}}_X = \tilde{g}_2.$$

31. See, for example, the papers by Harrison and Rubinfeld; Linneman; McDougall; Nelson; and Witte, Sumka, and Erekson cited in note 4.

32. The following discussion is taken from J. Brown and H. Rosen (1981). Harvey S. Rosen deserves equal credit for the points that follow.

33. One would expect such coefficients to be near zero if Witte et al. had nearly reproduced their marginal price function.

References

Alonso, W. 1964. *Location and land use*. Cambridge, Mass.: Harvard University Press.

Atrostic, B. K. 1982. The demand for leisure and nonpecuniary job characteristics. *American Economic Review* 72, no. 3: 428–40.

Becker, G. S. 1965. A theory of the allocation of time. *Economic Journal* 75: 493–517.

Blomquist, G., and L. Worley. 1981. Hedonic prices, demands for urban housing amenities, and benefit estimates. *Journal of Urban Economics* 9: 212–21.

Brown, C. 1980. Equalizing differences in the labor market. *Quarterly Journal of Economics* 94: 113–34.

Brown, G., and R. Mendelsohn. 1980. The hedonic-travel cost method. University of Washington, Department of Economics. Paper presented at the American Economic Association meeting, Denver, Colorado, 1980.

Brown, J., and H. S. Rosen. 1981. On the estimation of structural hedonic price models. Princeton University, Econometric Research Program Research Memorandum no. 284. (An abbreviated version of the paper appears in *Econometrica* 50: 765–68.)

Court, L. M. 1941. Entrepreneurial and consumer demand theories for commodity spectra. *Econometrica* 9: 135–62, 241–97.

Dhrymes, P. J. 1974. *Econometrics*. New York: Springer-Verlag.

Epple, D. 1980. Hedonic prices and implicit markets: Estimating demand and supply functions for differentiated products. Graduate School of Industrial Administration, Carnegie-Mellon University. Typescript.

Freeman, A. M. III. 1974. On estimating air pollution control benefits from land value studies. *Journal of Environmental Economics and Management* 1: 74–83.

———. 1979. The hedonic approach to measuring demand for neighborhood characteristics. In *The economics of the neighborhood*, ed. David Segal, 191–217. New York: Academic Press.

Griliches, Z. 1961. Hedonic price indexes for automobiles: An econometric analysis of quality change. In *The price statistics of the federal government*. General Series no. 73, 137–96. New York: National Bureau of Economic Research.

Griliches, Z., ed. 1971. *Price indexes and quality change*. Cambridge, Mass.: Harvard University Press.

Harrison, D., and D. Rubinfeld. 1978. Hedonic housing prices and the demand for clean air. *Journal of Environmental Economics and Management* 5: 81–102.

Houthakker, H. S. 1952. Compensated changes in quantities and qualities consumed. *Review of Economic Studies* 19: 155–64.

Lancaster, K. J. 1966. A new approach to consumer theory. *Journal of Political Economy* 74: 132–56.

Lewis, H. G. 1969. Employer interests in employee hours of work. *Cuadernos de Economia* (Catholic University, Chile) 18: 38–54.

Linneman, P. 1980. An empirical methodology for analyzing the properties of public goods. *Economic Inquiry* 18: 600–616.

———. 1981. The demand for residence-site characteristics. *Journal of Urban Economics* 9: 129–48.

Lucas, R. E. B. 1975. Hedonic price functions. *Economic Inquiry* 13: 157–78.

McDougall, G. S. 1976. Hedonic prices and the demand for local public goods. *Public Finance* 31: 265–77.

Muth, R. F. 1966. Household production and consumer demand functions. *Econometrica* 34: 699–708.

Nelson, J. P. 1978. Residential choice, hedonic prices, and the demand for urban air quality. *Journal of Urban Economics* 5: 357–69.

Rosen, S. 1974. Hedonic prices and implicit markets: Product differentiation in pure competition. *Journal of Political Economy* 82: 34–55.

Roy, A. D. 1950. The distribution of earnings and of individual output. *Economic Journal* 60: 489–505.

Sattinger, M. 1975. Comparative advantage and the distribution of earnings and abilities. *Econometrica* 43: 455–68.

Sider, H. 1981. Work-related accidents and the production process. BLS Working Paper 117 (April). Washington, D.C.: U.S. Bureau of Labor Statistics, Office of Research and Evaluation.

Smith, A. 1937. *An inquiry into the nature and causes of the wealth of nations*. New York: Modern Library.

Smith, R. S. 1974. The feasibility of an "injury tax" approach to occupational safety. *Law and Contemporary Problems* 38: 730–44.

———. 1979. Compensating wage differentials and public policy: A review. *Industrial and Labor Relations Review* 32: 339–52.

Tiebout, C. M. 1956. A pure theory of local expenditure. *Journal of Political Economy* 64: 416–24.

Tinbergen, J. 1956. On the theory of income distribution. *Weltwirtschaftliches Archiv* 77, no. 2: 155–75.

Witte, A. D., H. J. Sumka, and H. Erekson. 1979. An estimate of a structural hedonic price model of the housing market: An application of Rosen's theory of implicit markets. *Econometrica* 47: 1151–73.

Woodbury, S. A. 1983. Substitution between wage and nonwage benefits. *American Economic Review* 73, no. 1: 166–82.

4 Analysis of Labor Cost: Data Concepts and Sources

Joseph R. Antos

Economists face an all too familiar dilemma in carrying out conceptual and empirical work on labor cost: Data capable of supporting tests of sophisticated theoretical propositions are often inaccessible or nonexistent. Data development cannot proceed, however, without guidance from economic theory on the types of variables to be collected and the method of collection. It is thus important that researchers devise projects that illuminate the conceptual basis for the measurement of labor cost and find ways to test competing theories on currently available data sources.

In this paper I discuss a variety of data sources from the Bureau of Labor Statistics (BLS) which have considerable potential for the study of labor cost. A number of these series have been used in previous labor market research, most often in studies of employee compensation, but some are new and have yet to be fully exploited. The discussion of available data series is general, intended to give a flavor for the research potential that exists. Emphasis is placed on the prospects for analytically integrating BLS data for a more complete view of labor market activity.

Both the economic researcher and the economic statistician are faced with a host of analytical and conceptual problems which should be resolved—at least tentatively—before proceeding to statistical problems. It seems appropriate, then, to introduce the discussion of specific data

Joseph R. Antos is acting director, Office of Economic Policy Analysis, U.S. Department of Labor, Washington, D.C. This paper was completed while he was senior economist with the Office of Research and Evaluation, U.S. Bureau of Labor Statistics, Washington, D. C.

The comments of economists responsible for the programs discussed in this paper contributed greatly to its completeness and accuracy. The views expressed are those of the author and do not necessarily reflect the policies of the Bureau of Labor Statistics or any other agency of the Department of Labor.

sources by considering briefly what is meant by labor cost and what is needed to develop a measurable labor cost concept. Since the conceptual issues are far from settled, the discussion is confined to three themes on which some speculation seems warranted and which are central to the task of measurement. These themes are:

1. What should be included in labor cost measures, and what is the relationship between labor cost and traditional measures of employee compensation?
2. What is the appropriate unit of observation (e.g., the worker, the job, the firm, the collective bargaining contract, or the industry) and the appropriate time dimension (e.g., hourly, weekly, or some longer time period) for measuring labor cost?
3. What additional variables are necessary to explain observed variations in labor cost?

In discussing some of the factors which should influence the design of either a data collection or a data analysis project on labor cost, examples of the treatment of these issues in BLS statistical series are provided as a guide to the analytical potential (and pitfalls) of currently available data.

4.1 Measurement Issues

A distinction is maintained here between labor cost and employee compensation. Labor cost is viewed as the full cost to the firm of employing labor as a factor of production. Employee compensation, on the other hand, represents the stream of income (broadly defined to include nonwage forms of income) that accrues to an individual in payment for labor services. The two concepts are closely related, and parallel analytical problems are encountered in developing measures of labor cost and employee compensation. I turn first to a brief discussion of some of those problems related to compensation measures.

In its simplest form, the behavioral model that underlies most of the literature on compensation is that of a utility-maximizing individual who determines his level of labor supply, and, consequently, the amount of total income he has available to spend on consumption goods. Since consumption is time-consuming[1] and leisure is valued in its own right, there is a trade-off between hours of work (or its complement, leisure) and income (or, equivalently, goods consumption). More sophisticated models may incorporate decisions on occupational choice and other utility-relevant variables, and they may widen the focus from individual to family decision making. In any event, the representative individual (or family) of this model is assumed to have "nicely shaped" indifference curves which represent preferences stable over time. Factors other than the ones of most direct concern to the labor market problem at hand are also considered stable or fixed, such as the relative prices of consumption goods or nonlabor sources of income.

The resulting analysis of compensation is frequently, and often implicitly, a comparison of market alternatives assuming a fixed level of utility. For example, the goal of much of the voluminous literature on union pay impacts is to estimate pure wage differentials purged of other factors which imply a compensating payment (such as differences in individual productivity characteristics or working conditions). Of course, compensation analysis is conducted at various levels of aggregation, but a model of individual behavior provides the necessary theoretical underpinnings of even the most aggregative study. The assumptions outlined here provide a common basis for reducing the scope of the analytical problem, but a variety of issues remain to be settled in developing an adequate data base for empirical work which flows from the model.

The measurement of even the most commonly studied component of compensation, wages, can be troublesome. Variation in payment patterns across workers impedes wage comparisons, so a standardized wage measure in terms of both the time period of observation and the kinds of wage payments included in that measure is often desirable. Most economists compute an average hourly or weekly pay rate to impose some comparability on diverse samples. This procedure risks introducing systematic errors into the data, especially when the content of the underlying wage information is not fully specified. For example, the Current Population Survey (CPS), which has been widely used in studies of labor compensation, provides wage information on the basis of three questions:

i. How many hours per week does . . . [employed household member] USUALLY work at this job?

ii. (For those paid by the hour) How much does . . . earn per hour?

iii. (For all respondents) How much does . . . USUALLY earn per week at this job BEFORE deductions? Include any overtime pay, commissions, or tips usually received.[2]

There is a potential for error in combining the reported hourly rate for workers paid by the hour (question ii) with a computed hourly rate (using questions i and iii) for other workers. The reported rate probably represents the gross straight-time wage rate and excludes adjustments for overtime, commissions, and tips. The CPS interviewer's manual (U.S. Bureau of Census 1980) indicates that the intended response to question ii should exclude overtime, commissions, and tips. There is no attempt to clarify this point for the respondent, however.[3] Consequently, the result obtained depends on how the respondent himself interprets the question. The computed hourly rate, on the other hand, probably includes the adjustments to pay listed in question iii.

In actual practice, there does not seem to be much difference in reported and computed hourly earnings rates for respondents paid by the hour who answer all three questions. The reported rate appears to run about .5 to .75 percent below the computed rate for these workers, and the discrepancy does not greatly affect the estimated coefficients in common wage equation specifications. This somewhat surprising result seems to reflect conflicting errors in the measures. Although the weekly earnings figure is intended to include payroll deductions, some respondents (especially proxy respondents who respond for someone else in the household) may report by mistake net earnings. There is also probably some underreporting of overtime pay, commissions, and tips, which brings the computed and reported rates closer together. In addition, usual hours worked are subject to reporting error. A forty-hour week may be reported even when typical weekly workhours are less than forty. Many workers are paid on a forty-hour basis but regularly work less than forty hours. Some workers on rotating shifts work fewer hours on the night shift, but are paid at a constant nominal hourly wage rate for a constant nominal workweek.

Whichever hourly earnings measure is used, reporting errors aside, a comparability problem remains because there is no direct adjustment in the CPS for paid hours not worked. While some respondents may estimate average hours worked per week over the past year with a rough adjustment for the average accrual of paid leave hours, most probably report average hours worked during recent weeks without such an adjustment.[4] It is again impossible to know exactly how respondents answered the hours question. Since no further information is available from CPS to control for variations in paid leave, computed wage rates are thus not fully comparable across workers. Such data problems related to variations in survey or questionnaire design are not unique to the CPS, of course. This particular problem does not obviate the usefulness of CPS data for many empirical applications, but it does call for caution in the interpretation of resulting estimates and in comparisons with results from alternative data sources.

Even when there is less ambiguity in the underlying data, an hourly or weekly pay rate based on observations covering short time periods—as is usually the case—is not always the appropriate measure. This wage measure ignores the impact on earnings and worker behavior of unemployment patterns that are typical of particular occupations and industries. As part of an implicit labor contract, workers expect a certain level of job stability and plan their labor market and consumption activities accordingly. An annual earnings measure, corrected for employment duration and intensity, provides a better indicator of relative incomes for workers in diverse occupational and industrial settings. Such data are, however, probably subject to greater measurement error than weekly or hourly wage rates because of the greater reliance on the long-term memory of respondents and because of the complexity of the annual measure, which incorporates both price and quantity considerations.

Employee compensation includes nonmonetary forms of income as well as wages. Fringe benefits (such as pension and health insurance coverage) have become such a significant proportion of compensation that it is probably a misnomer to refer to them as "fringes."[5] Variations in working conditions and other conditions of employment must also be accounted for in explaining worker behavior. Such factors as the tediousness of the job, the risk of bodily injury, and, as just mentioned, the stability of employment (and of the income stream) all directly influence the wage level necessary to clear the market for particular jobs and ought to be included in measures of employee compensation.

Measuring nonpecuniary forms of compensation is difficult and evidently requires either direct quantity measurement of working conditions or benefits, or measures of their value to workers. Direct measurement is often not possible, but analytical means have been explored (in the hedonic labor market literature)[6] to infer the value of nonpecuniary job characteristics. A major limiting factor has been the paucity of information on fringe benefits and employment characteristics. Surveys of individuals have begun to provide such job-specific data, but they are generally limited to measures of the incidence (rather than the value or quantity) of fringe benefits and to a few largely impressionistic measures of conditions on the job. The CPS, for example, now provides information on pension and health insurance coverage (but not the value of that coverage) in its regular March supplement. A number of establishment surveys provide detailed measures of benefit incidence or cost, but are limited in their coverage of worker characteristics. One of the most comprehensive surveys providing fringe benefit costs is the Employer Expenditure for Employee Compensation Survey (EEEC), which has been successfully used in conjunction with the CPS and other data sources to explore compensation issues.[7]

When fringe benefit costs are available, their interpretation as compensation to workers is not always clear. Smeeding (this volume), for example, observes that scale economies may account for differences in the cost of firm-provided insurance plans and privately purchased plans. If costs for a given benefit plan vary across firms, say according to firm size, measures of the per worker cost of such plans may not accurately reflect the true level of benefits provided. Similarly, Schiller and Weiss (1980) have found evidence that the cost of pension plans may not be borne equally by all plan participants in a firm. Wage rigidities, especially in collective bargaining situations, may result in a shifting of the cost of plan improvements toward younger (low-tenure) workers. Firm-specific measures of fringe benefit costs may thus be incorrect indicators of their net value to individual workers within the firm.

The measurement problems associated with employee compensation are compounded when the relevant concept shifts to labor cost. The appropriate model for labor cost issues is firm cost minimization, subject to a production constraint. Analogous to the compensation model, a representative firm is posited which faces a stable production technology. It is usually necessary to assume that labor input is a separable factor or that the levels of other inputs are fixed. Empirical analysis involves the measurement of unit labor costs which standardize for qualitative and quantitative differences in labor inputs, assuming a fixed level of production.

Corresponding to the individual worker as decision maker in the compensation model, the decision making unit for the analysis of labor cost is the firm. Unlike the former analysis, however, there are practical difficulties in identifying the appropriate firm decision making level for measurement purposes. The modern firm is characterized by a complex organizational structure, and interrelated economic decisions are made at various levels within the firm. Moreover, a given decision may not be made at identical organizational levels across firms. For example, while some hiring decisions may be made at the plant or establishment level, decisions on wage rates and benefit levels may be determined at a company-wide level. Similarly, although short-run hiring may be determined at the plant level, long-run decisions about the general expansion of production (which affects long-run hiring plans) are made higher in the corporate structure. Complication is added by the existence of different sizes of firms with different types of organization structures.

For some research purposes, it may be valid to abstract from the specific firm decision making level and focus on individual jobs. This allows the use of survey data on individuals, but forces the analyst to ignore how individual workers are combined into effective labor input by the firm. Since a firm's labor cost depends on the composition of its work force and the joint productivity of a number of workers, data from a random cross section of individuals may not adequately represent the actual pattern of labor cost. Data from firms that include detail on the pay and productive characteristics of their employees are not generally available. Surveys of individuals rarely provide information that allows grouping by employer. Surveys of establishments occasionally provide some detail on individual workers or groups of workers, but the range of variables collected is always small. For example, the Area Wage Surveys (AWS) provide detailed wage information for individuals in selected occupations, by establishment, as well as information on fringe benefit incidence and a variety of data on establishment characteristics. The only demographic variable that can be obtained is sex. Other surveys, including EEEC, report wage or benefit data by occupation but are silent on worker characteristics.

Research with an institutional bent may call for other types of observational units. Studies of collective bargaining costs, for example, focus on the span of contract coverage, rather than the worker or the firm, as the appropriate unit of observation. This span may include part or all of a firm's (or several firms') employment and is not uniform from contract to contract. Since most collective bargaining contracts are multiyear agreements, account should be taken of any adjustments in the work force or employment conditions that may gradually occur in reaction to negotiated contract changes. Comparisons of the cost of collective bargaining settlements are also complicated by differences in the timing of settlements and the possibility of discontinuous jumps in costs from one contract to the next.

The existence of fixed labor costs places another burden on data collection. As Oi (1962) points out, hiring and training costs are likely to be significant, especially for highly skilled workers. In a steady state world, fixed labor costs would be approximately proportional to the rate of labor turnover measured over a relatively short time interval. Labor cost measured over a short time span is adequate under these circumstances. In a world characterized by business cycles, such a short-term measurement would be misleading for some purposes. During business downturns, firms tend to retain highly skilled (and highly paid) workers and labor productivity tends to drop, indicating a reduction in work intensity. Any labor cost indicator measured over a short time interval could thus under- or overstate the firm's average labor cost over the cycle. Moreover, comparisons of short-run labor costs over the cycle should also take account of the cyclical pattern of productivity. Intertemporal comparisons are facilitated by surveys like the Employment Cost Index (ECI), a Laspeyres index of labor costs. By standardizing for variations in the occupational mix and costing out a fixed set of labor inputs, the ECI attempts to distinguish price changes from labor force quantity changes.[8]

Whatever unit of observation and time dimension are deemed appropriate, labor cost measures should expand beyond the usual measures of compensation more commonly investigated in the literature. Everyone acknowledges that a comprehensive measure of labor cost would include wages and the cost of fringe benefits. However, a number of other direct costs, relating to hiring and training activities and labor negotiations, should also enter the calculation. Data on hiring and training costs are rarely available, but a proxy such as turnover rates can be included in the analysis. Similarly, direct collective bargaining costs are rarely reported. Indicators of strike activity can be developed, and are especially useful in analyzing labor cost across strike-prone and strike-free firms or industries. For most applications it is also desirable to control analytically for variations in working conditions and other job characteristics which influence wage demands. Finally, since the labor cost measure should represent the cost of producing a given level of output and labor manhours are not homogeneous, analytical control is necessary for the level of work intensity and variations in the quality of labor input. Given the assumptions of the behavioral model underlying the labor cost concept, human capital measures and hours worked (measured either for individuals or at a more aggregated level) may be useful in controlling for such variations.

The data requirements for analyzing labor cost are obviously high. The BLS offers a number of data sources on which empirical work in this area may be usefully based. I turn next to a brief discussion of those series.

4.2 Synopsis of BLS Data Sources

This section provides a description of selected BLS data sources appropriate for the analysis of various aspects of labor cost and labor compensation. Roughly similar types of surveys are grouped together. Unless specifically mentioned, the statistical programs have been in place (and data are available) for an extended period of time. The lowest level of aggregation available in each survey (e.g., the individual worker, the firm, or the collective bargaining contract) is emphasized, but each statistical program also provides data products at higher levels of aggregation. Because of confidentiality restrictions, not all programs release public use microdata files. Those that do release those files are specifically mentioned. Some censoring is customarily necessary to insure confidentiality, and special arrangements are necessary to develop microdata files for particular research uses.

The discussion is intended to give a sense of the research potential of these data series without being an exhaustive description. Additional information is available in selected publications from the U.S. Bureau of Labor Statistics (1976, 1977, 1980*b*, 1981) and the U.S. Bureau of Census (1977).

4.2.1 Current Population Survey (CPS)

The CPS is a monthly survey of about 60,000 households which obtains the labor force status, usual weekly hours and earnings, and demographic information for individuals. These data have been widely used for research and policy purposes and are the basis for national labor force and unemployment rate estimates. CPS microdata are available in addition to more aggregated data tabulations.

In addition to the regular survey questions, supplementary questions on numerous topics are included in the survey. Three supplements relevant to labor cost of compensation studies are included on an annual basis:

1. The work experience and income supplement, conducted every March, provides data on the extent of employment and unemployment in the population, and data on work experience, earnings, and household income during the previous year. Other data are collected on family characteristics, household composition, and population migration.

2. The multiple jobholding and premium pay supplement, conducted every May through 1981, provides data on the characteristics of multiple jobholders, the receipt of premium pay for overtime, scheduled work-hours, and union membership status. Current plans are to discontinue this supplement.

3. The school enrollment supplement, conducted every October, provides more information than the regular survey on educational attainment and labor force status, and it occasionally covers future educational plans.

Other supplements on a variety of topics are included on an irregular basis. Three of these special supplements are especially noteworthy:

1. The job search supplement, conducted in May 1976, provides information on the methods and intensity of job search and the reasons for that search activity. A short follow-up questionnaire on job search was conducted in May 1977.

2. The pension supplement, conducted in May 1979 for the Labor Management Services Administration and the Social Security Administration, provides information on employee participation in private pension and health insurance plans, as well as firm employment size data.

3. The job tenure supplement, conducted in January 1981, provides information on occupational mobility and length of employment at the current job. A more modest version of this supplement was conducted in January 1978.

The CPS has a rotating sample design, with households (addresses, strictly speaking) in the survey four months, out eight, and back in for four more months. Prior to 1979, the usual weekly hours and earnings questions (discussed in detail earlier) were asked of all respondents as part of the May supplement. Since then, the questions have been asked each month, but only of the two outgoing rotation groups (that is, respondents in their fourth or their eighth, and final, month in the sample). Consequently, a sample of over ten thousand employed persons reporting hours and earnings information is available each month from the CPS. These data are aggregated and reported on a quarterly basis.

The sample design allows observations to be linked in a longitudinal fashion over time spans as long as sixteen months. CPS matched files, which are available from the BLS, permit a greater range of empirical investigation than possible with a series of independent cross sections.

Mellow (1981), for example, uses year-to-year matched data to investigate the wage change of workers changing union status. Matched data also allow more intensive use of the supplements by increasing the size of the sample for which a full range of information is available. Matching individuals participating in both the May and June 1979 surveys, for example, roughly doubles the sample of observations that report both earnings and fringe benefit data.

A test of the accuracy of CPS earnings data was conducted as part of the January 1977 survey.[9] In this test, individuals in their final month of the survey (that is, one-eighth of the CPS sample) were asked a series of questions on the frequency of payment and amounts. The employers of those individuals were then asked the same questions, and the results were compared. The earnings validation study contains 4,166 cases with complete data from the individual respondent and his employer, about 60 percent of the eligible responses. Statistically significant differences were found between the individual and employer responses. Compared to the employers' responses, individuals overstated their workhours by an average of 3.6 percent and understated both their hourly rate of pay (by 5.2 percent) and their usual weekly earnings (by 11.7 percent). There is some evidence, however, that confusion on the part of some respondents inflated the discrepancy noted in usual weekly earnings. Moreover, the comparison of individual with employer responses is not an unambiguous test of the accuracy of individual responses, since the employer data are also subject to error.[10] The test results do indicate the need for caution in analyzing CPS earnings data, but do not invalidate their use.

The CPS is unquestionably the richest source of data relevant to labor compensation research available from BLS. Since it is a household survey, it is limited in what can be provided on employer characteristics and fringe benefits. The May 1979 pension supplement demonstrates that some of this information is collectible in household surveys, however, and the March demographic supplement now includes questions on pension and health insurance plan coverage.

4.2.2 Employer Expenditures for Employee Compensation (EEEC)

The EEEC was a biennial establishment survey conducted between 1959 and 1977. Between 1959 and 1966 the survey was restricted to manufacturing production workers; subsequently, production and office workers in all industries were covered. The most recent EEEC survey, conducted in 1977, provides information from 3,223 nonfarm establishments on their expenditures for wages and fringe benefits, total hours worked, and total hours paid for over the year. The 1977 survey is the largest nationwide survey of recent vintage providing detailed information on employers' outlays by fringe benefit category. The costs of nineteen separate benefit items are reported, including overtime and shift pay, paid leave, insurance benefits, retirement and savings benefits, and legally required benefits (principally social security and unemployment insurance). The data are reported separately for production workers and for office workers, and microdata are available.

EEEC, like the other establishment surveys discussed here, is incomplete in its data coverage for many research purposes. Consequently, it has been augmented in most studies with auxiliary information on worker characteristics, often from the CPS. In spite of this deficiency, the EEEC survey is extremely valuable because fringe benefit cost data are rarely available from other sources.

4.2.3 Employment Cost Index (ECI)

The ECI is a quarterly measure of the change in the rate of employee compensation, based on a sample of about two thousand establishments. About five occupations are sampled in each establishment, and data are collected on straight-time average hourly earnings and the cost of fringe benefits for those workers. Data are collected on about twenty specific occupations, each with about one hundred observations. Data collection was initiated in 1975, but benefit data have been collected only since 1980. The benefit types covered are essentially those mentioned in the discussion of EEEC, section 4.2.2.

The index derived from the ECI survey is a Laspeyres index using occupation weights from the 1970 census to standardize for employment patterns. By pricing out a fixed set of labor inputs, the index attempts to measure the pure change in the cost of employment over time, free from shifts in the composition of employment. Data on quarterly changes in compensation are limited to six broad occupation and industry categories. Corresponding data on wage changes are available for a variety of occupations, industries, regions, union/nonunion, and metropolitan/nonmetropolitan breakdowns.

4.2.4 Area and Industry Wage Surveys (AWS and IWS)

AWS surveys over twelve thousand establishments in seventy labor market areas on an annual basis, collecting information on the wage rates paid to workers in occupations common to a variety of industries. Every third year, on a staggered basis, additional information is collected on work schedules, paid vacation and holiday practices, fringe benefit coverage, and union status, reported separately for office and production workers. Many responding establishments provide a detailed listing of the wages paid to individual workers in the sampled occupations.

IWS surveys establishments in fifty manufacturing and twenty nonmanufacturing industries on a three- or five-year cycle. Data are collected on the methods and rates of wage payment for occupations considered peculiar to a particular industry. Like AWS, additional information is available on a variety of pay and benefit practices and union status, for broad occupational groups.

Microdata files are available for both AWS and IWS.

4.2.5 National Survey of Professional, Administrative, Technical, and Clerical Pay (PATC) and Level of Benefits Survey (LOB)

The PATC and LOB surveys are designed to provide a basis for federal white-collar pay setting. The pay-setting process attempts to establish comparable pay levels between employees in the federal and private sectors. Consequently, the surveys are directed toward selected occupations and industries which correspond to federal white-collar employment, and the samples are not nationally representative of white-collar employment.

PATC samples four thousand establishments annually to determine the salary rates for about ninety work-level categories in approximately twenty white-collar occupations. The work levels correspond roughly to particular pay grades within the federal white-collar pay system. This survey has been conducted since 1961.

LOB is a companion survey to PATC designed to provide a basis for adding federal-private sector differences in fringe benefits into the pay comparability process. The first LOB survey was conducted in 1979 on a sample of five hundred establishments drawn as a subsample of firms covered by PATC. Extraordinarily detailed data on the provisions of various benefit plans and their distribution across occupational groups were collected through a complex process of personal interviews and careful analysis of company provided brochures. Benefits covered include: paid lunch and rest periods; paid leave; life, accident, sickness, health, and long-term disability insurance; and private pension plans. For the purpose of pay comparability, the costs of these benefits are imputed by the Office of Personnel Management using an actuarial model. In this way estimates are made of the hypothetical private sector cost of providing benefits to a labor force with the characteristics of the federal labor force, rather than the actual cost of private sector benefits.

Microdata are available for both surveys. In the case of LOB, data are provided by benefit type and cannot be matched across types to create a profile of benefits provided by each establishment. While this is limiting for some purposes, the data still provide a uniquely detailed view of the structure of particular fringe benefits.

4.2.6 Wage Distribution Survey (WDS)

WDS is an establishment survey conducted between 1978 and 1980 for the Minimum Wage Study Commission and the Employment Standards Administration by the BLS. Observations on the pay and employment characteristics of individual nonsupervisory workers are available, including the straight-time hourly pay rate, paid weekly hours, bonus and commission pay, tips status, age, and sex. This basic survey was collected in all three years, with nearly 8,500 establishment responses in 1978 and 1980. In 1979 the basic survey had 4,500 responses, but was supplemented by a one-year panel survey covering 2,100 establishments which had participated in the 1978 survey. The panel survey includes additional establishment-level information on total employment and payroll, establishment receipts, collective bargaining coverage, overtime pay practices, and the incidence of twenty-one fringe benefits. The benefit information is particularly interesting because the survey indicates what benefits were added or deleted from 1978 to 1979, and because it picks up a number of infrequently measured benefits (including paid rest periods, subsidized meals, clothing allowance, laundering of uniforms, merchandise discounts, and educational benefits). A microdata file is available and has been used in the analysis conducted by the Minimum Wage Study Commission (1981).

4.2.7 Collective Bargaining Data

Three major BLS programs focus specifically on collective bargaining: Current Wage Developments (CWD), Work Stoppages (WS), and the Collective Bargaining File (CBF).

CWD is, in essence, two data programs. The first provides monthly information on general changes in newly negotiated wage and benefit contract provisions for specific bargaining situations, covering both private and public sector contract settlements. The universe for this program consists of 2,200 major collective bargaining units. Of course, in any given month a small fraction of those agreements are subject to negotiation and thus eligible for reporting in CWD. The general information provided on a monthly basis is derived primarily from secondary sources, such as newspapers and trade publications.

The second program under CWD analyzes on a quarterly basis the cost of wage and benefit changes under bargaining agreements. Wage information is collected for all agreements covering one thousand or more employees, about 1,900 agreements in all. Wage and benefit information is restricted to agreements covering five thousand or more employees, about 350 agreements. CWD is not a sample survey, so data are collected on all agreements affecting the stated number of workers.

This second data base is unique in that contract provisions affecting base wage rates, cost-of-living escalators, and numerous types of benefits are cost out on a consistent basis for the agreements covered by the survey. The estimation procedure attempts to measure the costs associated with the actual characteristics of the work force affected by the settlements, not the costs for a hypothetical employee group. Actual pricing procedures are complex, but changes in the cost of contract provisions are associated with specific average hourly earnings rates in as much detail as possible. Detailed occupational employment weights are used to compute average cost figures for each contract, which are reported as changes over the quarter. The weights are held constant (at the levels observed at the time of settlement) over the time period the contract is in force.

Because of the small number of observations in the universe, and because of the sensitive nature of the cost data, average percentage changes in wages and benefits are reported only in highly aggregated form. Wage change data are available for three industry breaks (manufacturing, nonmanufacturing, and construction), but wage and benefit change data are available only at national levels.

The other BLS collective bargaining programs can be described briefly. The work stoppages program covers all strikes and lockouts continuing for at least one full day (or shift) involving six or more workers. Information is collected on indicators of the magnitude of the stoppage, including the percentage of available work time lost, and on the issues in dispute and the methods for resolving the dispute. Data are tabulated for the nation and by selected industries. The BLS also maintains a public file of current bargaining agreements and issues reports on various features of those agreements. The file includes all private sector contracts affecting one thousand or more employees, as well as many public sector contracts.

4.2.8 Establishment Employment and Payroll (790 Survey) and Employment and Wages Covered by Unemployment Insurance Laws (ES-202 Program)

The 790 survey is the largest establishment survey conducted by the BLS, covering 160,000 establishments every month. Over 135,000 of those establishments, constituting 450 industries, provide data on the payroll, total employment, and hours of production or nonsupervisory workers. Data on overtime hours are also collected in 320 manufacturing industries. The 790 survey is the basis for BLS industry estimates of employment and earnings and is used to construct the BLS Hourly Earnings Index. Data are also available in the form of detailed industry tabulations.

The ES-202 program is an administrative data base, consisting of quarterly tax reports submitted to state unemployment security agencies by employers subject to unemployment insurance (UI) programs. About 4.6 million reporting units provide information on their monthly employment and quarterly payrolls and employer contributions to UI. The ES-202 is used by BLS as the sampling universe for its establishment data collection programs, and it also serves as the annual benchmark for the 790 survey's employment estimates. Data from this program are available in the form of tabulations by industry and state.

The strengths and weaknesses of both the 790 survey and the ES-202 program for research are similar. Both have untapped longitudinal capabilities. The 790 survey uses a link relative estimator which requires month-to-month observations on establishments. The ES-202 program is a virtual census of establishments every quarter. The sample sizes available in each case are extremely generous. On the other hand, the range of data collected is very limited in each case. Even if BLS could find the financial resources to resolve the technical problems which impede the longitudinal use of this data, the potential usefulness for most research on labor cost would be low. The 790 survey's research potential could improve, however, if extensive changes are made to that program during the multiyear revision that has recently been initiated.

4.2.9 Average Hourly Compensation (AHC)

The AHC program measures total compensation per hour with some industry detail on an annual basis, and by major sector on a quarterly basis. AHC includes as compensation: wages and salaries, other forms of direct payment (commissions, tips, bonuses, and some payments in kind), and supplements (employer expenditures on social insurance, private pension and health plans, workmen's compensation, doctor's fees, and pay for military leave). The AHC is estimated by combining data from numerous surveys and applying various definitional adjustments and imputations. Data for detailed industries are derived primarily from the Economic Census and Annual Surveys of Manufactures. Compensation data for major sectors are developed from Bureau of Economic Analysis data, supplemented by estimates of the labor share of proprietors' income, as part of the National Income Accounts. Other data sources for AHC include the ES-202 (wage information), the 790 survey (hours adjustment for nonfarm production workers), and the CPS (hours adjustment for other workers).

4.3 Integrating BLS Data

Although BLS and other data sources provide a basis for empirical investigation of labor cost, no single data source provides the range of information needed for thorough analysis of a broad range of issues. Just as the long run never arrives, however, the ideal data set will never be available because the target keeps advancing. As data are developed to meet one set of analytical needs, conceptual work continues, resulting in a new set of data requirements. The best that we can hope for is that data development does not lag too far behind theoretical development.

Deficiencies in existing data sources can be surmounted through a judicious focusing of empirical work and the development of statistical methodologies to accommodate certain of those deficiencies. Another approach is to integrate data sources with complementary strengths and weaknesses, and thus open the range of empirical issues that can be analyzed. Data integration is a particularly promising way of more fully exploiting already existing data sources at relatively low cost.

Most attempts to integrate data involve a statistical matching procedure of some sort, and that statistical process can introduce error into the resulting analysis. We are rarely lucky enough to find information sufficient to exactly identify respondents between surveys. CPS month-to-month matched files, for example, are often treated by researchers as exact matches. While the matching procedure used here is quite accurate, there is still a potential for error because the CPS is essentially a survey of street addresses rather than specific individuals. Consequently, demographic characteristics (rather than the names or social security numbers of individuals) must be used to match individuals observed at a given address in different months, and there is no guarantee that all matches are accurate. In other cases, especially when matching is attempted across dissimilar surveys, the probability of introducing error increases. Especially in these cases, it is important to examine the statistical properties of the resulting integrated data base. Sims's (1972) comments on the assumptions implicitly made concerning the joint distributions of variables in matched samples are especially helpful in this regard.

A variety of specific analytical problems are encountered during the course of most data integration projects. Often the units of observation across data sources are inconsistent. For labor cost problems we are often in the position of attempting to match individual or household data with establishment or firm data. The appropriate unit of observation must then be selected on the basis of the primary topic of research. Freeman (1981), for example, adds industry aggregates of CPS-measured demographic information to establishment-level data from EEEC in his study of union effects on fringe benefits. Smeeding (this volume), on the other hand, assigns EEEC and ECI compensation data computed as industry averages to data on individuals from the CPS because his focus is on the economic welfare of individual workers.

Problems associated with the unit of observation are also encountered when matching across surveys of the same generic type. Establishment surveys do not always adhere to identical definitions for what entity constitutes an establishment. In some surveys a very tight definition is enforced, while in other surveys responses from a variety of organizational levels are acceptable. AWS, for example, requires that respondents report only for a single physical location, even when the firm has a number of separate establishments. EEEC data refer to a broader range of possible observational units, with responses covering a single establishment or a number of establishments (in the AWS sense of the term).

Simply combining several years of data from a single survey can lead to problems, depending on the design of the survey. The CPS rotational pattern implies, for example, that a substantial number of individuals are included more than once in a data set constructed by amalgamating successive months or years of the survey. Even without a rotating sample design, this problem of double counting is likely in amalgamating establishment survey data, especially for large firms. It is necessary to ascertain in the context of a given analysis whether such double counting is harmless, or whether it introduces significant sample selectivity problems or spurious levels of estimated precision.

Survey definitions and reporting patterns also change over time, and care must be taken to insure consistency. Establishments may report sudden shifts in employment, for example, because of a corporate realignment which has no economic significance for the workers at a given location. Survey statisticians frequently try to improve the survey instrument by changing the placement or wording of questions, and those changes often affect the proper interpretation of the data. Even when the questionnaire is not changed, revisions in instructions to the data collector in the field may influence the nature of the information collected.

It is often difficult to determine the integration potential of various data series because there is rarely an easy way to determine overlaps in series coverage. Two of my former colleagues in the Office of Research and Evaluation, Joe Stone and Ollie Ballard, have constructed the first comprehensive guide to major statistical series which can be used to identify such overlapping coverage. This guide (which is reproduced as Appendix A in this volume) describes BLS establishment data collection programs for wage, price, and productivity statistics. Prepared in matrix form, it provides for each major statistical program information on industry coverage (at the three-digit level), publication status and frequency of data availability, and historical availability over the past thirty years. The matrix refers to the availability of data *tabulated* by three-digit industries. It is possible to find observations for additional industries for some series when using the microdata files, but the coverage is generally inadequate for tabulation purposes.

Scanning the wage-price-productivity matrix reveals a considerable stock of information collected from establishments in the goods-producing sector. The service sector, which has a higher proportion of small establishments, is less adequately represented. Although the general pattern is not surprising, it is useful to know specifically where coverage is available. For industry-level studies, the matrix is an invaluable guide to data resources.

The prospects for developing an integrated data base at finer levels of aggregation are less certain, although the matrix does provide some general guidance. There is unfortunately little chance that these data series will be integrated at the establishment level. Not only are all the technical problems related to survey comparability in force, but confidentiality requirements restrict the range of information that can be provided at the establishment level. Consequently, the public use microdata files for individual establishment surveys do not permit cross-survey matching. If the BLS were to develop an establishment matching capability, only selected data from such matches would be provided publicly. This problem is inherent in the use of firm-side information and is less of a difficulty for household data, as the ongoing CPS matching program attests.

4.4 Conclusion

A wealth of statistical information is collected every year by and for government agencies, and it is often difficult to get a sense of which data series are suitable for particular research purposes. This paper provides an overview of BLS data resources applicable to the analysis of labor cost and labor compensation and does not cover surveys available elsewhere. Nonetheless, the array of statistical series discussed here is impressive.

The distinction between labor cost and labor compensation concepts implies important differences in the corresponding statistical measures and the data requirements for their analysis. The measurement problems discussed in this paper are encountered to some degree in BLS and other data series, and that discussion should serve as a general admonition on the use of survey data. It should be remembered that academic research uses of the data are frequently a secondary goal of survey progams. From a research point of view, it sometimes seems that measurement problems have been designed into the surveys. In many cases, those problems are the result of the technical requirements of the survey's principal programmatic or policy functions. In other cases, the expense of resolving a particular measurement problem cannot be met within budget restrictions. For example, the Level of Benefits survey could be redirected to collect the costs of benefits as well as their incidence, but this is not the function of the survey as prescribed by its sponsor, the President's Pay Agent.[11] Fortunately, many of the data quality problems (such as sample selectivity, nonresponse, and measurement error) and the data coverage problems (lack of measurement rather than mismeasurement) are amenable to econometric analysis. Some problems are clearly intractable, however, short of developing the financial support for new and better surveys.

In spite of inevitable measurement problems and data gaps, a statistical foundation exists for empirical research on labor cost. That body of statistical information in its present form could be better utilized, and it can be improved in the future. Continued interchange between the research community and the statistical community can help insure progress on both fronts.

Notes

1. See Becker (1965).

2. Prior to October 1978, the prompting in question iii on what to include in usual weekly earnings was excluded and the order of questioning was changed so that the hourly rate question (ii) was asked last.

3. Except in the rare instance when the respondent indicates his uncertainty about the question.

4. "Usual" is defined in the CPS interviewer's manual (U.S. Bureau of Census 1980) as the most frequent schedule during the past four or five months. This definition is not provided to the respondent unless he insists on a specific explanation of the question.

5. In 1977 money wages accounted for 76.7 percent and benefits for 23.3 percent of total compensation in the private nonfarm economy. See U.S. Bureau of Labor Statistics (1980*a*), table 1.

6. Rosen (1974) provides a theoretical basis for most subsequent applications of hedonic theory to labor market analysis. Brown (1980) reviews much of the relevant empirical literature.

7. See, for example, Freeman (1981) and Antos (1981). EEEC is no longer an active survey; see section 4.2.2.

8. As with all base-weighted indexes, comparisons over long periods of time may be inappropriate. Substitution occurs between labor inputs as relative prices change over time. Moreover, the assumption of a constant technology may also become less valid. Thus the ECI may overstate labor costs over the long run.

9. See Carstensen and Woltman (1979) for a more complete description of the CPS earnings validation study.

10. One possible indication of establishment reporting error is the proportion of employers reporting hourly wage rates *below* the minimum wage—4.4 percent, for the full sample. It is unlikely that such a high proportion of hourly workers in the sample were not covered by the minimum wage, or that enforcement was loose enough in 1977 to detect such a proportion in a voluntary government survey.

11. The President's Pay Agent includes the Director, Office of Management and Budget, the Director, Office of Personnel Management, and the Secretary of Labor. Stelluto (1979) describes the decision-making process involved in setting federal white-collar pay levels.

References

Antos, Joseph R. 1981. Wages and compensation of white-collar workers. BLS Working Paper 123. Washington, D.C.: U.S. Bureau of Labor Statistics.

Becker, Gary S. 1965. A theory of the allocation of time. *Economic Journal* 75: 493–517.

Brown, Charles. 1980. Equalizing differences in the labor market. *Quarterly Journal of Economics* 94: 113–34.

Carstensen, Larry, and Henry Woltman. 1979. Comparing earnings data from the CPS and employers records. *Proceedings of the Social Statistics Section of the American Statistical Association*, pp. 168–73.

Freeman, Richard B. 1981. The effect of unionism on fringe benefits. *Industrial and Labor Relations Reveiw* 34: 489–509.

Mellow, Wesley. 1981. Unionism and wages: A longitudinal analysis. *Review of Economics and Statistics* 63: 43–52.

Minimum Wage Study Commission. 1981. *Report of the Minimum Wage Study Commission*. Washington, D.C.: Government Printing Office.

Oi, Walter Y. 1962. Labor as a quasi-fixed factor. *Journal of Political Economy* 70: 538–55.

Rosen, Sherwin. 1974. Hedonic prices and implicit markets: Product differentiation in pure competition. *Journal of Political Economy* 82: 34–55.

Schiller, Bradley R., and Randall D. Weiss. 1980. Pensions and wages: A test for equalizing differences. *Review of Economics and Statistics* 62: 529–38.

Sims, Christopher A. 1972. Comment. *Annals of Economic and Social Measurement* 1: 343–46.

Stelluto, George L. 1979. Federal pay comparability: Facts to temper the debate. *Monthly Labor Review* 102, no. 6: 18–28.

U.S. Bureau of Census. 1977. *The Current Population Survey: Design and methodology*. Census Technical Paper 40. Washington, D.C.: Government Printing Office.

———. 1980. *Current Population Survey: Interviewers reference manual*. CPS-250. Washington, D.C.: Government Printing Office.

U.S. Bureau of Labor Statistics. 1976. *BLS handbook of methods for surveys and studies*. Bulletin 1910. Washington, D.C.: Government Printing Office.

———. 1977. *BLS measures of compensation*. Bulletin 1941. Washington, D.C.: Government Printing Office.

———. 1980*a*. *Employee compensation in the private nonfarm economy, 1977*. Summary 80-5. Washington, D.C.: Government Printing Office.

———. 1980*b*. *Major programs: Bureau of Labor Statistics*. Report 552. Washington, D.C.: Government Printing Office.

———. 1981. *BLS machine-readable data and tabulating routines*. Report 620. Washington, D.C.: Government Printing Office.

Comment F. Thomas Juster

The Antos paper has three principal parts:

1. What can we learn from theory about the kind of measurements that need to be included in labor cost?
2. What are the principal series now produced by the Bureau of Labor Statistics that can be used to analyze labor cost?
3. How can researchers make more effective use of existing BLS data?

Labor Cost Theory and Measurements

Three general questions are posed in the theory section of the paper. First, what elements should be included in labor cost, and what is the relation between labor cost and labor compensation? Second, what is the appropriate unit of observation for the measurement of labor cost (the worker, the job, the firm, etc.) and what is the appropriate time dimension for the measurement of labor cost (hourly, weekly, annually, business cycle units, etc.)? Finally, what factors ought to be included in data sets relating to labor cost because they can be used to explain variation in costs?

The first part of the initial section is concerned with an analysis of the elements that ought to go into measures of labor compensation. Antos argues that analysis of labor compensation ought to focus on the value of various wage elements to workers, while the analysis of labor cost, in contrast, should focus on elements that represent costs to the firm regardless of their value to workers.

Before examining the elements that Antos argues should be included in compensation, and the degree to which existing BLS data satisfies appropriate analytical requirements, it may be useful to register a basic disagreement with part of the underlying framework which underpins most analyses of labor supply. Almost all such analyses start with what is clearly an article of faith among economists—as Antos expresses it, "consumption is time-consuming and leisure is valued in its own right." There is therefore a trade-off between the benefits of work (consumption goods or services) and the benefits of leisure.

The presumption that leisure is valued in its own right while work is not is basic to conventional notions about how to analyze well-being. For example, the Nordhaus-Tobin economic welfare measure would be negatively affected by the combination of a decline in housework hours and a rise in workhours, total market output held constant. The analysis below calls that proposition into question. I believe there is a basic flaw in the conventional welfare function, which causes difficulties for the labor supply models displayed at this conference and elsewhere.

F. Thomas Juster is the director of the Institute for Social Research and a professor of economics at the University of Michigan, Ann Arbor.

The problem is that, while leisure is clearly valued in its own right (intrinsic benefits), there is significant evidence that work is valued in its own right as well, quite apart from the consumption power produced by earnings from labor.[1] Economists have always recognized that jobs have intrinsic nonmonetary benefits, and there is an extensive literature in the labor supply area which examines the degree to which different kinds of jobs are thought to have greater or lesser amounts of nonpecuniary benefits, and therefore lower or higher wage rates as workers maximize both pecuniary and nonpecuniary benefits at the margin. Thus, jobs like collecting garbage are thought to be highly paid because they are distasteful, while jobs like arranging flowers are thought to be paid poorly because they are pleasant.

While the nonpecuniary aspects of jobs have been recognized in much analysis of job choice and compensation level, that has not been true for analysis of work/leisure choices. There, the conventional analysis sounds as if people believe that work is distasteful and leisure "tasteful," and that consumers therefore trade off positively valued leisure for negatively valued work.

It is possible to subject that presumption to empirical testing. In 1975–76, in the context of conducting a study of time-use focused on nonmarket activities, we obtained a series of what we call "process benefits"—the subjectively assessed intrinsic rewards from a comprehensive set of activities—working for pay, working in the home, going to plays or movies, taking care of children, and so forth. Conventional labor supply theory generally predicts that leisure would have higher intrinsic rewards than work. At the margin, conventional theory is a bit fuzzy—it surely must say that the combination of extrinsic and intrinsic rewards from work are equal to the combination of extrinsic and intrinsic rewards from leisure. If one assumes that leisure has no *extrinsic* rewards, then theory says that at the margin the intrinsic rewards from leisure must be higher than those from work (since work provides both extrinsic as well as intrinsic rewards). If leisure carries extrinsic rewards, it is not clear what thoery would predict about process benefits at the margin.

While the data we obtained in 1975–76 do not contain marginal intrinsic rewards, they do reflect what we judge to be average intrinsic rewards. Unless the functions are very differently shaped,[2] labor economists would expect the average intrinsic rewards from work to be lower than the intrinsic rewards from leisure. The data say that is not true. Of some twenty-two activities ranked according to intrinsic rewards on a ten through one scale, work ranked just about fifth—below a set of child care activities, below social entertainment at home, but above every other activity, including almost all leisure activities.

Moreover, these results are quite general across almost all kinds of jobs. If one classifies jobs into a simple eleven-category occupational code (professional, managerial, etc.), it turns out that the intrinsic rewards from work in each occupation are higher than the intrinsic rewards from most leisure activities: The sole exception is the female laborer group, where intrinsic rewards from work are lower than most leisure activities.

All this is more suggestive than definitive. But I suspect that analyses of labor supply, especially of decisions to participate in the labor market, will fail to meet the test of predicting behavioral responses if they ignore the fact that work seems to be a very highly valued activity by most people who participate in it. In particular, I expect that the intrinsic rewards from work explain a good bit of the rise in female labor force participation, and that the real cause of that rise is not, as many labor economists have argued, differentially changing productivity in the market and the home. Needless to say, failure to take account of this kind of analysis is hardly Antos's fault—the relevant data and analyses have just begun to get into the public domain, and he can hardly be faulted for ignoring it.

The Antos paper discusses the role of fringe benefits in compensation calculations and focuses mainly on fringe benefits that have a well-defined monetary value—health insurance, pension plans, and so forth. That is, of course, an area where the data are more readily available, but there is a wide range of fringe benefits—job flexibility, health and safety in the workplace—which are more difficult to value but which may be just as important. Most of these qualitative measures are not available from conventional BLS sources, but tend to be available in private sources of data dealing with labor supply, such as the Michigan Panel Study of Income Dynamics, the Quality of Working Life surveys, and the Michigan Time-Use studies referred to earlier.

The question of what time unit to use to measure labor compensation is an interesting one. Antos talks about the differences between hourly, weekly or some longer time span with which to measure wage rates, and pays little attention to what seems to me a serious source of difference between conventional and actual measures of labor compensation per hour. The source of the problem is that most measures of hours, including those obtained by BLS from the Current Population Survey, estimate hours with a set of questions that clearly overstate actual hours spent at the workplace. Again, I will call on the Michigan Time-Use studies for documentation.

In the 1975–76 study, we found that a comparison of diary estimates of time of arrival at work and time leaving the workplace produce an estimate of actual elapsed hours at the workplace that was some 15 percent lower than estimates fo workhours obtained from CPS-type measures included in the same survey.[3] That is, not only is there doubt about what people actually do while at work, but there is clear evidence that people spend less time at the workplace than they report on survey-type measures of the sort used in the CPS. And the differential between actual elapsed hours and conventionally reported hours has been growing between the mid-1960s and the mid-1970s, judging from comparisons using the Time-Use studies.

The same set of data suggests that even elapsed hours are not necessarily a good measure of labor compensation—at least not of compensation for current productive effort. People spend time at the workplace in learning and training activities, as well as in leisure activities, neither of which are an input into current production. And for analysis of labor supply, it turns out to be quite important to distinguish between productive time (time spent at the workplace less training and leisure) and elapsed time: for example, the age pattern of time spent at the workplace does not conform well to predictions from theory, if one uses total elapsed time to measure time input, but it conforms substantially better if one uses actual productive time.

The last issue in this area relates to how one actually measures the compensation available to workers in fringe benefit areas, like pensions. The problem is that most calculations distribute a pension entitlement equally across all eligible workers employed by the firm, while the likelihood (and perhaps the expected value) of pension rights may vary quite a lot depending on characteristics of both the pension plan and the worker.

Finally, Antos notes the way in which the Current Population Survey measures wage rates—there is a fairly simple set of questions which do not make any explicit distinction between regular hours or overtime hours. Independent evidence suggests that there are measurement errors in these wage rate estimates, although the errors seem not to be very serious.

Labor Costs

Antos asks whether it is more sensible to focus on the labor costs associated with individuals, jobs, or the firm as a whole when it comes to the measurement of labor cost. Those are interesting and important issues, and he is quite right to focus on those distinctions. One question which may be of analytic interest is whether there are subunits within a firm where the relevant variable is the labor cost associated with some particular function—the payroll department, for example—and whether labor cost measures for those kinds of working group subunits may be more relevant for analysis of costs than either individual, job, or firm estimates.

The paper also notes that estimates of labor cost clearly have to take account of factors like training and hiring costs, the seasonal pattern of employment, the average work pace, and so forth. In short, the calculation of labor cost is far from a simple exercise of adding up a set of wage and fringe benefit payments to either individual workers, particular jobs, or collections of workers. Rather, it is a subtle calculation in which turnover, cyclical phase, and work pace have an important role to play.

BLS Data Series

The second part of the paper summarizes the kind of information provided by the Bureau of Labor Statistics in its current reporting program. I will touch only briefly on some of the elements that seem to me to warrant discussion in Antos's extensive and useful description of BLS data sources.

CPS. The Current Population Suvery provides what can be described as extremely useful but not highly reliable estimates of hours and wage rates, along with a set of personal characteristics associated with those labor market variables. CPS is thought of as a household survey, in that labor force participation data and characteristics are obtained for each member of the household over the age of 14. However, it is really a survey of individuals, in that all the data for the household are typically obtained from a single reporter for the household. There is a good bit of experience suggesting that proxy reporters are not very accurate, especially for population subgroups like teenagers and women, and for work circumstances which are erratic and part-time rather than conventional and full-time. Whether it is worth the cost of fixing proxy reports is a difficult question to answer—the data would clearly be better, and models that are heavily dependent on the reliability of the data are likely to be in some difficulty if they use CPS-type estimates for modeling household labor supply. The CPS also has a variety of useful supplements that are obtained on an annual basis (e.g., income) and others that are obtained less frequently (e.g., pension coverage).

ECI. The Employment Cost Index focuses on a set of occupations, in contrast to a set of people with some set of skills, experience, and job responsibility. That is, ECI costs out jobs rather than people. The potential problem with that measure may relate more to slippage of occupational definitions and to changes in the mix of skill levels of the people who are categorized as being in a particular occupation.

AWS, IWS, PATC and WDS surveys. These are all a collection of special purpose wage surveys—Area Wage Surveys, Industry Wage Surveys, Professional, Administrative, Technical, and Clerical Wage Surveys, and Wage Distribution Surveys. It is clear enough from the description that they were all originally designed to answer particular policy needs as seen by either the Congress or the Administration—people want to know what the wage rates are in Cleveland, not in the United States, they want to know whether public and private employment have different wages for the same function, and they are concerned with the nature and characteristics of jobs close to the minimum wage.

Although these surveys presumably came into being as a consequence of clearly perceived policy needs, it is important to ask whether they continue to provide those needs, and whether the same objectives could be served, perhaps somewhat less well, at substantially lesser costs. The issues that these special purpose surveys were designed to illuminate are ones that could of course be handled by a lower cost and more general purpose survey of wage rates from a representative sample of establishments, including public ones. Such a survey would necessarily be less efficient for the particular purposes underlying these special surveys. The question then becomes: is the increased variance that users have to live with too great a price to pay? My general inclination as an academic user rather than a public policy user, would be to go with general purpose wage surveys rather than special purpose ones, living with somewhat greater variance for any particular purpose.

Collective bargaining data. BLS collects comprehensive data on a variety of collective bargaining agreements, including universe data for major agreements. Moreover, BLS practice is to do a careful job of costing out various collective bargaining contracts. Antos notes that the data thus collected are published only in rather broad industry groups (manufacturing, for example), since more refined disaggregation would violate the confidentiality of the information that had been collected. The reason appears to be that, although these collective bargaining agreements are in the public domain, BLS collects some information from contractees on a confidential basis, and these data are used to provide estimates of the cost of some contractual provisions. The experience of other researchers with attempts to produce comparable estimates without the detailed and confidential contractee data (relayed in a private communication from Jack Triplett of the BLS) suggests that it is extremely difficult for outsiders to replicate the BLS procedures for disaggregated industry groups.

The 790 survey and the ES-202 survey program. These two surveys are, respectively, the largest establishment survey conducted by the BLS (790) and an administrative data base consisting of quarterly reports submitted to state unemployment security agencies by employers subject to UI programs (ES-202). As Antos notes, these are enormously large data bases and have the deficiency often found in such data bases—they have very large numbers of observations but very few useful variables that can be used for analysis. The logical question is, of course, would not both BLS and the general user community be better served by a more parsimonious sample and a somewhat richer collection of analytic variables attached to that smaller sample? As an academic user, my answer of course would be yes, but then I am not responsible for having to provide states with estimates of the level of unemployment, nor having to provide other users in the government with estimates of hourly earnings by industry to go into various statistical estimates. I would still argue that it may be better to live with more variance and more analytical potential.

Reflections on the BLS Program Generally

Antos's paper provides a very useful and detailed summary of BLS procedures in collecting the information that provides for analysis of labor cost and compensation issues. In addition, he provides a very useful appendix which organizes these data resources so that the user can see what is available for what time period. The paper is understandably short on asking: What *should* the BLS do, if it didn't have any constraints other than those imposed by a budget and a mandate to provide data of maximal usefulness both for the policy community and to the research community?

Let me note some general principles that seem to me to be relevant to the question: What should the BLS do? First, my judgment is that the most useful data on earnings come from households rather than from establishments. The basic reason is that collecting such data from households permits, at modest cost, the addition of a whole set of demographic and worker characteristics from which a number of interesting and useful analyses can be done, while establishment data will inevitably suffer from the defect of lacking many of the relevant analytic variables. Moreover, labor supply characteristics like the training and leisure components of work can be obtained at least as reliably from household surveys as from establishment surveys. Finally, the most important advantage of establishment surveys—the presumed greater reliability of the financial data—may be much less of an advantage now than it used to be. Households will often tend to have records in the form of payroll forms or check stubs, and those records contain quite accurate information on hours actually worked, gross pay, and various other relevant labor supply variables.

Second, for a program designed to analyze the behavior of labor compensation and costs, the relevant data should be based on households rather than individuals. While it is true that the CPS data do relate to households, it is also true that proxy reporting may be a serious problem with the CPS data on the hours and earnings of household members other than the person doing the reporting.

Finally, if one asks what are the most important types of data that need to be obtained from establishments, it seems to me that the answer is data relating to the demand for labor, not data relating to the supply. What BLS does in its largest establishment surveys (the 790 and 202) is to collect data on workers and jobs which could in principle be obtained from households but which are obtained either from much larger samples or with greater presumed accuracy from establishments. In short, BLS is collecting labor supply-type data from the demanders of labor rather than from the suppliers because in many cases it is convenient to do so.

But there is an important set of questions dealing with labor market problems that relate to the demand side of the market for labor for which there is no other possible source but the establishment or the firm. Here, the current BLS program, as I understand it, seems to be totally lacking. For example, it would be nice to know something about hiring policies—where do firms look for new employees? It would be nice to know how firms evaluate worker productivity and decide on promotions, raises, firings, and so forth. It would be nice to know how firms behave with respect to training on the job and so on. None of these data can be obtained from households, and all seem to be needed to permit a better understanding of the way in which labor markets function.

I would make the judgment that the BLS program would be better if it collected data from fewer units of observation generally, but measured more variables for those same units. The basic reason is that I would be prepared to live with somewhat more sampling variance, if the benefits were a substantially enhanced analytic potential. And I would tend to worry more about designing a smaller number of efficient general purpose surveys of both households and establishments and not worry so much about the details of industry, area, and occupation. With an efficient national sample design one can always extract those details, although at the cost of a greater degree of variance than if one designs special purpose surveys with particular coefficients of variation for specific industries, areas, or occupations.

Finally, a discussion of data sources for the analysis of labor problems would be seriously incomplete without noting the existence of a set of nonfederal sources of data on these issues. The ones I know best are ones available at the Institute for Social Research at Michigan, although there are widely used and well-known data resources produced by other organizations such as the National Opinion Research Center at Chicago. At ISR, the most useful series relating to labor problems are clearly the Panel Study of Income Dynamics, a fifteen-year longitudinal panel of households and individuals within households which tracks movements in income, hours, and earnings for identical people; the Quality of Working Life surveys conducted in 1969, 1973, and 1977, which focus more on the conditions of work for a sample of employed adults than on hours and wage rates; and the Time-Use studies—a new and relatively small sample study which has produced some interesting results on labor supply issues, as I noted in the first part of this discussion. At NORC, the principal sources of information on labor supply are the National Longitudinal Surveys, begun quite a number of years ago with a set of panels of people of various age groups and recently augmented by the addition of two panels of younger workers.

These nonfederal data sources all have a set of common characteristics which make them highly complementary to the data resources described in the Antos paper. In principle, they provide enormous richness in variables relevant for the explanation of labor market behavior, while generally being substantially thinner than the BLS sources on sample size. They cannot generally be used for anything other than the grossest regional analyses, mainly because the samples are too small. But they provide a rich variety of data for a number of analytic purposes, and they probably tend to be underexploited just as the Antos paper suggests is true of the BLS data.

Notes

1. The argument is spelled out in F. Thomas Juster, Paul Courant, and Greg Dow. 1981. A framework for the measurement and analysis of well-being. In *Social accounting systems: Essays on the state of the art*, ed. F. T. Juster and K. Land. New York: Academic Press.

2. One could make a reasonable case that the functions are differently shaped—marginal intrinsic rewards for work might decline rather rapidly for hours in excess of a normal workweek. The occupational evidence is consistent with the view that people are not necessarily excited by what they do on the job but more by the generalized work environment. A full-time or even part-time job would fulfill this requirement. In contrast, excess work might be valued primarily because the work itself was interesting.

3. See Greg Duncan and Frank Stafford. 1980. The use of time and technology by households in the United States. In *Research in labor economics*, vol. 3, ed. R. G. Ehrenberg. Greenwich, Conn.: JAI Press.

PART

II Measures of Aggregate Labor Cost in the United States

5 Sectoral Measures of Labor Cost for the United States, 1948–1978

Frank M. Gollop and Dale W. Jorgenson

5.1 Introduction

The objective of this paper is to construct measures of labor cost for each industrial sector of the United States for the period 1948–78. The purpose of our measures of labor cost is to deal with the heterogeneity of labor input. Measures of labor cost based on average hourly earnings or average hourly compensation are derived by dividing payrolls by an unweighted sum of hours worked. The total of hours worked is estimated by combining, for example, the hours of hospital orderlies with the hours of brain surgeons. The resulting measures of labor cost do not adequately reflect the difference between the marginal productivity of a hospital orderly and the marginal productivity of a brain surgeon.

To solve the problem posed by the enormous heterogeneity of labor input we construct very detailed index numbers of labor cost and labor input. For this purpose we have developed a methodology based on an explicit model of production. This model is based on a production function for each sector giving output as a function of intermediate, capital, and labor inputs, and time. An important innovation in our methodology is that at the sectoral level we distinguish among components of labor input that differ in marginal productivity. Labor input is represented as a function of types of labor input broken down by characteristics of individual workers such as sex, age, education, employment status, and occupation.

A second important innovation in our methodology is that we treat the price and quantity of labor input symmetrically. In our sectoral models of

Frank M. Gollop is an associate professor of economics at Boston College, Chestnut Hill, Massachusetts. Dale W. Jorgenson is with the Department of Economics, Harvard University.

production we combine the production function and intermediate, capital, and labor inputs as functions of their components with necessary conditions for producer equilibrium. In equilibrium the share of each input in the value of output is equal to the elasticity of output with respect to that input. These conditions make it possible to identify the marginal product of each input with the ratio of the corresponding input price to the price of output. Similarly, the share of each component of labor input is equal to the elasticity of labor input with respect to that component. We can identify the marginal product of each component with the ratio of its cost to the cost of labor input as a whole.

Our methodology generates price and quantity index numbers for labor input. These index numbers are employed in constructing measures of labor cost and labor input for each industrial sector. To disaggregate labor input into components that differ in marginal productivity, we measure wage rates as well as hours worked broken down by characteristics of individual workers. We consider specific forms for the functions giving sectoral labor inputs in terms of their components. We take these functions to be translog in form, so that labor input is an exponential function of linear and quadratic terms in the logarithms of the components. Given translog labor inputs for all sectors, we can generate the corresponding translog quantity index numbers for labor input. The change in the logarithms of labor input between any two periods is a weighted average of changes in the logarithms of its components. Weights are given by the average share of each component in sectoral labor compensation for the two periods. The corresponding indexes of labor cost are defined as ratios of labor compensation to the translog quantity indexes.

To construct measures of labor cost and labor input that are consistent with the U.S. National Income and Product Accounts (Bureau of Economic Analysis 1977), we have controlled these data to industry totals based on establishment surveys. To disaggregate labor cost and labor input by industrial and demographic charcteristics of the work force, we have exploited the detail on employment, hours worked, weeks paid, and compensation available from household surveys. To achieve consistency between establishment and household survey data, we have used the household survey results to distribute industry totals based on establishment surveys.

We have disaggregated labor cost and labor input for all employed persons into cells cross-classified by the two sexes, eight age groups, five educational groups, two employment classes, ten occupational groups, and fifty-one industries listed in table 5.1. This breakdown of labor input characteristics is based on the groupings employed by the U.S. Bureau of the Census in reporting data from household surveys. The Census data provide the only source of consistent time series on the work force

Table 5.1 Characteristics of Labor Input

SEX:
Male
Female

AGE:
14–15 years
16–17 years
18–24 years
25–34 years
35–44 years
45–54 years
55–64 years
65 years and over

EDUCATION:
1–8 years grade school
1–3 years high school
4 years high school
1–3 years college
4 or more years college

EMPLOYMENT CLASS:
Wage and salary worker
Self-employed/unpaid family worker

OCCUPATION:
Professional, technical, and kindred workers
Farmers and farm managers
Managers and administrators, except farm
Clerical workers
Sales workers
Craftsmen and kindred workers
Operatives
Service workers, including private household
Farm laborers
Laborers, except farm

INDUSTRY:
Agricultural production
Agricultural services, horticultural services, forestry and fisheries
Metal mining
Coal mining
Crude petroleum and natural gas extractions
Nonmetallic mining and quarrying, except fuel
Contract construction
Food and kindred products
Tobacco manufacturers
Textile mill products
Apparel and other fabricated textile products
Paper and allied products
Printing, publishing, and allied industries
Chemicals and allied products
Petroleum and coal products
Rubber and miscellaneous plastic products
Leather and leather products
Lumber and wood products, except furniture
Furniture and fixtures
Stone, clay, and glass products
Primary metal industries
Fabricated metal industries
Machinery, except electrical
Electrical machinery, equipment, and supplies
Transportation equipment (except motor vehicles) and ordnance
Motor vehicles and motor vehicle equipment
Professional photographic equipment and watches
Miscellaneous manufacturing industries
Railroads and railway express services
Street railway, bus lines, and taxicab service
Trucking service, warehousing, and storage

Table 5.1 (continued)

Water transportation
Air transportation
Pipelines, except natural gas
Transportation services
Telephone, telegraph, and miscellaneous communication services
Radio broadcasting and television
Electric utilities
Gas utilities
Water supply, sanitary services, and other utilities
Wholesale trade
Retail trade
Finance, insurance, and real estate
Services
Private households
Nonprofit institutions
Federal public administration
Federal government enterprises
Educational services, government (state and local)
State and local public administration
State and local government enterprises

cross-classified by industrial, occupational, and demographic characteristics.

Data on labor cost and labor input for the fifty-one industry groups listed in table 5.1 also are available from establishment surveys employed in constructing the U.S. national income and product accounts. No existing household or establishment survey, including the recently expanded Current Population Survey, is designed to provide annual data on the distribution of workers among the 81,600 cells of a matrix cross-classified by the characteristics given in table 5.1. However, existing surveys do provide marginal totals cross-classified by two, three, and sometimes four characteristics of labor input. These marginal distributions, available for each year from 1948 to 1978, provide the basis for our estimates of labor cost and labor input.

Our first task is to construct annual matrices cross-classified by the industrial, occupational, and demographic characteristics listed in table 5.1 for employment, hours worked, weeks, and compensation, the four components required for measures of labor cost and labor input. We have employed all the published information on marginal totals for each component of labor cost and labor input available from the Census of Population and the Current Population Survey. A complete listing of the sources for the data on employment, hours, weeks, and labor compensation we have employed is given in the appendix to this chapter. The procedures we have adopted in constructing the matrices that underlie our index numbers for labor cost and labor input are outlined by Gollop and Jorgenson (1980).

A useful but much more costly alternative to our approach would be to compile data on hours worked and labor compensation per hour directly from the individual records underlying the Census of Population and the Current Population Survey. For example, the one in a thousand sample from the 1960 and 1970 Censuses could be used to compile data for the 81,600 entries of each matrix we require for these two years. This approach would not be feasible for data from the Current Population Survey, since the number of entries in each cell would be too small to provide the needed reliability. We have employed published data from the Census of Population rather than the one in a thousand sample in order to reduce costs. If resources were to become available that would make it possible to employ the individual records from this sample, the resulting tabulations would provide a useful check on the approach we have employed. These tabulations also could be used to benchmark our data on hours worked and labor compensation.

Data on labor cost and labor input cross-classified by characteristics such as employment class, occupation, and industry are required in studies of labor demand; data cross-classified by characteristics such as sex, age, and education are required in studies of labor supply. Our data base can be used to generate indexes of labor cost and labor input cross-classified by each of the characteristics we have employed in compiling data on hours worked and compensation per hour. The indexing methodology is described in the following section. We present indexes of labor cost and labor input for each of the fifty-one industries listed in table 5.1.

The desirability of disaggregating labor cost and labor input by industrial, occupational, and demographic characteristics of the work force has been widely recognized, for example, by Denison (1961, 1962), Griliches (1960), Jorgenson and Griliches (1967), Kendrick (1961), and others. Kendrick has developed measures of labor cost and labor input disaggregated by industry for much of the postwar period, but his measures do not incorporate a cross-classification of labor cost and labor input by age, sex, education, or other demographic characteristics of the work force. Denison has developed measures of labor cost and labor input for the U.S. economy as a whole based on data disaggregated by sex, age, education, and employment status, but not by occupation or industry.[1]

5.2 Indexes of Sectoral Labor Cost and Labor Input

We have outlined the development of data on annual hours worked and labor compensation per hour for each industrial sector. Both annual hours and compensation data are cross-classified by sex, age, education, employment class, and occupation of workers. To construct indexes of labor cost and labor input for each industrial sector, we assume that sectoral labor input, say $\{L_i\}$, can be expressed as a translog function of its individual components, say $\{L_{\ell i}\}$. The corresponding index of sectoral labor input is a translog quantity index of individual labor inputs:

$$\ln L_i(T) - \ln L_i(T-1) = \sum_{\ell} \bar{v}^i_{L\ell} [\ln L_{\ell i}(T) - \ln L_{\ell i}(T-1)], \quad (i = 1, 2, \ldots, n),$$

where weights are given by average shares of each component in the value of sectoral labor compensation:

$$\bar{v}^i_{L\ell} = \frac{1}{2} [v^i_{L\ell}(T) + v^i_{L\ell}(T-1)], \qquad (i = 1, 2, \ldots, n; \ \ell = 1, 2, \ldots, q),$$

and

$$v^i_{L\ell} = \frac{p^i_{L\ell} L_{\ell i}}{\sum_{\ell} p^i_{L\ell} L_{\ell i}}, \qquad (i = 1, 2, \ldots, n; \ \ell = 1, 2, \ldots, q).$$

The value shares are computed from data on hours worked $\{L_{\ell i}\}$ and compensation per hour $\{p^i_{L\ell}\}$ for each component of sectoral labor input, cross-classified by sex, age, education, employment class, and occupation of workers. Labor compensation for the sector as a whole, $\sum_{\ell} p^i_{L\ell} L_{\ell i}$, is controlled to labor compensation by industry from the U.S. national income accounts.

For each of the components of labor input into an industrial sector $\{L_{\ell i}(T)\}$ the flow of labor services is proportional to hours worked, say $\{H_{\ell i}(T)\}$:

$$L_{\ell i}(T) = Q^i_{L\ell} H_{\ell i}(T), \qquad (i = 1, 2, \ldots, n; \ \ell = 1, 2, \ldots, q),$$

where the constants of proportionality $\{Q^i_{L\ell}\}$ transform hours worked into a flow of labor services. The translog quantity indexes of sectoral labor input $\{L_i\}$ can be expressed in terms of their components $\{L_{\ell i}\}$ or in terms of the components of hours worked $\{H_{\ell i}\}$:

$$\begin{aligned} \ln L_i(T) - \ln L_i(T-1) &= \sum \bar{v}^i_{L\ell} [\ln L_{\ell i}(T) - \ln L_{\ell i}(T-1)] \\ &= \sum \bar{v}^i_{L\ell} [\ln H_{\ell i}(T) - \ln H_{\ell i}(T-1)], \\ &\qquad (i = 1, 2, \ldots, n). \end{aligned}$$

We form sectoral indexes of labor input from data on hours worked by industry, cross-classified by sex, age, education, employment class, and occupation. Changes in the logarithms of hours worked for each component are weighted by average shares in sectoral labor compensation.

We can define *sectoral hours worked*, say $\{H_i(T)\}$, as the unweighted sum of its components,

$$H_i(T) = \sum_{\ell} H_{\ell i}(T), \qquad (i = 1, 2, \ldots, n).$$

Similarly, we can define *sectoral indexes of the quality of hours worked*, say $\{Q_L^i(T)\}$, that transform sectoral measures of hours worked into the translog indexes of labor input:

$$L_i(T) = Q_L^i(T)H_i(T), \qquad (i = 1, 2, \ldots, n).$$

The sectoral indexes of the quality of hours worked can be expressed in the form:

$$\ln Q_L^i(T) - \ln Q_L^i(T-1) = \sum_{\ell} \bar{v}_{L\ell}^i[\ln H_{\ell i}(T) - \ln H_{\ell i}(T-1)] - [\ln H_i(T) - \ln H_i(T-1)], \quad (i = 1, 2, \ldots, n),$$

so that these indexes reflect changes in the composition of hours worked within each sector.[2] Sectoral labor quality remains unchanged if all components of hours worked within a sector are growing at the same rate. Sectoral quality rises if components with higher flows of labor input per hour worked are growing more rapidly and falls if components with lower flows per hour worked are growing more rapidly.

The product of price and quantity indexes of labor input must be equal to the value of total labor compensation for each sector. We can define the price index corresponding to the translog quantity index of labor input as the ratio of the value of total labor compensation into the sector to the translog quantity index. The resulting price index does not have the form of a translog price index, but it can be determined from data on prices and quantities of the components of labor input at any two discrete points of time. The price index of labor input becomes our index of labor cost.

We have generated price and quantity indexes of labor input for each industrial sector listed in table 5.1. There are 1600 categories of labor input for each industry and a total of fifty-one industries. Average annual rates of growth of the translog indexes of sectoral labor cost and labor input are presented for 1948–78 for seven subperiods for all fifty-one industries in tables 5.2 and 5.3. Indexes of labor cost and labor input and indexes of the quality of hours worked are presented in appendix B of this volume on an annual basis for the period 1948–78 for each industry. Annual data for employment, weekly hours per person, hourly compensation, hours worked, and labor compensation are also presented for each industry in appendix B.

To identify differences in patterns of growth in labor cost among subperiods more precisely, we present classifications of rates of growth by subperiod in table 5.4. The overall pattern of labor cost increases across subperiods coincides with variations in the rate of inflation during the postwar period. In every period more than 90 percent of the industries experienced growth rates of labor cost within a range of six percentage

Table 5.2 Sectoral Labor Cost: Rates of Growth

Industry	Price Index of Labor Input (average annual rates of growth) 1948–53	1953–57	1957–60	1960–66	1966–69	1969–73	1973–78
Agricultural production	−0.0405	0.0516	0.0503	0.0956	0.0572	0.1801	0.0675
Agricultural services	0.0439	0.0436	0.0285	−0.0125	0.0861	0.1045	0.0634
Metal mining	0.0709	0.0453	0.0276	0.0277	0.0501	0.0894	0.1126
Coal mining	0.0667	0.0425	0.0362	0.0239	0.0734	0.0808	0.0913
Crude petroleum and natural gas	0.0353	0.0346	0.0237	0.0298	0.0539	0.0649	0.0915
Nonmetallic mining and quarrying	0.0552	0.0515	0.0494	0.0277	0.0589	0.0791	0.0745
Contract construction	0.0560	0.0484	0.0397	0.0371	0.0616	0.0644	0.0613
Food and kindred products	0.0459	0.0497	0.0424	0.0321	0.0535	0.0656	0.0861
Tobacco manufacturers	0.0622	0.0603	0.0436	0.0364	0.0788	0.0685	0.1183
Textile mill products	0.0335	0.0248	0.0285	0.0368	0.0590	0.0603	0.0814
Apparel and other fabr. textile prod.	0.0314	0.0301	0.0183	0.0308	0.0703	0.0451	0.0702
Paper and allied products	0.0493	0.0453	0.0329	0.0327	0.0537	0.0713	0.0934
Printing and publishing	0.0415	0.0472	0.0110	0.0389	0.0524	0.0624	0.0651
Chemicals and allied products	0.0533	0.0486	0.0240	0.0339	0.0531	0.0698	0.0853
Petroleum and coal products	0.0546	0.0430	0.0275	0.0258	0.0528	0.0581	0.1012
Rubber and misc. plastic products	0.0469	0.0447	0.0289	0.0256	0.0525	0.0540	0.0791
Leather and leather products	0.0360	0.0376	0.0283	0.0325	0.0661	0.0434	0.0731
Lumber and wood prod., ex. furniture	0.0569	0.0548	0.0327	0.0394	0.0616	0.0653	0.0950
Furniture and fixtures	0.0464	0.0428	0.0380	0.0258	0.0627	0.0554	0.0744
Stone, clay, and glass products	0.0527	0.0488	0.0251	0.0322	0.0576	0.0690	0.0850
Primary metal industries	0.0613	0.0603	0.0372	0.0254	0.0538	0.0762	0.1019
Fabricated metal industries	0.0521	0.0428	0.0318	0.0302	0.0582	0.0637	0.0863
Machinery, ex. electrical	0.0583	0.0434	0.0360	0.0301	0.0597	0.0590	0.0845

Elec. machinery, eqpt., and supplies	0.0434	0.0398	0.0441	0.0260	0.0676	0.0562	0.0831
Trans. eqpt. + ord., ex. motor vehicles	0.0388	0.0499	0.0581	0.0346	0.0643	0.0641	0.0807
Motor vehicles and equipment	0.0716	0.0547	0.0288	0.0392	0.0645	0.0777	0.0917
Prof. photographic eqpt. and watches	0.0537	0.0480	0.0310	0.0283	0.0589	0.0569	0.0738
Misc. manufacturing industries	0.0494	0.0496	0.0213	0.0267	0.0642	0.0539	0.0683
Railroads and rail express services	0.0630	0.0472	0.0449	0.0217	0.0552	0.0989	0.0904
Street rail., bus lines, and taxicabs	0.0314	0.0337	0.0116	0.0430	0.0556	0.0463	0.0853
Trucking services and warehousing	0.0690	0.0499	0.0456	0.0306	0.0537	0.0883	0.0834
Water transportation	0.0759	0.0386	0.0351	0.0361	0.0657	0.0681	0.0808
Air transportation	0.0563	0.0404	0.0506	0.0472	0.0739	0.0924	0.0958
Pipelines, ex. natural gas	0.0398	0.0299	0.0263	0.0324	0.0302	0.0787	0.0989
Transportation services	0.0555	0.0657	0.0391	0.0207	0.0411	0.0747	0.0886
Tel. and tel. and misc. comm. services	0.0557	0.0311	0.0447	0.0369	0.0485	0.1189	0.1012
Radio broadcasting and television	0.0518	0.0518	0.0309	0.0315	0.0343	0.0502	0.0795
Electric utilities	0.0585	0.0422	0.0406	0.0409	0.0523	0.0807	0.0901
Gas utilities	0.0665	0.0550	0.0519	0.0280	0.0434	0.0771	0.0901
Water supply and sanitary services	0.0766	0.0688	0.0687	0.0508	0.0709	0.0728	0.0844
Wholesale trade	0.0339	0.0560	0.0192	0.0330	0.0646	0.0605	0.0765
Retail trade	0.0320	0.0498	0.0214	0.0499	0.0640	0.0616	0.0739
Finance, insurance, and real estate	0.0221	0.0528	−0.0064	0.0611	0.0853	0.0778	0.0549
Services	0.0421	0.0739	0.0329	0.0645	0.0779	0.0692	0.0765
Private households	0.0516	0.0460	0.0447	0.0381	0.0730	0.0560	0.0847
Nonprofit institutions	0.0478	0.0354	0.0142	0.0288	0.0451	0.0741	0.0631
Federal public administration	0.0509	0.0441	0.0554	0.0395	0.0548	0.0962	0.0696
Federal government enterprises	0.0442	0.0387	0.0442	0.0464	0.0626	0.1035	0.0890
State and local educ. services	0.0397	0.0489	0.0456	0.0507	0.0799	0.0689	0.0704
State and local public admin.	0.0366	0.0424	0.0410	0.0379	0.0752	0.0766	0.0704
State and local govt. enterprises	0.0504	0.0438	0.0507	0.0527	0.0628	0.0810	0.0667

Table 5.3 Sectoral Labor Input: Rates of Growth

Industry	Translog Index of Labor Input (average annual rates of growth)						
	1948–53	1953–57	1957–60	1960–66	1966–69	1969–73	1973–78
Agricultural production	−0.0320	−0.0505	−0.0251	−0.0495	−0.0242	−0.0077	−0.0176
Agricultural services	0.0178	−0.0098	−0.0350	0.0492	0.0400	0.0412	0.0433
Metal mining	0.0220	0.0035	−0.0454	−0.0070	0.0159	−0.0187	0.0091
Coal mining	−0.1040	−0.0568	−0.1224	−0.0189	−0.0117	0.0498	0.0843
Crude petroleum and natural gas	0.0491	0.0332	−0.0318	−0.0046	0.0123	−0.0030	0.1015
Nonmetallic mining and quarrying	0.0318	0.0159	−0.0136	0.0178	−0.0145	−0.0029	0.0178
Contract construction	0.0224	−0.0003	−0.0020	0.0325	0.0285	0.0235	0.0167
Food and kindred products	0.0027	−0.0081	−0.0014	0.0025	0.0048	−0.0120	0.0012
Tobacco manufacturers	0.0131	−0.0166	0.0079	−0.0083	−0.0197	0.0042	−0.0291
Textile mill products	−0.0259	−0.0392	−0.0087	0.0159	0.0076	0.0075	−0.0265
Apparel and other fabr. textile prod.	0.0069	−0.0119	0.0102	0.0228	−0.0017	0.0024	−0.0061
Paper and allied products	0.0327	0.0174	0.0231	0.0264	0.0244	−0.0052	−0.0004
Printing and publishing	0.0217	0.0137	0.0362	0.0139	0.0253	−0.0023	0.0150
Chemicals and allied products	0.0452	0.0234	0.0210	0.0270	0.0327	−0.0070	0.0231
Petroleum and coal products	0.0252	0.0045	−0.0306	−0.0161	0.0160	0.0043	0.0328
Rubber and misc. plastic products	0.0402	0.0138	0.0122	0.0566	0.0457	0.0307	0.0120
Leather and leather products	−0.0070	−0.0113	−0.0101	0.0046	−0.0278	−0.0313	−0.0261
Lumber and wood prod., ex. furniture	−0.0175	−0.0427	−0.0033	0.0120	0.0098	0.0213	−0.0008
Furniture and fixtures	0.0177	−0.0040	−0.0014	0.0370	0.0016	0.0182	−0.0017
Stone, clay, and glass products	0.0144	0.0055	0.0193	0.0176	0.0081	0.0130	0.0020
Primary metal industries	0.0216	−0.0055	−0.0309	0.0284	0.0005	−0.0047	−0.0076
Fabricated metal industries	0.0520	−0.0033	−0.0132	0.0378	0.0253	−0.0039	0.0003
Machinery, ex. electrical	0.0354	−0.0045	−0.0184	0.0548	0.0131	0.0076	0.0214

Elec. machinery, eqpt., and supplies	0.0727	0.0074	0.0396	0.0434	0.0141	0.0015	0.0076
Trans. eqpt. + ord., ex. motor vehicles	0.1923	−0.0004	−0.0545	0.0454	0.0029	−0.0684	0.0147
Motor vehicles and equipment	0.0540	−0.0420	−0.0147	0.0393	0.0044	0.0234	0.0057
Prof. photographic eqpt. and watches	0.0850	0.0165	0.0151	0.0364	0.0266	0.0080	0.0324
Misc. manufacturing industries	0.0078	−0.0212	0.0030	0.0233	−0.0010	0.0047	0.0057
Railroads and rail express services	−0.0421	−0.0408	−0.0714	−0.0174	−0.0269	−0.0273	−0.0176
Street rail., bus lines, and taxicabs	−0.0205	−0.0325	−0.0183	−0.0116	−0.0006	−0.0201	−0.0210
Trucking services and warehousing	0.0474	0.0184	0.0195	0.0339	0.0258	0.0218	0.0114
Water transportation	−0.0127	0.0070	−0.0355	0.0097	−0.0217	−0.0301	0.0105
Air transportation	0.0617	0.0851	0.0440	0.0461	0.1042	0.0042	0.0150
Pipelines, ex. natural gas	−0.0026	−0.0074	−0.0302	−0.0334	0.0102	−0.0295	0.0456
Transportation services	0.0150	−0.0149	0.0140	0.0470	0.0418	0.0239	0.0714
Tel. and tel. and misc. comm. services	0.0222	0.0288	−0.0084	0.0227	0.0440	0.0254	0.0057
Radio broadcasting and television	0.0702	0.0410	0.0306	0.0341	0.0509	0.0298	0.0394
Electric utilities	0.0207	0.0102	0.0110	0.0108	0.0253	0.0179	0.0093
Gas utilities	0.0261	0.0179	0.0196	0.0144	0.0252	0.0180	0.0094
Water supply and sanitary services	0.0169	0.0063	0.0044	0.0189	0.0244	0.0289	0.0151
Wholesale trade	0.0151	0.0128	0.0269	0.0233	0.0203	0.0215	0.0228
Retail trade	0.0118	0.0015	0.0143	0.0074	0.0130	0.0177	0.0179
Finance, insurance, and real estate	0.0421	0.0333	0.0392	0.0292	0.0390	0.0340	0.0368
Services	0.0181	0.0262	0.0335	0.0328	0.0350	0.0310	0.0347
Private households	−0.0257	0.0068	−0.0002	−0.0285	−0.0401	−0.0365	−0.0345
Nonprofit institutions	0.0470	0.0429	0.0878	0.0458	0.0527	0.0013	0.0304
Federal public administration	0.0539	−0.0060	0.0055	0.0280	0.0263	−0.0169	0.0179
Federal government enterprises	0.0282	0.0091	0.0287	0.0226	0.0268	−0.0087	−0.0038
State and local educ. services	0.0535	0.0586	0.0629	0.0535	0.0432	0.0374	0.0218
State and local public admin.	0.0434	0.0430	0.0270	0.0394	0.0334	0.0409	0.0289
State and local govt. enterprises	0.0647	0.0022	0.0647	0.0204	0.0408	0.0314	0.0386

Table 5.4 Classification of Rates of Growth of Sectoral Labor Cost by Subperiod, 1948–78

Average Rate of Growth of Labor Cost	1948–53	1953–57	1957–60	1960–66	1966–69	1969–73	1973–78
<0%	1	0	1	1	0	0	0
0–2%	0	0	5	0	0	0	0
2–4%	12	11	26	39	2	0	0
4–6%	28	35	18	8	25	12	1
6–8%	10	5	1	2	22	27	20
8–10%	0	0	0	1	2	8	25
>10%	0	0	0	0	0	4	5

points. The pattern varies among subperiods, depending on the rate of inflation during the period. For the subperiods 1948–53 and 1953–57, average rates of growth in labor cost for most industries ranged from 2 to 8 percent per year. For the subperiods 1957–60 and 1960–66, rates of growth in labor cost averaged 0–6 percent for most industries. The range moved up to 2–8 percent for the subperiod 1966–69, 4–10 percent for the subperiod 1969–73, and the highest of the postwar period, at 6–12 percent, for the subperiod 1973–78.

Our next objective is to identify the industrial sectors that experienced persistently rapid increases in labor cost during the postwar period. We focus on growth rates of labor cost that exceeded 4 percent in the first two subperiods (1948–53 and 1953–57), 2 percent in the following two subperiods (1957–60 and 1960–66), and 4, 6, and 8 percent in the subperiods 1966–69, 1969–73, and 1973–78 respectively. The industries with persistently rapid increases in labor cost include metal and coal mining, food, tobacco, paper, and chemicals among nondurables manufacturing; lumber and wood, stone, clay, and glass, primary and fabricated metal, and motor vehicles among durables manufacturing; railroads, trucking, air transportation, and transportation services among the transportation industries; electric utilities, gas utilities, and water supply and sanitary services among the utilities. We conclude that these industries are distributed among the major groups of the fifty-one industries included in our study.

Agricultural production stands out as the industry most subject to fluctuations in growth rates of labor cost. During the period 1948–53 the growth rate of labor cost was −4.05 percent per year. For the periods 1953–57 and 1957–60 the growth rate of labor cost was 5.16 and 5.03 percent per year. During the subperiod 1960–66 labor cost growth jumped to 9.56 percent annually; this was followed by growth at 5.72 percent per year for the subperiod 1966–69. Labor cost grew at rates of 18.01 and 6.75 percent per year during the final two subperiods, 1969–73 and 1973–78, respectively. This relatively erratic pattern reflects the important role of self-employment income in the agricultural sector and the sizable fluctuations in farm income due to variations in supply conditions.

We have presented six-percent ranges that include 90 percent of our fifty-one industrial sectors for each of seven subperiods. A useful perspective on rates of increase in labor cost is provided by identifying the industries that fall outside the six-percent ranges for each subperiod. During the period 1948–53 agricultural production experienced a decline in labor cost. During the period 1953–57 no industry had a growth rate of labor cost that fell below 2 percent or exceeded 8 percent.

The subperiod 1957–60 was characterized by a slower rate of growth of labor cost than the two preceding subperiods. Finance, insurance, and real estate experienced a decline in labor cost during this period, while water supply and sanitary services underwent a growth of labor cost of 6.87 percent per year. During the following period, 1960–66, the growth rate of labor cost for agricultural services fell to −1.25 percent annually, while the growth rate of labor cost in agricultural production was close to 10 percent per year. The subperiod 1966–69 resulted in more rapid growth of labor cost for most industries. The growth rate of labor cost was 8.61 percent per year for agricultural services and 8.53 percent per year for finance, insurance, and real estate.

The acceleration of growth in labor cost continued during the period 1969–73. Growth rates exceeded 10 percent annually for four industries—agricultural production, agricultural services, telecommunications, and federal government enterprises. The most rapid increases in labor cost during the postwar period took place during the final subperiod, 1973–78. The growth rate of labor cost exceeded 10 percent per year for six industry groups, while growth of labor cost in finance, insurance, and real estate lagged all other industries at 5.49 percent per year.

We next consider differences in patterns of growth in labor input among subperiods, based on rates of growth of labor input by subperiod in table 5.5. The overall pattern of labor input within and across all subperiods conforms well with general impressions of economic activity in the postwar period. In every period more than half of the fifty-one industries experienced a positive average annual rate of growth in labor input. The pattern varies over time and depends on the relative strength of growth during the period. Considering the subperiods in chronological order, the number of industries with positive average annual changes in quality adjusted hours worked are 41, 29, 27, 41, 40, 32, and 38, respectively.

The immediate postwar period (1948–53), the two periods capturing the surge of economic activity relating to the Vietnam War (1960–66 and 1966–69), and the final period (1973–78) stand out. So does the 1957–60 subperiod when 24 of 51 industries experienced declines in labor input. Both agricultural sectors, all four mining industries, construction, seven of eleven durable goods industries, and four of seven transportation sectors led the downward trend. This contrasts with the 1948–53, 1960–66, and 1966–69 subperiods when construction and nearly all durable goods sectors experienced increases in labor input. In the 1960–66 subperiod, both construction and all eleven durable goods industries experienced positive average annual rates of growth.

The comparative analysis of the economic activity in the seven subperiods generates much sharper conclusions when we narrow our focus to those sectors which experienced annual rates of growth in labor input greater than 6 percent or rates of decline less than −4 percent. The

Table 5.5 Classification of Rates of Growth of Sectoral Labor Input by Subperiod, 1948–78

Average Rate of Growth of Labor Input	1948–53	1953–57	1957–60	1960–66	1966–69	1969–73	1973–78
< −4%	2	5	4	1	1	1	0
−4 to −2%	4	3	7	2	4	6	5
−2 to 0%	4	14	13	7	6	12	8
0–2%	12	19	13	12	15	15	21
2–4%	12	5	10	20	16	14	12
4–6%	11	4	1	9	8	3	2
>6%	6	1	3	0	1	0	3

period as a whole was characterized by a dramatic decline in the dispersion of growth rates of labor input. During the subperiods 1948–53, 1953–57, and 1957–60, a total of eight, six, and seven industries, respectively, experienced decline in labor input at rates exceeding 4 percent or growth in labor input at rates greater than 6 percent. By contrast only a single industry exceeded these limits in the two subperiods 1960–66 and 1969–73, only two industries exceeded the limits in the subperiod 1966–69, and three industries fell outside the limits in 1973–78. It is important to emphasize that both rapid gains and losses in sectoral labor input took place during the period ending in 1960 as the U.S. economy was reshaped to meet postwar conditions.

Considering specific sectors that underwent rapid declines in labor input, we find that labor input declined at 10.4 percent annually in coal mining and at 4.21 percent annually in railroads in the subperiod 1948–53. During the subperiod 1953–57 labor input declined at rates exceeding 4 percent in agriculture, coal mining, lumber and wood products, and railroads. During 1957–60 declines exceeded 4 percent in metal mining, coal mining, transportation equipment excluding motor vehicles, and railroads. During 1960–66 only agriculture experienced decline in labor input at a rate exceeding 4 percent, during 1966–69 only private households declined more rapidly than 4 percent, while during 1969–73 only transportation equipment excluding motor vehicles declined at this rate. Our overall conclusion is that very rapid reductions of labor input were concentrated in agriculture, coal mining, and railroads.

Turning to increases in labor input at rates of growth exceeding 6 percent annually, there were six industries undergoing rapid growth during the subperiod 1948–53—electrical machinery, transportation equipment excluding motor vehicles, professional equipment, air transportation, broadcasting, and state and local government enterprises. Labor input in air transportation grew at 8.51 percent during the subperiod 1953–57 and at 10.42 percent during the subperiod 1966–69. During the subperiod 1957–60 nonprofit institutions, state and local educational services, and state and local government enterprises all experienced annual growth rates in excess of 6 percent. Finally, during the subperiod 1973–78, growth rates of coal mining, crude petroleum and natural gas, and transportation services exceeded 6 percent. Our overall conclusion is that very rapid growth in labor input was limited to air transportation and state and local government enterprises. Transportation equipment excluding motor vehicles grew rapidly during the Korean mobilization and declined rapidly during Korean and Vietnam demobilizations. Coal mining declined rapidly through 1960 and began to grow rapidly during the subperiod 1969–73.

Our earlier observation of strong economic growth during the subperiods 1948–53 and 1960–66 is borne out by the number of industries with rates of growth in labor input in excess of 2 percent—twenty-nine in both subperiods. By contrast labor grew at rates exceeding 2 percent in only ten industries during 1953–57. During the subperiods 1966–69, 1969–73, and 1973–78, twenty-five, seventeen, and seventeen industries, respectively, surpassed this limit. Finally, during 1957–60 fourteen industries experienced growth rates of labor input greater than 2 percent. Our overall conclusion from the data presented in tables 5.3 and 5.5 is that the postwar period was characterized by persistent growth in labor input; growth rates were high in 1948–53 and 1960–66 and low in 1953–57; finally, there was a sharp decline in dispersion of sectoral growth rates after 1960.

The growth rates of labor input for most of the fifty-one industries listed in table 5.3 exhibit no continuous postwar trend. Labor input increased over some periods and decreased over others. The exceptions, however, are notable. Labor input has persistently declined in agriculture, railroads, and local transportation sectors. The rates of growth vary over the periods but are consistently negative. The leather and private household sectors follow closely with declining labor input occurring over six of the seven subperiods. The full list includes no surprises. The principal explanations are changes in technology and tastes, the rising availability of domestic and imported substitute goods, and the reorganization of some sectors as part of government enterprises.

The list of industries with persistent positive trends is much longer. The following sectors had positive average annual growth in labor input over all seven subperiods: rubber, stone, clay, and glass, electrical machinery, professional equipment, trucking, air transportation, broadcasting, electric utilities, gas utilities, water supply and sanitary services, wholesale trade, retail trade, finance, insurance, and real estate, services, nonprofit institutions, and all three state and local government sectors. Not surprisingly all service sectors except private households are included. Noticeably absent are construction, all mining, and most manufacturing industries.

Not only has labor input in some industries persistently increased over the full 1948–78 period, but it has done so at average annual rates consistently exceeding 2 percent. This distinction is shared by the broadcasting industry, finance, insurance, and real estate, state and local educational services, and state and local public administration. Three other sectors—services, nonprofit institutions, and state and local public government enterprises—had increases in labor input in all seven subperiods and increases greater than 2 percent in six of the seven subperiods.

Second, trends in two industries have been significantly reversed. After experiencing a rather stagnant history over the 1948–60 period, labor input in agricultural services has increased at more than a 4 percent average annual rate between 1960 and 1978. More dramatically, the long decline in labor input in the coal mining industry which reached 10 and 12 percent annual rates in the 1948–53 and 1957–60 periods, respectively, has been reversed in the 1969–73 period when labor input increased at a 4.98 percent annual rate and in the 1973–78 period when the increase was 8.43 percent.

Third, the tobacco industry appears to have the most stable level of employment from peak to peak while the transportation equipment industry appears to be the most volatile. Growth rates in the former oscillate between positive and negative values but decline at more than a 2 percent annual rate only during the period 1973–78. Indeed, the average annual rate of growth or decline is less than one percent in three periods. In the transportation equipment industry, the level of labor input exhibits severe changes. The subperiod averages in chronological order are 19.23, −.04, −5.45, 4.54, .29, −6.84, and 1.47 percent. Interestingly, the positive average annual rate in 1948–53 is more than twice the positive growth rate during that period found in any other industry. Similarly, the negative rate in the 1969–73 period is almost twice the next largest negative rate reported for private households, the next most rapidly declining sector.

5.3 Alternative Measures of Sectoral Labor Compensation

Measures of sectoral labor compensation are important in many areas of economic research. Among these are the measurement and analysis of productivity growth. To provide additional perspective on our approach to measuring labor compensation, we find it useful to compare our methodology and data sources with alternative approaches found in the literature on productivity. We evaluate the alternative approaches against the requirements of economic theory. Wherever possible, we test the assumptions implicit in the alternative models. Our comparison begins with the measurement of hours. Since it is common practice to measure the wage rate as the ratio of the wage bill to some measure of hours, the treatment of hours affects the measurement of labor compensation. To measure payments to labor from the point of view of the producer, as required in productivity research and all studies of labor demand, the appropriate measure is labor compensation per hour worked.

Bureau of Labor Statistics data on hours paid are frequently employed in productivity studies.[3] It is important to recognize that measures of labor compensation based on hours paid data may be biased in two nontrivial ways. First, the time trend in hours paid data will be different from that of hours worked. Since time paid but not worked has increased significantly since 1948, the BLS hours paid estimates have a higher rate of growth than estimates of hours worked. The growth rates for the resulting measures of hourly wages are biased downward relative to the growth rates of the cost of an hour worked from the point of view of the employer. Second, the estimates of hourly wages in all nonmanufacturing sectors will be biased, since the BLS assigns the same number of hours to supervisory as to nonsupervisory workers.

The description in the *BLS Handbook of Methods* (1971) makes clear that separate hours series are developed for production and nonproduction workers only in the manufacturing sectors. According to the *Handbook*, manufacturing production worker hours are taken directly from the data in the BLS Area Wage Surveys and the study of employer expenditures published by the Bureau of Labor Statistics (1963). For the nonmanufacturing industries the hours paid series collected in the Consumer Expenditure Survey (CES) program relate to nonsupervisory workers only. The Bureau of Labor Statistics assumes that these hours apply to all wage and salary workers.[4]

The different demographic mix of the supervisory and nonsupervisory occupations and different average hours worked recorded for the demographic classes make suspect the assumption that supervisory workers in each nonmanufacturing industry are paid for the same average number of hours per week as are nonsupervisory workers. For example, according to the Census of Population, the 1970 female to male ratio was .87 in nonsupervisory occupations in the nonmanufacturing sector and only .22 in supervisory occupations.[5] Furthermore, female nonsupervisory workers in 1970 worked, on average, 34.5 hours while their male counterparts worked 41.5 hours.[6] Given that women in 1970 worked fewer weekly hours than men and were proportionately underrepresented in supervisory occupations, it is highly unlikely that supervisory laborers in the postwar period were paid for the same number of weekly hours as were nonsupervisory laborers, an assumption implicit in the BLS hours paid totals. A similar analysis could be based on age or education compositions. The conclusion would be the same.

The evidence suggests that estimates of hourly wages constructed from total wage bill and BLS hours paid data are biased for all nonmanufacturing sectors. More important, shifts in the demographic composition of the supervisory and nonsupervisory occupational groups over time will bias any estimates of the time trend in hourly labor costs. The direction of the bias is uncertain. It depends both on the difference in the composition of each industry's supervisory and nonsupervisory labor force and on the differential rates at which those compositions change.

Differences in the measurement of annual hours aside, measures of hourly labor compensation depend on the measurement of the annual wage bill. In the productivity literature it is common to employ earnings data for this purpose. Denison, for example, uses Bureau of the Census data on earnings to construct weights for use in aggregating distinct categories of hours both in his original *Sources of Economic Growth* (1962) and in his more recent works on productivity (1974, 1979). He discusses the assumptions underlying his use of earnings in the following excerpts from his 1979 book:

> Calculating such an index (of total hours) requires two types of information: distributions of hours worked by age and sex, and appropriate weights. Hourly earnings are used as weights. Their use rests on the assumption that average earnings in the ten age-sex groups distinguished are proportional to the marginal products of labor, per hour worked, of these groups. If this assumption is correct, it is necessary and legitimate to consider an average hour worked by a demographic group whose average hourly earnings are twice as high as those of another group to represent twice as much labor input. . . .
>
> My assumption that average earnings are proportional to marginal products of labor implies that an average hour's work by males 35 to 64 years of age, for example, was 2.3 times as valuable in the 1970's as an average hour's work by females 20 to 24 years of age (100 ÷ 44). The assumption is valid insofar as earnings differentials among age-sex groups reflect differences in the value of the work that is actually performed.[7]

The principal problem with using Census earnings data to measure marginal productivity is that reported earnings exclude all supplements to wages and salaries and include the return to capital invested by self-employed workers. As Denison correctly points out, earnings can be used only if the average earnings for workers cross-classified by education or by age and sex are proportional to the corresponding marginal products. However, given the way supplements, particularly social security and unemployment insurance, are charged to employers, reported earnings do not proportionately reflect employers' labor outlay. If supplements are neglected, only those ratios of hourly labor earnings among groups of laborers with annual incomes below the lowest base for supplements will be unbiased estimates of relative wages as viewed by employers.

Using Denison's example, if the average 35–64-year-old male has an annual labor income above either the social security or unemployment insurance tax bases, while the average 20–24-year-old female's labor earnings are below either base, then the male to female ratio of average hourly earnings is biased upward relative to the relative wages of males and females from the point of view of the employer. Supplements add to the employers' outlay for both males and females but, in this example, supplements add proportionately more to the employers' outlay for females than for males. Based on 1969 earnings reported in the decennial Census, employed 35–64-year-old males had mean annual earnings ($10,008) well above either the social security ($7800) or unemployment insurance ($3000) tax bases in 1969. Females 18–24 years of age, however, had mean labor income of $2960.[8] Ratios of male (35–64 years old) to female (18–24 years old) hourly wage costs excluding supplements are upward biased estimates of relative labor costs experienced by employers.

The inclusion of the return to noncorporate capital in measured earnings leads to an additional bias in the same direction. The assumption of proportionality between earnings and labor outlay among different sex-age groups is valid only if the ratio of noncorporate property income to total earnings is constant across these groups. However, if the representative 35–64-year-old male has a larger fraction of his earnings being generated from capital invested in noncorporate enterprises than does the representative 20–24-year-old female, then earnings based estimates for the relative valuation of an hour's work by males to an hour's work by females is upward biased. Unfortunately, we cannot test this hypothesis directly. Data measuring the noncorporate property income of workers classified by demographic characteristics are not available. However, the reasonableness of this assumption can be evaluated by comparing the distribution of employment in wage and salary versus self-employed activities across sex and age groups.

We again refer to data published in the 1970 Census. We construct ratios of self-employed persons to total employment for sixteen age groups for both males and females. The ratios, reported in table 5.6, vary

Table 5.6 Ratios of Self-Employed Persons to Total Employment by Age and Sex, 1970[a]

Age	Males	Females
14–15	.044	.026
16–17	.016	.009
18–19	.014	.005
20–24	.029	.011
25–29	.052	.024
30–34	.078	.033
35–39	.101	.038
40–44	.114	.041
45–49	.124	.045
50–54	.137	.053
55–59	.154	.060
60–62	.166	.062
63–64	.183	.073
65–69	.243	.093
70–74	.300	.118
75 and over	.336	.133

Source: Bureau of the Census (1973*b*), table 47.
[a]Total employed excludes unpaid family workers.

significantly across sex-age groups. For both males and females, the ratios generally increase with age; for any given age group, the ratio for males is more than twice the ratio for females. Continuing with our example, the ratios for older males are considerably higher than the similar ratios for young females. The relevant ratio for 35–64-year-old males is .130; the corresponding ratio for 20–24-year-old females is .011. Compared to young females, older males apparently allocate a greater proportion of their labor effort to self-employed activities.

From this we infer that earnings for a representative male include a higher percentage of returns to noncorporate capital than do the earnings for a representative female, even after controlling for age. In short, relative earnings are inadequate measures of relative marginal products. The wage and salary income of wage and salary workers adjusted for supplements is a more appropriate starting point for a measure of labor compensation.

The issues discussed in this section do not exhaust the problems that arise in measuring labor compensation in productivity studies. However, they are sufficient to illustrate two principles for measuring sectoral wages that follow directly from economic theory. First, any study of labor demand requires measures of wages and labor input from the producers' point of view. Second, measures of wages and labor input require data on labor compensation and hours worked for all categories of labor that are characterized by differences in marginal productivity.

5.4 Conclusion

In this paper we have developed measures of labor cost and labor input for each of fifty-one industrial sectors. Components of labor input that differ in marginal productivity are treated separately in measuring labor cost and labor input for each sector. In particular, we have constructed data on hours worked and labor compensation for 1600 types of labor input for each sector in each year from 1948 to 1978.

We have measured labor compensation from the producers' point of view, including wages and salaries, payroll taxes, and supplements paid by producers. We have employed data on labor compensation based on establishment surveys from the U.S. National Income and Product Accounts to provide control totals for labor compensation in each sector. Finally, we have allocated labor compensation among components of labor input on the basis of household surveys from the Census of Population and the Current Population Survey.

Similarly, we have controlled hours worked for each industrial sector to total employment and hours worked from establishment surveys. Hours worked have been distributed among components of labor input on the basis of household surveys. For both labor compensation and hours worked we have allocated data from establishment based surveys by using data from household surveys cross-classified by characteristics of individual workers.

On the basis of data from establishment and household surveys we have allocated labor compensation and hours worked among the two sexes, eight age groups, five education groups, two employment classes, and ten occupational groups for each industrial sector in each year from 1948 to 1978. Measurement of labor input from multiple job holders, self-employed individuals, and unpaid family workers has necessitated the use of supplementary survey data on hours worked and labor compensation for these workers.

Our data on labor input and hourly compensation have been compiled to facilitate the incorporation of new data from establishment and household surveys as they become available. Our classification of hours worked and labor compensation is consistent with the most recent reports from the Current Population Survey. We have reconciled the classifications of data on labor input from earlier surveys with the classification used in current reports. Our control totals for hours worked and labor compensation are consistent with data from the current version of the U.S. National Income and Product Accounts.

We have employed our data on hours worked and labor compensation to construct price and quantity indexes of labor input for each of the fifty-one industrial sectors included in our study. Our data also can be employed to construct indexes of hourly wages or labor input for either aggregates over these sectors or components within industrial sectors. For example, it would be possible to construct hourly wage and labor input indexes for each of the ten occupational groups within an industrial sector. These indexes, for example, could be employed in studies of the impact of changes in relative wages on the composition of demand for labor input by occupational groups.

Appendix
Data Sources for Labor Input

Introduction

This appendix lists the sources of the detailed labor data used to construct the sectoral measures of labor input described in the text. The following sections present tables identifying the particular sources of the employment, hours worked, weeks paid, and compensation data, respectively. The tables within each section are ordered similarly. Tables describing the data sources relevant to each benchmark year are presented first; a summary table for all intermediate years follows. Additional tables identifying the sources of various supporting data conclude each section. The formats introduced in the next section are adopted throughout the appendix.

Employment

Tables 5.A.1 through 5.A.6 list the sources of the data used to generate the employment matrices. All data for each of the benchmark years are taken from the decennial censuses conducted by the Bureau of the Census, U.S. Department of Commerce. Identifying publication codes for the population subject reports and detailed table titles and numbers are presented for the 1950, 1960, and 1970 data in tables 5.A.1 through 5.A.3, respectively.

The data sources for the nonbenchmark or intermediate years are arranged in table 5.A.4 so that the subscripted variables at the head of each column indicate the extent of cross-classification available in those data sources listed directly below. Each variable derives its name from the first letter of the labor dimension it represents: industry (I), sex (S), employment class (C), age (A), education (E), or occupation (O). Each subscript indicates the maximum number of discrete divisions available in the data tables. Absence of a subscript suggests that the tables' divisions for that variable match exactly with the characteristic groups listed in table 5.1. Blank lines within any column imply that the particular data series are not available for the corresponding years.[9]

The three-part entry for each data source listed in table 5.A.4 should be interpreted as follows. The first entry indicates the parent publication series, the second identifies the relevant volume within the series, and the third specifies the number of the appropriate table. For convenience, publication titles have been abbreviated as follows:

SLFR: *Special Labor Force Reports*, Bureau of Labor Statistics, U.S. Department of Labor

E/E: *Employment and Earnings*, Division of Manpower and Employment Statistics, Bureau of Labor Statistics, U.S. Department of Labor

P–20: *Series P–20 Current Population Reports—Population Characteristics*, Bureau of the Census, U.S. Department of Commerce

P–50: *Series P–50, Current Population Reports—Labor Force*, Bureau of the Census, U.S. Department of Commerce

P–60: *Series P–60, Current Population Reports—Consumer Income*, Bureau of the Census, U.S. Department of Commerce

The employment model requires two additional sets of employment data. The data tables necessary to build the second 1960 labor matrix based on the employed U.S. population exclusive of those persons working in either Alaska or Hawaii are listed separately under their state titles

Table 5.A.1 **U.S. Census Employment Data: 1950**

Population Subject Report	Table	
	Number	Title
P–E No. 1B	4	Age of the experienced civilian labor force, by detailed occupation and sex, for the U.S.: 1950.
P–E No. 1B	5	Age of wage and salary workers in the experienced civilian labor force, by detailed occupation and sex, for the U.S.: 1950.
P–E No. 1B	6	Age of employed persons, by detailed occupation and sex, for the U.S.: 1950.
P–E No. 1C	2	Detailed occupation of employed persons, by detailed industry and sex, for the U.S.: 1950.
P–E No. 1D	3	Age of employed persons, by detailed industry and sex, for the U.S.: 1950.
P–E No. 1D	4	Age of employed wage and salary workers, by detailed industry and sex, for the U.S.: 1950.
P–E No. 1D	6	Major occupation group of employed persons, by detailed industry and sex, for the U.S.: 1950.
P–E No. 1D	7	Major occupation group of employed wage and salary workers, by detailed industry and sex, for the U.S.: 1950.
P–E No. 5B	11	Major occupation group: persons 14 years old and over, by years of school completed, age, color, and sex, for the U.S., by regions: 1950.

Table 5.A.2 U.S. Census Employment Data: 1960

Population Subject Report	Table	
	Number	Title
PC(2)–5B	8	Major occupation group—persons 14 years old and over in the experienced civilian labor force, by years of school completed, age, color, and sex, for the U.S., by type of residence, and by regions: 1960.
PC(2)–7A	4	Age of the experienced civilian labor force, by detailed occupation and sex, for the U.S.: 1960.
PC(2)–7A	5	Age of wage and salary workers in the experienced civilian labor force, by detailed occupation and sex, for the U.S.: 1960.
PC(2)–7A	6	Age of employed persons, by detailed occupation and sex, for the U.S.: 1960.
PC(2)–7A	36	Industry group of employed persons, by occupation, color, and sex, for the U.S.: 1960.
PC(2)–7C	1	Major occupation group of employed persons, by major industry group, age, and sex, for the U.S.: 1960.
PC(2)–7C	2	Detailed occupation of employed persons, by detailed industry and sex, for the U.S.: 1960.
PC(2)–7F	4	Age of employed persons, by detailed industry and sex, for the U.S.: 1960.
PC(2)–7F	5	Age of employed wage and salary workers, by detailed industry and sex, for the U.S.: 1960.
PC(2)–7F	21	Years of school completed by the experienced civilian labor force, by detailed industry and sex, for the U.S.: 1960.
PC(2)–7F	28	Class of workers and color of the experienced civilian labor force, by agriculture and nonagricultural industries, years of school completed, and sex, for the U.S.: 1960.

Table 5.A.3 U.S. Census Employment Data: 1970

Population Subject Report	Table	
	Number	Title
PC(2)–5B	11	Major occupation group of employed persons 14 years old and over, by years of school completed, age, race, and sex: 1970.
PC(2)–7B	3	Years of school completed by the experienced civilian labor force by detailed industry and sex: 1970.
PC(2)–7B	34	Age of employed persons by detailed industry and sex: 1970.
PC(2)–7B	37	Class of worker of employed persons by detailed industry and sex: 1970.
PC(2)–7B	47	Age of employed persons by class of worker, agriculture and nonagricultural industries, race, Spanish origin, and sex: 1970.
PC(2)–7C	1	Industry group of employed persons by occupation, age, and sex: 1970.
PC(2)–7C	5	Industry group of employed wage and salary workers by occupation, race, and sex: 1970.
PC(2)–7C	6	Industry group of self-employed workers by occupation, race, and sex: 1970.
PC(2)–7C	8	Detailed occupation of employed persons by detailed industry and sex: 1970.

Table 5.A.4 **Employment Data for Nonbenchmark Years**

Year	SCI_2	SC_1I_{37}	SCI_2A	SI_{17}	$SI_{18}A_5$
1948	P–50,#13,T–9,10				
1949	P–50,#19,T–9				
1950	P–50,#31,T–9				
1951	P–50,#40,T–9				
1952	P–50,#45,T–9				
1953	P–50,#59,T–C9			P–50,#50,T–5	
1954	P–50,#59,T–A9				
1955	P–50,#67,T–12				
1956	P–50,#72,T–12				
1957	P–50,#85,T–12				
1958	P–50,#89,T–13				
1959	SLFR,#23,T–C4	SLFT,#11,T–B			SLFR,#4,T–C10
1960	SLFR,#23,T–C4	SLFR,#19,T–A2			
1961	SLFR,#23,T–C4	SLFR,#25,T–A2			SLFR,#23,T–C10
1962	SLFR,#69,T–C4	SLFR,#38,T–A2			SLFR,#31,T–C10
1963	SLFR,#69,T–C4	SLFR,#48,T–A2			SLFR,#43,T–C10
1964	SLFR,#69,T–C4	SLFR,#62,T–A2			SLFR,#52,T–C10
1965	SLFR,#69,T–C4	SLFR,#76,T–A2			SLFR,#69,T–C10
1966	E/E,Jan.'67,T–14	SLFR,#91,T–A2			
1967		SLFR,#107,T–A2	E/E,Jan.'68,T–A16		
1968		SLFR,#115,T–A2	E/E,Jan.'69,T–A18		
1969		SLFR,#127,T–A2	E/E,Jan.'70,T–A18		
1970		SLFR,#141,T–A2	E/E,Jan.'71,T–A18		
1971			E/E,Jan.'72,T–A18		
1972		SLFR,#162,T–A2	SLFR,#152,T–A19		
1973			SLFR,#163,T–A21		
1974			SLFR,#178,T–A20		
1975			SLFR,#185,T–20		
1976			SLFR,#199,T–21		
1977			SLFR,#212,T–24		
1978			SLFR,#218,T–24		

Table 5.A.4 (continued)

Year	SI_7A	SI_6A_6	SI_2A	$S_1I_{13}A$	$SI_{42}E$
1948			P–50,#13,T–5,6	P–50,#75,T–4	
1949			P–50,#19,T–5,6		
1950	P–50,#31,T–E		P–50,#31,T–5,6	P–50,#75,T–4	
1951	P–50,#40,T–E		P–50,#40,T–5,6		
1952	P–50,#45,T–E		P–50,#45,T–5,6	P–50,#75,T–4	
1953			P–50,#59,T–C5,6		
1954	P–50,#67,T–F		P–50,#59,T–A5,6	P–50,#75,T–4	
1955	P–50,#67,T–F		P–50,#67,T–8,9		
1956	P–50,#72,T–G		P–50,#72,T–8,9	P–50,#75,T–4	
1957			P–50,#85,T–9,10		
1958		P–50,#89,T–18	P–50,#89,T–9,10		
1959			SLFR,#31,T–C2,3		
1960			SLFR,#31,T–C2,3		
1961			SLFR,#31,T–C2,3		
1962			SLFR,#31,T–C2,3		
1963			SLFR,#69,T–C2,3		
1964			SLFR,#69,T–C2,3		
1965			SLFR,#69,T–C2,3		
1966			E/E,Jan.'67,T–A13		
1967					
1968					SLFR,#103,T–N
1969					SLFR,#125,T–N
1970					SLFR,#125,T–N
1971					SLFR,#140,T–N
1972					SLFR,#148,T–N
1973					
1974					
1975					
1976					
1977					
1978					

Table 5.A.4 (continued)

Year	$I_{12}O$	SAE	SA_5E	SAO	SA_6O
1948					
1949					
1950					
1951					
1952			P–50,#49,T–2		
1953					
1954					
1955					
1956					
1957			P–50,#78,T–2		
1958					P–50,#89,T–16
1959	SLFR,#4,T–C9	SLFR,#1,T–D		SLFR,#4,T–C8	
1960	SLFR,#14,T–C9			SLFR,#14,T–C8	
1961	SLFR,#23,T–C9			SLFR,#23,T–C8	
1962	SLFR,#31,T–C9	SLFR,#30,T–D		SLFR,#31,T–C8	
1963	SLFR,#43,T–C9			SLFR,#43,T–C8	
1964	SLFR,#52,T–C9	SLFR,#53,T–D		SLFR,#52,T–C8	
1965	SLFR,#69,T–C9	SLFR,#65,T–D		SLFR,#69,T–C8	
1966		SLFR,#83,T–D			
1967		SLFR,#92,T–D			
1968		SLFR,#103,T–D			
1969		SLFR,#125,T–D			
1970		SLFR,#125,T–D			
1971		SLFR,#140,T–D			
1972		SLFR,#148,T–D			
1973		SLFR,#161,T–D			
1974		SLFR,#175,T–D			
1975		SLFR,#186,T–D			
1976		SLFR,#193,T–D			
1977		SLFR,#209,T–E,T–L			
1978		SLFR,#225,T–E,SLFR,#218,T–3			

Table 5.A.4 (continued)

Year	SA_5O	SA_2O	S_1A_6O	SEO	SO
1948				P–50,#14,T–5	P–50,#13,T–15
1949					P–50,#19,T–14
1950		P–50,#32,T–4			P–50,#31,T–14
1951		P–50,#41,T–4			P–50,#40,T–14
1952				P–50,#49,T–4	P–50,#45,T–14
1953		P–50,#51,T–4			P–50,#67,T–25
1954		P–50,#58,T–3			P–50,#59,T–A10
1955		P–50,#64,T–3			P–50,#67,T–13
1956		P–50,#71,T–3			P–50,#72,T–13
1957	P–20,#80,T–4	P–50,#83,T–3		P–50,#78,T–7	P–50,#85,T–13
1958		P–50,#90,T–3			P–50,#89,T–14
1959		SLFR,#6,T–G	P–20,#104,T–8	SLFR,#1,T–1	
1960		SLFR,#16,T–G			
1961		SLFR,#22,T–G			
1962		SLFR,#34,T–G		SLFR,#30,T–I	
1963		SLFR,#42,T–G			
1964		SLFR,#55,T–G		SLFR,#53,T–I	
1965		SLFR,#68,T–F		SLFR,#65,T–I	
1966		SLFR,#87,T–F		SLFR,#83,T–I	
1967		SLFR,#98,T–G	P–20,#171,T–10	SLFR,#92,T–I	
1968		SLFR,#111,T–E	P–20,#188,T–9	SLFR,#103,T–I	
1969		SLFR,#124,T–E	P–20,#193,T–9	SLFR,#125,T–I	
1970		SLFR,#135,T–E	P–20,#210,T–9	SLFR,#125,T–I	
1971		SLFR,#147,T–E	P–20,#235,T–9	SLFR,#140,T–I	
1972		SLFR,#158,T–E		SLFR,#148,T–I	
1973		SLFR,#163,T–E		SLFR,#161,T–I	
1974		SLFR,#178,A–18		SLFR,#175,T–I	
1975		SLFR,#185,A–18		SLFR,#186,T–I	
1976		SLFR,#199,A–18		SLFR,#193,T–I	
1977		SLFR,#211,T–21,T–38		SLFR,#209,T–J	
1978		SLFR,#218,T–21,T–38		SLFR,#225,T–J	

Table 5.A.5 **U.S. Census Employment Data for Alaska and Hawaii: 1960**

Characteristics of the Population	Table	
	Number	Title
Vol. 1, part 3, Alaska	122	Occupation of the experienced civilian labor force by color, of the employed by race and class of worker, and of persons not in labor force with work experience by sex, for the state: 1960.
Vol. 1, part 3, Alaska	123	Age of employed persons, by occupation, color, and sex, for the state: 1960.
Vol. 1, part 3, Alaska	125	Industry group of the employed by occupation and sex, for the state: 1960.
Vol. 1, part 3, Alaska	126	Detailed industry of the experienced civilian labor force and of the employed by sex, for the state: 1960.
Vol. 1, part 3, Alaska	128	Age of employed persons by industry and sex, for the state: 1960.
Vol. 1, part 3, Hawaii	122	Occupation of the experienced civilian labor force by color, of the employed by race and class of worker, and of persons not in labor force with work experience by sex, for the state and for standard metropolitan statistical areas of 250,000 or more: 1960.
Vol. 1, part 13, Hawaii	123	Age of employed persons by occupation, color, and sex, for the state and for standard metropolitan statistical areas of 250,000 or more: 1960.
Vol. 1, part 13, Hawaii	125	Industry group of the employed by occupation and sex, for the state and for standard metropolitan statistical areas of 250,000 or more: 1960.
Vol. 1, part 13, Hawaii	127	Detailed industry for the employed by sex, for the state and for standard metropolitan statistical areas of 100,000 or more: 1960.
Vol. 1, part 13, Hawaii	128	Age of employed persons by industry and sex, for the state and for standard metropolitan statistical areas of 250,000 or more: 1960.

Table 5.A.6 **Monthly Labor Survey Employment Data: 1966**

Table 8	Employed persons by age and sex, Monthly Labor Survey—Current Population Survey comparisons, annual average 1966.
Table 11	Employed persons by class of worker and occupation group, Monthly Labor Survey—Current Population Survey comparisons, annual average 1966.

Source: Stein (1967).

in table 5.A.5. Table 5.A.6 identifies the published sources of the data compiled by the Monthly Labor Survey's 1966 study of employed persons under the then newly conceived Census definitions.

Hours Worked

The sources of the data on hours worked are listed in tables 5.A.7 through 5.A.12. Sources of the data for each decennial census year are presented in tables 5.A.7 through 5.A.9. For an explanation of the format underlying the presentation of the data sources for each intermediate year in table 5.A.10 consult the explanation before the source tables in the preceding section.

Using formats similar to that used in table 5.A.10, tables 5.A.11 and 5.A.12 list the data sources relating to the hours and employment series, respectively, for multiple job holders. The letter enclosed in parentheses and appended to the variable list at the head of each column indicates whether the recorded sources report data referring to the multiple job holders' demographic and occupational characteristics in their primary (P) or secondary (S) industry of employment.

Weeks

We require data on weeks paid per person to convert data measuring average compensation per person to estimates of average compensation per job. The necessary data sources are listed in tables 5.A.13 through 5.A.16. The weeks paid data used to construct the benchmark year series for this research are taken from the 1950, 1960, and 1970 decennial

Table 5.A.7 U.S. Census Hours Worked Data: 1950

Population Subject Report	Table	
	Number	Title
P–E No. 1A	13	Hours worked during census week: employed persons by age, color, and sex, for the U.S., urban and rural: 1950.
P–E No. 1B	14	Hours worked during the census week by employed persons, by detailed occupation and sex, for the U.S.: 1950.
P–E No. 1B	15	Hours worked during the census week by employed wage and salary workers, by detailed occupation and sex, for the U.S.: 1950.
P–E No. 1D	10	Hours worked during the census week by employed persons, by detailed industry and sex, for the U.S.: 1950.
P–D No. 1D	11	Hours worked during the census week by employed wage and salary workers, by detailed industry and sex, for the U.S.: 1950.

Table 5.A.8 U.S. Census Hours Worked Data: 1960

Population Subject Report	Table Number	Table Title
PC(2)–6A	12	Hours worked by employed persons, by marital status, presence of own children, age, color, and sex, for the U.S., urban and rural: 1960.
PC(2)–7A	13	Hours worked by employed persons, by detailed occupation and sex, for the U.S.: 1960.
PC(2)–7F	9	Hours worked by employed persons, by detailed industry and sex, for the U.S.: 1960.
PC(2)–7F	10	Hours worked by employed wage and salary workers, by detailed industry and sex, for the U.S.: 1960.
PC(2)–7F	23	Hours worked and color of employed persons, by class of worker, agriculture and nonagricultural industries, and sex, for the U.S.: 1960.

censuses. Since the "weeks paid" responses of those interviewed are based on their work experience during the previous year, the benchmark years for the weeks data are those immediately preceding the decennial census years. The specific data sources are listed in tables 5.A.13 through 5.A.15.

For an explanation of the abbreviations and format used in table 5.A.16 to present the sources for the weeks data of the intermediate years, consult the discussion immediately preceding the source tables in the second section of this appendix.

Compensation

Tables 5.A.17 through 5.A.21 identify data sources for labor compensation. All the compensation tables for the benchmark years 1949, 1959, and 1969 are presented in tables 5.A.17 through 5.A.19 are derived from the 1950, 1960, and 1970 decennial censuses, respectively. The one-year lag is explained by the fact that the census respondent declares his annual compensation for the previous year. The payroll tax tables, 5.A.20 and 5.A.21, are taken directly from Pechman (1977, pp. 264–65).

Table 5.A.9 **U.S. Census Hours Worked Data: 1970**

Population Subject Report	Table	
	Number	Title
PC(2)–6A	17	Hours worked of employed persons, by marital status, presence of own children, age, race, and sex, for the U.S., urban and rural: 1970.
PC(2)–7A	45	Employed persons by hours worked, detailed occupation, and sex: 1970.
PC(2)–7B	39	Employed persons by hours worked, detailed industry, and sex: 1970.
PC(2)–7B	48	Hours worked of employed persons by class of worker, agriculture and nonagricultural industries, race, Spanish origin, and sex: 1970.

Table 5.A.10 **Hours Worked Data for Nonbenchmark Years**

Year	SA	SA_6	SA_5	SO_8	C
1948					
1949					
1950					
1951					
1952					
1953					
1954					
1955					
1956	P–50,#72,T–18				
1957	P–50,#85,T–18				
1958	P–50,#89,T–24				
1959		SLFR,#4,T–D7			
1960		SLFR,#14,T–D7			
1961		SLFR,#23,T–D7			
1962		SLFR,#31,T–D7			
1963		SLFR,#43,T–D7			
1964		SLFR,#52,T–D7			
1965		SLFR,#69,T–D7			
1966		E/E,Jan.'67,T–22			
1967			E/E,Jan.'68,T–A21	E/E,Jan.'68,T–A22	E/E,Jan.'68,T–A20
1968			E/E,Jan.'69,T–A23	E/E,Jan.'69,T–A24	E/E,Jan.'69,T–A22
1969			SLFR,#116,T–A24	SLFR,#116,T–A25	SLFR,#116,T–A23
1970			SLFR,#129,T–A24	SLFR,#129,T–A25	SLFR,#129,T–A23
1971			SLFR,#142,T–A24	SLFR,#142,T–A25	SLFR,#142,T–A23
1972			SLFR,#152,T–A24	SLFR,#163,T–A27	SLFR,#152,T–A23
1973			SLFR,#163,T–A26	SLFR,#163,T–A27	SLFR,#163,T–A25
1974	SLFR,#178,T–1		SLFR,#178,T–A25,T–20	SLFR,#178,T–A26	SLFR,#178,T–A24
1975	SLFR,#185,T–1		SLFR,#185,T–A25,T–20	SLFR,#185,T–26	SLFR,#185,T–24
1976	SLFR,#199,T–1,T–33		SLFR,#199,T–31,T–21	SLFR,#199,T–32	SLFR,#199,T–30
1977	SLFR,#212,T–3,T–37		SLFR,#212,T–35,T–24	SLFR,#212,T–36,T–22	SLFR,#212,T–34
1978	SLFR,#218,T–3,T–37		SLFR,#218,T–35,T–24	SLFR,#218,T–36,T–21	SLFR,#218,T–34

Table 5.A.10 (continued)

Year	CI_2	C_1I_9	C_1I_8	C_1I_6	C_1I_5
1948					P–50,#61,T–8
1949					P–50,#61,T–8
1950					
1951			P–50,#40,T–G		
1952			P–50,#45,T–H		
1953					P–50,#61,T–8
1954					P–50,#61,T–8
1955					P–50,#67,T–17
1956					P–50,#67,T–17
1957					P–50,#85,T–21
1958	P–50,#89,T–22			P–50,#89,T–26	
1959	SLFR,#4,T–D2			SLFR,#4,T–D3	
1960	SLFR,#23,T–D2			SLFR,#14,T–D3	
1961	SLFR,#23,T–D2			SLFR,#23,T–D3	
1962	SLFR,#31,T–D2			SLFR,#31,T–D3	
1963	SLFR,#43,T–D2			SLFR,#43,T–D3	
1964	SLFR,#52,T–D2			SLFR,#52,T–D3	
1965	SLFR,#69,T–D2			SLFR,#69,T–D3	
1966	E/E,Jan.'67,T–22			E/E,Jan.'67,T–19	
1967		E/E,Jan.'68,T–A20			
1968		E/E,Jan.'69,T–A22			
1969		SLFR,#116,T–A23			
1970		SLFR,#129,T–A23			
1971		SLFR,#152,T–A23			
1972		SLFR,#152,T–A23			
1973		SLFR,#163,T–A25			
1974		SLFR,#178,T–A24			
1975		SLFR,#185,T–A24			
1976		SLFR,#199,T–30,T–24			
1977		SLFR,#212,T–31,T–27			
1978		SLFR,#218,T–34,T–27			

Table 5.A.10 (continued)

Year	I_2	O	O_8
1948			
1949			
1950			
1951			
1952		P–50,#45,T–H	
1953			
1954			
1955	P–50,#67,T–16		
1956	P–50,#72,T–17		
1957	P–50,#85,T–17		
1958		P–50,#89,T–27	
1959		SLFR,#4,T–D6	
1960		SLFR,#14,T–D6	
1961		SLFR,#23,T–D6	
1962		SLFR,#31,T–D6	
1963		SLFR,#43,T–D6	
1964		SLFR,#52,T–D6	
1965		SLFR,#69,T–D6	
1966			E/E,Jan.'67,T–20
1967	E/E,Jan.'68,T–A18		
1968	E/E,Jan.'69,T–A20		
1969	SLFR,#116,T–A21		
1970	SLFR,#129,T–A21		
1971	SLFR,#142,T–A21		
1972	SLFR,#152,T–A21		
1973	SLFR,#163,T–A21		
1974	SLFR,#178,T–A22		
1975	SLFR,#185,T–A22		
1976	SLFR,#199,T–30		
1977	SLFR,#212,T–32		
[illegible]	[illegible]		

Table 5.A.11 Hours Worked Data for Multiple Job Holders

Year	$CI_2(P)$	$CI_2(S)$	$C_1I_{12}(P)$	$C_1I_{12}(S)$	$C_1I_{11}(P)$	$C_1I_{11}(S)$
1948						
1949						
1950						
1951						
1952						
1953						
1954						
1955						
1956						
1957						
1958						
1959						
1960	SLFR,#18,T–G	SLFR,#18,T–H			SLFR,#18,T–G	SLFR,#18,T–H
1961						
1962	SLFR,#29,T–F	SLFR,#29,T–G			SLFR,#29,T–F	SLFR,#29,T–G
1963	SLFR,#39,T–F	SLFR,#39,T–G			SLFR,#39,T–F	SLFR,#39,T–G
1964	SLFR,#51,T–F	SLFR,#51,T–G			SLFR,#51,T–F	SLFR,#51,T–G
1965	SLFR,#63,T–G	SLFR,#63,T–H			SLFR,#63,T–G	SLFR,#63,T–H
1966	SLFR,#90,T–G	SLFR,#90,T–H			SLFR,#90,T–G	SLFR,#90,T–H
1967						
1968						
1969	SLFR,#123,T–H	SLFR,#123,T–I	SLFR,#123,T–H	SLFR,#123,T–I		
1970	SLFR,#139,T–H	SLFR,#139,T–I	SLFR,#139,T–H	SLFR,#139,T–I		
1971	SLFR,#139,T–H	SLFR,#139,T–I	SLFR,#139,T–H	SLFR,#139,T–I		
1972	SLFR,#166,T–H	SLFR,#166,T–I	SLFR,#166,T–H	SLFR,#166,T–I		
1973	SLFR,#166,T–H	SLFR,#166,T–I	SLFR,#166,T–H	SLFR,#166,T–I		
1974	SLFR,#177,T–H	SLFR,#177,T–I	SLFR,#177,T–H	SLFR,#177,T–I		
1975	SLFR,#182,T–H	SLFR,#182,T–I	SLFR,#182,T–H	SLFR,#182,T–I		
1976	SLFR,#194,T–B8	SLFR,#194,T–B9	SLFR,#194,T–B4	SLFR,#194,T–B9		
1977	SLFR,#194,T–B8	SLFR,#211,T–H	SLFR,#194,T–B4	SLFR,#211,T–H,T–L		
1978	SLFR,#194,T–B8	SLFR,#221,T–H	SLFR,#194,T–B4	SLFR,#221,T–C,T–H		

Table 5.A.12 Employment Data for Multiple Job Holders

Year	$CI_2(P)$	$CI_2(S)$	$C_1I_{16}(P)$	$C_1I_{16}(S)$	$C_1I_{12}(P)$
1948					
1949					
1950	P–50,#30,T–2	P–50,#30,T–2			
1951					
1952					
1953					
1954					
1955					
1956	P–50,#74,T–2	P–50,#74,T–2			
1957	P–50,#80,T–6	P–50,#80,T–6	P–50,#80,T–6	P–50,#80,T–6	
1958	P–50,#88,T–6	P–50,#88,T–6	P–50,#88,T–6	P–50,#88,T–6	
1959	SLFR,#9,T–2	SLFR,#9,T–B			
1960	SLFR,#18,T–3	SLFR,#18,T–3			
1961					
1962	SLFR,#29,T–2	SLFR,#29,T–2			
1963	SLFR,#39,T–2	SLFR,#39,T–2			
1964	SLFR,#51,T–4	SLFR,#51,T–4			
1965	SLFR,#63,T–3	SLFR,#63,T–3			
1966	SLFR,#90,T–3	SLFR,#90,T–3			
1967					
1968					
1969	SLFR,#123,T–B	SLFR,#123,T–B			SLFR,#123,T–B
1970	SLFR,#139,T–B	SLFR,#139,T–B			SLFR,#139,T–B
1971	SLFR,#139,T–B	SLFR,#139,T–B			SLFR,#139,T–B
1972	SLFR,#166,T–B	SLFR,#166,T–B			SLFR,#166,T–B
1973	SLFR,#166,T–B	SLFR,#166,T–B			SLFR,#166,T–B
1974	SLFR,#177,T–C	SLFR,#177,T–C			SLFR,#177,T–C
1975	SLFR,#182,T–C	SLFR,#182,T–C			SLFR,#182,T–C
1976	SLFR,#194,T–B3	SLFR,#194,T–B3			SLFR,#194,T–B3
1977	SLFR,#221,T–C	SLFR,#221,T–C			SLFR,#211,T–C
1978	[illegible]	[illegible]			[illegible]

Table 3.A.12 (continued)

Year	$C_1I_{12}(S)$	$C_1I_{11}(P)$	$C_1I_{11}(S)$	$C_1I_9(P)$	$C_1I_9(S)$
1948					
1949					
1950					
1951					
1952					
1953					
1954					
1955					
1956					
1957					
1958					
1959				SLFR,#9,T–2	SLFR,#8,T–B
1960		SLFR,#18,T–3	SLFR,#18,T–3		
1961					
1962		SLFR,#39,T–2	SLFR,#29,T–2		
1963		SLFR,#39,T–2	SLFR,#39,T–2		
1964		SLFR,#51,T–4	SLFR,#51,T–4		
1965		SLFR,#63,T–3	SLFR,#63,T–3		
1966		SLFR,#90,T–3	SLFR,#90,T–3		
1967					
1968					
1969	SLFR,#123,T–B				
1970	SLFR,#139,T–B				
1971	SLFR,#139,T–B				
1972	SLFR,#166,T–B				
1973	SLFR,#166,T–B				
1974	SLFR,#177,T–C				
1975	SLFR,#182,T–C				
1976	SLFR,#194,T–B3				
1977	SLFR,#221,T–C				
1978	SLFR,#221,T–C				

Table 5.A.13 **U.S. Census Weeks Paid Data: 1949**

Population Subject Report	Table Number	Title
P–E No. 1A	14	Weeks worked in 1949 by labor force status: persons by age, color, and sex, for the U.S., urban and rural: 1950.
P–E No. 1B	16	Weeks worked in 1949 by the experienced civilian labor force, by detailed occupation and sex, for the U.S.: 1950.
P–E No. 1B	17	Weeks worked in 1949 by wage and salary workers in the experienced civilian labor force by detailed occupation and sex, for the U.S.: 1950.
P–E No. 1D	12	Weeks worked in 1949 by the experienced civilian labor force, by detailed industry and sex, for the U.S.: 1950.
P–E No. 1D	13	Weeks worked in 1949 by wage and salary workers in the experienced civilian labor force, by detailed industry and sex, for the U.S.: 1950.
P–E No. 1D	21	Weeks worked in 1949 by the experienced civilian labor force, by class of worker and sex, for the U.S.: 1950.

Table 5.A.14 **U.S. Census Weeks Paid Data: 1959**

Population Subject Report	Table Number	Title
PC(2)–6A	15	Employment status, by weeks worked in 1959, age, color, and sex, for the U.S., urban and rural: 1960.
PC(2)–7A	14	Weeks worked in 1959 by the experienced civilian labor force, by detailed occupation and sex, for the U.S.: 1960.
PC(2)–7A	17	Weeks worked in 1959 by wage and salary workers in the experienced civilian labor force, by detailed occupation and sex, for the U.S.: 1960.
PC(2)–7F	11	Weeks worked in 1959 by the experienced civilian labor force, by detailed industry and sex, for the U.S.: 1960.
PC(2)–7F	13	Weeks worked in 1959 by wage and salary workers in the experienced civilian labor force, by industry, wage or salary income in 1959, and sex, for the U.S.: 1960.
PC(2)–7F	24	Weeks worked in 1959 and color of the experienced labor force, by class of worker, agriculture and nonagricultural industries, and sex, for the U.S.: 1960.

Table 5.A.15 U.S. Census Weeks Paid Data: 1969

Population Subject Report	Table Number	Table Title
PC(2)–6A	22	Employment status by weeks worked in 1969, age, race, Spanish origin, and sex: 1970.
PC(2)–7A	11	Weeks worked in 1969 by the experienced civilian labor force by detailed occupation and sex: 1970.
PC(2)–7A	14	Weeks worked in 1969 by wage and salary workers 16 years old and over in the experienced civilian labor force by the selected occupations and sex: 1970.
PC(2)–7B	6	Weeks worked in 1969 by the experienced civilian labor force, by detailed industry and sex: 1970.
PC(2)–7B	9	Weeks worked in 1969 by wage and salary workers in the experienced civilian labor force by industry and sex: 1970.

Table 5.A.16 Weeks Paid Data for Nonbenchmark Years

Year	SC_1I_{36}	SC_1I_9	SC_1I_8	SA	SO
1948					
1949					
1950			P–50,#35,T–4	P–50,#35,T–1	P–50,#35,T–3
1951			P–50,#43,T–4	P–50,#43,T–1	P–50,#43,T–3
1952			P–50,#48,T–4	P–50,#48,T–1	P–50,#48,T–3
1953		P–50,#54,T–3		P–50,#54,T–1	
1954		P–50,#59,T–B2		P–50,#59,T–1	
1955		P–50,#68,T–2		P–50,#68,T–1	P–50,#68,T–3
1956		P–50,#77,T–2		P–50,#77,T–1	P–50,#77,T–3
1957		P–50,#86,T–B		P–50,#86,T–1	P–50,#86,T–3
1958	P–50,#91,T–2,1			P–50,#91,T–1	P–50,#91,T–3
1959	SLFR,#11,T–B,A			SLFR,#11,T–A	SLFR,#11,T–C
1960	SLFR,#19,T–A2,A1			SLFR,#19,T–A1	SLFR,#19,T–A4,A1
1961	SLFR,#25,T–A2,A3			SLFR,#25,T–A1	SLFR,#25,T–A4,A1
1962	SLFR,#38,T–A2,A3			SLFR,#38,T–A1	SLFR,#38,T–A4,A1
1963	SLFR,#48,T–A2,A3			SLFR,#48,T–A1	SLFR,#58,T–A4,A1
1964	SLFR,#62,T–A2,A3			SLFR,#62,T–A1	SLFR,#62,T–A5,A1
1965	SLFR,#76,T–A2,A3			SLFR,#76,T–A1	SLFR,#76,T–A5,A1
1966	SLFR,#91,T–A2,A3			SLFR,#91,T–A1	SLFR,#91,T–A5,A1
1967	SLFR,#107,T–A2,A3			SLFR,#107,T–A1	SLFR,#107,T–A5
1968	SLFR,#115,T–A2,A3			SLFR,#115,T–A1	SLFR,#115,T–A5
1969	SLFR,#127,T–A2,A3			SLFR,#127,T–A1	SLFR,#127,T–A5
1970	SLFR,#141,T–A2,A3			SLFR,#141,T–A1	SLFR,#141,T–A5
1971	SLFR,#162,T–A2,A3			SLFR,#162,T–A1	SLFR,#162,T–A5
1972	SLFR,#162,T–A2,A3			SLFR,#162,T–A1	SLFR,#162,T–A5
1973	SLFR,#171,T–A2,A3			SLFR,#171,T–A1	SLFR,#171,T–A5
1974	SLFR,#181,T–A2,A3			SLFR,#181,T–A1	SLFR,#181,T–A5
1975	SLFR,#192,T–B2,B3			SLFR,#192,T–B1	SLFR,#192,T–B6
1976	SLFR,#201,T–B2,B3			SLFR,#201,T–B1	SLFR,#201,T–B6
1977	SLFR,#224,T–B2,B3			SLFR,#224,T–A1	SLFR,#224,T–A5
1978	SLFR,#236,T–B2,B3			SLFR,#236,T–A1	SLFR,#236,T–A5

Table 5.A.17 U.S. Census Labor Compensation Data: 1949

Population Subject Report	Table Number	Table Title
P–E No. 1B	19	Income in 1949 of the experienced civilian labor force, by detailed occupation and sex, for the U.S.: 1950.
P–E No. 1B	22	Wage and salary income in 1949 of wage and salary workers in the experienced civilian labor force, by detailed occupation and sex, for the U.S.: 1950.
P–E No. 1D	15	Income in 1949 of the experienced civilian labor force, by detailed industry and sex, for the U.S.: 1950.
P–E No. 1D	17	Wage and salary income in 1949 of wage and salary workers in the experienced civilian labor force, by detailed industry and sex, for the U.S.: 1950.
P–E No. 5B	12	Income in 1949, persons 14 years old and over, by years of school completed, age, color, and sex, for the U.S., by regions: 1950.

Table 5.A.18 U.S. Census Labor Compensation Data: 1959

Population Subject Report	Table Number	Table Title
PC(2)–5B	6	Total income—males 14 years old and over with income in 1959, by years of school completed, age, and color, for the U.S., by type of residence, and by regions: 1960.
PC(2)–5B	7	Total income—females 14 years old and over with income in 1959, by years of school completed, age, and color, for the U.S., by type of residence, and by regions: 1960.
PC(2)–5B	9	Occupation and earnings—persons 18 to 64 years old in the experienced civilian labor force with earnings in 1959, by years of school completed, age, and sex, for the U.S.: 1960.
PC(2)–7A	25	Income in 1959 of the experienced civilian labor force, by detailed occupation and sex, for the U.S.: 1960.
PC(2)–7A	27	Wage and salary income in 1959 of wage and salary workers in the experienced civilian labor force, by detailed occupation and sex, for the U.S.: 1960.
PC(2)–7F	15	Income in 1959 of the experienced civilian labor force, by detailed industry and sex, for the U.S.: 1960.
PC(2)–7F	17	Wage or salary income in 1959 of wage and salary workers in the experienced civilian labor force, by detailed industry and sex, for the U.S.: 1960.
PC(2)–7F	18	Earnings in 1959 of the experienced civilian labor force, by detailed industry and sex, for the U.S.: 1960.

Table 5.A.19 U.S. Census Labor Compensation Data: 1969

Population Subject Report	Table Number	Table Title
PC(2)–5B	7	Total income of males 14 years old and over with income in 1969, by years of school completed, age, and race: 1970.
PC(2)–5B	8	Total income of females 14 years old and over with income in 1969, by years of school completed, age, and race: 1970.
PC(2)–7A	24	Wage and salary earnings in 1969 of wage and salary workers, 16 years old and over, in the experienced civilian labor force, by detailed occupation and sex: 1970.
PC(2)–7B	12	Earnings in 1969 of the experienced civilian labor force by detailed industry and sex: 1970.
PC(2)–7B	16	Earnings in 1969 of the experienced civilian labor force by years of school completed, industry, and sex: 1970.
PC(2)–7B	20	Wage and salary earnings in 1969 of wage and salary workers in the experienced civilian labor force by industry and sex: 1970.
PC(2)–8B	1	Earnings and occupation of total and white males 25 to 64 years old in the experienced civilian labor force with earnings in 1969, by work experience in 1969, years of school completed, and age: 1970.
PC(2)–8B	5	Earnings and occupation of males 18 to 24 years old in the experienced civilian labor force with earnings in 1969, by work experience in 1969, years of school completed, race, and Spanish origin: 1970.
PC(2)–8B	6	Earnings and occupation of males 65 years old and over in the experienced civilian labor force with earnings in 1969, by work experience in 1969, years of school completed, race, and Spanish origin: 1970.
PC(2)–8B	7	Earnings and occupation of total and white females 25 to 64 years old in the experienced labor force with earnings in 1969, by work experience in 1969, years of school completed, and age: 1970.
PC(2)–8B	11	Earnings and occupation of females 18 to 24 years old in the experienced civilian labor force with earnings in 1969, by work experience in 1969, years of school completed, race, and Spanish origin: 1970.

Table 5.A.20 History of Social Security Tax Rates

Year	Maximum Taxable Wages[a] (dollars)	Tax Rate (percentages)		
		Employer	Employee	Self-Employed
	Old-Age, Survivors, Disability, and Health Insurance			
1937–49	3,000	1.0	1.0	[b]
1950	3,000	1.5	1.5	[b]
1951–53	3,600	1.5	1.5	2.25
1954	3,600	2.0	2.0	3.0
1955–56	4,200	2.0	2.0	3.0
1957–58	4,200	2.25	2.25	3.375
1959	4,800	2.5	2.5	3.75
1960–61	4,800	3.0	3.0	4.5
1962	4,800	3.125	3.125	4.7
1963–65	4,800	3.625	3.625	5.4
1966	6,600	4.2	4.2	6.15
1967	6,600	4.4	4.4	6.4
1968	7,800	4.4	4.4	6.4
1969–70	7,800	4.8	4.8	6.9
1971	7,800	5.2	5.2	7.5
1972	9,000	5.2	5.2	7.5
1973	10,800	5.85	5.85	8.0
1974	13,200	5.85	5.85	7.9
1975	14,100	5.85	5.85	7.9
1976	15,300	5.85	5.85	7.9
1977	16,500	5.85	5.85	7.9
1978	17,700	6.05	6.05	8.1

Source: Social Security Administration (1980), p. 35.

[a]Maximum taxable wages is in dollars per year for OASDHI.

[b]Not covered by the program until January 1, 1951.

Table 5.A.21 **History of Unemployment Insurance Tax Rates**

Year	Covered Wages[a] (dollars)	Statutory Range of Rates[b] (percentages)	Actual Rate Paid[c] (percentages)
	Federal Unemployment Insurance[d]		
1936	All wages	—	1.0
1937	All wages	—	2.0
1938	All wages	—	3.0
1939–60	3,000	—	3.0
1961	3,000	—	3.1
1962	3,000	—	3.5
1963	3,000	—	3.35
1964–69	3,000	—	3.1
1970–71	3,000	—	3.2
1972	4,200	—	3.2
1973	4,200	—	3.28
1974–76	4,200	—	3.2
1977	4,200	—	3.4
1978	6,000	—	3.4

Source: Pechman (1977), p. 312.

[a]Covered wages are in dollars per year for federal unemployment insurance.

[b]For federal unemployment insurance, employers are taxed by the states on the basis of an experience rating determined by past unemployment records. All employers are permitted to take the maximum credit allowed against the federal unemployment tax, even though they may, in fact, pay a lower rate because of a good experience rating. In 1969, the effective tax rate on covered wages ranged from 0.4 percent in Texas and Illinois to 2.9 percent in Alaska (U.S. Congress 1969, p. 183).

[c]For federal unemployment insurance, credit up to 90 percent of the tax is allowed for contributions paid into a state unemployment fund. Beginning in 1961, credits up to 90 percent are computed as if the tax rate were 3 percent.

[d]Applicable to employers of eight persons or more between 1936 and 1956, to employers of four persons or more from 1956 through 1971, and to employers of one person or more in 1972 and later years.

Notes

1. Kendrick purposely avoids disaggregating the employed population by demographic or occupational characteristics. Any difference in the productivity of an hour worked by laborers of differing personal characteristics should, in Kendrick's view, be captured not in a measure of factor input, but in an index of productivity change. By contrast, Denison posits that disaggregation by personal characteristics is essential in measuring labor input. In his view, however, any shifting composition by industrial and occupational characteristics does not reflect changes in the level of labor input, but should be included in the measure of productivity change.

2. Detailed discussions of quality indexes and applications to disaggregated labor data can be found in doctoral dissertations by Barger (1971) and Chinloy (1974). Chinloy (1980, 1981) presents an application to U.S. aggregate data.

3. Kendrick (1961, 1973), relies occasionally on Bureau of Labor Statistics (1973) data on hours paid. See Kendrick (1973), p. 156. In the more recent study, Kendrick and Grossman (1980) rely on BLS hours paid data for all laborers except proprietors and unpaid family workers. See Kendrick and Grossman (1980), p. 25.

Denison (1967, 1974, 1979) begins from the BLS hours paid series when constructing his hours estimates for wage and salary workers. He converts the average hours paid per job to average hours worked per job, using "unpublished BLS ratios of 'hours at work' to 'hours paid for.'" These ratios, extrapolated from data collected for a single year, 1966, were developed by BLS for the 1952–74 period. Based on the trends in the 1952–74 series, Denison (1979) further extrapolates his hours worked series back to 1947 and forward to 1976. See Denison (1979), p. 155.

4. Bureau of Labor Statistics (1971), pp. 214–15.

5. Bureau of the Census (1972), table 5. The Census occupational category for "managers" best identifies the group of nonsupervisory workers underlying BLS estimates. The occupations of nonsupervisory workers are defined in the technical note to Bureau of Labor Statistics [1976], p. 774.

6. Bureau of the Census (1973*c*), table 45. Also see note 5.

7. Denison (1979), pp. 32–33.

8. Bureau of Census (1973*a*), tables 1 and 11.

9. The reader should note that while entries appear in table 5.A.4 for the three benchmark years, these sources are listed only for completeness sake. The data reported in tables 5.A.1 through 5.A.3 are used to generate the 1950, 1960, and 1970 employment matrices.

References

Bacharach, Michael. 1965. Estimating non-negative matrices from marginal data. *International Economic Review* 6, no. 3: 294–310.

Barger, William J. 1971. *The measurement of labor input: U.S. manufacturing industries, 1948–1966*. Ph.D. diss., Harvard University.

Bureau of the Census. 1972. *Census of population: 1970, occupation by industry*. Final Report PC(2)-7C. Washington, D.C.: U.S. Department of Commerce.

———. 1973*a*. *Census of population: 1970, earnings by occupation and education*. Final Report PC(2)-8B. Washington, D.C.: U.S. Department of Commerce.

———. 1973*b*. *Census of population: 1970, industrial characteristics*. Final Report PC(2)-7B. Washington, D.C.: U.S. Department of Commerce.

———. 1973*c*. *Census of population: 1970, occupational characteristics*. Final Report PC(2)-7A. Washington, D.C.: U.S. Department of Commerce.

Bureau of Economic Analysis. 1977. *The national income and product accounts of the United States, 1929–1974: Statistical tables*, Washington, D.C.: Government Printing Office.

Bureau of Labor Statistics. 1963. *Manufacturing industries 1962: Employer expenditures for selected supplementary compensation practices for production and related workers*. Bulletin 1428. Washington, D.C.: U.S. Department of Labor.

———. 1971. *BLS Handbook of methods for surveys and studies*. Bulletin 1711. Washington, D.C.: U.S. Department of Labor.

———. 1973. Historical productivity measures. Working paper (March). Productivity and Technology Division. Washington, D.C.: U.S. Department of Labor.

———. 1976. *Employment and earnings, United States, 1909–75*. Bulletin 1312–10. Washington, D.C.: U.S. Department of Labor.

Chinloy, Peter T. 1974. *Issues in the measurement of labor input*. Ph.D. diss., Harvard University.

———. 1980. Sources of quality change in labor input. *American Economic Review* 70, no. 1: 108–19.

———. 1981. *Labor productivity*. Cambridge, Mass.: Abt Books.

Deming, W. E., and F. F. Stephan. 1940. On least squares adjustment of a sampled frequency table when the expected marginal totals are known. *Annals of Mathematical Statistics* 11: 427–44.

Denison, Edward F. 1961. Measurement of labor input: Some questions of definition and the adequacy of data. In *Output, input, and productivity measurement*. Conference on Research in Income and Wealth, 347–72. Princeton, N.J.: Princeton University Press.

———. 1962. *Sources of economic growth in the United States and the alternatives before us*. New York: The Committee for Economic Development.

———. 1967. *Why growth rates differ*. Washington, D.C.: The Brookings Institution.

———. 1974. *Accounting for United States economic growth: 1929 to 1969*. Washington, D.C.: The Brookings Institution.

———. 1979. *Accounting for slower economic growth: The United States in the 1970's*. Washington, D.C.: The Brookings Institution.

Gollop, Frank M., and Dale W. Jorgenson. 1980. U.S. productivity growth by industry, 1947–73. In *New developments in productivity measurement and analysis*, ed. J. W. Kendrick and B. Vaccara. Conference on Research in Income and Wealth: Studies in Income and Wealth, vol. 41, 17–136. Chicago: University of Chicago Press for the National Bureau of Economic Research.

Griliches, Zvi. 1960. Measuring inputs in agriculture: A critical survey. *Journal of Farm Economics* 42, no. 4: 1411–27.

Jorgenson, Dale W., and Zvi Griliches. 1967. The explanation of productivity change. *Review of Economic Studies* 34, no. 99: 249–83.

Kendrick, John W. 1961. *Productivity trends in the United States*. Princeton, N.J.: Princeton University Press.

———. 1973. *Postwar productivity trends in the United States, 1948–1969*. New York: National Bureau of Economic Research.

Kendrick, John W., and Elliot S. Grossman. 1980. *Productivity in the United States: Trends and cycles*. Baltimore and London: the Johns Hopkins University Press.

Pechman, Joseph A. 1977. *Federal tax policy*. Rev. ed. Washington, D.C.: The Brookings Institution (1st ed., 1966).

Social Security Administration. 1980. *Social security bulletin, annual statistical supplement, 1977–79*. Washington, D.C.: Government Printing Office.

Stein, Robert L. 1967. New definitions for employment and unemployment. *Employment and Earnings and Monthly Report on the Labor Force* 13, no. 8: 3–27.

Stone, R., and J. A. C. Brown. 1962. *A computable model of economic growth (a programme for growth 1)*. London: Chapman & Hall.

U.S. Congress. House. Committee on Ways and Means. 1969. *Hearings on unemployment compensation*. 91st Cong. 1st sess. October 1–7.

6 The Size Distribution of Wage and Nonwage Compensation: Employer Cost versus Employee Value

Timothy M. Smeeding

6.1 Introduction

The issue of total employee compensation is important both to applied labor economists and to economists interested in the size distribution of labor income and workers' economic well-being. Unfortunately, neither group has been afforded the luxury of a nationally representative data set for individual workers which allowed them to measure and value all major components of wage and nonwage compensation.

In empirical studies of the return to labor effort, commonly utilized household surveys, such as the Current Population Survey (CPS), the National Longitudinal Survey (NLS), and the Panel Study of Income Dynamics (PSID), have only recently begun to record individual worker's benefit recipiency information for major types of nonwage compensation, such as pension rights and health insurance. But none of these data bases records the dollar amount which employers "contribute" on behalf of employees.[1] On the other hand, the Bureau of Labor Statistics (BLS) has conducted several establishment surveys, such as the 1977 Employer's Expenditure for Employee Compensation Survey (EEEC) and the 1977 Employment Cost Index Survey (ECI) which provide

Timothy M. Smeeding is associate professor of economics at the University of Utah, Salt Lake City.

This research was completed while the author was an American Statistical Association Research Fellow at the U.S. Bureau of the Census. However, this paper should in no way be interpreted as the official position of the Census Bureau. The assistance of Angela Feldman, John Coder, Donald Woods, Enrique Lamas, Ben Stephens, Lillian Wilson, and Judith Norvell is gratefully appreciated. The author benefited from conversations with Steven Sheingold, Tom Swartz, Olivia Mitchell, and Joseph Antos; from comments by Jack Triplett and Janet Johnson on an earlier draft; and from seminars given at Cornell University and the Congressional Budget Office. The author retains all responsibility for the errors, omissions, and processes found herein.

aggregate employer outlays for several detailed types of wage and nonwage compensation, such as vacation and holiday pay and pensions, but no information on their distribution across individual workers.

In this paper we present the initial results of assigning recipiency and dollar values for various types of wage and nonwage compensation from BLS establishment surveys to individuals in the March 1980 CPS, using microdata simulation techniques.[2] This new data base is used to answer three questions:

1. How do the employer cost and employee value of fringe benefits differ between themselves and between other measures of worker compensation for different types of workers?
2. How do fringe benefits affect the size distribution of total compensation as compared to the size distribution of wages and salaries?
3. How does the definition of employee compensation affect the results of a standard human capital model or "earnings function" of the type employed in much of the empirical labor economics literature?

Section 6.2 presents the definitions of compensation, fringe benefits, and other terms used in this paper, along with data on their aggregate value and growth, and the limitations of this study. Section 6.3 briefly outlines a heuristic model of the employer-employee compensation determination process which establishes the difference between employer cost and employee value. Empirical proxies for employer cost and employee value are presented in section 6.4. Section 6.5 presents the empirical results which suggest answers to the three questions listed above, while section 6.6 summarizes the results and discusses the application of this technique for future research in related areas. The appendix contains a detailed discussion of the simulation procedures used to match the BLS data to the CPS.

6.2 Definitions of Terms: Fringe Benefits and Their Growth and Importance

Fringe benefits will be defined as the amount of total employee hourly compensation not received as pay for time worked, but paid by employers to employees for time not worked, or paid by employers to intermediaries on behalf of employees.[3] Payments for time not worked include vacation and holiday pay and other payments for nonproduction bonuses, for paid sick leave, and for severance pay. These items are already included in the money wages, salaries, or earnings (we use these interchangeably below) usually recorded in household surveys, along with pay for time worked: straight time pay, overtime pay, and shift differential. Payments made to intermediaries, such as insurance companies, are termed nonwage compensation or supplements to wages and salaries. These supplements are of two types: First, legally required payments, such as social security payroll taxes, unemployment insurance, and workers' compensation contributions, are included in supplements to wages and salaries. Second, supplements in the form of deferred compensation, such as employer pension and retirement contributions and employer contributions to thrift or savings plans are included here, as are insurance contributions for health, life, and sickness or accident insurance. Altogether wages and salaries (including both pay for time worked and pay for time not worked) plus supplements equals total compensation.

Table 6.1 presents estimates of the aggregate value of total employee compensation, as we have defined it, for the private nonfarm economy from 1966 to 1979. The 1966 and 1976 estimates are taken from the *Handbook of Labor Statistics 1978* (1979), while the 1979 estimates are taken from the 1977 EEEC, adjusted to 1979 using the ECI. These 1979 figures are the aggregate control values used in the microsimulation model. Both sets of data are normalized to indicate various components of compensation as a percent of aggregate wages and salaries in each year.

Several interesting patterns are suggested by table 6.1. The overall average difference between the most narrow measure of labor compensation (pay for time worked) and the broadest measure (total compensation) has grown from 18.9 percentage points as recently as 1966, to 29.5 percentage points by 1979. While pay for time worked has fallen slightly as a fraction of wages and salaries, mainly because of the increasing fraction of wages and salaries attributed to vacation and holiday pay, supplements have been growing at a more rapid rate. Legally required benefits have increased by 3.4 percentage points or nearly 60 percent from 1966 to 1979, largely due to the 2.2 percentage point increases in social security and railroad retirement payroll taxes (in parentheses in table 6.1), but also due to increases in unemployment insurance contributions. In terms of percentage change from 1966 to 1979, the two most rapidly rising elements of compensation are insurance contributions and deferred compensation which grew by 2.9 and 2.4 percentage points (or by 126.1 and 98.1 percent), respectively, over this period. As several researchers (Kennedy and Vogel 1979; Woodbury 1981; Clotfelter 1981) have noted, rising marginal tax rates, rising income, and other factors discussed more fully below have led employees to favor these nontaxable forms of compensation over wages and salaries.[4] Due to growth in these supplements, total compensation was almost 20 percent larger than wages in 1979.

While table 6.1 indicates a rapid rate of growth both in fringe benefits and, particularly, in supplements to wages and salaries, these figures only represent aggregate employer contributions as a percent of aggregate wages and salaries. Such estimates mask the variance in benefits, even

Table 6.1 **Change in Relative Components of Total Compensation in the Private Nonfarm Economy: 1966–1979**

Component of Total Compensation	Components of Total Compensation as Percentage of Wages and Salaries		
	1966	1976	1979
Pay for time worked[a]	92.0%	90.6%	90.1%
Vacations and holidays[b]	5.6	7.2	7.4
Other payments[c]	2.4	2.2	2.5
Total wages and salaries[d]	100.0	100.0	100.0
Supplements to wages and salaries:			
Legally required contributions[e]	5.7	8.1	9.1
(Social security/railroad retirement)	(3.4)	(5.1)	(5.6)
Insurance contributions[f]	2.3	4.8	5.2
Deferred compensation[g]	2.9	5.3	5.3
Total compensation[h]	110.9	118.2	119.6

Sources: 1966, 1976: *Handbook of Labor Statistics* (1979), table 113. 1979: 1977 EEEC adjusted to 1979 using the ECI; adjusted March 1980 CPS data tapes.

[a]Pay for time worked includes straight time wages and salaries, overtime, and shift differentials.

[b]Vacations and holidays include vacation and holiday pay and other paid leave, except for sick leave.

[c]Other payments include nonproduction bonuses, sick leave, and severance pay.

[d]Total wages and salaries includes all direct (before tax) payments to workers, i.e., the sum of pay for time worked, vacations and holidays, and other payments as recorded on household income surveys such as the CPS.

[e]Legally required contributions include employer contributions for social security and railroad retirement, unemployment insurance, workers' compensation, and other mandatory payments.

[f]Insurance contributions include employer payments for life, accident, private disability, and health insurance.

[g]Deferred compensation includes employer contributions for pension plans, retirement plans, and savings and thrift plans.

[h]Total compensation includes all listed components of total worker compensation: wages and salaries plus all supplements.

the benefit variance which can be observed on as simple a level as average increases in compensation for those actually receiving these benefits as compared to those who do not. For instance, pension and retirement plan contributions make up 95 percent of deferred compensation. Of all wage and salary workers in the private nonfarm economy, 44.6 percent were covered in 1979 by a pension plan to which their employer or union contributed.[5] For these covered workers, the average employer contribution was 11.4 percent of wages and salaries. Following a similar procedure for health insurance (which makes up roughly 80 percent of total insurance contributions) indicates an average employer contribution of

7.4 percent for those with subsidized health insurance coverage. Thus, while these two components of compensation average 9.2 percent of wages and salaries across all workers during 1979, they average more than twice as large an amount, or 18.8 percent, for the 37.8 percent of workers covered by both types of plans, even before taking account of intraindustry and intraoccupational differences in the level of pension and health insurance contributions. Other data sources suggest even wider differentials across specific groups of firms and workers (e.g., Chamber of Commerce of the United States 1980). To the extent that the microsimulation model used in this paper can capture these differentials, it appears that different measures of employee compensation will produce substantial differences between various types of workers as well as large dollar differences between various measures of compensation.

Before we begin our analysis it is important to keep the limitations of this effort in mind. First and most importantly, the measure of "total" compensation used in this paper does not include fringe benefits in-kind, such as free or employer subsidized meals, parking, personal use of cars, entertainment, travel, and so on; nor does it include other job amenities, such as office size or location and flexibility of work schedule. At this time there are limited data on even aggregate values of these forms of compensation, much less indicators of the types of workers who receive such "perks" or the distribution of their dollar value across various recipients.[6] Second, due to lack of appropriate data self-employed persons and all government workers are excluded from our analysis.

6.3 A Heuristic Model of Employer-Employee Benefit Determination

The decision to accept a job involves a worker who provides a given amount of labor services in exchange for an employer's compensation. In general this compensation can be broken into four components: wage goods, i.e., market purchased goods, W; fringe benefit goods, B; working conditions, i.e., job amenities not included in fringe benefits, A; and leisure, L.[7] The value of a job, or the utility derived from a job, to a worker can therefore be expressed as:

$$U = U(W, B, A, L). \qquad (1)$$

In the model which follows we examine the trade-off between W and B, largely ignoring A and L.[8]

In accepting a job, a worker in effect makes a tied purchase of a given set of W, B, A, and L. In general, following the work of Rosen (1974), the choice is made according to a worker's subjective evaluation of the objectively measure characteristics of this package. This hedonic model of the labor market is characterized by a set of firms offering various compensation packages in hopes of attracting a worker whose productive characteristics (training, appearance, physical and mental abilities, etc.) most closely match those sought by the firm. In the job bargaining process firms compete with one another for workers by offering different compensation packages or adjusting those which are already available. Adjustments in compensation packages are not costless and so, ceteris paribus, employers only provide more of a given compensation component, e.g., time off with pay or more generous pension plans, in lieu of lesser quantities of other components, e.g., shared offices or lower wages (e.g., see Rice 1966; Lester 1967; Steuerle 1979; Atrostic 1982). Employees evaluate the available packages and choose the package that maximizes equation (1). In a competitive economy, this interaction of workers and employers and the compensation package adjustment process results in a locus of job matches which trace out the rate at which the market trades off wage goods and benefits for various groups of workers at the margin. These marginal rates of exchange represent the implicit hedonic prices of various job and compensation package components.

Income tax advantages and two types of "scale" factors, economies of scale in pension funds and economies of scale and group rating for insurance, increase the value of untaxed benefits (or lower their implicit price) to employees, relative to their cost to employers. Employees can avoid personal income taxation for most employer provided supplements, particularly insurance and pensions—and also for such items as employer social security contributions. Scale economies allow the employer to either lower the cost of a given benefit or to offer a higher level of benefits for a given outlay. However, because employers do not, in general, avoid corporate or personal income taxation by rearranging their mix of benefits and wages, while employees do enjoy such advantages, we assume that the relative value of benefits to employees rises above the employers' cost of providing benefits.

Finally, we must admit the possibility of nonoptimal situations, at least for some workers. For instance, due to immobility, rigidities, customs, or habit, available wage-benefit packages may force some workers to accept some type(s) of fringe benefits whose characteristics they value below market prices. A good example might be duplicate fully employer funded family health insurance policies for two working spouses, whereby (ignoring the chance of layoff) one spouse's policy is virtually worthless. Such cases are not unlike the situation faced by many in-kind transfer recipients, e.g., low-income elderly who benefit from costly medicare and medicaid insurance. In both this latter situation and in the case of the doubly insured family, the beneficiary would accept a different wage-benefit package (or a lesser amount of cash transfers) and remain equally as well off, or better off, than at present. Thus we cannot ignore the possibility of a "cash equivalent" problem. While in-kind transfers valued by recipients below their market value may persist indefinitely, if, for instance, donor (taxpayer) preferences insisted upon such transfers, labor market disequilibriums of this sort should soon disappear as employers realize that, by offering workers some choice between current types of health insurance policies and other less costly wage or benefit packages which do not include health insurance, they can lower their compensation costs while still making workers better off.

In summary, because of tax advantages for fringe benefits and the savings from scale economies and group rating economies, any given mix of compensation characteristics carries with it two distinct dollar value measures: employer cost and employee value. The next section presents empirical proxies for these and other measures of employer compensation.

6.4 Empirical Measures of Fringe Benefits and Other Forms of Compensation

Empirical measures of the value of total compensation and its components can be readily derived. For any employer, let:

$$C(\mathrm{TC}) = \sum_{i=1}^{n} P_{B_i} \cdot B_i + P_W \cdot W, \tag{2}$$

where the employer cost of total compensation for any given employee, $C(\mathrm{TC})$, is equal to the sum total of dollar amounts of benefits, $P_{B_i} \cdot B_i$, for any given benefit $i(i = 1, 2, \ldots, n)$, and wages, $P_W \cdot W$, where P_{B_i} and P_W are the prices of benefits (B_i) and wage goods (W).

We define the employee value of the compensation package, $V(\mathrm{TC})$ for any employee as:

$$V(\mathrm{TC}) = \sum_{i=1}^{n} P_{B_i} \cdot B_i \cdot (t + S_i) + P_W \cdot W, \tag{3}$$

where t and S_i capture tax and scale advantages, respectively, by converting the value of benefits into equivalent pretax wages through their effect on relative prices. And $t = 1/(1 - t_m)$, where t_m is the marginal federal personal income tax rate on wages and other taxable money income for any given worker.[9]

Because $t_m \leq 1$, $t \geq 1$. The t factor estimates the additional amount of taxable wages necessary to leave the employee with after-tax income sufficient to purchase the same level of benefits which he now enjoys, at competitive market prices.[10] $S_i > 0$ also, indicating that, even in the absence of tax advantages, an employee could not purchase the same package of benefits at the same price as the employer, because group rating and scale economies lower prices to employers. Thus S_i represents the differentially higher prices that an employee would have to pay to purchase this same level of benefits. Together, the factor $(t + S_i) \geq 1$ then, indicating that $V(\mathrm{TC}) \geq C(\mathrm{TC})$ because the ratio of employer prices (r subscript) for wage goods to benefits, P_{Wr}/P_{Bir}, differs from the employee price ratio (e subscript), P_{We}/P_{Bie}, due to the fact that $P_{We} = P_{Wr} \cdot (t + S_i)$.

Each of these measures of total compensation can be compared to wages and salaries (WSAL) alone for each worker:

$$\text{(4)} \qquad \mathrm{WSAL} = P_W \cdot W,$$

or to pay for time worked (PTW) where:

$$\text{(5)} \qquad \mathrm{PTW} = \mathrm{WSAL} - \mathrm{VHOL} - \mathrm{OP},$$

and VHOL is vacation and holiday pay, and OP is equal to other (severance, bonus, and sick) pay included in wages, as defined in section 6.2.

Wages and salaries are a relevant point of comparison for both $V(\mathrm{TC})$ and $C(\mathrm{TC})$ because it is often used as a proxy for either (or both) of these measures of compensation. Pay for time worked is, however, less appealing as a measure of the employee value of compensation. But in order to examine the size distribution of fringe benefits as we have defined them, pay for time worked must be subtracted from the employee value (or employer cost) of compensation. Further, in models of household work behavior where time and subsidized leisure become important variables, pay for time worked may be a more relevant measure of "earnings" than wages and salaries. To the extent that lesser amounts of vacations and holidays can be substituted for higher hourly rates of pay, hourly money wages for various workers may be quite different if measured on a pay for time worked basis as compared to a wage and salary basis. Workers whose wages and salaries differ least from pay for time worked, as measured in equations (4) and (5), respectively, receive less benefits in the form of time off with pay and other types of wage compensation than do those with the largest differences.

In equations (2) and (3) the value of benefits, $P_{B_i} \cdot B_i$, will be measured by the individual components of supplements: insurance, deferred, and legally required contributions. However, readers may prefer to differentiate between these types of compensation. Insurance and deferred compensation are bargained upon by workers and employers and differ widely across firms. On the other hand, legally required benefits are nonnegotiable components of compensation. Moreover, in calculating the employee value, $V(\mathrm{TC})$, we will not be able to estimate the extent of nonoptimal situations at this time. The data needed to establish a worker's marginal rate of substitution between wage goods and benefits are not available. Assuming that hedonic prices or benefits levels adjust to competitive equilibrium, we would not find such situations to be widespread. For instance, the growth of "cafeteria" plans which allow workers to choose from various equal-cost bundles of benefits is a manifestation of this hedonic adjustment process. But in the case of legally required contributions, no adjustments can be made. In particular, due to the vagaries and long-run prospects for social security, younger workers may value employer (and employee) contributions far below their cost. On the other hand, Burkhauser and Turner (1981) have recently demonstrated that older workers may value these contributions in excess of an equal amount of wages due to the current social security benefit formulas (e.g., rules for spouse's benefits). Similarly, workers in cyclical industries may place a high value on unemployment insurance contributions while those in more stable job situations may find them virtually worthless. Because experience rating does not fully compensate for these differences (see Feldstein 1978), employees in cyclical industries may put a value on unemployment insurance above the employer cost. Because we have no estimates of the marginal rate of substitution between wage goods and benefits, and because labor markets cannot easily adjust these forms of compensation to suit employee and employer preferences, we will compute a second measure of the employee value of total compensation:

$$V(\mathrm{TC})X = V(\mathrm{TC}) - \mathrm{LR} \cdot t, \tag{6}$$

and a second measure of the employer cost of total compensation:

$$C(\mathrm{TC})X = C(\mathrm{TC}) - \mathrm{LR}, \tag{7}$$

which simply measure the value of total compensation, $V(\mathrm{TC})X$, or the employer cost, $C(\mathrm{TC})X$, disregarding employers' legally required contributions (LR).

In total, we will analyze the six measures of worker compensation indicated in equations (2)–(7). In addition, we will examine two measures of the value of fringe benefits alone: either fringe benefits valued at employer cost, $[C(\mathrm{TC}) - \mathrm{PTW}]$, or at employee value, $[V(\mathrm{TC}) - \mathrm{PTW}]$. More benefit-specific definitions for these variables, including the schedule of scale effects for pension contributions, and scale and group rating effects for health, life, and sickness or accident insurance, and a detailed explanation of the simulation methodologies employed to estimate the various components of employee compensation can be found in the appendix.

6.5 Results

The measures of compensation described above were used to answer three different questions: What are the differences between employer cost and employee value of fringe benefits and other measures of compensation? What is the effect of fringe benefits on the size distribution of earnings? What is the importance of different definitions of compensation in a standard human capital framework? We shall treat each in turn.

6.5.1 Comparing Employer Cost and Employee Value

Tables 6.2 through 6.5 present median levels of total compensation in the private nonfarm economy in 1979 for workers of different race, sex, and work status groups (tables 6.2 and 6.3); and for different occupational groups of workers (tables 6.4 and 6.5). In order to separate the effects of averaging measures of compensation for those with substantial levels of benefits and those without, tables 6.3 and 6.5 contain median compensation measures only for workers who receive both pension and health insurance benefits. In the private nonfarm economy, 37.8 percent of all workers, and 54.6 percent of all full-year full-time workers, receive both employer provided health insurance and pension benefits. In addition, workers with both types of benefits are more likely to receive other types of insurance coverage, sick pay, and other benefits than are other workers. Six measures of compensation are presented: wages and salaries (the standard measure of earnings); pay for time worked; the employer cost of total compensation (with and without legally required contributions); and the employee value of total compensation (with and without legally required benefits). In addition, we have calculated median levels of fringe benefits (total compensation minus pay for time worked) valued at employer cost and at employee value.

Median fringe benefits measured at employee value were $3099 (or 34.5 percent of wages) for all workers and $5208 (or 37.5 percent of wages) for full-year full-time workers in 1979 (table 6.2). Restricting the universe to employees with both health insurance and pension benefits in table 6.3 raises overall median benefits at employee value to $6866 (or 44.0 percent of wages and salaries) for all such workers and to $7239 (or 42.8 percent of wages and salaries) for all such full-year full-time workers. Workers with health insurance and pension benefits received more than twice as high a dollar amount in benefits ($6866 vs. $3099) and 9.5 more percentage points in total benefits relative to wages than did the overall average worker. Because workers with health insurance and pension benefits (table 6.3) are included among all workers (table 6.2) much wider differences would be found if we were to calculate median benefits for the 35.6 percent of workers with neither health insurance nor pension benefits.

Considering all workers in table 6.2, men received a higher dollar amount and a higher percent of salary in fringe benefits than did women. The ratio of female to male salary is 47.0 percent, while their ratio of fringe benefits at employee value is only 39.5 percent. However this substantial percent difference disappears totally when restricting the universe to all full-year full-time workers in table 6.2. Moreover, when

Table 6.2 **Different Measures of Median Compensation by Sex, Race, and Work Status in 1979**

Sex/Race	Wages and Salary	Pay for Time Worked	Total Compensation		Total Compensation without Legally Required		Total Fringe Benefits	
			Employer Cost	Employee Value	Employer Cost	Employee Value	Employee Value	Employer Cost
All workers:								
Both sexes	$ 8,974	$ 8,100	$10,667	$11,208	$ 9,590	$ 9,927	$3,099	$2,557
Males	13,047	11,883	15,789	16,594	14,472	14,909	4,711	3,906
Females	6,154	5,480	7,064	7,342	6,462	6,589	1,862	1,584
(female/male · 100)	(47.0)	(46.1)	(44.7)	(44.7)	(44.2)	(44.7)	(39.5)	(40.6)
Blacks	7,681	6,924	9,086	9,424	8,185	8,345	2,500	2,161
Whites	9,208	8,279	10,916	11,462	9,925	10,178	3,138	2,637
(black/white · 100)	(83.4)	(83.6)	(83.2)	(82.2)	(82.5)	(82.0)	(78.5)	(81.9)
Full-year full-time[a] *workers only:*								
Both sexes	13,884	12,327	16,596	17,535	15,248	15,842	5,208	4,269
Males	17,148	15,301	20,505	21,667	19,107	19,798	6,366	5,204
Females	9,784	8,561	11,598	12,229	10,649	10,990	3,668	3,037
(female/male · 100)	(57.1)	(56.0)	(56.5)	(56.4)	(55.7)	(55.5)	(56.6)	(58.4)

Source: Adjusted March 1980 CPS data tapes.

[a]Full-year full-time workers work thirty-five or more hours per week for fifty weeks or more per year.

Table 6.3 **Different Measures of Median Compensation by Sex, Race, and Work Status for Workers with Both Health Insurance and Pension Coverage in 1979**

Sex/Race	Wages and Salary	Pay for Time Worked	Total Compensation		Total Compensation without Legally Required		Total Fringe Benefits		Percent of All Workers with Health Insurance and Pension
			Employer Cost	Employee Value	Employer Cost	Employee Value	Employee Value	Employer Cost	
All workers:									
Both sexes	$15,577	$13,775	$19,180	$20,461	$17,637	$18,598	$6,866	$5,405	37.8%
Males	18,546	16,440	22,460	24,486	20,926	21,852	8,046	6,020	46.3
Females	10,352	9,044	12,791	13,709	11,744	12,325	4,665	3,747	27.0
(female/male · 100)	(55.8)	(55.0)	(57.0)	(56.0)	(56.1)	(56.4)	(58.0)	(62.2)	
Blacks	12,218	10,958	15,418	16,408	14,122	14,735	5,450	4,460	34.8
Whites	15,394	14,127	19,642	20,891	18,074	19,059	6,764	5,515	38.2
(black/white · 100)	(79.4)	(77.6)	(78.5)	(78.5)	(78.1)	(77.3)	(80.6)	(80.9)	
Full-year full-time[a] workers only:									
Both sexes	16,899	14,966	20,715	22,205	19,366	20,251	7,239	5,749	54.6
Males	19,761	17,236	23,856	25,821	21,973	23,173	8,585	6,620	59.8
Females	11,408	9,873	14,144	15,071	13,002	13,749	5,198	4,271	44.8
(female/male · 100)	(57.7)	(57.3)	(59.3)	(58.4)	(59.2)	(59.3)	(60.5)	(64.5)	

Source: Adjusted March 1980 CPS data tapes.

[a]Full-year full-time workers work thirty-five or more hours per week for fifty weeks or more per year.

looking only at workers with health insurance and pension benefits, the ratio of median female to median male fringe benefits, 58.0 percent, is now *higher* than their wages and salary ratio of 55.8 percent in table 6.3. This anomaly is explained by the fact that only 27.0 percent of all female workers received both health insurance and pension benefits as compared to 46.3 percent of males (table 6.3, final column). Thus female non-full-year non-full-time workers do less well than similar males, while fringe benefits reduce male-female compensation differentials for those females with both health insurance and pension benefits. Overall, blacks do not do quite as well as whites (table 6.2) when comparing median levels of benefits as a percentage of wages, but do slightly better than whites on this same basis for workers with both health insurance and pension benefits. It appears that much of the overall differences in benefits between males and females (and to a lesser extent blacks and whites) can be explained by the existence of benefits in a given job as compared to differences in benefit levels for those workers of each type with a given benefit package.

Across all workers (table 6.2), employers spend $1693 on supplements to wages and salaries (the difference between the employer cost of compensation and wages and salaries, not separately shown in tables 6.2 and 6.3) which employees then valued at $2234 (employee value of compensation minus wages and salaries). Excluding legally required benefits, these supplements were $725 and $953, respectively. Thus tax and scale advantages result in a difference in medians of $541 between employee value and employer cost of supplements including legally required benefits and $228 excluding these benefits. Both differences were approximately 32.0 percent of employer cost.

For workers with both health and pension benefits in table 6.3, the median level of supplements to salary including legally required benefits was $3603 in terms of employer cost and $4884 at employee value, producing a difference of $1281 or 35.6 percent of employer cost for these workers alone. Excluding legally required benefits, median insurance and deferred contributions alone were $2060 measured at employer cost and $3021 in employee value terms, leaving a difference of $961 or 46.5 percent of employer cost. Clearly the differences between employer cost and employee value of compensation are not insignificant at this time, particularly for workers who receive both health insurance and pension benefits.

The aggregate difference between employer cost and employee value of compensation was $67.43 billion or 7.71 percent of total wages and salaries with almost 95 percent of this difference due to the tax advantages of nonwage compensation alone. The aggregate gain in employee value due to tax advantages of $63.9 billion was 37.0 percent, as large as total supplements. Excluding legally required contributions, these differences fall to $43.25 billion or 4.94 percent of aggregate salaries. Thus the employee advantages of excluding employer provided benefits from income taxation are quite large. In this day and age of social security funding crises, it is interesting to note that if deferred contributions and insurance benefits were subject to payroll taxation by the employer, an additional $4.5 to $5.0 billion of social security payroll tax revenue would have been collected in 1979; double this amount if these benefits were also subject to employee payroll taxation.

While relative median compensation levels and measures of benefits vary by only a small amount for a given measure of compensation when comparing the groupings shown in tables 6.2 and 6.3, these estimates mask considerable differences across occupation groups, as seen in tables 6.4 and 6.5. In table 6.4, median fringe benefits vary from $5345 for craft and kindred workers to $709 for service workers, measured at employee value. As a percentage of wages the differences ranged from 36.9 percent for nontransport operatives to 20.8 percent for service workers at employee value and from 31.0 to 18.9 percent at employer cost. The most highly unionized occupations (e.g., craft and kindred workers and operatives) enjoyed the largest amount of fringe benefits as a percentage of wages and salaries (confirming the results of Freeman and Medoff [1980] and Antos [1981]) along with professional, technical, and kindred workers. Restricting the universe to employees with both health insurance and pension benefits (table 6.5) considerably reduces this variance. Now fringe benefits vary only from about 40 percent of wages for sales or service workers to roughly 46 percent for managers and the highly unionized groups when benefits are counted at employee value and from about 32 to 37 percent of wages when valued at employer cost. Major differences across occupations in table 6.4 are therefore explained largely by the fraction of each occupational group who receive both health insurance and pension benefits. The percent of all workers with both types of benefits is only 21.0 percent for service workers as compared to 51.4 percent for managers and administrators. This explains why overall service workers' fringe benefits of $642 at employer cost rise to $2970 for those with both types of benefits.

In summary, tables 6.2 through 6.5 indicate a series of interesting differences between the dollar level of different measures of compensation and benefits for any given set of workers. As expected, both full-year full-time workers and workers with health insurance and pension coverage benefit more than other groups in dollar terms and as a percentage of wages and salaries. Both male-female and interoccupational differences between wages and salaries and other measures of compensation are fairly substantial when measured across all workers. Tables 6.3 and 6.5 show that these differences are more a matter of benefit recipiency status than of benefit levels per se. For instance females (or service workers)

Table 6.4 **Different Measures of Median Compensation by Occupation in 1979**

Occupation	Wages and Salary	Pay for Time Worked	Total Compensation		Total Compensation without Legally Required		Total Fringe Benefits	
			Employer Cost	Employee Value	Employer Cost	Employee Value	Employee Value	Employer Cost
Prof./tech. & kind.	$14,327	$12,645	$16,895	$17,724	$15,523	$16,079	$5,079	$4,160
Mgr. & admin.	16,853	15,020	19,844	20,828	18,308	18,993	3,975	4,824
Sales	6,393	5,826	7,278	7,545	6,639	6,718	1,719	1,452
Clerical & kindred	7,539	6,753	8,945	9,496	8,152	8,354	2,653	2,192
Craft & kindred	14,981	13,351	17,666	18,693	16,219	16,743	5,345	4,315
Operating (ex. trans.)	8,846	8,012	10,754	11,277	9,690	9,945	3,265	2,742
Trans/equip. oper.	12,188	11,212	14,774	15,581	13,486	13,845	4,367	3,562
Laborers	5,570	5,003	6,391	6,621	5,784	5,859	1,618	1,388
Service	3,401	3,063	3,705	3,772	3,458	3,465	709	642
Total	8,974	8,110	10,677	11,208	9,699	9,927	3,099	2,557

Source: Adjusted March 1980 CPS data tapes.

Table 6.5 **Different Measures of Median Compensation by Occupation for Workers with Both Health Insurance and Pension Coverage in 1979**

Occupation	Wages and Salary	Pay for Time Worked	Total Compensation		Total Compensation without Legally Required		Total Fringe Benefits		Percent of All Workers with Health Insurance and Pension
			Employer Cost	Employee Value	Employer Cost	Employee Value	Employee Value	Employer Cost	
Prof./tech. & kind.	$18,900	$16,348	$22,544	$24,996	$21,080	$22,110	$8,646	$6,196	50.9%
Mgr. & admin.	21,693	18,962	25,832	28,162	24,150	25,321	9,200	6,870	51.4
Sales	15,976	14,249	19,355	20,616	17,796	18,817	6,367	5,106	22.5
Clerical & kindred	11,188	9,681	13,976	14,844	12,784	13,587	5,163	4,295	35.5
Craft & kindred	19,074	16,919	23,029	25,209	21,246	22,355	8,290	6,110	50.7
Operating (ex. trans.)	13,050	11,718	16,504	17,676	15,176	15,922	5,958	4,786	44.4
Trans/equip. oper.	16,786	15,166	20,588	21,979	19,113	20,010	6,813	5,422	45.4
Laborers	13,352	12,122	17,010	18,129	15,428	16,054	6,007	4,888	27.8
Service	9,298	8,356	11,326	12,115	10,469	10,848	3,759	2,970	12.0
Total	15,577	13,775	19,180	20,461	17,637	18,598	6,866	5,405	37.8

Source: Adjusted March 1980 CPS data tapes.

who are in jobs with both pension and health benefits receive levels of those benefits which are not dissimilar to males (or to those of other occupations). The inequality problem is largely explained by the relatively low fractions of females and service workers who are in jobs with both types of benefits. Additional tabulations not presented here indicate that the various measures of total compensation examined above have little effect on age-earnings profiles or on regional differences in measures of total compensation.

6.5.2 Fringe Benefits and Compensation Inequality

The second question we pose concerns itself with the impact of fringe benefits and supplements on the size distribution of total earnings. To begin with, table 6.6 investigates the way in which the various measures of total compensation are spread across wage and salary classes. All workers are ranked by wage level, and the percentage of workers in each bracket is shown. Mean levels of each additional measure of compensation and mean levels of benefits are then calculated, maintaining this same wage or salary ranking. These measures of mean compensation are recorded in part A of table 6.6, and as a percentage of wages and salaries by income bracket in part B. Additional information is provided for full-year full-time workers and part-year part-time workers as well. Because of their disequalizing effect, benefits which are distributed in a largely prorich pattern will be termed regressive, while those which provide a larger fraction of wages and salaries at low wage and salary levels will be referred to as progressive benefit structures.

In table 6.6, pay for time worked declines as a percentage of earnings as wages rise, indicating that paid leisure (vacations and holidays) and other benefits included in salary increase with earnings. These percentages range from 97.0 percent of salary in the lowest income class to 87.7 percent for those with salary levels in excess of $50,000 a year. Part-year part-time workers receive very little in the way of these benefits as compared to full-year full-time workers. The employer cost of total compensation, excluding legally required benefits, increases as a percentage of salaries as earnings levels increase from 104.2 percent in the lowest bracket to 112.8 percent at the $20,000 level, declining above this point, while the employer cost of total compensation including legally required benefits follows the same pattern but rises by a much lesser amount, from 116.0 to 121.6 percent of salaries, peaking at roughly the same point. It appears that legally required benefits exert an equalizing influence on compensation, so much so that the employer cost of compensation is actually a lesser percentage of salaries at levels of $50,001 or more than at earnings levels of $2000 or less.

Moving to employee value of compensation, we find that tax and scale advantages, which generally increase with earnings due to increasing

Table 6.6 Mean Levels of Compensation and Fringe Benefits by Wage or Salary Level in 1979

Annual Wage or Salary Level	(Percent of All Workers)	Wages and Salary	Pay for Time Worked	Total Compensation		Total Compensation without Legally Required		Total Fringe Benefits	
				Employer Cost	Employee Value	Employer Cost	Employee Value	Employee Value	Employer Cost
				A. Mean Compensation					
$2,000 or less	(15.2)	$ 875	$ 849	$ 1,014	$ 1,030	$ 912	$ 917	$ 181	$ 165
2,001–5,000	(15.3)	3,308	3,149	3,870	3,968	3,478	3,512	919	721
5,001–7,500	(12.6)	6,149	5,710	7,365	7,678	6,636	6,772	1,968	1,655
7,501–10,000	(11.0)	8,538	7,840	10,340	10,856	9,357	9,597	3,016	2,500
10,001–15,000	(18.1)	11,998	10,857	14,529	15,377	13,301	13,766	4,520	3,672
15,001–20,000	(12.6)	16,986	15,300	20,621	22,034	19,025	19,852	6,734	5,321
20,001–25,000	(7.8)	21,769	19,407	26,471	28,543	24,558	25,839	9,136	7,064
25,001–30,000	(3.8)	26,597	23,631	31,810	34,442	29,821	31,501	10,811	8,179
30,001–50,000	(3.4)	35,318	31,114	41,138	45,074	39,157	41,845	13,960	10,024
50,001 or more	(.8)	64,864	56,894	71,694	81,209	69,833	77,204	24,325	14,810
All workers	(100.0)	10,983	9,907	13,238	14,053	12,151	12,696	4,146	3,331
All full-year full-time workers	(56.2)	15,854	14,122	19,117	20,433	17,660	18,529	6,308	4,995
Part-year part-time workers	(14.0)	4,844	4,789	5,623	5,934	5,159	5,278	1,145	834

B. Mean Compensation as a Percentage of Wages and Salary

$2,000 or less	(15.2)	100.0%	97.0%	116.0%	117.7%	104.2%	104.8%	20.7%	18.0%
2,001–5,000	(15.3)	100.0	95.2	117.6	120.0	105.1	106.2	24.8	21.8
5,001–7,500	(12.6)	100.0	92.9	119.8	124.9	107.9	110.1	32.0	26.9
7,501–10,000	(11.0)	100.0	91.8	121.1	127.1	109.6	112.4	35.3	29.3
10,001–15,000	(18.1)	100.0	90.5	121.1	128.2	110.9	114.7	37.7	30.6
15,001–20,000	(12.6)	100.0	89.1	121.6	129.7	112.8	116.9	39.6	31.3
20,001–25,000	(7.8)	100.0	89.1	119.6	131.1	112.1	118.7	42.0	32.5
25,001–30,000	(3.8)	100.0	88.8	119.6	129.5	112.1	118.4	40.7	30.8
30,001–50,000	(3.4)	100.0	88.1	116.5	127.6	110.9	118.5	39.5	28.4
50,001 or more	(.8)	100.0	87.7	111.5	123.0	108.7	119.0	35.3	23.8
All workers	(100.0)	100.0	90.1	120.3	128.0	110.7	115.7	38.1	30.6
Full-year full-time workers	(56.2)	100.0	89.1	120.6	128.8	111.4	116.9	39.7	31.5
Part-year part-time workers	(14.0)	100.0	98.9	116.4	122.5	106.5	109.0	23.6	17.2

Source: Adjusted March 1980 CPS data tapes.

marginal tax rates, magnify these differentials below the $25,000 level. At higher levels of earnings, tax and scale advantages increase the employee value of supplements greatly, offsetting a large part of the decline in employer cost of compensation due to the earnings ceilings on most forms of legally required benefits. These advantages are large enough that, excluding legally required benefits, the employee value of compensation generally increases as a percentage of earnings throughout the earnings range. In comparison, employer cost excluding required benefits declines as a percent of wages above the $20,000 level. As expected, full-year full-time workers receive larger benefits, as a percentage of salaries, than do part-year part-time employees.

The final two columns of table 6.6 summarize these trends by presenting fringe benefits measured at employer cost and at employee value. These figures clearly indicate a regressive distribution of fringe benefits. In general, the 43.1 percent of workers at salary levels below $7500 receive lesser amounts of benefits as a percentage of salary than do higher salary workers. Employer cost of fringe benefits peaks at 32.5 percent of wages in the $20,000–$25,000 range, falling by a substantial amount above that level. In terms of employee value, we find a similar pattern with the 42.0 percent peak in this same earnings bracket. However, tax advantages again help maintain employee value at higher levels of wages and salaries.

Finally, levels of fringe benefits among part-year part-time workers are substantially below those for full-year full-time workers, and for all workers combined. Whereas the employer cost of benefits for a full-year full-time worker averages 31.5 percent of wages and salaries, a part-year part-time employee receives benefits which average only 17.2 percent.

The reasons for these patterns in benefits by earnings level are more apparent in table 6.7. Here we have disaggregated fringes as a percentage of wages and salaries by component. The percentages are formed by summing the component of benefits over all workers and dividing by aggregate wages in each income bracket. In part A the components of benefits are measured for all workers at employer cost and in part B at employee value. Parts C and D present similar decompositions for full-year full-time workers and part-year part-time workers, respectively.

In general, overall levels of benefits and their pattern by income class mask significantly different patterns in the individual components of compensation. As expected, those components of benefits already included in wages, i.e., vacations, holidays, and other payments (or pay for time not worked), in columns (1) and (2) are quite regressively distributed, each of them increasing consistently and substantially with earnings. These differences mirror the treatment of part-time vs. full-time workers at the very bottom of table 6.7.[11] These estimates are the same in parts A and B of table 6.7 because tax and scale advantages do not apply in this case.

The decomposition of nonwage compensation in the form of supplements to wages and salaries in columns (4) through (7) reveal several interesting patterns. Deferred compensation which consists almost wholly of pension contributions, increases greatly with earnings. Because pensions are calculated as a constant percentage of earnings for all workers within each industry, this pattern is mainly due to the pattern of pension plan coverage reported on the CPS. Tax advantages and economies of scale in pension fund management increase employee value (part B of table 6.7) by 45 percent relative to employer cost, further magnifying this pattern. In column (5) insurance contributions, of which health insurance premiums are roughly 80 percent, are fairly proportionate to salaries running from 3.7 percent at the lowest earnings level to a peak of 6.2 percent and then declining to 2.9 percent in the highest earnings group when measured at employer cost. Tax and scale advantages (part B) make these contributions slightly more regressive when counted at employee value. Taken together, insurance and deferred contributions (column [6]) generally rise with wages when measured at employer cost, and are quite regressive when counted at employee value, mirroring the patterns evident in table 6.6

In sharp contrast to other elements of compensation, legally required benefits (column [7] in table 6.7) are progressively distributed for two reasons: First, because they benefit virtually all workers. Second, because employer contributions are a constant percentage of wages up to a ceiling earnings level. For instance, the maximum employer social security contribution in 1979 was $1405 at $22,900. Above this level the fixed contribution declines as a fraction of wages. A similar but even more sharply progressive employer contribution schedule affects other legally required social insurance programs. Contribution ceilings for unemployment insurance and workers' compensation peak below $10,000. Because of this pattern, legally required benefits have a leveling effect on total nonwage compensation, tending to cancel out the regressive distribution of nonlegally required supplements. At the very bottom of table 6.7 we find that legally required benefits are the only form of compensation which provides a larger percent of wages for part-year part-time workers than for full-year full-time workers. The net effect (column [8]) reveals a slightly peaked distribution of total additions to wages when measured at employer cost. At employee value, tax and scale advantages reduce the decline in these estimates after their peak at the $25,000 level.

Finally, column (9) combines supplements and pay for time not worked to arrive at a measure of total fringe benefits. Because of the steeply regressive distribution of pay for time not worked, overall fringe benefits

Table 6.7 Components of Fringe Benefits as a Percentage of Wages and Salaries by Wage and Salary Level in 1979

	Fringe Benefits Included in Wages and Salaries			Supplement to Wages and Salaries					
Annual Wage and Salary	Other Payments[a] (1)	Vacation and Holiday Pay (2)	Total (3) = (1) + (2)	Deferred Compensation (4)	Insurance Compensation (5)	Subtotal (6) = (4) + (5)	Required Contributions (7)	Total Supplements (8) = (6) + (7)	Total Fringe Benefits (9) = (3) + (8)
A. Benefits Measured at Employer Cost, All Workers									
$2,000 or less	1.2%	1.7%	2.9%	.4%	3.7%	4.1%	11.8%	15.9%	18.8%
2,001–5,000	1.4	3.2	4.6	1.1	4.0	5.1	11.9	17.0	21.6
5,001–7,500	1.9	5.1	7.0	2.3	5.6	7.9	11.9	19.8	26.8
7,501–10,000	2.2	6.3	8.5	3.2	5.7	8.9	11.5	20.4	28.9
10,001–15,000	2.3	7.0	9.3	4.8	6.2	11.0	10.2	21.2	30.5
15,001–20,000	2.2	7.4	9.6	6.1	5.9	12.0	9.4	21.4	31.0
20,001–25,000	2.2	8.3	10.5	7.1	5.6	12.7	8.8	21.5	32.0
25,001–30,000	2.4	8.5	10.9	7.3	4.9	12.2	7.5	19.7	30.6
30,001–50,000	2.5	9.1	11.6	7.0	3.9	10.9	5.6	16.5	28.1
50,001 or more	2.7	10.8	13.7	7.2	2.9	10.1	2.3	12.4	26.1
Overall mean	2.2	7.4	9.6	5.4	5.3	10.7	9.1	19.8	29.4

B. Benefits Measured at Employee Value, All Workers									
$2,000 or less	1.2	1.7	2.9	.5	4.2	4.7	12.9	17.6	20.5
2,001–5,000	1.4	3.2	4.6	1.3	4.8	6.1	13.8	19.9	24.5
5,001–7,500	1.9	5.1	7.0	2.9	7.2	10.1	14.7	24.8	31.8
7,501–10,000	2.2	6.3	8.5	4.2	7.4	11.6	14.6	26.2	34.7
10,001–15,000	2.3	7.0	9.3	6.5	8.3	14.8	13.4	28.2	37.5
15,001–20,000	2.2	7.4	9.6	8.5	8.3	16.8	12.9	29.7	39.3
20,001–25,000	2.2	8.3	10.5	10.3	8.4	18.7	12.4	31.1	41.6
25,001–30,000	2.4	8.5	10.9	11.0	7.5	18.5	11.0	29.5	40.4
30,001–50,000	2.5	9.1	11.6	11.8	6.7	18.5	9.2	27.7	39.2
50,001 or more	2.7	10.8	13.7	14.0	5.1	19.1	4.6	23.7	37.4
Overall mean	2.2	7.4	9.6	7.9	7.6	15.6	12.4	28.0	37.6
C. Full-Year Full-Time Only									
Employer cost	2.3	7.8	10.1	5.6	5.4	11.0	9.0	20.0	30.1
Employee value	2.7	7.8	10.0	8.4	7.7	16.1	12.3	28.4	38.5
D. Part-Year Part-Time Only									
Employer cost	.9	0.0	.9	1.9	3.5	5.4	11.0	16.4	17.3
Employee value	.9	0.0	.9	2.7	4.7	7.4	13.6	21.0	21.9

Source: Adjusted March 1980 CPS data tapes.

[a]Includes severance pay, sick pay, and bonuses.

are decidedly prorich, even in terms of employer cost. Tax and scale advantages only strengthen this pattern in part B. For instance, benefit levels for the 30.5 percent of workers in the lowest two brackets are only slightly more than half as large, in percentage terms, as are benefit levels for the 15.8 percent of workers in the highest four brackets once tax and scale advantages are taken into account.

Based on the results presented in tables 6.6 and 6.7, one might suspect that conventional summary measures of the size distribution of employee compensation would tend toward greater inequality once fringe benefits were included. Table 6.8 confirms these suspicions. First, in part A of table 6.8 we find that the income share of the bottom quintile falls from 2.4 to 2.1 percent while the top quintile share increases from 47.3 to 48.4 percent when moving from left to right. These movements are confirmed by a 3.1 percent increase in the Gini coefficient, from .4529 to .4667, between these measures of compensation. In contrast, the size distribution pay for time worked is more equal than the size distribution of wages and salaries because of the fact that a much larger proportion of wages takes the form of vacation and holiday pay for higher income groups. Thus vacation and holiday pay exacerbates earned income inequality, as we would expect based on tables 6.6 and 6.7. Altogether the Gini rises by 4.5 percent or from .4466 to .4667, moving from pay for time worked—the most equally distributed measure of compensation—to the employee value of total compensation, excluding required benefits—the least equally distributed measure. Including legally required benefits only slightly tempers this conclusion. Similar patterns can be found for males and females. In part B of table 6.8 a similar pattern is evident for full-year full-time workers. Though size distributions of compensation for full-year full-time workers are considerably more equal than for all workers, even larger differences between the size distributions of total compensation can be noted. For males, the employee value Gini (excluding required benefits) exceeds the pay for time worked Gini by 6.1 percent, and for females by 9.5 percent (i.e., .2584 vs. .2359). In both parts of this table the distributional summary measures of the employer cost of compensation differ little from wages. Thus it is mainly the tax and scale advantages captured in the employee value measures which produce these differences.

Based on these tabulations it is fair to conclude that more full measures of compensation, such as those presented in this paper, indicate a more unequal size distribution of total employee compensation than the distribution of wages and salaries alone. Moreover, if we could include measures of other job perks and noncash compensation normally enjoyed by high-wage professionals, managers, and administrators in our estimates (see note 6), we strongly suspect that an even more unequal distribution of compensation would result. The major equalizing compo-

Table 6.8 **The Size Distribution and Degree of Inequality of Various Measures of Total Compensation in 1979 (measures of annual compensation)**

	Wages and Salaries	Pay for Time Worked	Total Compensation		Total Compensation Excluding Legally Required Contributions	
			Employer Cost	Employee Value	Employer Cost	Employee Value
A. All Workers						
Quintile shares of compensation:						
(Lowest) First quintile	2.4%	2.5%	2.2%	2.1%	2.2%	2.1%
Middle quintiles	50.3	50.8	50.8	50.0	50.1	49.5
(Highest) Fifth quintile	47.3	46.7	47.0	47.9	47.7	48.4
Gini coefficients:						
All workers	.4529	.4466	.4535	.4626	.4594	.4667
Males	.4027	.3944	.3984	.4081	.4068	.4144
Females	.4239	.4189	.4336	.4430	.4347	.4431
B. Full-Year Full-Time Workers						
Quintile shares:						
(Lowest) First quintile	8.0%	8.1%	7.9%	7.6%	7.8%	7.4%
Middle quintiles	53.2	53.7	54.0	53.5	53.4	53.1
(Highest) Fifth quintile	38.0	38.2	38.1	38.9	38.8	39.5
Gini coefficients:						
All workers	.3099	.3036	.3043	.3134	.3128	.3202
Males	.2852	.2679	.2760	.2858	.2860	.2939
Females	.2415	.2359	.2455	.2554	.2490	.2584

Source: Adjusted March 1980 CPS data tapes.

[a]Full-year, full-time workers work thirty-five or more hours per week for fifty weeks per year or more.

nents of fringe benefits in the private nonfarm labor market are legally required benefits which, some may argue, may have a fairly low value for persons on whose behalf such contributions are made. Finally, both the relatively low incidence of benefits and the low levels of benefits among part-year part-time workers appears to reduce the relative cost of this type of employee. If employers tend to favor these types of employees for cost reasons, hiring and laying off part-time workers on a regular basis, some portion of the recent pattern of labor market instability in the United States may be attributable to the relatively low employer compensation cost for these workers.

6.5.3 Measures of Compensation and Regression Models

The final issue to be investigated involves the question of the biases involved in empirical labor market research which relies only on wages and salaries as a proxy for total compensation. If regressors have widely different values for different measures of total compensation, biases in the effect of, for instance, education on compensation levels will likely be present. In this section we present a basic human capital model of the type suggested by Mincer (1974) and Blinder (1973). The dependent variable is the log hourly compensation measure, that is, the given measure of compensation divided by total hours worked. The log-linear format allows for straightforward comparison across the categories of total compensation with each coefficient capturing the approximate percentage change in the measure of hourly compensation, given a unit change in the independent variable. In the case of dummy variables (all variables but experience and experience squared) the coefficients can be interpreted as the percentage change in the dependent variable due to a change in the variable in question.[12] Regression results are shown for all workers (table 6.9) and the 47.9 percent of workers with both pension and health insurance benefits (table 6.10); standard errors are shown in parentheses. Also included in the final column is the hourly fringe benefit rate at employee value (i.e., fringe benefits divided by hours worked). These final figures can thus be compared to the other measures of compensation.

In general, the coefficients for virtually all independent variables (except for education) do not vary a great deal in either table 6.9 or 6.10. An extra year of "potential" experience (age minus years of education minus 6) has about a 2 percent greater impact on fringe benefits than on wages or pay for time worked in table 6.9, but not in table 6.10. Similarly, female fringe benefits are about 40.5 percent less than male fringe benefits compared to a 35.4 percent difference in wages in table 6.9. But restricting the universe to workers with both pension and health insurance benefits (table 6.10) reverses this finding. Here fringe benefits are about 36.4 percent less for females while wages are 41.4 percent less. Thus, if workers with both pension and health insurance benefits are considered, fringe benefits reduce female labor market disadvantages. As noted earlier, labor market disadvantages in table 6.9 then reflect the fact that females are more likely to be in jobs which do not offer both types of benefits.

The most significant differences in these models deal with the impact of education and work status. In the case of education there are only small (2–3 percent) differences between the measures of total compensation in terms of return to higher education levels. But comparing these to benefits reveals large differences for all workers. For instance, in table 6.9 some college (13–15 years of education) increases wages by 19.7 percent, but increases the employee value of benefits by roughly 32.4 percent. Similarly college graduates earn about 45.0 percent more than high school graduates in wage and salary terms, but receive approximately 59.6 percent more in fringe benefits in table 6.9. These effects are not, however, apparent in table 6.10. For workers with health insurance and pension benefits, the impact of fringe benefits is almost identical to the impact of education on the various measures of compensation. Thus again it appears that major differences in fringe benefits are due to the type of job which a worker has, i.e., their occupation and industry, which in turn affects their probability of having health insurance or pension benefits.

The coefficient for non-full-year full-time workers is interesting. For instance, in table 6.9, all else constant, on a pay-for-time-worked basis it appears that non-full-year full-time workers receive a higher rate of hourly compensation for actual hours worked than do full-year full-time workers. In table 6.9, for all workers, this difference averages 12.1 percent with a small standard error. In table 6.10, for workers with health and pension benefits, the differences are only 2.0 percent with a high standard error.[13] The final column in table 6.9 indicates that non-full-year full-time workers receive 51.6 percent less fringe benefits per hour, compared to full-year full-time workers. Based on these results, it appears highly probable that hourly rates of pay for non-full-year full-time workers compensate, to some extent, for their dearth of benefits. For instance, on the March 1980 CPS, only 5.1 percent of all part-year part-time workers received both health insurance and pension benefits as compared to 55.6 percent of all full-year full-time workers. This compensation-wage effect for non-full-year full-time workers who receive some vacation and holiday pay may at least partially offset the conclusion that part-year part-time workers are relatively cheap labor, as suggested earlier.[14] As expected, these differences are reduced to insignificance (table 6.10) once those workers with only health insurance and pension

Table 6.9 **Comparative Human Capital Regression Results for All Private Economy Nonfarm Workers in 1979 (standard errors in parentheses)**

	Dependent Variable, Log of Hourly						
			Total Compensation		Total Compensation Excluding Legally Required		
Variable	Wages and Salary	Pay for Time Worked	Employer Cost	Employee Value	Employee Value	Employer Cost	Fringe Benefits at Employee Value
Constant	1.423	1.232	1.574	1.575	1.466	1.457	1.061
	(.015)	(.015)	(.015)	(.015)	(.015)	(.015)	(.019)
Experience	.031	.029	.032	.034	.035	.033	.051
	(.001)	(.001)	(.001)	(.005)	(.006)	(.005)	(.001)
Experience^2	−.001	−.001	−.001	−.001	−.001	−.001	−.001
	(.000)	(.000)	(.000)	(.000)	(.000)	(.000)	(.000)
Race	−.086	−.089	−.082	.086	−.084	−.082	−.082
	(.008)	(.008)	(.008)	(.008)	(.008)	(.007)	(.001)
Sex	−.354	−.358	−.364	−.367	−.368	−.364	−.405
	(.006)	(.005)	(.005)	(.005)	(.005)	(.005)	(.001)
Region	−.084	−.082	−.085	.087	−.089	−.087	−.096
	(.006)	(.005)	(.005)	(.005)	(.005)	(.005)	(.007)
Residence	−.098	−.093	−.092	−.096	−.102	−.099	−.101
	(.005)	(.005)	(.004)	(.005)	(.005)	(.005)	(.006)

Education (years)							
Less than 7	−.140	−.147	−.139	−.142	−.150	−.143	−.112
	(.016)	(.016)	(.016)	(.017)	(.017)	(.017)	(.021)
8–11	−.044	−.045	−.042	−.041	−.043	−.042	−.025
	(.011)	(.010)	(.010)	(.011)	(.011)	(.011)	(.014)
13–15	.197	.178	.198	.211	.211	.206	.324
	(.010)	(.009)	(.009)	(.010)	(.010)	(.010)	(.012)
16 or more	.450	.421	.429	.458	.470	.458	.596
	(.011)	(.011)	(.011)	(.011)	(.011)	(.011)	(.014)
Veteran status	.113	.107	.116	.119	.126	.121	.145
	(.007)	(.007)	(.007)	(.007)	(.007)	(.001)	(.009)
Non-full-year non-full-time	−.189	.121	−.201	−.213	−.225	−.212	−.516
	(.007)	(.006)	(.006)	(.007)	(.007)	(.007)	(.009)
R^2	.300	.283	.315	.325	.330	.323	.415

Definitions of Variables:
Experience = age minus years of education minus six.
Race = 1 if black; 0 otherwise.
Sex = 1 if female; 0 otherwise.
Region = 1 is South; 0 otherwise.
Residence = 1 is nonmetropolitan; 0 otherwise.
Veteran status = 1 if veteran; 0 otherwise.
Non-full-year non-full-time = 1 for all workers who did not work thirty-five or more hours per week and who also did not work fifty or more weeks per year.

Table 6.10 **Regression Results for All Private Economy Nonfarm Workers with Both Pension and Health Benefits (standard errors in parentheses)**

	Dependent Variable, Log of Hourly					
			Total Compensation		Total Compensation Excluding Legally Required	
Variable	Wages and Salary	Pay for Time Worked	Employer Cost	Employee Value	Employee Value	Employer Cost
Constant	1.775	1.558	2.036	2.054	1.931	1.063
	(.031)	(.031)	(.030)	(.030)	(.031)	(.033)
Experience	.030	.029	.028	.030	.031	.032
	(.001)	(.001)	(.001)	(.001)	(.001)	(.001)
Experience^2	−.001	−.001	−.001	−.001	−.001	−.001
	(.000)	(.000)	(.000)	(.000)	(.000)	(.000)
Race	.106	−.103	−.097	−.103	−.103	−.102
	(.007)	(.007)	(.007)	(.007)	(.007)	(.008)
Region	−.072	−.070	−.066	−.068	−.069	−.064
	(.007)	(.007)	(.006)	(.007)	(.007)	(.007)
Residence	−.089	−.084	−.081	−.084	−.091	−.083
	(.006)	(.006)	(.006)	(.006)	(.006)	(.007)
Education (years)						
Less than 7	−.096	−.093	−.091	−.099	−.105	−.100
	(.025)	(.025)	(.023)	(.024)	(.024)	(.026)
8–11	−.023	−.021	−.025	−.028	−.029	−.031
	(.015)	(.015)	(.014)	(.014)	(.015)	(.016)
13–15	.155	.147	.139	.147	.151	.157
	(.015)	(.015)	(.014)	(.014)	(.015)	(.016)
16 or more	.395	.374	.352	.369	.384	.370
	(.016)	(.016)	(.015)	(.016)	(.016)	(.017)
Veteran status	.055	.051	.057	.058	.060	.072
	(.008)	(.007)	(.007)	(.007)	(.008)	(.008)
Non-full-year full-time	−.054	−.020	−.037	−.036	−.021	−.148
	(.001)	(.010)	(.010)	(.010)	(.010)	(.011)
R^2	.300	.298	.304	.300	.306	.269

Definition of Variables: Same as table 6.9.

benefits are included in the analysis. For this group, non-full-year full-time status only reduced fringe benefits by 14.8 percent as compared to full-year full-time employees.

In conclusion, based on tables 6.9 and 6.10, it does not appear that the wage and salary measure of total compensation, chosen for the most part by necessity in human capital studies, creates any significant bias in the results of those studies. However, two notes of caution must be added. First of all, the nondifferences in the coefficients in these tables may be a reflection of the simulation methodology used to allocate fringe benefits to CPS workers. As with all simulations, our methodology compresses the variance in benefit levels below that which would be obtained if individuals had reported actual benefit levels. But the Leibowitz paper in this volume, which is based on actual employer provided data for individual workers and not on imputed benefit amounts, supports these results based on Leibowitz's interpretation of her coefficients. Still, while the impact of education, experience, sex, etc., on chosen measures of compensation do not vary by a great deal, the same coefficients for fringe benefits themselves do exhibit some substantial differences, for example, those with some college and for college graduates. Further, there does appear to be some substantial difference between full-year full-time workers and other workers which is partially compensated for by higher nominal market wage rates for hours actually worked for non-full-year full-time workers.

Second, more complete specification of such models, for example, a model which includes occupation- or industry-specific differences in fringe benefits (the major differences which our simulation procedures directly controlled for), may produce differences in the effect of the independent variables on hourly compensation rates. Moreover, it appears that studies of sexual differences in rates of compensation may produce different coefficients, and possibly then different measures of the degree of labor market compensation differences between the sexes, than would studies based on wages and salaries alone. In both table 6.9 and 6.10, 5 percent differentials between fringe benefits and salaries for men and women were noted with the differences running in opposite directions in the two tables. However, until formal studies of this nature are actually completed, the extent of such biases—if there really are such biases—remain to be seen.

6.6 Summary and Conclusions

This paper has presented several measures of employee compensation, including measures of the employer cost and employee value of such benefits. A substantial differential between employer cost and full employee value was noted for various groups of workers. We were not able to estimate employee preferences for various types of benefits and thus could not adjust for nonoptimal situations. To the extent that an employee is forced to accept a benefit package with some components of that package valued below employer cost, the employee value measure used here may overstate the true employee value of compensation. Research on the determination of these preferences, for instance using studies of employer benefit package adjustments when employees are presented with a "cafeteria" plan, should be undertaken.

In many ways, the results of this endeavor seem promising, while in other ways they are disappointing. The regression results do not suggest that the different measures of compensation used in these regressions would substantially affect the previously determined impact of various explanatory variables on hourly wages and salaries. To the extent that more detailed outside data on the distribution of various types of benefits across different groups of workers become available, more sophisticated and accurate benefit simulation models may produce different results. While at this time we are not optimistic, we are working on new data sources which will improve the quality of these estimates.

On the other hand, several interesting patterns of benefit distribution across different demographic groups (male-female) and different income classes were noted. It appears that, as we have measured them, fringe benefits increase earned income inequality with this difference mainly due to the substantial tax and scale economy advantages of employer provided fringe benefits.

Appendix
Construction of March 1980 CPS Data Base

The March 1980 CPS contains wage and salary income data for a large group of U.S. workers. For the first time, the March CPS also asked workers about employer or union pension plan coverage and health insurance coverage. Respondents indicated whether the employer had a pension or health insurance plan, whether or not they were covered by their employer's plan, whether the employer subsidized the health insurance plan if they were covered, and whether they had individual or family coverage. No other information concerning nonwage compensation was obtained. The BLS 1977 EEEC survey and 1977 ECI survey both collected establishment data on employer outlays for various types of fringe benefits according to industry (EEEC) and occupation (ECI). The 1977 EEEC data tapes were combined into fifty-three industry groups, and aggregate outlays for various types of benefits as a percentage of WSAL were tabulated (see table 6.1). These tabulations provide the basic value of benefit data which was assigned to CPS workers. The ECI data were used in two ways: first, to update fringe benefit values to 1979, and second, after the EEEC based imputation, as a check against the occupation-specific consistency of the imputed CPS benefit value data.

In assigning benefit values to each individual worker, several different microsimulation techniques were employed. This appendix contains an explanation of the simulation methodology used to estimate the various components of the six measures of total compensation developed for this paper. We begin with definitions of each measure and then proceed to explain how each variable was created. The numbers in parentheses preceding each definition correspond to the equations which described these variables in the paper. Each mnemonic variable is explained below.

(4): WSAL = WSAL.

(5): PTW = WSAL − OP − VHOL.
OP = SKSAL + BOSAL + SEV PAY.
VHOL = VAC + HOL.

(2): C(TC) = WSAL + DC + IC + LR.
DC = PERT + SVTHR.
IC = LI + S/AI + HI.
LR = SSRR + OR.

(3): V(TC) = WSAL + DC$(t + S_1)$ + IC$(t + S_2)$ + LR(t).

(6): V(TC)X = V(TC) − LR(t).

(7): C(TC)X = C(TC) − LR.

WSAL = CPS wages and salaries, all private nonfarm workers. WSAL was \$874.066 billion in 1979.

PTW = pay for time worked, derived by subtracting VHOL and OP from WSAL. It includes straight time, wages, overtime pay, and shift differentials. PTW was \$790.370 billion in 1979.

OP = other nonPTW and non VHOL payments included in WSAL. These include:

SKSAL = sick pay. Workers were randomly assigned sick pay recipiency based on industry-specific probabilities of being covered as derived from the Battelle Employment Related Health Benefits (ERHB) Survey (Malhotra et al. 1980). Sick pay was then treated as an insurance policy, with an equal proportion of earnings assigned to each participant within each of the fifty-three EEEC industry groupings for which separate dollar amounts were available. Altogether SKSAL was .95 percent of WSAL or \$8.628 billion in 1979.

BOSAL = nonproduction bonus. Distributed across all non-part-year part-time workers by industry group in proportion to their wage and salary level.

SEV PAY = severance pay and contributions to severance pay funds not realized in 1979. These were distributed across all full-time workers in proportion to their wage and salary level within each of the fifty-three EEEC industry groups. The decision to exclude part-time workers was based on the AWS and LOB surveys and discussions with the BLS officials who take these surveys.

Together BOSAL and SEV PAY totaled \$10.740 billion in 1979, which when combined with SKSAL produces a total value of \$19.368 billion for OP in 1979.

VHOL = vacation and holiday pay. VHOL was estimated by assigning numbers of weeks of vacation (and numbers of holidays) to workers based on their industry, occupation, and firm-specific experience level. While firm-specific tenure data were not available in the March 1980

CPS, they were available on an earlier May 1979 CPS special supplement. Months of experience were assigned March 1980 CPS workers with a given level of tenure based on a regression model for estimating experience similar to that employed by Corcoran and Duncan (1979) and van der Gaag, Haveman, and Smeeding (1980). Separate estimates were obtained from the May 1979 CPS for males and females further separated by full-time or part-time work status. Having assigned a level of experience to March 1980 CPS workers, we next employed two BLS surveys: the 1977 Area Wage Survey (AWS) and the 1979 Level of Benefits (LOB) survey to determine how vacations and holidays were divided among specific types of workers according to experience, industry, and occupation. Using these data, a certain number of vacation days and a certain number of holidays were assigned to CPS workers with a given level of tenure. Using information on hours and weeks worked, all full-year workers, and all full-time but part-year workers were given a value for vacation and holiday pay based on their average hourly wages and salaries as reported on the CPS and prorated for employees working less than full year (fifty weeks) or working less than full time (thirty-five hours per week). Part-year part-time workers were not assigned these benefits. Once these values were determined, employees were aggregated into the fifty-three industry groupings consistent with EEEC, and the percentage of aggregate wages and salaries assigned to CPS workers was checked against industrywide totals (adjusted from 1977 to 1979 using the ECI), and scaled up or down by the same fraction for each worker in an industry grouping to reach the correct level of aggregate vacation and holiday benefits in each industry grouping. Altogether the March 1980 CPS includes $64.329 billion in VHOL for 1979.

C(TC) = employer cost of compensation, and includes DC, IC, and LR:

DC = deferred compensation which includes pensions and retirement pay (PERT) and employer savings or thrift plan contributions (SVTHR). PERT makes up in excess of 96 percent of DC. Equal percentage amounts of DC were assigned to workers reporting (or assigned) pension coverage on the March 1980 CPS. Dollar aggregates for determining these pensions were taken from the fifty-three industry-specific EEEC groupings for 1977, scaled up to 1979 by the change in PERT noted in the ECI. No acceptable alternative to this admittedly crude pension benefit assignment technique is currently available. For this reason it is not possible to use this data set and regression technique to estimate wage-pension trade-offs (as in Schiller and Weiss 1980). Other data which provide a more detailed breakdown of pension benefit information (e.g., data from the President's Commission on Pension Policy) are not available at this time. Altogether DC totaled $47.259 billion in 1979.

IC = insurance compensation which includes life insurance (LI), sickness or accident insurance (S/AI), and health insurance (HI). Each type of payment was imputed by a complicated procedure which can only be outlined here. First, the EEEC data do not separate the components of IC, recording all insurance payments in one lump sum amount. Fortunately the 1977 ECI survey does separate these amounts by industry. These percentage breakdowns were used to divide the fifty-three EEEC industry groupings' estimates of IC into LI, S/AI, and HI. On average, 77 percent of IC is HI, 12 percent is LI, and 11 percent S/AI. But there are wide variances across industry groups.

In the case of HI, average weekly premiums were assigned to workers reporting employer subsidized HI on the March 1980 CPS, according to family or individual coverage status. Premium amounts were obtained from the ERHB. These benefit amounts varied by industry and occupation grouping, by family/individual coverage, by employer percentage of premium paid, and by total premium cost of the policy. Using this data, average premiums per employee for each type of plan (family or individual) were obtained along with the variance in employer-employee contributions and benefit levels within industry groups. These premium values were updated to 1979 using Health Insurance Association of America data and were distributed to preserve the intraindustry and intraoccupation benefit level differences noted in the ERHB. Next, workers whose employer paid all or part of the HI premium were estimated by occupation and industry. The employer percentage of premium paid was then either 100 percent or something less—depending on the type of coverage and industry as determined by the ERHB and the March 1980 CPS. Workers were then assigned a net employer contribution based on coverage status and number of weeks worked. Dollar amounts were again aggregated and scaled on an equal dollar per worker basis and again prorated for weeks worked, to meet EEEC industry-specific total dollar amounts, adjusted to 1979 using the ECI.

The Battelle ERHB Survey also contained information on the percentage of employees in various industries who benefited from life and sickness/accident insurance, paid sick leave, or none of these, divided into establishments with group health insurance plans and establishments without them. LI and S/AI were calculated by assigning coverage according to industry group specific probabilities estimated for those workers with and without health insurance according to the ERHB Survey. Once a worker was selected, LI was estimated by giving each covered worker the same percentage of salary in insurance protection, the percent determined by the ECI-adjusted EEEC total value of contribution divided by covered workers' total wages within an industry. S/AI was also estimated by assigning ERHB-based probabilities to determine coverage. However, equal weekly amounts of S/AI were calculated for workers in each EEEC industry group according to weeks worked, and average S/AI expenditures per week worked. Altogether IC totaled $46.355 billion in 1981.

LR = legally required contributions which consist of social security and railroad retirement contributions (SSRR) and other required contributions (OR) for workers' compensation, unemployment insurance, and other minor legally required payments. SSRR was calculated simply as .0613 percent of wages up to a maximum of $1405 at $22,900. Other payments were calculated by dividing EEEC industry-specific OR total amounts (adjusted to 1979) by total wages and salaries of all workers up to $10,000 per year per worker (the most common unemployment insurance payroll tax base) within that group. This same percent was applied to wages (up to $10,000) and assigned to OR for all workers within an industry. In total, $79.347 billion of LR was estimated for 1979.

Once all benefits were assigned, CPS amounts were aggregated according to occupation, region, or location and tabulated as a percentage of wages and salaries so that they were comparable to the ECI data. In all cases the resulting percentages either were identical to the ECI to three places after the decimal, or were within the range of error which separates the EEEC and ECI survey results to three places after the decimal.

In summary then, DC, IC, and LR added $172.961 billion to WSAL ($874.066 billion) producing an aggregate C(TC) of $1047.027 billion including LR, and $967.680 billion for C(TC)X excluding LR. V(TC) and V(TC)X involve the same compensation components at C(TC) and C(TC)X, but also involve t, S_1 (for DC), and S_2 (for IC):

t = one over one minus the marginal federal personal income tax rate. The CPS does not contain income tax information. However, following the income tax simulation model used by Mathematica (Doyle et al. 1980) and by Smeeding (1975), the Census Bureau has designed a tax simulation model by which CPS workers were grouped into tax filing units, assigned standard or itemized deduction status, and placed in a marginal federal personal income tax bracket.

S_1 = scale factor for pension plans. Pension plans enjoy economies of scale based on the size of the pension fund. While custodial (administrative overhead) fees decline by a small amount when comparing an Individual Retirement Account (IRA) or a Keough plan (for self-employed persons) to larger pension funds, the major economies are due to lower securities commissions for portfolio adjustments. As shown in table 6.A.1, custodial fees and securities commissions fall from 5.90 percent for an IRA (Keough) plan to 3.54 percent for large pension funds, yielding a maximum value of 2.36 percentage points for S_1 (Mahler and Hanson 1981). Pension fund size was estimated by total annual pension fund

Table 6.A.1 Scale Factor for Pension and Retirement Plans: S_1

Category of Aggregate Pension Plan Size[a]	Total Custodial and Securities Fees as a Percent of Aggregate Pension Value	S_1^b
IRA/Keough	5.90%	NA%
Small	4.43	1.47
Medium	4.13	1.77
Large	3.54	2.36

Source: Paul Mahler and William Hanson; Merrill, Lynch, Pierce, Fenner, and Smith Pension Fund Managers.

[a]Exact dollar values for determining small, medium, and large pension plans are not disclosed, as requested by Merrill, Lynch, Pierce, Fenner, and Smith, Inc.

[b]S_1 factors are calculated by subtracting the fee for given size pension plan from the IRA/Keough figure of 5.90 percent.

outlays divided by the total number of firms for each of nine industry groupings. Covered employees in each industry grouping received the S_1 factor for that grouping.

S_2 = scale and group rating factor for insurance contributions. Commercial employer group health insurance is significantly less expensive than individual coverage due to lower sales costs (economies of scale) and group rating advantages. The difference in total expenses as a percentage of total premium for commercial health insurance companies varies from 38.7 to 61.6 percent of premium for groups of one to three employees, to levels of 6.0 to 7.0 percent for employee groups of one thousand or more workers (Thexton 1978; Schuttinga 1981). However, these differences are much smaller for Blue Cross/Blue Shield (BC/BS) health plans where expenses run only from 12.0 percent for groups of one to three workers to 7.1 percent for groups of one thousand or more workers (Schuttinga 1981). Various factors account for these differences, including the nonprofit status of BC/BS and the fact that BC/BS cross-subsidizes small group plans at the expense of larger group plans. In any case, because individual BC/BS plans are available at lower rates than commercial policies, the lower BC/BS expense margins were assumed to capture the current differential savings between individual and group policies. These factors are shown in table 6.A.2 and were used to adjust medical, sickness or accident, and life insurance for economies of scale and group rating. Group size was estimated by the average number of covered workers per firm within a given industry group.

While these simulation methods have most certainly compressed the true variance in employer contributions, particularly for pension plans, we expect that the benefit imputation procedures were of a sufficiently sophisticated nature to capture a large fraction of the true variance in

Table 6.A.2 Scale Factors for Insurance Plans: S_2

Group Size	Total Expenses[a] as a Percent of BC/BS Premium	S_2^b
1–3	12.0%	NA%
4–9	11.0	1.0
10–19	10.3	1.7
20–49	9.2	2.8
50–100	8.5	3.5
100–249	8.0	4.0
250–499	7.6	4.4
500–999	7.4	4.6
1,000–4,999	7.1	4.9
5,000 or more	7.0	5.0

Source: James Schuttinga, U.S. Department of Health and Human Services. Estimates are for August 1, 1978.

[a]Total expenses include premium taxes, sales costs, claims processing costs, and other costs.

[b]S_2 is calculated by taking the difference between expenses for groups of 1–3, i.e., 12.0 percent, and the expense level in each group size bracket.

employer contributions for fringe benefits. More refined estimates of the value and distribution of benefits and greater variance in imputed benefits await the availability of new and more detailed data sources.

Notes

1. There are, however, recent surveys which provide at least some of the necessary information for a limited group of workers, e.g., the 1977 National Medical Care Expenditure Survey which will soon be available for public use.

2. Others (e.g., Antos 1981; Alpert 1980) have followed the opposite approach, aggregating CPS variables and using these aggregates in conjunction with BLS data to analyze components of total compensation on an establishment basis.

3. While fringe benefits are defined and were simulated in hourly wage terms, they can also be aggregated across all workers (as in table 6.1) or expressed in terms of annual earnings (as in section 6.5). One problem with breaking fringe benefits into hourly rates is the definition of hours—either hours actually worked, or hours worked plus vacation, holiday, and other hours paid for but not worked, could be used. In this paper we use the latter (Census) definition of hours.

4. With deferred compensation, an employee only postpones taxation. However, in most cases (pensions, for instance) taxes are lowered as well as deferred by postponing taxation of benefits until retirement. In addition to deferral of taxation, a nonaccretion based income tax also allows deferred taxes to add to the aggregate value of pension funds, producing a higher compound return to such investments as well.

5. These figures on pension coverage and the health insurance coverage questions which follow were taken directly from the March 1980 CPS. The 44.6 percent of all private nonfarm workers with pension coverage in 1979 exceeds the 43.7 percent of private nonfarm workers covered by pensions as reported in the May 1979 CPS (Beller 1981).

6. Clotfelter (1979) cited a recent survey which indicated that 53 percent of sample companies paid for country club memberships for some executives, 83 percent for physical examinations, and 25 percent for personal use of company planes. The survey showed that an executive earning $100,000 averaged $30,000 in these and other types of in-kind compensation. While it is often difficult to separate true "business" expenses (real costs of doing business) from pure "pleasure" (pure consumption and thus income or compensation) when dealing with travel and entertainment expenses and other perks, a strong argument can be made to include large proportions of these outlays in a more full measure of total employee compensation (Clotfelter 1981).

7. Leisure refers to hours not worked and not paid for by the employer. Paid time off from work for vacations and holidays is included in fringe benefits, while time used for home production is either ignored or, equivalently for our purposes, lumped with L.

8. In a similar fashion, Thaler and Rosen (1975), Antos and Rosen (1975), Quinn (1979), and Smith (1979) have examined the trade-off between W and A, ignoring B and L. Antos (1981) and Alpert (1980) examine the trade-off between W and B, ignoring L and A. Brown (1980) has added A, but not L, to B and W in his analysis of equalizing differences in the labor market. Atrostic (1982) has included all four elements in an analysis of labor supply behavior, though A and B are combined into one subjective measure.

9. Others (e.g., Leibowitz in this volume; Woodbury 1981) have chosen to express this relationship in terms of after-tax wages. Such a transformation can be accomplished by multiplying both sides of equation (3) by $(1 - t_m)$. However, for the purposes of this paper, i.e., for comparing employee value to employer cost, we chose to cast the analysis in terms of pretax wages to capture the fact that employees value nontaxed benefits in excess of their employer cost. In either case, the dollar value of fringe benefits is the same regardless of whether the analysis is presented in terms of pretax or after-tax wages.

10. Clearly, state specific marginal income tax rates should be included where applicable. Thus our t is really a lower bound estimate of the tax advantages afforded by nontaxable fringe benefits. Note that federal OASDHI payroll taxes do not apply in this case. Essentially, adding legally required employer contributions to employee wages and salaries indicates that we are treating social security as a form of deferred compensation, albeit possibly indirect and uncertain compensation, not as a "tax" per se.

11. In some ways these estimates of zero vacation and holiday pay in part D of table 6.7 are only a direct consequence of our decision not to allocate vacation and holiday pay to part-year part-time workers. But, according to the best available information, the vast majority of such workers do not benefit from paid holidays or paid vacations.

12. The coefficients of a log-linear regression are only rough approximations of percentage increases for coefficients larger than .10. However, in order to provide easy translation from the regression results to the text, we refer to these coefficients as being roughly equal to percentage changes.

13. This coefficient was statistically insignificant at the 95 percent level.

14. However non-full-year full-time workers in the regression model would include full-year part-time and part-year full-time workers who were allocated some vacation and holiday pay, as well as part-year part-time workers, who were not assigned these benefits. Pay for time worked differs from nominal wages for part-year part-time workers by only .9 percent (table 6.7). The other two groups of non-full-year full-time employees were allocated these benefits. Of the 41.8 million non-full-year full-time employees in 1979, only 31.7 percent (13.3 million) were part-year part-time workers. On the other hand, only part-year part-time workers were singled out in tables 6.6, 6.7, and 6.8.

References

Alpert, William. 1980. An economic analysis of private wage supplements. Washington University, St. Louis. Mimeo.

Antos, Joseph R. 1981. Wages and compensation of white-collar workers. U.S. Bureau of Labor Statistics. Mimeo.

Antos, Joseph R., and Sherwin Rosen. 1975. Discrimination in the market for public school teachers. *Journal of Econometrics* 3: 123–50.

Atrostic, B. K. 1982. The demand for leisure and nonpecuniary job characteristics. *American Economic Review* 72: 428–440.

Beller, Daniel J. 1981. Coverage patterns of full-time employees under private retirement plans. *Social Security Bulletin* 44: 3–11.

Blinder, Alan. 1973. Wage discrimination: Reduced form and structural estimates. *Journal of Human Resources* 8: 426–54.

Brown, Charles. 1980. Equalizing differences in the labor market. *Quarterly Journal of Economics* 97: 113–34.

Burkhauser, Richard, and John Turner. 1981. Is the social security payroll tax a tax? Vanderbilt University. Mimeo. April.

Chamber of Commerce of the United States. 1980. *Employee benefits 1979*. Washington, D.C.: Chamber of Commerce.

Clotfelter, Charles. 1979. Equity, efficiency, and the tax treatment of in-kind compensation. *National Tax Journal* 32: 51–61.

———. 1981. Business perks and tax-induced distortions: The case of travel and entertainment. Working paper. Duke University, Institute of Policy Sciences and Public Affairs.

Corcoran, Mary, and Greg Duncan. 1979. Work history, labor force attachment, and earnings differences between the races. *Journal of Human Resources* 14: 3–20.

Doyle, Mary P., David Edson, Norma Pappas, and William Boulding. 1980. *Creation of 1980 and 1984 data bases from the March 1978 CPS, volume 1, final report*. Washington, D.C.: Mathematica Policy Research.

Feldstein, Martin S. 1978. The effects of unemployment insurance on temporary layoff unemployment. *American Economic Review* 68: 834–46.

Freeman, Richard, and James Medoff. 1980. *What do unions do?* Cambridge: Harvard University Press.

Gagg, Jacques van der, Robert Haveman, and Timothy Smeeding. 1980. Determinants of wage inequality: The impact of model specification on the estimated contribution to wage variation. Paper presented to the World Congress of the Econometric Society, 1 September 1980, Aix-en-Provence, France. Mimeo.

Handbook of labor statistics 1978. 1979. U.S. Department of Labor, Bureau of Labor Statistics. Bulletin 2000. Washington, D.C.: U.S. Government Printing Office.

Kennedy, Peter E., and Ronald J. Vogel. 1979. A theory of the determinants of fringe benefits. U.S. Department of Health and Human Services, Health Care Finance Administration. Mimeo.

Lester, Richard A. 1967. Benefits as a preferred form of compensation. *Southern Economic Journal* 33: 488–95.

Mahler, Paul, and William Hanson. 1981. Telephone conversation, June 10.

Malhotra, Suresh, Kenneth M. McCaffree, John M. Wills, and Jean Baker. 1980. *Employment related health benefits in private nonfarm business establishments in the United States, volume 2, description of selected data*. Seattle, Wash.: Battelle Human Affairs Research Center.

Mincer, Jacob. 1974. *Schooling, experience, and earnings*. National Bureau of Economic Research. New York: Columbia University Press.

Quinn, Joseph F. 1979. Wage differentials among older workers in the public and private sectors. *Journal of Human Resources* 14: 41–62.

Rice, Robert G. 1966. Skill, earnings, and the growth of wage supplements. *American Economic Review* 56: 583–93.

Rosen, Sherwin. 1974. Hedonic prices and implicit markets: Product differentiation in pure competition. *Journal of Political Economy* 82: 34–55.

Schiller, Bradley, and Randall Weiss. 1980. Pensions and wages—A test for equalizing differences. *Review of Economics and Statistics* 62: 529–38.

Schuttinga, James. 1981. Telephone conversation, June 9.

Smeeding, Timothy M. 1975. Measuring the economic welfare of low-income households and the antipoverty effectiveness of cash and non-cash transfers. Ph.D. diss., University of Wisconsin-Madison.

Smith, Robert S. 1979. Compensating wage differentials and public policy: A review. *Industrial and Labor Relations Review* 32: 339–51.

Steuerle, Eugene. 1979. Efficiency and the valuation of fringe benefits. U.S. Department of the Treasury. Mimeo.

Thaler, Richard, and Sherwin Rosen. 1975. The value of saving a life: Evidence from the labor market. In *Household production and consumption*, ed. N. E. Terleckyj. Conference on Research in Income and Wealth: Studies in Income and Wealth, vol. 40. New York: National Bureau of Economic Research.

Thexton, Peter M. 1978. Letter to Morton B. Hess, Office of the Actuary, Social Security Administration.

Woodbury, Stephen A. 1981. Estimating preferences for wage and nonwage benefits. Conference Paper no. 102. Cambridge, Mass.: National Bureau of Economic Research.

Comment Martin David

I will focus my comments on four areas: the conceptual underpinnings for the measurement of total compensation, the simulation methodology, the value of the statistics presented, and the possibilities for improved data in future studies.

Conceptual Underpinnings

Smeeding's estimates recognize that measures of cash wages are no longer sufficient as a description of the compensation package received by employees (if they ever were). The estimates attempt to draw a distinction between employer cost and employee valuation. In criticizing Smeeding's efforts, I will argue that several conceptual gaps mar the distinction drawn and imply that superior estimates can be drawn from the data base at hand.

In presenting a utility function, Smeeding rightly points out that amenities and leisure serve as important arguments. Indeed, it is probably more accurate to think of equation (1) as an indirect utility function and observe that there is a maximum achievable utility for any given vector of wage rates, fringe benefits, and amenities offered by the employers to whom an individual worker has access. Focusing on this indirect utility function, one can observe that there are two measures of interest:

A. What is the utility gain associated with acceptance of employment on the terms offered?

B. What are the characteristics of the compensation vector (WG, FB, A) that are operative at the several margins affecting work effort? That is, the decision on work intensity (hours/per week), the decision on work experience (hours/year), and the decision as to length of working lifetime depend on current and expected future compensation vectors.

To answer question A, it is clear that amenities of the job cannot be ignored. The disutility of work depends heavily on a number of factors that contribute substantially to the well-being of the worker. In addition to the in-kind consumption benefits that Smeeding alludes to, workers benefit from employer investments in job safety, from control over working conditions and job planning, and employer investments in general training. The theory of compensating differentials makes clear that variation in amenities will induce corresponding inverse variations in cash wage payments. Sider (1980) offers an excellent analysis that demonstrates the existence of a frontier relating wages to job safety levels. Stafford and Duncan (1980) point to substantial consumptive uses of time during working hours that again lead to amenity values. To provide a meaningful measure of the utility gain (question A) one must either demonstrate that there is no correlation between amenities and other

Martin David is professor of economics at the University of Wisconsin, Madison.

forms of compensation or one must control on the level of amenity provided.

Thus it appears that the employee valuation of total compensation presented by Smeeding is at best a partial measure whose meaning is rendered ambiguous by the possibilities of compensating variations for some amenities and complementarities between cash and other forms of compensation in other cases.

The second question has been almost completely ignored in Smeeding's presentation. Table 6.10 gives a partial insight; the last row relates the effect of full-year, full-time status to the compensation package. This contrast should be elaborated to show the effect of weeks worked during the year and the effect of employees with hours of work in excess of normal working weeks, as opposed to those with temporary reductions in workhours or layoffs. If the fringe benefits prove to be a largely inframarginal form of compensation, we would have some important evidence on how the change in total compensation packages affects work incentives.

A third question that can be asked about employment is a question that is asked by the employer:

C. What is the resource cost of an additional employee? or additional employee hours? A question corresponding to the utility gain question for the individual is the social question:

D. What is the total resource cost of employment?

Clearly, both of these questions entail the resource costs that are encumbered by employers in creating amenities as well as cash compensation. I see no way of excluding such costs from consideration. Indeed, one might divide all resource costs of employment into four categories:

Provider	Costs Generating Consumption Goods for the Employee	Costs Complementary to Labor Services Provided in the Work Setting
Employer	1	3
3rd Party	2	4

It is clear that the employer provided goods in category 1 can be either cash or in-kind; the distinction of who is the provider may have little economic meaning. Some employers may choose to absorb the costs of a sick leave policy directly; others may prefer to negotiate and purchase a temporary disability insurance policy; mixtures of these extremes are common.

The point to be made is that the exclusion of costs under category 3 (provision of uniforms, safety devices, or subsidizing meals taken during working hours) excludes a significant and amenity-producing use of resources. As a result it is not possible to relate the total compensation estimates in this paper to meaningful measures of costs of employment.

Conceptually, Smeeding appears to have presented us with half a loaf. While half may be better than none, it seems that we should be extremely cautious about inferring either welfare or resource cost implications from the data at hand.

The tax rate margin. The principal source of difference between the employee and employer valuation of fringe benefits is the margin created by the assignment of a marginal tax rate to the wages and salaries reported (WSAL). The rate is used to inflate the imputed fringe benefits, according to $1/(1 - t_m)$. This procedure is wrong for at least two reasons. The increase in utility associated with total compensation is the value of goods and services that both cash and in-kind compensation provide for consumption. If the tax rate rises, the utility value of fringe benefits does not necessarily rise—the health insurance benefit continues to provide the same increment in health. Rather, what has happened is that the after-tax value of cash compensation falls as the tax rate rises. Thus the appropriate measure of V(TC) would include WAGSAL net of income and payroll taxes *plus* the full outlay for fringe benefits without adjustment (see figs. C6.1 and C6.2).

The implications are twofold. First, for any wage earner $V(\text{TC}) \gtrless C(\text{TC})$, depending on the excess of scale economies in the purchase of fringe benefits over the employee tax liabilities. Second, it is the cumulative effect of all tax brackets that determines the difference between disposable wage goods and wage goods paid by the employer. Thus the *average* tax rate determines the position of the employee's budget constraint relative to the employer's isocost level. This latter observation implies that the margin between V(TC) and C(TC) augmented by the scale economies will be considerably less than Smeeding has estimated.

A third aspect of the adjustment for taxes paid is fundamental to the meaning of the V(TC). If a fixed revenue requirement for government is assumed, it is not possible for all employers to increase fringe benefits relative to wages without an increase in the tax rates; the converse holds if all employers reduce fringe benefits relative to wages. This observation suggests that the budget constraint on which Smeeding bases his valuations can not hold in the aggregate. In the long run, it is likely that Smeeding's representative employee faces a budget constraint in which the difference between gross wages and purchasing power disposable for the purchase of goods and services remains constant, no matter what arrangements employers make for the provision of in-kind fringe benefits.

If this latter argument has validity, it suggests that tax considerations do not increase the consumption attainable by "typical" workers who trade wages for fringe benefits. For the typical worker the sole value of fringe benefits lies in the economies of scale attainable. At the same time,

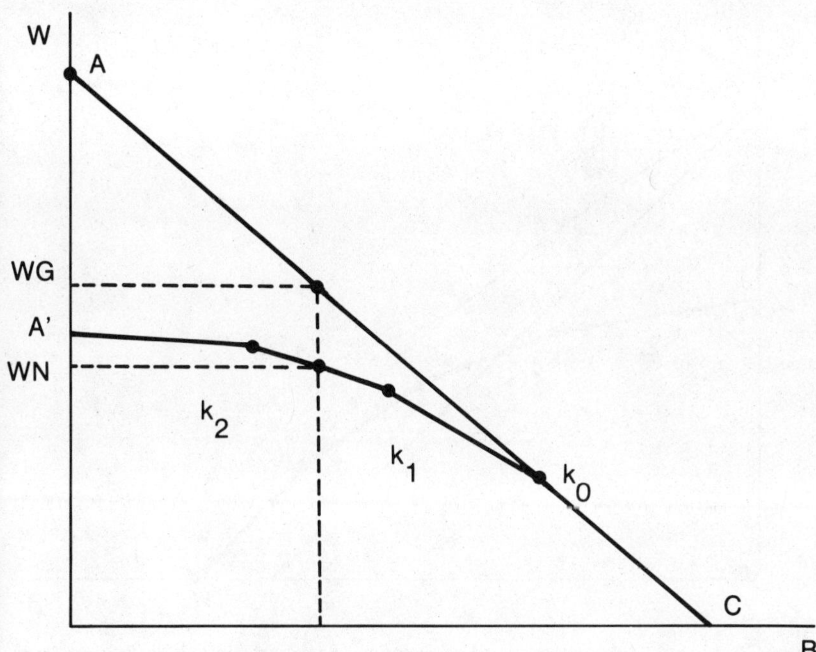

Fig. C6.1 AC = employer cost in the absence of scale advantages; $A'C$ = after-tax budget constraint; W = cash income tradable to all commodities; B = in-kind income; k_0, k_1, k_2 = bracket steps in federal income and payroll taxes including earned income tax credit.

of course, the existence of tax-exempt status for some fringe benefit payments may alter the progressiveness of the tax structure; increased use of fringe benefits by high-wage workers may cause tax rate changes for low-wage workers that leave them worse off.

Fortunately use of WSAL net of taxes plus employer costs provides the correct index of changes in worker utility over time as changes in tax rates will automatically be accounted for in the relevant way.

Simulation Methodology

The procedures used by Smeeding are similar to what many others have done to create synthetic data sets. The assumptions are neither more unreasonable nor is the execution less questionable than the work of others in creating CPS-IRS data sets or data sets that are used to estimate the scope of the welfare-eligible population. As a scientific profession, we must be extremely critical of all of these efforts on three grounds: (1) No measures of the variance associated with the imputation procedures are created; (2) the use of expectations reduces variance in

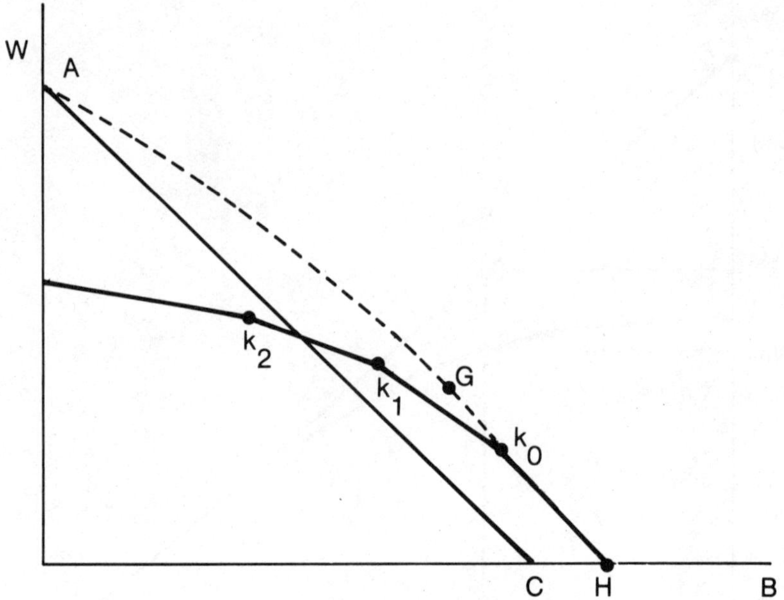

Fig. C6.2 AG = range of economies of scale in fringe benefit provision; Hk_0 = "zero" tax bracket; k_0k_1 = first tax bracket; k_1k_2 = second tax bracket.

the synthetic data set; and (3) the results are presented without information on the consequences of alternative imputation rules. Rubin (1980) gives us guidance on how each of these three objectives can be achieved by multiple imputation. How would this apply to the statistics at hand?

Smeeding's imputations are imputations at two levels. In some cases, a personal characteristic that is related to the payment of fringe benefits is missing from the CPS data base. In other cases, the value of a fringe benefit paid to an individual is not available, though information on some conditioning characteristics, including receipt of the benefit and occupation and industry, are known. In the latter case the imputation may be described as the creation of an index based on personal characteristics which is normalized to unity and then used to allocate the industrywide control on the aggregate of fringe benefits paid in that industry. (I hope this characterization is not too gross). The important element of variance that is suppressed by this procedure is the variance in the ratio of fringe benefits to wage and salary payments that exists among firms within an industry. This variance is estimable from the EEEC. To preserve variance, a value of the ratio would need to be drawn from the EEEC distribution and assigned to an appropriate number of employees; this would imply different levels of fringe benefits for persons with the same conditioning characteristics within an industry.

Let me elaborate. Health insurance varies substantially across employers with regard to types of services and costs that are reimbursable. Aside from the difference in proportion of premiums that are paid for by the employer, the amount of that premium will vary across firms. While Smeeding maintains variance in employer proportion contributed within an industry, as I understand the procedure, the same expected premium is used for all employers. This eliminated an important source of variance.

Failure to preserve the variance of the fringe benefit payments that exists in the universe renders Smeeding's conclusions on the Gini coefficient highly questionable. It also does violence to the regression findings since we can be sure that the covariance of personal characteristics with levels of fringe benefit payments is incorrect. This might not be so bad if we were sure that we understood the direction of bias in the covariance. However, as we have already suggested, one group of workers chooses among compensating differential cash payments; for them we expect an inverse relationship between cash and fringe benefits. For others in the population, as Smeeding strongly suggests, tax considerations imply a positive correlation between compensation in cash and fringe benefits. No prior grounds exist for asserting the population value of the covariance, and systematic understatement of the random variation in fringe benefits produces a meaningless result.

This same argument applies to the assignment of personal characteristics from other data sets to give the conditioning information that is required for the imputation.

Both preservation of variance and a measure of the variance associated with the imputation procedure can be obtained by the multiple imputation procedure advocated by Rubin. What is required is that two or more values be assigned to each data point, using a distribution of values conditional on individual (firm) characteristics. The variance of the stochastic component for like individuals then gives a measure of the variation due to the imputation procedure. In addition, the machinery for generating multiple imputations makes it easy to do sensitivity analysis of alternative imputation rules and their impact on the population statistics.

Value of the Imputations

Of the numbers presented, *C*(TC) appears the most useful. It adds to information that can be easily collected from household surveys. The accounting for employer costs other than WSAL appears well grounded in good measurements. The estimates related to *V*(TC) appear flawed, and if recomputed could tell us something about the relationship between employer costs of compensation and the movement of household budget constraints in different groups of workers.

The value of PTW is particularly obscure. PTW differs from WSAL largely because of VHOL; those imputations are particularly weak since appropriate information on employees was not available in the CPS to perform an allocation.

Tenure in the job had to be imputed before employer data could be used to assign expected number of paid holidays by occupation-industry class. (Loss of variance would appear to be particularly important as small and large firms in the same industry are unlikely to have the same vacation accruals.)

In addition, VHOL is primarily a technique for income averaging within the year and not subject to either the scale or tax questions nor to the in-kind consumption that dominate Smeeding's discussion.

The fringe benefits that are added to WSAL are valued as premiums paid to provide contingent income or benefits. The worker whose cancer treatment is paid by an employer contribution to health insurance does not receive a greater income than his healthy coworker. However, the amount of WSAL reported to CPS is *cash* realized from employment activities *including* sick pay. Thus the worker who receives cancer treatment *will* report a payment for time not worked while his healthy coworker does not. Smeeding estimates PTW by subtracting the same insurance premium for both workers from reported WSAL. This procedure preserves an appropriate expectation but gives extremely misleading estimates of the variance of PTW. The role of sick pay in maintaining WSAL for part-year workers is obscured, while for a majority of workers who draw no sick pay PTW is understated. It is extremely difficult to anticipate how this may bias computation of the change in Gini from PTW to WSAL—among covered workers those with smaller PTW will benefit because of the inverse correlation of PTW and sick pay. However, sick leave benefits may well be concentrated among those with higher PTW, offsetting the former effect. One would clearly prefer to use WSAL rather than PTW. Precisely because fringe benefits are highly variable across workers, the presentation of measures of variance should be added to the measures' central tendency in tables 6.2–6.7. Smeeding should provide tabulations where the value of CPS household and family characteristics is fully exploited.

Need for Additional Data

Smeeding comments that if imputation does not produce useful results, a large-scale survey involving both employers and employees would be required to produce information on total compensation. Smeeding has shown that some additional knowledge can be produced by imputation. However, the value of that knowledge would be much more secure if some small-sample data collections were undertaken from an appropriately structured sample of employers and employees. To validate the present results, one could start with a representative sample of employers and collect personal characteristics from a sample of their employees. This would be a validating procedure much like that of Ferber and his collaborators (1969) in testing the validity of household reports of savings and share holdings. Any information of this kind, and some is included in the Leibowitz paper in this volume, should be used in validating the simulation results.

I conclude:

1. This is a path-breaking effort. Census, BLS, and Smeeding are to be commended.

2. Correction of the tax factor will give us an enormously useful measure of employee valuation. Further work might well be undertaken to attach discounts (Z_{ij}) to health insurance benefits received by spouses who have overlapping coverage.

3. In any replication of this effort greater attention needs to be paid to preserving variance among employers and imparting that to the household data. The technique of multiple imputations appears ready to assist in that task, and its the task of assessing changes in variance that would be associated with alternative imputation procedures.

References

Ferber, R. et al. 1969. Validation of consumer financial characteristics: Common stock. *Journal of the American Statistical Association* 64: 415–32.

Rubin, D. B. 1980. Discussion. Section on survey methods. *Proceedings of the American Statistical Association*, 426–28.

Sider, H. 1980. Work-related accidents and the production process: An empirical analysis. Ph.D. diss. University of Wisconsin-Madison. Circulated as Work-related accidents and the production process. BLS Working Paper 117, April 1981. Washington, D.C.: U.S. Bureau of Labor Statistics.

Stafford, F., and G. J. Duncan. 1980. The use of time and technology by households in the United States. In *Research in labor economics*, vol. 3, ed. R. G. Ehrenberg, 335–75. Greenwich, Conn.: JAI Press.

7 New Measures of Labor Cost: Implications for Demand Elasticities and Nominal Wage Growth

Daniel S. Hamermesh

7.1 Introduction

No single measure of labor cost is appropriate for all purposes. Surely the measure appropriate to the employee relates his take-home pay plus the probability-weighted future stream of benefits deriving from his taxes to the disutility of the hours he works. This is clearly different from the measure that a profit-maximizing employer will use in hiring decisions. While I do not claim that the measures developed here are ideal descriptions of the aggregate variable characterizing the typical employer's decisions, they seem far better than the average hourly earnings data typically used in the voluminous literature that employs measures of labor cost either as indicators of the price of labor (see Hamermesh 1976) or (still less appropriately) as indicators of workers' well-being.

In section 7.2 I develop alternative quarterly time series of labor cost and show how their time paths over the past quarter century differ from that of average hourly earnings. Section 7.3 examines the general issue of whether replacing average hourly earnings by these labor cost measures in standard labor demand models affects the estimates of the demand elasticities that are produced. These models are estimated using payroll employment data for four major industries and for the entire private

Daniel S. Hamermesh is professor of economics at Michigan State University, East Lansing, Michigan. He is also a research associate of the National Bureau of Economic Research.

This paper is based partly on research done in fulfillment of the terms of contract no. J-9-M-0-0078 from the Minimum Wage Study Commission to the National Bureau of Economic Research. All findings and conclusions are those of the author alone and do not necessarily reflect the official views of the Commission or NBER. Helpful comments and essential data were provided by Curtis Gilroy, Ed Lazear, Walter Oi, and Jack Triplett. Charles Brown provided encouragement and guidance throughout the project. Excellent research assistance was given by Paul Koch and Paul Wendt.

nonfarm sector. Finally, section 7.4 examines the extent to which the insensitivity of the growth rate of nominal wages in the United States, to which others have pointed, is real or merely an artifact based on too narrow a measure of labor cost. Though sections 7.3 and 7.4 and the discussion in the concluding section 7.5 show the value and importance of using better measures of labor cost, such demonstrations are only part of my purpose here. Equally important is the construction of the new measures of labor cost themselves. To facilitate their use by others, I present the values of these series in Appendix C of this volume.

7.2 Measures of Labor Cost

Series on average hourly earnings (see *Employment and Earnings*, any issue) are based on all regular payrolls (including paid vacations, holidays, etc., but excluding irregular payments, such as Christmas and other bonuses) and required and nonmandatory fringe benefit charges. The measure is clearly quite far from an employer's average cost of an hour of labor input into production. Even the U.S. Bureau of Labor Statistics' measure of average hourly compensation (see Antos in this volume) only includes employers' payments for fringes such as social security, workers' compensation, health, retirement, and so on. Despite opinions in the literature to the contrary (see, e.g., Sachs 1979), the distinction between hours worked and hours paid for does not enter into the compensation measure, and bonuses are excluded:

> Hours of wage and salary workers in nonagricultural establishments refer to hours paid for all employees—production workers, nonsupervisory workers, and salaried workers.
>
> Compensation per hour includes wages and salaries of employees plus employers' contributions for social insurance and private benefit plans. (*Employment and Earnings*, February 1981, p. 181)

The user cost of training, which surely must be considered as part of the average cost of labor, also does not appear in either of these measures, nor does the net (after-tax) cost of labor.[1] In this section I develop a series of increasingly complex measures of labor cost that take account of these omissions from the commonly used series on wages and compensation. These include measures of the cost of an hour of work (COSTWK); that measure adjusted for the tax treatment of labor cost (COSTTAX); cost per hour worked plus the user cost of training (ECNT); and this last measure adjusted for the tax treatment of labor cost (EC). All the calculations are presented separately for manufacturing and the private business sector (because the U.S. Chamber of Commerce data, on which many of the calculations are based, have a sufficiently large sample of firms only in manufacturing among the individual industries analyzed).[2]

I start with the first three series whose trends are presented in table 7.1—straight-time average hourly earnings (AHE) (only in manufacturing); average hourly earnings (AHE), and compensation per hour (HCOMP).[3] The values of straight-time AHE for manufacturing, and for AHE and HCOMP for both sectors, as well as those of all the series derived in the present paper, are presented in this volume's Appendix C, tables C.1 and C.2. For both manufacturing and the private business sector, I present the growth in the trend of the latter two series between 1953:I and 1978:IV, and the actual growth between 1968:IV and 1978:IV.[4] The growth of each series in table 7.1 is in real terms: The deflator for manufacturing is the producers' price index of manufactured goods, that for private business is the deflator for output from the private business sector.[5]

Not surprisingly, given the sharp increases in mandatory social insurance payments and in bargained and unilaterally granted retirement and health benefits, real hourly compensation has increased far more rapidly, both in the entire postwar period and in the last decade, than have average hourly earnings. Clearly, even the slightly more comprehensive measure, hourly compensation, may produce substantially different views of phenomena relating to labor cost.

As the first step in modifying the existing cost series, I account for the existence of irregular payments, such as bonuses and the distinction between time paid and time worked. This latter distinction accounts for clean-up time, vacations, holidays, etc., though not for on-the-job leisure. I define the cost per hour worked as:

$$\text{COSTWK} = (\text{HCOMP} + \text{OTH} * \text{AHE})/(1 - s_1),$$

where HCOMP is the BLS compensation per hour paid; OTH is the fraction of payroll in the Chamber of Commerce surveys for irregular payments to labor; and s_1 is the fraction of payroll in the surveys that goes for time not worked.[6] COSTWK inflates the sum of compensation plus bonuses per hour paid for by the ratio of hours paid for to hours worked. As table 7.1 shows, this series has increased somewhat more rapidly than even hourly compensation (almost entirely because of increases in the length of paid vacations and the number of paid holidays). The differences between the trends in the two series seem fairly constant over the twenty-six-year period 1953–78. It is worth noting, though, that while the postwar trends in manufacturing and in the entire private business sector are nearly identical, real labor cost increased far more rapidly during the 1968–78 decade in the rest of the private business sector than in manufacturing.

Like interest payments and material costs, labor cost is an expense that corporations can deduct when calculating their profits for tax purposes. As such, a lower corporate income tax rate raises the net cost of labor to

Table 7.1 **Trend Growth, 1953:I–1978:IV, and Actual Growth, 1968:IV–1978:IV, Real Labor Cost Series (in percent)**

	Manufacturing		Private Business	
Labor Cost Measure	1953:I–1978:IV	1968:IV–1978:IV	1953:I–1978:IV	1968:IV–1978:IV
Straight-time AHE	53.8	1.8	—	—
AHE	55.4	1.6	66.5	11.5
Hourly compensation (HCOMP)	80.3	5.7	81.6	17.3
Cost/hour worked (COSTWK)	92.7	8.8	93.9	20.8
Cost/hour worked adjusted for taxes (COSTTAX)	123.7	10.7	124.8	23.1
Cost/hour worked adjusted for user cost of specific training (ECNT)	91.9	9.7	98.0	22.4
Cost/hour worked adjusted for taxes and user cost of specific training (EC)	121.4	11.2	127.7	24.3

the firm. (It will change the price of labor relative to that of capital, since capital costs cannot be expensed, so long as investment tax credits and allowable depreciation rates are not changed.) Since 1953 the highest marginal corporate tax rate has been steadily lowered: It was 52 percent from 1953 to 1963, 50 percent in 1964, and 48 percent from 1965 to 1978. This reduction has raised the net cost of labor by lowering the fraction of labor cost that can be subsidized through reduced taxes. I calculate COSTTAX as one minus the marginal corporate income tax rate times COSTWK.[7] The long-term and recent trends in COSTTAX are presented in the fifth row of table 7.1; they reflect the extra fillip to net labor costs that has been induced by the steady reduction in corporate income tax rates over the years.

When an employer hires a worker, the cost of hiring and training is presumably justified by the higher productivity expected. Insofar as the training is entirely general, the worker's earnings will reflect the cost of training. However, to the extent that the training is specific, the firm will bear part of the cost of training, and any measure that does not account for this will be incomplete.[8] Such costs must be included in an expanded labor cost measure. Materials costs obviously belong; and since the time of instructors is included in the denominator of COSTWK, though it does not add to production directly, it must be subtracted out implicitly by adding it to the cost per hour of those workers actually engaged in production. Essentially, instructors' time is a fixed cost to be allocated over that part of total hours worked accounted for by persons engaged in production.

The degree of bias resulting from ignoring this problem may have changed over time, both because the amount of training relative to the value of the raw labor may have changed, and because the time horizon over which the training cost can be amortized (the expected length of the worker's stay with the firm) may have changed. While we cannot measure changes in the relative cost of training and raw labor, we can account for changes that may have occurred in the time horizon. So too, we can adjust a training cost series to account for cyclical variations that do not affect long-term calculations of training cost.

The time horizon over which the employer's share of the cost of specific training can be amortized depends on the number of hours worked per time period and the expected length of the worker's stay with the firm. This latter in turn is a function of the expected quit rate. To derive measures of the firm's expectations about hours worked, H^*, and the quit rate, Q^*, I estimate:

(1a) $$Q = a_0 + a_1 t + a_2 U,$$

and

(1b) $$H = b_0 + b_1 t + b_2 U + b_3 \text{PTTIME},$$

where Q is the aggregate quit rate (measured as the fraction quitting), H is the length of the average workweek (in manufacturing or in the entire private business sector), t is a time trend, U is the unemployment rate of males 25–54 (a cyclical indicator), PTTIME is the fraction of workers (in manufacturing or the private business sector) who work part-time, and a_i and b_i are regression coefficients to be estimated.[9] Equation (1a) is estimated using quarterly data, 1953:I–1978:IV, for manufacturing only because of the lack of good data for most of nonmanufacturing. Because the data on part-time employment are not available before 1957, equation (1b) is estimated on quarterly data for manufacturing and private business, 1957:I–1978:IV.[10] The estimates are used to derive series on Q^* and H^* that are free of cyclical variations and changes induced by the changing part-time/full-time composition of the labor force. In particular, $Q^* = Q - \hat{a}_2(U - \bar{U})$, and $H^* = H - \hat{b}_2(U - \bar{U}) - \hat{b}_3\,(\text{PTTIME} - \overline{\text{PTTIME}})$, where the superior bar denotes the sample mean and the caret denotes an estimate. Q^* and H^* are thus the adjusted quit rate and average weekly hours, respectively.

The second input into the calculation of the user cost of training is a measure of the amount of specific training embodied in the average worker. We cannot derive a time series on the user cost, but we can measure it at a specific time for use with the time-varying Q^* and H^*. I rely on the assumption that the cost of specific training is split evenly between the worker and the employer, while general training cost is borne by, and all benefits reaped by, the worker. (The former is a reasonable outcome under certain symmetry assumptions about the underlying bilateral monopoly.) I estimate $S/(S + G)$, the ratio of specific to total (specific plus general) training, as the ratio of the effect of job tenure relative to that of total experience on the wage in a sample of typical workers. Using the estimates of Mincer and Jovanovic (1981) for a representative sample of male workers in 1975 from the Michigan Panel Study of Income Dynamics, the ratio of tenure to total experience is .324 at the mean wage.[11] Under the assumption that the cost of specific training is split evenly between the employer and the worker, the employer's share of total training cost for the typical worker is $.5\ S/(S + G)$, or .162. Assume that the amount of training can be derived as the difference in earnings between the average person with no experience and the average person. (To the extent that wages of inexperienced workers are depressed because they are paying for specific training, this will overstate its true cost.) The amount of annual earnings due to training is $.162\ (W - W_0)$, where W is the average annual earnings in a sample of workers, and W_0 is the earnings of the average worker with zero experience, both from Mincer's (1974) estimates for white, nonfarm males in 1959.

Assuming further that the rate of return to specific training equals the rate of return to education, the present value of the employer's return to the specific-training investment relative to average annual earnings is:

$$\tau = [.162(W - W_0)/r_e] \cdot \frac{1}{W},$$

where r_e is the rate of return to education (also from Mincer 1974). I calculate $\tau = 1.076$. In any given year, then, the value of the employer's cost of specific training of full-time worker equivalents is (2000τ) AHE_t. To find the cost of amortizing this investment, convert adjusted weekly hours, H_t^*, to monthly hours ($4.33\ H_t^*$) and divide it into the adjusted monthly quit rate, Q_t^*, to derive the fraction of the investment expected to disappear each hour. Then the employer's cost of specific training per hour paid for is:

$$T_t = \frac{Q_t^*}{4.33H_t^*}(2000\tau)\ \text{AHE}_t.$$

The cost of specific training, T_t, is multiplied by $(1 + s_1)$ to convert it to a per hour worked basis; the result is added to COSTWK_t to derive ECNT_t. These series reflect differences between hours paid and hours worked, all nonwage payments, and the user cost of training. The method of construction also implicitly includes any turnover cost that is specific to the firm (that raises wages in the firm more than does general experience). The long-term and recent trends in these series for manufacturing and for private business are presented in the penultimate row of table 7.1. The differences in the trends between these series and COSTWK are slight. It is interesting to note that ECNT has been rising more rapidly than COSTWK in manufacturing since 1968, though it rose less rapidly until 1968.

The fifth and final measure of labor cost simply takes the measures ECNT and multiplies them by one minus the marginal corporate income tax rate to derive after-tax employment cost measures, EC, that include the user cost of specific training. The last row of table 7.1 shows the trends in these series. Since they differ little from those in COSTTAX, they do not merit special comment.

Are these new measures consistent with ones that might be constructed from other sources of data? Consider the ratios in the two rows of table 7.2. Those in the first row are based on average values calculated from Appendix C, table C.2. (The data for 1979:II are based on updates of the series made possible when the 1979 Chamber of Commerce data became available.) The ratio shows the rapid rise in fringe benefits and the ratio of hours paid to hours worked. Most remarkably, it is strikingly close to the ratio of total compensation to pay for time worked based on the Employer Expenditures on Employee Compensation (EEEC) survey (calculated from Smeeding, in this volume). Not only are the increases very similar, but the levels are within 1.5 percent of each other. This suggests that the adjustments that led from AHE to COSTWK are reasonable, and that our new series are fairly free of errors that might result from the unrepresentative nature of the Chamber of Commerce sample. Unlike

Table 7.2 Comparison of the New Series to Alternatives Based on EEEC Data, Private Business Sector: 1966, 1976, 1979

	1966	1976	1979
New series			
COSTWK/AHE	1.213	1.323	1.334
Total compensation/ pay for time worked, EEEC data	1.205	1.305	1.327

series based on the EEEC data, which began in 1966, or the BLS Employment Cost Index, which makes adjustment for time not worked but only began in the mid-1970s, ours can be constructed beginning in the early 1950s.

7.3 Estimates of Labor Demand Elasticities Based on Alternative Measures of Labor Cost

Numerous studies have attempted to estimate "the" elasticity of demand for labor. (See Hamermesh 1976 for a review of this literature and Solow 1980 for a discussion of its importance in analyzing the behavior of the macroeconomy.) We know fairly conclusively that short-run (perhaps one-year) elasticities for all labor are quite low, perhaps no greater than .3; that the lags of employment behind changes in the demand for output are short—an average length less than six months; and that the lags in response to changes in factor prices are somewhat longer—average lags between six months and one year.

All of the studies that comprise this literature are based on measures of factor payments to labor that either consist simply of average hourly earnings or include the slightly broader definition, compensation per hour paid. Assuming, as seems reasonable, that productivity per hours worked has not increased proportionally, other things equal, as hours worked have declined relative to hours paid since 1954, on a priori grounds the broader measures can be expected to produce higher estimated elasticities. But, in fact, do the estimates depend very greatly on these definitions? That is, will a broader, and presumably more appropriate, definition produce sharply different estimates of these elasticities? Do the more theoretically appropriate measures explain variations in employment demand better than the simpler measures that have been used in the literature? This section examines these questions.

I use a fairly standard model of employment demand in which changes in output demand reflect a scale effect; changes in factor prices reflect substitution along an isoquant; and a time trend reflects changes in factor productivity. The basic equation is:

$$(2) \qquad E_t = \alpha_0 + \sum_{i=1}^{N_1} \beta_i Q_{t-i+1} + \sum_{i=1}^{N_2} \gamma_i W_{t-i+1} + \delta t + \epsilon_t,$$

where E is employment demand, Q is output, W is a labor cost measure, t is time, and ϵ is a disturbance term. No current wage or output terms are included to avoid any potential simultaneity; further lagged measures of wages and output are included to reflect the finding in the literature that there is a lagged response of employment to these. They are specified in relatively free form because of the consensus that the lags in the responses to changes in output and factor prices are not identical. The lengths of the lagged responses to changes in Q and W, N_1 and N_2, will be determined by varying these and finding the lengths that fit the data best. Though some studies have included a measure of the user cost of capital, we do not include it in this section. (This follows the finding of Clark and Freeman [1980] for the United States that its inclusion has little effect on the coefficients of the other variables in equation [2], apparently because of the large amount of measurement error in the user cost of capital included in previous studies. See also Kollreuter [1980] for West Germany.)

The labor cost series measure *average*, not *marginal*, costs. Fixed costs, such as the training included in ECNT and EC, and part of the social insurance, health insurance, and pension costs included in all the series other than AHE, are spread over all hours worked. A complete labor demand model would estimate the responses of demand for persons and hours separately and allow for asymmetry in the responses of each to changes in labor cost. Thus the short-run elasticities of demand for employees, γ_1, are not correctly estimated; but the long-run elasticities, $\Sigma\gamma_i$, on which I concentrate here, are.

The data are quarterly time series, 1953:I–1978:IV. Because of the need to allow sufficient observations to measure lagged adjustments, the first data points on E used in estimating equation (2) are from 1955:I. The data cover the private nonfarm sector; in addition, separate equations are estimated for the goods-producing sectors, manufacturing, transportation and public utilities, and mining and construction. (These latter two are aggregated because the time series on output was only available for this aggregate.) The employment measure in each case is payroll employment from the monthly BLS-790 data, averaged to produce a quarterly series.[12] Output is gross domestic product originating in the sector, and, except for manufacturing, this and the labor cost series are deflated by the implicit deflator for gross domestic product in the sector. (In manufacturing, I use the producers' price index for manufactured goods.) For each sector the estimates of equation (2) are produced separately for each of four labor cost series discussed in section 7.2: AHE_i, COSTWK_i, COSTTAX_i, and ECNT_i.[13] The latter three measures are in each case based on the average hourly earnings in the particular sector under study.[14]

Equation (2) is estimated using polynomial distributed lags to produce the coefficient estimates β_i and γ_i. Quadratics were used in all cases, and N_1 and N_2 were set equal to 4 and 8 alternatively.[15] Since in all cases I find that the shorter lag structure performed better than the longer, the results are presented for $N_1 = N_2 = 4$. The equations are estimated, adjusting for possible autocorrelation in the error structure of equation (2), using the Cochrane-Orcutt iterative technique.

The results of estimating (2) for the total private nonfarm sector, and for the three smaller aggregates separately, are presented in tables 7.3 through 7.6. Let us consider first the peripheral issues before concentrating on the two questions raised earlier in this section that provide the rationale for examining these results. I find in all cases that there is, as is usual in time-series studies of employment demand, substantial autocorrelation in the residuals *even when* a time trend is included. This suggests that those studies (the majority) that have failed to adjust for this problem have likely produced inefficient estimates of wage and output elasticities of employment demand. I also find, somewhat disturbingly, that there is no significant negative time trend in employment demand, ceteris paribus, in transportation and public utilities, and in the entire private nonfarm sector. Since I would expect labor-saving technical progress to have occurred in these sectors, and to see it reflected in a negative trend term, this result is disturbing. Perhaps, though, previous authors' findings

Table 7.3 **Payroll Employment, Private Nonfarm, 1955:I–1978:IV, with Different Labor Cost Series**

	Cost Measure			
	AHE	COSTWK	COSTTAX	ECNT
Time	−.00021 (−.27)	.00090 (.89)	.00054 (.57)	−.00099 (−1.33)
Output (sum of four lag terms)	.902 (15.35)	.905 (15.58)	.902 (15.53)	.852 (4.26)
Labor cost (sum of four lag terms)	−.400 (−2.50)	−.472 (−2.78)	−.336 (−2.69)	−.034 (−.45)
$\hat{\rho}$	.970 (39.21)	.970 (39.10)	.968 (37.90)	.972 (40.14)
$\hat{\sigma}_\epsilon$	.003993	.003990	.004016	.004084

Note: The numbers in parentheses here and in tables 7.4–7.6 are *t* statistics.

Table 7.4 **Payroll Employment, Manufacturing, 1955:I–1978:IV, with Different Labor Cost Series**

	Cost Measure			
	AHE	COSTWK	COSTTAX	ECNT
Time	−.00544	−.00453	−.00447	−.00550
	(−10.81)	(−7.82)	(−7.45)	(−7.31)
Output (sum of four lag terms)	.958	.938	.948	.920
	(14.84)	(17.83)	(18.18)	(16.32)
Labor cost (sum of four lag terms)	−.230	−.288	−.253	.008
	(−2.34)	(−3.27)	(−3.24)	(.08)
$\hat{\rho}$	.908	.891	.888	.956
	(21.14)	(19.10)	(18.81)	(31.57)
$\hat{\sigma}_\epsilon$	.006854	.006704	.006717	.006897

on this (see the survey in Hamermesh 1976) have been clouded by their failure to account carefully for serial correlation in the residuals.

Consider which of the labor cost measures produces the lowest standard error of estimate in the aggregate of the private nonfarm sector and in the three separate subaggregates. We see from table 7.3 that in the aggregate COSTWK gives the best fit, as it does in manufacturing.

Table 7.5 **Payroll Employment, Transportation and Public Utilities, 1955:I–1978:IV, with Different Labor Cost Series**

	Cost Measure			
	AHE	COSTWK	COSTTAX	ECNT
Time	.0025	.00090	.00080	−.0002
	(.22)	(.73)	(.61)	(−.02)
Output (sum of four lag terms)	.599	.598	.568	.497
	(6.24)	(6.54)	(6.28)	(5.88)
Labor cost (sum of four lag terms)	−.350	−.346	−.254	−.092
	(−1.78)	(−1.93)	(−1.57)	(−.85)
$\hat{\rho}$	.970	.970	.969	.971
	(38.82)	(38.56)	(38.52)	(39.36)
$\hat{\sigma}_\epsilon$	.007013	.00695	.007069	.006881

Table 7.6 Payroll Employment, Mining and Construction, 1955:I–1978:IV, with Different Labor Cost Series

	Cost Measure			
	AHE	COSTWK	COSTTAX	ECNT
Time	.00288	−.00244	−.00146	−.00334
	(−1.47)	(−1.10)	(−.66)	(−2.05)
Output (sum of four lag terms)	.954	.949	.982	.925
	(10.17)	(10.22)	(10.60)	(9.84)
Labor cost (sum of four lag terms)	−.219	−.218	−.355	−.081
	(−.80)	(−.90)	(−1.59)	(−.56)
$\hat{\rho}$	.975	.973	.975	.969
	(43.03)	(44.03)	(42.96)	(38.44)
$\hat{\sigma}_\epsilon$	.008954	.008962	.008762	.009149

COSTTAX produces the best fit in mining and construction, while ECNT gives the best results in transportation and public utilities. The differences in the fits across the equations using the different series are not great; nonetheless, it is apparent that, at the least, there are gains to basing the compensation measure on hours actually worked rather than on hours paid for to describe employers' labor demand.[16] While various of the labor cost measures perform best in the various sectors, in each case the measure that does best is based on hours worked. This suggests that the literature on labor demand, based as it is on measures of earnings or compensation per hour paid for, has problems.

If we view the incomplete measure of labor cost, AHE, as embodying an error of measurement, we should expect previous work to have underestimated the true elasticity. In fact, in the samples used here I find that, with the exception of transportation and public utilities (in which the wage terms are not significantly different from zero), using better measures of labor cost increases the absolute values of the wage elasticities. For example, in the private nonfarm sector the elasticity increases from .40 in the equation using AHE to .47 in the equation that gives the best fit, that using COSTWK. Similarly, in manufacturing the estimated elasticity increases from .23 to .29; in mining and construction the estimate goes from .22 to .36 in the best-fit equation, that based on COSTTAX. Though the differences are less than one standard error in all cases, it appears reasonable to conclude that labor-demand elasticities produced in previous time series studies are underestimates because of the failure to include a sufficiently comprehensive measure of labor cost.

Basing the equations on better measures of labor cost also affects the estimated trend terms and the employment-output elasticities. In the latter case, the effects are very minor. For example, in the private nonfarm sector and in mining and construction there is a tiny increase, while in manufacturing and transportation and public utilities there is a decrease. The time trend becomes more positive, except in transportation and public utilities, when the better labor cost measures are included; in manufacturing, though, the only industry in which this trend was significant, it remains negative.

Perhaps the best conclusion from this evidence is that there is some payoff to greater attention to the variables used to reflect labor cost in studies of employment demand. A more careful specification slightly improves the ability to track variations in employment, and it increases the estimated responses of employment demand to exogenous changes in labor cost. One would suppose in complete systems of factor demand equations, where incorrect data series might interact with powerful estimators to produce greater errors, that an even larger payoff would exist. This payoff is evident in the estimation of a system of equations for adult and teen labor in Hamermesh (1982).

7.4 Does Nominal Labor Cost in the United States Respond to Short-Term Price Variations?

Several authors (Sachs 1979; Grubb, Jackman, and Layard, 1982) have pointed to the apparent nonresponsiveness of nominal changes in labor cost in the United States as the rate of price inflation varies. Both narrowly define labor cost (the former, private nonfarm compensation per hour paid for, the latter, manufacturing average hourly earnings). It is claimed that this apparent rigidity in the growth rate of nominal wages has enabled the United States to maintain real wage flexibility when exogenous price shocks occur and thus to avoid the sharp increases in unemployment that plagued other Western nations in the mid- and late 1970s. Is this observation correct, though, or is it merely an artifact produced by defining labor cost too narrowly?

We can write the true cost per hour worked, C_t, as:

$$C_t = W_t(1 + M_t), \tag{3}$$

where W_t is a more narrowly defined measure of labor cost (wages or compensation per hour paid for), and M_t is the percentage by which true cost per hour of labor input differs at time t from the narrower measure. Taking logarithms and differentiating with respect to time:

$$\dot{c}_t \cong \dot{w}_t + \dot{m}_t, \tag{4}$$

where lowercase letters denote logs, and the dot denotes the time derivative. For the pattern of true labor cost to vary more closely with short-term price fluctuations than do earnings, the markup over earnings must itself change over time with the rate of price inflation. Is this likely to occur? Remembering that C and W differ by hours of paid leisure and (mostly untaxed) health, pension, and other contributions, a tentative affirmative answer seems reasonable. Given the nature of the U.S. tax structure in the 1970s, more rapid price inflation raised the marginal tax rate facing the average worker, thus lowering the price of nonwage elements of compensation. It has been shown that workers do react to the tax price of different components of compensation (Woodbury 1983); that being the case, we should not be surprised to see that $\dot{c}$ varies more closely with price changes than does the narrower $\dot{w}$.

Annual percentage changes in five labor cost series are presented in table 7.7 along with their coefficients of variation and changes in the CPI for the period beginning with the oil shock. Especially in manufacturing, AHE and HCOMP are far less variable than are the broader measures I have derived, as simple inspection of their values for 1975–78 and consideration of the standard deviation of these four values shows. More important, the broader measures seem to vary with changes in the CPI during this period substantially more closely than do hourly earnings or compensation per hour paid in manufacturing. In the entire private business sector even AHE and HCOMP do show some signs of varying with the CPI during the mid-1970s; however, their variability is less, and apparently less closely related to that of the CPI, than is the variation in the broader labor cost measures I have derived.

Additional light on the relation between $\dot{m}$ and inflation is shown by estimates of:

$$(5) \qquad \mathrm{CO\dot{S}TWK}_t - \mathrm{A\dot{H}E}_t = a + b\ \mathrm{C\dot{P}I}_t,\ t = 1973, \ldots, 1979.$$

For manufacturing, $\hat{b}$ from equation (5) is .28 ($t = 1.40$); for the private business sector it is .04 ($t = .47$). This provides some confirmation, though, perhaps because of the size of the postshock sample, hardly overwhelming evidence, of a positive relation between inflation and the divergence between growth in labor cost per hour and average hourly earnings.

My purpose here has not been to demonstrate that the coefficient on labor market slack, in an equation relating changes in labor cost to expected price changes and the extent of slack, increases when one defines labor cost more broadly (though I think that is the case). Rather, it has been the narrower one of pointing out the pitfalls of basing one's view of macroeconomic adjustment on inappropriate measures of labor cost. The rate of change of nominal labor cost may have been less responsive to price inflation in the United States than in other countries in

Table 7.7 **Percent Changes in Nominal Labor Cost Series and Consumer Prices (fourth quarter to fourth quarter), 1972–1980, and Their Coefficients of Variation**

	Manufacturing					Private Business					
Year	AHE	HCOMP	COSTWK	ECNT	EC	AHE	HCOMP	COSTWK	ECNT	EC	CPI (lagged one year)
1972–73	8.2	8.0	8.2	9.5	10.9	7.1	8.3	8.6	10.1	10.1	3.5
1973–74	10.1	12.7	14.0	10.5	11.5	10.1	10.7	11.3	7.6	8.3	8.4
1974–75	7.5	9.0	9.8	11.6	11.9	8.0	8.6	9.0	11.6	11.6	12.1
1975–76	8.4	9.0	8.6	7.8	7.5	8.0	8.7	8.5	7.5	7.5	7.2
1976–77	8.9	9.1	7.7	6.9	6.7	7.1	7.3	7.2	6.3	6.3	4.8
1977–78	9.0	8.7	8.6	9.3	9.2	9.2	9.0	9.2	9.7	9.6	6.7
1978–79	8.3	9.2	9.1	—	—	8.1	8.9	8.7	—	—	9.0
1979–80	10.6	12.1	12.7	—	—	10.1	10.5	10.7	—	—	12.7
Coefficient of variation:											
1972–78	.101	.177	.243	.185	.226	.143	.126	.149	.226	.215	
1972–80	.116	.175	.232	—	—	.142	.124	.142	—	—	

the 1970s, but its variability was greater than is indicated by commonly used measures of the demand price of labor.

7.5 Conclusions and Other Uses

There is no perfect measure of labor cost, but in this study I have presented calculations leading to the construction of easily usable alternative measures beyond the published ones on average hourly earnings and hourly compensation. These new series account for deviations of hours paid for from hours worked, for the tax treatment of wages under the corporate income tax, and for variations in the user cost of training. When used in place of the published series in regression equations describing the demand for labor in the United States, they generally produce slightly better fits and somewhat higher wage elasticities. This is to be expected insofar as they purge the published series of additive errors of measurement. The new series also provide a somewhat different view of the recent path of wage inflation in the United States, suggesting that nominal wage growth has been more responsive to variations in price inflation than the published labor cost series indicate.

I have not given the potential user of these series any guide about which one is in any sense the "best" to use for various purposes; in fact, no such guide is possible. However, the results on labor demand and a consideration of the concept of the employer's cost of labor suggest at the very least that a series that adjusts for the hours paid/hours worked distinction is required. Thus the series COSTWK, which adjusts hourly compensation and average hourly earnings to account for this distinction, would seem a good choice for use in any research requiring a measure of the demand price of labor. It has the additional virtue of being easy to update from readily available information using very simple techniques, as I have done in Appendix C of this volume for 1979 and 1980, and it is much "cleaner" than the more complex series I have constructed.

There are both substantial scope and need for using these new series or refined versions of them in other empirical work in labor economics. I have shown that they add to our ability to understand empirical aspects of labor demand. Though their effects in the simple equations I have presented are not major, they may well be far greater in the very closely specified equations (see Sargent 1978) that have used only the average earnings per hour paid for. Similarly, studies of the behavior of layoffs in the aggregate (e.g., Brechling 1981), which are important for analyzing the impact of unemployment insurance, for testing the theory of implicit contracts, and for examining unions' effects on the employment relation, should be based on these newer series rather than the earnings or compensation measures now used. Some of the complicated testing of recent theoretical results in macroeconomics, for example, tests of disequilibrium in aggregated markets (Rosen and Quandt 1978) or of the intertemporal substitution hypothesis (Altonji and Ashenfelter 1980), would be better examined using the new series derived here. Finally, though the conventional wisdom in the hoary debate of the cyclical behavior of real wages is that they are procyclical (Tobin 1980), not supported by the most recent empirical work (Chirinko 1980), the issue has not been examined using proper measures of the price per hour worked. In all these cases, then, there is a need for basing empirical work on a measure of labor cost more closely related to the concept being examined than are the average earnings or compensation measures that have been used. Though the trends in our series do not differ that greatly from those in the standard series, even slight differences are likely to have major impacts on estimates from tightly fitting time-series equations.

The measures are not true reflections of the price of an efficiency unit of labor, as they have not made two corrections. First, they do not account for changes in the composition of hours within industry aggregates because of changes in the occupational mix of employment. (This is done by the new Employment Cost Index series produced by the Bureau of Labor Statistics.) Second, they do not adjust for cyclical and secular changes in labor quality (nor does any other series). Thus, though representing an improvement over what is available, they must be viewed as a step on the road between the series now available and the ideal series.

Notes

1. Chinloy (1980) includes some fringe benefits, such as employer contributions for social insurance, in his calculation of labor cost, but ignores the distinction between hours paid and hours worked.

2. The source for these series is U.S. Chamber of Commerce, *Employee Benefits*, a biennial survey through 1977 that has been conducted annually since then. Though sample sizes were smaller in the early years of the survey, in 1978 the data are based on 497 manufacturing firms and 361 nonmanufacturing companies. These surveys clearly overrepresent large firms (though decreasingly so), for firms with fewer than one hundred employees are excluded. Since larger firms do offer higher fringe benefits relative to wages, the levels of the measures I produce are biased up from what a representative sample would produce. There is, though, no reason to expect their growth rates to be biased up for this reason, and the discussion below suggests this is the case.

3. Straight-time AHE and AHE are monthly published BLS data gleaned from the CITIBASE data file. These data were averaged to provide quarterly series for use in this study. Unpublished data on compensation per hour of employees were provided to me by Randy Norsworthy of the Bureau of Labor Statistics. Antos (this volume) describes all these series in greater detail.

4. These trends are derived from a bivariate regression of the logarithm of the labor cost series on a time trend.

5. The deflator and the producers' price index for manufacturing are taken from the CITIBASE data file. The latter series was averaged to put it on a quarterly basis.

6. Because the Chamber of Commerce data are available only biennially, I interpolated linearly between observations in this series, treating each observation as having been made in the middle of the calendar year to which the survey is attributed. (Thus I assume implicitly that the surveys were taken on July 1 of the years in question.)

7. I recognize that not all employers in the private business sector are incorporated; that not all corporations pay the highest marginal tax rate; and Lazear's point that the average tax rate may be more appropriate than the marginal for some purposes. Nonetheless, many of the largest employers do pay the highest rate; marginal rates paid by others are correlated with the top marginal rates; and average rates are likely to be correlated over time with marginal rates. I therefore base the COSTTAX series on the highest marginal corporate income tax rate payable in the calendar year. In doing so I also ignore any issue of tax incidence.

8. This distinction and the conclusions about the burdens of the cost of training of different types stem from Becker (1964).

9. Data on the number of voluntary part-time workers are from BLS, *Handbook of Labor Statistics*, Bulletin 2000, and *Employment and Earnings*, January 1979.

10. For manufacturing, the parameter estimates are: $a_0 = .0294$; $a_1 = .000047$; $a_2 = -.0037$; $b_0 = 43.59$; $b_1 = .028$; $b_2 = -.40$; $b_3 = -1.46$. The coefficients of determination for the two equations are .753 and .615. The equations were estimated by ordinary least squares. For the private business sector, the estimates are: $b_0 = 44.58$; $b_1 = -.0067$; $b_2 = -.21$; $b_3 = -.31$. The R^2 for this equation was .956.

11. W is calculated from Mincer's regression (1974, p. 92) as \$5636 and W_0 as \$1633. The implied rate of return to education is .107. In regressions from the National Longitudinal Survey (NLS) adult women's sample in Mincer and Jovanovic (1981), $S/(S + G)$ is .349, while in similar regressions for older males in the National Longitudinal Survey sample in 1973 the same calculation yields .638. I use the Michigan estimates because they are the only ones that are representative of the entire population of adult male workers.

12. Equations like (2) were estimated for man-hours also. The results in manufacturing were similar to those found for employment: The series based on AHE never fit as well as other series, and the wage elasticities produced with the more complex series were higher. For the private business sector the results were remarkably insensitive to the specification of the labor cost variables.

13. Since the equations using HCOMP or EC never produced a lower $\hat{\sigma}_\epsilon$ than those listed in the tables, and since I include equations based on AHE for comparison purposes, I do not present the equations using these two measures.

14. The inclusion of AHE_i, COSTWK_i, and ECNT_i is straightforward (though the calculation of ECNT_i for the nonmanufacturing sector requires that T_t be deflated by the ratio of the sector's AHE_t to manufacturing AHE_t).

15. Choosing the appropriate N reduces to finding the best fit, since the degrees of freedom in the regression are the same (dependent on the degree of the polynomial used) for any N.

16. The importance of the distinction between hours paid and hours worked has been stressed in the context of measuring cyclical changes in labor productivity by Fair (1969).

References

Altonji, Joseph, and Orley Ashenfelter. 1980. Wage movements and the labor market equilibrium hypothesis. *Economica* 47: 217–46.

Becker, Gary. 1964. *Human capital*. Princeton, N.J.: Princeton University Press.

Brechling, Frank. 1981. Layoffs and unemployment insurance. In *Studies in labor markets*, ed. Sherwin Rosen. Chicago: University of Chicago Press.

Chinloy, Peter. 1980. Sources of quality change in labor input. *American Economic Review* 70: 108–19.

Chirinko, Robert. 1980. The real wage rate over the business cycle. *Review of Economics and Statistics* 62: 459–61.

Clark, Kim, and Richard Freeman. 1980. How elastic is the demand for labor? *Review of Economics and Statistics* 62: 509–21.

Fair, Ray. 1969. *The short-run demand for workers and hours*. Amsterdam: North-Holland Press.

Grubb, David, Richard Jackman, and Richard Layard. 1982. Causes of the current stagflation. *Review of Economic Studies* 49: 707–30.

Hamermesh, Daniel 1976. Econometric studies of labor demand and their application to policy analysis. *Journal of Human Resources* 11: 507–25.

———. 1982. Minimum wages and the demand for labor. *Economic Inquiry* 20: 365–80.

Kollreuter, Christoph. 1980. Recent and prospective trends of the demand for labour in the FRG. In *Unemployment in Western countries*, ed. Edmond Malinvaud and Jean-Paul Fitoussi. London: St. Martin's Press.

Mincer, Jacob. 1974. *Schooling, experience, and earnings*. New York: Columbia University Press.

Mincer, Jacob, and Boyan Jovanovic. 1981. Labor mobility and wages. In *Studies in labor markets*, ed. Sherwin Rosen. Chicago: University of Chicago Press.

Rosen, Harvey, and Richard Quandt. 1978. Estimation of a disequilibrium aggregate labor market. *Review of Economics and Statistics* 60: 371–79.

Sachs, Jeffrey. 1979. Wages, profits, and macroeconomic adjustment. *Brookings Papers on Economic Activity* 10: 269–312.

Sargent, Thomas. 1978. Estimation of dynamic labor demand schedules under rational expectations. *Journal of Political Economy* 86:1009–44.

Solow, Robert. 1980. On theories of unemployment. *American Economic Review* 70: 1–11.

Tobin, James. 1980. *Asset accumulation and economic activity*. Chicago: University of Chicago Press.

Woodbury, Stephen. 1983. Substitution between wage and nonwage benefits. *American Economic Review* 73: 166–82.

Comment Edward P. Lazear

Hamermesh must be complimented on his examination of various definitions of labor cost and the way in which altering the definitions affects estimates based on them. It must be true that too little attention is paid to the construction of the variables on which we base our analyses and any attempt to investigate their validity should be applauded. Further, the issues on which Hamermesh focuses are important and difficult ones. That having been said, this reader remains unwilling to reject the more standard measures of labor cost in favor of those proposed by Hamermesh, despite the paper's claims of the new measures' superiority.

My apprehension is over two types of issues. First, I am not as convinced as the author that the new measures perform better even in the tests that he conducts. Second, I believe that some of the conceptual underpinnings of new measures are defective. Before discussing some of the more subtle theoretical issues, let us simply reexamine the results.

Hamermesh demonstrates the importance of the new measures by employing them in one of the most important applications of labor cost data—namely, estimating the elasticity of labor demand. I wholeheartedly support this approach to validating the new measures, but conclude that those tests suggest, at best, that new measures make no difference and at worst, that they simply add measurement error.

The relevant comparisons are derived from tables 7.3–7.6. First, the author suggests that the criterion to be used for comparison is the standard error of the estimate. By this criterion, the best measure is COSTWK, if we rely on the aggregate private nonfarm data (table 7.3). However, the traditional measure, AHE, is a very close second, and the two other new measures, COSTTAX and ECNT, are considerably poorer performers. The picture is more complicated if we look at the disaggregated estimates contained in tables 7.3–7.6. For mining and construction, the best measure by this criterion is the traditional AHE. The worst is ENCT with COSTWK third. For transportation and public utilities, the best is ECNT with COSTTAX performing worst. For manufacturing, the best is COSTWK with ECNT performing worst. To this reader, this is a pattern which effectively defies conclusion.

The point is even clearer if another criterion, namely examination of the actual labor cost coefficient, is adopted. The author points out that the absolute value of the coefficient is larger in the COSTWK equation than in the AHE equation (see table 7.2). But this difference, which is the largest one in the "right" direction in any table, amounts to less than one-half the standard error of any one coefficient. Further, there is hardly

Edward P. Lazear is professor of industrial relations, Graduate School of Business, University of Chicago, and a research associate with the National Bureau of Economic Research.

a consistent pattern of any definition's dominance over another in magnitude of the estimated coefficient. There is one exception to this: The coefficient on ECNT is as close to zero in all samples as one can imagine. This reflects the fact that it is almost pure noise as a measure of labor cost. Below, I will provide some theoretical reasons why this might be so.

The second source of apprehension stems from the lack of a coherent statement of what comprises a conceptually appropriate measure of labor cost. Measurement problems aside, it is important to know what one is looking for so that we can recognize its discovery. This does not negate that the appropriateness of a measure may well depend on the use to which it is applied. But the failure to be more specific about what one wants to find causes confusion. Consider an example:

The most creative measure that Hamermesh derives is ECNT, which takes into account the employer cost of specific human capital. Although I believe that there are some technical mistakes in its construction, let us for now assume that it measures exactly what it purports. My contention is that for most purposes, including the estimation of demand elasticities, it is inappropriate to take that cost into account.

Specific human capital makes the worker more productive when he is at the firm in question. So does the machine with which he works. Yet one would never argue that the amortized cost of the machine should be included into the cost of labor. But, one might argue, the machine is different because its cost is explicitly measured elsewhere whereas the cost of providing specific human capital is not. Yet even this is not correct. Specific human capital must be produced with other inputs currently at the firm. Consider the extreme case where the production of specific human capital requires only labor, e.g., a senior worker teaches a junior worker. The cost of this labor has already been taken into account in the reported earnings of the teacher. Accounting for the cost of specific human capital and the teacher's earnings counts cost twice without counting the output of the human capital. Thus, a firm which engages in a significant amount of training of junior workers would show up as a low productivity firm, not only because the output of human capital is not counted, but also because labor cost has been double counted.

Another example is useful. The author bemoans the fact that we are unable to take labor quality into account. At the same time, he argues that ignoring bonuses leads to an understatement of labor cost. But if it is labor per unit of quality that we are interested in, we might do better to ignore bonuses. For example, suppose that labor qualities are perfect substitutes in production. Then a worker who is worth one more dollar earns one more dollar. The bonus may reflect the premium paid to higher quality workers. We surely would not want to argue that workers who receive bonuses are necessarily more costly in efficiency units than those who do not. Yet accounting for bonuses without also adjusting for quality would lead us to this conclusion. In the context of estimating demand elasticities, an increase in the use of high quality workers who receive larger bonuses increases the "cost of labor" when bonuses are included in that cost measure. But the corresponding adjustment in the number of workers employed does not reflect a movement up the labor demand curve. Under these circumstances, we might do better to ignore bonuses altogether.

This discussion should not be interpreted to imply that corrections for specific human capital or bonuses should not be made. Rather, the intention is to point out how important it is to specify more concretely the definition of the conceptually appropriate measure before new measures can be constructed and evaluated.

In closing I wish to reiterate that, although I was not as convinced that this paper conclusively demonstrates the superiority of new measures of labor cost as the author, I share the author's enthusiasm for the issue. I also believe that this paper takes an important step toward a better understanding of labor cost, its uses and misuses.

8 Intermetropolitan Wage Differentials in the United States

George E. Johnson

8.1 Introduction

The purpose of this paper is to investigate the nature and causes of wage differentials between large metropolitan areas in the United States. Most of the recent literature on this subject has concerned the question of whether or not wages in the southern United States are lower than elsewhere.[1] The current consensus is that, although there is a wide disparity in *nominal* wage levels between the South and elsewhere, there is virtually no difference in *real* wage levels. The results in the present paper do not contradict this conclusion; indeed, real wage levels in Atlanta, Dallas, and Houston are estimated to be slightly higher in 1973–76 than wages in comparable cities in the North.

There is, however, considerable variation in wage rates in large metropolitan areas throughout the United States. For example, the estimated nominal wage of a private sector, nonunion, white, full-time male paid by the hour is 10 percent less in Boston than in Detroit (the real wage is 23 percent less). My purpose is to sort out why these differences exist. Are they best explained as a disequilibrium phenomenon, as the result of regional differences in the extent and nature of unionism, or as compensating differentials to reflect differences in the nonpecuniary attributes of areas?

The first task of the study is to estimate the "area effects" on nominal wages for four different types of workers (full-time male and female, hourly and salaried) from the May Current Population Survey data for 1973–76. These estimated area effects, which control for the standard human capital variables, race, unionism, and public sector employment,

George E. Johnson is with the Department of Economics, University of Michigan, Ann Arbor, and the National Bureau of Economic Research.

are then converted into real area effects by subtracting the logarithm of the price level for each area from the nominal area effect. For women the dispersion of area real wage levels across regions is smaller than the dispersion of nominal wages, but for men it is greater. There is, in addition, a positive correlation between both the nominal and real area effects for the four groups of workers. In other words, whatever set of factors makes wages high or low in a particular city for one group of workers also makes them high or low for other groups of workers.

There is some rather weak evidence that the size of the real nonunion area effect is negatively related to the extent of unionization in the area. This is consistent with the standard hypothesis that individuals will accept nonunion jobs in an area with a high degree of unionization at a lower wage than they would accept nonunion jobs in an area with a low degree of unionization. The reason for this is that their long-run income prospects may be better if they reside in an area with a greater probability of eventual attainment of a high-rent job. This runs counter to two hypotheses, which are reviewed in section 8.2, that predict that a large union sector will cause high union wages to "spill over" to the nonunion sector. The evidence on the distribution of real *nonunion* area effects is not encouraging to either of these hypotheses.

8.2 Conceptual Issues

Suppose we observe that nominal wage levels, after adjusting for human capital, in different areas across the United States are subject to substantial variation. To what could this phenomenon be attributed? Since, as will be shown subsequently, interarea wage levels *are* subject to variation that is both large and persistent, it is useful at the outset to state the various hypotheses that might explain it: (a) Wage differences represent a *compensating variation* to offset differences in price levels, nonpecuniary attributes, or both, and (b) wage differences are caused by *institutional rigidities*, primarily by differences in the nature and extent of unionism across areas.

8.2.1 Compensating Variation

If there are no differences in the assessments by individuals of the nonpecuniary attributes associated with residence in different areas, as well as no institutional impediments to the adjustment of relative wages, we would expect the "real" wage in all areas to be equal. In its most straightforward terms, this implies that

$$\frac{w_i}{w_j} = \frac{p_i}{p_j}, \tag{1}$$

where the w's are nominal wage levels and the p's are price levels for areas i and j. If, for example, we observed that the nominal wage in area i

were greater than that level that satisfies equation (1), we would expect that there would be migration into the area sufficient to drive w_i/p_i down to the nationwide value of the real wage rate $(w/p_i)*$.[2] Thus, by this simple specification, the long-run supply curve to an area is perfectly elastic at the $(w/p)*$. It is, therefore, a labor supply condition rather than a conventional particular supply curve.

In fact, the effect of price variation across areas on the equilibrium regional wage structure is slightly more complicated than this. The preceding discussion implies that, other things equal, a 1 percent increase in the cost of living in an area will increase the equilibrium wage in that area by 1 percent. This may not be true for two reasons: First, the nature of the tax and transfer system, and second, people have the option of retiring in areas with low price levels.

To take a simple case, assume that the utility of each person is a function of consumption during his working life (c_1) and during retirement (c_2) and that the utility function is Cobb-Douglas, i.e.,

$$U = \alpha \log c_1 + (1 - \alpha) \log c_2 . \tag{2}$$

Second, assume that federal income taxes may be approximated by a linear function, $t_f(w_i - X)$, where t_f is the marginal federal tax rate, w_i the gross earnings the individual earns in area i during his working life, and X the constant tax deduction (cumulated over his working life). In addition, the individual pays a proportional local income tax, $t_i w_i$, which is not deductible from his federal tax base. Finally, upon his retirement the individual receives a social security payment of S from the government, which is assumed to be independent of w_i. If the individual chooses to remain in area i during the years of his retirement, his lifetime budget constraint is

$$\begin{aligned} O &= [w_i(1 - t_f - t_i) + t_f X - p_i c_i] + \left(\frac{1}{1+z}\right)(S - p_i c_2) \\ &= V_i + V_T - p_i c_1 - \frac{p_i}{1+z} c_2 , \end{aligned} \tag{3}$$

where z is the interest rate (net of taxation, which is assumed to be solely federal), and p_i is the price level in the area (including local sales and property taxes). $V_i = w_i(1 - t_f - t_i)$ is the present value of net labor earnings (evaluated at the marginal rather than the average federal tax rate), and V_T is the present value of the income tax deduction and the social security payment.

Maximization of equation (2) with respect to c_1 and c_2 subject to equation (3) yields a utility-maximizing path of consumption over the life cycle. Plugging these values back into the utility function yields the utility associated with location in area i, and this depends on w_i and p_i as well as the various tax and transfer parameters. Labor supply equilibrium requires that the lifetime utility associated with all areas be equal. Of particular interest for present purposes is the effect of changes in the two parameters subject to interarea variation, p_i and t_i, on the eqilibrium area wage level. This can be shown to be

$$(4) \qquad d(\log w_i) = \frac{V_i + V_T}{V_i} d(\log p_i) + \frac{dt_i}{1 - t_f - t_i}.$$

The coefficient on $d(\log p_i)$ is *greater* than one if the tax system is progressive ($X>0$) or if there is a social security system (and the tax system not too regressive). The reason for this is that higher values of X and S diminish the relative importance of labor earnings in lifetime net income, thus requiring greater variation in w_i to compensate for a given variation in p_i. Variation in local (proportional) income taxes, however, have the same effect on w_i as one would expect on the basis of the equalization of after-tax wage rates.

The second complication arises from the fact that an individual may move from area i to area j (where $p_i > p_j$). Moving costs, which are incurred in period 2, are M, so for a person who does move the budget constraint becomes

$$(5) \qquad O = V_i + V_T - \frac{M}{1+z} - p_i c_i - \frac{p_j}{1+z} c_2.$$

Repeating the procedure followed above, the effect of variations in p_i on the equilibrium value of w_i is equal to ($\partial[\log w_i])/\partial t_i$ is the same as in equation [4])

$$(6) \qquad \frac{(\log w_i)}{(\log p_i)} = \alpha \left(\frac{V_i + V_T - \dfrac{M}{1+z}}{V_i} \right).$$

This may be greater or equal to one. If V_T and M were zero, it would simply equal the share of first-period consumption in the utility function, which is less than one. The more important transfers are and the more progressive the tax system is, the larger the effect of variations in area price levels is on the variation in area nominal wage levels.

A second source of variation in area real wage levels arises from the possibility that individuals may receive utility from specific nonpecuniary attributes of different areas. If, say, the San Francisco area is considered (over the relevant range) to be y more desirable in terms of climate, physical beauty, public services (net of taxes), and the like than the averge area in the country, then the equilibrium real wage in San Francisco would be $1 - y$ of the average real wage for all areas. The resultant supply curve would be horizontal at a lower real wage than that for the typical area (certainly lower than that of Buffalo). Compensation variations due to nonpecuniary attributes are subject to the modification arising from the possibility of locational change upon retirement that was discussed above with respect to price level differences. This merely implies that nonpecuniary differences are less important than if people never moved.

Another variant of the nonpecuniary model stresses that individuals have different tastes for different areas. For example, some individuals abhor climatic variation (and hence would sacrifice real income to live in San Diego) while others enjoy the "change of seasons" (and would, other things equal, prefer to live in Buffalo). This specification yields an upward-sloping equilibrium supply curve for each area that is the more elastic the less individuals' assessments of the nonpecuniary attributes of different areas vary. The general model makes no prediction about the eqilibrium wage structure—if real wages are high in area i, it is not viewed as an attractive area. The general specification, however, predicts that, given stability over time in the distribution of preferences, increases in the relative employment of an area, which arise due to relative shifts in the demand functions, will be associated with increases in relative wages. Both of the other specifications—nonpecuniary attributes are (a) not important or (b) evaluated identically by everyone—predict that there will be no relation between changes in relative wages and employment.

8.2.2 Institutional Rigidities

A second set of reasons why nominal and real wage levels may vary across areas is the failure of markets to adjust because of institutional rigidities. The primary candidate for such a rigidity is, of course, trade unionism—although the federal government and some local governments have wage structures that are a similar source of rigidity.[3]

Now if some areas were 100 percent unionized and unions were able to obtain a wage premium for their members, we would expect that the real wages of all the nonunion areas would be equal and the real wages of each union area to vary with the bargaining strength and success of the particular unions in that area. Labor mobility in this case would equilibrate the expected incomes (or utility) of each unionized area with that of the nonunion areas, and the equilibrating variable would be the unemployment rate in each unionized area.[4]

In fact, no areas are 100 percent unionized; there is not even a major metropolitan areas of the United States in which a majority of the labor force is unionized. Some areas (especially in the New York to Chicago industrial belt) are relatively heavily (25–45 percent) unionized, while other areas (especially in the South and Southwest) have very little unionization (10–15 percent). In this situation of *partial* unionization, we can observe equilibration through wage adjustment.

First, if individuals must live in an area to obtain a union job in that area, the equilibrium nonunion real wage in area i should depend negatively on the extent of unionism in that market. The reason for this is that the reservation wage of a person in a market with a high probability of future high wages will be lower than that in a market with a low probability of future rents. If, however, it is not possible to move from a nonunion to a union job (because unemployed persons are able to corner the search market), the nonunion wage rate in a heavily unionized labor market will not be influenced by the union wage. Instead, the nonunion wage will equal the nonunion wage in all other labor markets as well as the expected value of the income (or utility) associated with attaching oneself to the unionized sector.

Second, if individuals do not have to live in an area to obtain a union job in a highly unionized area, they can search for high-rent jobs (by, say, telephone or a two-day trip to Cleveland) without sacrificing their nonunion jobs in their initial area. In this circumstance, as in the case of the inability to move from a nonunion to a union job, there would be no tendency for nonunion jobs in highly unionized markets to offer real wages that are lower than those in relatively unionized markets.

The existence of a relatively high degree of unionization in an area may, therefore, lower the nonunion wage in an area or, under certain circumstances, have no effect on it. By the above arguments, however, it will not raise the nonunion wage. There are, however, two ways in which the existence of a large union sector could increase the nonunion wage above that in relatively unorganized labor markets.

First, assume that a nonunion employer could hire all the labor he wants at a wage of w_0. However, the probability that his firm will be organized (that an NLRB certification election will be held and won by the union) is $U = \phi(w/w_U, U)$, where w is the wage he offers and U is the extent of organization in the area as a whole.[5] Presumably, $\phi_1 < 0$ (the firm is more likely to be organized the lower its wage offer is relative to the prevailing union wage), $\phi_2 > 0$ (organization is more likely the greater the extent of unionization in the area), and $\phi_{12} < 0$ (the reduction in the threat of organization as w/w_U is increased the greater the extent of organization in the area). The expected wage rate that the firm will pay then depends on the wage it offers relative to the union wage, $R = w/w_U$, and the extent of unionization in the area, that is

(7) $$\bar{w} = w_U[\phi(R, U) + R(1 - \phi(R, U))],\ R \geq R_0.$$

If there is an interior solution (i.e., $d\bar{w}/dR > 0$ at $R = R_0$), the value of R satisfies

(8) $$1 - \phi(R, U) + (1 - R)\phi_1(R, U) = 0,$$

and, given that $\phi(1, U) = 0$, the cost-minimizing relative wage offer is between R_0 and 1.

An example of a functional form that satisfies the assumptions of the model is the quadratic:

$$\phi(R, U) = a_0 U(1 - R)^2 . \tag{9}$$

In this case the cost-minimizing relative wage offer is

$$R_* = 1 - \left(\frac{1}{3a_0 U}\right)^{1/2}, \tag{10}$$

which is binding so long as $R_* > R_0$ obviously increases as U increases; a decrease in a_0 (which would result from, say, passage of a right-to-work law in the area), would diminish the probability that the threat effect is operative.

To the extent that the threat effect is operative in *any* areas of the country, it should be most important in those areas with relatively high degrees of unionization. In those areas (if, again, there are any), the only way that the market can equate the attractiveness of the area with that of other markets is for excess normal unemployment to occur. Jobs will be rationed in both the union and nonunion sectors—although it is possible that the nonunion wage in a highly unionized area is still lower than that in a weakly unionized market. If the threat effect is operative, the nonunion wage is simply higher than that value that clears the market.

The threat effect model may have had great general relevance for wage determination in the United States during the 1930s and 1940s—and there are still large firms that reputedly pay union wages in order to stave off organization. It may, however, seem a trifle unrealistic to attempt to apply the model to the larger part of the nonunionized sector. The union movement in the United States, it could be argued, it not very interested in attempting to organize most currently unorganized firms that are small, pay low wages, and are characterized by rapid labor turnover. The marginal cost of servicing such bargaining units would, in most instances, be less than the marginal revenue.

An argument could be made, however, that wages in the union sector could, even in the absence of the threat of organization, have a direct influence on the wage levels of many nonunion firms. Suppose that a nonunion firm can hire as many workers as it wants at a wage w_0, but it realizes that the effort expended by the typical employee (a) will depend positively on the wage the firm offers relative to the nonunion wage,[6] say $a = \psi(R, U)$, where $\psi_1 > 0$, $\psi_2 < 0$, and $\psi_{12} > 0$. The cost of a unit of effort is then

$$c = \frac{Rw_U}{\psi(R, U)}, \quad R \geq R_0, \tag{11}$$

and it is *possible* that the cost-minimizing relative wage offer is between R_0 and 1. This will be the case if the elasticity of a with respect to R evaluated at R_0 exceeds unity.

This *contamination effect* model has roughly the same implications as the threat effect model. If there is anything at all to the hypothesis, the work effort of nonunion members will depend more significantly on their wage relative to the union wage in highly unionized areas than in those areas that have little unionization because high union wages are much more visible in the former than the latter. For example, the typical nonunion employee working in a highly unionized area is more likely to have held a high-rent union job (a higher wage for the same work) than is an equivalent person residing in an area with low unionization and thus would be more sensitive to the size of the union/nonunion differential.

8.2.3 Demand-Determined Versus Supply-Determined Area Wage Levels

To this point the discussion of area wage levels has been cast solely in terms of the supply side. A wage level in area i can deviate from that of other areas because a compensating variation is required or because of institutional considerations. For example, an area that is unattractive on nonpecuniary grounds will require high wage rates to attract workers. Given a finite long-run demand elasticity, the employment level in that area will be lower than if it were an attractive area, but there will still be a positive equilibrium employment level.

If, however, output were a function solely of labor and capital, the assumption of a finite demand elasticity would be wrong.[7] If the underlying production function were linear homogeneous, the condition of equal returns to capital would imply that all wage rates must be equal in the long run. If an area had a wage higher than any other area, its capital would flee and its employment would disappear. In other words, the demand curve, like the supply curve, would be horizontal.

On the other hand, suppose that the underlying production function is linear homogeneous in three factors: labor (E_i), capital (K_i), and resources (R_i^1). The last of these would include the industrial and commercial use of land, water, locally produced energy, and the like. Households, whose number is proportional to E_i, also demand resources—land for houses, water for swimming pools, etc., and the aggregate use of resources by households is R_i^2. I will assume, for the sake of simplicity, that each area has a fixed stock of resources (R_i) for both uses, i.e., $R_i = R_i^1 + R_i^2$.

The utility function for each household is given by $U_i = A_i\phi(c_i, r_i)$, where A_i is an area shift parameter reflecting the nonpecuniary attributes of the area, r_i is lifetime consumption of resources, and c_i lifetime consumption of all other goods. Ignoring taxes and area variations in the price of c_i (as well as the possibility of movement to low price level areas upon retirement), U_i is maximized subject to the budget constraint $w_i = c_i + b_i r_i$, where b_i is the price of a unit of resources. Thus, each household will demand $r(b_i, w_i)$ units of resources, and the total demand for resources by households in the area is

(12) $$R_i^2 = r(b_i, w_i)E_i,$$

where $\partial(\log r)/\partial(\log b_i) = -\eta_b$ and $\partial(\log r)/\partial(\log w_i) = \eta_w$ are the price and income elasticities of demand.

Equalization of net advantages of all areas implies that the total derivative of the utility function with respect to A_i, w_i, and b_i be equal to zero, or

(13) $$dU_i = \phi dA_i + A_i\phi_1(dw_i - r_i db_i) = 0.$$

Upon manipulation of this, we have

(14) $$d(\log w_i) = -\frac{1-\beta}{\theta} d(\log A_i) + \beta d(\log b_i),$$

where $\theta = c_i\phi_1/\phi$ is the elasticity of utility with respect to c_i and $\beta = b_i r_i/w_i$ is the share of household income going to the consumption of resources.

On the factor demand side, the aggregate production function for the area is $Q_i = F(E_i, K_i, R_i^1)$. It is assumed that F is linear homogeneous and, for simplicity, that the elasticities of substitution between each of the three factors are identical (σ). Thus, the logarithmic derivatives of the three factor prices are given by

(15) $$d(\log w_i) = -\frac{1-\alpha_1}{\sigma} d(\log E_i) + \frac{\alpha_2}{\sigma} d(\log K_i) + \frac{\alpha_3}{\sigma} d(\log R_i^1),$$

(16) $$O = \frac{\alpha_1}{\sigma} d(\log E_i) - \frac{1-\alpha_2}{\sigma} d(\log K_i) + \frac{\alpha_3}{\sigma} d(\log R_i^1),$$

and

(17) $$d(\log b_i) = \frac{\alpha_1}{\sigma} d(\log E_i) + \frac{\alpha_2}{\sigma} d(\log K_i) - \frac{1-\alpha_3}{\sigma} d(\log R_i^1),$$

where α_1, α_2, and α_3 are the three factor shares (which sum to one). The left-hand side of equation (16) is set equal to zero, reflecting the fact that the return to capital in all areas must be equal.

Since the fixed stock of resources in the area is divided between use by firms and households, i.e., $R_i = R_i^1 + R_i^2$, it follows that

(18) $$d(\log R_i) = kd(\log R_i^1) + (1-k)d(\log R_i^2),$$

where $k = R_i^1/R_i$ is the fraction used by firms. Differentiating (12) logarithmically,

(19) $$\alpha(\log R_i^2) = -\eta_b d(\log b_i) + \eta_w d(\log w_i) + d(\log E_i).$$

Substituting (19) into (18) and solving for (18), we obtain

$$(20)\ d(\log R_i^1) = \frac{1}{k} d(\log R_i) + \frac{1-k}{k} \eta_b d(\log b_i) - \frac{1-k}{k} \eta_w d(\log w_i) - \frac{1-k}{k} d(\log E_i).$$

R_i is allowed to vary to see how changes in the supply of resources in an area influence the other variables.

Equations (20), (14), (16), (17), and (18) can be manipulated to see how variations in the two exogenous variables, A_i and R_i, influence each of the five endogenous variables, w_i, b_i, E_i, K_i, and R_i^1. The determinant resultant system is

$$(21) \qquad \Delta = \frac{1}{\sigma^2}(\alpha_3 + \beta\alpha_1),$$

which is positive if $\alpha_3 > 0$ (firms use resources) or $\beta > 0$ (households use resources). This implies that there will be a unique solution of the endogenous variables of the model unless land, water, and the like are in infinite supply in each area.

An increase in the aggregate supply of resources in an area has no effect on the equilibrium levels of w_i and b_i. The two variable prices are only determined by the shift parameter A_i, that is

$$(22) \qquad \frac{\partial(\log w_i)}{\partial(\log A_i)} = -\frac{\alpha_3}{\alpha_3 + \beta_1} \frac{1-\beta}{\theta},$$

and

$$(23) \qquad \frac{\partial(\log b_i)}{\partial(\log A_i)} = \frac{\alpha_1}{\alpha_3 + \beta\alpha_1} \frac{1-\beta}{\theta}.$$

The effect of changes in the two exogenous variables on the level of employment is seen to be

$$(24) \qquad d(\log E_i) = -\frac{(1-k)(\alpha_1\eta_b + \alpha_3\eta_w) + k\sigma(\alpha_1 + \alpha_3)}{\alpha_3 + \beta\alpha_1} \frac{1-\beta}{\theta} d(\log A_i) + d(\log R_i).$$

Although w_i is an endogenous variable in the model, a quasi-elasticity of labor demand, $\partial(\log E_i)/\partial(\log w_i)$ holding R_i constant, can be obtained by dividing the coefficient on $d(\log A_i)$ in (24) by the negative of (22). This yields

$$(25) \qquad -\frac{\partial(\log E_i)}{\partial(\log w_i)} = -\frac{(1-k)(\alpha_1\eta_b + \alpha_3\eta_w) + k\sigma(\alpha_1 + \alpha_3)}{\alpha_3},$$

which is finite if $\alpha_3 > 0$, i.e., if firms use scarce natural resources as well as capital and labor.

The preceding model is merely an attempt to justify why I assume that there *could* be a regional labor market equilibrium with different area wage levels. It could also be extended in several directions—addition of variations in the prices of other goods due to transportation costs, taxes, the possibility of movement upon retirement, and the like.

8.3 Data and Initial Results

In order to estimate wage differentials between regions, it is necessary to adjust for the other factors that influence wages. To do this I shall employ the standard technique for analyzing the determinants of wages from cross-sectional data: the earnings function. The hourly wage of each worker is assumed to depend on four sets of variables: (a) *skill*, (b) *compensating*, (c) *discrimination*, and (d) *rent* variables. In terms of the CPS data I shall use in the analysis, the specification of the model is, for each sex,

$$\log w = \alpha_0 + \alpha_1 S + \alpha_2 X + \alpha_3 X^2 + \alpha_4 \mathrm{BL} + \alpha_5 \mathrm{OTH} + \alpha_6 U + \alpha_7 \mathrm{PUB} + \alpha_8 U \times PUB + \sum_{i=1}^{I-1} \gamma_i \mathrm{AR}_i + \sum_{j=1}^{J-1} \mu_j \mathrm{IND}_j + \sum_{k=1}^{K-1} \gamma_k \mathrm{OCC}_k + \epsilon, \tag{26}$$

where:

W = hourly nominal wage rate of a person
S = years of schooling attended
X = years of potential labor market experience (age $- S - 5$)
BL = one/zero dummy variable for blacks
OTH = dummy variable for race other than black or white
U = dummy variable for union membership
PUB = dummy variable for public employment
AR_i = set of dummy variables for geographic location
IND_j = set of dummy variables for industry
OCC_k = set of dummy variables for occupation.

The skill variables are proxies for the individual's stock of human capital and typically include S, X and its square, as well as some measure of innate ability. The Current Population Survey data set, however, includes no estimate of ability. $\alpha_1 = \partial(\log W)/\partial S \approx (W_S - W_{S-1})/W_{s-1}$ is (approximately) the rate of return to schooling without allowance for its resource cost. Past earnings function estimates have always found that

$\alpha_2 > 0$ and $\alpha_3 > 0$, presumably reflecting a diminishing rate of investment in human capital over the life cycle.

The compensating variables include several factors. First, W is measured in nominal terms, so, other things equal, wages should vary more or less in proportion to the price level of the region of residence of the worker. Second, some jobs are more onerous or dangerous than others, and persons in the "bad" jobs should receive a compensating differential. Similarly, employment in certain industries is subject to severe seasonal (e.g., construction) or cyclical (e.g., durable goods manufacturing) fluctuations, so persons in these industries should receive a higher hourly wage than persons in industries with secure employment. Third, areas that are attractive in terms of climate, physical characteristics, the net quantity and quality of public services, and the like should offer lower wages, ceteris paribus, than unattractive places.

In terms of the CPS data set, the second set of factors may be proxied (albeit somewhat imperfectly) by the industry and occupational dummy variables (IND and OCC). To a certain extent, however, these variables, especially the latter, are proxies for skill and luck, and I will present estimates of the major coefficients based on a *basic model* (without IND and OCC) and a *full model* (including them).

The first and third sets of factors are related to the interpretation of the set of coefficients that is central to this paper, those on the AR variables. The coefficient γ_i is the logarithmic difference, after accounting for the influence of the other variables, between the wage level in area i and the (arbitrarily excluded) area I. Thus, the ratio of what a person would earn in area i relative to area i' is $W_i/W_i' = \exp(\gamma_i - \gamma_i')$. The *nominal* area effect is γ_i, and the *real* area effect is γ_i minus some function of the area price level, p_i. The discussion in section 8.2 suggested that, in the absence of either government transfers or the possibility of postretirement migration, the appropriate function is $\log p_i$. If one used $\log W - \log p_i$ instead of $\log W$ in the earnings function, the area coefficients would be interpreted in real rather than in nominal terms—exactly what one would get by subtracting $\log p_i$ from the estimated nominal area effects. Since it is useful to hold open the question of how variations in area prices influence equilibrium area wage levels, I will estimate the earnings function in nominal terms.

The discrimination variables are represented in the United States by sex and race. Because (1) the preferences for different types of jobs may differ between men and women and (2) the potential experience variable is a much worse proxy for actual experience for women than for men, the model is estimated separately for the two sexes. Some of the difference between the predicted earnings of men and women for a given set of values of the independent variables may represent direct labor market discrimination against women, but it is impossible to tell how much.

Similarly, differences in the area coefficients between the sexes are consistent with both differential degrees of labor market discrimination against women and differences in the tastes of men and women for particular areas.

The coefficients on BL and OTH in equation (26) represent the logarithmic difference between the wages of each group relative to whites, other factors held constant. Thus, blacks earn $\exp(\alpha_4)$ of the wages of whites with the same observed qualifications, or, by one interpretation, employers behave as if they taxed black workers by $1 - \exp(\alpha_4)$ of their wage bill. This specification assumes that the proportional black/white differential is identical in all regions.[8]

The principal rent variable is unionism, and much attention in labor economics has focused on estimation of the union/nonunion relative wage advantage, $\exp(\alpha_6) - 1$, for private sector employees. In addition, it is possible that public employees earn more or less than their private sector counterparts, and the union/nonunion wage differential may be different in the public and private sectors. These last two possibilities can be tested by seeing if α_7 and α_8 in (26) are significantly different from zero. As with the case of the race variables, equation (26) assumes that unionism has the same proportionate impact on the wage in all areas. It is possible, however, that unions create a national wage scale, implying that the coefficients will vary less for union workers than for nonunion workers. To test this hypothesis, the model can be run separately for union and nonunion workers.

The data on which equation (26) is estimated are from the Current Population Survey for May of 1973 through 1976. The sample consists of all persons during each sample week who were (a) employed (but not self-employed or farmers), (b) between the ages of 17 and 72, inclusive, (c) had a positive wage, (d) were employed on a full-time basis, and (e) resided in one of the thirty-four large Standard Metropolitan Statistical Areas (SMSA) that are identifiable in the data set. In testing for the consistency of the results for the two wage measures, it became clear that for both men and women the estimated parameters of the basic model differed greatly with respect to the method by which the individual was paid (hourly versus salaried). Thus, the total sample of 43,940 persons during the four years was divided into four subsamples: (A) male hourly, (B) female hourly, (C) male salaried, and (D) female salaried.

The estimated coefficients of the basic model (that does not include industry and occupational dummy variables) are presented in table 8.1. These regressions do include thirty-three dummy variables for SMSA (Detroit is the excluded area), and these coefficients are discussed below. The results on the skill variables suggest that schooling and potential experience have a greater effect on the earnings of salaried workers than on those of hourly workers. As expected on the basis of several past

Table 8.1 Estimated Coefficients for Basic Model (estimated standard errors in parentheses)

	Hourly		Salaried	
Variables	(A) Men	(B) Women	(C) Men	(D) Women
S	.039	.052	.074	.069
	(.001)	(.002)	(.001)	(.002)
X	.030	.014	.042	.022
	(.001)	(.001)	(.001)	(.001)
X^2	−.00049	−.00022	−.00067	−.00038
	(.00002)	(.00002)	(.00002)	(.00002)
BL	−.146	−.028	−.158	−.088
	(.009)	(.011)	(.012)	(.012)
OTH	−.167	−.057	−.174	−.045
	(.025)	(.028)	(.024)	(.026)
U	.252	.184	.019	.078
	(.006)	(.010)	(.010)	(.015)
PUB	.151	.145	−.013	.136
	(.014)	(.014)	(.010)	(.010)
PUB × U	−.178	−.012	.007	−.050
	(.018)	(.026)	(.017)	(.021)
$D74$	.079	.095	.062	.072
	(.008)	(.011)	(.009)	(.010)
$D75$	.150	.165	.134	.137
	(.008)	(.011)	(.009)	(.010)
$D76$	.204	.237	.201	.208
	(.008)	(.011)	(.009)	(.010)
Constant	.627	.276	.325	.245
	(.02)	(.03)	(.03)	(.03)
R^2	.353	.277	.344	.330
SEE	.31	.31	.39	.35
N	12,191	6,760	15,355	9,634

studies, experience is a much more important determinant of earnings for men than for women. The estimated differential between the wages of white and nonwhite workers is larger for men than women.

The estimated effect of union membership on the earnings of full-time workers is quite large (a 28.7 percent advantage for men and a 20.2 percent advantage for women in the private sector), but it is much smaller for full-time salaried workers (1.9 percent for men and 8.1 percent for women). Being employed in the public sector increases the wages of women workers and male hourly workers by approximately 15 percent, but it has no effect on the earnings of salaried males. The estimated impact of public sector unions on wages, the sum of the coefficients on U and PUB × U, is, for full-time workers, greater for women than men and for hourly than salaried workers.

The predicted hourly wage rates of a typical worker—white, private sector, twelve years of schooling, age 35—in Detroit in 1973 in each of the four subsamples are as follows:

	Predicted Hourly Wage		Percent Private
	Nonunion	Union	Sector Unionized
A. Full-time hourly male	4.31	5.54	56
B. Full-time hourly female	2.90	3.49	22
C. Full-time salaried male	5.67	5.78	17
D. Full-time salaried female	3.78	4.09	9

Notice that the only group which private sector union membership is extensive is A, hourly males. In fact, whereas group A workers compose only 28 percent of total private sector employment, they have 58 percent of total private sector union membership. The impact of unionism on the wage rates of this group is such that a unionized male hourly worker has almost as high a wage as a salaried male worker.

8.4 Differences in Wage Levels between Areas

The four regressions in table 8.1 also include thirty-three dummy variables for SMSA of residence of the individual. The null hypothesis that the presence of these does not add sufficiently to the explanation of log w to justify the sacrifice of 33 degrees of freedom—i.e., that nominal wage levels for each of the groups do not differ among the thirty-four areas—is decisively refuted for the four groups (F values between 9 and 15 compared to $F_{.05}(33, \infty) = 1.44$).

Table 8.2 reports the point estimates of the coefficients on the area variables for the four groups of full-time employees. The "basic" model refers to the standard earnings functions, whose other coefficients were given in table 8.1, and the "full" model includes dummy variables for both industry and occupation at the one-digit aggregation. Each of the coefficients represents the estimated logarithmic deviation of the area effect for that area less that for Detroit. Thus, from the basic model, male hourly workers in New York, given their education, experience, race, union membership, and public/private status, earn $\exp(-.109) = 89.7$ percent of what comparable workers in Detroit earn. They earn $\exp(-.109 + .249) = 115.0$ percent of what comparable workers in Tampa earn. The estimated standard errors of the differences in the area coefficients range from a low of about .015 for areas with large samples of a subgroup to almost .050 for areas with very small samples. For example, the New York/Detroit relative for group A workers has a standard error

Table 8.2 Estimated Logarithmic Difference between Wage Levels in Thirty-four SMSA's and Detroit for Full-Time Hourly and Salaried Workers, by Sex, 1973–76

	Hourly				Salaried			
	Men		Women		Men		Women	
SMSA	Basic	Full	Basic	Full	Basic	Full	Basic	Full
East								
1. New York	−.109	−.116	.031	−.049	−.144	−.104	−.005	−.015
4. Philadelphia	−.082	−.116	−.071	−.180	−.128	−.117	−.160	−.172
8. Boston	−.103	−.146	−.016	−.020	−.158	−.129	−.077	−.090
9. Nassau-Suffolk	.020	−.033	.008	−.088	−.033	.002	−.046	−.047
10. Pittsburgh	−.183	−.187	−.172	−.129	−.188	−.164	−.172	−.184
15. Newark	−.110	−.124	−.087	−.078	−.094	−.086	−.139	−.140
23. Paterson	−.048	−.085	.010	−.118	.016	.032	−.033	−.025
25. Buffalo	−.161	−.143	−.098	−.149	−.230	−.200	−.264	−.248
Midwest								
3. Chicago	−.009	−.036	.018	−.026	−.056	−.034	−.049	−.066
5. Detroit	.000	.000	.000	.000	.000	.000	.000	.000
11. St. Louis	−.058	−.088	−.096	−.121	−.117	−.120	−.178	−.172
13. Cleveland	−.075	−.097	−.097	−.149	−.081	−.072	−.164	−.160
16. Minneapolis	.000	−.038	−.025	−.087	−.059	−.044	−.137	−.143

20. Milwaukee	−.038	−.051	−.021	−.022	−.089	−.081	−.117	−.135
22. Cincinnati	−.119	−.145	−.096	−.202	−.227	−.209	−.261	−.234
27. Kansas City	−.083	−.107	−.132	−.166	−.192	−.168	−.226	−.211
30. Indianapolis	−.080	−.116	−.068	−.054	−.127	−.124	−.214	−.201
South								
7. D.C.	.071	−.012	.003	−.015	.018	.007	−.032	−.135
12. Baltimore	−.070	−.116	−.038	−.050	−.151	−.138	−.150	−.146
14. Houston	−.031	−.120	−.167	−.116	−.060	−.057	−.215	−.216
17. Dallas	−.168	−.202	−.098	−.189	−.115	−.103	−.239	−.218
21. Atlanta	−.073	−.111	−.040	−.142	−.112	−.096	−.126	−.130
26. Miami	−.149	−.179	−.141	−.132	−.285	−.232	−.190	−.179
32. New Orleans	−.115	−.190	−.227	−.144	−.142	−.140	−.290	−.274
33. Tampa	−.249	−.283	−.216	−.264	−.300	−.278	−.303	−.290
West								
2. Los Angeles	−.103	−.109	−.015	−.076	−.115	−.087	−.087	−.050
6. San Francisco	.024	.020	.034	.061	−.089	−.058	−.044	−.049
18. Seattle	−.066	−.077	−.075	−.094	−.093	−.082	−.169	−.135
19. Anaheim	−.053	−.073	−.060	.004	−.069	−.063	−.120	−.128
24. San Diego	−.089	−.127	−.105	−.079	−.187	−.168	−.158	−.149
28. Denver	−.028	−.083	−.081	−.082	−.144	−.141	−.143	−.133
29. San Bernardino	−.071	−.099	−.146	−.175	−.212	−.059	−.227	−.186
31. San Jose	.011	−.003	.017	.053	−.071	−.076	−.061	−.045
34. Portland	−.067	−.075	−.074	.000	−.182	−.146	−.163	−.131

NOTE: Numbers before SMSAs indicate population ranking in 1976.

of 1.7 percent, the New York/Tampa relative a standard error of 2.9 percent.

To adjust these estimated nominal wage effects for prices, I used the BLS index of comparative living costs for an "intermediate" living standard for 1974.[9] Most of the variation in this price index is due to variations in housing costs and taxes.[10] The elasticity of the equilibrium wage level in a region with respect to the local price level may be, as shown in section 8.2, greater or less than one, but I initially constrained its impact to be one. Thus, the estimated real area effect is the estimated nominal effect less the logarithm of the price level, and these are shown for hourly workers in table 8.3. (For salaried workers the real area effect can be calculated by taking the nominal area effect in table 8.2 and subtracting the natural logarithm of the price level—normalized at one rather than 100.) To obtain the estimated average area effect, one averages the union and nonunion wage levels, which is done by adding the estimated coefficient on union membership (.25 for men and .18 for women) times the proportion of hourly private sector workers who are unionized. This is then exponentiated and normalized at Detroit equal to 100.

One index of the dispersion of area wage rates is the (weighted) standard deviation of the logarithm of the area effects. This is shown in table 8.4 for the nonunion area effect and the average (i.e., including unionism) for both nominal and real area effects. (Since unionism has little direct impact on the wages of salaried workers, the dispersion of average wages of salaried workers is not reported.) One might suspect that the dispersion of real area effects would be lower than the dispersion of nominal area effects if workers move between areas to equalize net returns. In fact, this is true for both groups of women workers, but it is *greater* for both groups of men workers.

What this implies is difficult to tell. First, the dispersion of real area effects will only be lower than the dispersion of nominal area effects if the slope coefficient of a regression of the nominal area effect on the log of area price level is greater than .5.[11] As shown in section 8.2, $\partial(\log w_i)/\partial(\log p_i)$ can be less than one even in a world of real income-maximizing suppliers of labor. Further, to the extent that area price levels are measured with error, the implicit coefficient of $\log w_i$ on $\log p_i$ will be biased down, thus increasing the estimated variance of $\log(w_i/p_i)$.

If there are no threat or contamination effects, the nonunion wage for a group for which there is a significant union effect will depend negatively on the extent of unionism in the area. Since the estimated union/nonunion effect is positively only for hourly workers, we would therefore expect that the extent of unionism would have a negative effect on the area effect for nonunion wages. On the other hand, if either the threat or contamination effect were operative, we would expect that the relation between the nonunion area effect and unionism would be much weaker—posibly even positive. For male hourly workers the coefficient of the logarithm of the real area effect for nonunion workers on the extent of unionism is −.15 (.09). This implies that the real nonunion wage level is about 9 percent lower in a heavily unionized area (about 75 percent) than in a weakly

Table 8.3 **Estimated Real Wage Levels (*w/p*) for Private Sector Hourly Workers in Thirty-three SMSA's (Detroit = 100)**

		Men		Women	
SMSA	Price Level	Nonunion Wage	Average Wage	Nonunion Wage	Average Wage
East					
1. New York	116	77	85	76	90
4. Philadelphia	103	89	88	85	90
8. Boston	117	77	71	84	81
9. Nassau-Suffolk	116	88	84	87	86
10. Pittsburgh	97	86	87	86	86
15. Newark	116	77	75	79	81
23. Paterson	116	82	79	87	88
25. Buffalo	107	80	85	79	83
Midwest					
3. Chicago	103	96	99	94	98
5. Detroit	100	100	100	100	100
11. St. Louis	97	97	98	94	93
13. Cleveland	102	91	89	90	88
16. Minneapolis	104	96	94	92	93
20. Milwaukee	105	92	93	90	92
22. Cincinnati	96	92	88	95	91
27. Kansas City	97	95	89	92	89
30. Indianapolis	99	93	94	90	92
South					
7. D.C.	105	102	98	93	93
12. Baltimore	100	93	89	96	93
14. Houston	90	108	97	87	91
17. Dallas	90	94	95	83	97
21. Atlanta	91	102	91	106	102
26. Miami	89	97	87	98	94
32. New Orleans	90	99	91	89	85
33. Tampa	89	88	76	91	87
West					
2. Los Angeles	98	92	86	101	99
6. San Francisco	106	97	98	95	99
18. Seattle	101	93	92	92	92
19. Anaheim	98	97	89	96	93
24. San Diego	98	93	89	92	89
28. Denver	95	102	95	97	94
29. San Bernardino	98	95	92	88	84
31. San Jose	106	95	90	96	94

NOTE: Numbers before SMSAs indicate population ranking in 1976.

Table 8.4 **Standard Deviation of Estimated Area Wage Effects for Four Subgroups**

	Average Wage		Average Wage	
	Nominal	Real	Nominal	Real
Male hourly	.066	.084	.085	.082
Female hourly	.070	.061	.080	.057
Male salaried	.077	.085	—	—
Female salaried	.084	.069	—	—

unionized area (about 15 percent), but this estimate is subject to a large standard error. For female hourly workers this coefficient is $-.20$ (.10), which, given the range of the extent of unionism, is actually a smaller effect.

One implication of both the threat and contamination effect models of the spillover of union wages to the nonunion sector is that the nonunion wage will depend positively on the extent of organization only when the extent of unionism is fairly large. The threat or contamination effect should be fairly small (or nonexistent) until unionism reaches a certain proportion—then they will be rather extensive. To test this I added quadratic terms so that the logarithm of the nonunion real area effect was a function of U and U^2 for both men and women hourly workers. The above argument would suggest that their coefficients would be negative and positive, respectively. The results, for both men and women, were the opposite—although the negative coefficient on the U^2 term dominates the positive coefficient on U. Adding dummy variables for certain "troublesome" areas (specifically, Detroit, which seems to be a special case, and Washington, D.C., which is dominated by a high-rent public sector), did nothing to upset the conclusion that there is little to the spillover hypotheses.

Notes

1. See, e.g., Scully (1969), Coelho and Ghali (1971), Bellante (1979), and Goldfarb and Yeager (1981).

2. It is, of course, possible that this migration takes a long time to occur so that there is at any time a large *disequilibrium* component in any observed distribution of regional wages. In the United States, however, there is a considerable amount of interarea labor mobility. For example, between March 1969 and March 1979, 2.9 percent of the male population from 35 to 44 years of age moved between states; for males ages 45 to 64 the mobility rate was 1.5 percent. Now even if some of this mobility is not related to economic migration (e.g., a move from Cos Cob, Connecticut to Short Hills, New Jersey), there appears to be enough movement to eliminate disequilibrium rather quickly.

3. Specifically, the federal government offers wage rates that are considerably in excess of the reservation prices of potential employers. For an empirical study of this phenomenon, see Smith (1976).

4. The original application of the Harris-Todaro framework to the explanation of regional differentials in unemployment was Hall (1970).

5. The original formulation of the "threat effect" model was done by Rosen (1969).

6. For a discussion of some further implications of the assumption of "interdependence" of different workers' utility functions, see Hamermesh (1975).

7. This point is stressed in Richard Muth's comment on this paper. The following section is a reply to that part of his comments.

8. It is, of course, likely that this assumption is not correct, as indeed has been demonstrated with respect to broad regional groups by Kiefer and Smith (1977). I did run my basic regressions separately for blacks and whites, but, despite the fact that estimated differentials between blacks and whites were somewhat larger in southern SMSA's than elsewhere, it made very little difference in the estimation of area effects.

9. The price levels for New York, Nassau-Suffolk, Newark, and Paterson are the New York/New Jersey rate; Miami and Tampa are assigned the level for Orlando; Anaheim and San Bernadino, the Los Angeles level (which equals the San Diego level); New Orleans, the Baton Rouge level; and San Jose, the San Francisco/Oakland level. No price level was available for Portland, Oregon.

10. The standard deviation of the logarithm of the housing component of the index for 1974 was .132; for taxes it was .204. All other categories—except medical, which had a relatively low weight—varied by .06 or less.

11. Let A_i and N_i be the real and nominal area effects and p_i the logarithm of the area price level. Then $A_i = N_i - p_i$, and $\text{var}(A_i) = \text{var}(N_i) + \text{var}(p_i) - 2\,\text{cov}(N_i, p_i) = \text{var}(N_i) + \text{var}(p_i)(1 - 2b_{N\cdot p})$. Thus, $\text{var}(A_i) < \text{var}(N_i)$ only if $b_{N\cdot p} > .5$.

References

Bellante, Don. 1979. The North-South differential and the migration of heterogeneous labor. *American Economic Review* 69: 166–75.

Coelho, Philip R. P., and Moheb A. Ghali. 1971. The end of the North-South wage differential. *American Economic Review* 61: 932–37.

Freeman, Richard B., and James L. Medoff. 1979. New estimates of private sector unionism in the U.S. *Industrial and Labor Relations Review* 32: 143–74.

Goldfarb, Robert S., and Anthony Yeager. 1981. Has the North-South wage differential really disappeared?—Some new evidence. George Washington University. Mimeo.

Hall, Robert E. 1970. Why is the unemployment rate so high at full employment? *Brookings Papers on Economic Activity* 3:369–402.

Hamermesh, Daniel S. 1975. Interdependence in the labor market. *Economica* 42: 420–29.

Kiefer, Nicholas M., and Sharon P. Smith. 1977. Union impact and wage discrimination by region. *Journal of Human Resources* 12:521–34.

Rosen, Sherwin. 1969. Trade union power, threat effects, and the extent of organization. *Review of Economic Studies* 36: 185–96.

Scully, Gerald W. 1969. Interstate wage differentials: A cross-section analysis. *American Economic Review* 59: 757–73.
Smith, Sharon P. 1976. Pay differentials between federal government and private sector workers. *Industrial and Labor Relations Review* 29: 179–97.

Comment Richard F. Muth

George Johnson's paper is the most thorough, carefully done study of intercity wage differentials that I have seen. Because of the great detail in the data set he uses, Johnson is able to eliminate the effects of a variety of other influences on wages and salaries which other studies have only partially controlled for. Among these other factors are schooling, potential labor force experience, race, union membership, public employment, industry, and occupation. Moreover, separate regressions are run for men and women and for hourly and salaried workers. The area effects which Johnson estimates are therefore remarkably free from the effects of possible correlation with omitted variables.

Yet, because of the attention given earlier in the paper to the effects of intercity differences in the prices of consumer goods on nominal wage levels in equilibrium, I was somewhat surprised that Johnson didn't include the BLS intercity living cost index as an explanatory variable in his nominal wage regressions. Earlier he argues correctly that progressive taxation of nominal earnings and social security payments upon retirement may make the partial derivative of the equilibrium wage rate with respect to consumer goods prices greater than unity. The option of retirement to a low-price area coupled with moving costs can make this partial derivative either greater or less than one. Surely then, it is not correct to divide the estimated area effect on nominal wages by the area's price index to obtain the real area effect, as Johnson does. Indeed, his finding of a greater area dispersion of real area effects for men than for nominal effects may merely reflect the fact that the former were incorrectly estimated.

In the earlier part of his paper, Johnson devotes considerable space to the effect of nonpecuniary advantages and disadvantages on equilibrium wage levels. I would have found it interesting if measures of such effects had been included among the explanatory variables and their effects on area wage levels calculated. A variety of such variables have been included in various spatial studies, especially studies of intermetropolitan migration. Variables related to weather, such as heating degree days (essentially the absolute difference between average temperature and

Richard F. Muth is professor of economics at Stanford University.

some level such as 50 degrees Fahrenheit if the former is smaller summed over the year), cooling degree days (similarly defined), humidity, and annual rainfall, are obvious candidates for inclusion. Other such variables might include proximity to oceans and to mountains and the presence of a symphony orchestra, or, if my tastes are indicative, a professional football team. Not only would the effects of such factors on (supposedly equilibrium) wage levels be of considerable interest but any remaining areal effects would approximate disequilibrium wage differences.

My greatest single criticism of Johnson's paper, however, is its neglect of demand-side variables. Implicit in the paper, it seems to me, is the hypothesis that area demand curves for labor are downward sloping to the right. This would be the case if products produced in a particular place were either unique or sold to a limited market area surrounding the city in which they are produced. If such were the case and there were no important differences among workers in the value placed upon nonpecuniary advantages, long-run horizontal labor supply curves would fix equilibrium wage levels. Forces influencing the area's demand curve for labor would then affect its total population and employment but would have no influence on long-run equilibrium wage levels. The above, it seems to me, is the predominant view among urban and regional economists, and Johnson's paper is certainly consistent with it.

There is an alternative view, however, attributable to Borts and Stein (1964), which suggests demand factors are all important in determining areal wage levels. Suppose that in any urban area there exist firms in significant numbers which, in the aggregate, have a negligible effect on the prices for their products which prevail on national or world markets. Furthermore, let the rental values of capital be fixed by external conditions to firms in the urban area, a condition most urban and regional economists would accept. Then, if production functions are homogeneous of degree one in labor and capital,[1] there exists a fixed nominal wage level in the urban area consistent with equilibrium for producers facing fixed product prices and selling in outside markets. Competition for labor would require that firms producing for domestic consumption or others facing downward sloping product demand schedules pay the same wage. The latter would be affected only by changes in capital rental values or changes in f.o.b. export prices of firms facing perfectly elastic product demand schedules, and not by the total level of employment. Factors affecting labor supply schedules, which would have to be upward sloping for equilibrium to be determinate, would, under these conditions, influence only an area's total population and employment; they would have no impact on nominal wages. Admittedly, this alternative view is a minority one among urban and regional economists. My own work (Muth 1968), though, suggests it more closely approximates the U.S. economy during the 1950s than the more conventional view sketched above.

Johnson certainly can't be faulted for not having studied intermetropolitan wage differences over time, for the basic data to be used probably don't exist. Yet, changes in wage differentials over time are of even greater interest than their level at a moment in time. One of the most striking features of the U.S. economy is the convergence of per capita incomes over time, especially the increase in the South relative to the rest of the United States. My earlier analysis of Easterlin's data (Perloff et al. 1960, chap. 28) together with more recent examinations of Census earnings data for white urban males for 1950–70 suggest that regional earnings differentials have been remarkably constant for half a century. Rising relative per capita incomes in the South would appear to have resulted primarily from a declining relative importance of agriculture in southern states. It would be nice, though, if we had a study as well done as Johnson's for some earlier period, such as 1950, from which we could better appraise the influence of changes in wage differentials on the regional covergence of per capita incomes.

Note

1. In the revised version of his paper, Johnson correctly argues that resources as an input into production make the demand for labor less than perfectly elastic. If resources as an input into the production of exportable commodities are relatively unimportant, however, the less than perfectly elastic demand may be of little practical significance.

References

Borts, George H., and Jerome L. Stein. 1964. *Economic growth in a free market.* New York: Columbia University Press.

Muth, Richard F. 1968. Differential growth among large U.S. cities. In *Papers in quantitative economics*, ed. James P. Quirk and Arvid M. Zarley. Lawrence, Kansas: The University Press of Kansas.

Perloff, Harvey S. et al. 1960. *Regions, resources, and economic growth.* Baltimore: The Johns Hopkins Press.

9 Imputing Income in the CPS: Comments on "Measures of Aggregate Labor Cost in the United States"

Donald B. Rubin

9.1 Introduction

Three of the four papers in this section (Gollop and Jorgenson, Smeeding, and Johnson) base conclusions on income data from the Census Bureau's Current Population Survey (CPS). The CPS is a major source of income data for economic research even though the nonresponse rate on income items is about 15–20%. This level of nonreporting of income, especially if concentrated among special types of individuals, should be of substantial concern to researchers in economics. Most published economic research, however, ignores this problem when using CPS data. The major reason that researchers can ignore this nonreporting of income is that before CPS public-use tapes are released, the Census Bureau imputes (i.e., fills in) missing income data (as well as other data). Although imputed data are flagged to distinguish them from real data, it is evidently easy for researchers to be seduced into ignoring this distinction and treating all values, imputed and real, on the same basis.

Three recent articles on income imputation in the CPS address the adequacy of current imputation procedures. They are Lillard, Smith, and Welch (1982, hereafter LSW), Greenlees, Reece, and Zieschang (1982, hereafter GRZ), and Herzog and Rubin (1983, hereafter HR). My comments here are designed to highlight relevant issues arising from the existence of income nonreporters in the CPS, especially in the context of work presented in these articles and other recent literature.

Donald B. Rubin is professor, Department of Statistics and Department of Education, University of Chicago.

This research was sponsored by the United States Army under contract DAAG29-80-C-0041 while the author was visiting professor with the Mathematics Research Center at the University of Wisconsin, Madison.

After characterizing income nonreporters in section 9.2 and describing the Census Bureau's hot deck procedure in section 9.3, in section 9.4 I point out the need for multiple imputation if uncertainty due to nonresponse is to be properly reflected in an imputed data set. Section 9.5 provides definitions of ignorable and nonignorable nonresponse, while section 9.6 describes the selection model used in LSW and GRZ and emphasizes that external information is needed to justify the acceptance of such a model or any other particular model for nonresponse as an accurate reflection of reality. Finally, section 9.7 briefly describes the CPS-SSA-IRS Exact Match File, which both GRZ and HR use to help provide such external information.

9.2 Who Are the Nonrespondents on Income Questions?

Of central importance for determining whether the 15–20% nonresponse rate on income questions is of major concern is the extent to which income nonreporters are different from income reporters. If the nonreporters were just a simple random sample from the population of reporters and nonreporters, the loss in efficiency of estimation created by ignoring the nonreporters altogether would be of little concern.

There is a great deal of evidence, however, that nonreporters do differ from reporters in important ways. One such piece of evidence that LSW presents is especially interesting. Apparently, if we were to plot "probability of nonresponse on income items" versus "amount of actual income," the relationship would be U-shaped: moderate nonresponse at low incomes, low nonresponse at moderate incomes, and very high nonresponse at high incomes. Moreover, LSW's evidence suggests that this U-shaped relationship is created by the existence of two primary types of income nonreporters. The first type is called "general nonreporters" because they have a high nonresponse rate on many CPS questions, not just income questions. These people tend to have low incomes and approach CPS questions in a generally reluctant manner. The second type of income nonreporter is called "specific nonreporters" because on most CPS questions, that is nonincome questions, they have low nonresponse rates, whereas on income questions their nonresponse rates are very high (e.g., over 30%). The specific nonreporters tend to be professionals with high incomes, for example, doctors, lawyers, and dentists.

If we accept this interesting picture as relatively accurate, it seems to me natural and desirable to try to build a nonresponse model that explicitly recognizes the U-shaped relationship and the two types of income nonreporters. The LSW and GRZ selection models, however, do not exploit this structure and instead use models for nonresponse asserting that, conditional on some predictor variables (such as years of education), the relationship between probability of nonresponse on income items and income is monotonic. Of course, one can criticize virtually any analysis for not fully exploiting some interesting features found in subsequent analyses. Consequently, my comment on this point should be viewed more as offering a suggestion for further study than as criticizing the work presented in LSW and GRZ.

9.3 The Census Bureau's Hot Deck Imputation Scheme

The Census Bureau's procedure for imputation, the hot deck, has been used since the early 1960s. The hot deck is a matching algorithm in the sense that for each nonrespondent, a respondent is found who matches the nonrespondent on variables that are measured for both. The variables used for the matching are all categorical, with varying numbers of levels (e.g., "gender" has two levels, "region of country" has four levels). If a match is not found, categories are collapsed and variables are deleted so that coarser matches are allowed. Eventually, every nonrespondent finds a match; the matching respondent is often called (by hot deck aficionados) "the donor" because the donor's record of values is donated to the nonrespondent to fill in all missing values in the nonrespondent's record.

The number of variables used for matching and their level of detail has expanded over the years, and imputed income can be sensitive to such rule changes. For example, between 1975 and 1976, years of education was added to the list of matching variables, and as a consequence, the imputed incomes of nonrespondents with many years of education increased substantially from 1975 to 1976. Such changes can create problems when comparing income data in different periods of time. A related problem is that even though the ideal match that is possible under the hot deck is closer now than it was years ago, many nonrespondents fail to find donors at this ideal level of detail. For one example, only 20% find donors in the same region of the country. For a second example, judges with ideal matches are imputed to earn approximately $30,000 more than judges without ideal matches.

The hot deck, by trying for exact multivariate categorical matches, is trying to control all higher order interactions among the matching variables. This task is very difficult with many matching variables when using a categorical matching rule, even if there is a large pool of potential matches for nonrespondents. For example, suppose all the matching variables are dichotomous and independent, with 50% of the population at each level of each variable. If p is the number of matching variables $(.5)^p$ is the probability of two randomly chosen units matching each other on all p variables. Since $.5^{10} < .001$, it is obvious that finding exact matches with many matching variables, even in this ideal setting, requires very large pools of potential matches.

Related work on matching methods in observational studies investigates categorical matching methods and offers alternative matching methods (e.g., Cochran and Rubin 1973; Rubin 1976*a*, 1976*b*, 1980*a*; Rosenbaum and Rubin 1983). I suspect that some of the more recent work (e.g., Rosenbaum and Rubin 1983) may have useful suggestions for an improved hot-deck-like procedure. Neither LSW nor GRZ suggests modifying the matching algorithm but rather suggests using explicit statistical models for imputation. HR considers both explicit models and hot deck procedures.

9.4 Imputation and the Need for Multiple Imputation

LSW and GRZ both suggest a model-based alternative to hot deck imputation: (a) build an explicit model, specifically, a selection model (cf. Heckman 1979) where the probability of nonresponse on income increases with income (see section 9.6 for details), (b) estimate the parameters of this model by maximum likelihood, and (c) impute one value for each missing value by randomly drawing observations from this model with unknown parameters replaced by their maximum likelihood estimates.

I have several general comments to make on imputation whether based on implicit models like the hot deck or explicit models like the selection model.

First, for the data producer, some form of imputation is almost required and often desirable even if not required. I believe the Census Bureau feels it cannot produce public-use files with blanks. Also, I believe it feels, and rightly so, that it knows more about the missing data than the typical user of public-use files. Furthermore, the typical user of public-use files will not have the statistical sophistication needed to routinely apply model-based methods for handling nonresponse, such as those reveiwed by Little (1982). Of course, in any public-use file, all imputed values must be flagged to distinguish them from real values.

Second, imputation based on explicit modeling efforts may require much more work than implicit models, such as the hot deck (or some other matching method for imputation), that can impute all missing variables at once no matter what the pattern of missing variables. Of course, this does not mean that explicit models should be avoided: explicit model-based methods are, in principle, the proper ones to handle nonresponse.

Third, when drawing values to impute, in order to obtain inferences with the correct variability, parameters of models must not be fixed at estimated values but must be drawn in such a way as to reflect uncertainty in their estimation.

Fourth, one imputation for each missing value, even if drawn according to the absolutely correct model, will lead to inferences that underestimate variability (e.g., underestimate standard errors).

Fifth, there exists a need to display sensitivity of answers to plausible models for the process that creates nonresponse since the observed data alone cannot determine which of a variety of models is correct.

These points are all leading to the suggestion to use multiple imputation as proposed in Rubin (1978*a*) and expanded upon in Rubin (1980*b*). Whether using an implicit model, such as the hot deck, or an explicit model, such as employed in LSW and GRZ, if imputation is used to handle nonresponse, multiple imputation is generally needed to reach the correct inference.

Multiple imputation replaces each missing value by a pointer to a vector, say of length m, of possible values; the m values reflect uncertainty for the correct value. Imputing only one value can only be correct when there is no uncertainty, but if there were no uncertainty, the missing value would not be missing; consequently, multiple imputation rather than single imputation is needed when there are missing data.

The m possible values for each of the missing data result in m complete data sets, and these can be analyzed by standard complete-data methods to arrive at valid inferences. Suppose, for example, that the m imputations were all made under one model for nonresponse, such as the LSW selection model, and suppose that with complete data we would form the estimate $\hat{Q}$ with associated standard error S. Let $\hat{Q}_i$ and S_i, $i = 1, \ldots, m$, be their values in each of the data sets created by miltiple imputation. Then the resultant multiple imputation estimate is simply $\bar{Q} = \Sigma \hat{Q}_i / m$ with standard error

$$\sqrt{\Sigma(\hat{Q}_i - \bar{Q})^2/(m-1) + \Sigma S_i^2/m}.$$

If the m imputations are from k different models, then those imputations under each model should be combined to form one inference under each model, and then the comparison across the k resulting inferences displays sensitivity of inference to the k different models.

HR applies multiple imputation to the CPS and compares the results with single imputation answers. Both an explicit model and a hot deck procedure are considered. In contrast to both LSW and GRZ, the income variable being imputed in HR is not total income, but rather social security benefits. Also, the model used in HR is not a selection model, but rather a two-stage log-liner/linear model, where the log-linear model is used to predict the existence of social security benefits (a 0-1 variable), and the linear model is used to predict the amount of benefits (actually, log benefits), given that some benefits were received. This work illustrates that multiple imputation can play an important practical role.

9.5 The Distinction between Ignorable Nonresponse and Nonignorable Nonresponse

An important distinction between the LSW and GRZ selection models and the HR two-stage model involves underlying assumptions. Models for survey nonresponse can be classified into ones assuming "ignorable" nonresponse and those assuming "nonignorable" nonresponse, the terminology being from Rubin (1976*c*, 1978*b*). I believe that LSW's use of "random nonresponse" is intended to convey essentially the same notion, although I find the LSW use of this phrase somewhat inconsistent. Both GRZ and HR use the ignorable/nonignorable classification.

Under ignorable nonresponse models, respondents and nonrespondents that are exactly matched with respect to observed variables have the same distribution of missing variables. The Census Bureau hot deck operates under this assumption, although it does not have to do so. For example, having found a donor for a nonrespondent, instead of imputing the donor's income, the hot deck algorithm could be instructed to impute the donor's income *plus* 10 percent. If we accept the Census Bureau's hot deck as currently implemented, then we implicitly accept the hypothesis that nonresponse is ignorable, and then there is no need to be concerned with selection models, such as used in LSW and GRZ. Instead, under ignorable nonresponse, all energy should be focused on modeling the conditional distribution of missing variables given observed variables for respondents, since, by assumption, this conditional distribution is the same for nonrespondents and respondents. The explicit model in HR posits ignorable nonresponse and focuses on predicting, for respondents, the amount of social security benefits.

When missing values are to be replaced by imputed values, however, whether these values arise from implicit or explicit models, a single imputation generally will underestimate variability. Consequently, the LSW statement accepting the hot deck if operating at its most detailed level is not entirely appropriate if valid inferences are desired, even if nonresponse is ignorable. Both GRZ and HR explicitly acknowledge this point, and HR uses multiple imputation under ignorable nonresponse models to address it.

Under nonignorable nonresponse models, respondents and nonrespondents perfectly matched on observed variables have different distributions on unobserved variables. The example of the modified hot deck which imputes donor's income plus 10 percent is an implicit nonignorable nonresponse model; the LSW and GRZ selection models are explicit nonignorable models since the probability of nonresponse increases with income. When nonignorable nonresponse is possible, as with income nonreporting in the CPS, it is crucial to expose sensitivity of answers to different models, all of which are consistent with the data. An important contribution of LSW is that it defines and illustrates the use of an expanded collection of such models. Specifically, LSW extends the GRZ selection model in which log(total income) is normally distributed to a selection model in which some Box-Cox (1964) transformation of total income is normally distributed, where the transformation is to be estimated.

Within the context of imputation for missing values, sensitivity to models can only be exposed through the use of multiple imputation, where for each missing value there are imputations under each model being considered (e.g., two imputations under the ignorable hot deck, two imputations under the nonignorable [plus 10 percent] model, and two imputations under the GRZ nonignorable selection model). Again, such multiple imputations are necessary to reach valid inferences under each model and to expose sensitivity of answers to population features not addressable by the observed data.

9.6 An Explicit Nonignorable Model: Caveats and Results

Let Y be earnings, which is sometimes missing in the CPS, and let X be a vector of predictor variables (e.g., education, work experience), which for simplicity is assumed to be always observed in the CPS. Define Y^* to be the Box-Cox (1964) transformed earnings ($Y^* = [Y^\theta - 1]/\theta$), Z to be an unobserved, hypothetical variable such that Y is missing if $Z > 0$, and suppose (Y^*, Z) given X is bivariate normal with correlation ρ. Since CPS income is "top coded" at $50,000, if Y is greater than $50,000 and $Z \leq 0$, then the observed income is $50,000. The parameters of the regression of (Y^*, Z) on X as well as θ and ρ are unknown and to be estimated.

If $\rho = 0$, nonresponse is ignorable, whereas if $\rho \neq 0$, nonresponse is nonignorable; as $|\rho| \rightarrow 1$, the extent of nonignorable nonresponses becomes more serious in the sense that the distribution of Y^* residuals for respondents becomes less normal and more skewed. This defines the LSW model, and LSW obtains maximum likelihood estimates for all parameters, explicitly recognizing the truncation of Y at $50,000 in the CPS. Essentially the same model with the restriction that $\theta = 0 (Y^* = \log[Y])$ is used in GRZ. The extension to other θ is certainly interesting and potentially quite useful. Of particular importance, it gives users a broader range of models for nonresponse to which sensitivity of estimation can be investigated.

It must not be forgotten, however, that the estimation of parameters is relying critically on the assumed normality of the regression of (Y^*, Z) on X: both θ and ρ are chosen by maximum likelihood to make the residuals in this regression look as normal as possible. If in the real world there is no (θ, ρ) that makes this regression like a normal linear regression, then there is no real reason to believe that the answers that are obtained by maximizing θ and ρ lead to better real world answers. A small artificial example I've used before (Rubin 1978*a*) illustrates this point in a simpler context:

> Suppose that we have a population of 1000 units, try to record a variable Z, but half of the units are nonrespondents. For the 500 respondents, the data look half-normal. Our objective is to know the

> mean of Z for all 1000 units. Now, if we believe that the nonrespondents are just like the respondents except for a completely random mechanism that deleted values (i.e., if we believe that mechanisms are ignorable), the mean of the respondents, that is, the mean of the half-normal distribution, is a plausible estimate of the mean for the 1000 units of the population. However, if we believe that the distribution of Z for the 1000 units in the population should look more or less normal, then a more reasonable estimate of the mean for the 1000 units would be the minimum observed value because units with Z values less than the mean refused to respond. Clearly, the data we have observed cannot distinguish between these two models except when coupled with prior assumptions. (p. 22)

Notwithstanding the above caveats, suppose we put our faith in the normal linear model for the bivariate regression of (Y^*, Z) on X. LSW produces some interesting results using white males, 16–65 years old, in the 1970, 1975, 1976, and 1980 CPS. One interesting, but not surprising, result is that fixing θ at 1 ($Y^* = Y$) produces very different answers from fixing θ at 0 ($Y^* = \log[Y]$); if $\theta = 1$, nonrespondents are imputed to earn less than matching respondents, whereas if $\theta = 0$, nonrespondents are imputed to earn more than matching respondents. With θ fixed, the asymmetry in the Y^* given X residuals addresses the correlation ρ and so determines the extent to which the nonresponse is nonignorable. Thus, we have learned that the Y given X residuals are skewed left and the $\log(Y)$ given X residuals are skewed right. Further study shows that $\theta = .45$ provides a better fit to the data than either $\theta = 0$ or $\theta = 1$, but that the residuals are still skewed right; under $\theta = .45$ we find that nonrespondents are imputed to earn more than similar respondents; $\theta = .45$ leads to a 10% increase in average earnings over the CPS hot deck values, \$18,000 versus \$16,000.

But we must remember that if the distribution of $Y^{(.45)}$ given X really has the right asymmetry that is observed when $Y^{(.45)}$ is regressed on X, then the adjustment created by assuming a selection effect on Z is entirely inappropriate, and (just as with the artificial half-normal example) the data cannot distinguish between the ignorable and nonignorable alternatives. More precisely, suppose first that, in the population, $Y^{(.45)}$ has a linear regression on X with a skew distribution of residuals like that observed when we regress $Y^{(.45)}$ on X for the CPS data and that nonresponse is ignorable; such a model would generate data just like those we have observed, and then we should *not* be imputing higher incomes for nonrespondents than respondents with the same X values.

In contrast, suppose that $Y^{(.45)}$ in the population really has a normal linear regression on X and that the stochastic censoring implied by the LSW nonresponse model is correct, that is, nonresponse is nonignorable with this particular form; then, as LSW shows, we should be imputing higher incomes for nonrespondents than respondents with the same X

values. There is no way that the observed data can distinguish between these two alternatives; if we really believe Y^* given X in the population is *normal* for some θ, then we can correctly assert that the CPS hot deck procedure is biased. If we admit the possibility that Y^* given X is not normal or even symmetric for any θ, then we cannot legitimately assert that the LSW answers are better than the CPS hot deck answers.

In the same vein, LSW's checking the accuracy of the LSW model by checking the prediction of respondents' values does not adequately check the imputations of the model for nonrespondents. In particular, both the ignorable and nonignorable nonresponse models discussed above will accurately reproduce the observed data for respondents, even though they predict very different amounts for nonrespondents. In order to address which model is more appropriate, we need data from nonrespondents or some external information about the distribution of reported incomes in the entire population.

9.7 The CPS-SSA-IRS Exact Match File

There is a data set that provides data relevant to accessing the differences in distributions of incomes between CPS nonrespondents and respondents. This data set is the CPS-SSA-IRS (SSA = Social Security Administration; IRS = Internal Revenue Service) Exact Match File (Aziz, Kilss, and Scheuren 1978). The exact match file is based on a sample of 1978 CPS interviews with incomes obtained from SSA and IRS administration records. Thus, this file is a data set consisting of CPS respondents and nonrespondents with administrative income always observed. By treating CPS nonrespondents' administrative income as missing and applying specific methods for handling nonresponse, we do in fact obtain some evidence for the adequacy of these specific techniques for adjusting for nonresponse bias, although admittedly for administrative income rather than CPS reported income. Both HR and GRZ compare results of their imputations to the administrative data for nonrespondents from the exact match file.

HR compares the imputations for social security benefits from a version of the CPS hot deck and those from an explicit two-stage log-linear/linear model and also evaluates the utility of multiple imputation for obtaining proper inferences. Since HR's objective is to predict social security benefits rather than total income, its results do not address the same kind of income nonresponse as studied in LSW.

GRZ, however, like LSW, studies earned income using maximum likelihood on essentially the same selection model as LSW with the restriction $\theta = 0$ (i.e., income is lognormal) and compares these predictions of nonrespondents' administrative income to their actual administrative income. Interesting conclusions of GRZ include: (a) the model predicts nonrespondent income rather well; (b) the true residuals in the log scale for the entire population, although not normal, are approximately symmetric; and (c) the CPS hot deck underestimates income by about 7 percent. These results lend modest, although mixed, support to the utility of LSW/GRZ-type selection models for CPS income data.

The results of combining the efforts of LSW and GRZ by applying the extended LSW selection model to the exact match file would certainly be of interest. Of particular importance, such an application would help investigate which model for nonresponse is truly appropriate for CPS income data. Any such study would ideally include the use of multiple imputation so that variability can be properly assessed.

References

Aziz, F., B. Kilss, and F. Scheuren. 1978. *1973 current population survey—Administrative record exact match file codebook, part I, Code counts and item definitions*. Washington, D.C.: U.S. Department of Health, Education, and Welfare.

Box, G. E. P., and D. R. Cox. 1964. An analysis of transformations. *Journal Royal Statistical Society B* 26: 211–52.

Cochran, W. G., and D. B. Rubin. 1973. Controlling bias in observational studies: A review. *Sankhya – A, 35*, 4: 417–46.

Greenlees, J. S., W. S. Reece, and K. D. Zieschang. 1982. Imputation of missing values when the probability of response depends upon the variable being imputed. *Journal of the American Statistical Association* 77: 251–61.

Heckman, J. 1979. Sample selection bias as a specification error. *Econometrica* 47: 153–61.

Herzog, T. N., and D. B. Rubin. 1983. Using multiple imputations to handle nonresponse in sample surveys. In *Incomplete data and sample surveys*, vol. 2, *Theory and bibliographics*. D. B. Rubin, W. G. Medow, and I. Olkin (eds.), pp. 209–45. New York: Academic Press.

Lillard, L., J. P. Smith, and F. Welch. 1981. What do we really know about wages: The importance of non-reporting and census imputation. University of California at Los Angeles, unpublished paper.

Little, R. J. A. 1982. Models for response in sample surveys. *Journal of the American Statistical Association* 77: 237–50.

Rosenbaum, P. R., and D. B. Rubin. 1983. The central role of the propensity score in the analysis of observational studies for causal effects. *Biometrika* 70, no. 1: 41–55.

Rubin, D. B. 1976*a*. Multivariate matching methods that are equal percent bias reducing, I: Some examples. *Biometrics* 32, no. 1: 109–20. Printer's correction note p. 955.

———. 1976*b*. Multivariate matching methods that are equal percent bias reducing, II: Maximums on bias reduction for fixed sample sizes. *Biometrics* 32, no. 1: 121–32. Printer's correction note p. 955.

———. 1976*c*. Inference and missing data. *Biometrika* 63: no. 3: 581–92.

———. 1978*a*. Multiple imputations in sample surveys—A phenomenological Bayesian approach to nonresponse. With discussion and reply. *Proceedings of the Survey Research Methods Section of the American Statistical Association*, 20–34. Also in *Imputation and editing of faulty or missing survey data*. U.S. Department of Commerce, 1–23.

———. 1978*b*. Bayesian inference for causal effects: The role of randomization. *Annals of Statistics* 7, no. 1: 34–58.

———. 1980*a*. Bias reduction using Mahalanobis' metric matching. *Biometrics* 36, no. 2: 295–98. Printer's correction p. 296.

———. 1980*b*. *Handling nonresponse in sample surveys by multiple imputations*. U.S. Department of Commerce, Bureau of the Census Monograph.

PART

III Pensions and Benefits as Labor Cost Components

10 Estimating Wage-Fringe Trade-Offs: Some Data Problems

Robert S. Smith and Ronald G. Ehrenberg

Fringe benefits are a growing component of total compensation, and their growth presents a number of challenges to economists on both the scientific and policymaking level. For example, when the government passes legislation requiring that pensions be made more generous or more widely available, it is natural to ask just who will pay the cost. Economic theory, as we will show, is quite clear on this point. It suggests that when pensions increase wages will decrease, other things equal, thus implying that it is workers themselves who will pay the cost of pension reform legislation. The view that wages and pensions are negatively related (if other things are held constant) is not widely held among noneconomists, however. Casual observation, in fact, yields quite the opposite view. The highest-wage workers receive the best pensions, and high-wage firms are the very ones with the most generous pensions. Even sophisticated studies that attempt to control for the "other things" influencing total compensation sometimes estimate that wages and pensions are positively related (Blinder, Gordon, and Wise 1979).

To take another example, federal/private sector wage comparability studies have historically ignored fringe benefits. If increases in earnings and increases in fringe benefits are roughly *proportional* within each sector, then changes in earnings may serve as an adequate index (given the cost of acquiring fringe benefit data) for changes in total compensation. However, if, as economists suspect, earnings and fringe benefits are

Robert S. Smith and Ronald G. Ehrenberg are with the New York State School of Industrial and Labor Relations, Cornell University, Ithaca, New York.

An earlier version of this study was done for the President's Commission on Pension Policy, but the views presented herein are solely those of the authors. The authors wish to thank Dan Sherman for his invaluable assistance on this project. The paper has also benefited from excellent comments by Charles Brown and Jack Triplett on earlier drafts.

inversely related within each sector, other things equal, then comparability studies that ignore fringes could be seriously deficient.

Finally, many labor market studies that *should* be measuring and analyzing total compensation focus instead on wages or earnings owing to the general paucity of fringe benefit data. If marginal changes in wages and fringe benefits are proportionally related, other things equal, these studies may not contain fatal biases; however, if such changes can be shown to be inversely related, then problems of unknown magnitude could arise in such important areas as judging sectors with labor surpluses and shortages, assessing the existence and size of compensating wage differentials, measuring the returns to human capital investments, and measuring the "unexplained residual" for minorities and women.

Common to the above examples is the problem of estimating the trade-off between wages and fringe benefits. While estimating this trade-off might appear on the surface to be a straightforward matter of obtaining data on fringe benefits, we will show in this paper that it is not. Instead, there are potentially serious biases that arise when standard data sets are used. Thus, if we are to successfully shed light on the important issues of wage-fringe trade-offs, some rather unique data requirements must be met.

This paper represents an inquiry into some of the data related difficulties inherent in estimating wage-fringe trade-offs, and it explores the usefulness of a particular source of data in meeting these difficulties.

In section 10.1 we briefly present the theory underlying economists' notions about the trade-offs between wages and fringe benefits. Section 10.2 discusses the unique data required to test this theory, and section 10.3 describes a test using such data. In section 10.4 tests for wage-fringe trade-offs using conventional data are described and analyzed for the purpose of assessing the extent of any biases that arise when such data are used. The paper concludes with a section on data recommendations.

10.1 The Theory of the Wage-Fringe Relationship

Economic theory of the relationship between wages and fringe benefits in competitive markets starts with the notion that it is *total compensation* that matters to employers. They are trying to maximize profits and, in so doing, will endeavor to assemble a labor force of sufficient quality and size to enable them to produce output that they can sell at competitive prices. To attract the desired quantity and quality of labor requires that they offer a compensation bundle the total value of which is at least as good as other employers are offering. However, if they offer total compensation that is too high, they will find their costs are such that they cannot compete in the product market. The result of these forces is that they will offer total compensation that is no more or less than is offered by other employers to workers in the same labor market. In short, for every type of worker or skill grade, there will be a "going rate" of total compensation that firms must pay.

Employees, on the supply side of the market, will of course want to obtain offers that are as large as possible. They will find, however, that firms are unwilling to offer compensation packages that are more in total value than the going rate. Their problem, then, is to choose the package whose *composition* best suits their tastes.

The employer and employee sides of the market, discussed above, are summarized graphically in figure 10.1, using pensions as an example of a

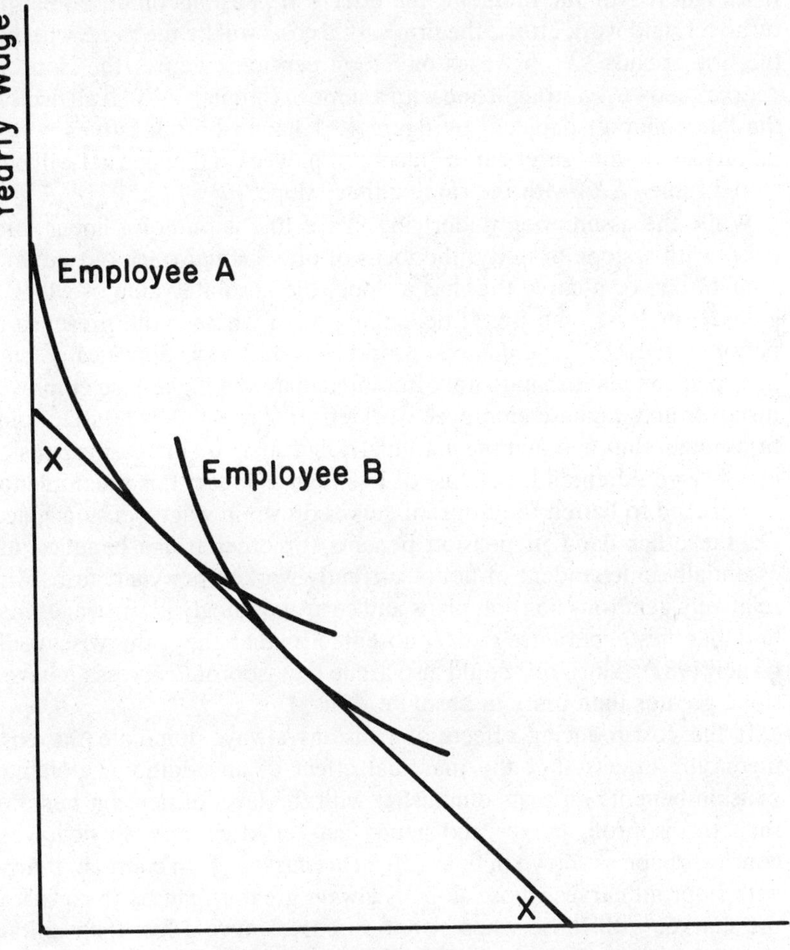

Fig. 10.1 The trade-off between wages and promised pension benefits.

fringe benefit. This graph depicts the relationship between pensions and wages, and it implicitly assumes all *other* job characteristics and elements of compensation are already determined. We have argued that employers must pay the "going rate" in terms of total compensation, and that at this compensation level they will be competitive in both the labor and product markets. The employer side of the labor market can thus be represented by an "isoprofit curve"—a curve along which any combination of wages and pensions yields equal profits to the firm. The isoprofit curve shown, XX, is the zero-profit (competitive) curve, and it implies that the firm must pay $\$X$ in total compensation to be competitive in the labor market. If we ignore, for the moment, the effects of pensions on absenteeism, turnover, and work effort, the firm's total costs will be the same whether the firm spends $\$X$ on wages or $\$X$ on pensions; hence, the isoprofit "curve" shown is a straight line with a slope of (minus) unity. If all firms in the labor market depicted by figure 10.1 have isoprofit curves with a unitary slope, the "offer curve" facing employees in that market will be a straight line (XX) with the same unitary slope.

While the assumption underlying figure 10.1 is one of a linear offer curve with a slope of unity, the locus of offers *could* trace out either a straight line or a curve that has a slope, the absolute value of which is greater (or less) than unity, depending upon whether the presence of pensions reduces (or enhances) worker productivity. Specifically, suppose pension plans that do not offer immediate vesting reduce employee turnover and increase employee work effort (Lazear 1979, 1981). Some firms might thus find that the marginal dollar spent on increasing pension benefits would entail a net cost of less than a dollar; this phenomenon would tend to flatten the isoprofit curves drawn in wage-pension space. On the other hand, if pension benefits (or other fringe benefits) are essentially independent of hours currently worked per year, firms with relatively generous pension plans and correspondingly lower wages may find that they experience greater absenteeism than they otherwise would (Allen 1981). Thus, one could also argue that isoprofit curves can have a slope greater than unity in absolute value.

If the cost-reducing effects of pensions always dominate the cost-increasing effects, but the marginal effect of an additional dollar of pension benefits on costs diminishes with the level of pension benefits, then the isoprofit curve, and hence market offer curve, will have a concave shape as shown in figure 10.2 (the curve yy). In contrast, if firms with isoprofit curves whose slope is always greater than unity coexist in the market with those whose isoprofit curves have a less than unitary slope, the locus of offers to employees could fall along a convex curve—$QRST'$ as shown in figure 10.3.

The above arguments concerning the offer curve, which are derived from an analysis of the employer side of the market, suggest that the

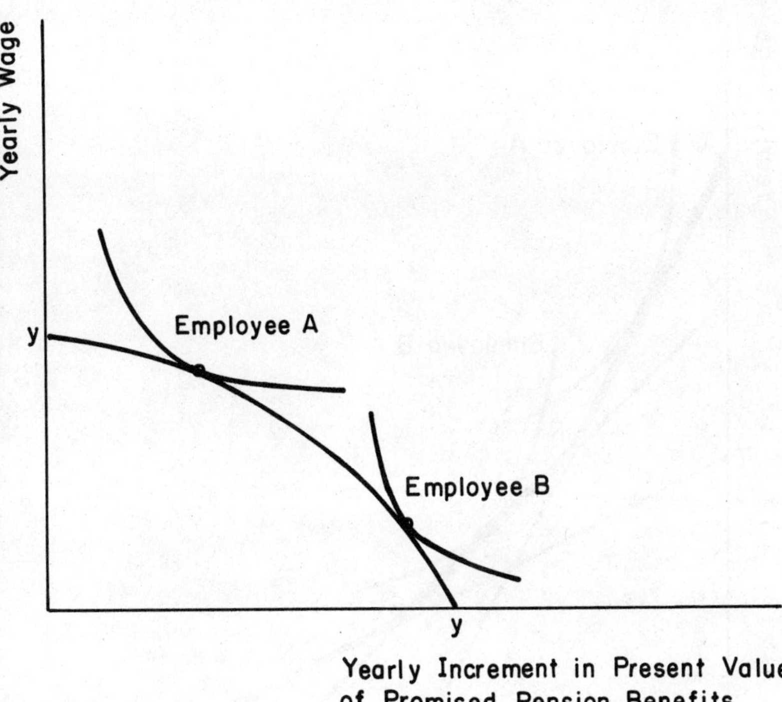

Fig. 10.2 A concave offer curve resulting from diminishing marginal effects of pensions on costs.

problem facing employees is one of choosing the compensation package that maximizes utility. That is, the observed compensation packages in a given labor market will trace out the offer curve that exists at any point in time, and the package chosen by any employee will reflect his or her utility function. The *exact* shapes of employee indifference curves in wage-pension space are not critical to our analysis, although linear or concave indifference curves would in general lead to corner solutions (in which case a variety of wage/pension "mixes" would *not* be observed in a given market). We have thus drawn the indifference curves in figures 10.1, 10.2, and 10.3 as convex. Are there other reasons to suppose these indifference curves are convex?

In the life cycle context, workers could be viewed as maximizing a lifetime stream of utility; thus, different wage-pension combinations could simply be viewed as different asset portfolios. However, given one's tastes, the marginal rate of substitution between wage goods and pensions is likely to be diminishing. As wages are *increased* and pensions are *reduced*, more of one's total compensation becomes taxable (at

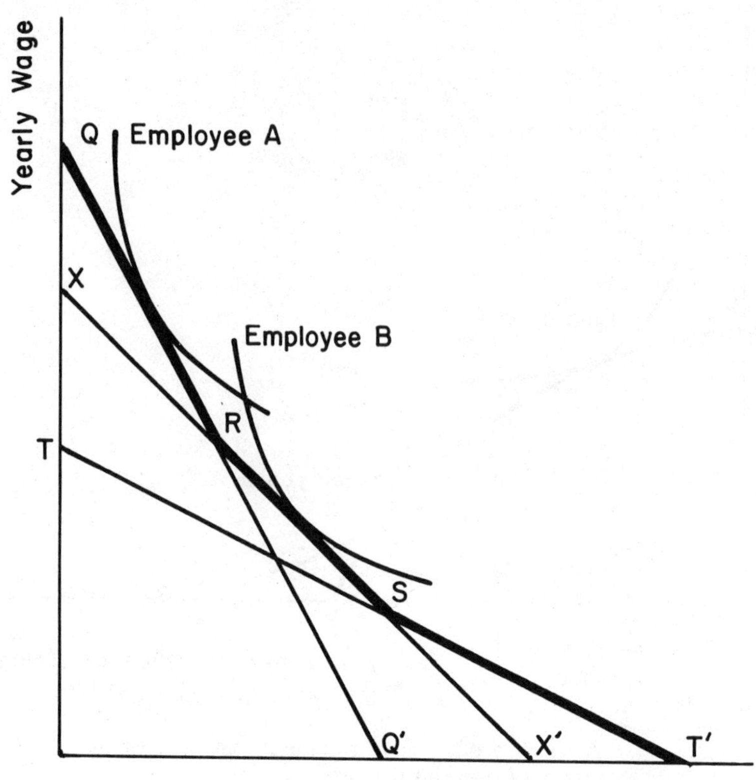

Fig. 10.3 A convex offer curve: XX', pensions do not change productivity; TT', pensions increase productivity; QQ', pensions reduce productivity.

progressively increasing rates) at the relatively high tax rates that prevail during one's working years. These relatively high and increasing rates tend to progressively increase the amount of pretax wages employees would require to compensate them for successive reductions in pension benefits. Conversely, as wages are *reduced* and pension benefits are *increased*, less of one's total compensation becomes accessible for current expenditure—a fact suggesting that workers will be willing to accept ever-smaller wage reductions in return for progressive increases in pension benefits.[1] Thus convex indifference curves in wage-pension space seem likely to exist.

Figures 10.1, 10.2, and 10.3, and the associated theory behind them suggest three things about the relationship between wages and pensions.

First, they suggest that employees pay for their own pensions through a lowered wage. That is, there should be a negative wage-pension relationship once other things that affect compensation have been controlled for (as they have by assumption in all figures). Second, theory also suggests that the above negative trade-off might be close to (or fluctuate around) unity. Third, the observed trade-off could be linear, convex, or concave.

Similar reasoning about how labor markets work leads us, more generally, to expect that the trade-off between wages and *any* fringe benefit, ceteris paribus, will be negative. Moreover, when such benefits are expressed in terms of employer cost, the trade-off we can observe should be close to unitary. Thus, companies with a more generous fringe benefit package will tend to pay lower wages, other things equal.

The theoretical considerations noted here suggest the outlines of an empirical study wherein the determinants of wages could be estimated by an equation such as

$$W = a_0 + a_1 P + a_f F + a_x X + e, \tag{1}$$

where W is the wage or salary paid to workers, P is the present value of yearly per worker pension accruals ("normal cost"),[2] F is the employer cost of other fringe benefits per worker, X is a vector of all other factors that influence wages or salaries, and e is a random error term. The coefficients a_i are to be estimated, and it is predicted that a_1 and a_f will be negative and close to unitary in absolute value.[3]

10.2 Data Requirements

While equation (1) appears to offer a rather simple empirical test, to estimate it requires data that do not normally exist in standard household or firm surveys. In particular, equation (1) imposes three data requirements that are difficult to meet. First, the variables P and F require the availability of data on employers' costs of fringe benefits. That is, we need to have access to estimates of "normal pension cost" and the cost of other fringe benefits—which in many cases requires actuarial estimates that take into account employee turnover and other factors affecting the probability that they will be eligible for, or choose to receive, a given benefit. These data can only be found in *employer*-based data sets—and even there only rarely.

Second, many fringe benefits are explicitly stated as a function of wages, so that detailed information on the determinants of their actuarial value are required to estimate equation (1) in an unbiased way. W and P in equation (1), for example, are closely related for more than the *behavioral* reason suggested by theory. They are related in a very *technical* sense, because pension benefits are normally calculated as some fraction of wages. We are interested in the behavioral relationship, not the technical one, but the latter relationship (which is a *positive* one) may obscure the former (which we hypothesize to be negative). We must therefore find a way to filter out the technical from the behavioral relationship.

One very simple filtering process consists of specifying that P (normal cost) is a linear function of W and a vector (Z) of all pension characteristics (vesting, replacement rates, COLA adjustments, etc.):

$$P = b_0 + b_1 W + b_z Z + u. \tag{2}$$

One could then proceed to estimate equations (1) and (2) using a two-stage least-squares estimator. What this essentially involves is regressing P on all independent variables in (1) and (2) except W. Using these regression estimates, an instrument for P (call it $\hat{P}$) is calculated and entered as an independent variable in equation (1), replacing P.[4] The variable $\hat{P}$ is an estimate of normal cost that is "purged" of the effects of wages. Using $\hat{P}$ in equation (1) thus would allow us to observe the behavioral relationship.

Variables that belong in vector Z are thus necessary to an unbiased estimate of equation (1). Like actuarial estimates of the cost of fringe benefits, these variables are not commonly found in data sets; however, when they can be had, they are found only in *employer* data sets.

The third need is for measures of the variables in vector X—the "other things" that influence wages. Economists normally use data on education, age, race, sex, marital status, and so forth, to control for these things, but such variables are not usually found in *employer* data sets. Thus, we must either find ways to match employer and household data sets or take pains to address some rather severe problems inherent in employer data.

In particular, it is likely that a firm—through its use of hiring standards and a particular compensation package—will assemble a fairly homogeneous work force. However, its work force will tend to systematically vary from the work force in other firms in characteristics that are very difficult to measure: motivation, dependability, competence, and aggressiveness. In using employer based data, the problem created by firms' employment of homogeneous workers who differ in unmeasurable ways from those employed by other firms is the classic one of "omitted variables bias." Firms that offer higher total compensation will in general be able to select employees with higher motivation, dependability, etc. High-ability workers thus receive higher wages and higher fringe benefits, so that unless data on ability are available, the fringe benefit variables in equation (1) will pick up the effects of ability. A positive bias on the coefficients of the fringe benefit variables is thus distinctly possible when one is using a data set in which worker quality is unobservable and potentially varies across firms.

Previous studies we have done on the wage-pension trade-off in the public sector do not appear to have suffered much from the above problem of omitted variables bias (Ehrenberg and Smith 1981). The local government employers in those data sets were hiring workers—police, firefighters, and nonuniformed employees—who all worked in the same "industry" and had very similar duties across cities; thus, it is unlikely that employee quality varied substantially across cities. However, when one moves to tests for wage-fringe trade-offs in the *private* sector, homogeneity of worker quality across employers is much less likely. The managers of a company producing sophisticated technical equipment are likely to have different characteristics from those in a trucking firm, and those in highly competitive industries are likely to differ from those in a public utility. One purpose of this paper is to inquire into the significance of, and a solution to, this problem of unmeasured heterogeneity of workers across firms.

10.3 Estimating Wage-Fringe Trade-Offs

We were able to obtain an employer based data set that generally met the requirements outlined in the previous section. These data were provided to us by Hay Associates, a large compensation consulting firm. Hay conducts its own survey of cash and noncash compensation within client firms and was able to provide us with a sample of roughly two hundred usable observations. The sample has several rather unique characteristics.

10.3.1 Controls for Other Influences on Wages

First, salary and fringe benefit data were provided to us for three different white-collar job grades within each company. Hay evaluates every job within a client company using three principal criteria: required "know-how," accountability, and the degree of problem solving involved. It assigns point values to each job characteristic, totals them, and uses these "Hay Point" evaluations as points of reference when comparing compensation within and across firms.

We were interested in obtaining the compensation associated with given Hay Point levels as one means of controlling for the "other things" that influence wages. Thus, we asked Hay to provide us with data at three different Hay Point levels in each of the firms: 100 Hay Points (entry level white-collar job for someone with a Bachelor's degree), 200 Hay Points (supervision of a small staff section), and 400 Hay Points (lower middle management position or a department head in a small organization). It normally takes three to six years to go from a 100 to a 200 Hay Point job, and seven to fifteen years to go from a 100 to a 400 point position within an organization.

Another crucial advantage to obtaining data on different job grades within each company is that it permits one to employ a procedure that, in effect, controls for the firm-specific effects of unmeasured worker characteristics. For example, suppose that salaries at the 100 Hay Point level are given by the following variant of equation (1):

$$W_{100} = a_0 + a_1 P_{100} + a_f F_{100} + a_x X + a_m M + e, \tag{3}$$

where M stands for the unmeasured worker characteristics, and X contains other measurable variables that influence wages. Suppose also that a similar equation describes wages at, say 400 Hay Points:

$$W_{400} = a_0' + a_1 P_{400} + a_f F_{400} + a_x' X + a_m M + e'. \tag{4}$$

The assumptions underlying equations (3) and (4) are that the wage-fringe trade-offs (a_1 and a_f) are the same at each Hay Point level, but that the intercept terms (a_0 and a_0') differ. We also assume that the coefficients on the variables in the X vector differ, but that the X variables (firm size and industry, for example) are the *same* at each Hay Point level within a firm. Finally we assume that the unobservable worker characteristics (M) are constant within a firm and that their marginal effects (a_m) are the same in each equation (in effect, they add a constant absolute amount to compensation at each job level within a given firm).

Subtracting equation (3) and (4), we arrive at an equation that explains the *difference* in salaries across Hay Point levels *within* each firm:

$$\begin{aligned} W_{400} - W_{100} = {} & (a_0' - a_0) + a_1 (P_{400} - P_{100}) \\ & + a_f (F_{400} - F_{100}) + (a_x' - a_x) X + e''. \end{aligned} \tag{5}$$

One can note from equation (5) that the unobservable effects of worker quality drop out of the equation (we are explaining *within-firm* wage profiles now). Thus, having access to compensation data at different job grades within firms should allow us to work around at least some of the problems of omitted variables bias.

10.3.2 Employer Cost Data on Fringe Benefits

The second unique feature of our data set is that it contains actuarial estimates of employers' costs of all privately provided fringe benefits—pensions, paid vacations and holidays, medical-dental plans, death and disability benefits, and capital accumulation plans (profit sharing or stock options). The means of each element in total compensation (excluding government mandated items) are displayed for each Hay Point level in table 10.1. In the case of pensions, death and disability benefits, and

Table 10.1 **Means of Hay Compensation Data Per Year**

	Hay Point Level		
	100	200	400
Salary	$13,434	$20,646	$34,862
Pension value	816	1,450	2,870
Value of vacations and holidays	1,334	2,057	3,490
Death benefit value	234	346	595
Disability benefit value	447	694	1,221
Capital accumulation value	385	600	1,034
Medical-dental plan value (same for all H.P. levels)	1,114	1,114	1,114

NOTE: The range (standard deviation) of the salary data are as follows:
100 H.P.: 8,200–26,100 (2,407)
200 H.P.: 13,700–31,000 (2,972)
400 H.P.: 24,700–50,700 (4,749)

capital accumulation plans, values shown indicate the present value of the estimated increase in firm liabilities accruing during a year.

10.3.3 Data on Pension Characteristics

A third feature of our data set is that it contains information on several important pension characteristics: the effects of social security benefits on the pension benefits promised by the firm, eligibility and vesting provisions, replacement rates, cost-of-living adjustments to benefits, death benefits, and retirement age. The means of several of these pension characteristics are summarized in table 10.2. These data permit us to estimate wage equations using the instrumental variables procedure outlined in section 10.2—the purpose of which is to purge the wage equation of the technical dependence of pension costs on wages.

Unfortunately, the actuarial calculations of capital accumulation and death/disability benefit values were highly complex and we were not provided with sufficient data to meaningfully purge them of their technical dependence on wages. Our solution to this problem was to *assume* a

Table 10.2 **Summary Statistics on Selected Pension Plan Characteristics**

Percent of plans with full vesting after 10 years	72%
Percent integrated with social security	87%
Percent with formal or informal COLA	45%
Mean replacement rate for 30-year employee with a salary base of $25,000	56%
Mean replacement rate for 30-year employee with a salary base of $50,000	47%
Percent with disability retirement	32%

one-for-one trade-off between them and wages and move the values of these three fringe benefits from the F vectors to the left-hand side of equation (5)—adding them to salaries (W_{100} and W_{400}) to form W'_{100} and W'_{400}, respectively.

10.3.4 The Estimating Equations

The wage equations we ultimately estimated had the form

$$(6) \quad \Delta W' = a''_0 + a_1 (\Delta P) + a_3 \Delta F + a_4 (S) + a_5 (T) + a_d D + e'' ,$$

where $\Delta W'$ is the change in salaries plus death, disability, and capital accumulation fringe benefits from one Hay Point level to another within a firm; ΔP is the change in pension value from one Hay Point level to another (an instrumental variable, $\Delta \hat{P}$, was substituted for ΔP as noted above); ΔF is the change in days of paid leave from one Hay Point level to another (the value of medical-dental plans dropped out of the vector F because it was constant across Hay Point levels within a firm); and the observed firm characteristics variables are firm size (S), a dichotomous variable taking the value of 1 if the firm has a mandatory retirement policy and 0 if it does not (T), and vector of industry dummy variables (D). The mandatory retirement variable, (T), is included because firms with mandatory retirement may well have steeper earnings profiles than those that do not (Lazear 1979). The average company size in this sample was 12,360 employees, and 50% were in manufacturing industries. No firm in the sample required pension contributions of its employees.

Equation (6) was estimated using the two-stage least-squares procedure outlined in section 10.2. To simultaneously estimate the "normal cost" function approximated by equation (2) in the context of explaining salary differentials across job grades within firms, we had to reformulate the equation as follows:[5]

$$(7) \quad \Delta P = b_0 + b_1 \Delta W' + b_z Z + u .$$

The variables in Z include the replacement rate (assuming workers retire at age 65 with thirty years of service), whether or not employees are immediately members of the pension plan, whether or not the plan fully vests after ten years of service, whether or not benefits are adjusted to reflect cost-of-living increases, whether or not disability retirement provisions are present, the degree to which retirement benefits are offset by social security benefits, and whether or not an assumption of future salary increases was made in the actuarial calculation of normal pension cost.

Three versions of equation (6) were estimated: differences between 200 and 100 Hay Points, differences between 400 and 200 Hay Points, and differences between 400 and 100 Hay Points. The results are presented in table 10.3. (Results of the first-stage estimation are presented in table 10.A.1 in the appendix.)

Table 10.3 **Estimates of Equation (6) Determinants of the Change in Salary Plus Selected Fringe Benefits across Hay Point Levels within Firms (method: two-stage least squares)**

	Coefficients (standard errors) of Independent Variables		
	400–100 H.P.	200–100 H.P.	400–200 H.P.
Change in paid holidays (days)	109.49(186.81)	−220.32(176.16)	80.88(149.85)
Change in pension value (dollars)	−.106(.466)	−.445(.642)	.085(.472)
Presence of mandatory retirement	−187.46(586.65)	41.07(239.26)	−229.04(421.04)
Firm size (number of employees)	.021(.009)	.009(.004)	.012(.006)
Industrywide effects (financial, insurance, real estate omitted):			
Durable mfg.	643.32(757.78)	79.47(309.64)	513.50(546.93)
Nondurable mfg.	3,229.67(803.63)	957.80(327.40)	2,210.88(581.30)
Transportation, communications, and public utility	1,036.58(1,015.00)	802.47(413.89)	354.80(732.21)
Service	−415.23(1,143.15)	−227.06(464.46)	−220.83(824.07)
Firms with missing data on firm size	1,216.80(791.45)	565.70(320.08)	620.65(568.46)
Constant	22,019.01(1,097.47)	7,546.97(447.87)	14,468.68(784.09)
R^2	.14	.13	.12
Number of observations	193	193	193

The results of most interest for our current purposes, of course, are the estimated coefficients on the pension and paid leave variables. Theory led us to expect that the coefficient on the pension variable should be roughly -1 in magnitude, and that the coefficient on the paid leave variable should be approximately equal to the negative of the change in the daily wage from one Hay Point level to another (which was about \$30 for 100 to 200 Hay Points, \$57 for 200 to 400 Hay Points, and \$87 for 100 to 400 Hay Points). Of the six estimated coefficients, only three have the expected negative sign. While none is significantly different from its expected magnitude, the estimates are so imprecise that none is significantly different from zero either. Thus, the results of this test give no support for our theory of the wage-fringe relationship.

Two possible explanations for these disappointing results must be considered. First, it is possible, as noted earlier, that our procedure for finding an instrument for ΔP in equation (6) is too crude, so that the relationship between ΔP and $\Delta \hat{P}$ is not very close. This seems unlikely, however, because, as can be seen from table 10.A.1 in the appendix, the variables in the first stage of our estimating procedure explain 55–60% of the variance in ΔP.

Second, our assumption that unmeasured employee characteristics add a constant dollar amount to total compensation at each Hay Point level may be incorrect. A tractable alternative assumption is that these unobserved characteristics affect total compensation *equiproportionally* at each Hay Point level.[6] Suppose, for example, that total compensation at any Hay Point level can be expressed as

$$(8) \qquad W(1 + p + f) = Ae^{(a_0 + a_x X + \phi M + u)},$$

where p and f are employers' costs of pensions and other fringe benefits expressed as a fraction of wages, and ϕ is the fraction by which marginal changes in unmeasured employee characteristics increase total compensation. Taking logs and using the fact that $\ln(1 + r) \approx r$, when r is small, equation (8) can be approximated by

$$(9) \qquad \ln W = a_0' + a_x X + \phi M + a_1 p + a_f f + u,$$

where a_1 and a_f are predicted to be negative and equal to unity in absolute value.

The effects of unmeasured employee characteristics, ϕM, can be eliminated by differencing equation (9) across Hay Point levels within a firm to obtain

$$(10) \qquad \Delta(\ln W) = \mathrm{a}_0'' + a_1(\Delta p) + a_f(\Delta f) + \mathrm{a}_x'' X + u'',$$

where Δ indicates the change in the relevant variables across Hay Point levels. Because Δp will in general depend on changes in salaries across Hay Point levels, equation (10) was estimated using the instrumental variables approach analogous to that explained earlier.[7] The results of major interest are shown in table 10.4.

As with the results presented in table 10.3, those in table 10.4 offer no support for the theory outlined in section 10.1. We will return to a brief discussion of these negative findings in section 10.5. However, before doing so, it will be instructive to consider the biases that could exist if alternative procedures or data were used.

10.4 The Potential Biases Using Standard Data Sets

Sections 10.2 and 10.3 emphasized two potential biases in estimating wage-fringe trade-offs using conventional data sets. First, unless account is taken of the *technical* dependence of many fringe benefits on wages, the behavioral trade-off will be obscured. We dealt with this potential bias by using an instrumental variables approach. Second, it is possible that workers in roughly the same jobs will differ widely in certain unmeasurable characteristics across firms; that is, workers *within* firms may be fairly homogeneous, while *across* firms they may not be. The procedure we adopted in section 10.3 to deal with this problem was to purge the estimating equations of firm-specific "fixed effects" of these unmeasured characteristics by analyzing within-firm salary changes. In this section we analyze these two potential biases by investigating what happens when the above problems cannot be circumvented owing to lack of data.

10.4.1 Ordinary Least-Squares Estimates of Equations (6) and (10)

Suppose that we had data on employers' "normal cost" of pensions, but that we did not have information on the characteristics of the pension plan. This lack of data would preclude our use of the instrumental variables approach described in section 10.3, and we might be forced to use an ordinary least-squares estimating procedure. What would be the consequences of this defect in our data set?

The ordinary least-squares estimates of the coefficients of major interest in equations (6) and (10) are given in table 10.5. These estimates demonstrate very clearly the strong positive bias that emerges when one is unable to control for the technical dependence of pensions on wages.

Table 10.4 Estimated Wage-Fringe Trade-Offs, Equation (10)

	Estimated Coefficient (standard error)	
Equation	Pensions (a_1)	Paid Holidays (a_f)
400–100 H.P.	.359(.687)	−.362(1.555)
200–100 H.P.	.136(1.049)	1.615(2.553)
400–200 H.P.	.373(.682)	−.175(.958)

Table 10.5 **Estimates of the Wage-Fringe Trade-Off Using Ordinary Least Squares to Estimate Equations (6) and (10)**

		Estimated Coefficient (standard error)	
		Pension (a_1)	Paid Holidays (a_f)
Equation (6):	400–100 H.P.	1.513 (.323)	60.809 (174.922)
	200–100 H.P.	2.391 (.379)	−318.369 (153.482)
	400–200 H.P.	1.609 (.324)	40.730 (141.333)
Equation (10):	400–100 H.P.	1.247 (.501)	−.585 (1.538)
	200–100 H.P.	2.268 (.714)	−.185 (2.415)
	400–200 H.P.	.926 (.451)	−.259 (.951)

Estimated coefficients on the pension variables, which were close to zero and smaller than their standard errors in tables 10.3 and 10.4, are all strongly positive here. Thus, data sets that do not permit the researcher to disentangle the technical from the behavioral relationship between wages and pension costs will yield biased estimates of the trade-off.

10.4.2 Estimates Ignoring Firm-Specific Fixed Effects

Suppose now that we had access to data on employers' fringe benefit costs and pension plan characteristics, but that we had only one observation per firm. Lacking the data required to filter out the "fixed effects" of unmeasured worker quality within a firm, one would have to attempt to estimate trade-offs across firms at a fixed skill level. Estimates of equations like (3), (4), and (9) at each of the three Hay Point levels, using our instrumental variables approach described earlier, but of course omitting the variable M, were made in the course of our research. The results of major interest are reported in table 10.6.

In equations using the levels of salaries and fringe benefits, one can see (by comparing tables 10.3 and 10.6) that ignoring the fixed effects of

Table 10.6 **Estimates of the Wage-Fringe Trade-Off Ignoring the "Fixed Effects" of Unmeasured Worker Quality**

	Estimated Coefficient (standard error)	
Dependent Variable	Pensions (a_1)	Paid Holidays (a_f)
Salary level at 100 H.P.	−.006 (.686)	140.291 (75.550)
200 H.P.	−.059 (.512)	330.955 (102.806)
400 H.P.	−.126 (.480)	529.145 (146.000)
Log of salary at 100 H.P.	.506 (.590)	2.445 (1.386)
200 H.P.	−.187 (.509)	2.284 (1.227)
400 H.P.	−.635 (.451)	2.403 (1.034)

unmeasured worker characteristics does not alter the size or quality of the estimated wage-pension trade-off. However, ignoring these effects imparts a very definite positive bias to the trade-off between wages and paid holidays. Further, the fact that the estimated coefficient grows more positive as one moves up the Hay Point scale tends to suggest the effects of unmeasured characteristics may also tend to grow absolutely larger as workers are promoted. Generally, similar observations can be made by comparing the results of our logarithmic specification in table 10.4 with the corresponding results in table 10.6. Thus, there is clear evidence that omitted variables bias associated with unobserved worker characteristics is a problem that must be addressed when generating a data set for the purpose of estimating wage-fringe trade-offs.

10.5 Data Recommendations

This paper has attempted to identify the data needed to estimate trade-offs between wages and fringe benefits, and it has sought to explore the usefulness of one particular data set in this context. We have stressed that meaningful estimates of these trade-offs require data possessing three somewhat unique characteristics. First, estimates of the *magnitude* of any trade-offs require employer cost data—which, for many fringe benefits, entail actuarial estimation. Thus, researchers must have access to employer based data of a detailed nature.

Second, because pensions and many other fringe benefits are actuarial functions of wages or salaries, this technical relationship must be accounted for when estimating the behavioral relationship of interest. The data required to do this properly are those *other* variables also affecting the actuarial value of fringe benefits. In the case of pensions, data on replacement rates, vesting, COLA adjustments, the existence of death or disability benefits, and the like are required. We have demonstrated that ignoring this issue can result in seriously biased estimates.

Finally, heterogeneity of employees across employers presents researchers using employer based data with potentially severe problems of omitted variables bias. Unmeasured within-firm worker characteristics will tend to affect wages and fringes in the same direction, thus imparting a positive bias to the estimated coefficients on fringe benefits. We attempted to circumvent this by obtaining multiple observations per firm and analyzing within-firm compensation changes. While these procedures eliminated the countertheoretical estimates of a strong positive trade-off between wages and paid holidays, they did not allow us to find the predicted trade-off between wages and fringe benefits. In point of fact, we found no evidence in our data set to support the predictions of theory.

Explaining our negative findings cannot be done with certainty at this point. It may be that the theory is wrong, or at least not predictive of "real world" behavior. Given our earlier findings for the public sector, we are reluctant to embrace this explanation—at least until the weight of replicative findings mounts up. It may also be that our theory is correct, but that it is difficult to isolate the wage-fringe trade-off in the private sector; other nonpecuniary job characteristics (e.g., working conditions) may vary systematically.

A third possible explanation is that in our data set, skill level and fringe benefits were measured with so much error that estimates of existing negative trade-offs were biased toward zero. This possibility receives support from some of the errors we encountered in using the data and from the wide, overlapping ranges of salary levels at each of the three Hay Point levels (see the note to table 10.1). It may be that the Hay system of job rating is so arbitrary that across-firm comparisons are rendered essentially meaningless—and that the actuarial estimates of fringe benefit costs are so crude as to be unreliable. However, the Hay Point system of job evaluation is perhaps the foremost rating system of its kind in the world, the company is large and employs a battery of actuaries and other specialists, and the data we used were derived from a routine survey used and paid for by its clientele. It is hard to reconcile the hypothesis of sloppy or meaningless comparisons with the reputation and continued prosperity of the Hay company. If their work is of poor quality, would not they be punished by the market?

While we cannot answer the preceding question, there remains a fourth possible explanation. Perhaps the lack of data on employee characteristics caused the poor results. It could be that, despite our best efforts, we were really not able to completely avoid the positive biases associated with the problem of unmeasured worker characteristics. If this explanation is correct, it would suggest that some means must be found to include *employee* characteristics into employer based data sets. It suggests, in other words, that unless the employer based data that researchers must use contain information on the education, experience, training, etc., of employees, unbiased estimates of wage-fringe trade-offs may not be possible. We recommend, then, that to the three data requirements discussed at length in this paper, a fourth be added. Namely, employer based data sets should either include measures of average employee characteristics directly, or they should contain sufficient identification so that they can be cross-referenced to employee based data sets.

Appendix

Table 10.A.1 Estimated Coefficients Produced by Regressing ΔP on All Exogenous Variables in Equations (6) and (7)

Variable	Estimated Coefficients (standard errors)		
	400–100 H.P.	200–100 H.P.	400–200 H.P.
Paid holidays	26.65(28.06)	27.07(23.42)	26.39(22.98)
Firm size ÷ 1000	.02(1.33)	.41(.47)	.38(.98)
Firm size missing (0, 1)	210.89(122.12)	87.37(42.77)	123.41(89.66)
Durable mfg. (0, 1)	−25.84(122.62)	−22.57(43.77)	−3.04(90.41)
Nondurable mfg. (0, 1)	147.69(128.57)	46.45(45.80)	101.46(94.74)
Trans., public utility (0, 1)	−39.38(161.87)	75.29(56.90)	−114.61(118.69)
Service industry (0, 1)	221.33(173.21)	91.94(61.27)	129.58(127.27)
Mandatory retirement (0, 1)	82.83(85.94)	33.62(30.27)	49.19(63.05)
Pension replacement rate	.21(.03)	.07(.01)	.13(.02)
Immediate membership in plan (0, 1)	157.32(90.80)	63.59(31.99)	93.73(66.59)
Full vesting at ten years (0, 1)	−85.73(101.23)	−22.60(35.74)	−63.19(74.27)
COLA provided to benefits (0, 1)	467.12(92.12)	118.35(32.37)	348.79(67.45)
Disability retirement allowed (0, 1)	67.18(93.36)	13.64(33.31)	53.41(68.56)
Social security offset, flat %	.56(.53)	.09(.19)	.48(.39)
Social security offset, yearly level	14.61(17.02)	.67(5.98)	13.93(12.48)
Social security offset capped by max.	3.86(4.59)	.88(1.61)	2.98(3.37)
Social security offset by step rate (0, 1)	187.97(144.84)	23.24(51.48)	164.58(106.14)
Actuarial assumption of rising salaries (0, 1)	12.38(94.63)	24.82(33.32)	−12.56(69.67)
Intercept	218.19(163.65)	59.10(57.67)	159.06(119.89)
R^2	.60	.54	.58

Notes

1. While in theory people could borrow against their future pension promises, capital markets are not likely to be so perfect that they can do so without facing interest rates that rise with the size of the desired loan.

2. "Normal cost" is the actuarial value (in the present) of the increase in pension liabilities incurred during the current year—or the yearly contribution to the pension fund needed to keep it fully funded.

3. Equation (1), of course, restricts the wage-fringe trade-offs to be constant (linear). Alternative specifications of this "basic" equation would allow the trade-offs to be nonlinear, as suggested by our discussions of figures 10.2 and 10.3. While for the sake of convenience our analysis of the data and estimation problems will center on equation (1), we will briefly discuss our results using other functional forms.

4. Equation (2) can be viewed as a linear approximation to the complex way in which pension benefits are actually computed. There is no reason, of course, to think that a linear approximation is sacred, and future researchers might use more complex forms (e.g., higher order polynomials) to increase the precision of the instrument for P that is obtained. We should note, however, that this linear approximation has been used with some success in prior research (Smith 1981).

5. Equation (7) is derived by assuming that the following equations hold for, say the 400 and 100 Hay Point levels:

$$P_{400} = b_0'' + b_1 W_{400}' + b_z'' Z + u'' , \tag{7a}$$

$$P_{100} = b_0' + b_1 W_{100}' + b_z' Z + u' . \tag{7b}$$

Subtracting (7b) from (7a) results in equation (7), where

$$b_0 = b_0'' - b_0'; \ \Delta W' = W_{400}' - W_{100}'; \ b_z = b_z'' - b_z'; \text{ and } u = u'' - u' .$$

6. We are indebted to Charles Brown for this suggestion.

7. For reasons discussed earlier, fringe benefits except "paid days off" were added to the salary variable.

References

Allen, Steven G. 1981. Compensation, safety, and absenteeism: Evidence from the paper industry. *Industrial and Labor Relations Review* 34: 207–18.

Blinder, Alan S., Roger H. Gordon, and Donald E. Wise. 1979. Market wages, reservation wages, and retirement decisions. Paper read at the NBER Workshop on Social Security, 28–29 December 1979, Stanford University. Mimeo.

Ehrenberg, Ronald G., and Robert S. Smith. 1981. A framework for evaluating state and local government pension reform. In *Public sector labor markets*, ed. Peter Mieszkowski and George Peterson. COUPE Papers on Public Economics, no. 4. Washington, D.C: The Urban Institute Press.

Lazear, Edward P. 1979. Why is there mandatory retirement? *Journal of Political Economy* 87: 1261–84.

———. 1981. Agency, earnings profiles, productivity, and hours restrictions. *American Economic Review* 71: 606–20.

Smith, Robert S. 1981. Compensating differentials for pensions and underfunding in the public sector. *Review of Economics and Statistics* 63: 463–68.

Comment Charles Brown

Smith and Ehrenberg have brought an interesting source of data (compensation information from a major compensation consulting firm) to an interesting question (do workers pay for fringe benefits by receiving lower wages?). The paper is, in my view, no less interesting because the results do not support the theoretical model, which predicts that fringe benefits will generate compensating differentials in the wage rate.

The theory outlines an interesting special case of the general compensating differentials model. If one neglects the impact of pensions on worker productivity, etc., *each* firm's isoprofit curve for wages and pensions has a slope of minus one. Thus, in equilibrium the observed wage-pension locus will also have a slope of minus one, even though workers are not continually indifferent between equally costly wage-pension mixes.

Once the restriction that pensions have no effect on productivity is relaxed, this strong conclusion no longer holds. Indeed, with linear isoprofit curves with different slopes, the market wage-pension locus will be convex. This may establish a *loose presumption* that the market locus will be convex if not linear, but (as Smith and Ehrenberg indicate) this is not a *necessary* result without further assumptions. If individual isoprofit curves are concave, the market wage-pension curve could be concave too.

My comments on the empirical work fall into two groups. The first group concerns what they did to test their hypothesis. These are minor points, in the sense that they do not lead me to doubt their basic finding. I then consider why they didn't find the hypothesized trade-off between wages and fringes.

In estimating this locus, they use an instrumental variable estimate $\hat{P}$ instead of actual pension expense P, in order to remove the "technical" dependence of P on W. Unfortunately, this does not remove all correlation between P and the error term in equation (1). Smith and Ehrenberg clearly recognize this but don't explain why it is so: Part of this error term corresponds to omitted worker quality, and this is surely correlated with

Charles Brown is associate professor of economics, University of Maryland, College Park, and a research associate of the National Bureau of Economic Research.

the pension characteristic Z's in equation (2). This is why differencing across Hay Point levels is necessary and omitted quality problems assume a large role in the discussion at the end of the paper.

The specification with $\Delta \ln W$ as dependent variable (eq. [10]) is preferable to that using ΔW (eq. [6]) apart from the handling of the firm-specific effects (which the authors emphasize). Equation (6) assumes that $\partial W/\partial F$, the earnings loss from each day off, is constant at different salary levels. Equation (10), in contrast assumes that $\partial \ln W/\partial f$ is constant, where f is the ratio of vacation cost to wages. If workers are in fact paid for the time they work, $\partial W/\partial F$ equals minus the daily wage (and cannot be constant across job levels), but $\partial \ln W/\partial f$ will equal -1 (see eq. [8]) at all job levels. Unfortunately, as table 10.4 (which uses eq. [10]) shows, my "preferred" specification only shows that neither $a_1 = -1$ *nor* $a_f = -1$ are supported by the data.

Finally, if the firm effects ($a_M M$ in eq. [3]–[4] or ϕM in eq. [9]) are really fixed across job levels, deviating all variables from their firm-specific means and estimating the model with the transformed data would give us single estimates of a_1 and a_f, rather than the trio of nonindependent estimates in tables 10.3 and 10.4. This "pooling" should give slightly tighter standard errors than does differencing, since each differenced equation leaves out the information for one job level. This would not alter the basic conclusions (though it might allow us to reject $a_1 = -1$ or $a_f = -1$ more decisively than the standard errors in table 10.4 permit).

What went wrong? If one thinks the compensating differentials hypothesis is plausible (as I do), why is there so little evidence for it in the data?

The compensating differential hypothesis is usually supported with the argument that a firm which has a good pension, generous vacations, and the like will be able to pay a lower wage (to attract a given quality of labor). A more institutional story is that a firm which offers a good pension and high wages gets the "pick of the litter" of job applicants; only firms offering equally attractive pension-wage packages will end up with comparably able workers. This rephrasing makes it clear that unions, custom, or other institutional forces *do not* undercut what I take to be the essential prediction of the compensating differential argument, whatever their effect on wage flexibility may be.

This rephrasing also makes more apparent the plausibility of Smith and Ehrenberg's suggestion that omitted worker characteristics are important. If we were to fix P and W with the sort of positive correlation we observe, and told *each* firm to hire the best workers it could attract, we might still find no evidence of a negative relationship between P and W among "comparable" workers—unless we knew (nearly) all the characteristics firms use in choosing among workers. Even with the easily observed personal characteristics, such as schooling or age-experience, we would still have workers who are equivalent to the researcher but not equivalent to firms. Indeed, it may well be higher levels of effort (or "esprit de corps," Clague 1977) rather than of worker quality that firms offering the best compensation packages are buying. If so, the omitted variable problem could be murderous even with ideal measures of worker quality.

A second explanation is based on the fact that, after differencing across job levels in a sample of firms, the estimates are based on comparisons across job levels in the same firm. Is there really any reason to think, if firms have relatively stable promotion ladders, that the theory should hold at each job level rather than over a career? Suppose P_{400} is high in one firm relative to others. Should I expect W_{400} to be low? Or should I expect $P_{100} + W_{100}$ to be lower? Suppose one "pays" for the prospect of generous pension additions as a 400-level worker by accepting lower *wages* as a 100-level worker. Then $W_{400} - W_{100}$ will be positively correlated with $P_{400} - P_{100}$, even if there are no variations in worker quality and the theory is, in a fundamental sense, true. This is consistent with Lazear's (1979) argument that compensation can differ systematically from marginal product, with young workers underpaid and old workers overpaid. Schiller and Weiss (1980) suggest a cross-age adjustment of this sort in discussing their rather mixed findings for pensions and wages.

Unfortunately, this explanation will not persuade the noneconomist Smith and Ehrenberg mention in their introduction. He will recognize what we're saying: The theory is so true that we can't show you any evidence for it! This is not *quite* true—in principle, the problem could be solved with whole career data on pensions and wages. But the very real problems one points to when one gets wrong-signed estimates leaves on wondering whether the *magnitude* of right-*signed* coefficients in the literature shouldn't be viewed more skeptically.

References

Clague, Christopher. 1977. Information costs, corporate hierarchies, and earnings inequality. *American Economic Review* 67: 81–85.

Lazear, Edward P. 1979. Why is there mandatory retirement? *Journal of Political Economy* 87: 1251–84

Schiller, Bradley R., and Randall D. Weiss. 1980. Pensions and wages: A test for equalizing differences. *Review of Economics and Statistics* 62: 529–37.

11 Fringe Benefits in Employee Compensation

Arleen Leibowitz

11.1 Introduction

Although economists generally measure employees' compensation by money wages, money wages account for a shrinking proportion of total employee compensation. In 1977 only 76.7 percent of employee compensation in the private, nonfarm economy was in the form of direct payment for time worked (U.S. Bureau of Labor Statistics 1980*b*, p. 8). Paid leave (vacations and holidays) accounted for 6.1 percent of compensation, employer contributions to social security and other retirement programs for 8.5 percent, employer expenditures for life, accident, and health insurance, for 4 percent, and expenditures for sick leave, unemployment, and bonuses accounted for the remainder. Between 1966 and 1977 nonwage compensation or fringe benefits grew at a faster rate than pay for time worked.

In spite of the importance of fringe benefits, labor supply models typically treat only the wage portion of compensation, while it is clear that total compensation is the relevant variable affecting labor supply. How much does this distort our conclusions? Clearly, if wages are only a part of labor compensation and, in fact, are negatively related to benefits, wages alone may be a very error-prone measure of compensation. This would tend to bias toward zero the measured labor supply elasticities.

We show below that at higher tax rates, employees desire a greater proportion of their total income in the form of nontaxable benefits. Therefore, earnings functions which look at the wage portion of compensation will underestimate the total earnings of employees facing high marginal tax rates. Since more highly educated workers may face higher marginal tax rates, they may take a greater percentage of their remunera-

Arleen Leibowitz is an economist at the Rand Corporation, Santa Monica, California.
This chapter, originally published as Rand Corporation Publication N-1827-HHS, is reprinted by permission of the Rand Corporation.

tion in the form of benefits. We would therefore underestimate the rate of return to schooling, because we measure a decreasing proportion of total compensation at higher wage levels. Earnings functions often show rates of return at high schooling levels which are low compared to market rates of return on capital (Freeman 1977). This could result from the unobserved returns in the form of benefits. If men and women receive different proportions of compensation in the form of benefits, we will also distort earnings comparisons between these groups.

Clearly, measuring the effect that ignoring fringe benefits has on estimates of labor supply and earnings functions requires data on factors affecting individuals' productivity and personal characteristics as well as on wages and fringe benefits. Some studies have considered how the amounts of fringe benefits supplied by employers vary with industry or employer but not employee characteristics (e.g, Goldstein and Pauly 1976). A recent survey of health care coverage (Taylor and Lawson 1981) does contain the requisite demographic data but does not include information on the employer's payments for health insurance or other fringes. Data sets with both employee characteristics and employer fringe benefit payments can be constructed by linking data from separate employer and employee surveys (e.g., Smeeding, this volume). By using means, however, we lose the data on individual characteristics which would allow us to hold productivity constant.

The present paper, instead of using establishment data, uses data on individuals which is supplemented by employer reports of those individuals' benefits. Data collected as part of the Health Insurance Study (Newhouse 1974) are used to examine how the benefits received vary with *employee* characteristics. The HIS has cost data only for health insurance and vacation pay. It has data on individuals' *receipt* of other benefits, but not their value. These values, conditional on receipt of benefits, are estimated from the 1972 BLS survey of firm compensation practices.

The paper is organized as follows: Section 11.2 presents a simple model of the division of compensation between wages and benefits. Section 11.3 presents findings from the 1972 BLS survey. Section 11.4 describes the HIS data. Section 11.5.1 compares the HIS data with a large national sample. Section 11.5.2 shows how fringe benefits vary with full-time work status, sex, and race, and also presents earnings function estimates. Section 11.6 gives conclusions and data recommendations.

11.2 Trade-offs between Wages and Benefits

11.2.1 Wage Benefit Trade-offs in Theory

Consider a model of the labor market where remuneration for a given worker consists not only of money wages, but also of benefits paid directly by the employer. Employers will be indifferent to the composition of total compensation between money wages and benefits.

Employees have preferences between wages and benefits. Many benefits are characterized by their nonmarketability. They can only be consumed as a tie-in to employment, and they are not transferable—for example, an employee cannot resell his health insurance or accept bids for his sick leave. However, employees are free to choose employers whose benefit mix maxmimizes their utility. Thus, on-the-job benefits can be considered local public goods, and Tiebout-like, employees search out employers who have a benefit mix which "fits" their utility function (see Goldstein and Pauly 1976). Employers, too, will have an incentive to adjust their mix to the expected tastes of their potential employees. Thus, public school systems offer generous sick leave for their largely female work force, while universities offer free tuition to their education-minded employees.

We distinguish three types of benefits from the employee's point of view. First, there are nontaxable substitutes for private consumption expenditures (such as employer-financed health insurance or subsidized lunches in the company cafeteria). Second, there are taxable substitutes for private consumption which the employer can provide at low cost because of quantity discounts (such as life insurance). Third, there are "paid vacations" and sick leave which also are taxable. We assume that the employer is indifferent to the composition of benefits among the three types.

Even from this cursory taxonomy of the on-the-job benefits it is evident why some classes of benefits exist: given positive marginal tax rates, employers can purchase nontaxable benefits which are worth more to their employees than an equivalent expenditure on wages.

It can be shown (see Leibowitz 1982) that the greater the marginal tax rate, the lower the effective price of benefits. Thus, nontaxable benefits are most valuable to the highest wage employees. Further, because of group rates, employers may effect economies of scale in providing even taxable benefits. Sick leave is a kind of disability insurance where the employer self-insures. Typically, for extended sick leave the employer reinsures with a commercial agency or relies on government coverage. Vacation as a fringe benefit is harder to understand since providing "paid vacation" is equivalent to providing a wage increase. Perhaps "paid vacation" is more of a benefit for the employer than the employee since it is a mechanism whereby employers limit the amount of unscheduled unpaid leave employees can take.

11.2.2 Wage-Benefit Trade-offs in Practice

Ceteris paribus, there should be a negative relationship between wages and benefits. The problem for estimation is to hold productivity constant *in practice*. Establishment data, such as have been used in previous studies, have only the crudest indicators of productivity—production or white-collar worker, union status, and type of industry. With such data, one is likely to pick up changes in benefits across levels of worker productivity, rather than trade-offs between wages and benefits for a given employee. For this reason, it is not possible to obtain a meaningful hedonic benefits function from this type of data.

With disaggregated data on individuals, it is possible to control sufficiently for productivity that a wage benefit trade-off could be observed. Then wages and benefits should be negatively related. However, if there are unobserved factors affecting productivity, it is no longer true that observed wages and benefits will be negatively correlated since benefits may be related to the unobserved productivity factors, which shift the entire wage-benefit locus.

If benefits accounted for the same share of remuneration at all productivity levels, rate of return calculations would not be affected by not fully controlling for productivity. Since we expect higher proportions of benefits at higher tax brackets, the expansion path may veer toward benefits as wages increase. However, at some point, the demand for benefits may become saturated, as the marginal utility of benefits falls to zero. Government regulations may also limit the amount of benefits an employee can receive with favored tax treatment.

In this paper we can provide some evidence about the bias resulting from the omission of fringe benefits in computing the increase in earnings due to additional schooling and in comparing earnings of men and women. There are insufficient numbers of blacks in the sample to make meaningful racial comparisons.

In the next section, findings from a 1972 BLS survey are presented. The following two sections describe the HIS data base and present some empirical estimates.

11.3 Fringes and Wages in a National Sample

A 1972 BLS survey of firm compensation practices provides data on employers' expenditures for various categories of benefits and for wages (U.S. Bureau of Labor Statistics 1975). The survey, a stratified probability sample of establishments covered by state employment insurance laws, included 5031 firms. The strata are classified by industry, location, and number of employees, with the probability of inclusion in the sample roughly proportional to employment size.

Table 11.1 presents data on averge hourly wages and benefits for office and nonoffice workers. The data are averages over the 4632 firms who reported complete information and have been weighted to be representative of covered employees in these industries nationwide. The nominal wage for working hours reflects the usual use of the term "wage rate"—

Table 11.1 Hourly Wages and Benefits of Office and Nonoffice Workers—1972

Compensation	Office Workers[a] $/hr	Office Workers[a] %	Nonoffice Workers[b] $/hr	Nonoffice Workers[b] %	Correlation between Nominal Wage and Ratio of Benefit to Nominal Wage
Nominal wage for working hours	4.94	82.9	3.18	84.4	—
Vacation	.46	7.7	.17	4.5	.15
Pension	.16	2.7	.06	1.6	.30
Social security	.20	3.4	.17	4.5	−.59
Unemployment	.08	1.3	.12	3.2	−.22
Insurance	.12	2.0	.07	1.9	.15
Total compensation	5.96	—	3.77	—	.15

Source: Calculated from U.S. Bureau of Labor Statistics (1975).

[a]Office workers are defined as: all employees in executive, administrative, and management positions above the working supervisory level; supervisory and nonsupervisory professional employees and their technical assistants; office clerical workers; salespersons whose sales activities are primarily performed outside the establishment (e.g., real estate salesmen, door-to-door salesmen).

[b]Nonoffice workers are defined as: all employees, except office employees, in nonsupervisory, nonprofessional positions, including employees engaged in fabricating, processing, assembling, building, mining, repairing, warehousing, trucking, retail sales, etc. Proprietors, members of unincorporated firms, and unpaid family workers are excluded from the survey.

that is, direct payments for hours worked. It includes payments for shift differentials but does not include overtime pay. Wage rates were calculated by dividing employer expenditures for time worked by the number of hours worked.

Hourly benefits were calculated by dividing each employer's expenditures on benefits by the number of hours worked. Employer payments for health, life, and accident insurance accounted for 2.0 percent of office employees' total compensation, and 1.9 percent for nonoffice employees. Including vacation pay, pensions, insurance, and social security payments, office workers gained, on average, \$1.02 per hour and nonoffice workers, \$.59 per hour from the various fringe benefits.

In spite of the substantial increase in compensation per hour represented by fringe benefits, the correlation of total compensation (wages plus fringes) with base wage rate is 0.98. However, as wages increase, fringe benefits grow as a fraction of total compensation, as seen by the positive correlation between wages and percentage of compensation accounted for by fringe benefits. The last column shows the correlation across firms in the 1972 BLS survey of nominal wages with the ratio of fringe benefits to nominal wages. Over all, there is a low positive correlation (0.15) between base wage rates and the share of fringe benefits in wage rates.

As postulated above, benefits increase as a share of total compensation at higher productivity levels. However, it appears that nontaxable as well as taxable benefits increase with productivity. The share of nontaxable, private pensions, in total compensation, is more highly correlated with wages (0.30) than the share of taxable leave time (vacation, holidays, sick leave, and personal leave). Both leave time's share and that of insurance benefits are correlated 0.15 with nominal wages. Benefits mandated by law, such as employer contributions to social security and unemployment insurance, account for a smaller share of wages at higher compensation levels, largely because there is a ceiling on the income subject to employer and employee taxes. In general, however, benefits represent a larger share of compensation at higher wage levels. To see whether this leads to underestimates of rates of return, we turn to data from the Health Insurance Study.

11.4 The Health Insurance Study

Data for this section were collected by the Health Insurance Study (HIS) which is being carried out under a grant from the Department of Health and Human Services (previously Health, Education, and Welfare) to The Rand Corporation. The purpose of the HIS is to address questions of health care financing by experimentally enrolling families in a variety of health insurance plans which vary in the amount they reimburse families for medical expenditures, and monitoring their subsequent health and health-care expenditures. (The study design is described in Newhouse [1974].) As part of this effort, data on wages, income, and fringe benefits were also collected. Beginning in 1974, a total sample of 7706 individuals in 2756 families have been enrolled at six sites: Dayton, Ohio; Seattle, Washington; Fitchburg, Massachusetts; Franklin County, Massachusetts; Charleston, South Carolina; and Georgetown County, South Carolina. Participants were enrolled for a period of either three years or five years. Early results on the response of medical expenditures to variation in reimbursement are reported in Newhouse et al. (1981).

Eligibility for participants is quite broad. The only ineligible people are those 62 years of age and older at the time of enrollment, and persons with special health-care options such as members of the military, persons in prisons, recipients of disability medicare or veterans with service connected disabilities. In addition, low-income families were slightly oversampled, and those with incomes in excess of $25,000 (in 1973 dollars) were not eligible. Families in the experiment are representative of families in their site, although because of the income restriction, they do not represent a random sample. The sample as a whole is not a random sample of the U.S. population, but the sites do cover a mix of urban and rural northern, southern, and western sites. This allows estimation of regional and city-size effects.

Over the life of the study, data are collected on demographic and economic variables, health status, utilization of health services, type of health services received, and type of providers utilized. Demographic and economic data are elicited at baseline interviews prior to actual enrollment.

Income data are updated annually, when respondents are asked to copy from their income tax forms information on earnings, interest, dividends, federal, state, and local taxes paid, tax credits, and nontaxable income. From these data, marginal tax rates are calculated. Wage and labor supply data are updated at four- to six-month intervals. Each person over age 16 fills in a mailed questionnaire with employment data. A flexible format allows respondents to report hourly, daily, weekly, biweekly, monthly, or annual earnings. For this study all earnings were reduced to an hourly basis using data supplied in the same questionnaire on weekly hours of work and weeks worked per year. Wage data were obtained for a primary and secondary job, but only the wage data for the first job are used in this paper. The periodic employment report also asked whether the respondent was eligible at his first job for "employer-paid accident insurance" and "employer-paid life insurance." "Employer-paid" was defined as insurance for which the employer paid any part. The amount of the premium paid on behalf of the employee is not known.

Vacation and sick leave data were obtained directly from employers by means of the sick leave abstraction form. Employers were identified from the preceding periodic employment report. Employers reported the number of hours, days, or weeks of vacation for which each of their employees in the HIS was eligible. Employers supplied a great deal of detail about sick leave: whether it accrued with length of service, or was a fixed amount per illness or per period of time, or was given at the employer's discretion. Whether the employee received full or partial pay for sick days, whether benefits began on the first day of illness, and whether sick leave could be accumulated were also determined. Sick leave data were not obtained for persons who were self-employed, so they have been eliminated from this analysis.

Vacation and sick leave plans were obtained from employers in 1978. Wage data corresponding to the same time period were obtained from periodic employment reports administered in March 1978 for Dayton and in September 1978 for the Seattle, Massachusetts, and South Carolina sites.

Health insurance benefits could not be obtained for the identical time period because after enrollment all HIS subjects received their HIS-assigned insurance package. Therefore, the health insurance measure relates to the benefits workers received before enrollment in the HIS. Because many workers had changed jobs in the several years between enrollment in the study and the time at which we obtained wage data, the available sample size was smaller for analyses using health insurance data. The sample was further reduced because data were only available for a subsample of employees. For those with data, the measure is the annual employer contribution to health insurance premiums, as reported by the employer. The HIS data base also contains detailed information on the provisions of health insurance held by employees in our study prior to their enrollment in the experimental HIS plans. Marquis (1981) describes how these data were obtained by abstracting descriptive booklets provided by employers. She also finds that most families were well informed about some aspects of their health insurance coverage, but many lacked detailed knowledge of benefits covered. Some knowledge about the generosity of health insurance coverage (and other fringe benefits) is essential if employees are to effectively trade off benefits for money wages.

11.5 Empirical Estimates

11.5.1 Characteristics of Fringe Benefits Data

In order to assess the quality of the HIS fringe benefits data, we begin by comparing fringe benefits data collected by the HIS in 1978 with the 1979 Level of Benefits (LOB) Survey (U.S. Bureau of Labor Statistics 1980*a*). The LOB data were collected by the Bureau of Labor Statistics in 1979 as a pilot survey. The survey, conducted for the Office of Personnel Management, will be used to develop cost estimates for providing federal employees' benefits comparable to those in private industry.

While the LOB and HIS fringe benefits surveys occurred within a relatively short time span, the LOB sample differs in several ways from the HIS sample. The LOB obtained information from 1253 large establishments in the continental United States. Establishments with few employees (the minimum number of employees varied between 50 and 250, depending on the industry) were not surveyed. Responding establishments were asked to provide benefits data for three classes of workers: professional-administrative, technical-clerical, and production. The LOB survey excluded executive management employees and part-time, seasonal, and temporary employees.

The HIS sample, by contrast, was defined as including employed individuals who were enrolled in the HIS, and therefore subject to its sampling rules. The data represent plans applicable for a given individual. No exclusions were made on the basis of occupation, part-time employment, or establishment size. The HIS data can be aggregated to the occupation categories in the LOB for comparison. However, because of the noted differences between the two samples, the data obtained from the two sources may not correspond exactly.

The benefit rates reported in the LOB tend to exceed the rates in the HIS because LOB excludes seasonal and temporary workers and smaller employers. The percentage of employees covered by life insurance is similar in the two surveys, but the percentage covered by health insurance is lower in the HIS. While LOB reports that 96 percent of full-time employees receive health insurance benefits, HIS data indicate 87 percent do so. The HIS number matches well with National Center for Health Statistics (NCHS) data which show 86–91 percent of workers in firms with health insurance plans. The same document shows that over 90 percent of employees in firms with more than twenty-five workers have health insurance plans available, while only 55 percent of workers in firms with twenty-five or fewer employees do (Taylor and Lawson 1981, p. 4). The exclusion of smaller employers and part-time workers causes the LOB estimates to exceed the average for all firms and workers. This is a probable explanation for the reported differences in paid vacation and sick leave. The HIS data seem to correspond well to national data, where the comparison group is similar, as in the NCHS survey.

The multivariate analysis will use only data on full-time workers, but we can use the HIS data to determine how the various benefits vary with part-time/full-time status. Table 11.2 shows that fewer than half of the HIS sample part-time employees receive each of the benefit types, except health insurance. The percent of the HIS sample of full-time employees

Table 11.2 **Benefits of Part-Time and Full-Time Employees**

	Percent Receiving Benefit		
	Part-Time	Full-Time	
Benefit	HIS[a]	HIS[a]	LOB[b]
Sick leave	36%*	47%	56%
Paid vacation	30%*	56%	100%
Accident insurance (noncontributory)	43%*	79%	55%[c]
Life insurance	31%*	73%	77%
Health insurance[d]	75%*	87%	96%

[a]HIS data from 1978 Sick leave Abstraction and Periodic Employment Reports (III for Dayton, IV for other sites), see Leibowitz (1982).

[b]U.S. Bureau of Labor Statistics (1980*a*), table 1, p. 4.

[c]Accident and sickness insurance, noncontributory.

[d]HIS data based on a subsample at baseline.

*Differences between HIS full- and part-time employees significant at the 0.001 level.

receiving benefits is nearly twice as high as for part-time in each category except sick leave and health insurance.

Table 11.3 shows that even among full-time employees, benefits vary by race and sex. The top panel shows what percentage of employees received benefits of various types. The bottom panel shows the wage increase implied by two types of benefits. These two fringe benefits are the only ones where the HIS data have actual employer expenditures. Female employees were significantly more likely to receive paid sick leave and vacation than male employees, while men were more likely to receive both accident and life insurance. Male and female workers were equally likely to receive health insurance through their employment. Black-white differences should be interpreted with caution, since blacks accounted for only 4 percent of the sample. Further, a majority of the blacks resided in South Carolina, where all workers have lower benefit levels. Given these interpretive caveats, the data show that white workers were more likely to receive sick leave, accident and life insurance, but no more likely to receive health insurance or paid vacation.

The bottom panel of table 11.3 shows the percentage increase in compensation due to employer-paid health insurance premiums and due

Table 11.3 **Benefits of Full-Time Employees by Race and Sex**

Benefit	White	Black	Male	Female
	Percent Receiving Benefits			
Sick leave	47[b]	34	40[c]	60
Paid vacation	57	44	53[d]	62
Accident insurance	81[a]	47	84[c]	70
Life insurance	73[a]	53	75[d]	68
Health insurance	87	85	87	86
Number of observations (first four benefits)	856	32	587	301
Number of observations (health insurance)	443	21	165	299
	Percentage Increase in Compensation due to Benefit			
Employer-paid health insurance	*	*	4.4%	4.5%
Paid vacation	3.4	2.5	3.0%[c]	4.0%
Paid vacation plus holidays	6.1[a]	5.0	5.5%[c]	7.2%

[a]Difference between whites and blacks is significantly different at 1% level; however, these differences may be peculiar to our sample.

[b]Difference between whites and blacks is significantly different at 10% level; however, these differences may be peculiar to our sample.

[c]Difference between males and females is significantly different at 1% level.

[d]Difference between males and females is significantly different at 5% level.

*Insufficient observations to compute.

to paid vacation and holidays.[1] For full-time workers in this sample, paid vacation added 3 percent to men's salaries and 4 percent to women's. Thus women were not only more likely to receive vacation, but also had a significantly greater share of compensation as vacation benefits. Including paid holidays makes the differences appear even larger, since even among full-time workers, men have longer average workweeks than women. These numbers correspond well to the 6.1 percent of compensation attributable to vacations and holidays in 1977 reported by the BLS (1980*b*). The percentage increase in wages attributable to health insurance, for those who had health insurance, is 4.4 percent for men and 4.5 percent for women. When we allow for the fact that not all workers have health insurance benefits and that life and accident insurance premiums are likely to be small, this number is quite consistent with the 4 percent of employers' expenditures for life, accident, and health insurance (U.S. Bureau of Labor Statistics 1980*b*). Thus the HIS data are quite comparable to national averages.

The differences by sex indicate that significant variation exists within the group of full-time employees. Table 11.3 shows that at least in terms of sick leave and vacation, women are more likely to receive benefits than men. To see whether this offsets some of the male-female differential in direct monetary compensation, we must use multivariate methods to control for productivity differences. Because of the richness of complementary data on wages and demographic characteristics, we should be able to determine to what extent employees trade off wages and benefits.

11.5.2 Multivariate Analyses

In this section hedonic wage functions are estimated. We expect a negative relationship between wages and benefits if productivity is effectively held constant. A single method such as this does not capture the simultaneous nature of the wage-benefit trade-off. However, it does solve a data problem posed by having employer costs for some benefits, but only a dichotomous indicator of whether benefits were received for others.

Table 11.4 presents regressions for the entire sample of full-time workers (those who worked thirty-five hours or more a week) for whom wage and fringe benefits data referred to the same employer. Regressing the log of hourly earnings on the usual productivity measures, we find that the implied rate of return to schooling is 4.1 percent. The rate of return estimate falls in the low end of the range reported in the literature. A consumer price index[2] as well as dummy variables for the sites are included in the regression, but not shown. This regression accounts for one-quarter of the variance in log hourly earnings.

Men's median earnings were estimated to be 49 percent greater than women's, and union workers earn 17 percent greater wages. Separate

Table 11.4 **Wage Regressions for Full-Time Workers (*t*-values in parentheses)**

Dependent Variable:	Log Hourly Wage			Log Vacation Days	Log Hourly Wage Plus Benefits	Log of after Tax Wages Plus Benefits	Log of Ratio before and after Tax Wages Plus Benefits
Sample:	All Full Time (1)	Males (2)	Females (3)	All Full Time (4)	All Full Time (5)	All Full Time[b] (6)	All Full Time[b] (7)
Independent Variables:[a]							
Intercept	1.098	1.482	.997	−.330	1.114	1.004	.110
	(7.94)	(9.35)	(4.59)	(−.96)	(10.3)	(9.61)	(5.17)
Education (years)	.041	.041	.043	.067	.043	.038	.005
	(6.67)	(5.33)	(4.31)	(4.24)	(8.79)	(7.99)	(5.41)
Experience (years)	.009	.0154	−.003	.022	.021	.018	.003
	(1.48)	(2.07)	(−.31)	(1.50)	(4.44)	(3.95)	(3.15)
Experience squared (years × 10^{-2})	−.006	−.017	.012	−.023	−.036	−.033	−.003
	(−.42)	(−.99)	(.57)	(−.66)	(−3.42)	(−3.20)	(−1.54)
Sex	.399			−.081	.367	.370	−.003
	(9.29)			(−.74)	(11.1)	(11.60)	(−.44)
Union	.127	.151	.058	−.272	.146	.133	−.013
	(2.73)	(2.65)	(.73)	(−2.27)	(4.18)	(3.93)	(−1.92)
R^2	.25	.17	.16	.07	.38	.36	.14
Number of observations	595	389	206	595	595	515	515

[a]Prices and sites were also controlled in the regressions.

[b]After tax regression has smaller sample because of missing income tax forms.

regressions for men and women had significantly different sets of coefficients. ($F = 24.5$ with 14 and 580 degrees of freedom.) While the rates of return were similar, men's wages increased more with experience and were positively related to union membership, while women's wages were not.

A significant share of employees' fringe benefits is in the form of paid vacation. What does "vacation earnings function" look like? Column (4) in table 11.4 shows how the log of vacation days is related to productivity determinants, just as wages are. Vacation days increase significantly more rapidly with education than do money wages,[3] even though there is no tax advantage in receiving vacation pay. This result is consistent with the finding from the 1972 data reported in table 11.1. Union status is associated with shorter paid vacations, but higher wages. In contrast to the results for money wages, sex does not affect vacation benefits significantly, once experience and other factors are accounted for.

How would the rate of return to schooling be affected by including compensation in the form of fringe benefits in total compensation? The wage data used in columns (1)–(3) were augmented to account for the implicit increase due to vacation pay, for sick leave (based on the sex-adjusted average number of days lost from work due to sickness by men and women), and on price-adjusted, occupation-specific expenditures for health, life, and accident insurance, given that an individual received insurance.[4] Hourly wages, including vacation pay, sick leave, and insurance, averaged \$6.70 compared to \$6.25 before benefits were added, an increase of 7 percent. This increase falls within the range reported above for office and nonoffice workers. The earnings function explains a substantially greater percent of the variance of wages plus benefits than of wages alone.

If a greater percentage of compensation is given in the form of benefits to workers with certain characteristics (those with more education or experience, for example), then earnings functions which excluded benefits would bias the coefficients of these variables. To see which characteristics would be significantly biased by omitting benefits, the ratio of full compensation to wage compensation was regressed on the independent variables included in table 11.4. The results show that there is no systematic relationship between the independent variables and the ratio of wage to wages plus benefits. This is equivalent to stating that the sets of coefficients in columns 1 and 5 in table 11.4 differ only in the intercept.[5]

The benefits accounted for here are largely taxable, and the correlations using BLS data show these rise less rapidly with productivity than nontaxable benefits. However, it is clear that the omission of taxable benefits from earnings functions does not lead to significant bias in rate of return to schooling estimates, or to male-female or union-nonunion comparisons. In column (6) of table 11.4 the family marginal tax rate (derived from data on actual income taxes paid) and social security tax rate are applied to wages to obtain an earnings function for after-tax wages plus benefits.

The regression shows that accounting for taxes has a greater effect on the coefficients than including benefits. The ratio of before-tax wage plus benefits to after-tax wage plus benefits is significantly related to both education and labor market experience, as the last column shows, while we found no significant change in coefficients due to adding benefits to raw wages. The positive coefficients in column (7) indicate that the rate of return to schooling and experience appear to be significantly more positive when marginal tax rates are ignored. The bias amounted to a difference in the rate of return of 0.5 percent. The ratio of after-tax wage plus benefit to hourly wages (e.g., comparing columns 7 and 1) is not significantly related to either education or experience, since the positive effect of schooling on benefits is counterbalanced by the positive relationship of schooling and marginal tax rates.

Using this basic earnings function framework, we next estimate an hedonic wage function to determine in what way employees trade off wages for benefits. Table 11.5 presents hedonic wage equations in which benefits are added to the basic earnings function. If employees are trading off wages for benefits, we expect these benefit variables to have negative signs. There are four dummy variables indicating whether or not benefits are received. Receipt of paid vacation, sick leave, and accident insurance is associated with lower wages, but only vacation benefits lower wages significantly. However, the receipt of life insurance is positively related to wages. While not receiving any vacation or sick leave is compensated by higher wages, among those who do receive the benefit, wages are positively related to the amount of benefit received.

The LOB study gives a clue as to why this happens. Their data show that within occupation types, the number of vacation days and sick leave days increase with years of service (U.S. Bureau of Labor Statistics 1980*a*, pp. 5 and 6). But wages also increase with years of service or experience. Borjas (1981) found that workers with greater employer-specific tenure had significantly higher wages at later ages. While the regression controls for labor market experience, it does not perfectly control for years of service with a given employer. Thus the unobserved variable, years of employer-specific experience, which is positively related to both wages and vacation and sick leave benefits, biases the continuous benefit coefficients.

Separate regressions for men and women were found to differ significantly from each other.[6] Both men's and women's wages react similarly to vacation benefits, but they differ in the response to sick leave. Sick leave has little effect on men's wages. For women, however, receiving any sick leave is compensated by lower wages, but among women who

Table 11.5 Hedonic Wage Equations for Full-Time Workers (*t*-values in parentheses)

	Dependent Variable: Log Hourly Wage			
Independent Variables[a]	All Full-Time	Full-Time Males	Full-Time Females	Sample with Health Insurance
Education	.04	.04	.04	.07
	(5.60)	(4.49)	(3.48)	(2.90)
Receives vacation	−.34	−.44	−.34	.19
	(−1.97)	(−1.78)	(−1.46)	(.26)
Receives sick leave	−.12	.01	−.31	.31
	(−.80)	(.06)	(−1.29)	(.59)
Receives accident insurance	−.04	−.05	−.07	.02
	(−.72)	(−.54)	(−.89)	(.09)
Receives life insurance	.15	.19	.10	.10
	(2.66)	(2.61)	(1.29)	(.56)
Log of annual vacation days	.15	.18	.11	−.05
	(2.22)	(1.95)	(1.26)	(−.18)
Log of annual sick leave	.04	−.03	.19	−.22
	(.73)	(−.40)	(1.87)	(−1.03)
Log of health insurance premium	—	—	—	.14
				(1.50)
R^2	.26	.17	.15	.12
Number of observations	595	389	206	136

Source: HIS data.

[a]Prices, sites, experience, experience squared, and union status were also controlled for.

receive sick leave, higher-wage women receive more. Sick leave may have greater importance for women because of greater sickliness or because of their responsibilities for sick children. Whereas 5.1 percent of women employed full-time lost time from work due to illness in May 1978, only 3.4 percent of men employed fully were absent from work in that month. This represented a loss of 2.8 percent of working time for women and 2.1 percent for men, since men had lengthier absences for each incidence (Taylor 1979, p. 57). Table 11.3 also showed that women were significantly more likely than men to receive any sick leave.

What the regressions suggest is that full-time employees can choose jobs with benefits or jobs without benefits, which are compensated at a higher rate. Thus workers can be thought of as regular employees receiving benefits or as working on contract to provide certain services, without receiving benefits. However, among employees who receive benefits, the amount of these benefits is positively related to wages. This may occur because an unobserved job tenure variable relates wages and benefits indirectly, or because the benefit is tied directly to wage levels. The LOB reports, for example, that 63 percent of the job-related life insurance plans insure employees for a multiple of their earnings rather than for a flat amount or one based on years of service (U.S. Bureau of Labor Statistics 1980*a*, p. 14).

One of the most costly benefits is health insurance. The last column of table 11.5 presents some results using the smaller sample on which health insurance benefits are available in the HIS sample. The health insurance variable is a measure of the amount the employer paid for health insurance. There are only 136 observations for this regression because data were only available for a subsample of HIS participants, and because workers who had changed jobs in the interval between the collection of health insurance data at baseline and the collection of wage data in 1978 were eliminated from the sample. Although the coefficients lack precision due to the small sample size, it is clear that employer-paid premiums are positively rather than negatively related to wages.

The rate of return to schooling for this subsample is 0.052 when benefits variables are not included in the regression, but increases to 0.07 when benefits are included. However, the small sample size prevents any firm conclusions about bias.

11.6 Conclusions

Fringe benefits data from the HIS showed that there are significant differences by sex and race in the probability of receiving benefits. However, there was little evidence in the multivariate analyses that omitting benefits from earnings functions would systematically affect comparisons among sex or union groups.

Hedonic wage equations showed that employees earned compensating differentials when benefits were not provided on the job. However, among those receiving any benefits, the level of benefits was positively related to wage rates. While both men and women who did not receive paid vacations have higher wages, men seem not to pay any significant price in terms of lost earnings for receiving sick leave. Accident insurance affected wages insignificantly for both groups, perhaps because the total expenditure is small. Life insurance was positively related to wages. In the subsample for whom health insurance data were available, the amount of employer-paid premiums was positively related to wages.

These results indicate that lack of data on employee-specific taxable benefits does not greatly bias either rate of return estimates or earnings comparisons between men and women. Accounting for marginal tax rates had a greater effect on rates of return than accounting for fringe benefits. However, comparisons with LOB employer supplied data show that it is nonetheless true that benefits vary with employee characteristics. For comparisons of relative earnings, lack of benefits data does not seem crucial. However, the exclusion of nontaxable benefits, such as pensions, which rise more rapidly than taxable benefits with earnings, may pose a problem for relative earnings comparisons. While for relative wage comparisons taxable fringe benefits have little effect, for comparison of absolute total compensation, ignoring benefits would lead to underestimates.

The exclusion of part-time and seasonal employees from national benefits surveys may result in overestimates of fringe benefits coverage among workers. One way employees may choose a package of low benefits is to choose to work part-time, since many employers pay benefits only to full-time employees. Thus, total compensation may have a discontinuity at the number of hours at which employees become eligible for benefits.

More realistic models of labor supply should incorporate fringe benefits as part of the compensation for work and acknowledge explicitly that hours worked respond to the discontinuity in compensation schedules due to providing fringe benefits only for full-time employees. The results presented here indicate that employees do trade off wages for the option to receive benefits. Surely this option affects hours of work as well.

Notes

1. We assume six paid holidays per year, in order to compare HIS data to data in BLS (1980*b*).

2. The price index used is based on BLS data (U.S. Bureau of Labor Statistics 1978) on the autumn cost of living for an urban intermediate family of four in 1975–78, and on price data collected by the HIS. It is fully documented in Manning and Duan (1981). Only two of our sites (Dayton and Seattle) coincided with sites used by BLS. Because the remaining sites were not specifically reported in BLS data, in all sites we sampled prices for a subset of thirty-three items in the BLS list of more than four hundred items. The data for Dayton and Seattle, where both sets of estimates were available, were used to calibrate HIS cost-of-living to BLS cost-of-living estimates. The constructed indices were validated by comparing the HIS price index with data for available BLS sites (comparing Fitchburg, Massachusetts, site with Boston; Franklin County, Massachusetts, with Northeast Nonmetropolitan; Charleston with Atlanta; Georgetown County, South Carolina, with Southern Nonmetropolitan).

3. Since the two dependent variables are regressed on the same set of independent variables, the appropriate test involves restricting some or all of the two sets of coefficients to be identical in the two regressions. The F value is 4.12 for the education variable, with 1 and 586 degrees of freedom, which is significantly different from zero at better than the 5 percent level. An equivalent test involves regressing the differences between the two dependent variables on the set of independent variables. Since the dependent variables are in logs, this is equivalent to the log of the ratio

$$\ln W - \ln V = \ln\left(\frac{W}{V}\right) = f(X_i),$$

where W and V are the wage rates and vacation days, respectively, and X_i are the independent variables. A significant education coefficient indicates the ratio of wages to vacation falls with education, implying vacation rises more rapidly with education than wages do.

4. To estimate sick leave taken, as contrasted with the maximum entitlement reported in the HIS data, the mean number of days of sick leave taken by male and female workers nationally was used (Taylor 1979, p. 51). Price adjustment was by means of the price index described in note 1. Mean expenditures for life, health, and accident insurance in occupations were calculated from BLS (1975) and matched by occupation to the sample data if the individual received such employer-paid insurance.

5. The test described in note 2 was used. The F value was 0.71, with 8 and 586 degrees of freedom, which is not significant at the 5 percent level. It is, however, difficult to find significant differences when comparing to the raw wage rate equation, which lacks statistical precision.

6. The F value was 12.5 with 26 and 502 degrees of freedom.

References

Borjas, George. 1981. Job mobility and earnings over the life cycle. *Industrial and Labor Relations Review* 34, no. 3: 365–76.

Freeman, Richard B. 1977. The decline in the economic rewards to college education. *Review of Economics and Statistics* 59: 18–27.

Goldstein, Gerald S., and Mark V. Pauly. 1976. Group health insurance as a local public good. In *The role of health insurance in the health services sector*, ed. Richard N. Rosett. Universities-Bureau Conference Series, no. 27. New York: National Bureau of Economic Research.

Leibowitz, Arleen. 1983. Fringe benefits in employee compensation. The Rand Corporation, N-1827-HHS.

Manning, Willard G., and Naihua Duan. 1981. Cost-of-living analysis. The Rand Corporation, unpublished memo, SM-9522.

Marquis, Susan M. 1981. *Consumers' knowledge about their health insurance coverage*. The Rand Corporation, R-2753-HHS.

Newhouse, J. P. 1974. A design for a health insurance experiment. *Inquiry*. 11: 5–27.

Newhouse, J. P. et al. 1981. Some interim results from a controlled trial of cost sharing in health insurance. *New England Journal of Medicine* 305: 1501–7.

Taylor, Amy K., and Walter R. Lawson, Jr. 1981. Employer and employee expenditures for private health insurance. *U.S. Public Health Service Data Preview*, 7 June.

Taylor, Daniel E. 1979. Absence from work—measuring the hours lost, May 1978. BLS Special Labor Force Report no. 229. Washington, D.C.: U.S. Bureau of Labor Statistics.

U.S. Bureau of Labor Statistics. 1975. Employee compensation in the private nonfarm economy, 1972. BLS Bulletin 1873. Washington, D.C.: U.S. Department of Labor.

———. 1978. Autumn urban family budgets and comparative indexes for selected urban areas. Supplement to BLS Bulletin 1570-5. Washington, D.C.: U.S. Department of Labor.
———. 1980*a*. Employee benefits in industry: A pilot survey. BLS Report no. 615. Washington, D.C.: U.S. Department of Labor.
———. 1980*b*. Employee compensation in the private nonfarm economy, 1977. BLS Summary 80-S. Washington, D.C.: U.S. Department of Labor.

Comment B. K. Atrostic

The other papers presented in this session (Burkhauser and Quinn, and Smith and Ehrenberg) show that estimation of labor cost and trade-offs among wages, fringe benefits, and employment characteristics requires data on employer and employee characteristics, as well as detailed data on fringe benefit plans and expenditures, and information on personnel policies, such as mandatory retirement. Leibowitz appears to have, in the Health Insurance Survey (HIS), just such data. Demographic and economic data collected from households are matched with employer records of fringe benefit expenditures. The importance of having fairly complete measures of labor cost and worker characteristics can be highlighted by laying out clearly the model whose hypotheses Leibowitz tests, and comparing her results with those obtained by estimating the same model with a data set which permits a more complete measure of labor cost.

The wage and compensation equations relevant to Leibowitz's investigation can be stated formally as:

(1) $\ln(W) = A_1X + e_1,$

(2) $\ln(W + B_T) = A_2X + e_2,$

(3) $\ln(W + B_T + B_{NT}) = A_3X + e_3,$

where B_T and B_{NT} are taxable and nontaxable benefits, W is wages, and X is a vector of pay determining characteristics (education, sex, region, etc.). Assuming that the X vector and the dependent variables are correctly specified and measured, a series of hypotheses about the A vectors can be tested. If taxable benefits are paid in proportion to wages, coefficients A_1 and A_2 will be equal, except for the intercept. If nontax-

B. K. Atrostic is an economist in the Office of Research and Evaluation, U.S. Bureau of Labor Statistics, Washington, D.C.

The views expressed are those of the author and do not reflect the official position of the Bureau of Labor Statistics.

able benefits are lower priced than taxable benefits, or if the proportion of nontaxable benefits in total compensation varies with elements of the X vector, A_3 will not equal A_1 or A_2. Leibowitz frames the hypothesis that "employers can purchase nontaxable benefits which are worth more to their employees than an equivalent expenditure on wages," and therefore "higher proportions of benefits at higher tax brackets" would be expected. The implied hypothesis tests are

$$H_0\colon A_1 = A_2,$$

and

$$H_0\colon A_1 = A_3.$$

Equations (2) and (3) are not estimated separately. Instead, the benefit measures in the HIS data (vacation and sick leave, and health insurance), described as "largely taxable" are combined with wages to form an earnings variable,[1] so that a limited form of equation (3) is actually estimated:

$$\text{(3a)} \qquad \ln(W + B_T + B_{NT}^*) = A_{3a} X + e_{3a},$$

where B_T is vacation and sick leave, and B_{NT}^* includes only health insurance (and no other nontaxable benefits). The hypothesis that *can* be tested by comparing coefficient estimates in columns (1) and (5) of Leibowitz's table 11.4 is thus:

$$H_0\colon A_1 = A_{3a}.$$

Additionally, Leibowitz tests the importance of the nontaxability of most benefits by including the marginal and social security tax rates directly and estimating:

$$\text{(3b)} \qquad \ln[(W + B_T)(1 - t) + B_{NT}] = A_{3b} X + e_{3b},$$

where $(W + B_T)(1 - t)$ is after-tax income from wages and taxable benefits. Two hypotheses are tested: that A_{3b} is equal to A_3, and that A_{3b} is equal to A_1:

$$H_0\colon A_1 = A_{3b},$$

$$H_0\colon A_{3b} = A_3.$$

B_{NT}^* rather than B_{NT} is also used in estimating equation (3b) and its coefficients, A_{3b}.

Estimates of equations (1), (3a), and (3b) are presented in columns (1), (5), and (6), respectively, of Leibowitz's table 11.4. There is little difference in coefficient estimates for union, sex, education, or experience variables between regressions where the dependent variable is wages, or ones where it is wages plus fringe benefits, or after-tax wages plus fringe benefits. Leibowitz's empirical results support the hypothesis that

$A_1 = A_{3b} = A_{3a}$. From this, she concludes that there is "little evidence" that "omitting benefits from earnings functions would systematically affect comparisons among sex or union groups," and therefore that employee-specific benefit data are not required for unbiased rate of return, sex, or union comparisons.[2] She has not shown, however, that $A_1 = A_2 = A_3 = A_{3b}$.

As equation (3a) makes clear, Leibowitz's actual left-hand-side variables for her columns (5) and (6) are not those implied by equations (3) and (3b). Substantial benefit expenditure categories are omitted, notably pensions and legally required benefits (primarily employer contributions for social security, unemployment compensation, and workmen's compensation). These two categories accounted for 15 percent of employer expenditures for employee compensation in 1977, or over half of the 23 percent of compensation that was paid as benefits (U.S. Bureau of Labor Statistics 1980, table 1). This omission will be shown to have serious consequences for Leibowitz's conclusions.

Additionally, the hypothesis that workers in higher marginal tax brackets receive more of their compensation in the form of nontaxable fringe benefits, thus biasing estimates that use only wages or that fail to account for the differential taxability of different fringe benefits, cannot be tested with the HIS data and the above methodology. There is not enough data on major expenditure categories of nontaxable benefits, even were equations (2) and (3) to be estimated separately.

The effect of the shortcomings of the HIS data generally and of the benefits measures in particular is shown below, using estimates of sex, union, and occupation parameter estimates based on employer-employee exact match data from two BLS establishment surveys. Wages, sex, and union coverage are reported directly for individual workers in selected occupations in one survey, and fringe benefits expenditures for each worker are calculated from the other survey.[3] These data were collected between 1976 and 1978, roughly the same span as the HIS data, collected from 1974 to 1978. Measures of education and experience are not collected in these data, but detailed occupational specifications give some indication of relative human capital attainment. Alternative estimates of equations (1), (3), and (3a), using the BLS matched employer-employee data set, are reported in table C11.1. Column (1) presents a regression using only wages as the dependent variable, as in equation (1). Column (2) presents a regression whose dependent variable corresponds to Leibowitz's "wage plus fringe benefits" in column (5) of her table 11.4; that is, the benefits portion of compensation includes only sick leave, vacation, and life, accident, and health insurance expenditures. This corresponds to equation (3a) above. Finally, column (3) reports a regression whose dependent variable is expanded to include the other benefit categories available in the Employer Expenditure for Employee Com-

Table C11.1 Full-Time Office Workers: Labor Cost Regressions ($N = 20544$)

	ln (Wage) (1)	ln (Labor $Cost_L$) (2)	ln (Labor $Cost_A$) (3)
Union (office workers)	.0828	.0934	.1125
	(.0042)	(.0041)	(.0044)
Male	.0410	.0381	.0441
	(.0051)	(.0049)	(.0053)
Percentage female in occupations surveyed	−.1142	−.1095	−.0545
	(.0115)	(.0112)	(.0121)
Office workers as percentage of total	−.0847	−.2249	−.2232
	(.0134)	(.0131)	(.0141)
Part of larger firm	.0527	.0749	.0957
	(.0033)	(.0110)	(.0047)
Employment 5,000+	.2865	.3227	.4637
	(.0112)	(.0110)	(.0118)
Employment 1,000–4,999	.1727	.2090	.3144
	(.0110)	(.0108)	(.0116)
Employment 500–999	.0290	.0631	.0946
	(.0129)	(.0126)	(.0136)
System analyst	.8215	.7858	.7967
	(.0082)	(.0080)	(.0086)
Secretary	.3515	.3301	.3493
	(.0066)	(.0065)	(.0070)
File clerk	−.0446	−.0400	−.0187
	(.0088)	(.0086)	(.0093)
$\bar{R}^2$	.6973	.7156	.7077

NOTES: The regressions contain other occupation dummies, and also include industry and region dummies. See Atrostic (1983) for a detailed description of the data.

Labor $Cost_L$ = Sum of employer expenditures for each worker on wages, sick leave, vacation pay, and life, accident, and health insurance. Corresponds to "Wage plus benefits" in column (5), table 11.4, in Leibowitz's paper. Labor $Cost_A$ = Sum of employer expenditures on all wages and fringe benefits for which data are collected in the Employer Expenditures for Employee Compensation Survey. Includes all fringe benefits in Labor $Cost_L$, plus pensions and legally required benefits.

Standard errors are in parentheses.

pensation data (primarily pensions and legally required benefits), corresponding to equation (3). These estimations do not exactly duplicate Leibowitz's, as the data sets do not contain identical information about employer and employee characteristics, but the differences in empirical findings nonetheless are highly suggestive.

A comparison of columns (1) and (2) yields results similar to Leibowitz's: the addition of (selected) fringe benefits has little effect on estimates of sex, union, or occupational differentials. A comparison of columns (1) and (3) or columns (2) and (3), however, yields quite different results. Male premiums remain at about 4 percent.[4] Union coefficients increase substantially from 8 to 12 percent. The discount associated with increasing the percentage of females in the occupation falls from 12 to 6 percent. Occupational differentials narrow: the system analyst premium decreases by about 9 percentage points, while the file clerk discount decreases by about 2 percentage points. Additionally, estimates of the effect of employer characteristics, such as establishment size, differ between specifications. Statistical tests of the hypotheses that $A_1 = A_3$, $A_1 = A_{3a}$, and $A_3 = A_{3a}$ lead to rejection of these hypotheses at the 0.0001 level.[5] Thus the completeness of benefits data included in the dependent variable substantially alters estimates of labor market differentials. Additionally, the adjusted R^2 values in table C11.1 are higher for regressions using some measure of fringe benefits in the dependent variable (this is also true of Leibowitz's table 11.4).

Other problems with the data and analysis in Leibowitz's paper suggest that its conclusions should be viewed with caution. The censoring problem in the HIS study (a $25,000 income cutoff in 1973 dollars) is a liability for studying the effect of the differential taxability of fringe benefits. Her estimated union and sex differentials are not compared with those estimated elsewhere in the human capital or wage determination literature. Leibowitz does not include variables such as establishment size, occupation, and industry, which have proven important in other studies.

In conclusion, Burkhauser and Quinn show changes in estimated labor supply effects from expanding the concept of labor cost. Smith and Ehrenberg and Leibowitz fail to find expected differences in estimates of labor market parameters, and both results are attributable to the use of incomplete data. Consideration of the complete set of benefits that are relevant to Leibowitz's study makes the data recommendations of this session unanimous: detailed employer-employee data *are* needed for accurate estimates of the determinants of labor cost.

Notes

1. Although Leibowitz states in section 11.2.1 that health insurance expenditures are *not* taxable, in section 11.5.2 she describes this group of fringes as "largely taxable." Health insurance, one of the "most costly" fringe benefit expenditures, was about 4 percent of compensation in 1977, while sick leave and vacation pay comprise 6.9 percent of compensation, according to the 1977 Employer Expenditures for Employee Compensation Survey (U.S. Bureau of Labor Statistics 1980, table 1). These three benefits are "largely taxable" only in the sense that 58 percent of them are taxable.

2. What is meant, it would appear, is that omitting *taxable* benefits does not bias comparisons, for these otherwise contradictory statements then follow: the "exclusion of nontaxable benefits . . . may pose a problem for relative earnings comparisons," and that "ignoring benefits would lead to underestimates." Neither of these statements is supported by the empirical results.

3. The data, and the Area Wage Surveys and Employer Expenditures for Employee Compensation Survey from which the data are derived, are described more fully in Atrostic (1983).

4. The percentage is given by: exp(coefficient) − 1.

5. The appropriate test for equality of (some or all) parameters of regression equations

in which alternative dependent variables are employed is described in Rao (1973, pp. 543–56), and implemented in the SAS statistical package (SAS Institute Inc. 1981). Rao's test assumes that the ratios of the variances of the residuals with respect to the various dependent variables are unknown. Leibowitz's test—entering the difference between alternative specifications as the dependent variable in a regression, and testing whether the coefficients thus estimated are equal to zero—is correct for the case of two alternative dependent variables. I am indebted to Richard J. McDonald for discussions on this point.

For the data presented in this comment, both Leibowitz's test and Rao's test were applied, with essentially equivalent results: the hypotheses that $A_1 = A_3$, $A_1 = A_{3a}$, and $A_3 = A_{3a}$ should not be accepted.

References

Atrostic, B. K. 1983. Alternative pay measures and labor market differentials. BLS Working Paper 127 (revised). Washington, D.C.: U.S. Department of Labor, Bureau of Labor Statistics.

Rao, C. Radhakrishna. 1973. *Linear statistical inference and its applications*. 2d ed. New York: John Wiley and Sons.

SAS Institute Inc. 1981. SAS 79-5 changes and enhancements. SAS Technical Report P-115. Cary, North Carolina: SAS Institute Inc.

U.S. Bureau of Labor Statistics. 1980. Employee compensation in the private nonfarm economy, 1977. Summary 80-5. Washington, D.C.: U.S. Department of Labor.

12 The Effect of Pension Plans on the Pattern of Life Cycle Compensation

Richard V. Burkhauser and Joseph F. Quinn

Mandatory retirement is one means of enforcing long-term contracts between employees and firms to insure that earnings over a worker's tenure equal the value of that worker's marginal product. In this paper, we argue that pension plans provide an alternative way to enforce these contracts. In section 12.1, we discuss the implications of using pension plans as a mechanism for adjusting compensation to induce job exit. In section 12.2 we use actual earnings and pension data from the Retirement History Study to show the importance of pension benefits in labor compensation. In section 12.3, we show the effect of pension and social security rules on the pattern of net wage earnings for workers nearing "traditional" retirement age and consider their use as an alternative to mandatory retirement.

12.1 The Effect of Pension Plans on Net Wages

The passage of the 1977 Amendments to the Age Discrimination in Employment Act increased from 65 to 70 the minimum age at which a worker could be terminated for reasons of age alone. Some people have proposed that mandatory retirement be eliminated entirely. Edward Lazear has argued, however, that even in a competitive labor market, mandatory retirement may yield advantages to both labor and manage-

Richard V. Burkhauser is an associate professor with the Department of Economics and a research associate with the Institute for Public Policy Study at Vanderbilt University, Nashville, Tennessee. Joseph F. Quinn is an associate professor with the Department of Economics, Boston College, Chestnut Hill, Massachusetts.

This research was funded in part by the Department of Labor, Labor-Management Services Administration. The authors wish to thank Richard Fendler and Irene Powell for valuable research assistance, and Cordelia Reimers and Jack Triplett for extremely helpful comments.

ment (Lazear 1979, p. 1264). He argues that while the 1977 Amendments will aid the current group of older workers, the total elimination of mandatory retirement would reduce economic efficiency.

Lazear provides an important example of a life cycle approach to labor agreements. Once it is recognized that there is a multiperiod contract, it can be shown that the usual efficiency condition—that the wage equals the value of the marginal product (VMP)—is no longer a necessary characteristic of a competitive market. Though it is true that a worker's VMP over his tenure with a firm must equal his wage earnings over that period, wage earnings need not equal VMP during each period. "Other things equal, a worker would be indifferent between a wage path which paid him a constant dollar amount over his lifetime and another one which had the same present value but paid him less when he was young and more when he was old" (Lazear 1979, p. 1264). Other things equal, firms also would be indifferent between the two. As Lazear suggests, however, other things may not be equal, and it may pay both firms and workers to agree to long-term earning streams which pay workers less than their VMP when young and more than their VMP when old. This arrangement is superior because turnover and its attendant costs are decreased, and workers are induced to cheat less and work harder on the job (Lazear 1979, p. 1266). A necessary condition of such an agreement, however, is a mechanism for fixing a time after which the worker is no longer entitled to receive wage earnings greater than VMP. Lazear argues that mandatory retirement provides this mechanism.

Clearly, mandatory retirement rules are one means of forcing older workers to leave a job after some mutually agreed upon age. In this paper, however, we suggest that it is only one such mechanism. Firms can also use pension plans either to induce exit from the job or to reduce net earnings (as defined below) after some age. When a pension plan is part of a total compensation package, long-term contracts can be enforced through pension rules which effectively penalize workers who stay on the job "too long."

Employer pension plans are an extremely important component of the financial environment for many older Americans. These plans are complex and differ in many aspects, such as coverage criteria, age of earliest eligibility, age of full eligibility, benefit amount, and inflation protection after retirement. In empirical work on the impact of these plans on worker behavior, it is necessary to ignore many of the specifics of the plans (which are often unknown to the researcher in any case) and to summarize the plans along very simple dimensions.

The wealth equivalent of pension rights provides an excellent summary statistic of the magnitude of a plan. At any moment in time, the value of a pension to a worker is equal to the present discounted value of all anticipated future payments:

$$\text{WEALTH}(s) = \sum_{i=s}^{n} \frac{p_i B_i(s)}{(1+r)^i}, \tag{1}$$

where s refers to the time period in which pension benefits are first claimed. WEALTH(s) is actually a vector of asset values for a pension initially taken at different periods (s), all evaluated in present discounted value terms adjusted to period 0. P_i is the probability of living through the ith period, and $B_i(s)$ is the benefit stream associated with a pension accepted in period s. The discount rate is r, and n denotes the age at the end of benefit receipt (arbitrarily chosen to be 100 in this research).

Pension wealth is higher, the earlier one is eligible to accept benefits, the higher the benefits upon receipt, and the lower the relevant discount rate. The discount rate has two components: the real rate of interest (reflecting the fact that one would prefer a real dollar now to one in the future) and the expected rate of inflation (since nominal dollars in the future will buy less than they do today). In cases where plans are fully indexed (such as social security and federal government employee retirement benefits), the inflation component disappears. Where future benefits are only partly indexed (as with many state and local government plans), only the uncovered portion of inflation is included.

By structuring pensions so that their value falls when receipt is postponed past some age, employers can ensure either job exit or a reduction of real wages of workers who remain on the job past that age. We define DELTA as the change in pension wealth from period 0 to period 1 plus $C(0)$—the *worker's* contribution to the pension during the period (which is 0 in noncontributing plans):

$$\begin{aligned} \text{DELTA} &= \text{WEALTH}(0) - \text{WEALTH}(1) + C(0) \\ &= \sum_{i=0}^{n} \frac{p_i B_i(0)}{(1+r)^i} - \sum_{i=1}^{n} \frac{p_i B_i(1)}{(1+r)^i} + C(0). \end{aligned} \tag{2}$$

The sign and magnitude of DELTA depend on how the benefit stream changes when one delays receipt. There are two possible sources of a change in B_i: the benefit calculation formula and the postponed benefit adjustment formula. In a defined contribution pension system, yearly benefits are based on employer and employee contributions paid into the system. A worker continuing on his job until period 1 would increase $B_i(s)$ in the future because of increased contributions by him or the firm. Most pension systems are defined benefit plans, however, in which there is no direct relationship between yearly contributions and benefits. In such a case, $B_i(s)$ will increase on the basis of other criteria, like years of service, average earnings, or age.

Actuarial adjustments are additional changes in $B_i(s)$ which compensate workers for postponing acceptance. $B_i(s)$ increases by some percentage for each year benefits are postponed. Thus, pension wealth is sensitive to the method in which benefits are adjusted, either directly by increased contributions or by some defined benefit rule, or because of an actuarial supplement for postponed receipt.

It is important to recognize the difference between pension wealth and the pension income available in a single year. Two workers both eligible to receive \$5,000 in annual pension benefits if they left their jobs today may act quite differently if the first worker, by delaying acceptance, receives a substantially larger yearly pension in the future, while the second worker receives no increase in benefits. In the first case, the increase in future benefits offsets the loss in pension benefits this year, while in the latter case, postponed benefits are lost forever.

How then does a typical pension affect life cycle earnings? For simplicity, we assume in figure 12.1 that the VMP of a worker on the job and in all other activities is constant across life, but that the employer and employee find that it is optimal to agree on a lower yearly salary at younger ages. Total yearly compensation (what we define as net earnings) equals wages and salary minus DELTA, the loss in pension wealth.[1] In this example, we assume the worker is vested at age A, first starts to receive total compensation above VMP at age B, and reaches peak total earnings and pension wealth at P. After that age, decreases in the asset value of the pension reduce net earnings until at S^* they just equal VMP.

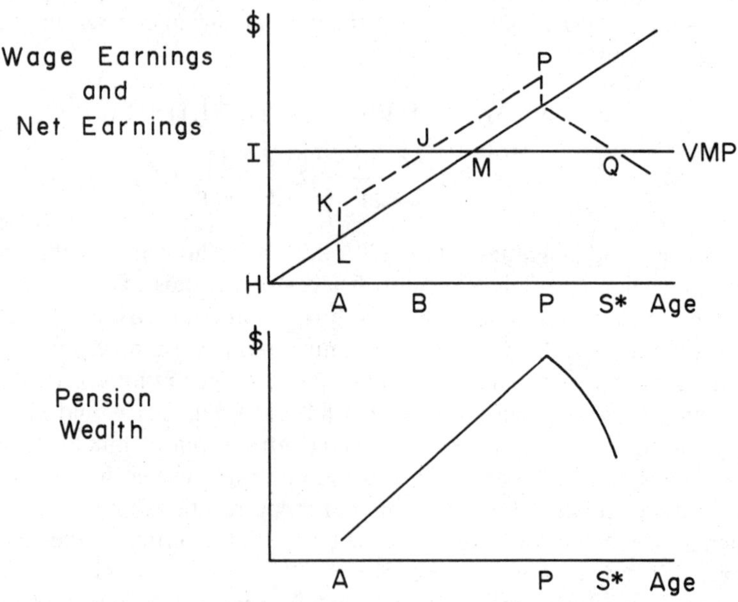

Fig. 12.1 Life cycle gross and net earnings of a worker in a given firm.

Notice, however, that lifetime earnings also equal lifetime marginal product. Hence, the area (*HIJKL*) equals the area (*JPQ*) (in present discounted value terms). The ability to mix pension benefits and salary enables the employer to decrease actual net earnings, even as wage earnings (the size of the paycheck) continue to increase. We argue that changes in pension wealth can have a significant effect on the actual net earnings of older workers and can provide employers with an alternative means of enforcing long-term labor contracts.

12.2 The Importance of Retirement Income Plans

Pension wealth is important in the retirement decision in two ways. First, it has a wealth effect as does any asset. The higher the pension wealth, ceteris paribus, the higher the probability of labor force withdrawal. But equally important, pension wealth is not a constant, it varies with the age at which the pension is claimed. This concept of wealth change (DELTA) is central to this paper, and we treat this change as a component of current compensation. When positive, DELTA represents a wealth loss—a cost to continued work, or equivalently, an earnings reduction. When negative, the present discounted value is increasing by more than the employee contributions, and net earnings are higher than they appear.

Both the WEALTH and DELTA values for workers around retirement age can be substantial. We use data from the Social Security Administration's Retirement History Study (RHS) to estimate these values. (A description of the data and the derivation of these variables appears in the appendix.) Table 12.1 shows pension WEALTH values for full-time, private sector, male workers (not self-employed) aged 63 to 65 in 1974, using 5 and 10 percent discount rates.[2] Almost two-thirds of the sample has some pension wealth (either from their current job or a previous job). Using the lower discount rate, over 5 percent of our sample (9 percent of those with pensions) has over \$50,000 (in 1974 dollars) in pension wealth, and one-third of the entire sample (over one-half of those with pensions) has benefits in excess of \$20,000. One measure of the value of a pension for the group is that the median pension wealth value for those with pensions—about \$21,000—is over twice the value of median annual wage earnings for this group (\$9,400). At the higher 10 percent discount rate, pension wealths are lower, but the median is still over \$15,000—one and a half times the average annual earnings.

DELTA values for these same respondents are shown in table 12.2. These values are positive when the wealth value of a pension falls over the year. While we know the yearly pension benefit of workers in the RHS, we do not know the method used by each private pension to derive these

Table 12.1 **Percentage Distribution of Pension WEALTH for Full-Time Employed Men, Aged 63 to 65, by Age and Discount Rate (5% and 10%), 1974**

Age	0	$1–5,000	$5,001–10,000	$10,001–20,000	$20,001–30,000	$30,001–50,000	$50,001–75,000	$75,001+	*N*	Median[a]
Discount Rate = 5%										
63	36.5	4.8	13.2	12.1	12.2	13.8	7.4	0.0	189	$21,500
64	36.2	5.5	11.0	18.1	16.5	11.0	1.6	0.0	127	$17,813
65	38.6	4.0	2.0	17.8	11.9	14.9	6.9	4.0	101	$26,250
Discount Rate = 10%										
63	36.5	11.1	13.2	16.4	9.5	11.6	1.6	0.0	189	$15,000
64	36.2	11.0	12.6	24.4	12.6	3.1	0.0	0.0	127	$12,708
65	38 6	4.0	10.9	14.9	12.9	14.9	3.0	1.0	101	$20,417

Source: (for all tables): Retirement History Study, 1969–75.

[a]Median of those with positive pension WEALTH. Medians calculated on intervals of $2,500.

Table 12.2 Percentage Distribution of Pension DELTAs[a] for Full-Time Employed Men, Aged 63 to 65, by Age and Discount Rate (5% and 10%), 1974

Age	$−2,000 to −1,000	$−999 to −1	0[b]	$1–1,000	$1,001–2,000	$2,001–3,000	$3,001–4,000	$4,001–5,000	$5,001+	*N*	Median[c]
Discount Rate = 5%											
63	3.2	21.7	43.4	20.1	4.8	2.6	1.6	0.5	2.1	189	$148
64	0.0	3.9	46.5	18.9	15.0	11.0	0.0	3.9	0.8	127	$1,156
65	0.0	1.0	47.5	10.9	13.9	12.9	4.0	4.0	5.9	101	$2,062
Discount Rate = 10%											
63	1.6	18.0	43.4	13.8	12.2	5.3	3.2	0.0	2.6	189	$482
64	0.0	3.1	46.5	15.7	16.5	10.2	3.1	2.4	2.4	127	$1,393
65	0.0	1.0	47.5	8.9	13.9	12.9	4.0	4.0	7.9	101	$2,208

[a]The difference in pension wealth when the pension is postponed one year from 1974 to 1975. See the appendix for a fuller explanation of this variable.

[b]Some respondents have positive pension WEALTH but no DELTA because the pension was earned on a previous job. DELTA refers only to the changes in pension wealth on the *current* job, since this is the only wealth affected by current labor supply decisions.

[c]Median of those with nonzero pension DELTA. Median calculated on intervals of $250.

benefits or to change them over time. Therefore, we have used data from the Bureau of Labor Statistics' Level of Benefits Study to assign pension characteristics to workers in our sample based on their industry and occupation. Since years of service is the dominant method of calculation in defined benefits programs, we assume benefit increases are based on years of service, a value available in the RHS, and use industry and occupation averages to calculate actuarial adjustments. (A fuller discussion of our methodology is found in the appendix.)

For workers aged 63, DELTAs (discounting at 5 percent) are closely split between positive and negative values. For those aged 64 and 65, pension wealth falls with continued work for most workers. The median loss at age 65 is over $2,000—almost 20 percent of the median wage of workers aged 65 who are in jobs with pensions. For those aged 64 it is $1,156 or 12 percent, while for those aged 63 it is only $148. With the 10 percent rate, future gains are discounted more heavily, and the resultant DELTA values are slightly larger.

Using a very different methodology (data on actual pension plans are applied to hypothetical individuals), Lazear reaches similar conclusions, that the expected present value of pension rights generally declines as retirement is postponed (Lazear 1981, p. 20). He interprets this as a modern form of severance pay—a bonus to those who retire early. The terminology is different from ours, but the basic point is the same—beyond some age workers are penalized financially by their pension plans for continued work.

The incentives implicit in the social security system can be summarized in analogous fashion, although there are two complications. The first involves spouse's and dependent's benefits in the event of the respondent's death. These are important aspects of social security coverage and should be considered. In this work, we have ignored children's benefits, but have augmented social security wealth by considering the probability of the spouse outliving the respondent (using the age of each and survival tables) and collecting benefits on her own, at two-thirds of the combined rate.

The second complication concerns an option open to workers under social security, but not under private pension plans—to continue working at the same job *and* collect benefits. A worker who stays at a given job cannot at the same time receive a private pension from that job. This is not the case with social security, which exempts a certain amount of earnings ($2400 in 1974) and then reduces benefits by $1.00 for every $2.00 of wage earnings. Since we are interested in discrete changes in labor force behavior (withdrawal from a given job), and because we are primarily interested in the impact of pensions on net earnings in a given job, we have ignored this option and have defined social security DELTAs in the same manner as above—the difference between current social security wealth and the wealth following an incremental year of work, plus employee social security taxes during that year. The more difficult it is for a worker to adjust his hours within a job, the more likely it is that discrete changes in labor force behavior will be the response to social security incentives. To the extent that workers receive benefits during that year and remain in their same job, this calculation overstates the social security cost of that employment and the disincentive to remain on the job. To minimize that problem, we have restricted our sample to those who are employed full-time and who are, therefore, least likely to combine work in the same job with social security receipt.

Tables 12.3 and 12.4 illustrate the magnitude of social security WEALTH and DELTA value to workers nearing traditional retirement age. Social security WEALTH is substantial for our subsample of full-time workers. Coverage is almost universal, and over 70 percent of this sample has over $50,000 in social security rights (1974 dollars—5 percent real discount rate). At the lower 2 percent real rate, two-thirds of this sample has over $70,000 in social security wealth. Wealth values rise or fall over time depending on whether the benefits lost by delay are outweighed by the future increments due to the recalculation of average earnings and the actuarial adjustment.

Prior to age 65, whether the actuarial adjustment and benefit recalculation outweigh the benefits lost through postponement of acceptance depends on the discount rate used (see table 12.4). When a 5 percent rate is employed, about 80 percent of the 63 and 64 year olds in our sample gain by delay. The median values of the wealth increases for those eligible for social security are $1852 (for those aged 63) and $857 (for those aged 64). When a 10 percent rate is used, only 41 percent of the 63 year olds and less than 20 percent of the 64 year olds gain, and the median wealth *losses* associated with a year's delay are $115 and $937, respectively.[3]

At age 65, when the actuarial adjustment drops to 1 percent (3 percent as of 1982), nearly everyone loses with delay, and the losses are substantial. Even with a 5 percent discount rate, the median loss in our sample is over $3000. At 10 percent, it is slightly higher.

That industrial pensions and social security benefits are a major source of wealth for workers on the verge of retirement is clearly shown in tables 12.1 and 12.3.[4] That this wealth will vary to an important degree across potential retirement ages is seen in tables 12.2 and 12.4. As we will see in the next section, ignoring the effect of these changes will lead to a significant overstatement of the actual net earnings of older workers.

12.3 An Empirical Look at Net Earnings

In this section we calculate the net earnings of men aged 59–65 who are full-time wage and salary workers in the private sector. It is this group of

Table 12.3 **Percentage Distribution of Social Security WEALTH, Full-Time Employed Men, Aged 63 to 65, by Age and Discount Rate (2% and 5%), 1974**

Age	0	$1–30,000	$30,001–40,000	$40,001–50,000	$50,001–60,000	$60,001–70,000	$70,001–80,000	$80,001–90,000	*N*	Median[c]
					Discount Rate = 2%					
63	36.5	4.8	13.2	12.1	12.2	13.8	7.4	0.0	189	$21,500
64	36.2	5.5	11.0	18.1	16.5	11.0	1.6	0.0	127	$17,813
65	38.6	4.0	2.0	17.8	11.9	14.9	6.9	4.0	101	$26,250
					Discount Rate = 5%					
63	5.8	5.3	7.9	12.2	68.8	0.0	0.0	0.0	189	$54,216
64	3.1	2.4	8.7	12.6	44.1	29.1	0.0	0.0	127	$56,818
65	5.9	2.0	7.9	7.9	20.8	55.5	0.0	0.0	101	$62,278

[a]Median of those with positive social security WEALTH. Calculated on intervals of $2,000.

Table 12.4 **Percentage Distribution of Social Security DELTAs,[a] Full-Time Employed Men, Aged 63 to 65, by Age and Discount Rate (5% and 10%), 1974**

Age	–$6,000 to –3,000	–$2,999 to –1,500	–$1,499 to –750	–$749 to –1	0	$1–750	$751–1,500	$1,501–3,000	$3,001–6,000	*N*	Median[b]
					Discount Rate = 5%						
63	3	51	15	14	6	11	1	0	0	189	–$1,852
64	1	34	16	29	3	12	4	1	0	127	–$857
65	0	0	0	1	6	1	2	43	48	101	$3,044
					Discount Rate = 10%						
63	0	1	3	37	6	24	24	5	0	189	$115
64	0	0	1	18	3	28	31	19	0	127	$937
65	0	0	0	0	6	0	3	28	63	101	$3,586

[a]Social security DELTA is the change in social security wealth if receipt is postponed one year (from 1974 to 1975), plus employee social security taxes paid during that year. Because of the peculiar technique used by the social security system to adjust postponed benefits, 5 and 10 percent discount rates were used in this table rather than the 2 and 5 percent rates used for social security WEALTH. (See note 3 and Burkhauser and Turner 1981).

[b]Median of those with nonzero social security DELTA.

men nearing "traditional" retirement age who were expected to benefit most from the change in the mandatory retirement law. Using the first four waves of the RHS (1969–75), we study men who were aged 59–61 in 1970 and these same men aged 63–65 in 1974.[5] All the men in our sample remained on their same full-time jobs from 1969 to 1973. We analyze the effect of the private pension system on the net earnings of these men and, more importantly, on the relationship between the net earnings of workers with and without pensions and mandatory retirement.

Table 12.5 presents the median earnings and median net earnings (earnings minus private pension DELTA) at various ages for three subsamples defined by pension and mandatory retirement status. (A fourth group, those without pensions but with mandatory retirement, was too small for analysis.) As can be seen, workers with pension plans have higher earnings than those without such plans regardless of mandatory retirement.

What then is the effect of pension rules on net earnings in this age group? How do pensions relate to mandatory retirement as a method of assuring that lifetime contracts are enforced? In table 12.6, we calculate the ratio of earnings net of pension DELTA to unadjusted earnings for those who are eligible for pensions.[6] (For those not eligible for pensions, the ratio (as defined so far) would be 1.) The impact of age can be seen in two ways. The median ratios decrease monotonically, and decline to 0.83 by age 65. In addition, the display of the distribution illustrates the shift from ratios above 1 at the younger ages to below 1 later on. At ages 59 and 60, for example, most of these workers are enjoying a slight supplement to pay because of increasing pension asset values. By 64 and 65, however, nearly all are losing, and a substantial proportion is experiencing a pay decrement of over 20 percent.

Table 12.7 shows another interesting result. Here we compare the median net earnings of those with pensions to that of those without. We disaggregate the pension sample by mandatory retirement status and simply create ratios from the columns in table 12.5. For those without mandatory rules, we find that the median net earnings of the pension subsample has dropped to precisely that of those without pensions by age 65 (i.e., the final ratio in the first column is 1.00).[7] For those with a pension and with mandatory retirement, the ratio also falls, but only to 1.19.

These results are preliminary and are based on small samples. But they strongly suggest that pension systems do eventually reduce the true earnings of older men who continue on their same job. In fact, the difference in earnings between workers with and without pension plans narrows dramatically as workers approach age 65, and for those in our sample, it disappears entirely for workers not subject to mandatory retirement.

Table 12.5 **Median Earnings and Earnings Net of Pension DELTA[a] by Age and by Pension and Mandatory Retirement Status**

	Without Mandatory Retirement Without Pension Benefits			Without Mandatory Retirement With Pension Benefits			With Mandatory Retirement With Pension Benefits		
Age	Wage Earnings	Net Wage Earnings	*N*	Wage Earnings	Net Wage Earnings	*N*	Wage Earnings	Net Wage Earnings	*N*
59	$6,292	$6,292	66	$ 8,250	$ 8,188	38	$ 8,700	$ 8,583	69
60	5,750	5,750	50	7,750	8,250	32	8,312	8,188	36
61	6,594	6,594	42	7,833	8,167	19	10,027	10,292	34
63	7,750	7,750	66	10,250	10,458	38	11,250	10,786	69
64	6,521	6,521	50	10,075	9,479	32	9,791	8,441	36
65	7,813	7,813	42	9,750	7,833	19	12,250	9,321	34

[a]Pension DELTA with 5 percent discount rate. Earnings are in 1970 dollars for ages 59–61, and in 1974 dollars for ages 63–65. Medians based on intervals of $500.

Table 12.6 **Percentage Distribution of Ratio of Earnings Net of Pension DELTA to Earnings for Those with Pensions, by Age and Mandatory Retirement Status**

Age	Less than .80	.80–.90	.91–.95	.96–1.00	1.01–1.05	1.06–1.10	1.11–1.20	1.21–1.30	Median Ratio
Without Mandatory Retirement									
59	11	0	5	5	39	39	0	0	1.04
60	3	9	6	9	44	16	9	3	1.03
61	16	0	5	11	53	5	5	5	1.03
63	11	8	11	18	37	13	3	0	1.00
64	28	28	25	16	3	0	0	0	0.88
65	42	21	11	26	0	0	0	0	0.83
With Mandatory Retirement									
59	7	3	1	13	41	26	9	0	1.03
60	7	3	0	19	50	17	3	3	1.02
61	6	6	15	24	29	21	0	0	1.00
63	9	9	20	23	23	13	3	0	0.98
64	25	42	8	14	8	3	0	0	0.86
65	35	53	6	3	3	0	0	0	0.83

Table 12.7 **Ratio of Median Net Earnings of Those with Pensions, by Mandatory Retirement Status, to Median Net Earnings of Those without Pensions**

Age	Without Mandatory Retirement	With Mandatory Retirement
59	1.30	1.36
60	1.43	1.42
61	1.24	1.56
63	1.35	1.39
64	1.45	1.29
65	1.00	1.19

Source: Net wage medians in table 12.5.

The net earnings of workers subject to mandatory retirement also decreased as they neared age 65. Nevertheless, their net earnings were still about 20 percent greater than net income of those not subject to mandatory retirement rules. In fact, this may be the reason why mandatory retirement was a necessary part of the personnel strategy in these firms.

In table 12.8, we add the effect of social security DELTAs, using a 5% discount rate. As mentioned above, workers can continue on their job and receive social security benefits. For workers who do both, the DELTAs used here exaggerate the losses. Nevertheless, the results are provocative. Here we calculate the ratio of earnings net of both pension and social security DELTAs to current earnings for those with and without pensions. The medians suggest that pensions and social security on average provide a slight wage increase up to age 65. These medians hide a considerable amount of dispersion, however. Among those 59–61, for example, between a sixth and a third of those with pensions lose retirement wealth if they continue to work. At age 65, the median ratio is about two-thirds for those without pensions and nearly down to one-half for those with a pension. Thus, measures of compensation which do not take the effect of pensions and social security into consideration dramatically overestimate the value of continued work at this age. For the median workers in our sample eligible for both social security and pension benefits at age 65, unadjusted wages overstate true earnings by almost 100 percent.

In this paper, we have described and estimated some of the work (or retirement) incentives implicit in current pension and social security rules. But we do not estimate the impact of these incentives on labor supply. In a related paper, however, we do and find that changes in pension and social security wealth are significant explanators of the labor supply behavior of older Americans (Burkhauser and Quinn 1983). The

Table 12.8 Percentage Distribution of Ratio of Earnings Net of Pension and Social Security DELTA to Earnings, by Age and Pension Status

Age	.70 and less	.71–.90	.91–.95	.96–1.00	1.01–1.05	1.06–1.10	1.11–1.20	1.21–1.30	1.31+	Median Ratio
Without Pensions										
59	0	0	0	6	23	41	24	6	0	1.07
60	0	0	0	0	22	44	30	2	2	1.08
61	0	0	2	7	19	33	31	7	0	1.08
63	0	3	6	11	12	11	24	23	11	1.13
64	6	4	8	10	16	6	32	10	8	1.10
65	74	17	2	7	0	0	0	0	0	0.65
With Pensions										
59	6	4	1	3	17	29	35	7	0	1.08
60	4	1	3	7	12	29	35	3	4	1.09
61	6	8	4	13	11	23	32	2	2	1.07
63	6	1	6	12	7	11	34	17	7	1.12
64	15	18	13	9	15	4	22	4	0	0.97
65	92	6	2	0	0	0	0	0	0	0.52

larger the DELTA values, the higher the probabilities that respondents leave their jobs over a two-year transition period. In fact, these variables do a better job of predicting transition behavior than do simple eligibility dummies. This is evidence that these incentives are important and that workers both understand their general nature and respond to them.

12.4 Conclusions and Data Needs

Mandatory retirement is one method of enforcing long-term contracts so that the earnings of a worker over his tenure with a firm will just equal the value of his marginal product. In this paper, we suggest that it is not the only method of enforcing such contracts. Pension plans which vary in value across life enable employers to reduce earnings at older ages even when wage and salary payments as traditionally measured are increasing.

Using data from the RHS we show that pension WEALTH is an important component of a worker's wealth portfolio and that pension DELTAs significantly affect net earnings as workers approach traditional retirement age. In fact, a measure of compensation which includes pension DELTAs shows that workers in our sample who are not subject to mandatory retirement earn approximately the same amount for work at age 65 regardless of whether or not they are eligible for a pension. For those who are subject to mandatory retirement, earnings net of pension DELTAs fall as they approach age 65 yet still exceed the net earnings of those without pensions and mandatory retirement. Thus, firms do appear to have some motive to use mandatory retirement to enforce job exit. But adjustments to pensions also are used and appear to be an important alternative method of enforcement. Once social security is considered it is even less likely that workers will continue to work past the traditional retirement age.

There are at least two implications of these findings with respect to mandatory retirement. The first is that mandatory retirement is less important than a simple comparison of workers with and without these provisions would suggest. This is because mandatory retirement often occurs at precisely the time that these strong social security and pension incentives go into effect. A simple comparison implicitly attributes the impacts of all of these factors to mandatory retirement, and thereby exaggerates its effect. In our paper (Burkhauser and Quinn 1983), we estimate that approximately half of the raw differential in quit behavior can be attributed to factors other than mandatory retirement.

The second implication concerns the labor market repercussions to be expected from changing the age of mandatory retirement (as Congress has done) or from eliminating it altogether (as has been suggested). Our research indicates that the effect will depend dramatically on the extent to which employers can change other aspects of the employment agreement, particularly the details of the pension system. With enough leeway, we would argue, firms can bring about retirement patterns very similar to those observed with mandatory retirement.

A major shortcoming of this research is the lack of knowledge about respondents' pension plans—how benefits are determined and how they change over time. This knowledge is needed for two reasons. It is required in order to calculate DELTA values more precisely and to judge more accurately the impact of these incentives on retirement behavior. In addition, it is important baseline data from which to measure changes in pension rules in response, partly, to changes in mandatory retirement options.

Specific data on individual pension plans are collected by the Department of Labor and have been used by researchers (Lazear 1981 and Urban Institute 1982). But such data are not generally available about the respondents who appear in large microeconomic surveys, such as the Retirement History Study. In other words, we have longitudinal microdata sets with superb demographic and economic data, but with very little detail on pension plans, and we have excellent pension data with little or no personal data on the individuals covered.[8] That we do not have both is particularly unfortunate because there is considerably more diversity across pension plans than across social security. A much larger proportion of the population is not covered, and for those workers who are, the variation in benefit levels is extreme.[9] Linking these two types of information is not a simple process. Asking individuals about the details of their pension plans (beyond information like age of eligibility and amount expected) is probably fruitless. Using existing Department of Labor files on pension plans has not been successful. And even asking firms may not always be the answer, because often they do not administer their own pension plans. The cost of gathering this institutional information is high. But so, we would argue, is the benefit. In the meantime, we must continue to use broad industrial and occupational averages for the benefit calculation rules, as we have done in this paper, and accept the biases which such measurement error entails.

Appendix

The data for this research are taken from the first four waves of the Retirement History Study (RHS)—a ten-year longitudinal analysis of the retirement process undertaken by the Social Security Administration. The study began with over 11,000 men and nonmarried women aged 58–63 in 1969. The respondents were reinterviewed at two-year intervals. By 1975, the last wave available when this research was undertaken, the sample was down to approximately 8,600 due to the death, institutionalization, mobility, or noncooperation of some respondents. Our work is based on a subsample of these 8,600 respondents. (For more detail on the RHS, see Irelan [1976].)

Social security and pension WEALTH and DELTA variables were calculated for each worker for 1970 and for 1974. This was a relatively simple process for social security because RHS data include actual social security records, and because we knew the rules on which benefits are based. For 1970–71, for example, we calculated

(i) WEALTH(0), the present discounted value, in 1970 dollars, of the social security benefit stream if the individual claimed benefits in 1970 (see eq. [1] in the text), and

(ii) WEALTH(1), the present discounted value, in 1970 dollars, of the stream which would begin in 1971, after the individual worked another year. Following the zero value for social security receipt in 1970, $B(1)$ would exceed $B(0)$ both because of the actuarial adjustment past age 62 and because of the change in average monthly wages due to increased wage earnings. We assume real wages for 1970–71 would equal the actual 1969–70 wages for all workers. Because these calculations are sensitive to the interest rate, we use a 2, 5, and 10 percent rate, both here and in the pension estimates.

As described in the text (eq. [2]), social security DELTA is this change in the WEALTH value if acceptance is postponed one year plus the employee's social security contributions during that hypothetical year of additional work. This same process is then repeated for the entire sample in 1974.

Pension WEALTH and DELTA estimates for 1970 and 1974 were more difficult to obtain, since annual benefits had to be derived from individual questionnaire responses. As with social security, knowing a yearly pension is only the first step in estimating WEALTH and DELTA values. Because we had no details on the structure of pension plans, the following assumptions were made:

(a) The yearly benefits described by the workers did not include a joint and survivor provision, though some private pension plans do provide for actuarial adjustments for survivors' benefits.

(b) The benefit amount ($B[s]$) is based on years of service, so that an additional year of work increases the benefit by $1/n$, where n is the number of years with the firm.

(c) For those currently eligible for reduced but not full benefits, the benefit amount also increases because of an actuarial adjustment. Since we do not know these actuarial adjustment factors for the individual pension plans, we used very rough industry averages. (These averages were taken from Urban Institute [1982], which used data from the BLS Level of Benefits Study).

The procedure was then the same as is described above and in equations (1) and (2) for both 1970 and 1974. We calculated two values of pension wealth (with and without an additional year of work), and defined DELTA as the difference. The derivations were again done with 2, 5, and 10 percent discount rates. A fuller discussion of the problems associated with all the variables used in our analysis is available (Burkhauser and Quinn 1983).

Notes

1. A comprehensive definition of compensation is obviously broader than this, and should include other fringe benefits (such as medical, disability and life insurance, paid vacations, etc.) as well as nonpecuniary aspects of the job, like working conditions and employment security. These are not included here because they are not the focus of the paper and because we have no data on them for the respondents in our sample. Changes in these other dimensions of compensation after a particular age (for example, a cessation of medical benefits after age 65) could certainly be important, and would have the same type of effect as would a decrease in pension wealth.

In this paper, DELTA is defined to equal the loss in pension wealth plus employee contributions during the year. For ease of exposition, the latter phrase is often dropped. Operationally, for employer pensions we assumed $C(0)$ was zero; for social security we used employee payroll taxes in a given year.

2. Private pensions include all employer pensions, but do not include social security, which is considered separately. Most private sector pensions are not automatically indexed for inflation after retirement, so a nominal rate of interest should be used in discounting. The early 1970s were a transitionary period for inflationary expectations, so we use two discount rates, 5 and 10 percent. When we consider social security benefits below, we use lower real rates (2 and 5 percent) since benefit adjustments have traditionally been greater than or equal to the cost of living—previously by congressional action and now by law.

3. Due to a quirk in the social security law prior to 1977, we employ higher discount rates for the social security DELTA than for social security WEALTH. From 1961 to 1977, the *absolute* cost of living raises given to those who retired early at actuarially reduced amounts were the same as the increments to those who claimed benefits at 65 (Burkhauser and Turner 1981). The penalty for early retirement was therefore a constant *dollar* amount, not a constant percentage. One discounts a constant dollar amount with the nominal rate of interest, not the real rate used with social security wealth.

It should be remembered that social security DELTA contains both the change in wealth (usually a loss at age 65) plus the employee's social security contribution during the year. The full-time workers in our sample are disproportionately high wage earners, so their DELTAs are generally higher than those in the general population.

4. This point is confirmed in a related paper, in which pension and social security wealth are explicitly compared to other more traditional forms of wealth—financial assets and net equity in the home, business, or real estate (Quinn 1983). It is found that for many workers in this age group the asset value of retirement rights dominate all other forms of wealth, including the value of the home.

5. The Retirement History Study reinterviewed the sample at two-year intervals (1969, 1971, 1973, and 1975), and these are the four snapshots we have. We assumed that respondents maintained their initial labor force status until the middle of each two-year interval and then made whatever transitions we observed in the subsequent interview. Hence, we refer to men aged 59–61 in 1970 and 63–65 in 1974.

6. We are grateful to Cordelia Reimers for suggestions on the restructuring of tables 12.6 and 12.8.

7. Since the magnitude of the pension DELTA values increases with age, we suspect that the pattern illustrated in table 12.7 is actually smoother than it appears, and the decline in the ratio more gradual. Unfortunately, our particular sample of respondents with neither mandatory retirement nor pensions includes one age group (60 in 1970 and 64 in 1974) with particularly poor earnings (see table 12.5). When they are compared with the subsamples with pensions, the ratios are very high. We suspect that this would not be the case in a larger sample.

8. The Department of Labor has a data source which combines information on the details of several hundred plans with the social security data on approximately 400,000 individuals in these plans. With respect to demographic and other economic variables, however, the research is limited to the very sparse detail on the social security earnings record. There have been proposals to combine this source with current microsurveys (such as the Survey of New Beneficiaries or the Exact Match File), but so far this has not been done.

9. For example, using 1975 data on 244 pension plans from the Bankers Trust Study of Corporate Pension Plans, and a 10 percent discount rate, Lazear finds pension wealth for hypothetical individuals ranging from about $400 to over $400,000 (Lazear 1981, p. 19).

References

Burkhauser, Richard V., and Joseph F. Quinn. 1983. Is mandatory retirement overrated? Evidence from the 1970's. *Journal of Human Resources* 18: 337–53.

Burkhauser, Richard V., and John Turner. 1981. Can twenty-five million Americans be wrong? A response to Blinder, Gordon, and Wise. *National Tax Journal* 34: 467–72.

Irelan, Lola M. 1976. Retirement history study: Introduction. In *Almost 65: Baseline data from the retirement history study*. Social Security Administration, Office of Research and Statistics, Research Report no. 49. Washington, D.C.: Government Printing Office.

Lazear, Edward P. 1979. Why is there mandatory retirement? *Journal of Political Economy* 87: 1261–84.

———. 1981. Severance pay, pensions, mobility, and the efficiency of work incentives. University of Chicago. Mimeo.

Quinn, Joseph F. 1983. The importance of pension and social security rights in the wealth portfolios of older Americans. In *Economic resources for the elderly: Prospects for the future*, Christopher Garbacz (ed.). Boulder, CO: Westview Press, forthcoming.

Urban Institute. 1982. *Financial retirement incentives in private pension plans*. Report to the U.S. Department of Labor. January 1982. Washington, D.C. (Contract no.: J-9-P-0-0163).

Comment Cordelia W. Reimers

This paper opens up a large terrain for future investigation. The basic insight about changes in the asset value of pensions being a component of net earnings—one that these authors have written about before—is unassailable, and the empirical work is sufficient to establish the practical importance of pension rules as a mechanism for reducing the net earnings of older workers and, presumably, encouraging retirement. Burkhauser and Quinn have clearly put their collective finger on an alternative mechanism to mandatory retirement.

The actual numbers they report are, as they are the first to say, preliminary, based on very small and restricted samples and hampered by the lack of information on respondents' pension plans that plagues most research on retirement behavior. I would therefore not make too much of the exact numbers reported here, but would urge Burkhauser and Quinn, and others, to try to refine these estimates further.

For instance, if we are to believe these numbers, DELTA (even taking private pensions alone) does not appreciably reduce median net earnings before age 64; and social security appears to *increase* median net earnings before age 65. Yet most men currently retire before that age. Mandatory retirement cannot be the reason, either, so it appears that we have still not got a satisfactory explanation of observed retirement behavior.

But there are several ways the numbers might be improved upon, even with existing data, before abandoning the hypothesis. I shall discuss four problem areas: the calculation of the private pension DELTAs; the model of the retirement decision; the use of the median earnings of those without pensions as evidence on the alternative wage; and the biases involved in the choice of samples for study.

I can't say much about the way the private pension DELTAs were calculated, because the appendix is too vague on this point. But one question does arise regarding these DELTAs. To get around the lack of information in the Retirement History Study about benefit formulas, the authors use industry-occupation averages for certain pension plan characteristics. To evaluate this strategy, it is important to know how much pension plans vary among firms, *within* an industry and occupation. How much of the true variation in DELTA is being lost by this imputation? If industry-occupation averages are much alike, but firms vary a great deal, Burkhauser and Quinn's method will produce a much narrower distribution of private pension DELTAs than actually exists. Then the distributions of private pension DELTAs and of the net earnings/current wage ratios would be more spread out in reality than appears in tables 12.2,

Cordelia W. Reimers is associate professor of economics at Hunter College of the City University of New York.

12.6, and 12.8 of the paper. How this might affect the medians is anybody's guess.

On a related point about measurement, these net earnings/current wage ratios should of course be measured, insofar as possible, net of taxes and inclusive of other fringe benefits—especially those that change with age. It's not clear that taxes have been netted out of the numbers reported in the paper.

I now turn to the way Burkhauser and Quinn model the retirement decision and use the numbers as evidence bearing on the hypothesis that pension rules induce retirement. First, their model of the retirement decision, while a major improvement over one that simply compares the current period's wage and pension benefit, is still too myopic. There is no more reason for a worker to consider only his current period wage than only his current period pension benefit. The optimal timing of retirement involves comparison of the present values of the entire *streams* of future wages, alternative wages (or values of nonmarket time), and pension benefits. To use a one-period wage comparison in modeling retirement, one must assume that once net earnings dip below the alternative wage, they remain there forever after. (To see this, ask yourself why we do not expect a man of 35 to retire from the labor force just because he has a spell of disability or unemployment that drastically, but temporarily, reduces his market wage.) We may be perfectly comfortable making this assumption for older men, but we ought to be explicit about it.

Second, the numbers in table 12.7 of the paper appear to be presented as evidence about whether the private pension DELTAs are large enough to induce retirement. But there are several difficulties in interpreting them that way. If we are trying to explain retirement, we will want to know how a man's net earnings compare with his own alternative, or reservation, wage. If we know how much pension DELTAs reduce net earnings, one additional piece of information is needed: how the net earnings compare with the alternative wage. Burkhauser and Quinn seem to interpret their table 12.7 as if it contained that sort of information. What it does show is the ratio of median net earnings of those *with* a pension to median earnings of those *without* a pension, allowing for the private pension DELTA only.

To interpret these ratios as containing any evidence at all about whether pensions reduce net earnings enough to enforce job exit requires four assumptions about the median alternative wage: (1) that it is the same for those with and without a private pension; (2) that it is the same for those with and without mandatory retirement; (3) that it is equal to the median current wage of those who have no private pension; and (4) that the distributions of individuals' net earnings and alternative wages just happen to be related in such a way that the ratio of the medians is equal to the median ratio.

Given these four assumptions, we could conclude from table 12.7 of the paper that, for those without mandatory retirement, the private pension plan alone is sufficient to reduce net earnings to the alternative wage level for half the sample at age 65. We could also conclude that, where it exists, mandatory retirement is needed because the private pension plan does not sufficiently reduce median net earnings. These are, in fact, the conclusions drawn by Burkhauser and Quinn.

However, I think it highly unlikely, first of all, that the median alternative wage is the same across pension-mandatory retirement status, or is equal to the no-pension wage. The idea of comparing net earnings of people with and without pensions to get a comparison of a person's net earnings and alternative wage would be justified by a model in which people are randomly assigned to pension-mandatory retirement status and are identical in other respects—in particular, their alternative wage. Moreover, those without pensions would have to be in a spot labor market, where wage = VMP at all times. But this model violates the basic fact that pension-mandatory retirement status is not random, but results from a selection process such as Walter Oi discusses in his paper in this volume.

For one thing, we know private pension coverage is positively correlated with education. Besides, workers will tend to sort themselves among firms on the basis of mandatory retirement and their own preferences for leisure (i.e., their reservation wages). Furthermore, even on most jobs without pension plans the wage probably includes some return to firm-specific human capital and therefore is above the alternative wage. Some effort to standardize for education and other determinants of the alternative wage should be made before comparing net earnings across pension and mandatory retirement categories. Moreover, Burkhauser and Quinn's table 12.7 completely ignores social security, and it is the *combined* effect of social security and a private pension plan that determines whether mandatory retirement is necessary to end the period when $W > \text{VMP}$.

Even if we could accept assumptions (1) through (3), however, and take the median no-pension wage as a measure of the median alternative wage for those with pensions, there is a serious problem with using the ratio of these medians as evidence on the distribution of the ratio of the two variables. Individual workers' net earnings/alternative wage ratios are the variable of interest; yet what Burkhauser and Quinn report is not, even under assumptions (1) through (3), the median ratio, but the ratio of median net earnings to the median alternative wage. This may be quite misleading. Suppose, for example, net earnings were distributed as in figure C12.1A, and the distribution of alternative wages looked like figure C12.1B, with everyone's rank order being preserved. Then the *ratio of medians* = 1, but the *median ratio* is clearly much greater than 1.

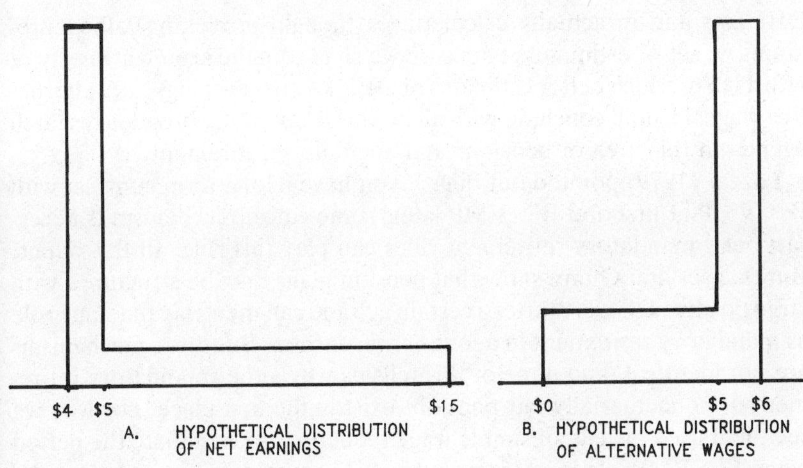

Fig. C12.1

(In fact, it would be about 1.8.) It is obvious that we cannot, in general, learn much of value about the median ratio by looking at the ratio of the medians.

Turning now to the authors' choice of samples for study: is it really necessary to confine the samples to *full-time* workers, and in some cases to those who were in the *same full-time* job in 1969 and 1974? If the hypothesis underlying the paper is correct, men over 60 with large positive DELTA are more likely to retire, other things being equal. This presumably biases the samples toward those men with small or negative DELTA (though the bias, in fact, depends on the correlations among DELTA, wages, and reservation wages). This could explain the authors' finding that median net earnings are not appreciably reduced by private pensions before age 64.

Burkhauser and Quinn are concerned that people who take social security benefits while keeping the same job would bias their estimates of the social security DELTA upward, if they included part-time workers. They could presumably determine from the Retirement History Survey how widespread this practice is. My guess is that it's rare, because it is hard to adjust hours drastically on the same job, and that the downward bias of DELTA from selecting only full-time workers is more serious. This bias question is further complicated by the information in note 3 of the paper, that the social security DELTAs are biased *upward* because the sample members tend to be high wage earners.

Those are the main things that bother me about this paper. These criticisms should not obscure the useful contribution that Burkhauser and Quinn have made in emphasizing the potential importance of pension

DELTAs and in actually calculating a thought-provoking, albeit preliminary, set of estimates. I am sure we shall soon be seeing a variety of efforts to produce better estimates of DELTA, net earnings, and alternative wages. I shall conclude with a few words about the broader research agenda in this area of pensions and mandatory retirement.

Lazear (1979) pointed out that, if you have a long-term contract with $W<$ VMP at first and $W>$ VMP later, some cutoff mechanism is necessary, and mandatory retirement rules can play this role. In this paper, Burkhauser and Quinn show that pension plans may be structured with large positive DELTAs after a certain age and can then play the same role as mandatory retirement in a long-term contract. But these mechanisms are not identical, and none of this tells us why either mandatory retirement or nonactuarially fair pensions exist in the first place, nor why we see them used instead of simple wage reductions to terminate the period when $W>$ VMP in a long-term contract. There may be some clues in the types of firms and workers that do and don't have mandatory retirement and pensions with large DELTAs. Perhaps one mechanism is more efficient than another, depending on the circumstances. Perhaps they act in different ways to sort workers among firms according to workers' preferences about how long to work. The costs associated with the various cutoff mechanisms need investigating before we will know the true costs of raising or abolishing the mandatory retirement age. Burkhauser and Quinn make a start in opening up this important subject.

Reference

Lazear, Edward P. 1979. Why is there mandatory retirement? *Journal of Political Economy* 87: 1261–84.

PART

IV Labor Cost Measures and Economic Policy Analysis

13 Measuring Labor Compensation in Controls Programs

J. Stuart McMenamin and R. Robert Russell

13.1 Introductory Remarks

It is commonly said that wage control programs are much easier to formulate and to administer than price control programs. The reasons given are that consumer and producer products and services are much more heterogeneous than labor inputs, and pricing practices are much more diverse than pay structures. While there is much truth to these comparisons, the difficulties of formulating an effective and workable program on the pay side are easily underestimated. The formulation of pay change measurement rules is complicated by two major factors: (1) the existence, and increasing relative size, of many types of labor compensation other than straight hourly pay and (2) the existence of many types of salary structures and plans.

These complications create problems for any economic analysis requiring measurement of labor cost. They are, however, especially problematical in the formulation of wage limitations in a controls program. Whether the program is voluntary or mandatory (more realistically, regardless of where it is located on the voluntary-to-mandatory spectrum), issues of equity and universal comprehension of the rules of the game are paramount. If such issues could be ignored, the straightforward economic objective of such programs—controlling labor cost[1]—would be adequately served by a definition of labor compensation that is no dif-

J. Stuart McMenamin is a lecturer in the Department of Economics, University of California, San Diego, and is associated with Criterion Incorporated in San Diego. R. Robert Russell is a professor of economics and director of the C. V. Starr Center for Applied Economics at New York University.

The authors wish to acknowledge the helpful comments of Bruno Stein, Haig Nalbantian, and the conference participants, especially Erwin Diewert and Jack Triplett.

ferent from that employed in any other economic analysis; there would be no special measurement issues and no purpose for this paper.

This objective, however, is inevitably compromised by the need to eclicit and to maintain public support and cooperation, which require at least the appearance of equitable treatment of different employee groups (e.g., management/nonmanagement and union/nonunion). Equity considerations are central to "incomes policies" (controls on types of incomes—labor compensation, profit, rent, and interest) commonly employed in Western European countries, and they have also inevitably crept into the price and wage control programs adopted in the United States. Indeed, neutrality with respect to labor/nonlabor income shares was a basic tenet of all three programs of the last two decades: the Kennedy/Johnson guideposts, the Nixon controls, and the Carter pay/price standards.

Employer cooperation also requires that the rules stipulate a clear goal that can be attained through standard compensation-administration procedures. Requiring firms to control costs that are substantially beyond their control can erode cooperation.

These issues of equity and administrative workability interact with the two pay program complications listed above (multiple types of compensation and multiple types of salary structures) in a way that makes the measurement of labor cost more problematical in a controls program than in other types of labor market analyses and programs. Controls programs confront all of the usual measurement problems, plus many others. These measurement problems provide the focus of this paper.[2]

In the following discussion, we relate the resolution of the measurement issues in Phase II of the Nixon administration's Economic Stabilization Program (ESP) and the first year of the Carter administration's Pay and Price Standards Program.[3] The first program was administered by the tripartite Pay Board and was constrained by legislative mandate, whereas the Carter administration's program was based on an executive order and therefore was, at least initially, relatively unconstrained by external factors. We ignore the two ESP freezes. We also devote little attention to Phases III and IV of the ESP and the second year of the Carter program, since they essentially constitute periods of gradual decontrol (the first administered by the Cost of Living Council and the second, in effect, engineered by the Pay Advisory Committee).

In section 13.2, the labor cost measurement concept in a controls program is placed in the context of the cost-push theory of inflation and the theory of production and cost minimization. In section 13.3, we discuss issues involving the coverage and treatment of nonwage compensation. In section 13.4, we deal with the index number issues that arise in choosing a method for calculating compensation rate changes. Section 13.5 contains a few concluding remarks.

13.2 Modeling Controls

13.2.1 Cost-Push Inflation and Measurement Rules

The objective of the labor cost controls programs adopted in the United States has been to mitigate cost-push pressures on product prices. The underlying behavioral description of the firm is typically based on a proportional markup of prices over unit costs,[4] which in turn can be based on the theory of production and cost minimization. The cost function, C, of an input-price-taking firm is defined by[5]

$$(1) \qquad C(w, r, q) = \min_{\ell, z} [w \cdot \ell + r \cdot z \mid q \leq F(\ell, z)],$$

where w is a vector of compensation rates for different types of labor, r is a vector of prices of other inputs (e.g., rental rates for capital and prices of intermediate goods), q is output, ℓ is the vector of labor inputs, z is the vector of nonlabor inputs, and F is the production function.

Our exposition can be simplified without loss of any essential aspects if we assume that the production function is homogenous of degree one, in which case the cost function can be structured into the multiple of output and a unit cost function, c (Shephard 1970):

$$(2) \qquad C(w, r, q) = c(w, r) \cdot q.$$

The markup theory of price behavior is then described by the following equation:

$$(3) \qquad p = \alpha \cdot c(w, r),$$

where α is a markup factor. By converting to logs,

$$(4) \qquad \ln p = \ln \alpha + \ln \tilde{c} (\ln w, \ln r),$$[6]

and differentiating with respect to time, we obtain the corresponding expression for the rate of inflation:

$$(5) \qquad \frac{\dot{p}}{p} = \frac{\dot{\alpha}}{\alpha} + \sum_i s_i(w, r) \frac{\dot{w}_i}{w_i} + \sum_j s_j(w, r) \frac{\dot{r}_j}{r_j},$$

where a dot over a variable indicates a time derivative (i.e., $\dot{p}/p$ is the rate of change of the product price), and $s_i(w, r)$ and $s_j(w, r)$ are, respectively, the shares of types of labor inputs and nonlabor inputs in total costs.[7]

Equation (5), in the spirit of the cost-push theory of inflation, allocates the rate of increase of price to rates of increase of cost components, as well as the rate of change of the markup factor. A comprehensive controls program would therefore place an upper limit on the rate of change of each of the cost components and the markup factor. Alternatively, a control could be placed on some of the input prices (e.g., labor compensation rates) as well as the rate of increase of price itself, $\dot{p}/p$, in which case the other (nonlabor) cost components would implicitly be controlled by the limitation on price increases. In either case, one possible guideline for labor cost is

$$\frac{\dot{w}_i}{w_i} \leq \beta \, \forall \, i. \tag{6}$$

The principal problem with the control rule (6) is that it does not provide flexibility for relative compensation rates to change; for all rates for which the constraint is binding, relative compensation rates must remain fixed. This inflexibility exacerbates the problem of induced inefficiencies, particularly in the case of occupational shortages. Of course, one could adopt different upper bounds for different types of labor inputs, but the task of deciding on all of these limitations would be exceedingly difficult for anything but a trivial partition of the labor force. Reflecting these facts, controls program have typically placed restrictions on some aggregate measure of labor cost. Permitting firms to comply with a limitation on an index of labor cost affords them the opportunity to change relative compensation rates in response to changing market conditions while meeting the control objective of limiting total labor cost.

The question is: Where does this index of labor cost come from? A natural measure is the second set of terms in equation (5), with the share weights normalized to sum to unity:

$$\sum_i s_i^L(w, r) \frac{\dot{w}_i}{w_i} < \beta, \tag{7}$$

where

$$s_i^L(w, r) = \frac{s_i(w, r)}{\sum_i s_i(w, r)}$$

is the share of labor-type i in total labor cost.

There does not in general exist an aggregate labor compensation rate (a theoretically consistent aggregation rule for compensation rate levels) corresponding to the continuous measure of change in (7); integration of the left-hand side of (7) results in a function of both w and r. An aggregated compensation rate exists if and only if the unit cost function can be written as

$$c(w, r) = \hat{c}[W(w), r]. \tag{8}$$

In this representation, the function W can be interpreted as the aggregation rule (or index specification), and $W(w)$ is the aggregate compensation rate. This construction is possible if and only if compensation rates of various types of labor are separable from prices of other inputs—i.e., if and only if labor price frontiers are independent of the prices of other inputs (Blackorby, Primont, and Russell 1978, p. 70). Under homotheticity—but only in this case—this condition is equivalent to separability of labor inputs from other inputs in the production function (Blackorby, Primont, and Russell 1978, p. 89). This in turn requires that technical rates of substitution between labor inputs are independent of the quantities of other inputs. Needless to say, this is a strong restriction.

If the conditions for aggregation across compensation rates are satisfied, the cost-push equation can be written as

$$\frac{\dot{p}}{p} = \frac{\dot{\alpha}}{\alpha} + S_L[W(w), r]\frac{\dot{W}(w)}{W(w)} + \sum_j s_j(w, r)\frac{\dot{r}_j}{r_j}, \tag{9}$$

where

$$\frac{\dot{W}(w)}{W(w)} = \sum_i s_i^L(w)\frac{\dot{w}_i}{w_i}, \tag{10}$$

$s_L[W(w), r]$ is labor's share of total costs, and $s_i^L(w)$ is the share of the ith labor input in total labor cost. The aggregate compensation rate control rule is then

$$\frac{\dot{W}(w)}{W(w)} \leq \beta. \tag{11}$$

The difference between control rules (7) and (11) is that the share weights in (7) depend on nonlabor input prices as well as labor compensation rates. Thus, in principle inequality (7) requires more information than (11); however, the required information about all price levels is embodied in the share weights, and in both cases data on shares of individual types of labor inputs suffice to construct the aggregate rate of change—in the continuous case. In practice, however, aggregate compensation changes must be constructed from discrete data. If the aggregation condition in (8) is satisfied, such constructions are naturally and trivially given by

$$W[w(t_1)]/W[w(t_0)] - 1 \leq \beta, \tag{12}$$

where $w(t_0)$ and $w(t_1)$ are the compensation rate vectors in the base period and terminal period, respectively.

Alternatively, the discrete time control rule can be constructed by taking a discrete approximation to (7) or (11). In general, however, such discrete approximations may not themselves be derivable from a well-behaved cost function; moreover, discrete indexes of the form (12) are not in general functions of share weights and percentage rates of change of individual compensation rates. (See section 13.4 for additional discussion of these issues.) In any event, the exposition that follows is somewhat more evocative if we assume the existence of a labor cost aggregate,

W; the reader can easily modify the arguments for the case where this condition is not satisfied.

13.2.2 Technological Change

The exposition thus far has ignored the effect of technological change. If the state of technology is not invariant, the markup rule is

$$p = \alpha \cdot c(w, r, \tau), \tag{13}$$

where τ is an index of the state of technology (i.e., total factor productivity) and c is decreasing in τ. If compensation rates are separable not only from other input prices but also from the state of technology, then the unit cost function can be written as

$$c(w, r, \tau) = \hat{c}[W(w), r, \tau]. \tag{14}$$

Under the maintained assumption of homogeneity, this separability condition is eqivalent to Hicks neutrality of technological change with respect to labor inputs (Blackorby, Lovell, and Thursby 1976). In this case, introduction of technological progress simply adds a term to the cost-push equation (9).

If the neutrality/separability condition is not satisfied, the unit cost function image is

$$c(w, r, \tau) = \hat{c}[W(w, \tau), r, \tau]. \tag{15}$$

In this case, the change in the aggregate compensation rate is given by

$$\frac{\dot{W}(w)}{W(w)} = \sum_i s_i^L(w, \tau)\frac{\dot{w}_i}{w_i} + \epsilon(w, \tau)\frac{\dot{\tau}}{\tau}, \tag{16}$$

where $\epsilon(w, \tau)$ is the elasticity of labor costs with respect to the state of technology. Thus, a rule of the type in inequality (11) would allow larger compensation increases in those firms with larger elasticities or more rapid rates of technological change, since the second term on the right-hand side of equation (16) is negative when there is technological progress.

Indeed, many argue that the allowable compensation change should be sensitive to rates of productivity growth. To the extent, however, that disparities in rates of technological progress are attributable to differential rates of capital formation and to differences in the potential scope of innovation, this approach is inequitable and distortionary; with competitive labor and product markets, high productivity growth rates tend to be reflected in lower rates of price increases rather than higher rates of wage increases.

On the other hand, to the extent that the disparities reflect differences in workers' or unions' resistance to labor-saving technological innovations, an aggregate labor cost control rule that limited (16) might be more appropriate. In a practical vein, however, there is no way that controllers can discern those cases in which larger wage increases were granted in return for acceptance of labor-saving technological progress.

13.2.3 Incentive Pay

More vexing are the problems raised when rates of labor compensation include some form of incentive pay. There are two general types of such programs: (1) group productivity plans and (2) individual worker incentive plans (such as piecework pay).

In a group productivity plan, the hourly compensation of a group member depends on measured group performance, and group performance depends on the level of group effort and the state of technology. Thus, a simplified statement of the group compensation rate is

$$w_i(\omega_i, \gamma_i, \tau_i) = \omega_i + b_i[\gamma_i e_i(\gamma_i), \tau_i], \tag{17}$$

where ω_i is the hourly wage rate, b_i is the hourly productivity bonus function, γ_i is the incentive rule parameter, $e_i(\gamma_i)$ is the level of group effort, and τ_i is a group-specific measure of technology.[8] The presumption of such plans is that effort, $e_i(\gamma_i)$, and therefore group productivity is increasing in γ_i. Further, if the increased worker efficiency induced by the plan outweighs the additional compensation generated by the plan, unit costs are reduced by its introduction; that is, the unit cost function is decreasing in γ_i, at least over some interval, and in particular unit costs are lower for some positive γ_i than when $\gamma_i = 0$.

Over time, the hourly wage rate, the incentive rule parameter, the level of effort, and technology may all change. The rate of change of hourly compensation for a group is

$$\frac{\dot{w}_i}{w_i} = \frac{1}{w_i}\left(\dot{\omega}_i + \frac{\partial b_i}{\partial \gamma_i}\dot{\gamma}_i + \frac{\partial b_i}{\partial e_i}\frac{de_i}{\partial \gamma_i}\dot{\gamma}_i + \frac{\partial b_i}{\partial \tau_i}\dot{\tau}_i\right), \tag{18}$$

and the change in the aggregate labor compensation rate is

$$\frac{\dot{W}(w)}{W(w)} = \sum_i \frac{s_i^L(w)}{w_i}\left(\dot{\omega}_i + \frac{\partial b_i}{\partial \gamma_i}\dot{\gamma}_i + \frac{\partial b_i}{\partial e_i}\frac{de_i}{d\gamma_i}\dot{\gamma}_i + \frac{\partial b_i}{\partial \tau}\dot{\tau}_i\right).^9 \tag{19}$$

Corresponding to this decomposition of $\dot{W}(w)/W(w)$, there are several possible control rules, three of which are

$$\frac{\dot{W}(w)}{W(w)} \leq \beta, \tag{20}$$

$$\sum_i \frac{s_i^L}{w_i}\left(\dot{\omega}_i + \frac{\partial b_i}{\partial \gamma_i}\dot{\gamma}_i + \frac{\partial b_i}{\partial \tau}\dot{\tau}\right) \leq \beta, \tag{21}$$

and

$$\sum_i s_i^L \frac{\dot{\omega}_i}{\omega_i} \leq \beta . \tag{22}$$

The first of these rules is typically the strictest, charging employee units for all increased bonus payments as well as hourly wage gains; the second charges against the guideline only those increases in bonuses that are attributable to changes in technology and in the incentive plan parameters, forgiving those that are attributable to increased group effort; the last ignores all changes in compensation rates attributable to the group productivity plan and hence is the most liberal of the three rules.

Choosing among these three rules was a matter of great controversy in both the Nixon controls program and the Carter standards program. The issue centers on the apparent conflict between the objectives of promoting economic efficiency and productivity growth (for minimizing induced inefficiencies) on the one hand, and the objective of controlling labor costs on the other. To the extent that the group productivity plan induces workers to become more efficient and to the extent that the resultant bonuses do not overcompensate for those gains, the increases generated by the plan should be excluded from the measurement of labor compensation. Under these conditions, the most liberal rule, inequality (22), would still be effective in controlling unit costs (and hence prices under the markup rule [3]).

There are, however, two problems with this rule. First, there is good reason to be skeptical about the incentive effects of group productivity plans, because of the free rider phenomenon. Improvements in group productivity attributable to the increased diligence of any one member of the group are shared among all members, and each member benefits from group productivity improvements whether or not he makes a contribution. Consequently, looked at from the perspective of individual self-interest, there may be little reason for such plans to improve group productivity. The counterargument is that individual workers are likely to respond to peer group pressure to perform effectively. Clearly, the severity of the free rider problem is sensitive to the size of the group. Unfortunately, there is little empirical evidence about the effectiveness of such plans; most of the evidence is anecdotal.

Second, there are economic arguments suggesting that the increased productivity attributable to technological change should be charged against the standard. In most industries, growth in total factor productivity is an ongoing phenomenon because of technological change and capital investment. As noted above, providing higher allowable compensation rate increases for workers in industries with more rapid technological progress and more capital investment is inequitable and fails to simulate market processes (in which relatively rapid rates of productivity growth tend to be reflected in relatively slower rates of inflation rather than relatively higher rates of growth of labor compensation). If it were possible to separate the productivity gains attributable to induced group effort from those attributable to technological progress and capital investment, there would be no problem, and rule (21) could be used. In practice, however, such distinctions are impractical; trained econometricians could construct models and perform experiments that could be used to infer such dichotomizations, but it is not possible to construct a reasonable set of rules that companies can follow in distinguishing between the two sources of productivity gains.[10]

For these two reasons—the free rider problem and the measurement problem—no exception was provided for group productivity plans in the Carter Pay and Price Standards Program. Immense lobbying pressure—both directly and through the Congress—pressured the Council on Wage and Price Stability into the formulation of a tightly worded exception for group productivity plans (i.e., one that required a reasonable assurance that the bonuses were conditional on increased worker effort), but its promulgation was effectively blocked by the Pay Advisory Committee. In any event, the issue of exemptions for group productivity plans in today's economy is not of critical importance, because these plans are uncommon. (Much more common are incentive plans for which the performance criterion is not in terms of physical output; see section 13.3.) Such plans were even more uncommon in 1972, when the Congress mandated an exception for them in the ESP.

A feature of the control rules (21) and (22) is that, despite the exclusion of compensation increases attributable to productivity improvements, the base compensation rate, $w_i(\omega_i, \gamma_i, \tau_i)$, includes all compensation, including base group productivity bonuses. This makes sense. The purpose of these exclusions is to encourage future productivity gains, and punishing workers for past gains in productivity would be inequitable. Moreover, workers may well in the past have given up fixed wage increases in return for the incentive plan. (This is, of course, less likely to be true for unions, which traditionally resist any type of incentive pay. At any rate, such plans are rare for union workers.)

One of the two problems associated with group productivity exceptions is eliminated in the case of individual worker incentive plans, such as piecerate compensation payments. Such programs can be modeled by

$$w_{ij}(\omega_i, \gamma_i, \tau_i) = \omega_i + b_i[\gamma_i, e_{ij}(\gamma_i), \tau_i], \tag{23}$$

where w_{ij} is the total hourly compensation rate for the jth worker in the ith group, and e_{ij} is the level of effort of that worker induced by the incentive rate for the ith group, γ_i. If all compensation is in the form of piecework pay, the first term of (23) vanishes, and if the worker receives only fixed compensation, the second term vanishes.

In this case, assuming sufficient structure to aggregate across employees within each group, the rate of change in the group compensation rate is given by

$$\frac{\dot{w}_i}{w_i} = \sum_j \frac{s^L_{ij}}{w_{ij}} \left(\dot{\omega}_i + \frac{\partial b_i}{\partial \gamma_i} \dot{\gamma}_i + \frac{\partial b_i}{\partial e_{ij}} \frac{de_i}{d\gamma_i} \dot{\gamma}_i + \frac{\partial b_i}{\partial \tau_i} \dot{\tau}_i \right), \tag{24}$$

where s^L_{ij} is the share of worker j in the total labor cost for group i. Further aggregation is then possible, using equation (10).

As in the case of group productivity plans, three possible control rules are obtained by (1) controlling all four terms in (24), (2) eliminating the third term, or (3) eliminating the last three terms. The first of these rules is the most stringent, charging all compensation increases against the guidelines; the last is the most lenient, excluding all changes in incentive payments; the second is intermediate, excluding increases in compensation attributable to demonstrable increases in individual worker productivity, but counting against the guideline increases attributable to changes in the piecework formula and changes attributable to technological advance.

Although the free rider problem does not exist for individual worker incentive programs, the problem of separating productivity improvements attributable to increased worker effort from those attributable to the ongoing process of capital investment and technological change is still relevant. All piecework payments were legislatively excluded from the purview of the ESP. The Carter program excluded compensation increases demonstrably attributable to increased output per hour.

Additional measurement problems, which are complicated by the control program imperatives of equity considerations and the need to make the rules understandable and workable, are created by two factors: (1) the need to define precisely the compensation rates, w, taking into account the diverse types of compensation payment, and (2) the need to specify an aggregation technique. These two measurement problems are discussed respectively in sections 13.3 and 13.4.

13.3 Treatment of Nonwage Compensation

In the preceding section, we dealt with compensation as a single numerical entity. In fact, compensation comes in many diverse forms. In this section, we discuss three major types of compensation other than hourly wages and the measurement issues that arise in designing control rules to cover them. The first major category is incentive pay, including bonuses and profit-sharing plans (usually associated with management groups). A second category, future value compensation, includes long-term incentive plans involving the issuance of awards where cost and value will not be known until some future time. The final and most important category is fringe benefits, such as medical insurance and pension plans.

13.3.1 General Issues

Administrators of controls programs face three general issues in the treatment of nonwage compensation: (1) whether a particular item should be covered, (2) whether the item should be measured in terms of employer costs or employee benefits, and (3) whether the rule should be applied separately to each component or to their aggregate. In the context of the simple model described in section 13.2, the answers tend to be obvious; when the control issues of equity and workability are taken into account, however, the answers are not so obvious.

As noted in section 13.2, the issue of whether to include certain types of incentive pay is a real one. The issue turns on whether the incentive pay induces commensurate productivity improvements that offset the effect of higher labor compensation. In the context of the simple model of section 13.2, however, any rise in the aggregate compensation rate that does not have offsetting productivity effects should be covered, since it results in higher price. Moreover, so long as the constraint is binding, any uncovered item would provide an escape mechanism, and the induced substitution toward the uncovered form of compensation would be undesirable from the perspective of economic efficiency as well as program effectiveness. Finally, exclusion of selected types of compensation can undermine public support for the program, particularly if executives appear to benefit most from the exclusions (as is the case for many types of nonwage compensation).

On the other hand, inclusion of some of these items requires complex rules, thereby increasing the administrative and reporting burden on firms and the monitoring burden on government administrators. In addition, some forms of pay are, to a greater or lesser extent, beyond the control of employers, and their inclusion can undermine support for the program.

The general approach of both the Pay Board and CWPS was to cover all forms of compensation. Both, however, excluded employer contributions to social security, because they are beyond the control of employers and because the legislated increases have differential impacts across groups of employees. The Congress directed the Pay Board to exclude most fringe benefits from its measure of labor compensation but allowed for limits on such benefits if the contributions made to support them were "unreasonably inconsistent" with the standards for wage or price stability. The Pay Board translated this general principle into some specific restrictions on the excludable fringe benefits (see the discussion in section 13.3.4).

The second question is whether the nonwage items should be measured in terms of the value of the benefits received by the employees or by the cost to the employers. Of course, benefits and cost coincide in the case of wages and salaries, but they can diverge markedly for many types of fringe benefits (for example, changes in pension-funding laws or regulations can affect employer costs substantially without changing employee benefits). The fundamental objective of controlling labor cost is clearly served by focusing on employer costs rather than employee benefits. In those instances, however, where the employer does not control the cost of providing a particular benefit, this approach can cause either equity distortions across employee groups or administrative bottlenecks as firms request exceptions on equity grounds. The Pay Board regulations and the CWPS standards were designed to embody the general principle of measuring the employer's cost when that cost was directly controlled by the employer and measuring the value of employee benefits when the costs were not directly controlled.

The third question is whether the individual nonwage items should be treated under separate limitations or be aggregated with wages under a common limitation. Under a common aggregate rule, employers would have the flexibility to substitute from one compensation form to another without violating the overall standard. This flexibility would be absent if separate limitations were imposed on each compensation type, resulting in a stricter standard but one that would inhibit substitution. The general approach of both the Pay Board and CWPS was to place all compensation forms under an aggregate standard whenever possible.

13.3.2 Incentive Pay

A wide variety of incentive pay arrangements are used in the U.S. economy. In some, such as those discussed in section 13.2, nominal amounts are paid based on quantity measures of performance; examples are piecework pay, unit-based sales commission plans, and some employee group production incentive plans. Others proceed on a percent-of-value basis; examples are sales commission plans that are revenue based and profit-sharing bonus plans. Finally, some firms pay discretionary bonuses that are not tied to a specific performance-based formula.

These plans have two characteristics that make their treatment in a controls program problematical. The obvious one, discussed above, is the danger that controls will interfere with the salutary incentive effects of such programs. The second problem is that employer costs of these programs cannot be determined in advance. In fact, the primary rationale for such plans is that pay should be high when individual or company performance is good and low when it is not.

One measurement approach would be to charge the ex post employer payout in full. The objection that this approach would stifle performance incentives is most credible for those plans that provide direct incentives to individual employees, as in the case of piecework and commission pay and productivity plans modeled for small employee groups. The argument carries less weight for companywide plans, where the individual incentives are diluted. Moreover, in many cases the performance criterion bears little relationship to work performance—especially those that are based on revenues or profit rather than physical quantity or productivity.

On theoretical grounds, an ideal approach would be one that requires firms to design incentive compensation packages with an expected payout value that will meet the standard, where the expectations would be determined assuming a common base performance. This approach would leave incentives intact. In applying such a prospective rule, however, it would be necessary to quantify the concept of performance, and this need raises a new set of measurement problems for all but the most basic incentive pay programs.

As noted in section 13.2, the pay generated by productivity incentive plans was legislatively excluded in the Nixon program, whereas the CWPS standard allowed companies with sales commission or production incentive plans to assess compliance on the assumption of constant physical volume. All other forms of incentive pay were included at their actual value in the measure of labor compensation in both programs. The alternative of excluding these payments would have created a gaping loophole in the pay standard for managerial employees.[11] The Pay Board evaluated the plans prospectively on the assumption that its targets were fully achieved, whereas the CWPS standard evaluated them retrospectively. Because of the considerable volatility of profits, and hence of profit-based bonus plans, both programs allowed considerable flexibility in the choice of a bonus base.

13.3.3 Future Value Compensation

The salient characteristic of future value compensation is that its value will not be known until some future time. In most cases, this type of compensation is used to provide long-run incentives to upper level management. As such, it is relatively unimportant from the perspective of inflation impact. The justification for covering it in a controls program is based on equity considerations and promotion of public acceptance of the program by guaranteeing that management compensation is covered in all forms.

The problem posed by covering future value compensation, of course, is that of evaluating its cost. Consider, for example, a stock-option grant providing an option to buy 500 shares at $40 per share any time in the next five years. Until the option is exercised, the cost to the employer is unrealized and unknown. The employee may never benefit from such a grant if the stock price never exceeds $40 over the exercise period.

In theory, an ideal approach would be to assign a market value to such awards when they are granted. This would measure both the opportunity cost to the employer (who could sell the awarded units) and the compensation benefit to the employee. In practice, such an assignment is difficult because of the absence of markets. For example, stock options are actively traded for only a handful of major stocks, and the exercise periods of marketable options normally do not exceed one year. In contrast, option awards often have multiyear exercise periods and are often contingent on multiyear performance criteria, making the determination of a market value difficult to codify.

Because of these problems, future value awards under continuing plans were treated as a separate pay item with a separate numerical limitation under the CWPS standard. This was the only case where a compensation form was segregated rather than included under an aggregate limitation. Awards under newly introduced plans were to be assigned a "reasonable value" and included with other pay items.

The Pay Board treated qualified stock-option plans—those qualifying for preferred tax treatment under IRS rules—differently from nonqualified plans. A separate standard limited the issuance of options under existing qualified plans to the average number issued during the three fiscal years before Phase II. Nonqualified plans, on the other hand, were evaluated and added to wages and salaries. Issuances were evaluated at the difference between the option price and the market price (one IRS condition for qualification for preferential tax treatment is equality of option and market prices) plus 25 percent of the market value (the Board's estimate of the discounted value of an option). In addition, if the option was exercised during the control period at a price more than 25 percent below market value, the amount above 25 percent was charged to labor compensation.

13.3.4 Fringe Benefits

Fringe benefits have become an increasingly large component of employer costs over the last two decades. Here, we consider the two major benefits, employer contributions for health insurance coverage and pension plan funding.

Health insurance costs have risen rapidly for two reasons: the widespread improvement in the coverage provided and the rapid medical cost inflation. The first factor is controlled by firms but the latter is not. Further, the timing and magnitude of employer cost increases vary across plans and insurance providers, depending on plan experience and other factors. As a result, it is possible for two firms to have radically different cost changes in a particular measurement period, although the benefits to employees are identical and remain unchanged. If these costs are charged against an aggregate pay standard, the company with the larger insurance cost increases (after the program begins) would have to anticipate these increases and grant lesser wage changes to remain in compliance. If anticipations are correct, an equity problem across firms is created; if anticipations are incorrect, inadvertant noncompliance can result.

Similar comments apply to pension fund costs. Pension funds are of two basic types: defined contribution plans, where the employer contributes specified amounts to employee-specific accounts; and defined benefit plans, which specify the future benefits an employee will receive. For our purposes, defined contribution plans can be treated as current cash payments, like wages, salaries, and bonuses. However, for defined benefit plans, current employer costs are determined by actuarial computations based on planning assumptions about retirement ages, longevity after retirement, earnings growth rates, and rates of return. Thus, as with health insurance costs, the linkage between changes in employer costs and changes in employee benefits is broken. Further, a simple exclusion rule for unchanged plans will lead to obvious inequity problems, since some plans are indexed (terminal pay plans) whereas other plans pay fixed nominal amounts (flat rate plans).

Thus, for both health insurance and pension plans, the employer can control the benefit rules but cannot control the cost of providing the benefits. Under the CWPS rules, the increase in all employer costs was to be checked against the standard, but automatic exceptions were provided for excesses above the standard when benefit levels remained unchanged. This approach was equivalent to simply excluding these fringe benefit costs from the labor compensation calculation when plans were not improved and costs rose at least as much as the allowable pay increase. If pension or health-care costs rose less than the guideline, additional increases in other forms of compensation were allowed. The costs of all improvements in benefit levels were charged against the standard. Thus, the rule was a hybrid of an employer cost restriction and an employee benefit constraint.

As noted above, the Pay Board standards for pension and health benefits were looser than the wage and salary standard, because the Congress mandated exclusion unless this was "unreasonably inconsistent" with the anti-inflation objectives of the program. Companies were allowed to increase these benefits by 0.7 percent of the total hourly compensation base. On average, this amounted to a 7 percent standard for fringe benefits (since fringes then accounted for about 10 percent of total compensation), compared to a 5.5 percent standard for wages, salaries, and bonuses. The fringe benefit rules also allowed for employees' units to catch up when those units' benefit/total compensation ratios were below the national average and when their benefit increases for the previous three years were less than 1.5 percent of the compensation base.

13.4 Salary Structures and Index-Number Problems

The previous section discussed the issues entailed in construction of the vector of compensation rates, w, in the control rule (11). This section discusses the aggregation rule, W, and the concomitant index number construction, a discrete form of $\dot{W}/(w)/W(w)$—alternatively, a discrete approximation to inequality (7) or (11).

As discussed above, the formulation of workable rules regarding the construction of w is complicated by the existence of many types of compensation and the need to preserve the appearance of equity and the administrative workability of the program. Similarly, the formulation of aggregation rules is complicated by the wide variety of compensation practices and the varying dynamic situations firms experience; any chosen method will limit the compensation increases of different firms and different employees in vastly different ways.

Before proceeding to a discussion of the possible approaches, we briefly describe the main types of salary structures encountered in the economy. After analyzing the index number problems in section 13.4.2, we discuss the treatment of cost-of-living adjustment clauses and time weighting in sections 13.4.3 and 13.4.4.

13.4.1 Salary Structures

Company pay plans vary in terms of the timing of pay rate changes and the salary structures of the work force. In some companies, changes are irregular, but this is the exception. Most firms have annual or multiyear pay plans that are handled through salary administration branches of personnel departments. These are of three basic types. The first involves across-the-board adjustment of varying amounts granted to the entire work force at common times—for example, annually or semiannually. Equally common are anniversary plans, under which individual employees are evaluated on a staggered basis throughout the year, and changes are made consistent with a general salary objective for that year. Finally, there are multiyear plans under which increases are granted according to established formulas; these are usually associated with collective bargaining agreements.

Salary structures also take on several characteristic forms. Production workers typically are paid flat job rates once journeyman status is achieved, while less senior employees are paid according to formal entry-level-to-job-rate progressions.

Supervisory employees and management employees are typically paid according to salary ranges. In most cases, the ranges are adjusted regularly, and an individual employee's position in the applicable range is adjusted according to annual merit reviews, performance evaluations, and other factors. In contrast, most government salary structures entail semiautomatic progression (step increases) up a salary scale, sometimes referred to as longevity increases.

In all cases, individual employees move along salary scales or within salary ranges and shift from scale to scale as a result of promotions and demotions. Also, over time, the composition of the work force changes as work force adjustments are made. To design its salary program under a compensation standard, a firm must evaluate the dynamics of its work force in light of the way employee groups are to be defined and in light of the rules to be used in measuring average changes.

13.4.2 Indexing Methods

In principle, the natural index number to be used in calculating aggregate compensation rate changes would be determined by the structure of the unit cost functions (and hence the structure of the underlying production function) of individual firms. In particular, a discrete form of $\dot{W}(w)/W(w) \leq \beta$,

$$W[w(t_1)]/W[w(t_0)] - 1 \leq \beta, \tag{12}$$

which is specific to each firm, would be the appropriate construction.

The problems with this approach are obvious: First, the separability condition underlying the existence of such an aggregate is unlikely to be satisfied in most cases. Second, individual firms are unlikely to be able to ascertain the structure of their unit cost functions, even if this assumption were satisfied. Third, even if individual firms could construct the appropriate compensation rate, it would be virtually impossible for the government to monitor these constructions.

In short, allowing the individual firms to decide on the type of index to be used would offer them a wide number of alternatives, and firms would naturally choose those constructions that serve their own purposes; in particular, if a firm wanted to pay more than the standard, it could probably find a (bogus) index number construction that would allow it to do so. For this reason, controls programs typically stipulate the technique to be used in constructing changes in the aggregate compensation rate. The three approaches that have been used, graphically described as the "double-snapshot method," the "ice-cube method," and "the melting-ice-cube method," are in fact common calculation procedures.

The double-snapshot method is simply a unit value construction. This involves a comparison of average compensation rates (total compensation divided by total hours worked) for active employees at the beginning and end of the measurement period. This method is simplest, most easily understood, and least ambiguous of the three methods. Unfortunately, the limitations that this method imposes can be significantly affected by changes in the functional composition of the work force.

The ice-cube method adjusts for changes in the work force composition by using a fixed-weight index. There are, of course, a large number of possible specifications of fixed-weight indexes and a voluminous literature on the subject. The theoretical construct,

$$\frac{\dot{W}(w)}{W(w)} = \sum_i s_i^L(w) \frac{\dot{w}_i}{w_i}, \tag{10}$$

suggests a share-weighted index.

The index number (10) is called a Divisia index (Divisia 1926), and there are a number of ways to approximate it by a discrete index. One approach is to use base period shares; another is to use terminal period shares. The Törnqvist index uses the simple arithmetic average of the base period and terminal period shares as weights (Törnqvist 1936; Theil 1965). (Diewert 1976 has shown that the Törnqvist index can be derived from a homothetic translog aggregation function, W.) The problem with the terminal period weights or the Törnqvist index is that the weights are not known until the end of the control period. Consequently, the more common approach to the specification of index number calculations in a controls program is to use base period shares as weights.

One problem with the ice-cube method is that it requires companies to perform what they often consider to be complex calculations. Small companies especially find the very notion of index number construction, or mix adjustment, to be too esoteric. A simpler method for dealing with composition changes is the melting-ice-cube, or continuing employee, method. Using this method, a firm computes average salary changes for those employees who are in the work force throughout the measurement period. New entrants into the work force and terminated employees do not enter computations. Thus, this is a unit value technique applied to continuing employees. Using this method to make the melting-ice-cube comparable with the other methods, it is necessary to exclude those portions of compensation rate increases attributable to legitimate promotions and qualification changes.

The characteristics of these three types of measurement techniques can be best illustrated by example. Consider a work force with four jobs, Job 1 to Job 4, each with its own salary range (see table 13.1). Assume, for simplicity, that there is initially one person in each job, Person A to Person D. At the beginning of the measurement period, each person is near the top of the salary range for his or her respective job and no salary range increases are made. During the measurement period, Person A retires, and Persons B, C, and D are promoted upward sequentially into vacated positions, with salaries set at the lower end of each range. A new employee, Person E, is hired into the vacated position in Job 4. There are no changes in the salary structure—i.e., no general compensation rate

Table 13.1 Jobs and Salary Ranges

Job	Salary Ranges
1	$30,000–35,000
2	25,000–30,000
3	20,000–25,000
4	15,000–20,000

increases. These movements and the before-and-after salaries are presented in table 13.2.

If the unit value method is used, the average pay rate is $26,000 at the beginning of the period and $22,000 at the end—a 15.5 percent decline. If the continuing employee method, applied to Persons B, C, and D, is used, these averages are $24,000 and $25,000, respectively, indicating a 4.2 percent increase. If the salary changes attributable to promotions are eliminated under the continuing employee method, the average compensation rate change is zero; this is the same result that would be obtained using an index defined on the salary ranges.

This example illustrates several points. First, in any company with salary ranges and a policy of promotion from within—the most common compensation structure for nonunion work forces—the double-snapshot method will tend to understate both the average increase granted to continuing employees and the weighted average salary-range adjustment. The tendency for the turnover and promotion process to reduce measured average changes is called "slippage" by compensation administrators, and slippage values of from 1 to 3 percent are common. Employee groups with wide salary ranges and high turnover tend to experience the greatest slippage, whereas slippage is relatively small for employee groups with flat job rates and little turnover.

Second, the downward bias of the double-snapshot technique is even more pronounced for growing firms, since new employees in the lower ends of salary brackets will further reduce unit value changes. On the other hand, work force reductions, which tend to be concentrated among

Table 13.2 Workforce and Salary Changes

Before						
Person	Job	Salary	Change	Person	Job	Salary
A	1	$34,000	Retires			
B	2	29,000	Promoted	B	1	$30,000
C	3	24,000	Promoted	C	2	25,000
D	4	19,000	Promoted	D	3	20,000
			Hired	E	4	15,000

low-tenure, low-paid workers in each range, work in the opposite direction.

Third, the continuing employee approach would tend to overstate average changes if there were no adjustment for promotions and qualification increases. With such adjustments, this method would appear to approximate the fixed-weight approach. Further, the continuing employee method provides a simple operational guideline (e.g., grant across-the-board increases that are consistent with the pay guideline and follow normal promotional practices), but its use raises the difficult problems of defining, tracking, and defending promotional increases in ex post compliance checks. (These problems are also serious from the controller's point of view, since, for example, a formal distinction must be drawn between promotions and longevity increases.)

Although there was much confusion about computational methods during Phase II, the Pay Board ultimately seemed to prescribe the ice-cube method for both union and nonunion employee groups. The CWPS rules mandated the ice-cube approach for multiyear collective bargaining units (essentially requiring the construction of a fixed-weight index of wage changes for jobs), but allowed companies to choose among the three methods for single-year contracts and nonunion employee units. This choice—particularly the option of choosing the double-snapshot method—undoubtedly allowed average increases substantially above the standard for many high-growth companies, but CWPS was not able to obtain a quantitative estimate of this effect.

13.4.3 Evaluating Cost-of-Living Adjustments

Cost-of-living adjustments (COLA), which have become increasingly prevalent over the last decade in response to high inflation rates, pose special problems for the measurement of labor compensation in a controls program: the actual COLA payouts depend on future inflation and are therefore unknown at the time a collective bargaining agreement is signed.

The Pay Board provided no special instructions for evaluating COLAs (other than time weighting, discussed below); thus, implicitly, such clauses could be evaluated retrospectively, and if unanticipated inflation threw an agreement out of compliance, a rollback could have been dictated by the board. Because the Pay Board evaluated only those contracts that were challenged by one of its members, there was no general need to make prospective evaluations. In fact, there was no challenge of a COLA clause during Phase II.

At the time the Carter administration's program was promulgated, however, COLAs were a much more important phenomenon, and it was decided that a rule for prospective evaluation of COLA clauses was required. The one adopted in the CWPS standards provided an inflation assumption to be used in evaluations of all such clauses. The problem with this approach is a matter of painful history. Because the actual inflation rate during the two years of the program substantially exceeded the rate stipulated in the rules for evaluating COLAs, complying workers protected by these clauses could receive much higher increases than nonprotected employee units.[12] CWPS estimated that this factor averaged 1½ percentage points for all collective bargaining contracts signed during the first program year and 1¾ percentage points in the second year. Because some 40 percent of union workers are not covered by COLAs, the average for collective bargaining units so covered was probably on the order of 3 percent. Indeed, the major collective bargaining agreements during the first year of the program did generate average annual increases of about 10 percent (using realistic inflation forecasts), three points above the pay standard.[13]

13.4.4 Time Weighting

The numerical wage standards in the Nixon and Carter programs essentially involved point-to-point comparisons of wage rates. That is, the restriction was on the percentage increase in the average compensation rate from the base period to the end of the control period. The path of compensation rates within the control period, i.e., the timing of increases, was irrelevant. In both cases, organized labor argued vigorously that time weighting of pay rate changes should be allowed. Under this approach, a 5 percent increase initiated on the first day of the year and maintained throughout the year would be judged equivalent to a 10 percent increase instituted halfway through the year. The essence of time weighting, therefore, is that any undershooting of the allowable pay rate path should be allowed to be "banked" and used later in the year.

Time weighting as a general approach was rejected in both programs because of the emphasis on the objective of controlling labor cost. To take an extreme example, a 365 percent increase in wages on the last day of a control year would be far more destructive to an anti-inflation effort than a 1 percent increase on the first day of the control period, but the two would be treated equivalently under time weighting.

Although the Pay Board rejected the notion of time weighting in general, it did ultimately allow time weighting of COLAs. This was justified on the ground that COLA payments are typically made with a lag, whereas fixed wage increases are typically paid up front, and this creates an inequity between units with COLAs and those without. In the Carter administration's program, however, time weighting was not allowed for COLAs or for fixed wage increases. In some instances, this approach undoubtedly promoted front loading, or acceleration of increases.

13.5 Concluding Remarks and Afterthoughts

On the basis of the above discussion of the problems of measuring labor compensation in a controls program and of our experience with the CWPS program, we offer a few concluding remarks:

1. If there is to be retroactive monitoring of pay increases and penalties for noncompliance with a guideline, an elaborate specification of rules and regulations is necessary. A simple numerical guideline worked well during the Kennedy/Johnson years because there was no systematic monitoring or enforcement; only one or two full-time equivalent professional employees (at the Council of Economic Advisors) were involved in the program, and intervention by the administration was for the most part limited to presettlement jawboning in a few major collective bargaining negotiations. For the vast majority of the work force, the guidepost was effectively self-administered by employers.

In the Nixon and Carter programs, however, the ambitious monitoring effort and the attention given to the use of sanctions—fines in the former and public stigmatization and debarment from government procurement contracts in the latter—resulted in a complex set of rules. Both began with relatively (indeed naively) simple notions of labor compensation measurement, but business insistence on more and more specificity led to an increasingly complicated body of regulations and case law. The need for more rules and rulings is boundless, as each resolution of an ambiguity begets new questions and as each closing of a loophole challenges business ingenuity to find a new way around the guideline. This is not uniquely a feature of controls programs; an increasingly lengthy, detailed, and complex body of tax law and IRS rulings has built up over the years for similar reasons. But while the collection of taxes is a generally accepted government activity, there is considerable dispute about the propriety of government programs to control wages and prices. The growing body of regulations in a controls program therefore comes to be perceived as unduly onerous and even as evidence of the ultimate futility of direct government intervention both in the marketplace and in collective bargaining for the purpose of arresting inflation. The weight of the rules and regulations becomes a burden that the program cannot bear—especially if it is proclaimed to be "voluntary."

2. An irony of an ambitious controls program is that an inordinate amount of effort is expended on the design of measurement rules for types of compensation that have but a trivial effect on inflation—especially many types of executive compensation. This is an implication of the paramount need to promote the appearance of equity—an impression that appears, from the experience of the Nixon program, to be as essential in a mandatory program as in a voluntary one for building and maintaining public support.

3. A set of measurement rules does not exist that would avert vociferous charges of inequity. Too many decisions about alternatives work to the advantage of some and the disadvantage of others. Both the Pay Board and CWPS were the subject of much criticism on this ground. Ultimately, feelings of inequitable treatment led, at least avowedly, to the labor walkout from the Pay Board and to erosion of the grudging business support for the Carter program.

4. A program that is equitable (by some definition) under certain assumptions can be indisputably inequitable under others. The best example is the underevaluation of COLA clauses in the Carter program. Had inflation rates been close to the administration's forecast at the time the standards program was promulgated, the approach to evaluating COLAs would have been defensible. As it was, the problem of underevaluation came to be seen as a severe union/nonunion inequity and, more than anything else, led to the erosion of business support for the program. (Although nonunion employee units had the advantage of slippage in the double-snapshot calculation methods, this advantage was not nearly as important quantitatively as the underevaluation of COLA.)

5. Any successful incomes policy in the future will have to come to grips with the problem of evaluating COLA. Perhaps the only effective approach is to provide a ceiling above which total pay increases, including COLAs, are not allowed. Thus, COLAs in contracts entered into during the program would be required to be "capped." This approach, however, amounts to the virtual abrogation of COLA clauses and would meet with extreme resistance from organized labor. It would seem that any attempt to enforce a ban on COLAs in a controls program would require legislation. Thus, any successful wage control program in the future is likely to be a legislatively mandated one.

Notes

1. The theoretical justifications for this goal are the need to retard inflationary expectations and to alter the (short-run) Phillips curve in order to lower the economic costs of anti-inflationary fiscal and monetary policies. These justifications can be elaborated on by appealing either to the theory of informational disequilibrium (e.g., Lucas and Prescott 1974; Phelps 1979) or to the theory of implicit contracts (e.g., Azariadis 1975; Baily 1974; Gordon 1976; Okun 1981), each of which can explain sluggish adjustment of wages and prices to new equilibria. Such elaboration, however, would take us far afield of the topic of this paper.

2. The focus on measurement rules avoids dealing with other important (and controversial) design issues, such as numerical standards vs. case-by-case review, economy-wide vs. sectoral guidelines, the treatment of special pay situations (such as tandem pay relationships and pattern bargaining), and exceptions criteria for such things as occupational labor shortages.

3. Our knowledge of the former is based on published materials; our knowledge of the latter is based on first-hand experience. The best sources for the ESP are Office of Economic Stabilization, Department of the Treasury (1974) and Weber and Mitchell (1978). (Also see Dunlop and Fedor 1977; Yoshe, Allams, Russell, and Atkin 1972; Mitchell and Azevedo 1976.) The best reference for the Kennedy/Johnson guideposts is Sheahan (1967). Ulman and Flanagan (1971) describe wage-restraint programs in other countries.

4. This theoretical predicate is not essential. Everything that follows could also be discussed in the context of a reduced form price equation that includes demand-side variables (such as income) in addition to input prices as explanatory variables.

5. It may seem peculiar to posit a model of input-price-taking behavior in the context of a controls program, since the controls would be expected to be applicable only in those cases where there is discretion in the setting of the input prices. This approach, however, makes sense in a market characterized by collective bargaining; once a contract is signed, compensation rates are effectively determined for the duration of the contract (typically three years in major negotiating situations), and the managers seek to minimize costs subject to predetermined compensation rates. Similarly, in the "wage-wage model" of the inflation process (see Hall 1974; Okun 1981, chap. 3), nonunion wages tend to follow the pattern set by major collective bargaining agreements. Whether the controls programs should apply to the nonunion labor markets as well as to major collective bargaining negotiations is a matter of contention among economists. Whether or not it makes sense from a strictly economic point of view to restrict the guidelines to major collective bargaining negotiations, political realities require that the program be much more comprehensive.

6. The function $\tilde{c}$ is defined by $\tilde{c}(\ln w, \ln r) = c(w, r)$.

7. That is,

$$s_i(w, r) = \frac{\partial \ln \tilde{c}(\ln w, \ln r)}{\partial \ln w_i} = \frac{\partial c(w, r)}{\partial w_i} \frac{w_i}{c(w, r)} = \frac{w_i \ell_i}{C(w, r, q)},$$

where the last identity follows from Hotelling's theorem (see Blackorby, Primont, and Russell 1978, p. 32):

$$\ell_i = \frac{\partial C(w, r, q)}{\partial w_i} = \frac{\partial c(w, r)}{\partial w_i} q.$$

8. For simplicity, we suppose that the group corresponds to a labor type, i; otherwise, the notation would be unduly cumbersome. We also ignore, in this formulation, the problem of distinguishing between work effort, $e(\gamma_i)$, and technology, τ_i—an important practical problem in the design of these plans. In practice, there are very few productivity plans that so explicitly relate labor compensation to the level of group productivity. Most so-called group productivity plans in the real world are in fact little different from profit-sharing plans, which can result in higher rates of compensation simply because of higher product prices. The treatment of these types of plans is discussed in section 13.3.

9. At this point, we adopt the reprehensible practice of writing notations for functions when we mean function images to keep the notation from getting out of hand.

10. Of course, an appropriately constructed group productivity plan might induce technological progress within a reasonably defined group. For the most part, however, such plans are designed to promote increased worker effort rather than technological progress.

11. The Carter administration's standard was applied separately to management and nonmanagement employee units; the ESP accorded firms sufficient flexibility in the choice of employee units to treat executives separately.

12. Recall, however, the computational advantage accorded many nonunion employee units by allowing them to calculate wage increases using the double-snapshot technique.

13. The COLA-costing assumption also promoted the design of COLA clauses tailored around the assumption, such as triggered or other nonlinear COLA formulas.

References

Azariadis, Costas. 1975. Implicit contracts and unemployment equilibria. *Journal of Political Economy* 83: 1183–1202.

Baily, Martin. 1974. Wages and employment under uncertain demand. *Review of Economic Studies* 41: 37–50.

Blackorby, Charles, C. A. Knox Lovell, and M. Thursby. 1976. Extended Hicks neutral technological change. *Economic Journal* 86: 845–52.

Blackorby, Charles, Daniel Primont, and R. Robert Russell. 1978. *Duality, separability, and functional structure: Theory and economic applications*. New York: North-Holland.

Diewert, W. Erwin. 1976. Exact and superlative index numbers. *Journal of Econometrics* 4: 115–45.

Divisia, F. 1926. *L'indice monétaire et la théorie de la monnaie*. Paris: Société Anonyme du Recueil Sirey.

Dunlop, John T., and Kenneth J. Fedor. 1977. *The lessons of wage and price controls—The food sector*. Boston: Division of Research, Graduate School of Business Administration, Harvard University.

Gordon, Donald F. 1976. A neo-classical theory of Keynesian unemployment. In *The Phillips curve and labor markets*, ed. Karl Brunner and Allen H. Meltzer. Amsterdam: North-Holland.

Hall, Robert E. 1974. The process of inflation in the labor market. *Brookings Papers on Economic Activity* 2: 343–93.

Lucas, Robert E., Jr., and Edward C. Prescott. 1974. Equilibrium search and unemployment. *Journal of Economic Theory* 7: 188–209.

Mitchell, Daniel J. B., and Ross E. Azevedo. 1976. *Wage-price controls and economic distortions*. Los Angeles: Institute of Industrial Relations, University of California.

Office of Economic Stabilization, Department of the Treasury. 1974. *Historical working papers on the Economic Stabilization Program*. Washington, D.C.

Okun, Arthur M. 1981. *Prices and quantities: A microeconomic analysis*. Washington, D.C.: The Brookings Institution.

Phelps, Edmund S. 1979. Introduction: Developments in non-Walrasian theory. In *Studies in macroeconomic theory: Employment and inflation*, ed. Edmund S. Phelps, vol. 1. New York: Academic Press.

Sheahan, John. 1967. *The wage-price guideposts*. Washington, D.C.: The Brookings Institution.

Shephard, Ronald W. 1970. *Theory of cost and production functions*. Princeton, N.J.: Princeton University Press.

Theil, H. 1965. The information approach to demand analysis. *Econometrica* 33: 67–87.

Törnqvist, L. 1936. The Bank of Finland's consumption price index. *Bank of Finland Monthly Bulletin* 10: 1–8.

Ulman, Lloyd, and Robert J. Flanagan. 1971. *Wage restraint: A study of incomes policies in Western Europe*. Berkeley: University of California Press.

Weber, Arnold R., and Daniel J. B. Mitchell. 1978. *The Pay Board's progress: Wage controls in Phase II*. Washington, D.C.: The Brookings Institution.

Yoshe, Harry B., John F. Allams, Joseph E. Russell, and Barbara A. Atkin. 1972. *Stemming inflation*. Washington: Office of Energy Preparedness, Executive Office of the President.

14 Wage Measurement Questions Raised by an Incomes Policy

Donald A. Nichols

A wage stabilization program encounters many of the fundamental wage measurement problems that also face the Bureau of Labor Statistics and researchers who use wage data. Because millions of dollars are at stake in the administrative decisions made in an incomes program, enormous pressure is brought to bear to find solutions to these problems that are precise and simple, yet consistent. The record of such a program, then, provides an interesting perspective on wage measurement issues. Can we measure wages when there is money on the table? Which wage measurement problems were found to be insoluble by wage stabilization authorities in the past? Which definitions of wage increase were thought by these authorities to be consistent enough to stand up in court? What can we learn from the high-priced talent that scrutinized the proposed wage definitions for inconsistencies?

In this paper, I describe some of the wage measurement questions that arose during the Carter stabilization program of 1978–80 and the solutions to those issues that were adopted by the Council on Wage and Price Stability (CWPS).[1] Lessons for wage measurement are drawn. Many of these issues are also addressed in the paper by McMenamin and Russell (this volume), though from a slightly different perspective.

14.1 Problems with Wage Indexes

The CWPS pay standard permitted firms to give an average pay increase of no more than 7 percent. Within large employee groups, the total

Donald A. Nichols is professor of economics at the University of Wisconsin, Madison.

This research was supported by grant 99-0-2289-50-11 from the National Commission for Employment Policy and contract 20-06-08-11 from the Employment and Training Administration, U.S. Department of Labor. Jack Triplett provided helpful comments on an earlier draft.

increase permitted by this standard could be allocated over workers in any way the firm chose. CWPS defined three different indexes that could be used to compute this average rate of wage increase. These methods acquired the colorful titles of the "double snapshot," the "ice cube," and the "melting ice cube."

The double snapshot measured wage increases by simply dividing total compensation by total hours at two different times and computing the excess of one average over the other. The Antos paper in this volume describes the use of this method by the BLS in computing average hourly earnings. When the CWPS first proposed this index, critics noted that firms could evade the standard by increasing their fraction of low-wage workers. In this case existing employees could all be granted increases in excess of 7 percent, but the average would be kept down by adding low-wage workers at the bottom. On the other hand, firms expecting to change their employee mix toward high-wage workers felt this standard hurt them unduly. They might be found in violation of the standard even if none of their employees received an increase over 7 percent.

To satisfy this objection, other indexes were permitted. The ice cube was a fixed-weight index of wage rates paid for specific job descriptions where the weights were equal to the initial distribution of employment over those jobs. By definition, changes in the mix of employment could not affect this index since its weights were frozen at their initial levels. Wage levels were attached to jobs in this index, not to people. If a worker was promoted, his increase would not be counted as long as the wage rates for the job he left and the job he took remained unchanged. Firms had asked for this treatment of promotions to be able to retain their best employees who might otherwise be tempted to leave by offers of promotions from other firms.

The third index that was permitted, the melting ice cube, was an average of the increases granted to all employees who worked for the firm the entire period over which the wage increase was measured. This was also a fixed-weight index, but here the weights were based on workers, not jobs. These weights were also frozen, but the components of the index would melt away with employee turnover. In this index, increases granted for promotions had to be counted in the overall average. This made the melting ice cube less attractive than the ice cube for many firms. It was probably of greatest interest to small firms with poorly defined job descriptions that would have trouble distinguishing a promotion from a pay raise in any event.

While CWPS called the index of worker-specific wages a melting cube and the index of occupation-specific wages a plain cube, in practice, occupations can be discontinued (melt away) just as workers can leave a firm. New occupations can be added when production methods are revised, and the wage rates of these occupations will not appear in the occupational wage index. Similarly, the wages of new employees will not appear in the index of wage rates of continuing workers.

14.1.1 Wage Rates of Workers or Wage Rates for Jobs

The Antos paper notes the distinction between a worker-specific wage index and a job-specific index and points out that aggregate measures of both concepts are published in addition to the unweighted measure of average hourly earnings. Antos notes that the CPS measures the wages of individuals while the Employment Cost Index and the BLS occupational wage surveys measure the wages attached to particular jobs. Which is the correct measure of wages? The answer depends, of course, on the purposes of the data.

CWPS was forced to permit the use of a fixed-weight index of occupational wage rates as a measure of wage increase. This seems a sensible decision to me, since CWPS was interested in limiting labor cost rather than workers' incomes. As a measure of labor cost, what is needed is an index of the prices at which labor can be hired to perform specific tasks. These tasks are precisely defined for the occupational wage surveys through a set of occupational definitions. Regardless of how the wages of particular individuals may vary over time, labor cost will increase or decrease depending on the wages that must be paid for the performance of the specific tasks necessary for production. In the absence of productivity growth, an index of the wage rates paid for these tasks will capture changes in labor cost.

The sample rotation procedure of the Current Population Survey provides a subset of workers whose earnings are surveyed in two successive years or months. Their wage increases provide a sample of the wage increases of workers generally, whose average size may be quite different from the average wage increase paid for the sample of occupations noted above.

A simplified illustration of the difference between the two wage measures is found in the concept of a *job ladder*, which is a series of steps through which an individual might progress in the course of a career. Each step denotes a job or occupation defined by a set of assignments. Each step has a wage or a wage structure associated with it. Occupational wage statistics measure what is being paid at each rung of the ladder. Occupational wage increases rise when the wage paid at a particular rung increases regardless of who occupies the rung. Worker-specific wages, then, can change for two reasons: (1) the wage paid at the rung the worker occupies may change; or (2) the worker may take a step up (or down) the ladder to a higher (or lower) rung with a different wage.

CWPS permitted firms to report either the average amount by which the wage rates on their job ladders had risen (the ice-cube method) or the average amount of the increases received by their continuing workers, regardless of their rate of progress up the ladder (the melting ice-cube method). Since workers, on average, do move up the job ladder, an occupational index might normally be expected to increase less than the index of continuing workers' wages.

Nevertheless, since small firms are not likely to have precise job definitions, they may be forced to use a worker-specific index during an incomes program rather than a job-specific index. In small firms, work may be divided among existing workers according to ability. As a worker gains experience, more assignments may be added to his given job along with higher pay. Work then gets divided in a different way. This may be thought of as partly a promotion and partly a redefinition of the existing jobs. Because of the difficulty of linking the new wages to the old occupations, CWPS forced such firms to use either an index of wages paid to existing workers or the average hourly earnings measure which is not a fixed-weight index at all.

But how do we want BLS to treat these small firms in their occupational wage surveys? There appears to be no alternative to reclassifying each job each year. While this can add an element of error to each observation, there is no reason to believe it adds bias. For CWPS, such a procedure was impractical both because the number of firms was so much larger than their limited staff could handle and because the respondents' desires to make the reported data come out a certain way would bias their response. BLS, and researchers in general, do not face the problem of response bias that CWPS confronted.

The ability to use the occupational job ladder measure of wage rates for compliance purposes made promotions exempt from the wage standard. An issue similar to promotions is that of wage increases based on seniority, and these CWPS decided not to allow. At each rung of the ladder, there may be a whole schedule of wage rates based on experience of longevity. A worker might normally expect to progress through this schedule as he rests on the rung. Should the wage increases that result from progressing through such a preexisting schedule also be exempt? That is, if a firm raises its whole wage schedule by exactly 7 percent, including all the seniority premiums associated with each step of the ladder, should it be penalized for noncompliance simply because its workers age? On the other hand, should it be able to raise its wage schedule by more than 7 percent if many workers retire in a particular year to be replaced by junior workers at the bottom of the scale? CWPS answered yes to these questions by forcing firms to include longevity wage increases as part of the 7 percent permitted by the standard. This was done by permitting only one wage level for each job definition, with the original level being the average paid to all workers performing that job in the base year.

How would we want BLS to treat longevity increases when measuring labor cost? One issue of importance in answering this question is whether the seniority premiums generally reflect greater productivity or not. Medoff and Abraham (1980) found little relation between productivity and seniority for white-collar employees in two large manufacturing firms. If this result is typical of all occupations at all business firms, then it could be argued that seniority increases should be counted as wage increases and not simply as movements within a fixed-wage structure. The cost of production would increase with wage increases based on seniority in this case. If, on the other hand, productivity would normally be expected to increase along with pay, presumably because of the advantage of greater experience, it would be reasonable to ignore such increases and treat them as a change in the mix of employees. Obviously, to answer this question, more research is needed on the effect of seniority on productivity, and this research could be directed at the implications for wage measurement.

A more difficult issue is suggested by the question of why firms would pay such premiums if they do not reflect productivity. One possible answer is found in the length of the typical employer-employee relationship. This period's wage payment need not reflect this period's production alone but could represent, instead, an installment payment on a lengthy, possibly even a lifetime, contract. Japanese firms provide an excellent example of this with lifetime employment for some groups of workers who receive quite large longevity increases. Senior workers in Japan can earn much more than junior workers for performing the same task. The treatment given seniority increases when measuring the overall wage increase in Japan is crucial.

The seniority issue is but one manifestation of the general problem that the traits of workers and jobs evolve over time and that the mixes of jobs and workers' capacities change as well. Generally these changes lead to larger wage increases as measured by average hourly earnings than as measured by a fixed-weight index of occupations. "Wage drift" is the term given to this difference. Drift arises because of new occupations, changes in the mix of old occupations and, possibly, job downgrading. The last term refers to issues such as earlier promotion for people on career job ladders where the assigned tasks vary little with the level of the job. Academia provides a good example of this where earlier promotion to the rank of full professor could result in a higher average rate of wage increase for academics as a group, but that would not be reflected in an index of wages paid to each of the academic ranks. Indeed, because of the range of salaries available at each rank, an increase in promotions can reduce the average rate of pay of both associate and full professors by removing the highest paid associates and adding to the lowest paid group of full professors. This reduction in reported rates for each job could be accompanied by a higher average increase for each worker.

Job downgrading may be associated with demographic cycles, or it may be endemic to a democratic society that promises advancement to all. It leads to wage drift. It is a phenomenon we need to know more about. Are measureable performance standards lower today than they once were for given occupations? What is the average amount of wage drift to be expected in the United States?

Human capital theory provides one way to estimate job downgrading. The Gollop and Jorgenson paper in this volume classifies workers by education, among other traits. If, over time, a particular occupation were occupied by workers with less and less education, one might surmise that this particular job was being downgraded. On average, however, because of the increasing percentage of the population attending college, education may not provide an invariable measure of human capital. Indeed, educational downgrading may be taking place and this may permit—perhaps require—employers to upgrade the educational requirements they demand of job applicants. More typical, then, might be increasing amounts of human capital being found in particular occupations over time, if human capital is measured by education alone.

Over the long-run, downgrading and changes in the occupational mix can lead to quite different estimates of the overall rate of wage increase, depending on whether the wage rates surveyed are those associated with specific tasks, those associated with individuals, or simply the average wage paid to a changing mix of workers and occupations. This makes it hard to interpret what certain wage trends mean. Douty (1980) reports that the percentage by which the average hourly earnings of skilled workers in manufacturing exceeded that for unskilled workers fell from 105 percent in 1907 to 31 percent in 1976. He points out that this decline could represent a narrowing of differentials, or it could represent an upgrading of the skills expected of unskilled workers, or a downgrading of the skills expected by skilled workers. As an example of the possible upgrading of unskilled workers, he points out that seventy-five years ago they were not expected to read or be familiar with machinery; they worked with simple tools, if any, often using strength to move materials. Today's unskilled worker in manufacturing may perform work that would have been semiskilled seventy-five years ago. As old jobs were eliminated and new ones created, the very concept of unskilled work gradually changed until it is now quite different from before. There is no way to be sure which of the wage measures, including the unweighted average hourly earnings, provides the best measure of wage change over such long periods.

Over the business cycle, it is extremely important that a fixed-weight measure of occupational wage rates be reported. Macroeconomic theory and policy are sharply divided today over the issue of how flexible wages are. Empirical estimates of the cyclical variation of wages are found in the large-scale econometric models and have been used as a basis for policy by every administration since Nixon's. Most of these estimates are based on the Hourly Earnings Index which holds constant the weights of large manufacturing groupings and corrects for overtime premiums. But many changes in the composition of the work force take place over the cycle that can affect the rate of wage inflation reported by this index. In a recent paper, Nichols (1981), I showed that cyclical wage variation is substantially less in the wage indexes derived from the Professional, Administrative, and Clerical Wage (PATC) survey than it is in the Hourly Earnings Index.[2] Why this is true could not be resolved, but one possibility is that the fixed-weight PATC survey provides a more accurate measure of cyclical change than the unweighted Hourly Earnings Index. The issue of cyclical wage variability remains of crucial importance to macroeconomic policy, and macroeconomists should be prepared for the possibility that what they have come to regard as the normal response of wages to recession may simply be the result of the effect of the cycle on the weights of the Hourly Earnings Index. Short-run macroeconomic models may rely too heavily on the past behavior of average hourly earnings.

14.2 Nonhourly Compensation

Theoretical and empirical work in economics has been organized around the hour as a measure of labor input. Compensation is divided by hours worked to get a measure of the cost of each unit of labor input. Some forms of compensation do not lend themselves easily to such computations. Several are discussed here.

14.2.1 Incentive Pay

Incentive pay arrangements are quite common in manufacturing. They pose an enormous problem for wage measurement. They also pose a problem for a wage stabilization agency. In some occupations, technical progress or increases in the amount of capital used per worker permit great increases in productivity, while in other occupations no increase is possible. One would expect that competition would normally keep compensation at roughly equal levels for work of equal difficulty, and this means that those occupations paid on an incentive basis but with no chance for an improvement in productivity should get an annual enrichment of the incentive formula to keep them abreast of the occupations where compensation grows automatically with productivity. In other cases, improvements in production methods require the formulas to be revised downward periodically. The question arises how CWPS can tell in advance which occupations would normally expect an improvement in the incentive formula, which would expect a decline, and which would have no change.

CWPS denied all improvements in incentive formulas. On the other hand, they did not force any formulas to decline and, therefore, permitted any increase in compensation that took place as a result of an increase in productivity. This was clearly inequitable on the face of it, but it was felt there was really no option since the wage measurement issue was so difficult. Mills (1975) points out that the same decision was reached by wage stabilization authorities during World War II, the Korean War, and the Nixon controls. He concludes, "This review of historical experience suggests that, because incentive plans are very much specific to individual plants and industries, boards should handle them largely on a case-by-case basis." (Mills 1975, p. 201)

A case-by-case treatment may be feasible for a large controls program. It is not a sound approach for collecting wage data outside the purview of a controls program. The BLS must measure the increase in the wage rates attached to specific occupations, many of which are paid on an incentive basis. They cannot assign numbers by judgment to each observation in their sample. This is not a problem for the average hourly earnings measure of wages where total compensation is simply divided by total hours. But it is a problem for an index of occupational wages like the Employment Cost Index.

Research is needed on the nature of incentive compensation. How prevalent is it? How much of the normal increase in compensation earned by workers on incentive scales is due to an enrichment of the scales and how much to increased productivity? Can the variation in the source of these increases across different industries be attributed to any economic characteristics? The answers to these questions are of interest to those who measure wages for research purposes and to those who measure them for stabilization programs.

A less common form of incentive pay are bonuses linked to the firm's financial performance. CWPS treated these in the same way as piece rates—any enrichment of the bonus schedule was counted as a pay increase; any increase in compensation due to better performance of the firm was permitted. However, firms without well-defined formulas linking performance to bonuses were denied the chance to increase bonus compensation by more than 7 percent. Since the economy improved after the guidelines were installed in October 1978, many of these firms probably experienced an improvement in profits and under normal circumstances would have increased bonuses by more than 7 percent. But because of the element of discretion in their bonus procedure, this normal practice was denied by CWPS.

14.2.2 Future Value Compensation

Future value compensation poses two conceptual wage measurement issues: First, does an ex post measure of what is actually paid provide the desired measure of labor cost? Second, how should an ex ante measurement be made if one is necessary? CWPS could not use an ex post measurement since firms wished to be told in advance whether a compensation agreement they were about to sign was in compliance. And for benefits such as pensions, not only was it clearly impractical for CWPS to wait and count the payments that were actually collected by workers, but the BLS also needs to have a way of estimating their value in advance.

Pension agreements are of two major kinds: defined benefit and defined contribution. Defined contribution plans pose no measurement issue for CWPS or BLS. The firm agrees to put a defined amount of money aside for its workers who will collect the invested proceeds of this money at the time they retire. The amount of money being put aside under a defined contribution plan is clearly part of labor cost. But defined benefit plans have formulas that link the promised pension to the worker's employment and wage history. Actuarial assumptions, investment performance, and government regulations determine how much must be put aside today to meet the promises implied by the formula.

Query: Under a defined benefit plan, is labor cost increased when the firm enriches the formula or when it increases its rate of contribution into the fund that finances the given formula? CWPS permitted firms to use either method without penalty. Under its average hourly earnings measure of wage increase, all current outlays for benefits were counted as part of labor cost. A firm could adopt this method regardless of any changes made in its formula. But CWPS permitted an exception for firms that had to raise their rates of contribution as long as they didn't enrich their formulas. Such an increase could be due to a bad investment experience that caused the fund to fall below the level the actuaries deemed to be safe, or it could result from an ERISA regulation that required an increase so the fund could reach some minimum level, or it could be due to a change in actuarial methods or assumptions.

Examples of these possibilities pose interesting issues of labor cost measurement for the BLS or for researchers. If a company must raise its contribution rate because of bad investment experience on the pension fund's portfolio, is that an increase in compensation and labor cost? I propose that for research purposes, no labor cost increase should be counted in this case. The reason is that the firm can be viewed as being engaged in two activities: (1) making things with labor and (2) gambling on the securities market. Its losses in the second activity should not be counted as a cost for the first. The market price of labor is unchanged by this. New workers can still be hired at the old rates. It is only the amount the firm has to put aside to meet that price that has been increased.

An interesting complication of this example arises if the union runs a multiemployer pension fund and the firms merely contribute defined amounts to it. The Teamsters, for example, receive defined contributions from firms but promise defined benefits to their members. Successful investing is required if the contributions are to be sufficient to cover the benefits. But before the 1979 negotiations, the Teamsters had invested pension assets in Las Vegas real estate and lost some of the fund's money. Trucking firms were asked to raise their rate of contribution to the fund though employee benefits were not to be enriched by the increase. Query: Did Teamster compensation increase as a result of the increased contributions? CWPS, in a famous decision, said no, thereby permitting the Teamster contract to slide through the wage standard. What should BLS say in such a case?

I feel that a strong case can be made to keep all aspects of investment experience out of the measures of compensation. Profits or losses on a pension fund's investments should be treated like profits and losses in other activities of the firm. While they may appear in funds that have been segregated into an account for employees, as long as they do not affect the price the firm would have to pay to hire new labor, they are not a part of labor cost. Yet, in the Teamster case, a new employee would entail a higher pension cost under the new agreement even though this higher cost was necessary only to make up for past losses. Multiemployer funds are clearly a complicated issue.

A change in government regulation has more significance for CWPS than for researchers. During the CWPS program, a regulation came into effect defining equal pay for equal work to mean women had to receive the same pension formula promised to men despite their greater longevity. This meant that firms could expect to pay more to hire a woman than a man for the same job. Firms that had provided less generous pension formulas for women (though of equal expected value to those provided to men) had to increase their rate of contribution to the fund when women were promised the same formula as men. CWPS made these increased contributions exempt from the 7 percent standard. Since the increases raised both the expected cost to firms and the expected receipts of workers, they should be counted as increased labor cost by BLS. While standards of social equity might define equal pay to mean an identical formula of defined benefits, researchers should note that the expected pay of female workers was higher than that for men as a result of the regulation.

Changes in actuarial assumptions provide a similar problem. If the change is due to a new estimate of longevity, we might say that the old formula had been discovered to be more generous than expected. Maintaining this formula would then provide an increase in expected compensation. On the other hand, a change in actuarial methods might lead to an increased rate of contribution with no change in the expected benefits. This latter change is simply a change in the timing of payments into the fund and not in their expected value. They should not be counted as increases in compensation by CWPS or BLS.

Because pension payments will take place in the distant future, an estimate of their present value must be generated. Other future value compensation benefits have more immediate implications and pose a different problem. An employer who self-insures his medical benefits and is then caught by an epidemic in the town of his major plant finds his labor cost increased. Should researchers treat an increase in the hospitalization of workers' children as an increase in labor cost? The expected cost of hiring new labor in the market is unchanged. The compensation expected to be paid to existing workers after the epidemic is unchanged. Probably it is best to include only the expected value of medical benefits as a labor cost rather than the actual payment. Differences between the expected and actual costs can be attributed to the firm being in the medical insurance business rather than to its need to hire labor. It is a loss on another activity of the firm, and not a cost of hiring labor. Martin David's paper in this volume makes the same point.

14.2.3 Stock Options

Stock options, granted primarily to executives, combine several of these conceptual problems. The option is of uncertain future value, and the size of the option may vary with the firm's economic circumstances. In this case the option would combine the characteristics of incentive compensation with those of future value compensation. The expected value of the option would have to be computed in advance to know the amount of compensation for determining compliance with the pay standard. Since the option may extend for years into the future, even measures of compensation for the year past would have to have a way of estimating its value. Stock options of short-term duration are traded on exchanges, and their prices may provide a basis for an ex ante evaluation of the options granted to executives by firms. Formulas have been worked out for the actuarial value of an option, and these could be used to provide an ex ante estimate of the likely value of an untraded option.

14.2.4 Cost-of-Living Adjustments

Finally, cost-of-living adjustments (COLA) provide a knotty problem. The McMenamin-Russell paper claims that the COLA issue, more than any other, caused the downfall of the wage stabilization program. CWPS had to provide an ex ante evaluation of the COLA to determine compliance. This was done by using an estimate of 6 percent as the likely increase in the Consumer Price Index in future years. From the perspective of mid-1978, this estimate was not as bad as it appears with hindsight, since the December-to-December inflation rates for 1976 and 1977 had been 4.8 and 6.8 percent, respectively. A minor decline in inflation because of the program could have brought about a 6 percent inflation rate, a number thought to be consistent with the 7 percent wage standard. But what transpired was a 9 percent inflation rate in 1978 and a 13.3

percent rate in 1979. Workers who had bargained for a full COLA plus a 1 percent wage increase were credited with a total increase of 7 percent by CWPS, whereas the striking of such a bargain in December 1978 would have led to an actual wage increase of 14.3 percent. This inequity brought down the system.

How does the COLA issue effect wage measurement for purposes of research? The issue resembles those posed by other kinds of future value compensation. Workers have shifted an uncertainty over future events to employers who not only pay the workers an agreed wage but who insure them against inflation. Regardless of one's view of the process of inflation, there are two different ways a COLA can affect a worker's wage. First, there is the common equal increase in wage and price inflation that can take place as a result of an unanticipated increase in demand. In the absence of a COLA, a multiyear wage agreement would imply substantially different levels of real wages if different macroeconomic policies were followed subsequent to the signing of the agreement. The COLA insures both the worker and the firm against changes in overall inflation so that real compensation can be independent of it.

The second effect of a COLA is to insure a worker's future real wage regardless of changes in relative prices. A bad harvest, for example, normally reduces real wages. Macroeconomists might not agree whether this decline would normally be manifested in an increase in the rate of price inflation or a reduction in the rate of wage inflation. But whichever would transpire, a full COLA would guarantee a worker's real wage though it would not guarantee the real burden to be paid by the employer. In this second sense, a COLA is similar to medical insurance where variations in the worker's benefits are accompanied by variations in the firm's real labor cost. In this case, the worker is insured against the possibility of a bad harvest. Wage increases granted to keep up with a common wage-price inflation can be thought of as part of what the firm would have to pay for labor in the open market. Insurance against a bad harvest that temporarily causes food prices to be high is a benefit, like medical insurance, whose expected value might be counted as a part of the going price of labor, but whose actual payments also include a random element. I see no easy way to separate these two effects in practice.

14.3 Collective Bargaining Agreements

The percentage increase in compensation attributed to a single collective bargaining agreement requires, in many cases, a solution to the problems noted above. Evaluating an agreement in which shift, seniority, or skill differentials are changed, or in which incentive formulas are changed, perhaps in response to increased productivity under the old formulas, or in which fringe benefits of uncertain future value are changed, requires answers to the above questions. In principle, the percentage increase attributed to the agreement is an index of the increases for the various occupations whose wages and benefits are covered by the agreement. They do not measure wage increases of individuals moving up a job ladder but of the upward movement of the ladder itself.

BLS publishes statistics on new collective bargaining agreements without estimating the size of the COLA benefits. The agreements are classified into two groups, those with COLAs and those without. These statistics would be of greater use if estimates of the value of the COLAs were included. But what estimates of future inflation should BLS use in pricing COLAs? The experience of CWPS warns against the use of a single measure, particularly one with political significance. Instead, three or four estimates might be provided. An example would be of inflation at rates of 4, 8, or 12 percent and possibly at the actual rate of the preceding twelve months. The reader could then provide his own interpolation to arrive at an estimate corresponding to his own inflation forecast. Readers can't do this at present because of the complicated limitations on COLAs that exist—minima, maxima, partial coverage, and so on. If the alternative estimates were provided, researchers could generate forecasts of inflation in any way they wished to provide estimates of the expected wage increases contained in the contracts with COLAs.

14.4 Conclusion

I have pointed out a few issues raised by a wage stabilization program that are also of importance for wage measurement and, therefore, for research that makes use of wage data. Wage stabilization programs generate mountains of correspondence with the private sector. Indeed, I contributed several letters myself during the recent CWPS program containing questions that had been asked of me when I had lectured about the program to the private sector.

An interesting research project would be to search the CWPS file of correspondence for questions about how wages are to be measured for purposes of compliance. The record of CWPS' decisions on the issues raised by that correspondence, or, indeed, of any wage stabilization board's decisions, would provide insight into many subtle wage measurement issues whose resolution can have a fundamental effect on our view of how the economy works. Important among these questions are issues about the level of productivity and resource growth over time and the extent and nature of wage flexibility. These are among the fundamental research issues of our time. Accurate measurement is essential to their early and sound resolution.

Notes

1. The author participated in the design of the Carter wage and price standards in 1978 when he was deputy assistant secretary of labor for economic policy and research.

2. An example of the PATC wage indexes can be found in *Bureau of Labor Statistics* (1980), p. 7.

References

Bureau of Labor Statistics. 1980. *National survey of professional, administrative, technical, and clerical pay, March 1978*. Bulletin 2045. Washington, D.C.: Government Printing Office.

Douty, H. M. 1980. *The wage bargain and the labor market*. Baltimore: The Johns Hopkins University Press.

Medoff, James L., and Katherine G. Abraham. 1980. Experience, performance, and earnings. *Quarterly Journal of Economics* 95: 703–36.

Mills, Daniel Quinn. 1975. *Government, labor, and inflation: Wage stabilization in the United States*. Chicago: University of Chicago Press.

Nichols, Donald A. 1981. Macroeconomic determinants of wage adjustments in white collar occupations. *Review of Economics and Statistics*, forthcoming.

PART

V Data Appendixes

Appendix A
Current and Historical Availability of BLS Wage, Price, and Productivity Series by SIC Industries

Joseph R. Antos

I. DESCRIPTION

THIS IS A TABULATION ACCORDING TO 1972 STANDARD INDUSTRIAL CLASSIFICATION (SIC) CODES OF THE MAJOR WAGE, INDUSTRIAL PRICE, AND PRODUCTIVITY SERIES PRODUCED BY THE BUREAU OF LABOR STATISTICS. THE DATA SERIES INCLUDED IN THE TABLE ARE LABOR PRODUCTIVITY (OUTPUT PER EMPLOYEE-HOUR), INDUSTRY PRICE INDEXES, AND SEVERAL ALTERNATIVE MEASURES OF WAGES: AVERAGE HOURLY EARNINGS, AVERAGE HOURLY COMPENSATION, AND INDUSTRY WAGE SURVEY DATA.

FOR EACH SERIES, THE TABLE SHOWS THE CURRENT AND HISTORICAL AVAILABILITY OF DATA AT AGGREGATE AND FOUR-DIGIT SIC LEVELS. HISTORICAL AVAILABILITY IS SHOWN FOR 1947, 1958, AND 1972, AND SHOULD BE INTERPRETED AS FOLLOWS: ENTRIES FOR , E.G., THE 1978, 1972, AND 1958 COLUMNS WITH NO ENTRY FOR 1947 INDICATES THAT A CONTINUOUS TIME SERIES EXTENDS AT LEAST AS FAR AS 1958, BUT NOT TO 1947. ALSO SHOWN IN THE TABLE ARE THE QUARTERLY DATA ON PAYROLLS COVERED BY UNEMPLOYMENT INSURANCE LEGISLATION WHICH ARE AVAILABLE FOR VIRTUALLY ALL SIC CODES. THE BLS EMPLOYMENT COST INDEX HAS BEEN OMITTED FROM THE PRESENT TABULATION BECAUSE IT IS A RELATIVELY NEW SERIES AND BECAUSE IT HAS RELATIVELY LITTLE INDUSTRY DETAIL.

WITH THE EXCEPTION OF AVERAGE HOURLY COMPENSATION, A DESCRIPTION OF THE CONCEPT, MEASUREMENT METHOD, AND PUBLICATION SOURCE FOR EACH SERIES CAN BE FOUND IN THE BLS HANDBOOK OF METHODS (1976). MORE DETAILED INFORMATION CONCERNING WAGE MEASURES CAN BE FOUND IN BLS MEASURES OF COMPENSATION, BULLETIN 1941 (1977). THE AVERAGE HOURLY COMPENSATION MEASURE IS BASED ON DATA COMPILED BY THE BUREAU OF ECONOMIC ANALYSIS FOR THE NATIONAL ACCOUNTS AND IS NOT CURRENTLY PUBLISHED. EXCEPT FOR INDUSTRY WAGE SURVEY DATA, MACHINE-READABLE VERSIONS OF ALL PUBLISHED SERIES ARE AVAILABLE ON LABSTAT, THE BLS DATA-BANK (CONTACT BRENDA KYLE (202-523-1075) FOR INFORMATION).

THIS TABULATION WAS PREPARED BY JOE A. STONE AND OLLIE BALLARD OF THE OFFICE OF RESEARCH AND EVALUATION, JACK TRIPLETT, ASST. COMMISSIONER, IN COOPERATION WITH ISSUING OFFICES LISTED BELOW. FOR FURTHER INFORMATION ON THE TABLE, CONTACT MARK WILSON (202-523-1347).

II. DATA SOURCES

SERIES	HANDBOOK PAGES	ISSUING OFFICE	CONTACT
LABOR PRODUCTIVITY	219-32	PRODUCTIVITY & TECHNOLOGY (J. MARK, ASST. COMMISSIONER)	J. MARK (202-523-9294)
INDUSTRIAL PRICES	123-26	PRICES & LIVING CONDITIONS (J. LAYNG, ASST. COMMISSIONER)	C. HOWELL (202-272-5113)
AVERAGE HOURLY EARNINGS	26-42	EMPLOYMENT STRUCTURE AND TRENDS (T. PLEWES, ASST. COMMISSIONER)	C.M. UTTER (202-523-1461)
AVERAGE HOURLY COMPENSATION	(NOT IN HANDBOOK)	PRODUCTIVITY & TECHNOLOGY (J. MARK, ASST. COMMISSIONER)	J. MARK (202-523-9294)
INDUSTRY WAGE SURVEY	135-45	WAGES & INDUSTRIAL RELATIONS (G. STELLUTO, ASST. COMMISSIONER)	M. PERSONICK (202-523-1268)
UNEMPLOYMENT INSURANCE PAYROLL DATA	66-73	EMPLOYMENT STRUCTURE AND TRENDS (T. PLEWES, ASST. COMMISSIONER)	R. GREENE (202-523-1339)

III. CODES

PART/PT COVERAGE OF THE INDUSTRY IS PARTIAL OR COMBINED WITH OTHER RELATED INDUSTRIES.

U UNPUBLISHED DATA.

M DATA FOR THIS INDUSTRY AVAILABLE .... MONTHLY.

Q DATA FOR THIS INDUSTRY AVAILABLE .... QUARTERLY.

A DATA FOR THIS INDUSTRY AVAILABLE .... ANNUALLY.

P DATA FOR THIS INDUSTRY AVAILABLE .... PERIODICALLY, EITHER ON A SPECIAL STUDY BASIS WITH NO FINAL SCHEDULE, OR ON A MULTI-YEAR CYCLE.

IV. FOOTNOTES

1 PREPARED AND PUBLISHED ARE MEASURES OF PRODUCTIVITY AND HOURLY COMPENSATION FOR THE BUSINESS AND NONFARM SECTORS, WHICH DIFFER FROM THE TOTAL PRIVATE ECONOMY AND NONFARM ECONOMY IN THAT OWNER-OCCUPIED REAL ESTATE, PRIVATE HOUSEHOLDS AND NONPROFIT INSTITUTIONS ARE EXCLUDED FROM THE FORMER. ALSO PREPARED, BUT NOT PUBLISHED, ARE PRODUCTIVITY MEASURES, BASED ON BOTH THE CURRENT EMPLOYMENT STATISTICS AND THE CURRENT POPULATION SURVEY HOURS MEASURES, FOR THE TOTAL PRIVATE ECONOMY AND THE NONFARM ECONOMY.

2 ALSO PUBLISHED ARE PRODUCTIVITY AND HOURLY COMPENSATION MEASURES FOR NONFINANCIAL CORPORATIONS.

3 DATA FOR CROP AND LIVESTOCK AGRICULTURE ARE COMBINED IN MEASURES FOR THE FARM SECTOR. MEASURES ARE PREPARED FOR FARM, BOTH INCLUDING AND EXCLUDING THE RENTAL VALUE OF OWNER-OCCUPIED FARM HOUSING.

4 DATA FOR AGRICULTURE SERVICES, FORESTRY, AND FISHERIES ARE INCLUDED IN THOSE FOR THE SERVICES SECTOR

5 AS OF JAN. 1978, DATA FOR THIS INDUSTRY HAVE BEEN COMBINED WITH DATA FOR A RELATED INDUSTRY.

6 QUARTERLY MEASURES FOR DURABLE MANUFACTURING AND NONDURABLE MANUFACTERING ARE ALSO PUBLISHED SEPARATELY.

7 UNPUBLISHED QUARTERLY MEASURES ARE ALSO AVAILABLE FOR THIS INDUSTRY.

8 ANNUAL UNPUBLISHED MEASURES FOR TRANSPORTATION ARE PREPARED WHICH INCLUDE DATA FOR ALL INDUSTRIES 4000 TO 4789 EXCEPT 4300, POSTAL SERVICES.

9 PART OF SIC 4213.

0 EXCLUDES HOUSEHOLDS.

1 ALL UNPUBLISHED(U) DATA IN THIS SERIES ARE COLLECTED MONTHLY(M).

STANDARD INDUSTRIAL CLASSIFICATION	LABOR PRODUCTIVITY				INDUSTRIAL PRICES				AVERAGE HOURLY EARNINGS 11 (INDUSTRY EMPLOYMENT STATISTICS PROGRAM)				AVERAGE HOURLY COMPENSATION: TOTAL COMPENSATION				INDUSTRY WAGE SURVEY PROGRAM: WAGES & SALARIES				UNEMPLOYMENT INSURANCE DATA (ES202): TOTAL COVERED PAYROLL			
	1978	1972	1958	1947	1978	1972	1958	1947	1978	1972	1958	1947	1978	1972	1958	1947	1978	1972	1958	1947	1978	1972	1958	1947
TOTAL ECONOMY																					Q	Q	Q	Q
TOTAL PRIVATE ECONOMY	Q1,2	Q1,2	Q1,2	Q1,2									Q 1,2	Q 1,2							Q	Q	Q	Q
TOTAL PRIVATE NON-FARM ECONOMY	Q 1	Q 1	Q 1	Q1,2					M	M	A	A	Q 1	Q 1							Q	Q	Q	Q
AGRICULTURE	QU 3	QU 3	QU 3	QU 3									QU 3	QU 3							Q	Q	Q	Q
DURABLE MANUFACTURING	Q	Q	Q	Q					M	M	M	M	Q	Q							Q	Q	Q	Q
NONDURABLE MANUFACTURING	Q	Q	Q	Q					M	M	M	M	Q	Q							Q	Q	Q	Q
TRANSPORTATION	A 8	A 8	A 8	A 8									AU 8	A 8							Q	Q	Q	Q
GOVERNMENT ENTERPRISES	AU	AU	AU	AU									AU	A							Q	Q	Q	Q
A. AGRICUL FORESTRY & FISHING																								
100 AGRICUL PROD-CROPS	3	3	3	3									3	3							Q	Q	Q	Q
110 CASH GRAINS																					Q	Q	Q	Q
111 WHEAT																					Q	Q	Q	Q
112 RICE																					Q	Q	Q	Q
115 CORN																					Q	Q	Q	Q
116 SOYBEANS																					Q	Q	Q	Q
119 CASH GRAINS NEC																					Q	Q	Q	Q
130 FIELD CROPS EXC. CASH GRAINS																					Q	Q	Q	Q
131 COTTON																					Q	Q	Q	Q
132 TOBACCO																					Q	Q	Q	Q
133 SUGAR CROPS																					Q	Q	Q	Q
134 IRISH FOTATOES																					Q	Q	Q	Q
139 FIELD CROPS EXC. CASH GRAIN NEC																					Q	Q	Q	Q
160 VEG & MELONS																					Q	Q	Q	Q
161 VEG & MELONS																					Q	Q	Q	Q
170 FRUITS & TREE NUTS																					Q	Q	Q	Q
171 BERRY CROPS																					Q	Q	Q	Q
172 GRAPES																					Q	Q	Q	Q
173 TREE NUTS																					Q	Q	Q	Q
174 CITRUS FRUITS																					Q	Q	Q	Q
175 DECIDUOUS TREE FRUITS																					Q	Q	Q	Q
179 FRUITS & TREE NUTS NEC																					Q	Q	Q	Q
180 HORTICUL SPECIALTIES																					Q	Q	Q	Q
181 ORNAMENTAL NURSERY PROD																					Q	Q	Q	Q
182 FOOD CROPS GROWN UNDER COVER																					Q	Q	Q	Q
189 HORTICUL SPECIALTIES NEC																					Q	Q	Q	Q
190 GENERAL FARMS PRIMARILY CROP																					Q	Q	Q	Q
191 GENERAL FARMS PRIMARILY CROP																					Q	Q	Q	Q

STANDARD INDUSTRIAL CLASSIFICATION		LABOR PRODUCTIVITY				INDUSTRIAL PRICES				AVERAGE HOURLY EARNINGS 11 (INDUSTRY EMPLOYMENT STATISTICS PROGRAM)				COMPENSATION TOTAL COMPENSATION				INDUSTRY WAGE SURVEY PROGRAM WAGES & SALARIES				(ES202) TOTAL COVERED PAYROLL			
		1978	1972	1958	1947	1978	1972	1958	1947	1978	1972	1958	1947	1978	1972	1958	1947	1978	1972	1958	1947	1978	1972	1958	1947
210	LIVESTOCK EXC. DAIRY POULTRY																					Q	Q	Q	Q
211	BEEF CATTLE FEEDLOTS																					Q	Q	Q	Q
212	BEEF CATTLE EXC. FEEDLOTS																					Q	Q	Q	Q
213	HOGS																					Q	Q	Q	Q
214	SHEEP & GOATS																					Q	Q	Q	Q
219	GENERAL LIVESTOCK NEC																					Q	Q	Q	Q
240	DAIRY FARMS																					Q	Q	Q	Q
241	DAIRY FARMS																					Q	Q	Q	Q
250	POULTRY & EGGS																					Q	Q	Q	Q
251	BROIL FRY & ROASTER CHICKENS																					Q	Q	Q	Q
252	CHICKEN EGGS																					Q	Q	Q	Q
253	TURKEYS & TURKEY EGGS																					Q	Q	Q	Q
254	POULTRY HATCHERIES																					Q	Q	Q	Q
259	POULTRY & EGGS NEC																					Q	Q	Q	Q
270	ANIMAL SPECIALTIES																					Q	Q	Q	Q
271	FUR-BEARING ANIMALS & RABBIT																					Q	Q	Q	Q
272	HORSES & OTHER EQUINES																					Q	Q	Q	Q
279	ANIMAL SPECIALTIES NEC																					Q	Q	Q	Q
290	GENERAL FARMS PRIM LIVESTOCK																					Q	Q	Q	Q
291	GENERAL FARMS PRIM LIVESTOCK																					Q	Q	Q	Q
700	AGRICULTURAL SERVICES	4	4	4	4									4	4							Q	Q	Q	Q
710	SOIL PREPARATION SERV																					Q	Q	Q	Q
711	SOIL PREPARATION SERV																					Q	Q	Q	Q
720	CROP SERV																					Q	Q	Q	Q
721	CROP PLANTING & PROTECTION																					Q	Q	Q	Q
722	CROP HARVESTING																					Q	Q	Q	Q
723	CROP PREP SERV FOR MRKT																					Q	Q	Q	Q
724	COTTON GINNING																					Q	Q	Q	Q
729	GENERAL CROP SERV																					Q	Q	Q	Q
740	VET SERV									U	U														
741	VET SERV FARM LIVESTOCK																								
742	VET SERV SPECIALTIES																					Q	Q	Q	Q
750	ANIMAL SERV EXC. VET									U	U											Q	Q	Q	Q
751	LIVESTOCK SERV EXC. SPECIAL																					Q	Q	Q	Q
752	ANIMAL SPECIALTY SERV																					Q	Q	Q	Q
760	FARM LABOR & MANAGE. SERV																					Q	Q	Q	Q
761	FARM LABOR CONTRACT																					Q	Q	Q	Q
762	FARM MANAGE. SERV																					Q	Q	Q	Q
780	LANDSCAPE & HORTICUL SERV									U	U														
781	LANDSCAPE COUNSEL & PLAN																								
782	LAWN & GARDEN SERV																								
783	ORNAMENTAL SHRUB & TREE SERV																								
800	FORESTRY	4	4	4	4									4	4							Q	Q	Q	Q
810	TIMBER TRACTS																					Q	Q	Q	Q
811	TIMBER TRACTS																					Q	Q	Q	Q
820	FOREST NURSERY & SEED																					Q	Q	Q	Q

STANDARD INDUSTRIAL CLASSIFICATION		LABOR PRODUCTIVITY				INDUSTRIAL PRICES				AVERAGE HOURLY EARNINGS 11 (INDUSTRY EMPLOYMENT STATISTICS PROGRAM)				AVERAGE HOURLY COMPENSATION: TOTAL COMPENSATION				INDUSTRY WAGE SURVEY PROGRAM: WAGES & SALARIES				UNEMPLOYMENT INSURANCE DATA (ES202): TOTAL COVERED PAYROLL			
		1978	1972	1958	1947	1978	1972	1958	1947	1978	1972	1958	1947	1978	1972	1958	1947	1978	1972	1958	1947	1978	1972	1958	1947
821	FOREST NURSERY & SEED																					Q	Q	Q	Q
840	GATHER OF MISC. FOREST PROD																					Q	Q	Q	Q
843	EXTRACTION OF PINE GUM																					Q	Q	Q	Q
849	GATHERING OF FOREST PROD NEC																					Q	Q	Q	Q
850	FORESTRY SERV																					Q	Q	Q	Q
851	FORESTRY SERV																					Q	Q	Q	Q
900	FISHING HUNTING & TRAPPING	4	4	4	4									4	4							Q	Q	Q	Q
910	COMM FISHING																					Q	Q	Q	Q
912	FINFISH																					Q	Q	Q	Q
913	SHELLFISH																					Q	Q	Q	Q
919	MISC MARINE PROD																					Q	Q	Q	Q
920	FISH HATCHERIES & PRESS																					Q	Q	Q	Q
921	FISH HATCHERIES & PRESS																					Q	Q	Q	Q
970	HUNTING TRAPPING GAME PROPAG.																					Q	Q	Q	Q
971	HUNTING TRAPPING GAME PROPAG.																					Q	Q	Q	Q
	B. MINING	AU	AU	AU	AU					M	M	M	M	AU	A							Q	Q	Q	Q
1000	METAL MINING									M	M	M	M									Q	Q	Q	Q
1010	IRON ORES	A	A	A	A					M	M	M	M					P	P			Q	Q	Q	Q
1011	IRON ORES	A	A	A	A	M												P	P			Q	Q	Q	Q
1020	COPPER ORES	A	A	A	A					M	M	M	M					P	P			Q	Q	Q	Q
1021	COPPER ORES	A	A	A	A													P	P			Q	Q	Q	Q
1030	LEAD & ZINC ORES									U	U							P	P			Q	Q	Q	Q
1031	LEAD & ZINC ORES																	P	P			Q	Q	Q	Q
1040	GOLD & SILVER ORES									U PT	U PT											Q	Q	Q	Q
1041	GOLD ORES																					Q	Q	Q	Q
1044	SILVER ORES																					Q	Q	Q	Q
1050	BAUXITE & OTHER ALUMIN ORES									U PT	U PT											Q	Q	Q	Q
1051	BAUXITE & OTHER ALUMIN ORES																					Q	Q	Q	Q
1060	FERROALLOY ORE EXC. VANADIUM									U PT	U PT											Q	Q	Q	Q
1061	FERROALLOY ORE EXC. VANADIUM																					Q	Q	Q	Q
1080	METAL MINING SERV									U PT	U PT											Q	Q	Q	Q
1081	METAL MINING SERV																					Q	Q	Q	Q
1090	MISC METAL ORES									U PT	U PT											Q	Q	Q	Q
1092	MERCURY ORES					M																Q	Q	Q	Q
1094	URANIUM-RADIUM-VANADIUM ORE																	P				Q	Q	Q	Q
1099	METAL ORES NEC																					Q	Q	Q	Q
1100	ANTHRACITE MINING	A 5	A 5	A 5	A 5					M PT	M PT	M PT		5	5							Q	Q	Q	Q
1110	ANTHRACITE MINING	A 5	A 5	A 5	A 5									5	5							Q	Q	Q	Q
1111	ANTHRACITE																					Q	Q	Q	Q
1112	ANTHRACITE MINING SERV																					Q	Q	Q	Q

STANDARD INDUSTRIAL CLASSIFICATION		LABOR PRODUCTIVITY				INDUSTRIAL PRICES				EARNINGS 11 (INDUSTRY EMPLOYMENT STATISTICS PROGRAM)				TOTAL COMPENSATION				SURVEY PROGRAM WAGES & SALARIES				(ES202) TOTAL COVERED PAYROLL			
		1978	1972	1958	1947	1978	1972	1958	1947	1978	1972	1958	1947	1978	1972	1958	1947	1978	1972	1958	1947	1978	1972	1958	1947
1210	BITUM COAL & LIGNITE MINING	A 5	A 5	A 5	A 5																	Q	Q	Q	Q
1211	BITUM COAL & LIGNITE					M	M	A										P	P	P		Q	Q	Q	Q
1213	BITUM & LIGNITE MINING SERV																					Q	Q	Q	
1300	OIL & GAS EXTRACTION									M	M	M	M									Q	Q	Q	Q
1310	CRUDE PETRO & NATURAL GAS									M	M	M	M					P	P	P		Q	Q	Q	Q
1311	CRUDE PETRO & NATURAL GAS					M	M	A										P	P	P		Q	Q	Q	Q
1320	NATURAL GAS LIQUIDS									U	U											Q	Q	Q	Q
1321	NATURAL GAS LIQUIDS																					Q	Q	Q	Q
1380	OIL & GAS FIELD SERV									M	M	M										Q	Q	Q	Q
1381	DRILLING OIL & GAS WELLS																	P				Q	Q	Q	Q
1382	OIL & GAS EXPLORATION SERV																					Q	Q	Q	Q
1389	OIL & GAS FIELD SERV NEC																					Q	Q	Q	Q
1400	NONMETAL MINERAL EXC. FUEL	A	A	A	A					M	M	M	M									Q	Q	Q	Q
1410	DIMENSION STONE									U PT	U PT											Q	Q	Q	Q
1411	DIMENSION STONE																					Q	Q	Q	Q
1420	CRUSHED & BROKEN STONE	A	A	A	A					M	M	M										Q	Q	Q	Q
1422	CRUSHED & BROKEN LIMESTONE																					Q	Q	Q	Q
1423	CRUSHED & BROKEN GRANITE																					Q	Q	Q	Q
1429	CRUSHED & BROKEN STONE NEC																					Q	Q	Q	Q
1440	SAND & GRAVEL																					Q	Q	Q	Q
1442	CONST SAND & GRAVEL					M	M	A		U	U											Q	Q	Q	Q
1446	INDUST SAND																					Q	Q	Q	Q
1450	CLAY & RELATED MINERALS									U PT	U PT											Q	Q	Q	Q
1452	BENTONITE																					Q	Q	Q	Q
1453	FIRE CLAY																					Q	Q	Q	Q
1454	FULLER'S EARTH																					Q	Q	Q	Q
1455	KAOLIN & BALL CLAY					M																Q	Q	Q	Q
1459	CLAY & RELATED MINERALS NEC																					Q	Q	Q	Q
1470	CHEM & FERTILIZER MINERALS									U	U											Q	Q	Q	Q
1472	BARITE																					Q	Q	Q	Q
1473	FLUORSPAR																					Q	Q	Q	Q
1474	POTASH SODA & BORATE MINERALS																					Q	Q	Q	Q
1475	PHOSPHATE ROCK																					Q	Q	Q	Q
1476	ROCK SALT																					Q	Q	Q	Q
1477	SULFUR																					Q	Q	Q	Q
1479	CHEM & FERTILIZER MINING NEC																					Q	Q	Q	Q
1480	NONMETALLIC MINERALS SERV									U PT	U PT											Q	Q	Q	Q
1481	NONMETALLIC MINERALS SERV																					Q	Q	Q	Q
1490	MISC NONMETALLIC MINERALS									U PT	U PT											Q	Q	Q	Q
1492	GYPSUM																					Q	Q	Q	Q
1496	TALC SOAPSTONE & PYROPHYLLITE																					Q	Q	Q	Q
1499	NONMETALLIC MINERALS NEC																								
	C. CONSTRUCTION	AU	AU	AU	AU					M	M	M	M	AU	AU			A	A	A	A	Q	Q	Q	Q
1500	GENERAL BUILD CONTRACT									M	M	M						A	A	A	A	Q	Q	Q	Q

STANDARD	LABOR PRODUCTIVITY				INDUSTRIAL PRICES				AVERAGE HOURLY EARNINGS 11				AVERAGE HOURLY COMPENSATION				INDUSTRY WAGE SURVEY PROGRAM				UNEMPLOYMENT INSURANCE DATA (ES202)			
INDUSTRIAL									(INDUSTRY EMPLOYMENT STATISTICS PROGRAM)				TOTAL COMPENSATION				WAGES & SALARIES				TOTAL COVERED PAYROLL			
CLASSIFICATION	1978	1972	1958	1947	1978	1972	1958	1947	1978	1972	1958	1947	1978	1972	1958	1947	1978	1972	1958	1947	1978	1972	1958	1947
1520 RESIDENTIAL BUILD CONST									M	M							P	P			Q	Q	Q	Q
1521 SINGLE-FAMILY HOUSING CONST																								
1522 RESIDENTIAL CONST NEC																								
1530 OPERATIVE BUILDERS									M	M											Q	Q	Q	Q
1531 OPERATIVE BUILDERS																					Q	Q	Q	Q
1540 NONRES BUILD CONST									M	M							P	P			Q	Q	Q	Q
1541 INDUST BUILD & WAREHOUSE																								
1542 NONRES CONST NEC																								
1600 HEAVY CONST CONTRACTORS									M	M							A	A			Q	Q	Q	Q
1610 HIGHWAY & STREET CONST									M	M							A	A			Q	Q	Q	Q
1611 HIGHWAY & STREET CONST																	A	A			Q	Q	Q	Q
1620 HEAVY CONST EXC. HIGHWAY									M	M							A	A			Q	Q	Q	Q
1622 BRIDGE TUNNEL & ELEV HIGHWAY																					Q	Q	Q	Q
1623 WATER SEWER & UTILITY LINES																					Q	Q	Q	Q
1629 HEAVY CONST NEC																					Q	Q	Q	Q
1700 SPECIAL TRADE CONTRACTORS									M	M	M	M					A	A	A	A	Q	Q	Q	Q
1710 PLUMBING HEAT AIR COND									M	M	M						Q	Q	Q	A	Q	Q	Q	Q
1711 PLUMBING HEAT AIR COND																	Q	Q	Q	A	Q	Q	Q	Q
1720 PAINT PAPER HANG DECORATING									M	M	M						Q	Q	Q	A	Q	Q	Q	Q
1721 PAINT PAPER HANG DECORATING																	Q	Q	Q	A	Q	Q	Q	Q
1730 ELEC WORK									M	M	M						Q	Q	Q	A	Q	Q	Q	Q
1731 ELEC WORK																	Q	Q	Q	A	Q	Q	Q	Q
1740 MASONRY STONEWORK & PLASTER									M	M							Q	Q	Q	A	Q	Q	Q	Q
1741 MASONRY & OTHER STONEWORK																	Q	Q	Q	A	Q	Q	Q	Q
1742 PLASTER DRYWALL & INSULATION																	Q	Q	Q	A	Q	Q	Q	Q
1743 TERR TILE MARBLE MOSAIC WORK																	A	A	A	A	Q	Q	Q	Q
1750 CARPENTERING & FLOORING									M	M							Q	Q	Q	A	Q	Q	Q	Q
1751 CARPENTERING																	Q	Q	Q	A	Q	Q	Q	Q
1752 FLOOR LAY & FLOOR WORK NEC																	A	A	A	A	Q	Q	Q	Q
1760 ROOFING & SHEET METAL WORK									M	M	M						A	A	A	A	Q	Q	Q	Q
1761 ROOFING & SHEET METAL WORK																	A	A	A	A	Q	Q	Q	Q
1770 CONCRETE WORK									U	U							A	A	A	A	Q	Q	Q	Q
1771 CONCRETE WORK																	A	A	A	A	Q	Q	Q	Q
1780 WATER WELL DRILLING									U	U											Q	Q	Q	Q
1781 WATER WELL DRILLING																					Q	Q	Q	Q
1790 MISC. SPECIAL TRADE CONTRACT									U	U											Q	Q	Q	Q
1791 STRUCT STEEL ERECTION																	A	A	A	A	Q	Q	Q	Q
1793 GLASS & GLAZING WORK																	A	A	A	A	Q	Q	Q	Q
1794 EXCAVATING & FOUNDATION WORK																	A	A	A	A	Q	Q	Q	Q
1795 WRECKING & DEMOLITION WORK																	A	A	A	A	Q	Q	Q	Q
1796 INSTALL BUILD EQUIP NEC																	A	A	A	A	Q	Q	Q	Q
1799 SPECIAL TRADE CONTRACT NEC																	A	A	A	A	Q	Q	Q	Q

	INDUSTRIAL CLASSIFICATION	PRODUCTIVITY				PRICES				EARNINGS 11 (INDUSTRY EMPLOYMENT STATISTICS PROGRAM)				TOTAL COMPENSATION				SURVEY PROGRAM WAGES & SALARIES				(ES202) TOTAL COVERED PAYROLL			
		1978	1972	1958	1947	1978	1972	1958	1947	1978	1972	1958	1947	1978	1972	1958	1947	1978	1972	1958	1947	1978	1972	1958	1947
2000	FOOD & KINDRED PROD	AU	AU	AU						M	M	M	M	AU	AU							Q	Q	Q	Q
2010	MEAT PROD	AU	AU	AU						M	M	M	M	AU	AU							Q	Q	Q	Q
2011	MEAT PACKING PLANTS	AU	AU	AU		M	M			M	M	M	M	AU	AU			P	P	P		Q	Q	Q	Q
2013	SAUSAGE & OTHER PREP MEAT	AU	AU	AU		M	M			M	M	M		AU	AU			P	P	P		Q	Q	Q	Q
2016	POULTRY DRESSING PLANTS	AU 5	AU 5	AU 5		M	M	A		M	M			AU 5	AU 5							Q	Q	Q	Q
2017	POULTRY & EGG PROCESSING	AU 5	AU 5	AU 5						U	U			AU 5	AU 5							Q	Q	Q	Q
2020	DAIRY PROD	AU	AU	AU						M	M	M		AU	AU							Q	Q	Q	Q
2021	CREAMERY BUTTER	AU	AU	AU		M	M			U PT	U PT			AU	AU							Q	Q	Q	Q
2022	CHEESE NATURAL & PROCESSED	AU	AU	AU		M				M	M			AU	AU							Q	Q	Q	Q
2023	CONDENSED & EVAPORATED MILK	AU	AU	AU						U PT	U PT			AU	AU							Q	Q	Q	Q
2024	ICE CREAM & FROZEN DESSERTS	AU	AU	AU		M				U	U			AU	AU							Q	Q	Q	Q
2026	FLUID MILK	AU	AU	AU						M	M	M		AU	AU			P	P	P		Q	Q	Q	Q
2030	PRESERVED FRUITS & VEG	A	A	A	A					M	M			AU	AU							Q	Q	Q	Q
2032	CANNED SPECIALTIES	AU	AU	AU						M	M			AU	AU							Q	Q	Q	Q
2033	CANNED FRUITS & VEG	AU	AU	AU		M	M			M	M			AU	AU							Q	Q	Q	Q
2034	DEHYDRATED FRUITS VEG SOUPS	AU	AU	AU		M				U	U			AU	AU							Q	Q	Q	Q
2035	PICKLE SAUCE & SALAD DRESS	AU	AU	AU						U	U			AU	AU							Q	Q	Q	Q
2037	FROZEN FRUITS & VEG	AU 5	AU 5	AU 5						M	M			AU 5	AU 5							Q	Q	Q	Q
2038	FROZEN SPECIALTIES	AU 5	AU 5	AU 5						U	U			AU 5	AU 5							Q	Q	Q	Q
2040	GRAIN MILL PROD	A	A	A						M	M	M		AU	AU							Q	Q	Q	Q
2041	FLOUR & OTHER GRAIN MILL	A	A	A	A	M	M			M	M	M		AU	AU			P	P	P		Q	Q	Q	Q
2043	CEREAL BREAKFAST FOODS	A	A	A						U	U			AU	AU							Q	Q	Q	Q
2044	RICE MILLING	A	A	A		M	M	A		U PT	U PT			AU	AU			P				Q	Q	Q	Q
2045	BLENDED & PREPARED FLOUR	A	A	A						U PT	U PT			AU	AU			P				Q	Q	Q	Q
2046	WET CORN MILLING	A	A	A						U	U			AU	AU			P				Q	Q	Q	Q
2047	DOG CAT & OTHER PET FOOD	A 5	A 5	A 5						U	U			AU 5	AU 5							Q	Q	Q	Q
2048	PREPARED FEEDS NEC	A 5	A 5	A 5		M				M	M			AU 5	AU 5							Q	Q	Q	Q
2050	BAKERY PROD	A	A	A	A					M	M	M	M	AU	AU							Q	Q	Q	Q
2051	BREAD CAKE & RELATED PROD	AU	AU	AU						M	M	M		AU	AU							Q	Q	Q	Q
2052	COOKIES & CRACKERS	AU	AU	AU						M	M	M		AU	AU							Q	Q	Q	Q
2060	SUGAR & CONFEC PROD	AU	AU	AU						M	M	M	M	AU	AU							Q	Q	Q	Q
2061	RAW CANE SUGAR	A 5	A 5	A 5	A 5	M	M			M PT	M PT	M PT	M PT	AU 5	AU 5							Q	Q	Q	Q
2062	CANE SUGAR REFINING	A 5	A 5	A 5	A 5					M PT	M PT	M PT	M PT	AU 5	AU 5							Q	Q	Q	Q
2063	BEET SUGAR	A 5	A 5	A 5	A 5	M				M PT	M PT	M PT	M PT	AU 5	AU 5							Q	Q	Q	Q
2065	CONFEC PROD	A	A	A	A					M	M	M	M	AU	AU			P	P	P		Q	Q	Q	Q
2066	CHOCOLATE & COCOA PROD	AU	AU	AU						U PT	U PT			AU	AU							Q	Q	Q	Q
2067	CHEWING GUM	AU	AU	AU		M	M	A		U PT	U PT			AU	AU							Q	Q	Q	Q
2070	FATS & OILS	AU	AU	AU						M	M			AU	AU							Q	Q	Q	Q
2074	COTTONSEED OIL MILL	AU	AU	AU		M	M	A		U PT	U PT			AU	AU							Q	Q	Q	Q
2075	SOYBEAN OIL MILL	AU	AU	AU		M	M			U PT	U PT			AU	AU							Q	Q	Q	Q
2076	VEG OIL MILL NEC	AU	AU	AU						U PT	U PT			AU	AU							Q	Q	Q	Q
2077	ANIMAL & MARINE FATS & OILS	AU	AU	AU		M	M			U	U			AU	AU							Q	Q	Q	Q
2079	SHORTENING & COOKING OILS	AU	AU	AU						U	U			AU	AU							Q	Q	Q	Q
2080	BEVERAGES	AU	AU	AU						M	M	M	M	AU	AU							Q	Q	Q	Q
2082	MALT BEVERAGES	A	A	A	A					M	M	M	M	AU	AU							Q	Q	Q	Q
2083	MALT	AU	AU	AU		M	M			U PT	U PT			AU	AU							Q	Q	Q	Q
2084	WINE BRANDY & BRANDY SPIRIT	AU	AU	AU						U	U			AU	AU							Q	Q	Q	Q
2085	DISTIL LIQUOR EXC. BRANDY	AU	AU	AU		M				U	U			AU	AU							Q	Q	Q	Q
2086	BOTTLE & CAN SOFT DRINKS	A	A	A						M	M	M	M	AU	AU							Q	Q	Q	Q

STANDARD INDUSTRIAL	CLASSIFICATION	LABOR PRODUCTIVITY				INDUSTRIAL PRICES				AVERAGE HOURLY EARNINGS 11 (INDUSTRY EMPLOYMENT STATISTICS PROGRAM)				AVERAGE HOURLY COMPENSATION: TOTAL COMPENSATION				INDUSTRY WAGE SURVEY PROGRAM: WAGES & SALARIES				UNEMPLOYMENT INSURANCE DATA (ES202): TOTAL COVERED PAYROLL			
		1978	1972	1958	1947	1978	1972	1958	1947	1978	1972	1958	1947	1978	1972	1958	1947	1978	1972	1958	1947	1978	1972	1958	1947
2087	FLAVOR EXTRACT & SYRUPS NEC	AU	AU	AU						U PT	U PT			AU	AU							Q	Q	Q	Q
2090	MISC. FOODS & KINDRED PROD	AU	AU	AU						M	M			AU	AU							Q	Q	Q	Q
2091	CANNED & CURED SEAFOODS	AU	AU	AU		M				U	U			AU	AU							Q	Q	Q	Q
2092	FRESH OR FROZEN PACKAGE FISH	AU	AU	AU		M	M	A		U	U			AU	AU							Q	Q	Q	Q
2095	ROASTED COFFEE	AU 5	AU 5	AU 5		M				U	U			AU 5	AU 5							Q	Q	Q	Q
2097	MANUFACTURED ICE	AU	AU	AU						U PT	U PT			AU	AU							Q	Q	Q	Q
2098	MACARONI & SPAGHETTI	AU	AU	AU		M	M			U PT	U PT			AU	AU							Q	Q	Q	Q
2099	FOOD PREPARATIONS NEC	AU 5	AU 5	AU 5						U PT	U PT			AU 5	AU 5							Q	Q	Q	Q
2100	TOBACCO MANUFACTURES	AU	AU	AU						M	M	M	M	AU	AU							Q	Q	Q	Q
2110	CIGARETTES	A 5	A 5	A 5	A 5					M	M	M	M	AU 5	AU 5			P	P	P		Q	Q	Q	Q
2111	CIGARETTES	A 5	A 5	A 5	A 5	M	M	A		M	M	M	M	AU 5	AU 5			P	P	P		Q	Q	Q	Q
2120	CIGARS	A	A	A	A					U	U			AU	AU			P	P	P		Q	Q	Q	Q
2121	CIGARS	A	A	A	A	M	M	A		U	U			AU	AU			P	P	P		Q	Q	Q	Q
2130	CHEWING & SMOKING TOBACCO	A 5	A 5	A 5	A 5					U PT	U PT			AU 5	AU 5							Q	Q	Q	Q
2131	CHEWING & SMOKING TOBACCO	A 5	A 5	A 5	A 5	M	M	A		U PT	U PT			AU 5	AU 5							Q	Q	Q	Q
2140	TOBACCO STEMMING & REDRYING	AU	AU	AU						U PT	U PT			AU	AU							Q	Q	Q	Q
2141	TOBACCO STEMMING & REDRYING	AU	AU	AU						U PT	U PT			AU	AU							Q	Q	Q	Q
2200	TEXTILE MILL PROD	AU	AU	AU						M	M	M	M	AU	AU							Q	Q	Q	Q
2210	WEAVING MILL COTTON	AU	AU	AU						M	M	M		AU	AU			P	P	P		Q	Q	Q	Q
2211	WEAVING MILL COTTON	AU	AU	AU		M				M	M	M		AU	AU			P	P	P		Q	Q	Q	Q
2220	WEAVING MILL SYNTHETICS	AU	AU	AU						M	M	M		AU	AU			P	P	P		Q	Q	Q	Q
2221	WEAVING MILL SYNTHETICS	AU	AU	AU		M				M	M	M		AU	AU			P	P	P		Q	Q	Q	Q
2230	WEAVING & FINISH MILL WOOL	AU	AU	AU						M	M	M		AU	AU			P	P	P		Q	Q	Q	Q
2231	WEAVING & FINISH MILL WOOL	AU	AU	AU						M	M	M		AU	AU			P	P	P		Q	Q	Q	Q
2240	NARROW FABRIC MILL	AU	AU	AU						M	M	M		AU	AU							Q	Q	Q	Q
2241	NARROW FABRIC MILL	AU	AU	AU						M	M	M		AU	AU							Q	Q	Q	Q
2250	KNITTING MILL	AU	AU	AU						M	M	M	M	AU	AU							Q	Q	Q	Q
2251	WOMEN'S HOSIERY EXC. SOCKS	A 5	A 5	A 5	A 5	M				M	M	M		AU 5	AU 5			P	P	P		Q	Q	Q	Q
2252	HOSIERY NEC	A 5	A 5	A 5	A 5					M	M	M		AU 5	AU 5			P	P	P		Q	Q	Q	Q
2253	KNIT OUTERWEAR MILL	AU	AU	AU						M	M	M	M	AU	AU							Q	Q	Q	Q
2254	KNIT UNDERWEAR MILL	AU	AU	AU		M	M			M	M	M	M	AU	AU							Q	Q	Q	Q
2257	CIRCULAR KNIT FABRIC MILL	AU 5	AU 5	AU 5		M				M	M			AU 5	AU 5							Q	Q	Q	Q
2258	WARP KNIT FABRIC MILL	AU 5	AU 5	AU 5						U PT	U PT			AU 5	AU 5							Q	Q	Q	Q
2259	KNITTING MILL NEC	AU	AU	AU						U PT	U PT			AU	AU							Q	Q	Q	Q
2260	TEXTILE FINISH EXC. WOOL	AU	AU	AU						M	M	M	M	AU	AU			P	P	P		Q	Q	Q	Q
2261	FINISHING PLANTS COTTON	AU	AU	AU		M				M	M			AU	AU			P	P	P		Q	Q	Q	Q
2262	FINISHING PLANTS SYNTHETICS	AU	AU	AU		M				M	M			AU	AU			P	P	P		Q	Q	Q	Q
2269	FINISHING PLANTS NEC	AU	AU	AU						U	U			AU	AU							Q	Q	Q	Q
2270	FLOOR COVERING MILL	AU	AU	AU						M	M	M		AU	AU							Q	Q	Q	Q
2271	WOVEN CARPETS & RUGS	AU	AU	AU		M				M PT	M PT	M PT		AU	AU							Q	Q	Q	Q
2272	TUFTED CARPETS & RUGS	AU	AU	AU		M				M PT	M PT	M PT		AU	AU							Q	Q	Q	Q
2279	CARPETS & RUGS NEC	AU	AU	AU						M PT	M PT	M PT		AU	AU							Q	Q	Q	Q
2280	YARN & THREAD MILL	AU	AU	AU						M	M	M	M	AU	AU							Q	Q	Q	Q

STANDARD INDUSTRIAL	CLASSIFICATION	LABOR PRODUCTIVITY				INDUSTRIAL PRICES				AVERAGE HOURLY EARNINGS 11 (INDUSTRY EMPLOYMENT STATISTICS PROGRAM)				COMPENSATION TOTAL COMPENSATION				SURVEY PROGRAM WAGES & SALARIES				(ES202) TOTAL COVERED PAYROLL			
		1978	1972	1958	1947	1978	1972	1958	1947	1978	1972	1958	1947	1978	1972	1958	1947	1978	1972	1958	1947	1978	1972	1958	1947
2284	THREAD MILL	AU	AU	AU		M				U	U			AU	AU							Q	Q	Q	Q
2290	MISC TEXTILE GOOD	AU	AU	AU						M	M	M		AU	AU							Q	Q	Q	Q
2291	FELT GOOD EXC. WOVEN FELT	AU	AU	AU						U PT	U PT			AU	AU							Q	Q	Q	Q
2292	LACE GOOD	AU	AU	AU						U PT	U PT			AU	AU							Q	Q	Q	Q
2293	PADDINGS & UPHOL FILLING	AU	AU	AU						U PT	U PT			AU	AU							Q	Q	Q	Q
2294	PROCESSED TEXTILE WASTE	AU	AU	AU						U PT	U PT			AU	AU							Q	Q	Q	Q
2295	COATED FABRIC NOT RUBBERIZED	AU	AU	AU						U	U			AU	AU							Q	Q	Q	Q
2296	TIRE CORD & FABRIC	AU	AU	AU						U	U			AU	AU							Q	Q	Q	Q
2297	NONWOVEN FABRICS	AU 5	AU 5	AU 5						U PT	U PT			AU 5	AU 5							Q	Q	Q	Q
2298	CORDAGE & TWINE	AU	AU	AU		M				U	U			AU	AU							Q	Q	Q	Q
2299	TEXTILE GOOD NEC	AU 5	AU 5	AU 5						U PT	U PT			AU 5	AU 5							Q	Q	Q	Q
2300	APPAREL & OTHER TEXTILE PROD	AU	AU	AU						M	M	M	M	AU	AU							Q	Q	Q	Q
2310	MEN & BOY SUITS & COATS	AU	AU	AU						M	M	M	M	AU	AU			P	P	P		Q	Q	Q	Q
2311	MEN & BOY SUITS & COATS	AU	AU	AU		M	M	A		M	M	M	M	AU	AU			P	P	P		Q	Q	Q	Q
2320	MEN & BOY FURNISH	AU	AU	AU						M	M	M	M	AU	AU							Q	Q	Q	Q
2321	MEN & BOY SHIRTS & NIGHTWEAR	AU	AU	AU		M	M	A		M	M	M	M	AU	AU			P	P	P		Q	Q	Q	Q
2322	MEN & BOY UNDERWEAR	AU	AU	AU		M	M			U	U			AU	AU							Q	Q	Q	Q
2323	MEN & BOY NECKWEAR	AU	AU	AU		M				U	U			AU	AU							Q	Q	Q	Q
2327	MEN & BOY SEPARATE TROUSERS	AU	AU	AU		M	M			M	M	M	M	AU	AU			P	P			Q	Q	Q	Q
2328	MEN & BOY WORK CLOTHING	AU	AU	AU		M	M	A		M	M	M		AU	AU			P	P	P		Q	Q	Q	Q
2329	MEN & BOY CLOTHING NEC	AU	AU	AU						U	U			AU	AU							Q	Q	Q	Q
2330	WOMEN & MISS OUTERWEAR	AU	AU	AU						M	M	M	M	AU	AU							Q	Q	Q	Q
2331	WOMEN & MISS BLOUSES & WAIST	AU	AU	AU						M	M	M		AU	AU							Q	Q	Q	Q
2335	WOMEN & MISS DRESSES	AU	AU	AU		M				M	M	M		AU	AU			P	P	P		Q	Q	Q	Q
2337	WOMEN & MISS SUITS & COATS	AU	AU	AU						M	M			AU	AU			P	P	P		Q	Q	Q	Q
2339	WOMEN & MISS OUTERWEAR NEC	AU	AU	AU						M	M	M		AU	AU							Q	Q	Q	Q
2340	WOMEN & CHILD UNDERGARMENT	AU	AU	AU						M	M	M	M	AU	AU							Q	Q	Q	Q
2341	WOMEN & CHILD UNDERWEAR	AU	AU	AU		M				M	M	M	M	AU	AU							Q	Q	Q	Q
2342	BRASSIERES & ALLIED GARMENT	AU	AU	AU		M				M	M	M		AU	AU							Q	Q	Q	Q
2350	HATS CAPS & MILLINERY	AU	AU	AU						U PT	U PT			AU	AU							Q	Q	Q	Q
2351	MILLINERY	AU	AU	AU						U PT	U PT			AU	AU							Q	Q	Q	Q
2352	HATS & CAPS EXC. MILLINERY	AU	AU	AU						U PT	U PT			AU	AU							Q	Q	Q	Q
2360	CHILD'S OUTERWEAR	AU	AU	AU						M	M	M	M	AU	AU							Q	Q	Q	Q
2361	CHILD'S DRESSES & BLOUSES	AU	AU	AU						M	M	M		AU	AU							Q	Q	Q	Q
2363	CHILD'S COATS & SUITS	AU	AU	AU						U	U			AU	AU							Q	Q	Q	Q
2369	CHILD'S OUTERWEAR NEC	AU	AU	AU						U	U			AU	AU							Q	Q	Q	Q
2370	FUR GOOD	AU	AU	AU						U	U			AU	AU							Q	Q	Q	Q
2371	FUR GOOD	AU	AU	AU						U	U			AU	AU							Q	Q	Q	Q
2380	MISC APPAREL & ACCESS	AU	AU	AU						M	M			AU	AU							Q	Q	Q	Q
2381	FABRIC DRESS & WORK GLOVES	AU	AU	AU		M	M	A		U	U			AU	AU							Q	Q	Q	Q
2384	ROBES & DRESSING GOWNS	AU	AU	AU						U	U			AU	AU							Q	Q	Q	Q
2385	WATERPROOF OUTERGARMENTS	AU	AU	AU						U	U			AU	AU							Q	Q	Q	Q
2386	LEATHER & SHEEP LINED CLOTH	AU	AU	AU						U PT	U PT			AU	AU							Q	Q	Q	Q
2387	APPAREL BELTS	AU	AU	AU						U PT	U PT			AU	AU							Q	Q	Q	Q
2389	APPAREL & ACCESS NEC	AU	AU	AU						U PT	U PT			AU	AU							Q	Q	Q	Q
2390	MISC. FAB TEXTILE PROD	AU	AU	AU						M	M	M		AU	AU							Q	Q	Q	Q
2391	CURTAINS & DRAPERIES	AU	AU	AU						M	M			AU	AU							Q	Q	Q	Q
2392	HOUSE FURNISH NEC	AU	AU	AU						M	M			AU	AU							Q	Q	Q	Q

STANDARD INDUSTRIAL CLASSIFICATION		LABOR PRODUCTIVITY				INDUSTRIAL PRICES				AVERAGE HOURLY EARNINGS 11 (INDUSTRY EMPLOYMENT STATISTICS PROGRAM)				AVERAGE HOURLY COMPENSATION TOTAL COMPENSATION				INDUSTRY WAGE SURVEY PROGRAM WAGES & SALARIES				UNEMPLOYMENT INSURANCE DATA (ES202) TOTAL COVERED PAYROLL			
		1978	1972	1958	1947	1978	1972	1958	1947	1978	1972	1958	1947	1978	1972	1958	1947	1978	1972	1958	1947	1978	1972	1958	1947
2393	TEXTILE BAGS	AU	AU	AU						U	U			AU	AU							Q	Q	Q	Q
2394	CANVAS & RELATED PROD	AU	AU	AU		M				U	U			AU	AU							Q	Q	Q	Q
2395	PLEATING & STITCHING	AU 5	AU 5	AU 5						U	U			AU 5	AU 5							Q	Q	Q	Q
2396	AUTO & APPAREL TRIMMINGS	AU 5	AU 5	AU 5		M				M	M			AU 5	AU 5							Q	Q	Q	Q
2397	SCHIFFLI MACH EMBROIDERIES	AU	AU	AU						U PT	U PT			AU	AU							Q	Q	Q	Q
2399	FAB TEXTILE PROD NEC	AU	AU	AU						U PT	U PT			AU	AU							Q	Q	Q	Q
2400	LUMBER & WOOD PROD	AU	AU	AU						M	M	M	M	AU	AU							Q	Q	Q	Q
2410	LOG CAMPS & LOG CONTRACT	AU	AU	AU						M	M			AU	AU							Q	Q	Q	Q
2411	LOG CAMPS & LOG CONTRACT	AU	AU	AU						M	M			AU	AU			P	P	P		Q	Q	Q	Q
2420	SAWMILL & PLANING MILL	AU	AU	AU						M	M	M	M	AU	AU			P	P	P		Q	Q	Q	Q
2421	SAWMILL & PLANING MILL GEN.	A	A	A		M	M			M	M	M		AU	AU			P	P	P		Q	Q	Q	Q
2426	HARDWOOD DIMENSION & FLOOR	AU	AU	AU						M	M			AU	AU							Q	Q	Q	Q
2429	SPECIAL PROD SAWMILL NEC	AU	AU	AU						U	U			AU	AU							Q	Q	Q	Q
2430	MILL PLYWOOD & STRUCT MEM.	AU	AU	AU						M	M			AU	AU							Q	Q	Q	Q
2431	MILLWORK	AU 5	AU 5	AU 5						M	M			AU 5	AU 5							Q	Q	Q	Q
2434	WOOD KITCHEN CABINETS	AU 5	AU 5	AU 5						M	M			AU 5	AU 5			P	P	P		Q	Q	Q	Q
2435	HARDWOOD VENEER & PLYWOOD	A 5	A 5	A 5						M	M			AU 5	AU 5							Q	Q	Q	Q
2436	SOFTWOOD VENEER & PLYWOOD	A 5	A 5	A 5		M				M	M			AU 5	AU 5							Q	Q	Q	Q
2439	STRUCT WOOD MEMBERS NEC	AU 5	AU 5	AU 5		M				U	U			AU 5	AU 5							Q	Q	Q	Q
2440	WOOD CONTAINERS	AU	AU	AU						M	M			AU	AU							Q	Q	Q	Q
2441	NAILED WOOD BOXES & SHOOK	AU	AU	AU						U	U			AU	AU							Q	Q	Q	Q
2448	WOOD PALLETS & SKIDS	AU 5	AU 5	AU 5		M				U	U			AU 5	AU 5							Q	Q	Q	Q
2449	WOOD CONTAINERS NEC	AU	AU	AU						U	U			AU	AU							Q	Q	Q	Q
2450	WOOD BUILD & MOBILE HOME	AU	AU	AU						M	M			AU	AU							Q	Q	Q	Q
2451	MOBILE HOMES	AU 5	AU 5	AU 5		M				M	M			AU 5	AU 5							Q	Q	Q	Q
2452	PREFAB WOOD BUILDS	AU 5	AU 5	AU 5						U	U			AU 5	AU 5							Q	Q	Q	Q
2490	MISC WOOD PROD	AU	AU	AU						M	M			AU	AU							Q	Q	Q	Q
2491	WOOD PRESERVING	AU	AU	AU						U	U			AU	AU							Q	Q	Q	Q
2492	PARTICLEBOARD	AU 5	AU 5	AU 5		M				U PT	U PT			AU 5	AU 5							Q	Q	Q	Q
2499	WOOD PROD NEC	AU 5	AU 5	AU 5						U PT	U PT			AU 5	AU 5							Q	Q	Q	Q
2500	FURNITURE & FIXTURES	AU	AU	AU						M	M	M	M	AU	AU							Q	Q	Q	Q
2510	HOUSE FURN	A	A	A						M	M			AU	AU							Q	Q	Q	Q
2511	WOOD HOUSE FURN	A 5	A 5	A 5		M	M			M	M			AU 5	AU 5			P	P	P		Q	Q	Q	Q
2512	UPHOLSTERED HOUSE FURN	A	A	A		M	M			M	M			AU	AU							Q	Q	Q	Q
2514	METAL HOUSE FURN	A	A	A						M	M			AU	AU							Q	Q	Q	Q
2515	MATTRESSES & BEDSPRINGS	A	A	A		M	M			M	M	M	M	AU	AU							Q	Q	Q	Q
2517	WOOD TV & RADIO CABINETS	A 5	A 5	A 5						U PT	U PT			AU 5	AU 5			P	P	P		Q	Q	Q	Q
2519	HOUSE FURN NEC	AU	AU	AU						U PT	U PT			AU	AU							Q	Q	Q	Q
2520	OFFICE FURN	AU	AU	AU						M	M	M		AU	AU							Q	Q	Q	Q
2521	WOOD OFFICE FURN	AU	AU	AU		M	M	A		U	U			AU	AU							Q	Q	Q	Q
2522	METAL OFFICE FURN	AU	AU	AU						U	U			AU	AU							Q	Q	Q	Q
2530	PUBLIC BUILD & RELATED FURN	AU	AU	AU						M	M	M		AU	AU							Q	Q	Q	Q
2531	PUBLIC BUILD & RELATED FURN	AU	AU	AU						M	M			AU	AU							Q	Q	Q	Q
2540	PARTITIONS & FIXTURES	AU	AU	AU						M	M	M		AU	AU							Q	Q	Q	Q

	INDUSTRIAL CLASSIFICATION	PRODUCTIVITY				PRICES				EMPLOYMENT (INDUSTRY EMPLOYMENT STATISTICS PROGRAM)				TOTAL COMPENSATION				WAGES & SALARIES				TOTAL COVERED PAYROLL			
		1978	1972	1958	1947	1978	1972	1958	1947	1978	1972	1958	1947	1978	1972	1958	1947	1978	1972	1958	1947	1978	1972	1958	1947
2590	MISC FURN & FIXTURES	AU	AU	AU						M	M	M		AU	AU							Q	Q	Q	Q
2591	DRAPERY HARDWARE & BLINDS	AU	AU	AU						U	U			AU	AU							Q	Q	Q	Q
2599	FURN & FIXTURES NEC	AU	AU	AU						U	U			AU	AU							Q	Q	Q	Q
2600	PAPER & ALLIED PROD	AU	AU	AU						M	M	M	M	AU	AU							Q	Q	Q	Q
2610	PULP MILL	A 5	A 5	A 5	A 5					M PT	M PT	M PT		AU 5	AU 5			P	P	P		Q	Q	Q	Q
2611	PULP MILL	A 5	A 5	A 5	A 5	M				U PT	U PT			AU 5	AU 5			P	P	P		Q	Q	Q	Q
2620	PAPER MILL EXC. BUILD PAPER	A 5	A 5	A 5	A 5					M	M			AU 5	AU 5			P	P	P		Q	Q	Q	Q
2621	PAPER MILL EXC. BUILD PAPER	A 5	A 5	A 5	A 5	M				M	M			AU 5	AU 5			P	P	P		Q	Q	Q	Q
2630	PAPERBOARD MILL	A 5	A 5	A 5	A 5					M	M	M		AU 5	AU 5			P	P	P		Q	Q	Q	Q
2631	PAPERBOARD MILL	A 5	A 5	A 5	A 5	M				M	M	M		AU 5	AU 5			P	P	P		Q	Q	Q	Q
2640	MISC. CONVERTED PAPER PROD	AU	AU	AU						M	M	M		AU	AU							Q	Q	Q	Q
2641	PAPER COATING & GLAZING	AU	AU	AU						M	M			AU	AU							Q	Q	Q	Q
2642	ENVELOPES	AU	AU	AU						M	M			AU	AU							Q	Q	Q	Q
2643	BAGS EXC. TEXTILE BAGS	AU	AU	AU						M	M	M		AU	AU							Q	Q	Q	Q
2645	DIE-CUT PAPER & BOARD	AU	AU	AU						U	U			AU	AU							Q	Q	Q	Q
2646	PRESSED & MOLDED PULP GOOD	AU	AU	AU						U PT	U PT			AU	AU							Q	Q	Q	Q
2647	SANITARY PAPER PROD	AU 5	AU 5	AU 5		M	M			U	U			AU 5	AU 5							Q	Q	Q	Q
2648	STATIONERY PROD	AU 5	AU 5	AU 5						U PT	U PT			AU 5	AU 5							Q	Q	Q	Q
2649	CONVERTED PAPER PROD NEC	AU 5	AU 5	AU 5						U PT	U PT			AU 5	AU 5							Q	Q	Q	Q
2650	PAPERBOARD CONTAIN & BOXES	AU	AU	AU						M	M	M	M	AU	AU				P	P		Q	Q	Q	Q
2651	FOLDING PAPERBOARD BOXES	AU	AU	AU						M	M			AU	AU				P	P		Q	Q	Q	Q
2652	SET-UP PAPERBOARD BOXES	AU	AU	AU						U	U			AU	AU				P	P		Q	Q	Q	Q
2653	CORRUGAT & SOLID FIBER BOX	A	A	A						M	M	M		AU	AU			P	P	P		Q	Q	Q	Q
2654	SANITARY FOOD CONTAINERS	AU	AU	AU		M	M			M	M	M		AU	AU				P	P		Q	Q	Q	Q
2655	FIBER CAN DRUM & SIMIL. PROD	AU	AU	AU		M				U	U			AU	AU				P	P		Q	Q	Q	Q
2660	BUILD PAPER & BOARD MILL	A 5	A 5	A 5	A 5					M PT	M PT	M PT		AU 5	AU 5							Q	Q	Q	Q
2661	BUILD PAPER & BOARD MILL	A 5	A 5	A 5	A 5					M PT	M PT	M PT		AU 5	AU 5							Q	Q	Q	Q
2700	PRINTING & PUBLISHING	AU	AU	AU						M	M	M	M	AU	AU							Q	Q	Q	Q
2710	NEWSPAPERS	AU	AU	AU						M	M	M	M	AU	AU			P	A	A	A	Q	Q	Q	Q
2711	NEWSPAPERS	AU	AU	AU						M	M	M		AU	AU			P	A	A	A	Q	Q	Q	Q
2720	PERIODICALS	AU	AU	AU						M	M			AU	AU							Q	Q	Q	Q
2721	PERIODICALS	AU	AU	AU						M	M			AU	AU							Q	Q	Q	Q
2730	BOOKS	AU	AU	AU						M	M	M	M	AU	AU			P	A	A	A	Q	Q	Q	Q
2731	BOOK PUBLISHING	AU	AU	AU						M	M			AU	AU			P	A	A	A	Q	Q	Q	Q
2732	BOOK PRINTING	AU	AU	AU						M	M			AU	AU			P	A	A	A	Q	Q	Q	Q
2740	MISC PUBLISHING	AU	AU	AU						U	M			AU	AU							Q	Q	Q	Q
2741	MISC PUBLISHING	AU	AU	AU						M	M			AU	AU							Q	Q	Q	Q
2750	COMM PRINTING	AU	AU	AU						M	M	M		AU	AU			P	A	A	A	Q	Q	Q	Q
2751	COMM PRINTING LETTERPRESS	AU 5	AU 5	AU 5						M	M			AU 5	AU 5			P	A	A	A	Q	Q	Q	Q
2752	COMM PRINTING LITHOGRAPHIC	AU 5	AU 5	AU 5						M	M			AU 5	AU 5			P	A	A	A	Q	Q	Q	Q
2753	ENGRAVING & PLATE PRINTING	AU	AU	AU						U	M			AU	AU			P	A	A	A	Q	Q	Q	Q
2754	COMM PRINTING GRAVURE	AU 5	AU 5	AU 5						U	M			AU 5	AU 5			P	A	A	A	Q	Q	Q	Q
2760	MANIFOLD BUSINESS FORMS	AU	AU	AU						M	M			AU	AU							Q	Q	Q	Q
2761	MANIFOLD BUSINESS FORMS	AU	AU	AU						M	M			AU	AU							Q	Q	Q	Q
2770	GREETING CARD PUBLISHING	AU	AU	AU						U	U			AU	AU							Q	Q	Q	Q
2771	GREETING CARD PUBLISHING	AU	AU	AU						U	U			AU	AU							Q	Q	Q	Q

STANDARD INDUSTRIAL CLASSIFICATION		LABOR PRODUCTIVITY				INDUSTRIAL PRICES				AVERAGE HOURLY EARNINGS 11 (INDUSTRY EMPLOYMENT STATISTICS PROGRAM)				AVERAGE HOURLY COMPENSATION: TOTAL COMPENSATION				INDUSTRY WAGE SURVEY PROGRAM: WAGES & SALARIES				UNEMPLOYMENT INSURANCE DATA (ES202): TOTAL COVERED PAYROLL			
		1978	1972	1958	1947	1978	1972	1958	1947	1978	1972	1958	1947	1978	1972	1958	1947	1978	1972	1958	1947	1978	1972	1958	1947
2780	BLANKBOOKS & BOOKBINDING	AU	AU	AU						M	M	M		AU	AU							Q	Q	Q	Q
2782	BLANKBOOKS & LOOSELEAF BIND	AU	AU	AU						U	U			AU	AU			P	A	A	A	Q	Q	Q	Q
2789	BOOKBINDING & RELATED WORK	AU	AU	AU						U	U			AU	AU			P	A	A	A	Q	Q	Q	Q
2790	PRINTING TRADE SERV	AU	AU	AU						M	M			AU	AU			P	A	A	A	Q	Q	Q	Q
2791	TYPESETTING	AU	AU	AU						U	U			AU	AU			P	A	A	A	Q	Q	Q	Q
2793	PHOTOENGRAVING	AU	AU	AU						U PT	U PT			AU	AU			P	A	A	A	Q	Q	Q	Q
2794	ELECTROTYPE & STEREOTYPING	AU	AU	AU						U PT	U PT			AU	AU			P	A	A	A	Q	Q	Q	Q
2795	LITHOGRAPH PLATEMAKING SERV	AU 5	AU 5	AU 5						U PT	U PT			AU 5	AU 5			P	A	A	A	Q	Q	Q	Q
2800	CHEMICALS & ALLIED PROD	AU	AU	AU						M	M	M	M	AU	AU							Q	Q	Q	Q
2810	INDUST INORGANIC CHEM	AU	AU	AU						M	M			AU	AU			P	P	P		Q	Q	Q	Q
2812	ALKALIES & CHLORINE	AU	AU	AU		M				U	U			AU	AU							Q	Q	Q	Q
2813	INDUST GASES	AU	AU	AU						U	U			AU	AU							Q	Q	Q	Q
2816	INORGANIC PIGMENTS	AU	AU	AU						U	U			AU	AU							Q	Q	Q	Q
2819	INDUST INORGANIC CHEM NEC	AU 5	AU 5	AU 5						M	M			AU 5	AU 5							Q	Q	Q	Q
2820	PLASTIC MATER & SYNTHETICS	AU	AU	AU						M	M	M		AU	AU							Q	Q	Q	Q
2821	PLASTIC MATER & RESINS	AU	AU	AU		M				M	M			AU	AU				P	P		Q	Q	Q	Q
2822	SYNTHETIC RUBBER	AU	AU	AU		M	M	A		U	U			AU	AU							Q	Q	Q	Q
2823	CELLULOSIC MAN-MADE FIBERS	A 5	A 5	A 5						U	U			AU 5	AU 5			P	P	P		Q	Q	Q	Q
2824	ORGANIC FIBERS NONCELL	A 5	A 5	A 5		M	M			M	M			AU 5	AU 5			P	P	P		Q	Q	Q	Q
2830	DRUGS	AU	AU	AU						M	M	M	M	AU	AU							Q	Q	Q	Q
2831	BIOLOGICAL PROD	AU	AU	AU						U	U			AU	AU							Q	Q	Q	Q
2833	MEDICINALS & BOTANICALS	AU	AU	AU						U	U			AU	AU							Q	Q	Q	Q
2834	PHARMACEUTICAL PREPARATIONS	A	A	A						M	M	M		AU	AU							Q	Q	Q	Q
2840	SOAP CLEANERS & TOILET GOOD	AU	AU	AU						M	M	M		AU	AU							Q	Q	Q	Q
2841	SOAP & OTHER DETERGENTS	AU	AU	AU						M	M	M		AU	AU							Q	Q	Q	Q
2842	POLISHES & SANITATION GOOD	AU	AU	AU						M PT	M PT			AU	AU							Q	Q	Q	Q
2843	SURFACE ACTIVE AGENT	AU	AU	AU						M PT	M PT			AU	AU							Q	Q	Q	Q
2844	TOILET PREPARATIONS	AU	AU	AU						M	M	M		AU	AU							Q	Q	Q	Q
2850	PAINTS & ALLIED PROD	AU	AU	AU						M	M	M		AU	AU			P	P	P		Q	Q	Q	Q
2851	PAINTS & ALLIED PROD	A	A	A						M	M			AU	AU			P	P	P		Q	Q	Q	Q
2860	INDUST ORGANIC CHEM	AU	AU	AU						M	M			AU	AU			P	P	P		Q	Q	Q	Q
2861	GUM & WOOD CHEM	AU	AU	AU						M PT	M PT			AU	AU							Q	Q	Q	Q
2865	CYCLIC CRUDES & INTERMED.	AU	AU	AU						M	M			AU	AU							Q	Q	Q	Q
2869	INDUST ORGANIC CHEM NEC	AU	AU	AU						M PT	M PT			AU	AU							Q	Q	Q	Q
2870	AGRICUL CHEM	AU	AU	AU						M	M			AU	AU							Q	Q	Q	Q
2873	NITROGENOUS FERTILIZERS	AU 5	AU 5	AU 5		M				U	U			AU 5	AU 5			P	P	P		Q	Q	Q	Q
2874	PHOSPHATIC FERTILIZERS	AU	AU	AU		M	M			U	U			AU	AU			P	P	P		Q	Q	Q	Q
2875	FERTILIZERS MIXING ONLY	AU	AU	AU		M	M			U	U			AU	AU			P	P	P		Q	Q	Q	Q
2879	AGRICUL CHEM NEC	AU	AU	AU						U	U			AU	AU							Q	Q	Q	Q
2890	MISC CHEM PROD	AU	AU	AU						M	M			AU	AU							Q	Q	Q	Q
2891	ADHESIVES & SEALANTS	AU	AU	AU						U	U			AU	AU							Q	Q	Q	Q
2892	EXPLOSIVES	AU	AU	AU		M	M	A		U	U			AU	AU							Q	Q	Q	Q
2893	PRINTING INK	AU	AU	AU						U	U			AU	AU							Q	Q	Q	Q
2895	CARBON BLACK	AU	AU	AU						U PT	U PT			AU	AU							Q	Q	Q	Q
2899	CHEM PREPARATIONS NEC																								

STANDARD INDUSTRIAL CLASSIFICATION		PRODUCTIVITY				PRICES				EARNINGS 11 (INDUSTRY EMPLOYMENT STATISTICS PROGRAM)				TOTAL COMPENSATION				SURVEY PROGRAM WAGES & SALARIES				(ES202) TOTAL COVERED PAYROLL			
		1978	1972	1958	1947	1978	1972	1958	1947	1978	1972	1958	1947	1978	1972	1958	1947	1978	1972	1958	1947	1978	1972	1958	1947
2910	PETRO REFINING	A	A	A	A					M	M	M	M	AU	AU			P	P	P		Q	Q	Q	Q
2911	PETRO REFINING	A	A	A	A	M				M	M	M	M	AU	AU			P	P	P		Q	Q	Q	Q
2950	PAVING & ROOFING MATER	AU	AU	AU						M	M			AU	AU							Q	Q	Q	Q
2951	PAVING MIXTURES & BLOCKS	AU	AU	AU		M				U	U			AU	AU							Q	Q	Q	Q
2952	ASPHALT FELTS & COATINGS	AU	AU	AU		M				U	U			AU	AU							Q	Q	Q	Q
2990	MISC. PETRO & COAL PROD	AU	AU	AU						U	U			AU	AU							Q	Q	Q	Q
2992	LUBRICATING OILS & GREASES	AU	AU	AU						U	U			AU	AU							Q	Q	Q	Q
2999	PETRO & COAL PROD NEC	AU	AU	AU						U	U			AU	AU							Q	Q	Q	Q
3000	RUBBER & MISC. PLASTIC PROD	AU	AU	AU						M	M	M	M	AU	AU							Q	Q	Q	Q
3010	TIRES & INNER TUBE	A	A	A	A					M	M	M	M	AU	AU							Q	Q	Q	Q
3011	TIRES & INNER TUBE	A	A	A	A	M				M	M	M		AU	AU							Q	Q	Q	Q
3020	RUBBER & PLASTIC FOOTWEAR	AU	AU	AU						M	M			AU	AU							Q	Q	Q	Q
3021	RUBBER & PLASTIC FOOTWEAR	AU	AU	AU		M	M			M	M			AU	AU							Q	Q	Q	Q
3030	RECLAIMED RUBBER	AU	AU	AU						M PT	M PT			AU	AU							Q	Q	Q	Q
3031	RECLAIMED RUBBER	AU	AU	AU		M				M PT	M PT			AU	AU							Q	Q	Q	Q
3040	RUBBER & PLASTIC HOSE & BELT	AU 5	AU 5	AU 5						M PT	M PT			AU 5	AU 5							Q	Q	Q	Q
3041	RUBBER & PLASTIC HOSE & BELT	AU 5	AU 5	AU 5						M PT	M PT			AU 5	AU 5							Q	Q	Q	Q
3060	FAB RUBBER PROD NEC	AU 5	AU 5	AU 5						M	M			AU 5	AU 5							Q	Q	Q	Q
3069	FAB RUBBER PROD NEC	AU 5	AU 5	AU 5						M	M			AU 5	AU 5							Q	Q	Q	Q
3070	MISC PLASTIC PROD	AU 5	AU 5	AU 5						M	M	M		AU 5	AU 5			P	P	P		Q	Q	Q	Q
3079	MISC PLASTIC PROD	AU 5	AU 5	AU 5						M	M	M		AU 5	AU 5			P	P	P		Q	Q	Q	Q
3100	LEATHER & LEATHER PROD	AU	AU	AU						M	M	M	M	AU	AU							Q	Q	Q	Q
3110	LEATHER TANNING & FINISHING	AU	AU	AU						M	M	M	M	AU	AU			P	P	P		Q	Q	Q	Q
3111	LEATHER TANNING & FINISHING	AU	AU	AU		M				M	M	M	M	AU	AU			P	P	P		Q	Q	Q	Q
3130	BOOT & SHOE CUT STOCK & FIND	AU	AU	AU						U	U			AU	AU							Q	Q	Q	Q
3131	BOOT & SHOE CUT STOCK & FIND	AU	AU	AU						U	U			AU	AU							Q	Q	Q	Q
3140	FOOTWEAR EXC. RUBBER	A	A	A	A					M	M	M	M	AU	AU			P	P	P		Q	Q	Q	Q
3142	HOUSE SLIPPERS	AU	AU	AU		M				U	U			AU	AU							Q	Q	Q	Q
3143	MEN FOOTWEAR EXC. ATHLETIC	AU	AU	AU		M				M	M			AU	AU			P	P	P		Q	Q	Q	Q
3144	WOMEN FOOTWEAR EXC. ATHLETIC	AU	AU	AU		M	M			M	M			AU	AU			P	P	P		Q	Q	Q	Q
3149	FOOTWEAR EXC. RUBBER NEC	AU	AU	AU						U	U			AU	AU			P	P	P		Q	Q	Q	Q
3150	LEATHER GLOVES & MITTENS	AU	AU	AU						U PT	U PT			AU	AU							Q	Q	Q	Q
3151	LEATHER GLOVES & MITTENS	AU	AU	AU						U PT	U PT			AU	AU							Q	Q	Q	Q
3160	LUGGAGE	AU	AU	AU						M	M			AU	AU							Q	Q	Q	Q
3161	LUGGAGE	AU	AU	AU						M	M			AU	AU							Q	Q	Q	Q
3170	HANDBAGS & PERSONAL LEATHER	AU	AU	AU						M	M	.M		AU	AU							Q	Q	Q	Q
3171	WOMEN HANDBAGS & PURSES	AU	AU	AU		M				U	U			AU	AU							Q	Q	Q	Q
3172	PERSONAL LEATHER GOOD NEC	AU	AU	AU						U	U			AU	AU							Q	Q	Q	Q
3190	LEATHER GOOD NEC	AU	AU	AU						U PT	U PT			AU	AU							Q	Q	Q	Q
3199	LEATHER GOOD NEC	AU	AU	AU						U PT	U PT			AU	AU										
3200	STONE CLAY & GLASS PROD	AU	AU	AU						M	M	M	M	AU	AU							Q	Q	Q	Q
3210	FLAT GLASS	AU	AU	AU						M	M	M		AU	AU							Q	Q	Q	Q
3211	FLAT GLASS	AU	AU	AU		M	M			M	M	M		AU	AU							Q	Q	Q	Q
3220	GLASS, GLASSWARE PRESSED BLOWN	AU	AU	AU						M	M	M		AU	AU							Q	Q	Q	Q

STANDARD INDUSTRIAL CLASSIFICATION		LABOR PRODUCTIVITY				INDUSTRIAL PRICES				AVERAGE HOURLY EARNINGS 11 (INDUSTRY EMPLOYMENT STATISTICS PROGRAM)				AVERAGE HOURLY COMPENSATION: TOTAL COMPENSATION				INDUSTRY WAGE SURVEY PROGRAM: WAGES & SALARIES				UNEMPLOYMENT INSURANCE DATA (ES202): TOTAL COVERED PAYROLL			
		1978	1972	1958	1947	1978	1972	1958	1947	1978	1972	1958	1947	1978	1972	1958	1947	1978	1972	1958	1947	1978	1972	1958	1947
3221	GLASS CONTAINERS	A	A	A	A	M	M	A		M	M	M	M	AU	AU			P	P	P		Q	Q	Q	Q
3229	PRESSED & BLOWN GLASS NEC	AU	AU	AU						M	M	M	M	AU	AU			P	P	P		Q	Q	Q	Q
3230	PROD OF PURCHASED GLASS	AU	AU	AU						M	M			AU	AU							Q	Q	Q	Q
3231	PROD OF PURCHASED GLASS	AU	AU	AU						M	M			AU	AU							Q	Q	Q	Q
3240	CEMENT HYDRAULIC	A	A	A	A					M	M	M	M	AU	AU							Q	Q	Q	Q
3241	CEMENT HYDRAULIC	A	A	A	A	M	M	A		M	M	M	M	AU	AU							Q	Q	Q	Q
3250	STRUCT CLAY PROD	A	A	A						M	M	M	M	AU	AU			P	P	P		Q	Q	Q	Q
3251	BRICK & STRUCT CLAY TILE	A 5	A 5	A 5		M	M	A		U	U			AU 5	AU 5			P	P	P		Q	Q	Q	Q
3253	CERAMIC WALL & FLOOR TILE	A 5	A 5	A 5		M				U PT	U PT			AU 5	AU 5			P	P	P		Q	Q	Q	Q
3255	CLAY REFRACTORIES	A	A	A		M	M	A		U	U			AU	AU			P	P	P		Q	Q	Q	Q
3259	STRUCT CLAY PROD NEC	A 5	A 5	A 5		M	M	A		U PT	U PT			AU 5	AU 5			P	P	P		Q	Q	Q	Q
3260	POTTERY & RELATED PROD	AU	AU	AU						M	M	M	M	AU	AU							Q	Q	Q	Q
3261	VITREOUS PLUMBING FIXTURES	AU	AU	AU		M	M	A		U	U			AU	AU							Q	Q	Q	Q
3262	VITREOUS CHINA FOOD UTENS.	AU	AU	AU		M	M	A		U PT	U PT			AU	AU							Q	Q	Q	Q
3263	FINE EARTHENWARE FOOD UTENS.	AU	AU	AU		M	M	A		U PT	U PT			AU	AU							Q	Q	Q	Q
3264	PORCELAIN ELEC SUP.	AU	AU	AU						U	U			AU	AU							Q	Q	Q	Q
3269	POTTERY PROD NEC	AU	AU	AU		M				U	U			AU	AU							Q	Q	Q	Q
3270	CONCRETE GYPSUM & PLASTER	AU	AU	AU						M	M	M		AU	AU							Q	Q	Q	Q
3271	CONCRETE BLOCK & BRICK	A 5	A 5	A 5	A 5	M	M	A		M	M			AU 5	AU 5							Q	Q	Q	Q
3272	CONCRETE PROD NEC	A 5	A 5	A 5	A 5					M	M			AU 5	AU 5							Q	Q	Q	Q
3273	READY-MIXED CONCRETE	A	A	A		M	M	A		M	M			AU	AU							Q	Q	Q	Q
3274	LIME	AU	AU	AU		M				U PT	U PT			AU	AU							Q	Q	Q	Q
3275	GYPSUM PROD	AU	AU	AU		M	M	A		U PT	U PT			AU	AU							Q	Q	Q	Q
3280	CUT STONE & STONE PROD	AU	AU	AU						U	U			AU	AU							Q	Q	Q	Q
3281	CUT STONE & STONE PROD	AU	AU	AU						U	U			AU	AU							Q	Q	Q	Q
3290	MISC. NONMETALLIC MINERAL	AU	AU	AU						M	M			AU	AU							Q	Q	Q	Q
3291	ABRASIVE PROD	AU	AU	AU		M	M			M	M	M		AU	AU							Q	Q	Q	Q
3292	ASBESTOS PROD	AU	AU	AU						M	M			AU	AU							Q	Q	Q	Q
3293	GASKETS PACKING & SEALING	AU	AU	AU						U	U			AU	AU							Q	Q	Q	Q
3295	MINERALS GROUND OR TREATED	AU	AU	AU						U	U			AU	AU							Q	Q	Q	Q
3296	MINERAL WOOL	AU	AU	AU						U	U			AU	AU							Q	Q	Q	Q
3297	NONCLAY REFRACTORIES	AU	AU	AU		M				U PT	U PT			AU	AU							Q	Q	Q	Q
3299	NONMETALLIC MINERAL PROD NEC	AU	AU	AU						U PT	U PT			AU	AU							Q	Q	Q	Q
3300	PRIMARY METAL INDUSTRIES	AU	AU	AU						M	M	M	M	AU	AU							Q	Q	Q	Q
3310	BLAST FURNACE & BASIC STEEL	A 7	A 7	A 7	A 7					M	M	M	M	AU 7	AU 7			P	P	P		Q	Q	Q	Q
3312	BLAST FURNACES & STEEL MILL	AU	AU	AU		M	M	A		M	M	M		AU	AU							Q	Q	Q	Q
3313	ELECTROMETALLURGICAL PROD	AU	AU	AU		M				U	U			AU	AU							Q	Q	Q	Q
3315	STEEL WIRE & RELATED PROD	AU	AU	AU						U	U			AU	AU							Q	Q	Q	Q
3316	COLD FINISH OF STEEL SHAPES	AU	AU	AU		M	M			U	U			AU	AU							Q	Q	Q	Q
3317	STEEL PIPE & TUBE	AU	AU	AU		M	M			M	M			AU	AU							Q	Q	Q	Q
3320	IRON & STEEL FOUNDRIES	AU	AU	AU						M	M	M	M	AU	AU			P	P	P		Q	Q	Q	Q
3321	GRAY IRON FOUNDRIES	A	A	A		M	M			M	M	M	M	AU	AU			P	P	P		Q	Q	Q	Q
3322	MALLEABLE IRON FOUNDRIES	AU	AU	AU						M	M	M	M	AU	AU			P	P	P		Q	Q	Q	Q
3324	STEEL INVEST. FOUNDRIES	A 5	A 5	A 5						U	U			AU 5	AU 5			P	P	P		Q	Q	Q	Q
3325	STEEL FOUNDRIES NEC	A 5	A 5	A 5						M	M			AU 5	AU 5			P	P	P		Q	Q	Q	Q
3330	PRIMARY NONFER METALS	AU	AU	AU						M	M	M		AU	AU										

INDUSTRIAL CLASSIFICATION	PRODUCTIVITY				PRICES				EARNINGS II (INDUSTRY EMPLOYMENT STATISTICS PROGRAM)				TOTAL COMPENSATION				SURVEY PROGRAM: WAGES & SALARIES				TOTAL COVERED PAYROLL			
	1978	1972	1958	1947	1978	1972	1958	1947	1978	1972	1958	1947	1978	1972	1958	1947	1978	1972	1958	1947	1978	1972	1958	1947
3333 PRIMARY ZINC	A 5	A 5	A 5	A 5	M	M			U PT	U PT			AU 5	AU 5							Q	Q	Q	Q
3334 PRIMARY ALUMINUM	A	A	A	A	M	M			M	M			AU	AU							Q	Q	Q	Q
3339 PRIMARY NONFER METALS NEC	AU	AU	AU						U	U			AU	AU							Q	Q	Q	Q
3340 SECONDARY NONFER METALS	AU	AU	AU						U	U			AU	AU							Q	Q	Q	Q
3341 SECONDARY NONFER METALS	AU	AU	AU						U	U			AU	AU							Q	Q	Q	Q
3350 NONFER ROLLING & DRAWING	AU	AU	AU						M	M	M		AU	AU							Q	Q	Q	Q
3351 COPPER ROLLING & DRAWING	A	A	A	A	M	M	A		M	M	M	M	AU	AU							Q	Q	Q	Q
3353 ALUMINUM SHEET PLATE & FOIL	A 5	A 5	A 5		M				M	M			AU 5	AU 5							Q	Q	Q	Q
3354 ALUMINUM EXTRUDED PROD	A 5	A 5	A 5		M				U	U			AU	AU							Q	Q	Q	Q
3355 ALUMINUM ROLLING & DRAWING	A 5	A 5	A 5		M				U PT	U PT			AU 5	AU 5							Q	Q	Q	Q
3356 NONFER ROLLING & DRAWING	AU	AU	AU						U PT	U PT			AU	AU							Q	Q	Q	Q
3357 NONFER WIRE DRAWING & INSUL.	AU	AU	AU						M	M	M		AU	AU							Q	Q	Q	Q
3360 NONFER FOUNDRIES	AU	AU	AU						M	M	M	M	AU	AU			P	P	P		Q	Q	Q	Q
3361 ALUMINUM FOUNDRIES	AU	AU	AU						M	M	M		AU	AU							Q	Q	Q	Q
3362 BRASS BRONZE & COPPER FOUND	AU	AU	AU						U	U			AU	AU							Q	Q	Q	Q
3369 NONFER FOUNDRIES NEC	AU	AU	AU						U	U			AU	AU							Q	Q	Q	Q
3390 MISC PRIMARY METAL PROD	AU	AU	AU						U	U			AU	AU							Q	Q	Q	Q
3398 METAL HEAT TREATING	AU 5	AU 5	AU 5						U	U			AU 5	AU 5							Q	Q	Q	Q
3399 PRIMARY METAL PROD NEC	AU 5	AU 5	AU 5						U	U			AU 5	AU 5							Q	Q	Q	Q
3400 FABRICATED METAL PROD	AU	AU	AU						M	M	M	M	AU	AU							Q	Q	Q	Q
3410 METAL CANS & SHIP CONTAINERS	AU	AU	AU						U PT	M	M		AU	AU							Q	Q	Q	Q
3411 METAL CANS	A	A	A	A	M	M			M	M	M	M	AU	AU							Q	Q	Q	Q
3412 METAL BARRELS DRUMS & PAILS	AU	AU	AU						U	U			AU	AU							Q	Q	Q	Q
3420 CUTLERY HAND TOOL & HARDWARE	AU	AU	AU						M	M	M	M	AU	AU							Q	Q	Q	Q
3421 CUTLERY	AU	AU	AU						U	U			AU	AU							Q	Q	Q	Q
3423 HAND & EDGE TOOLS NEC	AU	AU	AU						M PT	M PT			AU	AU							Q	Q	Q	Q
3425 HAND SAWS & SAW BLADES	AU	AU	AU		M				M PT	M PT			AU	AU							Q	Q	Q	Q
3429 HARDWARE NEC	AU	AU	AU						M	M	M	M	AU	AU			P	P	P		Q	Q	Q	Q
3430 PLUMBING & HEAT EXC. ELECTRIC	AU	AU	AU						M	M			AU	AU							Q	Q	Q	Q
3431 METAL SANITARY WARE	AU	AU	AU		M	M	A		U	U			AU	AU							Q	Q	Q	Q
3432 PLUMBING FITTINGS & BRASS	AU	AU	AU						M	M			AU	AU							Q	Q	Q	Q
3433 HEAT EQUIP EXC. ELECTRIC	AU	AU	AU						M	M			AU	AU							Q	Q	Q	Q
3440 FAB STRUCT METAL PROD	AU	AU	AU						M	M	M	M	AU	AU							Q	Q	Q	Q
3441 FAB STRUCT METAL	AU	AU	AU						M	M	M		AU	AU			P	P	P		Q	Q	Q	Q
3442 METAL DOORS SASH & TRIM	AU	AU	AU						M	M	M		AU	AU							Q	Q	Q	Q
3443 FAB PLATE WORK (BOILER SHOP)	AU	AU	AU						M	M	M		AU	AU							Q	Q	Q	Q
3444 SHEET METAL WORK	AU	AU	AU						M	M	M	M	AU	AU							Q	Q	Q	Q
3446 ARCH METAL WORK	AU 5	AU 5	AU 5						M	M			AU 5	AU 5							Q	Q	Q	Q
3448 PREFAB METAL BUILDS	AU 5	AU 5	AU 5						U	U			AU 5	AU 5							Q	Q	Q	Q
3449 MISC METAL WORK	AU 5	AU 5	AU 5						U	U			AU 5	AU 5							Q	Q	Q	Q
3450 SCREW MACH PROD BOLTS ETC.	AU	AU	AU						M	M	M		AU	AU							Q	Q	Q	Q
3451 SCREW MACH PROD	AU	AU	AU						M	M	M		AU	AU							Q	Q	Q	Q
3452 BOLTS NUTS RIVETS & WASHERS	AU	AU	AU						M	M	M		AU	AU							Q	Q	Q	Q
3460 METAL FORGINGS & STAMPINGS	AU	AU	AU						M	M			AU	AU							Q	Q	Q	Q
3462 IRON & STEEL FORGINGS	AU	AU	AU						M	M	M	M	AU	AU							Q	Q	Q	Q
3463 NONFER FORGINGS	AU	AU	AU						U PT	U PT			AU	AU							Q	Q	Q	Q
3465 AUTO STAMPINGS	AU 5	AU 5	AU 5		M				M	M			AU 5	AU 5			P	P	P		Q	Q	Q	Q
3466 CROWNS & CLOSURES	AU 5	AU 5	AU 5						U PT	U PT			AU 5	AU 5							Q	Q	Q	Q

STANDARD INDUSTRIAL	CLASSIFICATION	LABOR PRODUCTIVITY				INDUSTRIAL PRICES				AVERAGE HOURLY EARNINGS 11 (INDUSTRY EMPLOYMENT STATISTICS PROGRAM)				AVERAGE HOURLY COMPENSATION: TOTAL COMPENSATION				INDUSTRY WAGE SURVEY PROGRAM: WAGES & SALARIES				UNEMPLOYMENT INSURANCE DATA (ES202): TOTAL COVERED PAYROLL			
		1978	1972	1958	1947	1978	1972	1958	1947	1978	1972	1958	1947	1978	1972	1958	1947	1978	1972	1958	1947	1978	1972	1958	1947
3469	METAL STAMPINGS NEC	AU 5	AU 5	AU 5						M	M			AU 5	AU 5							Q	Q	Q	Q
3470	METAL SERV NEC	AU	AU	AU						M	M	M		AU	AU							Q	Q	Q	Q
3471	PLATING & POLISHING	AU	AU	AU						M	M			AU	AU							Q	Q	Q	Q
3479	METAL COATING & ALLIED SERV	AU	AU	AU						M	M			AU	AU							Q	Q	Q	Q
3480	ORDNANCE & ACCESS NEC	AU	AU	AU						M	M			AU	AU							Q	Q	Q	Q
3482	SMALL ARMS AMMO	AU 5	AU 5	AU 5		M				U PT	U PT			AU 5	AU 5							Q	Q	Q	Q
3483	AMMO EXC. FOR SMALL ARMS NEC	AU 5	AU 5	AU 5						M	M			AU 5	AU 5							Q	Q	Q	Q
3484	SMALL ARMS	AU 5	AU 5	AU 5						U PT	U PT			AU 5	AU 5							Q	Q	Q	Q
3489	ORDNANCE & ACCESS NEC	AU 5	AU 5	AU 5						U PT	U PT			AU 5	AU 5							Q	Q	Q	Q
3490	MISC. FAB METAL PROD	AU	AU	AU						M	M			AU	AU							Q	Q	Q	Q
3493	STEEL SPRINGS EXC. WIRE	AU	AU	AU		M	M			U	U			AU	AU			P	P	P		Q	Q	Q	Q
3494	VALVES & PIPE FITTINGS	AU	AU	AU		M	M			M	M			AU	AU							Q	Q	Q	Q
3495	WIRE SPRINGS	AU	AU	AU						U	U			AU 5	AU 5							Q	Q	Q	Q
3496	MISC. FAB WIRE PROD	AU 5	AU 5	AU 5						M	M			AU 5	AU 5							Q	Q	Q	Q
3497	METAL FOIL & LEAF	AU 5	AU 5	AU 5						U PT	U PT			AU	AU							Q	Q	Q	Q
3498	FAB PIPE & FITTINGS	AU	AU	AU		M	M	A		U	U			AU	AU							Q	Q	Q	Q
3499	FAB METAL PROD NEC	AU	AU	AU						U PT	U PT			AU	AU							Q	Q	Q	Q
3500	MACHINERY EXC. ELECTRIC	AU	AU	AU						M	M	M	M	AU	AU			P	P	P		Q	Q	Q	Q
3510	ENGINES & TURBINES	AU	AU	AU						M	M	M		AU	AU							Q	Q	Q	Q
3511	TURBINES & TURBINE GEN. SETS	AU	AU	AU						M	M	M		AU	AU							Q	Q	Q	Q
3519	INTERNAL COMBUST ENGINES NEC	AU	AU	AU		M	M			M	M	M		AU	AU							Q	Q	Q	Q
3520	FARM & GARDEN MACH	AU	AU	AU						M	M			AU	AU							Q	Q	Q	Q
3523	FARM MACH & EQUIP	AU 5	AU 5	AU 5						M	M			AU 5	AU 5			P	P	P		Q	Q	Q	Q
3524	LAWN & GARDEN EQUIP	AU 5	AU 5	AU 5						U	U			AU 5	AU 5							Q	Q	Q	Q
3530	CONST & RELATED MACH	AU	AU	AU						M	M	M		AU	AU							Q	Q	Q	Q
3531	CONST MACH	AU	AU	AU		M				M	M			AU	AU			P	P	P		Q	Q	Q	Q
3532	MINING MACH	AU	AU	AU		M				M	M			AU	AU							Q	Q	Q	Q
3533	OIL FIELD MACH	AU	AU	AU		M	M	A		M	M	M		AU	AU							Q	Q	Q	Q
3534	ELEVATORS & MOVING STAIRWAYS	AU	AU	AU		M	M			U	U			AU	AU							Q	Q	Q	Q
3535	CONVEYORS & CONVEYING EQUIP	AU	AU	AU						M	M			AU	AU							Q	Q	Q	Q
3536	HOISTS CRANES & MONORAILS	AU	AU	AU						U	U			AU	AU							Q	Q	Q	Q
3537	INDUST TRUCKS & TRACTORS	AU	AU	AU						M	M			AU	AU							Q	Q	Q	Q
3540	METALWORKING MACH	AU	AU	AU						M	M	M	M	AU	AU							Q	Q	Q	Q
3541	MACH TOOLS METAL CUTTING	AU	AU	AU						M	M	M	M	AU	AU							Q	Q	Q	Q
3542	MACH TOOLS METAL FORMING	AU	AU	AU		M	M			M	M			AU	AU							Q	Q	Q	Q
3544	SPECIAL DIES TOOLS JIGS	AU	AU	AU						M	M	M		AU	AU			P	P	P		Q	Q	Q	Q
3545	MACH TOOL ACCESS	AU	AU	AU						M	M	M		AU	AU			P	P	P		Q	Q	Q	Q
3546	POWER DRIVEN HAND TOOLS	AU 5	AU 5	AU 5		M				M	M			AU 5	AU 5							Q	Q	Q	Q
3547	ROLLING MILL MACH	AU 5	AU 5	AU 5						U	U			AU 5	AU 5							Q	Q	Q	Q
3549	METALWORKING MACH NEC	AU 5	AU 5	AU 5						U	U			AU 5	AU 5							Q	Q	Q	Q
3550	SPECIAL INDUSTRY MACH	AU	AU	AU						M	M	M	M	AU	AU							Q	Q	Q	Q
3551	FOOD PROD MACH	AU	AU	AU						M	M	M		AU	AU							Q	Q	Q	Q
3552	TEXTILE MACH	AU	AU	AU		M	M			M	M	M		AU	AU			P	P	P		Q	Q	Q	Q
3553	WOODWORKING MACH	AU	AU	AU		M				U	U			AU	AU							Q	Q	Q	Q
3554	PAPER INDUSTRIES MACH	AU	AU	AU						U	U			AU	AU			P	P	P		Q	Q	Q	Q

	INDUSTRIAL CLASSIFICATION	PRODUCTIVITY				PRICES				EARNINGS 11 (INDUSTRY EMPLOYMENT STATISTICS PROGRAM)				TOTAL COMPENSATION				SURVEY PROGRAM: WAGES & SALARIES				(ES202) TOTAL COVERED PAYROLL			
		1978	1972	1958	1947	1978	1972	1958	1947	1978	1972	1958	1947	1978	1972	1958	1947	1978	1972	1958	1947	1978	1972	1958	1947
3561	PUMPS & PUMPING EQUIP	AU 5	AU 5	AU 5						M	M			AU 5	AU 5							Q	Q	Q	Q
3562	BALL & ROLLER BEARINGS	AU	AU	AU						M	M	M	M	AU	AU							Q	Q	Q	Q
3563	AIR & GAS COMPRESSORS	AU 5	AU 5	AU 5						M	M			AU 5	AU 5							Q	Q	Q	Q
3564	BLOWERS & FANS	AU	AU	AU						M	M			AU	AU							Q	Q	Q	Q
3565	INDUST PATTERNS	AU	AU	AU						U	U			AU	AU							Q	Q	Q	Q
3566	SPEED CHANGERS DRIVES & GEAR	AU 5	AU 5	AU 5						M	M			AU 5	AU 5							Q	Q	Q	Q
3567	INDUST FURNACES & OVENS	AU	AU	AU						U	U			AU	AU							Q	Q	Q	Q
3568	POWER TRANSMISSION EQUIP NEC	AU 5	AU 5	AU 5						M	M			AU 5	AU 5							Q	Q	Q	Q
3569	GENERAL INDUST MACH NEC	AU	AU	AU						U	U			AU	AU							Q	Q	Q	Q
3570	OFFICE & COMPUTING MACHS	AU	AU	AU						M	M	M		AU	AU							Q	Q	Q	Q
3572	TYPEWRITERS	AU 5	AU 5	AU 5						U	U			AU 5	AU 5							Q	Q	Q	Q
3573	ELECTRONIC COMPUTING EQUIP	AU 5	AU 5	AU 5						M	M			AU 5	AU 5							Q	Q	Q	Q
3574	CALCULATING & ACCT MACHS	AU 5	AU 5	AU 5						U	U			AU 5	AU 5							Q	Q	Q	Q
3576	SCALES & BALANCES EXC. LAB	AU	AU	AU		M	M	A		U PT	U PT			AU	AU							Q	Q	Q	Q
3579	OFFICE MACHS NEC	AU 5	AU 5	AU 5						U PT	U PT			AU 5	AU 5							Q	Q	Q	Q
3580	REFRIGERATION & SERV MACH	AU	AU	AU						M	M	M		AU	AU							Q	Q	Q	Q
3581	AUTOMATIC MERCHANDISING MACHS	AU	AU	AU						U	U			AU	AU							Q	Q	Q	Q
3582	COMM LAUNDRY EQUIP	AU	AU	AU						U	U			AU	AU							Q	Q	Q	Q
3585	REFRIG & HEAT EQUIP	AU	AU	AU						M	M	M		AU	AU							Q	Q	Q	Q
3586	MEASURING & DISPENSING PUMPS	AU	AU	AU						U PT	U PT			AU	AU							Q	Q	Q	Q
3589	SERV INDUSTRY MACH NEC	AU	AU	AU						U PT	U PT			AU	AU							Q	Q	Q	Q
3590	MISC. MACH EXC. ELEC	AU	AU	AU						M	M			AU	AU							Q	Q	Q	Q
3592	CARBS PISTONS RINGS VALVES	AU 5	AU 5	AU 5		M				M	M			AU 5	AU 5							Q	Q	Q	Q
3599	MACH EXC. ELEC NEC	AU 5	AU 5	AU 5						M	M			AU 5	AU 5			P	P	P		Q	Q	Q	Q
3600	ELECTRIC & ELECTRONIC EQUIP	AU	AU	AU						M	M	M	M	AU	AU							Q	Q	Q	Q
3610	ELECTRIC DISTRIBUTING EQUIP	AU	AU	AU						M	M	M		AU	AU							Q	Q	Q	Q
3612	TRANSFORMERS	AU	AU	AU		M	M			M	M	M		AU	AU							Q	Q	Q	Q
3613	SWITCHGEAR & SWITCHBOARD APP.	AU	AU	AU						M	M	M		AU	AU							Q	Q	Q	Q
3620	ELEC INDUST APPARATUS	AU	AU	AU						M	M	M		AU	AU							Q	Q	Q	Q
3621	MOTORS & GENERATORS	A	A	A						M	M	M		AU	AU							Q	Q	Q	Q
3622	INDUST CONTROLS	AU	AU	AU						M	M	M		AU	AU							Q	Q	Q	Q
3623	WELDING APPARATUS ELECTRIC	AU	AU	AU		M				U	U			AU	AU							Q	Q	Q	Q
3624	CARBON & GRAPHITE PROD	AU	AU	AU						U	U			AU	AU							Q	Q	Q	Q
3629	ELEC INDUST APP. NEC	AU	AU	AU						U	U			AU	AU							Q	Q	Q	Q
3630	HOUSE APPLIANCES	AU	AU	AU						M	M	M		AU	AU							Q	Q	Q	Q
3631	HOUSE COOKING EQUIP	A 5	A 5	A 5		M				U	U			AU 5	AU 5							Q	Q	Q	Q
3632	HOUSE REFRIG & FREEZERS	A 5	A 5	A 5		M				M	M			AU 5	AU 5							Q	Q	Q	Q
3633	HOUSE LAUNDRY EQUIP	A 5	A 5	A 5		M				M	M	M		AU 5	AU 5							Q	Q	Q	Q
3634	ELECTRIC HOUSEWARES & FANS	AU	AU	AU						M	M	M		AU	AU							Q	Q	Q	Q
3635	HOUSE VACUUM CLEANERS	AU	AU	AU		M	M			U PT	U PT			AU	AU							Q	Q	Q	Q
3636	SEWING MACHS	AU	AU	AU		M				U PT	U PT			AU	AU							Q	Q	Q	Q
3639	HOUSE APPLIANCES NEC	A 5	A 5	A 5						U PT	U PT			AU 5	AU 5							Q	Q	Q	Q
3640	ELECTRIC LIGHT & WIRE EQUIP	AU	AU	AU						M	M	M		AU	AU							Q	Q	Q	Q
3641	ELECTRIC LAMPS	A	A	A		M	M			M	M	M		AU	AU							Q	Q	Q	Q
3643	CURR-CARRYING WIRING DEVICE	AU	AU	AU						M	M			AU	AU							Q	Q	Q	Q
3644	NONCURR-CARRY WIRING DEVICE	AU	AU	AU		M				M	M			AU	AU							Q	Q	Q	Q
3645	RESIDENTIAL LIGHT FIXTURES	A 5	A 5	A 5						M	M			AU 5	AU 5							Q	Q	Q	Q
3646	COMM LIGHTING FIXTURES	A 5	A 5	A 5		M				U	U			AU 5	AU 5							Q	Q	Q	Q

Standard Industrial Classification		Labor Productivity				Industrial Prices				Average Hourly Earnings 11 (Industry Employment Statistics Program)				Average Hourly Compensation: Total Compensation				Industry Wage Survey Program: Wages & Salaries				Unemployment Insurance Data (ES202): Total Covered Payroll			
		1978	1972	1958	1947	1978	1972	1958	1947	1978	1972	1958	1947	1978	1972	1958	1947	1978	1972	1958	1947	1978	1972	1958	1947
3647	VEHICULAR LIGHTING EQUIP	A 5	A 5	A 5						U PT	U PT			AU 5	AU 5							Q	Q	Q	Q
3648	LIGHTING EQUIP NEC	A 5	A 5	A 5		M				U PT	U PT			AU 5	AU 5							Q	Q	Q	Q
3650	RADIO & TV RECEIVING EQUIP	AU	AU	AU						M	M	M		AU	AU							Q	Q	Q	Q
3651	RADIO & TV RECEIVING SETS	A	A	A						M	M			AU	AU							Q	Q	Q	Q
3652	PHONOGRAPH RECORDS	AU	AU	AU						U	U			AU	AU							Q	Q	Q	Q
3660	COMMUNICATION EQUIP	AU	AU	AU						M	M	M		AU	AU							Q	Q	Q	Q
3661	TELEPH & TELEGRAPH APPARATUS	AU	AU	AU						M	M	M	M	AU	AU							Q	Q	Q	Q
3662	RADIO & TV COMMUN EQUIP	AU	AU	AU						M	M	M		AU	AU							Q	Q	Q	Q
3670	ELECTRONIC COMPONENT & ACC	AU	AU	AU						M	M	M		AU	AU							Q	Q	Q	Q
3671	ELECTRON TUBE RECEIVING TYPE	AU	AU	AU		M	M			M PT	M PT	M PT		AU	AU							Q	Q	Q	Q
3672	CATHODE RAY TV PICTURE TUBE	AU	AU	AU						M PT	M PT	M PT		AU	AU							Q	Q	Q	Q
3673	ELECTRON TUBE TRANSMITTING	AU	AU	AU						M PT	M PT	M PT		AU	AU							Q	Q	Q	Q
3674	SEMICONDUCT & RELATED DEVICE	AU 5	AU 5	AU 5		M	M			M	M			AU 5	AU 5			P				Q	Q	Q	Q
3675	ELECTRONIC CAPACITORS	AU 5	AU 5	AU 5		M				U	U			AU 5	AU 5							Q	Q	Q	Q
3676	ELECTRONIC RESISTORS	AU 5	AU 5	AU 5		M				U PT	U PT			AU 5	AU 5							Q	Q	Q	Q
3677	ELECTRONIC COIL & TRANSFORM	AU 5	AU 5	AU 5						U	U			AU 5	AU 5							Q	Q	Q	Q
3678	ELECTRONIC CONNECTORS	AU 5	AU 5	AU 5		M				U PT	U PT			AU 5	AU 5							Q	Q	Q	Q
3679	ELECTRONIC COMPONENTS NEC	AU 5	AU 5	AU 5						M	M			AU 5	AU 5							Q	Q	Q	Q
3690	MISC. ELEC EQUIP & SUPPLY	AU	AU	AU						M	M	M		AU	AU							Q	Q	Q	Q
3691	STORAGE BATTERIES	AU	AU	AU						M	M			AU	AU							Q	Q	Q	Q
3692	PRIMARY BATTERIES DRY & WET	AU	AU	AU		M	M	A		U	U			AU	AU							Q	Q	Q	Q
3693	X-RAY APPARATUS & TUBE	AU	AU	AU						U	U			AU	AU							Q	Q	Q	Q
3694	ENGINE ELEC EQUIP	AU	AU	AU						M	M	M	M	AU	AU			P	P	P		Q	Q	Q	Q
3699	ELEC. EQUIP & SUPPLY NEC	AU	AU	AU						U	U			AU	AU							Q	Q	Q	Q
3700	TRANSPORTATION EQUIPMENT	AU	AU	AU						M	M	M	M	AU	AU							Q	Q	Q	Q
3710	MOTOR VEHICLES & EQUIP	A	A	A						M	M	M	M	AU	AU							Q	Q	Q	Q
3711	MOTOR VEHICLES & CAR BODIES	AU	AU	AU		M				M	M	M		AU	AU			P	P	P		Q	Q	Q	Q
3713	TRUCK & BUS BODIES	AU	AU	AU						M	M			AU	AU							Q	Q	Q	Q
3714	MOTOR VEHICLE PTS. & ACCESS	AU	AU	AU						M	M	M		AU	AU			P	P	P		Q	Q	Q	Q
3715	TRUCK TRAILERS	AU	AU	AU						M	M			AU	AU							Q	Q	Q	Q
3720	AIRCRAFT & PTS.	AU	AU	AU						M	M	M	M	AU	AU							Q	Q	Q	Q
3721	AIRCRAFT	AU	AU	AU						M	M	M	M	AU	AU							Q	Q	Q	Q
3724	AIRCRAFT ENGINE & ENGINE PTS.	AU 5	AU 5	AU 5						M	M			AU 5	AU 5							Q	Q	Q	Q
3728	AIRCRAFT EQUIP NEC	AU 5	AU 5	AU 5						M	M			AU 5	AU 5							Q	Q	Q	Q
3730	SHIP & BOAT BUILD & REPAIR	AU	AU	AU						M	M	M	M	AU	AU							Q	Q	Q	Q
3731	SHIP BUILD & REPAIR	AU	AU	AU						M	M	M	M	AU	AU			P				Q	Q	Q	Q
3732	BOAT BUILD & REPAIR	AU	AU	AU						M	M	M	M	AU	AU							Q	Q	Q	Q
3740	RAILROAD EQUIP	AU	AU	AU						M	M	M	M	AU	AU							Q	Q	Q	Q
3743	RAILROAD EQUIP	AU	AU	AU						M	M	M	M	AU	AU							Q	Q	Q	Q
3750	MOTORCYCLES BICYCLES & PTS.	AU	AU	AU						U	U			AU	AU							Q	Q	Q	Q
3751	MOTORCYCLES BICYCLES & PTS.	AU	AU	AU						U	U			AU	AU							Q	Q	Q	Q
3760	GUIDED MISS. SPACE VEH. PTS.	AU	AU	AU						M	M			AU	AU							Q	Q	Q	Q
3761	GUIDED MISS. & SPACE VEH.	AU	AU	AU						M	M			AU	AU							Q	Q	Q	Q
3764	SPACE PROPULSION UNITS	AU 5	AU 5	AU 5						U PT	U PT			AU 5	AU 5							Q	Q	Q	Q
3769	SPACE VEHICLE EQUIP NEC	AU 5	AU 5	AU 5						U PT	U PT			AU 5	AU 5							Q	Q	Q	Q

Standard Industrial Classification		Labor Productivity 1978	Labor Productivity 1972	Labor Productivity 1958	Labor Productivity 1947	Industrial Prices 1978	Industrial Prices 1972	Industrial Prices 1958	Industrial Prices 1947	Average Hourly Earnings 11 (Industry Employment Statistics Program) 1978	1972	1958	1947	Compensation: Total Compensation 1978	1972	1958	1947	Industry Wage Survey Program: Wages & Salaries 1978	1972	1958	1947	Insurance Data (ES202): Total Covered Payroll 1978	1972	1958	1947
3799	TRANS EQUIP NEC	AU	AU	AU						U PT	U PT			AU	AU							Q	Q	Q	Q
3800	INSTRUMENTS & RELATED PROD	AU	AU	AU						M	M	M	M	AU	AU							Q	Q	Q	Q
3810	ENGINEER & SCIEN INSTRUM	AU	AU	AU						M	M			AU	AU							Q	Q	Q	Q
3811	ENGINEER & SCIEN INSTRUM	AU	AU	AU						M	M			AU	AU							Q	Q	Q	Q
3820	MEASURE & CONTROL DEVICE	AU	AU	AU						M	M	M		AU	AU							Q	Q	Q	Q
3822	ENVIRONMENTAL CONTROLS	AU	AU	AU						M	M	M		AU	AU							Q	Q	Q	Q
3823	PROCESS CONTROL INSTRUM	AU 5	AU 5	AU 5						M	M			AU 5	AU 5							Q	Q	Q	Q
3824	FLUID METERS & COUNT DEVICE	AU 5	AU 5	AU 5						U	U			AU 5	AU 5							Q	Q	Q	Q
3825	INSTRUM TO MEASURE ELEC	AU	AU	AU						M	M			AU	AU							Q	Q	Q	Q
3829	MEASURE & CONTROL DEVICE NEC	AU 5	AU 5	AU 5						U	U			AU 5	AU 5							Q	Q	Q	Q
3830	OPTICAL INSTRUM & LENSES	AU	AU	AU						M	M			AU	AU							Q	Q	Q	Q
3832	OPTICAL INSTRUM & LENSES	AU	AU	AU						M	M			AU	AU							Q	Q	Q	Q
3840	MEDICAL INSTRUM & SUPPLY	AU	AU	AU						M	M	M		AU	AU							Q	Q	Q	Q
3841	SURGICAL & MEDICAL INSTRUM	AU	AU	AU						M	M			AU	AU							Q	Q	Q	Q
3842	SURGICAL APPLIANCE & SUPPLY	AU	AU	AU						M	M			AU	AU							Q	Q	Q	Q
3843	DENTAL EQUIP & SUPPLY	AU	AU	AU						U	U			AU	AU							Q	Q	Q	Q
3850	OPHTHALMIC GOOD	AU	AU	AU						M	M	M		AU	AU							Q	Q	Q	Q
3851	OPHTHALMIC GOOD	AU	AU	AU						M	M	M		AU	AU							Q	Q	Q	Q
3860	PHOTO EQUIP & SUPPLY	AU	AU	AU						M	M	M	M	AU	AU							Q	Q	Q	Q
3861	PHOTO EQUIP & SUPPLY	AU	AU	AU						M	M	M	M	AU	AU							Q	Q	Q	Q
3870	WATCHES CLOCKS & WATCHCASES	AU	AU	AU						M	M	M	M	AU	AU							Q	Q	Q	Q
3873	WATCHES CLOCKS & WATCHCASES	AU	AU	AU						M	M	M	M	AU	AU							Q	Q	Q	Q
3900	MISC MANUFACTURING INDUSTRY	AU	AU	AU						M	M	M	M	AU	AU							Q	Q	Q	Q
3910	JEWELRY SILVERWARE & PLATED	AU	AU	AU						M	M	M	M	AU	AU							Q	Q	Q	Q
3911	JEWELRY PRECIOUS METAL	AU	AU	AU						M	M			AU	AU							Q	Q	Q	Q
3914	SILVERWARE & PLATED WARE	AU	AU	AU						U	U			AU	AU							Q	Q	Q	Q
3915	JEWELERS' MATER & LAPIDARY	AU	AU	AU						U	U			AU	AU							Q	Q	Q	Q
3930	MUSICAL INSTRUM	AU	AU	AU						M	M	M		AU	AU							Q	Q	Q	Q
3931	MUSICAL INSTRUM	AU	AU	AU						M	M			AU	AU							Q	Q	Q	Q
3940	TOYS & SPORT GOOD	AU	AU	AU						M	M	M	M	AU	AU							Q	Q	Q	Q
3942	DOLLS	AU	AU	AU		M				M PT	M PT	M PT		AU	AU							Q	Q	Q	Q
3944	GAMES TOYS & CHILD VEHICLES	AU	AU	AU		M	M			M PT	M PT	M PT		AU	AU							Q	Q	Q	Q
3949	SPORT & ATHLETIC GOOD NEC	AU	AU	AU						M	M	M		AU	AU							Q	Q	Q	Q
3950	PEN PENCIL OFF & ART SUPPLY	AU	AU	AU						M	M	M		AU	AU							Q	Q	Q	Q
3951	PENS & MECHANICAL PENCILS	AU	AU	AU						U	U			AU	AU							Q	Q	Q	Q
3952	LEAD PENCILS & ART GOOD	AU	AU	AU						U	U			AU	AU							Q	Q	Q	Q
3953	MARKING DEVICES	AU	AU	AU						U PT	U PT			AU	AU							Q	Q	Q	Q
3955	CARBON PAPER & INKED RIBBON	AU	AU	AU		M				U PT	U PT			AU	AU							Q	Q	Q	Q
3960	COSTUME JEWELRY & NOTIONS	AU	AU	AU						M	M	M	M	AU	AU							Q	Q	Q	Q
3961	COSTUME JEWELRY	AU	AU	AU						M	M			AU	AU							Q	Q	Q	Q
3962	ARTIFICIAL FLOWERS	AU	AU	AU						U PT	U PT			AU	AU							Q	Q	Q	Q
3963	BUTTONS	AU	AU	AU						U PT	U PT			AU	AU							Q	Q	Q	Q
3964	NEEDLES PINS & FASTENERS	AU	AU	AU						U	U			AU	AU							Q	Q	Q	Q
3990	MISC MANUFACTURES	AU	AU	AU						M	M			AU	AU							Q	Q	Q	Q
3991	BROOMS & BRUSHES	AU	AU	AU						U	U			AU	AU							Q	Q	Q	Q
3993	SIGNS & ADVERTISING DISPLAY	AU	AU	AU						M	M			AU	AU							Q	Q	Q	Q

Standard Industrial Classification		Labor Productivity				Industrial Prices				Average Hourly Earnings 11 (Industry Employment Statistics Program)				Average Hourly Compensation: Total Compensation				Industry Wage Survey Program: Wages & Salaries				Unemployment Insurance Data (ES202): Total Covered Payroll			
		1978	1972	1958	1947	1978	1972	1958	1947	1978	1972	1958	1947	1978	1972	1958	1947	1978	1972	1958	1947	1978	1972	1958	1947
3995	BURIAL CASKETS	AU	AU	AU		M				U	U			AU	AU							Q	Q	Q	Q
3996	HARD SURFACE FLOOR COVERING	AU	AU	AU						U PT	U PT			AU	AU							Q	Q	Q	Q
3999	MANUFACT. INDUSTRIES NEC	AU	AU	AU						U PT	U PT			AU	AU							Q	Q	Q	Q
	E. TRANS & PUBLIC UTILITIES	8	8	8	8					M	M			8	8							Q	Q	Q	Q
4000	RAILROAD TRANSPORTATION	8	8	8	8					U	U			8	8										
4010	RAILROADS	A	A	A	A	PART																			
4011	RAILROADS LINE-HAUL OPERATE					PART	M			M	M	M	M												
4013	SWITCHING & TERMINAL SERV																								
4040	RAILWAY EXPRESS SERV					NA																			
4041	RAILWAY EXPRESS SERV					NA																			
4100	LOCAL & INTERURBAN TRANSIT	8	8	8	8					M	M			8	8							Q	Q	Q	Q
4110	LOCAL & SUBURBAN TRANS									M	M											Q	Q	Q	Q
4111	LOCAL & SUBURBAN TRANSIT																	A	A	A	A	Q	Q	Q	Q
4119	LOCAL PASSENGER TRANS NEC																					Q	Q	Q	Q
4120	TAXICABS									U	U											Q	Q	Q	Q
4121	TAXICABS																					Q	Q	Q	Q
4130	INTERCITY HIGHWAY TRANS									M	M											Q	Q	Q	Q
4131	INTERCITY HIGHWAY TRANS																					Q	Q	Q	Q
4140	TRANS CHARTER SERV									U PT	U PT											Q	Q	Q	Q
4141	LOCAL PASSENGER CHARTER SERV																					Q	Q	Q	Q
4142	CHARTER SERV EXC. LOCAL																					Q	Q	Q	Q
4150	SCHOOL BUSES									U	U											Q	Q	Q	Q
4151	SCHOOL BUSES																					Q	Q	Q	Q
4170	BUS TERMINAL & SERV FACILITY									U PT	U PT											Q	Q	Q	Q
4171	BUS TERMINAL FACILITIES																					Q	Q	Q	Q
4172	BUS SERV FACILITIES																					Q	Q	Q	Q
4200	TRUCKING & WAREHOUSING	8	8	8	8					M	M	M		8	8							Q	Q	Q	Q
4210	TRUCKING LOCAL & LONG DIST									M PT	M PT											Q	Q	Q	Q
4212	LOCAL TRUCKING WITHOUT STOR																	A	A	A	A				
4213	TRUCKING EXC. LOCAL	A 9	A 9	A 9										9	9										
4214	LOCAL TRUCKING & STOR																	A	A	A	A				
4220	PUBLIC WAREHOUSING									M	M	M										Q	Q	Q	Q
4221	FARM PROD WAREHOUSING & STOR																					Q	Q	Q	Q
4222	REFRIG WAREHOUSING																					Q	Q	Q	Q
4224	HOUSE GOOD WAREHOUSING																					Q	Q	Q	Q
4225	GENERAL WAREHOUSING & STOR																					Q	Q	Q	Q
4226	SPEC WAREHOUSING & STOR NEC																					Q	Q	Q	Q
4230	TRUCKING TERMINAL FACILITY									M PT	M PT											Q	Q	Q	Q
4231	TRUCKING TERMINAL FACILITY																					Q	Q	Q	Q

STANDARD INDUSTRIAL CLASSIFICATION		LABOR PRODUCTIVITY				PRICES				EARNINGS 11 (INDUSTRY EMPLOYMENT STATISTICS PROGRAM)				TOTAL COMPENSATION				SURVEY PROGRAM WAGES & SALARIES				(ES202) TOTAL COVERED PAYROLL			
		1978	1972	1958	1947	1978	1972	1958	1947	1978	1972	1958	1947	1978	1972	1958	1947	1978	1972	1958	1947	1978	1972	1958	1947
4311	U.S. POSTAL SERV																					Q	Q	Q	Q
4400	WATER TRANSPORTATION	8	8	8	8									8	8							Q	Q	Q	Q
4410	DEEP SEA FOREIGN TRANS									U PT	U PT											Q	Q	Q	Q
4411	DEEP SEA FOREIGN TRANS																					Q	Q	Q	Q
4420	DEEP SEA DOMESTIC TRANS									U PT	U PT											Q	Q	Q	Q
4421	NONCONTIGUOUS AREA TRANS																					Q	Q	Q	Q
4422	COASTWISE TRANS																					Q	Q	Q	Q
4423	INTERCOASTAL TRANS																					Q	Q	Q	Q
4430	GREAT LAKES TRANS									U PT	U PT											Q	Q	Q	Q
4431	GREAT LAKES TRANS																					Q	Q	Q	Q
4440	TRANS ON RIVERS & CANALS									U PT	U PT											Q	Q	Q	Q
4441	TRANS ON RIVERS & CANALS																					Q	Q	Q	Q
4450	LOCAL WATER TRANS									U PT	U PT											Q	Q	Q	Q
4452	FERRIES																					Q	Q	Q	Q
4453	LIGHTERAGE																					Q	Q	Q	Q
4454	TOWING & TUGBOAT SERV																					Q	Q	Q	Q
4459	LOCAL WATER TRANS NEC																					Q	Q	Q	Q
4460	WATER TRANS SERV									U	U											Q	Q	Q	Q
4463	MARINE CARGO HANDLING																					Q	Q	Q	Q
4464	CANAL OPERATION																					Q	Q	Q	Q
4469	WATER TRANS SERV NEC																					Q	Q	Q	Q
4500	TRANSPORTATION BY AIR	8	8	8						U	U			8	8							Q	Q	Q	Q
4510	CERTIFICATED AIR TRANS	A	A	A	A													P	P			Q	Q	Q	Q
4511	CERTIFICATED AIR TRANS	A	A	A	A													P	P			Q	Q	Q	Q
4520	NONCERTIFICATED AIR TRANS																					Q	Q	Q	Q
4521	NONCERTIFICATED AIR TRANS																					Q	Q	Q	Q
4580	AIR TRANS SERV																					Q	Q	Q	Q
4582	AIRPORTS & FLYING FIELDS																					Q	Q	Q	Q
4583	AIRPORT TERMINAL SERV																					Q	Q	Q	Q
4600	PIPE LINES EXC. NATURAL GAS	8	8	8	8					M	M	M		8	8							Q	Q	Q	Q
4610	PIPE LINES EXC. NATURAL GAS																					Q	Q	Q	Q
4612	CRUDE PETRO PIPE LINES	A 5	A 5	A 5	A 5									5	5							Q	Q	Q	Q
4613	REFINED PETRO PIPE LINES	A 5	A 5	A 5	A 5									5	5							Q	Q	Q	Q
4619	PIPE LINES NEC																					Q	Q	Q	Q
4700	TRANSPORTATION SERVICES	8	8	8	8									8	8							Q	Q	Q	Q
4710	FREIGHT FORWARDING									U	U											Q	Q	Q	Q
4712	FREIGHT FORWARDING																					Q	Q	Q	Q
4720	ARRANGEMENT OF TRANS									U	U											Q	Q	Q	Q
4722	PASSENGER TRANS ARRANGEMENT																					Q	Q	Q	Q
4723	FREIGHT TRANS ARRANGEMENT																					Q	Q	Q	Q
4740	RENT OF RAILROAD CARS									U PT	U PT											Q	Q	Q	Q
4742	RAILROAD CAR RENT WITH SERV																					Q	Q	Q	Q

STANDARD INDUSTRIAL CLASSIFICATION		LABOR PRODUCTIVITY				INDUSTRIAL PRICES				AVERAGE HOURLY EARNINGS 11 (INDUSTRY EMPLOYMENT STATISTICS PROGRAM)				AVERAGE HOURLY COMPENSATION: TOTAL COMPENSATION				INDUSTRY WAGE SURVEY PROGRAM: WAGES & SALARIES				UNEMPLOYMENT INSURANCE DATA (ES202): TOTAL COVERED PAYROLL			
		1978	1972	1958	1947	1978	1972	1958	1947	1978	1972	1958	1947	1978	1972	1958	1947	1978	1972	1958	1947	1978	1972	1958	1947
4743	RAILROAD CAR RENT W/O SERV																					Q	Q	Q	Q
4780	MISC TRANS SERV									U PT	U PT											Q	Q	Q	Q
4782	INSPECTION & WEIGHING SERV																					Q	Q	Q	Q
4783	PACKING & CRATING																					Q	Q	Q	Q
4784	FIXED FACIL FOR VEHICLE NEC																					Q	Q	Q	Q
4789	TRANS SERV NEC																					Q	Q	Q	Q
4800	COMMUNICATION	AU	AU	AU	AU					M	M	M		AU	AU							Q	Q	Q	Q
4810	TELEPH COMMUN	A	A	A						M	M	M	M					A	A	A	A	Q	Q	Q	Q
4811	TELEPH COMMUN	A	A	A														A	A	A	A	Q	Q	Q	Q
4820	TELEGRAPH COMMUN									U	U							A	A	A	A	Q	Q	Q	Q
4821	TELEGRAPH COMMUN																	A	A	A	A	Q	Q	Q	Q
4830	RADIO & TV BROADCASTING									M	M	M										Q	Q	Q	Q
4832	RADIO BROADCASTING																					Q	Q	Q	Q
4833	TV BROADCASTING																					Q	Q	Q	Q
4890	COMMUN SERV NEC									U	U											Q	Q	Q	Q
4899	COMMUN SERV NEC																					Q	Q	Q	Q
4900	ELECTRIC GAS & SANITARY SERV	AU	AU	AU	AU					M	M	M		AU	A							Q	Q	Q	Q
4910	ELECTRIC SERV	A 5	A 5	A 5	A 5					M	M	M	M	5	5			P	P	P		Q	Q	Q	Q
4911	ELECTRIC SERV																	P	P	P		Q	Q	Q	Q
4920	GAS PROD & DISTRIB	A 5	A 5	A 5	A 5					M	M	M		5	5			P	P	P		Q	Q	Q	Q
4922	NATURAL GAS TRANSMISSION																	P	P	P		Q	Q	Q	Q
4923	GAS TRANSMISSION & DISTRIB																	P	P	P		Q	Q	Q	Q
4924	NATURAL GAS DISTRIB																	P	P	P		Q	Q	Q	Q
4925	GAS PROD &/OR DISTRIB																	P	P	P		Q	Q	Q	Q
4930	COMBINATION UTILITY SERV	A 5	A 5	A 5	A 5					M	M	M		5	5							Q	Q	Q	Q
4931	ELEC & OTHER SERV COMBINED																	P	P	P		Q	Q	Q	Q
4932	GAS & OTHER SERV COMBINED																	P	P	P		Q	Q	Q	Q
4939	COMBINATION UTILITY SERV NEC																					Q	Q	Q	Q
4940	WATER SUPPLY									U	U											Q	Q	Q	Q
4941	WATER SUPPLY																					Q	Q	Q	Q
4950	SANITARY SERV									M	M											Q	Q	Q	Q
4952	SEWERAGE SYSTEMS																					Q	Q	Q	Q
4953	REFUSE SYSTEMS																					Q	Q	Q	Q
4959	SANITARY SERV NEC																					Q	Q	Q	Q
4960	STEAM SUPPLY									U PT	U PT											Q	Q	Q	Q
4961	STEAM SUPPLY																					Q	Q	Q	Q
4970	IRRIGATION SYSTEMS									U PT	U PT											Q	Q	Q	Q
4971	IRRIGATION SYSTEMS																					Q	Q	Q	Q
	F. WHOLESALE TRADE	AU	AU	AU	AU					M	M	M	M	AU	A							Q	Q	Q	Q
5000	WHOLESALE TRADE-DURABLE GOOD									M	M											Q	Q	Q	Q
5010	MOTOR VEHICLES & AUTO EQUIP									M	M	M										Q	Q	Q	Q

STANDARD INDUSTRIAL CLASSIFICATION		LABOR PRODUCTIVITY				INDUSTRIAL PRICES				AVERAGE HOURLY EARNINGS 11 (INDUSTRY EMPLOYMENT STATISTICS PROGRAM)				COMPENSATION: TOTAL COMPENSATION				INDUSTRY WAGE SURVEY PROGRAM: WAGES & SALARIES				INSURANCE DATA (ES202): TOTAL COVERED PAYROLL			
		1978	1972	1958	1947	1978	1972	1958	1947	1978	1972	1958	1947	1978	1972	1958	1947	1978	1972	1958	1947	1978	1972	1958	1947
5014	TIRES & TUBE																					Q	Q	Q	Q
5020	FURN & HOME FURNISH									M	M											Q	Q	Q	Q
5021	FURN																					Q	Q	Q	Q
5023	HOME FURNISH																					Q	Q	Q	Q
5030	LUMBER & CONST MATER									M	M											Q	Q	Q	Q
5031	LUMBER PLYWOOD & MILLWORK																					Q	Q	Q	Q
5039	CONST MATER NEC																					Q	Q	Q	Q
5040	SPORT GOOD TOYS & HOBBY GOOD									M	M											Q	Q	Q	Q
5041	SPORT & REC GOOD																					Q	Q	Q	Q
5042	TOYS & HOBBY GOOD & SUPPLY																					Q	Q	Q	Q
5043	PHOTO EQUIP & SUPPLY																					Q	Q	Q	Q
5050	METALS & MINERALS EXC. PETRO									M	M											Q	Q	Q	Q
5051	METALS SERV CENTERS & OFF																					Q	Q	Q	Q
5052	COAL & OTHER MINERALS & ORES																					Q	Q	Q	Q
5060	ELEC GOOD									M	M	M										Q	Q	Q	Q
5063	ELEC APPARATUS & EQUIP																					Q	Q	Q	Q
5064	ELEC APPLIANCES TV & RADIOS																					Q	Q	Q	Q
5065	ELECTRONIC PTS. & EQUIP																					Q	Q	Q	Q
5070	HARDWARE PLUMB. & HEAT EQUIP									M	M											Q	Q	Q	Q
5072	HARDWARE																					Q	Q	Q	Q
5074	PLUMBING & HYDRO HEAT SUPPLY																					Q	Q	Q	Q
5075	WARM AIR HEAT & AIR COND																					Q	Q	Q	Q
5078	REFRIGERATION EQUIP & SUPPLY																					Q	Q	Q	Q
5080	MACH EQUIP & SUPPLY									M	M											Q	Q	Q	Q
5081	COMM MACHS & EQUIP																					Q	Q	Q	Q
5082	CONST & MINING MACH																					Q	Q	Q	Q
5083	FARM MACH & EQUIP																					Q	Q	Q	Q
5084	INDUST MACH & EQUIP																					Q	Q	Q	Q
5085	INDUST SUPPLY																					Q	Q	Q	Q
5086	PROFESSIONAL EQUIP & SUPPLY																					Q	Q	Q	Q
5087	SERV ESTABLISHMENT EQUIP																					Q	Q	Q	Q
5088	TRANS EQUIP & SUPPLY																					Q	Q	Q	Q
5090	MISC DURABLE GOOD									M	M											Q	Q	Q	Q
5093	SCRAP & WASTE MATER																					Q	Q	Q	Q
5094	JEWELRY WATCHES & PRECIOUS																					Q	Q	Q	Q
5099	DURABLE GOOD NEC																								
5100	WHOLESALE TRADE-NONDUR. GOOD									M	M											Q	Q	Q	Q
5110	PAPER & PAPER PROD									M	M											Q	Q	Q	Q
5111	PRINTING & WRITING PAPER																					Q	Q	Q	Q
5112	STATIONERY SUPPLY																					Q	Q	Q	Q
5113	INDUST & PERSONAL SERV PAPER																					Q	Q	Q	Q
5120	DRUGS PROPRI & SUNDRIES									M	M											Q	Q	Q	Q
5122	DRUGS PROPRI & SUNDRIES																					Q	Q	Q	Q
5130	APPAREL PIECE GOOD & NOTIONS									M	M	M										Q	Q	Q	Q
5133	PIECE GOOD																								
5134	NOTIONS & OTHER DRY GOOD																								
5136	MEN CLOTHING & FURNISH																								
5137	WOMEN & CHILD CLOTHING																								

STANDARD INDUSTRIAL CLASSIFICATION		LABOR PRODUCTIVITY				INDUSTRIAL PRICES				AVERAGE HOURLY EARNINGS 11 (INDUSTRY EMPLOYMENT STATISTICS PROGRAM)				AVERAGE HOURLY COMPENSATION TOTAL COMPENSATION				INDUSTRY WAGE SURVEY PROGRAM WAGES & SALARIES				UNEMPLOYMENT INSURANCE DATA (ES202) TOTAL COVERED PAYROLL			
		1978	1972	1958	1947	1978	1972	1958	1947	1978	1972	1958	1947	1978	1972	1958	1947	1978	1972	1958	1947	1978	1972	1958	1947
5139	FOOTWEAR																								
5140	GROCERIES & RELATED PROD									M	M	M										Q	Q	Q	Q
5141	GROCERIES GENERAL LINE																					Q	Q	Q	Q
5142	FROZEN FOODS																					Q	Q	Q	Q
5143	DAIRY PROD																					Q	Q	Q	Q
5144	POULTRY & POULTRY PROD																					Q	Q	Q	Q
5145	CONFECTIONERY																					Q	Q	Q	Q
5146	FISH & SEAFOODS																					Q	Q	Q	Q
5147	MEATS & MEAT PROD																					Q	Q	Q	Q
5148	FRESH FRUITS & VEG																					Q	Q	Q	Q
5149	GROCERY & RELATED PROD NEC																					Q	Q	Q	Q
5150	FARM-PROD RAW MATER									U	U											Q	Q	Q	Q
5152	COTTON																					Q	Q	Q	Q
5153	GRAIN																					Q	Q	Q	Q
5154	LIVESTOCK																					Q	Q	Q	Q
5159	FARM-PROD RAW MATER NEC																					Q	Q	Q	Q
5160	CHEM & ALLIED PROD									M	M											Q	Q	Q	Q
5161	CHEM & ALLIED PROD																					Q	Q	Q	Q
5170	PETRO & PETRO PROD									M	M											Q	Q	Q	Q
5171	PETRO BULK STAT. & TERMINAL																					Q	Q	Q	Q
5172	PETRO PROD NEC																					Q	Q	Q	Q
5180	BEER WINE & DISTILLED BEV									M	M											Q	Q	Q	Q
5181	BEER & ALE																					Q	Q	Q	Q
5182	WINES & DISTILLED BEV																					Q	Q	Q	Q
5190	MISC NONDURABLE GOOD									M	M											Q	Q	Q	Q
5191	FARM SUPPLY																					Q	Q	Q	Q
5194	TOBACCO & TOBACCO PROD																					Q	Q	Q	Q
5198	PAINTS VARNISHES & SUPPLY																					Q	Q	Q	Q
5199	NONDURABLE GOOD NEC																					Q	Q	Q	Q
	G. RETAIL TRADE	AU	AU	AU	AU					M	M	M		AU	A							Q	Q	Q	Q
5200	BUILD MATERIAL & GARDEN SUPPLY									M	M											Q	Q	Q	Q
5210	LUMBER & OTHER BUILD MATER									M	M											Q	Q	Q	Q
5211	LUMBER & OTHER BUILD MATER																					Q	Q	Q	Q
5230	PAINT GLASS & WALLPAPER STORE									U	U											Q	Q	Q	Q
5231	PAINT GLASS & WALLPAPER STORE																					Q	Q	Q	Q
5250	HARDWARE STORE									M	M											Q	Q	Q	Q
5251	HARDWARE STORE																					Q	Q	Q	Q
5260	RETAIL NURSERY & GARDEN STORE									U	U											Q	Q	Q	Q
5261	RETAIL NURSERY & GARDEN STORE																					Q	Q	Q	Q
5270	MOBILE HOME DEALER									U	U											Q	Q	Q	Q
5271	MOBILE HOME DEALER																					Q	Q	Q	Q
5300	GENERAL MERCHANDISE STORES									M	M											Q	Q	Q	Q
5310	DEPARTMENT STORE									M	M	M						R	R			Q	Q	Q	Q

STANDARD INDUSTRIAL CLASSIFICATION		LABOR PRODUCTIVITY				INDUSTRIAL PRICES				AVERAGE HOURLY EARNINGS 11 (INDUSTRY EMPLOYMENT STATISTICS PROGRAM)				AVERAGE HOURLY COMPENSATION: TOTAL COMPENSATION				INDUSTRY WAGE SURVEY PROGRAM: WAGES & SALARIES				INSURANCE DATA (ES202): TOTAL COVERED PAYROLL			
		1978	1972	1958	1947	1978	1972	1958	1947	1978	1972	1958	1947	1978	1972	1958	1947	1978	1972	1958	1947	1978	1972	1958	1947
5331	VARIETY STORE																					Q	Q	Q	Q
5390	MISC. GENERAL MERCH STORE									M	M											Q	Q	Q	Q
5399	MISC. GENERAL MERCH STORE																					Q	Q	Q	Q
5400	FOOD STORES	A	A	A						M	M	M										Q	Q	Q	Q
5410	GROCERY STORE									M	M							P	P			Q	Q	Q	Q
5411	GROCERY STORE																	P	P			Q	Q	Q	Q
5420	MEAT MRKTS & FREEZER PROVIS									U	U											Q	Q	Q	Q
5422	FREEZER & LOCKER MEAT PROVIS																					Q	Q	Q	Q
5423	MEAT & FISH (SEAFOOD) MRKTS																					Q	Q	Q	Q
5430	FRUIT STORE & VEG MRKTS									U PT	U PT											Q	Q	Q	Q
5431	FRUIT STORE & VEG MRKTS																					Q	Q	Q	Q
5440	CANDY NUT & CONFEC STORE									U PT	U PT											Q	Q	Q	Q
5441	CANDY NUT & CONFEC STORE																					Q	Q	Q	Q
5450	DAIRY PROD STORE									U PT	U PT											Q	Q	Q	Q
5451	DAIRY PROD STORE																					Q	Q	Q	Q
5460	RETAIL BAKERY									M	M											Q	Q	Q	Q
5462	RETAIL BAKERY-BAKING & SELL																					Q	Q	Q	Q
5463	RETAIL BAKERY-SELLING ONLY																					Q	Q	Q	Q
5490	MISC FOOD STORE									U PT	U PT											Q	Q	Q	Q
5499	MISC FOOD STORE																					Q	Q	Q	Q
5500	AUTO DEALER & SERV STATIONS									M	M											Q	Q	Q	Q
5510	NEW & USED CAR DEALER	A	A	A						M PT	M PT	M PT						P	P	P		Q	Q	Q	Q
5511	NEW & USED CAR DEALER	A	A	A														P	P	P		Q	Q	Q	Q
5520	USED CAR DEALER									M PT	M PT	M PT										Q	Q	Q	Q
5521	USED CAR DEALER																					Q	Q	Q	Q
5530	AUTO & HOME SUPPLY STORE									M	M											Q	Q	Q	Q
5531	AUTO & HOME SUPPLY STORE																					Q	Q	Q	Q
5540	GASOLINE SERV STATIONS	A	A	A						M	M											Q	Q	Q	Q
5541	GASOLINE SERV STATIONS	A	A	A																		Q	Q	Q	Q
5550	BOAT DEALER									U PT	U PT											Q	Q	Q	Q
5551	BOAT DEALER																					Q	Q	Q	Q
5560	REC & UTILITY TRAILER DEALER									U PT	U PT											Q	Q	Q	Q
5561	REC & UTILITY TRAILER DEALER																					Q	Q	Q	Q
5570	MOTORCYCLE DEALER									U PT	U PT											Q	Q	Q	Q
5571	MOTORCYCLE DEALER																					Q	Q	Q	Q
5590	AUTO DEALER NEC									U PT	U PT											Q	Q	Q	Q
5599	AUTO DEALER NEC																					Q	Q	Q	Q
5600	APPAREL & ACCESSORY STORE									M	M	M	M									Q	Q	Q	Q
5610	MEN & BOY CLOTHING & FURNISH									M	M	M										Q	Q	Q	Q
5611	MEN & BOY CLOTHING & FURNISH																					Q	Q	Q	Q
5620	WOMEN READY-TO-WEAR STORE									M	M	M										Q	Q	Q	Q
5621	WOMEN READY-TO-WEAR STORE																					Q	Q	Q	Q
5630	WOMEN ACCESS & SPEC STORE									U	U											Q	Q	Q	Q
5631	WOMEN ACCESS & SPEC STORE																					Q	Q	Q	Q

STANDARD INDUSTRIAL CLASSIFICATION		LABOR PRODUCTIVITY				INDUSTRIAL PRICES				AVERAGE HOURLY EARNINGS 11 (INDUSTRY EMPLOYMENT STATISTICS PROGRAM)				AVERAGE HOURLY COMPENSATION: TOTAL COMPENSATION				INDUSTRY WAGE SURVEY PROGRAM: WAGES & SALARIES				UNEMPLOYMENT INSURANCE DATA (ES202): TOTAL COVERED PAYROLL			
		1978	1972	1958	1947	1978	1972	1958	1947	1978	1972	1958	1947	1978	1972	1958	1947	1978	1972	1958	1947	1978	1972	1958	1947
5640	CHILD & INFANT WEAR STORE									U	U											Q	Q	Q	Q
5641	CHILD & INFANT WEAR STORE																					Q	Q	Q	Q
5650	FAMILY CLOTHING STORE									M	M	M										Q	Q	Q	Q
5651	FAMILY CLOTHING STORE																					Q	Q	Q	Q
5660	SHOE STORE									M	M	M										Q	Q	Q	Q
5661	SHOE STORE																					Q	Q	Q	Q
5680	FURRIERS & FUR SHOP									U PT	U PT											Q	Q	Q	Q
5681	FURRIERS & FUR SHOP																					Q	Q	Q	Q
5690	MISC APPAREL & ACCESS									U PT	U PT											Q	Q	Q	Q
5699	MISC APPAREL & ACCESS																					Q	Q	Q	Q
5700	FURNITURE & HOME FURNISH STORE									M	M	M										Q	Q	Q	Q
5710	FURN & HOME FURNISH STORE									M	M	M										Q	Q	Q	Q
5712	FURN STORE																					Q	Q	Q	Q
5713	FLOOR COVERING STORE																					Q	Q	Q	Q
5714	DRAPERY & UPHOL STORE																					Q	Q	Q	Q
5719	MISC. HOME FURNISH STORE																					Q	Q	Q	Q
5720	HOUSE APPLIANCE STORE									M	M											Q	Q	Q	Q
5722	HOUSE APPLIANCE STORE																					Q	Q	Q	Q
5730	RADIO TV & MUSIC STORE									M	M											Q	Q	Q	Q
5732	RADIO & TV STORE																					Q	Q	Q	Q
5733	MUSIC STORE																					Q	Q	Q	Q
5800	EATING & DRINKING PLACES	A	A	A						M	M											Q	Q	Q	Q
5810	EATING & DRINKING PLACES																		P			Q	Q	Q	Q
5812	EATING PLACES																		P						
5813	DRINKING PLACES																		P						
5900	MISC RETAIL									M	M											Q	Q	Q	Q
5910	DRUG STORE & PROPRI STORE									M	M	M										Q	Q	Q	Q
5912	DRUG STORE & PROPRI STORE									U	U											Q	Q	Q	Q
5920	LIQUOR STORE																					Q	Q	Q	Q
5921	LIQUOR STORE																					Q	Q	Q	Q
5930	USED MERCHANDISE STORE									U	U											Q	Q	Q	Q
5931	USED MERCHANDISE STORE																					Q	Q	Q	Q
5940	MISC SHOPPING GOOD STORE									M	M											Q	Q	Q	Q
5941	SPORT GOOD & BICYCLE SHOP																					Q	Q	Q	Q
5942	BOOK STORE																					Q	Q	Q	Q
5943	STATIONERY STORE																					Q	Q	Q	Q
5944	JEWELRY STORE																					Q	Q	Q	Q
5945	HOBBY TOY & GAME SHOP																					Q	Q	Q	Q
5946	CAMERA & PHOTO SUPPLY STORE																					Q	Q	Q	Q
5947	GIFT NOVELTY & SOUVENIR SHOP																					Q	Q	Q	Q
5948	LUGGAGE & LEATHER GOOD STORE																					Q	Q	Q	Q
5949	SEW NEEDLEWORK & PIECE GOOD																					Q	Q	Q	Q
5960	NONSTORE RETAILERS									M	M											Q	Q	Q	Q

INDUSTRIAL CLASSIFICATION		PRODUCTIVITY				PRICES				EARNINGS 11 (INDUSTRY EMPLOYMENT STATISTICS PROGRAM)				TOTAL COMPENSATION				SURVEY PROGRAM WAGES & SALARIES				(ES202) TOTAL COVERED PAYROLL			
		1978	1972	1958	1947	1978	1972	1958	1947	1978	1972	1958	1947	1978	1972	1958	1947	1978	1972	1958	1947	1978	1972	1958	1947
5962	MERCHANDISING MACH OPERATORS																					Q	Q	Q	Q
5963	DIRECT SELLING ORGANS																					Q	Q	Q	Q
5980	FUEL & ICE DEALER									M	M	M										Q	Q	Q	Q
5982	FUEL & ICE DEALER NEC																					Q	Q	Q	Q
5983	FUEL OIL DEALER																					Q	Q	Q	Q
5984	LIQUIFIED PETRO GAS DEALER																					Q	Q	Q	Q
5990	RETAIL STORE NEC									M	M											Q	Q	Q	Q
5992	FLORISTS																					Q	Q	Q	Q
5993	CIGAR STORE & STANDS																					Q	Q	Q	Q
5994	NEWS DEALER & NEWSSTANDS																					Q	Q	Q	Q
5999	MISC RETAIL STORE NEC																					Q	Q	Q	Q
	H. FINANCE INSUR & REAL ESTATE	AU	AU	AU	AU					M	M			AU	AU							Q	Q	Q	Q
6000	BANKING									M	M	M						P	P	P		Q	Q	Q	Q
6010	FED RES BANK									U PT	U PT											Q	Q	Q	Q
6011	FED RES BANK																					Q	Q	Q	Q
6020	COMM & STOCK SAVE BANK									M	M											Q	Q	Q	Q
6022	STATE BANK FED RES																					Q	Q	Q	Q
6023	STATE BANK NOT FED RES FDIC																					Q	Q	Q	Q
6024	STATE BANK NOT F. R. NOT FDIC																					Q	Q	Q	Q
6025	NATIONAL BANK FED RES																					Q	Q	Q	Q
6026	NAT. BANK NOT FED RES FDIC																					Q	Q	Q	Q
6027	NATIONAL BANK NOT FDIC																					Q	Q	Q	Q
6028	PRIV BANK NOT INCORP NOT FDIC																					Q	Q	Q	Q
6030	MUTUAL SAVE BANK									U	U											Q	Q	Q	Q
6032	MUTUAL SAVE BANK FED RES																					Q	Q	Q	Q
6033	MUTUAL SAVE BANK NEC																					Q	Q	Q	Q
6034	MUTUAL SAVE BANK NOT FDIC																					Q	Q	Q	Q
6040	TRUST COMP NONDEPOSIT									U PT	U PT											Q	Q	Q	Q
6042	NONDEPOSIT TRUSTS FED RES																					Q	Q	Q	Q
6044	NONDEPOSIT TRUSTS NOT FDIC																					Q	Q	Q	Q
6050	FUNC CLOSELY RELATED TO BANK									U PT	U PT											Q	Q	Q	Q
6052	FOREIGN EXCHANGE ESTAB																					Q	Q	Q	Q
6054	SAFE DEPOSIT COMP																					Q	Q	Q	Q
6055	CLEARINGHOUSE ASSOC																					Q	Q	Q	Q
6056	CORP. FOR BANKING ABROAD																					Q	Q	Q	Q
6059	FUNC RELATED TO BANKING NEC																					Q	Q	Q	Q
6100	CREDIT AGENCY OTHER THAN BANK									M	M											Q	Q	Q	Q
6110	REDISCOUNT & FINANCING INST																					Q	Q	Q	Q
6112	REDISCOUNT NOT FOR AGRICUL																					Q	Q	Q	Q
6113	REDISCOUNTING FOR AGRICUL																					Q	Q	Q	Q
6120	SAVE & LOAN ASSOC									M	M											Q	Q	Q	Q
6122	FED SAVE & LOAN ASSOC																					Q	Q	Q	Q
6123	STATE ASSOC INSURED																					Q	Q	Q	Q
6124	STATE ASSOC NONINSURED FHLB																					Q	Q	Q	Q
6125	STATE ASSOC NONINSURED NEC																					Q	Q	Q	Q

STANDARD INDUSTRIAL CLASSIFICATION		LABOR PRODUCTIVITY				INDUSTRIAL PRICES				AVERAGE HOURLY EARNINGS 11 (INDUSTRY EMPLOYMENT STATISTICS PROGRAM)				AVERAGE HOURLY COMPENSATION TOTAL COMPENSATION				INDUSTRY WAGE SURVEY PROGRAM WAGES & SALARIES				UNEMPLOYMENT INSURANCE DATA (ES202) TOTAL COVERED PAYROLL			
		1978	1972	1958	1947	1978	1972	1958	1947	1978	1972	1958	1947	1978	1972	1958	1947	1978	1972	1958	1947	1978	1972	1958	1947
6130	AGRICUL CREDIT INST									U PT	U PT											Q	Q	Q	Q
6131	AGRICUL CREDIT INST																					Q	Q	Q	Q
6140	PERSONAL CREDIT INST									M	M											Q	Q	Q	Q
6142	FED CREDIT UNIONS																					Q	Q	Q	Q
6143	STATE CREDIT UNIONS																					Q	Q	Q	Q
6144	NONDEPOSIT INDUST LOAN COMP																					Q	Q	Q	Q
6145	LICENSED SMALL LOAN LENDERS																					Q	Q	Q	Q
6146	INSTALL SALES FINANCE COMP																					Q	Q	Q	Q
6149	MISC. PERSONAL CREDIT INST																					Q	Q	Q	Q
6150	BUSINESS CREDIT INST									U	U											Q	Q	Q	Q
6153	SHORT-TERM BUSINESS CREDIT																					Q	Q	Q	Q
6159	MISC. BUSINESS CREDIT INST																					Q	Q	Q	Q
6160	MORTGAGE BANKER & BROKER									U	U											Q	Q	Q	Q
6162	MORTGAGE BANKER & CORRESP																					Q	Q	Q	Q
6163	LOAN BROKER																					Q	Q	Q	Q
6200	SECURITY COMMOD BROKER & SERV									U	U											Q	Q	Q	Q
6210	SEC. BROKER & DEALER									U	U											Q	Q	Q	Q
6211	SEC. BROKER & DEALER																					Q	Q	Q	Q
6220	COMMOD CONTRACTS BROKER DEAL									U PT	U PT											Q	Q	Q	Q
6221	COMMOD CONTRACTS BROKER DEAL																					Q	Q	Q	Q
6230	SEC. & COMMOD EXCHANGES									U PT	U PT											Q	Q	Q	Q
6231	SEC. & COMMOD EXCHANGES																					Q	Q	Q	Q
6280	SEC. & COMMOD SERV									U PT	U PT											Q	Q	Q	Q
6281	SEC. & COMMOD SERV																					Q	Q	Q	Q
6300	INSURANCE CARRIERS									M	M											Q	Q	Q	Q
6310	LIFE INSUR									M	M							P	P	P		Q	Q	Q	Q
6311	LIFE INSUR																	P	P	P		Q	Q	Q	Q
6320	MEDICAL SERV & HEALTH INSUR									M	M											Q	Q	Q	Q
6321	ACCIDENT & HEALTH INSUR																					Q	Q	Q	Q
6324	HOSPITAL & MEDICAL SERV PLAN																					Q	Q	Q	Q
6330	FIRE MARINE & CASUALTY INSUR									M	M											Q	Q	Q	Q
6331	FIRE MARINE & CASUALTY INSUR																					Q	Q	Q	Q
6350	SURETY INSUR									U PT	U PT											Q	Q	Q	Q
6351	SURETY INSUR																					Q	Q	Q	Q
6360	TITLE INSUR									U PT	U PT											Q	Q	Q	Q
6361	TITLE INSUR																					Q	Q	Q	Q
6370	PENSION HEALTH & WELFARE FUND									U PT	U PT											Q	Q	Q	Q
6371	PENSION HEALTH & WELFARE FUND																					Q	Q	Q	Q
6390	INSUR CARRIERS NEC									U PT	U PT											Q	Q	Q	Q
6399	INSUR CARRIERS NEC																					Q	Q	Q	Q
6400	INSUR AGENT BROKER & SERVICE									U	U											Q	Q	Q	Q

STANDARD INDUSTRIAL CLASSIFICATION		LABOR PRODUCTIVITY				INDUSTRIAL PRICES				AVERAGE HOURLY EARNINGS 11 (INDUSTRY EMPLOYMENT STATISTICS PROGRAM)				COMPENSATION TOTAL COMPENSATION				INDUSTRY WAGE SURVEY PROGRAM WAGES & SALARIES				INSURANCE DATA (ES202) TOTAL COVERED PAYROLL			
		1978	1972	1958	1947	1978	1972	1958	1947	1978	1972	1958	1947	1978	1972	1958	1947	1978	1972	1958	1947	1978	1972	1958	1947
6500	REAL ESTATE									U	U											Q	Q	Q	Q
6510	REAL ESTATE OPER. & LESSOR									U	U											Q	Q	Q	Q
6512	NONRES BUILD OPERATORS																								
6513	APT BUILD OPERATORS																								
6514	DWELLING OPERATORS EXC. APTS																								
6515	MOBILE HOME SITE OPERATORS																								
6517	RAILROAD PROPERTY LESSORS																								
6519	REAL PROPERTY LESSORS NEC																								
6530	REAL ESTATE AGENT & MANAGER									U	U											Q	Q	Q	Q
6531	REAL ESTATE AGENT & MANAGER																					Q	Q	Q	Q
6540	TITLE ABSTRACT OFF																					Q	Q	Q	Q
6541	TITLE ABSTRACT OFF									U	U											Q	Q	Q	Q
6550	SUBDIVIDERS & DEVELOPERS									U	U											Q	Q	Q	Q
6552	SUBDIVIDERS & DEVELOPERS NEC																					Q	Q	Q	Q
6553	CEMETERY SUBDIV. & DEVELOPER																					Q	Q	Q	Q
6600	COMBINED REAL ESTATE INSUR									U	U											Q	Q	Q	Q
6610	COMBINED REAL ESTATE INSUR																					Q	Q	Q	Q
6611	COMBINED REAL ESTATE INSUR																					Q	Q	Q	Q
6700	HOLDING & OTHER INVEST. OFFICES									U	U											Q	Q	Q	Q
6710	HOLDING OFF									U	U											Q	Q	Q	Q
6711	HOLDING OFF																					Q	Q	Q	Q
6720	INVEST. OFF																					Q	Q	Q	Q
6722	MANAGE. INVEST. OPEN-END																					Q	Q	Q	Q
6723	MANAGE. INVEST. CLOSED-END																					Q	Q	Q	Q
6724	UNIT INVEST. TRUSTS																					Q	Q	Q	Q
6725	FACE-AMOUNT CERTIFICATE OFF																					Q	Q	Q	Q
6730	TRUSTS																					Q	Q	Q	Q
6732	EDUC. RELIGIOUS ETC. TRUSTS																					Q	Q	Q	Q
6733	TRUSTS NEC																					Q	Q	Q	Q
6790	MISC INVESTING																					Q	Q	Q	Q
6792	OIL ROYALTY TRADERS																					Q	Q	Q	Q
6793	COMMOD TRADERS																					Q	Q	Q	Q
6794	PATENT OWNERS & LESSORS																					Q	Q	Q	Q
6799	INVESTORS NEC																					Q	Q	Q	Q
	I. SERVICES	AU 4	AU 4	AU 4	AU 4					M	M			AU 4	AU 4							Q	Q	Q	Q
7000	HOTEL & OTHER LODGING PLACE									U	U											Q	Q	Q	Q
7010	HOTEL MOTEL & TOURIST COURT	A	A	A						M	M	M						P	P	P		Q	Q	Q	Q
7011	HOTEL MOTEL & TOURIST COURT	A	A	A														P	P	P		Q	Q	Q	Q
7020	ROOMING & BOARDING HOUSES									U PT	U PT											Q	Q	Q	Q
7021	ROOMING & BOARDING HOUSES																					Q	Q	Q	Q
7030	CAMPS & TRAILERING PARKS									U	U											Q	Q	Q	Q
7032	SPORT & REC CAMPS																					Q	Q	Q	Q

STANDARD INDUSTRIAL CLASSIFICATION		LABOR PRODUCTIVITY				INDUSTRIAL PRICES				AVERAGE HOURLY EARNINGS 11 (INDUSTRY EMPLOYMENT STATISTICS PROGRAM)				AVERAGE HOURLY COMPENSATION TOTAL COMPENSATION				INDUSTRY WAGE SURVEY PROGRAM WAGES & SALARIES				UNEMPLOYMENT INSURANCE DATA (ES202) TOTAL COVERED PAYROLL			
		1978	1972	1958	1947	1978	1972	1958	1947	1978	1972	1958	1947	1978	1972	1958	1947	1978	1972	1958	1947	1978	1972	1958	1947
7033	TRAILER PARKS FOR TRANSIENT																					Q	Q	Q	Q
7040	MEMBER-BASIS ORGAN HOTEL									U PT	U PT											Q	Q	Q	Q
7041	MEMBER-BASIS ORGAN HOTEL																					Q	Q	Q	Q
7200	PERSONAL SERVICES									U	U											Q	Q	Q	Q
7210	LAUNDRY CLEAN & GARMENT SERV	A	A	A						M	M	M										Q	Q	Q	Q
7211	POWER LAUNDRY FAMILY & COMM																		P	P					
7212	GARMENT PRESS & CLEAN AGENT																								
7213	LINEN SUPPLY																								
7214	DIAPER SERV																								
7215	COIN-OPER LAUNDRY & CLEAN																								
7216	DRY CLEAN PLANTS EXC. RUG																								
7217	CARPET & UPHOL CLEAN																								
7218	INDUST LAUNDERERS																								
7219	LAUNDRY & GARMENT SERV NEC																								
7220	PHOTO STUDIOS PORTRAIT									U	U											Q	Q	Q	Q
7221	PHOTO STUDIOS PORTRAIT																					Q	Q	Q	Q
7230	BEAUTY SHOP									M	M											Q	Q	Q	Q
7231	BEAUTY SHOP																					Q	Q	Q	Q
7240	BARBER SHOP									U	U											Q	Q	Q	Q
7241	BARBER SHOP																					Q	Q	Q	Q
7250	SHOE REPAIR & HAT CLEAN SHOP									U PT	U PT											Q	Q	Q	Q
7251	SHOE REPAIR & HAT CLEAN SHOP																					Q	Q	Q	Q
7260	FUNERAL SERV & CREMATORIES									U	U											Q	Q	Q	Q
7261	FUNERAL SERV & CREMATORIES																					Q	Q	Q	Q
7290	MISC PERSONAL SERV									U PT	U PT											Q	Q	Q	Q
7299	MISC PERSONAL SERV																					Q	Q	Q	Q
7300	BUSINESS SERVICES									M	M											Q	Q	Q	Q
7310	ADVERTISING									M	M											Q	Q	Q	Q
7311	ADVERTISING AGENCIES																					Q	Q	Q	Q
7312	OUTDOOR ADVERTISING SERV																					Q	Q	Q	Q
7313	RADIO TV PUBLISHER REPRESENT.																					Q	Q	Q	Q
7319	ADVERTISING NEC																					Q	Q	Q	Q
7320	CREDIT REPORT & COLLECTION									U	U											Q	Q	Q	Q
7321	CREDIT REPORT & COLLECTION																					Q	Q	Q	Q
7330	MAILING REPROD STENO																					Q	Q	Q	Q
7331	DIRECT MAIL ADVERTISING SERV									U	U											Q	Q	Q	Q
7332	BLUEPRINTING & PHOTOCOPYING																					Q	Q	Q	Q
7333	COMM PHOTOGRAPHY & ART																					Q	Q	Q	Q
7339	STENO & REPROD NEC																					Q	Q	Q	Q
7340	SERV TO BUILDS									M	M							P	P	P		Q	Q	Q	Q
7341	WINDOW CLEAN																					Q	Q	Q	Q
7342	DISINFECTING & EXTERMINATING																					Q	Q	Q	Q
7349	BUILD MAINTENANCE SERV NEC																					Q	Q	Q	Q
7350	NEWS SYNDICATES									U PT	U PT														

STANDARD INDUSTRIAL	CLASSIFICATION	LABOR PRODUCTIVITY				INDUSTRIAL PRICES				AVERAGE HOURLY EARNINGS 11 (INDUSTRY EMPLOYMENT STATISTICS PROGRAM)				COMPENSATION TOTAL COMPENSATION				INDUSTRY WAGE SURVEY PROGRAM WAGES & SALARIES				(ES202) TOTAL COVERED PAYROLL			
		1978	1972	1958	1947	1978	1972	1958	1947	1978	1972	1958	1947	1978	1972	1958	1947	1978	1972	1958	1947	1978	1972	1958	1947
7361	EMPLOYMENT AGENCIES																					Q	Q	Q	Q
7362	TEMPORARY HELP SUPPLY SERV																					Q	Q	Q	Q
7369	PERSONNEL SUPPLY SERV NEC																					Q	Q	Q	Q
7370	COMPUTER & DATA PROCESS SERV									M	M											Q	Q	Q	Q
7372	COMPUTER PROGRAM & SOFTWARE																	P				Q	Q	Q	Q
7374	DATA PROCESSING SERV																	P				Q	Q	Q	Q
7379	COMPUTER RELATED SERV NEC																					Q	Q	Q	Q
7390	MISC BUSINESS SERV									U PT	U PT											Q	Q	Q	Q
7391	RESEARCH & DEVELOP. LABS																					Q	Q	Q	Q
7392	MANAGE. & PUBLIC RELATIONS																					Q	Q	Q	Q
7393	DETECTIVE & PROTECTIVE SERV																					Q	Q	Q	Q
7394	EQUIP RENT & LEASING																					Q	Q	Q	Q
7395	PHOTOFINISHING LABS																					Q	Q	Q	Q
7396	TRADING STAMP SERV																					Q	Q	Q	Q
7397	COMM TESTING LABS																					Q	Q	Q	Q
7399	BUSINESS SERV NEC																					Q	Q	Q	Q
7500	AUTO REPAIR SERV & GARAGES									M	M											Q	Q	Q	Q
7510	AUTO RENTS WITHOUT DRIVERS									U	U											Q	Q	Q	Q
7512	PASSENGER CAR RENT & LEASE																					Q	Q	Q	Q
7513	TRUCK RENT & LEASING																					Q	Q	Q	Q
7519	UTILITY TRAILER RENT																					Q	Q	Q	Q
7520	AUTO PARKING									U	U											Q	Q	Q	Q
7523	PARKING LOTS																					Q	Q	Q	Q
7525	PARKING STRUCTURES																					Q	Q	Q	Q
7530	AUTO REPAIR SHOP									M	M											Q	Q	Q	Q
7531	TOP & BODY REPAIR SHOP																					Q	Q	Q	Q
7534	TIRE RETREAD & REPAIR SHOP																					Q	Q	Q	Q
7535	PAINT SHOP																					Q	Q	Q	Q
7538	GENERAL AUTO REPAIR SHOP																					Q	Q	Q	Q
7539	AUTO REPAIR SHOP NEC																					Q	Q	Q	Q
7540	AUTO SERV EXC. REPAIR									U	U											Q	Q	Q	Q
7542	CAR WASHES																					Q	Q	Q	Q
7549	AUTO SERV NEC																					Q	Q	Q	Q
7600	MISC REPAIR SERVICES									M	M											Q	Q	Q	Q
7620	ELEC REPAIR SHOP									U	U							P	P			Q	Q	Q	Q
7622	RADIO & TV REPAIR																					Q	Q	Q	Q
7623	REFRIGERATION SERV & REPAIR																					Q	Q	Q	Q
7629	ELEC REPAIR SHOP NEC																					Q	Q	Q	Q
7630	WATCH CLOCK & JEWELRY REPAIR									U PT	U PT											Q	Q	Q	Q
7631	WATCH CLOCK & JEWELRY REPAIR																					Q	Q	Q	Q
7640	REUPHOL & FURN REPAIR									U	U											Q	Q	Q	Q
7641	REUPHOL & FURN REPAIR																					Q	Q	Q	Q
7690	MISC REPAIR SHOP									U PT	U PT											Q	Q	Q	Q
7692	WELDING REPAIR																					Q	Q	Q	Q
7694	ARMATURE REWINDING SHOP																					Q	Q	Q	Q
7699	REPAIR SERV NEC																					Q	Q	Q	Q

STANDARD INDUSTRIAL CLASSIFICATION		LABOR PRODUCTIVITY				INDUSTRIAL PRICES				AVERAGE HOURLY EARNINGS 11 (INDUSTRY EMPLOYMENT STATISTICS PROGRAM)				AVERAGE HOURLY COMPENSATION TOTAL COMPENSATION				INDUSTRY WAGE SURVEY PROGRAM WAGES & SALARIES				UNEMPLOYMENT INSURANCE DATA (ES202) TOTAL COVERED PAYROLL			
		1978	1972	1958	1947	1978	1972	1958	1947	1978	1972	1958	1947	1978	1972	1958	1947	1978	1972	1958	1947	1978	1972	1958	1947
7800	MOTION PICTURES									M	M											Q	Q	Q	Q
7810	MOTION PICTURE PROD & SERV									M	M											Q	Q	Q	Q
7813	MOTION PICTURE PROD EXC. TV																					Q	Q	Q	Q
7814	MOTION PICTURE PROD FOR TV																					Q	Q	Q	Q
7819	SERV ALLIED TO MOTION PICT																					Q	Q	Q	Q
7820	MOTION PICTURE DISTRIB & SERV									U	U											Q	Q	Q	Q
7823	MOTION PICTURE FILM EXCHANGE																					Q	Q	Q	Q
7824	FILM OR TAPE DISTRIB FOR TV																					Q	Q	Q	Q
7829	MOTION PICTURE DISTRIB SERV																					Q	Q	Q	Q
7830	MOTION PICTURE THEATERS									U	U								P			Q	Q	Q	Q
7832	MOT. PICT. TH. EX DRIVE-IN																		P			Q	Q	Q	Q
7833	DRIVE-IN MOT. PICT. THEATER																		P			Q	Q	Q	Q
7900	AMUSEMENT & RECEATION SERV									M	M											Q	Q	Q	Q
7910	DANCE HALLS STUDIO & SCHOOL									U PT	U PT											Q	Q	Q	Q
7911	DANCE HALLS STUDIO & SCHOOL																					Q	Q	Q	Q
7920	PRODUCER ORCH. ENTERTAINER									U	U											Q	Q	Q	Q
7922	THEATRICAL PRODUCERS & SERV																					Q	Q	Q	Q
7929	ENTERTAINER & ENTER. GROUPS																					Q	Q	Q	Q
7930	BOWLING & BILLIARD ESTAB									U	U											Q	Q	Q	Q
7932	BILLIARD & POOL ESTAB																					Q	Q	Q	Q
7933	BOWLING ALLEYS																					Q	Q	Q	Q
7940	COMM SPORTS									U	U											Q	Q	Q	Q
7941	SPORTS CLUBS & PROMOTERS																					Q	Q	Q	Q
7948	RACING INCL. TRACK OPERATION																					Q	Q	Q	Q
7990	MISC. AMUSEMENT REC SERV									U PT	U PT											Q	Q	Q	Q
7992	PUBLIC GOLF COURSES																					Q	Q	Q	Q
7993	COIN-OPER. AMUSEMENT DEVICE																					Q	Q	Q	Q
7996	AMUSEMENT PARKS																					Q	Q	Q	Q
7997	MEMBER SPORTS & REC CLUBS																					Q	Q	Q	Q
7999	AMUSEMENT & REC NEC																					Q	Q	Q	Q
8000	HEALTH SERVICES									M	M											Q	Q	Q	Q
8010	OFF OF PHYSICIANS									M	M											Q	Q	Q	Q
8011	OFF OF PHYSICIANS																					Q	Q	Q	Q
8020	OFF OF DENTISTS									M	M											Q	Q	Q	Q
8021	OFF OF DENTISTS																					Q	Q	Q	Q
8030	OFF OF OSTEOPATHIC PHYSICIAN									U	U											Q	Q	Q	Q
8031	OFF OF OSTEOPATHIC PHYSICIAN																					Q	Q	Q	Q
8040	OFF OF OTHER HEALTH PRACT.									U	U											Q	Q	Q	Q
8041	OFF OF CHIROPRACTORS																					Q	Q	Q	Q
8042	OFF OF OPTOMETRISTS																					Q	Q	Q	Q
8049	OFF OF HEALTH PRACT. NEC																					Q	Q	Q	Q
8050	NURSE & PERS. CARE FACILITY									M	M								P	P			Q	Q	Q	Q

STANDARD INDUSTRIAL CLASSIFICATION		LABOR PRODUCTIVITY				INDUSTRIAL PRICES				AVERAGE HOURLY EARNINGS 11 (INDUSTRY EMPLOYMENT STATISTICS PROGRAM)				COMPENSATION TOTAL COMPENSATION				INDUSTRY WAGE SURVEY PROGRAM WAGES & SALARIES				(ES202) TOTAL COVERED PAYROLL			
		1978	1972	1958	1947	1978	1972	1958	1947	1978	1972	1958	1947	1978	1972	1958	1947	1978	1972	1958	1947	1978	1972	1958	1947
8060	HOSPITALS									M	M							P	P	P		Q	Q	Q	Q
8062	GENERAL MED. & SURG. HOSP.																					Q	Q	Q	Q
8063	PSYCHIATRIC HOSPITALS																					Q	Q	Q	Q
8069	SPECIALTY HOSP. EXC PSYCH																					Q	Q	Q	Q
8070	MEDICAL & DENTAL LABS									U	U											Q	Q	Q	Q
8071	MEDICAL LABS																					Q	Q	Q	Q
8072	DENTAL LABS																					Q	Q	Q	Q
8080	OUTPATIENT CARE FACILITIES									U PT	U PT											Q	Q	Q	Q
8081	OUTPATIENT CARE FACILITIES																					Q	Q	Q	Q
8090	HEALTH & ALLIED SERV NEC									U PT	U PT											Q	Q	Q	Q
8091	HEALTH & ALLIED SERV NEC																					Q	Q	Q	Q
8100	LEGAL SERVICES									M	M											Q	Q	Q	Q
8110	LEGAL SERV																					Q	Q	Q	Q
8111	LEGAL SERV																					Q	Q	Q	Q
8200	EDUCATIONAL SERVICES									U	U											Q	Q	Q	Q
8210	ELEMENTARY & SECOND. SCHOOL									U	U								P			Q	Q	Q	Q
8211	ELEMENTARY & SECOND. SCHOOL																		P			Q	Q	Q	Q
8220	COLLEGES & UNIVERSITIES									U	U								P			Q	Q	Q	Q
8221	COLLEGES & UNIVERSITIES NEC																		P			Q	Q	Q	Q
8222	JUNIOR COLLEGES																					Q	Q	Q	Q
8230	LIBRARIES & INFO CENTERS									U PT	U PT											Q	Q	Q	Q
8231	LIBRARIES & INFO CENTERS																					Q	Q	Q	Q
8240	CORRESPOND & VOCATION SCHOOL									U PT	U PT											Q	Q	Q	Q
8241	CORRESPOND SCHOOL																					Q	Q	Q	Q
8243	DATA PROCESSING SCHOOL																					Q	Q	Q	Q
8244	BUSINESS & SECRETARY SCHOOL																					Q	Q	Q	Q
8249	VOCATIONAL SCHOOL NEC																					Q	Q	Q	Q
8290	SCHOOL & ED. SERV NEC									U PT	U PT											Q	Q	Q	Q
8299	SCHOOL & ED. SERV NEC																					Q	Q	Q	Q
8300	SOCIAL SERVICES									U	U											Q	Q	Q	Q
8320	INDIVIDUAL & FAMILY SERV									U	U											Q	Q	Q	Q
8321	INDIVIDUAL & FAMILY SERV																					Q	Q	Q	Q
8330	JOB TRAINING & RELATED SERV									U	U											Q	Q	Q	Q
8331	JOB TRAINING & RELATED SERV																					Q	Q	Q	Q
8350	CHILD DAY CARE SERV									U	U											Q	Q	Q	Q
8351	CHILD DAY CARE SERV																					Q	Q	Q	Q
8360	RESIDENTIAL CARE									U	U											Q	Q	Q	Q
8361	RESIDENTIAL CARE																					Q	Q	Q	Q
8390	SOCIAL SERV NEC									U	U											Q	Q	Q	Q
8399	SOCIAL SERV NEC																					Q	Q	Q	Q
8400	MUSEUMS BOTAN. ZOOLOG. GARDENS																					Q	Q	Q	Q
8410	MUSEUMS & ART GALLERIES									U PT	U PT											Q	Q	Q	Q

STANDARD INDUSTRIAL CLASSIFICATION		LABOR PRODUCTIVITY				INDUSTRIAL PRICES				AVERAGE HOURLY EARNINGS 11 (INDUSTRY EMPLOYMENT STATISTICS PROGRAM)				AVERAGE HOURLY COMPENSATION: TOTAL COMPENSATION				INDUSTRY WAGE SURVEY PROGRAM: WAGES & SALARIES				UNEMPLOYMENT INSURANCE DATA (ES202): TOTAL COVERED PAYROLL			
		1978	1972	1958	1947	1978	1972	1958	1947	1978	1972	1958	1947	1978	1972	1958	1947	1978	1972	1958	1947	1978	1972	1958	1947
8411	MUSEUMS & ART GALLERIES																					Q	Q	Q	Q
8420	BOTANICAL & ZOOLOG. GARDEN									U PT	U PT											Q	Q	Q	Q
8421	BOTANICAL & ZOOLOG. GARDEN																					Q	Q	Q	Q
8600	MEMBER ORGANIZATIONS									U	U											Q	Q	Q	Q
8610	BUSINESS ASSOC									U	U											Q	Q	Q	Q
8611	BUSINESS ASSOC																					Q	Q	Q	Q
8620	PROFESSIONAL ORGANS									U	U											Q	Q	Q	Q
8621	PROFESSIONAL ORGANS																					Q	Q	Q	Q
8630	LABOR ORGANS									U	U											Q	Q	Q	Q
8631	LABOR ORGANS																					Q	Q	Q	Q
8640	CIVIC & SOCIAL ASSOC									U	U											Q	Q	Q	Q
8641	CIVIC & SOCIAL ASSOC																					Q	Q	Q	Q
8650	POLITICAL ORGANS									U PT	U PT											Q	Q	Q	Q
8651	POLITICAL ORGANS																					Q	Q	Q	Q
8660	RELIGIOUS ORGANS									U	U											Q	Q	Q	Q
8661	RELIGIOUS ORGANS																					Q	Q	Q	Q
8690	MEMBER ORGANS NEC									U PT	U PT											Q	Q	Q	Q
8699	MEMBER ORGANS NEC																					Q	Q	Q	Q
8800	PRIVATE HOUSES																					Q	Q	Q	Q
8810	PRIVATE HOUSES																					Q	Q	Q	Q
8811	PRIVATE HOUSES																					Q	Q	Q	Q
8900	MISC SERV									M	M											Q	Q	Q	Q
8910	ENGINEER & ARCH SERV									M	M											Q	Q	Q	Q
8911	ENGINEER & ARCH SERV																					Q	Q	Q	Q
8920	NONCOMM RESEARCH ORGANS									U PT	U PT											Q	Q	Q	Q
8922	NONCOMM RESEARCH ORGANS																					Q	Q	Q	Q
8930	ACCT AUDITING & BOOKKEEPING									M	M											Q	Q	Q	Q
8931	ACCT AUDITING & BOOKKEEPING																					Q	Q	Q	Q
8990	SERV NEC									U PT	U PT											Q	Q	Q	Q
8999	SERV NEC																					Q	Q	Q	Q
	J. PUBLIC ADMINISTRATION																					Q	Q	Q	Q
9100	EXECUTIVE LEGISLATIVE & GEN.																					Q	Q	Q	Q
9110	EXECUTIVE OFF																					Q	Q	Q	Q
9111	EXECUTIVE OFF																					Q	Q	Q	Q
9120	LEGISLATIVE BODIES																					Q	Q	Q	Q
9121	LEGISLATIVE BODIES																					Q	Q	Q	Q
9130	EXECUTIVE & LEGISLATIVE COMB																					Q	Q	Q	Q
9131	EXECUTIVE & LEGISLATIVE COMB																					Q	Q	Q	Q
9190	GENERAL GOVERNMENT NEC																					Q	Q	Q	Q
9199	GENERAL GOVERNMENT NEC																					Q	Q	Q	Q

STANDARD INDUSTRIAL CLASSIFICATION		LABOR PRODUCTIVITY				INDUSTRIAL PRICES				AVERAGE HOURLY EARNINGS 11 (INDUSTRY EMPLOYMENT STATISTICS PROGRAM)				COMPENSATION TOTAL COMPENSATION				INDUSTRY WAGE SURVEY PROGRAM WAGES & SALARIES				INSURANCE DATA (ES202) TOTAL COVERED PAYROLL			
		1978	1972	1958	1947	1978	1972	1958	1947	1978	1972	1958	1947	1978	1972	1958	1947	1978	1972	1958	1947	1978	1972	1958	1947
9210	COURT																					Q	Q	Q	Q
9211	COURT																					Q	Q	Q	Q
9220	PUBLIC ORDER & SAFETY																					Q	Q	Q	Q
9221	POLICE PROTECTION																	A	A			Q	Q	Q	Q
9222	LEGAL COUNSEL & PROSECUTION																					Q	Q	Q	Q
9223	CORRECTIONAL INST																					Q	Q	Q	Q
9224	FIRE PROTECTION																	A	A			Q	Q	Q	Q
9229	PUBLIC ORDER & SAFETY NEC																					Q	Q	Q	Q
9300	FINANCE TAX & MONETARY POLICY																					Q	Q	Q	Q
9310	FINANCE TAX & MONETARY POLICY																					Q	Q	Q	Q
9311	FINANCE TAX & MONETARY POLICY																					Q	Q	Q	Q
9400	ADMIN. OF HUMAN RESOURCES																					Q	Q	Q	Q
9410	ADMIN. OF ED. PROG																					Q	Q	Q	Q
9411	ADMIN. OF ED. PROG																					Q	Q	Q	Q
9430	ADMIN. OF PUBLIC HEALTH PROG																					Q	Q	Q	Q
9431	ADMIN. OF PUBLIC HEALTH PROG																					Q	Q	Q	Q
9440	ADMIN. OF SOC & MANPOWER PROG																					Q	Q	Q	Q
9441	ADMIN. OF SOC & MANPOWER PROG																					Q	Q	Q	Q
9450	ADMIN. OF VETERANS' AFFAIRS																					Q	Q	Q	Q
9451	ADMIN. OF VETERANS' AFFAIRS																					Q	Q	Q	Q
9500	ENVIRON. QUAL. & HOUSING																					Q	Q	Q	Q
9510	ENVIRONMENTAL QUALITY																					Q	Q	Q	Q
9511	AIR H2O & SOLID WASTE MANAGE.																					Q	Q	Q	Q
9512	LAND MINERAL WILDLIFE CONSER																					Q	Q	Q	Q
9530	HOUSING & URBAN DEVELOP.																					Q	Q	Q	Q
9531	HOUSING PROG																					Q	Q	Q	Q
9532	URBAN & COMMUNITY DEVELOP.																					Q	Q	Q	Q
9600	ADMIN. OF ECON PROGRAMS																					Q	Q	Q	Q
9610	ADMIN. OF GENERAL ECON PROG																					Q	Q	Q	Q
9611	ADMIN. OF GENERAL ECON PROG																					Q	Q	Q	Q
9620	REGULATION ADMIN. OF TRANS																					Q	Q	Q	Q
9621	REGULATION ADMIN. OF TRANS																					Q	Q	Q	Q
9630	REG. ADMIN. OF UTILITIES																					Q	Q	Q	Q
9631	REG. ADMIN. OF UTILITIES																					Q	Q	Q	Q
9640	REGULATION OF AGRICUL MRKT																					Q	Q	Q	Q
9641	REGULATION OF AGRICUL MRKT																					Q	Q	Q	Q
9650	REG. MISC. COMM SECTORS																					Q	Q	Q	Q
9651	REG. MISC. COMM SECTORS																					Q	Q	Q	Q
9660	SPACE RESEARCH & TECHNOLOGY																					Q	Q	Q	Q
9661	SPACE RESEARCH & TECHNOLOGY																					Q	Q	Q	Q
9700	NAT. SEC. & INTL. AFFAIRS																					Q	Q	Q	Q

STANDARD INDUSTRIAL CLASSIFICATION	LABOR PRODUCTIVITY				INDUSTRIAL PRICES				AVERAGE HOURLY EARNINGS 11 (INDUSTRY EMPLOYMENT STATISTICS PROGRAM)				AVERAGE HOURLY COMPENSATION: TOTAL COMPENSATION				INDUSTRY WAGE SURVEY PROGRAM: WAGES & SALARIES				UNEMPLOYMENT INSURANCE DATA (ES202): TOTAL COVERED PAYROLL			
	1978	1972	1958	1947	1978	1972	1958	1947	1978	1972	1958	1947	1978	1972	1958	1947	1978	1972	1958	1947	1978	1972	1958	1947
9710 NATIONAL SEC.																					Q	Q	Q	Q
9711 NATIONAL SEC.																					Q	Q	Q	Q
9720 INTERNATIONAL AFFAIRS																					Q	Q	Q	Q
9721 INTERNATIONAL AFFAIRS																					Q	Q	Q	Q
K. NONCLASSIFIABLE ESTAB									U	U											Q	Q	Q	Q
9900 NONCLASSIFIABLE ESTAB																					Q	Q	Q	Q
9990 NONCLASSIFIABLE ESTAB																					Q	Q	Q	Q
9999 NONCLASSIFIABLE ESTAB																					Q	Q	Q	Q

Appendix B
Sectoral Labor Input

Frank M. Gollop and Dale W. Jorgenson

YEAR	PRICE	QUANTITY	OUTLAY	QUALITY	EMPLOYMENT	WEEKLY HOURS PER PERSON	HOURLY COMPENSATION	HOURS WORKED
	LABOR INPUT							
				AGRICULTURAL PRODUCTION				
1948	0.353	53.643	19.021	0.884	8094	49.8	0.91	20950
1949	0.359	51.885	18.621	0.891	7900	48.7	0.93	20025
1950	0.361	51.655	18.648	0.911	7730	48.5	0.96	19500
1951	0.402	48.252	19.382	0.893	7271	49.2	1.04	18587
1952	0.314	47.190	14.839	0.908	7054	48.7	0.83	17871
1953	0.289	45.890	13.240	0.904	6814	49.3	0.76	17459
1954	0.274	44.935	12.327	0.909	6836	47.8	0.72	17006
1955	0.237	43.469	10.303	0.907	6643	47.7	0.63	16477
1956	0.281	40.610	11.398	0.909	6316	46.8	0.74	15362
1957	0.355	37.493	13.299	0.908	5988	45.6	0.94	14196
1958	0.425	36.011	15.305	0.913	5752	45.3	1.13	13561
1959	0.307	35.436	10.895	0.915	5605	45.7	0.82	13316
1960	0.412	34.778	14.343	0.950	5275	45.9	1.14	12590
1961	0.436	32.765	14.290	0.921	5218	45.1	1.17	12235
1962	0.442	32.314	14.282	0.933	5026	45.6	1.20	11908
1963	0.490	30.462	14.916	0.919	4727	46.4	1.31	11399
1964	0.515	28.697	14.786	0.930	4455	45.8	1.39	10610
1965	0.594	28.056	16.669	0.940	4242	46.5	1.62	10261
1966	0.732	25.847	18.914	0.964	3839	46.2	2.05	9218
1967	0.520	24.915	12.949	0.975	3681	45.9	1.47	8787
1968	0.591	24.738	14.620	0.978	3647	45.9	1.68	8700
1969	0.869	24.040	20.885	0.979	3501	46.4	2.47	8448
1970	0.839	24.305	20.402	1.028	3400	46.0	2.51	8130
1971	0.952	23.150	22.032	0.993	3339	46.2	2.75	8022
1972	1.000	23.140	23.140	1.000	3343	45.8	2.91	7958
1973	1.785	23.311	41.616	1.007	3323	46.1	5.23	7964
1974	1.263	22.819	28.815	0.999	3359	45.0	3.67	7852
1975	0.660	22.662	14.966	1.008	3304	45.0	1.94	7733
1976	1.579	21.951	34.655	1.004	3248	44.5	4.61	7517
1977	1.729	21.346	36.916	1.002	3106	45.4	5.04	7326
1978	2.502	21.346	53.412	1.008	3060	45.8	7.33	7283
				AGRICULTURAL SERVICES				
1948	0.412	1.584	0.652	0.856	345	37.2	0.98	668
1949	0.463	1.553	0.719	0.864	338	36.9	1.11	649
1950	0.477	1.613	0.769	0.906	337	36.7	1.20	643
1951	0.473	1.686	0.797	0.884	358	37.0	1.16	689
1952	0.494	1.759	0.869	0.899	370	36.8	1.23	707
1953	0.513	1.731	0.888	0.884	365	37.3	1.26	707
1954	0.544	1.723	0.937	0.878	368	37.0	1.32	709
1955	0.581	1.692	0.983	0.872	366	36.8	1.40	701
1956	0.596	1.681	1.002	0.866	370	36.4	1.43	701
1957	0.611	1.665	1.016	0.864	371	36.1	1.46	696
1958	0.698	1.632	1.140	0.859	365	36.1	1.66	686
1959	0.699	1.620	1.132	0.841	366	36.5	1.63	695
1960	0.665	1.409	0.997	0.771	372	36.3	1.42	702
1961	0.739	1.565	1.157	0.782	388	35.8	1.60	723
1962	0.675	1.669	1.127	0.815	395	36.0	1.52	740
1963	0.650	1.735	1.129	0.830	400	36.3	1.49	755
1964	0.738	1.824	1.347	0.854	413	35.9	1.75	771
1965	0.692	1.938	1.340	0.865	430	36.2	1.66	809
1966	0.617	2.013	1.242	0.898	433	36.0	1.53	810
1967	0.725	2.112	1.532	0.939	437	35.7	1.89	812
1968	0.721	2.211	1.594	0.964	446	35.7	1.92	828
1969	0.799	2.270	1.814	0.963	456	35.9	2.13	851
1970	0.651	2.228	1.451	0.933	460	36.0	1.68	862
1971	1.019	2.290	2.333	0.997	441	36.2	2.81	830
1972	1.000	2.464	2.464	1.000	466	36.7	2.77	890
1973	1.213	2.677	3.248	1.009	499	36.9	3.39	958
1974	1.375	2.639	3.629	1.015	512	35.3	3.86	939
1975	1.457	2.395	3.489	1.031	486	33.2	4.16	838
1976	1.518	2.698	4.094	1.072	521	33.5	4.51	909
1977	1.421	2.867	4.073	1.072	539	34.5	4.22	966
1978	1.666	3.323	5.536	1.071	629	34.2	4.94	1120
				METAL MINING				
1948	0.298	1.196	0.357	0.872	105	39.6	1.65	216
1949	0.315	1.083	0.341	0.875	98	38.3	1.75	195
1950	0.329	1.139	0.375	0.879	100	39.3	1.83	204
1951	0.362	1.258	0.455	0.883	107	40.3	2.03	224
1952	0.393	1.291	0.507	0.894	108	40.5	2.23	228
1953	0.425	1.335	0.567	0.900	112	40.2	2.43	234
1954	0.425	1.209	0.514	0.904	106	38.3	2.44	211
1955	0.453	1.284	0.582	0.907	109	39.4	2.61	223
1956	0.481	1.374	0.661	0.912	116	39.4	2.78	237
1957	0.509	1.354	0.690	0.920	117	38.2	2.97	232
1958	0.521	1.070	0.557	0.932	95	36.7	3.08	181
1959	0.551	1.004	0.553	0.936	86	37.8	3.27	169
1960	0.553	1.181	0.654	0.936	98	39.1	3.28	199
1961	0.575	1.109	0.637	0.944	92	38.7	3.44	185
1962	0.585	1.061	0.621	0.953	87	38.8	3.54	175
1963	0.603	1.007	0.607	0.955	83	38.6	3.65	166
1964	0.638	1.021	0.651	0.962	83	38.8	3.89	167
1965	0.636	1.076	0.684	0.962	87	39.0	3.88	176
1966	0.653	1.133	0.740	0.969	90	39.4	4.01	184
1967	0.680	1.035	0.703	0.975	82	39.3	4.20	167
1968	0.712	1.096	0.780	0.986	84	40.1	4.45	175
1969	0.759	1.188	0.902	0.990	92	39.5	4.77	189
1970	0.812	1.229	0.998	0.999	96	38.9	5.14	194
1971	0.896	1.118	1.001	1.002	90	37.6	5.69	176
1972	1.000	1.065	1.065	1.000	87	37.1	6.34	168
1973	1.086	1.102	1.197	0.986	90	37.7	6.79	176
1974	1.185	1.211	1.435	1.004	97	37.7	7.55	190
1975	1.386	1.154	1.600	1.016	94	36.6	8.94	179
1976	1.541	1.144	1.763	1.018	94	36.2	9.95	177
1977	1.711	1.128	1.929	1.015	93	36.2	11.01	175
1978	1.907	1.154	2.200	1.021	94	36.5	12.35	178

YEAR	LABOR INPUT PRICE	QUANTITY	OUTLAY	QUALITY	EMPLOYMENT	WEEKLY HOURS PER PERSON	HOURLY COMPENSATION	HOURS WORKED
COAL MINING								
1948	0.309	6.333	1.958	0.934	544	34.9	1.98	987
1949	0.313	4.871	1.524	0.934	485	30.1	2.01	759
1950	0.333	5.186	1.728	0.939	480	32.2	2.15	804
1951	0.386	4.903	1.893	0.938	452	32.4	2.49	761
1952	0.390	4.321	1.687	0.942	408	31.5	2.53	668
1953	0.432	3.765	1.625	0.940	353	31.8	2.79	583
1954	0.445	2.810	1.252	0.935	278	30.3	2.86	438
1955	0.442	2.995	1.325	0.933	261	34.4	2.83	467
1956	0.476	3.160	1.504	0.937	272	34.7	3.06	491
1957	0.511	2.999	1.534	0.938	266	33.6	3.30	465
1958	0.524	2.363	1.238	0.941	225	31.2	3.39	365
1959	0.552	2.228	1.230	0.944	199	33.2	3.58	344
1960	0.570	2.077	1.184	0.941	185	33.4	3.69	321
1961	0.562	1.872	1.052	0.944	165	33.6	3.64	289
1962	0.566	1.851	1.047	0.953	157	34.6	3.71	283
1963	0.575	1.871	1.075	0.952	152	36.2	3.76	286
1964	0.611	1.850	1.130	0.957	149	36.3	4.02	281
1965	0.626	1.857	1.163	0.959	146	37.1	4.13	282
1966	0.658	1.854	1.220	0.965	143	37.6	4.36	280
1967	0.694	1.860	1.291	0.974	142	37.7	4.64	278
1968	0.735	1.770	1.301	0.978	136	37.2	4.94	263
1969	0.820	1.790	1.468	0.983	138	37.0	5.53	265
1970	0.885	1.972	1.745	0.990	148	37.7	6.02	290
1971	0.951	2.009	1.910	0.999	150	37.5	6.52	293
1972	1.000	2.226	2.226	1.000	163	38.2	6.87	324
1973	1.133	2.185	2.474	1.002	163	37.4	7.80	317
1974	1.416	2.346	3.321	1.007	182	35.9	9.70	339
1975	1.512	2.890	4.368	1.018	216	36.8	10.58	413
1976	1.376	3.211	4.418	1.057	230	37.0	9.99	442
1977	1.731	3.162	5.473	0.954	242	38.3	11.34	483
1978	1.787	3.330	5.952	1.063	236	37.2	13.05	456
CRUDE PETROLEUM AND NATURAL GAS								
1948	0.403	2.478	0.998	0.801	278	38.0	1.81	550
1949	0.417	2.440	1.018	0.805	272	38.1	1.89	539
1950	0.424	2.514	1.066	0.813	275	38.5	1.94	550
1951	0.444	2.817	1.250	0.823	303	38.6	2.05	609
1952	0.467	3.062	1.430	0.843	321	38.7	2.21	646
1953	0.481	3.167	1.522	0.852	330	38.5	2.30	661
1954	0.496	3.217	1.596	0.857	336	38.2	2.39	668
1955	0.512	3.368	1.725	0.862	350	38.2	2.48	695
1956	0.537	3.554	1.909	0.871	363	38.4	2.63	726
1957	0.552	3.617	1.996	0.884	366	38.2	2.74	728
1958	0.557	3.403	1.897	0.900	339	38.1	2.82	672
1959	0.573	3.473	1.989	0.911	339	38.4	2.93	678
1960	0.593	3.288	1.948	0.914	323	38.1	3.05	640
1961	0.611	3.273	2.000	0.932	316	38.0	3.20	624
1962	0.622	3.289	2.046	0.947	311	38.2	3.31	618
1963	0.644	3.179	2.047	0.943	300	38.4	3.41	599
1964	0.658	3.218	2.118	0.955	299	38.5	3.54	599
1965	0.676	3.197	2.162	0.960	296	38.5	3.65	592
1966	0.708	3.198	2.265	0.969	292	38.7	3.86	587
1967	0.757	3.144	2.379	0.968	287	38.7	4.12	578
1968	0.794	3.181	2.526	0.973	288	38.8	4.34	582
1969	0.833	3.318	2.763	0.981	291	39.8	4.59	602
1970	0.882	3.226	2.844	0.997	280	39.5	4.94	576
1971	0.939	3.134	2.944	1.004	272	39.3	5.30	555
1972	1.000	3.176	3.176	1.000	272	39.9	5.62	565
1973	1.079	3.279	3.539	0.998	280	40.1	6.06	584
1974	1.155	3.830	4.424	1.009	310	41.9	6.55	675
1975	1.341	4.048	5.426	1.018	336	40.5	7.68	707
1976	1.451	4.240	6.152	0.995	359	40.6	8.12	758
1977	1.582	4.688	7.418	1.009	368	40.9	8.98	826
1978	1.705	5.446	9.288	1.020	444	41.1	9.79	949
NONMETALLIC MINING AND QUARRYING								
1948	0.294	1.062	0.312	0.916	102	41.0	1.44	217
1949	0.293	1.040	0.304	0.919	102	40.0	1.44	212
1950	0.328	1.081	0.355	0.921	104	40.7	1.61	220
1951	0.348	1.187	0.412	0.923	112	41.4	1.71	241
1952	0.361	1.217	0.439	0.932	114	41.3	1.79	245
1953	0.388	1.245	0.483	0.934	117	41.1	1.93	250
1954	0.404	1.228	0.495	0.933	117	40.5	2.01	247
1955	0.422	1.282	0.540	0.933	121	40.9	2.10	258
1956	0.453	1.356	0.614	0.933	128	41.0	2.25	273
1957	0.476	1.327	0.632	0.934	127	40.3	2.37	266
1958	0.501	1.285	0.644	0.941	123	40.0	2.52	256
1959	0.515	1.332	0.686	0.942	125	40.8	2.59	265
1960	0.552	1.274	0.704	0.935	122	40.2	2.76	255
1961	0.556	1.282	0.713	0.944	121	40.5	2.80	255
1962	0.569	1.299	0.740	0.956	120	40.8	2.90	255
1963	0.581	1.297	0.754	0.957	119	41.1	2.97	254
1964	0.618	1.324	0.817	0.965	119	41.6	3.18	257
1965	0.627	1.393	0.874	0.962	124	42.1	3.22	271
1966	0.652	1.417	0.924	0.971	125	42.1	3.38	273
1967	0.689	1.376	0.948	0.978	122	41.6	3.59	264
1968	0.726	1.358	0.986	0.983	120	41.5	3.81	259
1969	0.778	1.357	1.056	0.988	118	42.0	4.10	257
1970	0.838	1.334	1.117	0.988	118	41.3	4.41	253
1971	0.893	1.330	1.188	1.005	118	40.4	4.79	248
1972	1.000	1.276	1.276	1.000	115	40.0	5.33	239
1973	1.068	1.341	1.432	1.003	119	40.5	5.72	251
1974	1.145	1.419	1.625	1.000	124	41.3	6.11	266
1975	1.268	1.362	1.727	1.028	119	40.1	6.95	248
1976	1.315	1.379	1.814	1.025	120	40.4	7.19	252
1977	1.449	1.383	2.003	1.024	120	40.6	7.91	253
1978	1.551	1.465	2.272	1.028	126	40.8	8.50	267

YEAR	LABOR INPUT PRICE	QUANTITY	OUTLAY	QUALITY	EMPLOYMENT	WEEKLY HOURS PER PERSON	HOURLY COMPENSATION	HOURS WORKED
				CONTRACT CONSTRUCTION				
1948	0.299	33.760	10.082	0.910	3338	37.1	1.57	6440
1949	0.296	32.111	9.496	0.910	3202	36.8	1.55	6120
1950	0.325	34.738	11.303	0.911	3471	36.7	1.71	6616
1951	0.353	37.937	13.395	0.920	3705	37.2	1.87	7157
1952	0.370	38.887	14.393	0.930	3699	37.7	1.98	7253
1953	0.395	37.762	14.918	0.932	3643	37.1	2.12	7031
1954	0.412	36.263	14.954	0.937	3525	36.6	2.23	6717
1955	0.437	37.300	16.311	0.941	3622	36.5	2.37	6880
1956	0.450	39.091	17.599	0.939	3761	36.9	2.44	7224
1957	0.479	37.713	18.078	0.938	3680	36.4	2.59	6972
1958	0.484	36.450	17.657	0.942	3565	36.2	2.63	6712
1959	0.517	38.109	19.712	0.944	3703	36.4	2.81	7003
1960	0.540	37.488	20.243	0.941	3659	36.3	2.93	6911
1961	0.555	37.786	20.958	0.950	3635	36.5	3.04	6898
1962	0.564	39.362	22.216	0.965	3708	36.7	3.14	7076
1963	0.583	40.551	23.660	0.967	3779	37.0	3.25	7277
1964	0.613	42.180	25.872	0.977	3899	37.0	3.45	7492
1965	0.631	44.038	27.790	0.978	4050	37.1	3.56	7816
1966	0.674	45.547	30.722	0.987	4126	37.3	3.84	8004
1967	0.693	45.527	31.568	0.992	4084	37.5	3.97	7959
1968	0.756	46.920	35.488	0.999	4216	37.2	4.36	8145
1969	0.811	49.616	40.263	1.001	4409	37.5	4.68	8598
1970	0.861	48.001	41.323	0.999	4349	36.9	4.96	8338
1971	0.930	49.370	45.901	1.007	4437	36.9	5.40	8504
1972	1.000	50.624	50.624	1.000	4649	36.3	5.76	8783
1973	1.050	54.497	57.208	1.002	4969	36.5	6.06	9439
1974	1.122	53.732	60.263	1.002	4964	36.0	6.48	9305
1975	1.183	48.100	56.919	1.011	4449	35.7	6.89	8256
1976	1.295	49.486	64.090	1.010	4513	36.2	7.54	8504
1977	1.373	52.939	72.712	1.005	4871	36.1	7.96	9135
1978	1.427	59.245	84.515	1.005	5428	36.2	8.26	10227
				FOOD AND KINDRED PRODUCTS				
1948	0.332	17.499	5.815	0.933	1847	39.6	1.53	3798
1949	0.329	17.206	5.664	0.937	1827	39.2	1.52	3721
1950	0.347	17.430	6.048	0.935	1834	39.6	1.60	3775
1951	0.377	17.712	6.685	0.936	1878	39.2	1.74	3832
1952	0.393	17.796	7.000	0.945	1876	39.1	1.84	3813
1953	0.418	17.735	7.415	0.949	1877	38.8	1.96	3787
1954	0.439	17.501	7.684	0.952	1853	38.6	2.06	3723
1955	0.460	17.500	8.043	0.949	1851	38.8	2.15	3736
1956	0.489	17.519	8.567	0.946	1869	38.6	2.28	3750
1957	0.510	17.171	8.757	0.948	1844	38.2	2.39	3667
1958	0.532	16.737	8.911	0.955	1787	38.2	2.51	3551
1959	0.560	16.919	9.477	0.956	1798	38.3	2.64	3584
1960	0.579	17.097	9.903	0.958	1820	38.2	2.74	3616
1961	0.597	16.893	10.082	0.952	1805	38.3	2.81	3592
1962	0.611	17.035	10.410	0.965	1793	38.4	2.91	3576
1963	0.631	16.830	10.612	0.960	1779	38.4	2.99	3551
1964	0.663	16.929	11.230	0.965	1781	38.4	3.16	3553
1965	0.672	17.032	11.450	0.960	1796	38.5	3.19	3592
1966	0.702	17.360	12.193	0.971	1809	38.5	3.37	3622
1967	0.732	17.489	12.796	0.977	1820	38.3	3.53	3626
1968	0.772	17.578	13.579	0.982	1821	38.3	3.75	3624
1969	0.825	17.612	14.524	0.981	1827	38.3	3.99	3636
1970	0.887	17.371	15.416	0.992	1812	37.6	4.35	3547
1971	0.938	17.214	16.146	1.006	1777	37.5	4.66	3466
1972	1.000	16.903	16.903	1.000	1752	37.6	4.94	3423
1973	1.072	16.783	17.996	0.995	1746	37.6	5.27	3416
1974	1.166	16.848	19.640	1.003	1739	37.6	5.77	3401
1975	1.274	16.545	21.083	1.017	1690	37.5	6.40	3296
1976	1.404	16.663	23.395	1.015	1717	37.2	7.04	3325
1977	1.521	16.721	25.428	1.014	1739	36.9	7.62	3338
1978	1.649	16.881	27.837	1.016	1760	36.8	8.27	3366
				TOBACCO MANUFACTURERS				
1948	0.265	0.822	0.218	0.832	100	36.2	1.16	188
1949	0.284	0.821	0.233	0.835	102	35.2	1.24	187
1950	0.305	0.803	0.245	0.832	98	36.1	1.33	184
1951	0.320	0.877	0.281	0.835	106	36.3	1.40	200
1952	0.337	0.883	0.298	0.840	106	36.3	1.49	200
1953	0.362	0.878	0.317	0.844	106	35.9	1.60	198
1954	0.379	0.870	0.330	0.862	104	35.5	1.72	192
1955	0.391	0.876	0.343	0.864	102	36.4	1.78	193
1956	0.427	0.857	0.366	0.867	99	36.5	1.94	188
1957	0.460	0.822	0.378	0.873	95	36.2	2.11	179
1958	0.470	0.827	0.388	0.884	93	36.8	2.18	178
1959	0.488	0.841	0.410	0.889	93	37.2	2.28	180
1960	0.525	0.841	0.441	0.909	93	36.4	2.51	176
1961	0.531	0.826	0.438	0.903	90	37.2	2.52	174
1962	0.559	0.827	0.462	0.920	90	36.5	2.70	171
1963	0.581	0.817	0.475	0.920	89	36.5	2.81	169
1964	0.595	0.843	0.502	0.927	91	36.6	2.90	173
1965	0.634	0.802	0.508	0.931	88	35.8	3.10	164
1966	0.653	0.800	0.522	0.940	85	36.7	3.22	162
1967	0.674	0.815	0.549	0.951	86	36.4	3.37	163
1968	0.745	0.784	0.584	0.963	84	35.5	3.77	155
1969	0.827	0.754	0.624	0.970	81	35.1	4.21	148
1970	0.816	0.777	0.634	0.985	81	35.6	4.23	150
1971	0.924	0.747	0.691	1.001	77	35.5	4.87	142
1972	1.000	0.736	0.736	1.000	77	35.0	5.26	140
1973	1.087	0.767	0.834	1.000	79	35.5	5.71	146
1974	1.259	0.752	0.947	1.008	79	34.6	6.67	142
1975	1.377	0.705	0.971	1.024	73	34.5	7.42	131
1976	1.613	0.683	1.102	1.023	72	33.9	8.68	127
1977	1.790	0.666	1.193	1.022	70	34.1	9.62	124
1978	1.965	0.663	1.303	1.026	69	34.3	10.60	123

		LABOR INPUT						
YEAR	PRICE	QUANTITY	OUTLAY	QUALITY	EMPLOYMENT	WEEKLY HOURS PER PERSON	HOURLY COMPENSATION	HOURS WORKED
				TEXTILE MILL PRODUCTS				
1948	0.404	8.880	3.591	0.940	1333	37.7	1.38	2612
1949	0.414	7.688	3.186	0.942	1196	36.3	1.41	2255
1950	0.431	8.508	3.667	0.942	1260	38.1	1.47	2495
1951	0.463	8.217	3.808	0.941	1243	37.3	1.58	2412
1952	0.472	7.828	3.698	0.948	1168	37.6	1.62	2283
1953	0.478	7.800	3.730	0.948	1163	37.6	1.64	2273
1954	0.480	6.992	3.354	0.957	1053	36.9	1.66	2020
1955	0.484	7.343	3.554	0.954	1064	38.5	1.67	2128
1956	0.508	7.134	3.624	0.954	1043	38.1	1.75	2067
1957	0.528	6.669	3.522	0.957	990	37.4	1.83	1927
1958	0.536	6.250	3.347	0.964	927	37.2	1.87	1792
1959	0.561	6.688	3.750	0.963	954	36.7	1.95	1920
1960	0.575	6.498	3.738	0.978	931	37.9	2.04	1836
1961	0.586	6.299	3.691	0.969	902	38.3	2.06	1796
1962	0.599	6.558	3.926	0.981	913	38.9	2.13	1847
1963	0.619	6.435	3.985	0.977	900	38.9	2.19	1821
1964	0.653	6.507	4.248	0.977	902	39.3	2.31	1841
1965	0.683	6.841	4.670	0.973	935	40.0	2.40	1943
1966	0.717	7.147	5.128	0.974	974	40.0	2.53	2028
1967	0.750	6.989	5.240	0.977	971	39.2	2.65	1978
1968	0.803	7.316	5.871	0.980	1006	39.5	2.84	2064
1969	0.856	7.311	6.261	0.978	1016	39.1	3.03	2066
1970	0.899	7.022	6.313	0.994	989	38.0	3.23	1952
1971	0.942	7.016	6.610	1.003	965	38.5	3.42	1933
1972	1.000	7.414	7.414	1.000	1005	39.2	3.62	2049
1973	1.090	7.534	8.212	0.997	1036	38.8	3.93	2089
1974	1.207	6.938	8.375	1.003	990	37.2	4.38	1913
1975	1.281	6.176	7.915	1.018	872	37.0	4.72	1676
1976	1.394	6.646	9.264	1.014	921	37.8	5.11	1811
1977	1.516	6.611	10.022	1.013	915	37.9	5.56	1804
1978	1.638	6.599	10.806	1.007	916	38.0	5.97	1811
				APPAREL AND OTHER FABRICATED TEXTILE PRODUCTS				
1948	0.433	7.432	3.218	0.973	1234	34.9	1.44	2238
1949	0.428	7.232	3.092	0.975	1211	34.5	1.42	2175
1950	0.455	7.516	3.422	0.970	1234	35.4	1.51	2272
1951	0.492	7.396	3.638	0.967	1243	34.7	1.62	2243
1952	0.490	7.608	3.730	0.966	1258	35.3	1.62	2308
1953	0.507	7.693	3.899	0.962	1284	35.1	1.66	2344
1954	0.517	7.247	3.747	0.972	1221	34.4	1.71	2186
1955	0.523	7.566	3.955	0.964	1256	35.2	1.72	2301
1956	0.561	7.523	4.223	0.962	1260	35.0	1.84	2293
1957	0.572	7.334	4.192	0.963	1236	34.7	1.88	2233
1958	0.590	6.944	4.098	0.969	1180	34.2	1.95	2100
1959	0.599	7.473	4.480	0.966	1239	35.2	1.97	2269
1960	0.604	7.562	4.566	0.988	1252	34.5	2.04	2244
1961	0.633	7.290	4.611	0.968	1231	34.5	2.09	2207
1962	0.629	7.926	4.984	0.981	1281	35.5	2.11	2366
1963	0.648	7.935	5.141	0.974	1294	35.5	2.15	2388
1964	0.678	8.006	5.431	0.972	1314	35.3	2.25	2414
1965	0.697	8.366	5.831	0.968	1363	35.8	2.30	2534
1966	0.727	8.668	6.298	0.966	1414	35.8	2.40	2630
1967	0.769	8.559	6.579	0.968	1406	35.4	2.54	2591
1968	0.849	8.633	7.329	0.973	1421	35.2	2.82	2600
1969	0.897	8.623	7.736	0.970	1430	35.0	2.97	2605
1970	0.930	8.264	7.687	0.987	1381	34.2	3.13	2454
1971	0.955	8.334	7.962	1.004	1359	34.4	3.27	2433
1972	1.000	8.570	8.570	1.000	1389	34.8	3.41	2512
1973	1.074	8.707	9.354	0.996	1424	34.6	3.65	2564
1974	1.164	8.207	9.553	1.004	1366	33.7	3.99	2396
1975	1.221	7.719	9.425	1.023	1259	33.8	4.26	2212
1976	1.299	8.440	10.963	1.016	1346	34.8	4.50	2434
1977	1.417	8.319	11.791	1.016	1339	34.5	4.91	2400
1978	1.526	8.447	12.890	1.018	1357	34.5	5.30	2432
				PAPER AND ALLIED PRODUCTS				
1948	0.334	4.731	1.578	0.867	471	39.8	1.62	976
1949	0.347	4.475	1.554	0.870	454	39.0	1.69	920
1950	0.362	4.952	1.795	0.870	486	40.3	1.76	1016
1951	0.396	5.221	2.068	0.877	511	40.1	1.94	1065
1952	0.413	5.205	2.148	0.891	505	39.8	2.06	1045
1953	0.427	5.572	2.379	0.898	534	39.9	2.15	1109
1954	0.443	5.564	2.467	0.908	535	39.4	2.25	1096
1955	0.463	5.835	2.705	0.909	552	40.0	2.36	1148
1956	0.486	6.023	2.930	0.913	571	39.7	2.48	1180
1957	0.512	5.973	3.057	0.919	568	39.3	2.63	1162
1958	0.529	5.904	3.125	0.930	559	39.0	2.75	1135
1959	0.550	6.292	3.459	0.935	583	39.7	2.87	1204
1960	0.565	6.402	3.615	0.948	593	39.2	2.99	1208
1961	0.584	6.526	3.808	0.948	600	39.5	3.09	1231
1962	0.604	6.726	4.065	0.962	616	39.0	3.25	1250
1963	0.623	6.808	4.239	0.959	623	39.2	3.34	1269
1964	0.647	6.892	4.458	0.965	626	39.2	3.49	1277
1965	0.663	7.084	4.698	0.963	641	39.5	3.57	1315
1966	0.687	7.409	5.153	0.972	669	39.7	3.74	1380
1967	0.712	7.612	5.420	0.980	681	39.2	3.90	1389
1968	0.757	7.807	5.906	0.985	693	39.3	4.17	1417
1969	0.807	8.069	6.513	0.986	715	39.4	4.45	1464
1970	0.875	7.774	6.806	0.995	704	38.2	4.87	1397
1971	0.928	7.608	7.058	1.004	680	38.3	5.21	1354
1972	1.000	7.731	7.731	1.000	685	38.8	5.59	1382
1973	1.074	7.903	8.486	0.999	702	38.8	6.00	1415
1974	1.188	7.772	9.232	1.005	702	37.9	6.68	1382
1975	1.308	7.151	9.352	1.019	643	37.5	7.46	1254
1976	1.446	7.548	10.912	1.017	675	37.8	8.22	1327
1977	1.573	7.768	12.220	1.014	694	38.0	8.92	1370
1978	1.712	7.888	13.508	1.018	702	38.0	9.75	1386

LABOR INPUT

YEAR	PRICE	QUANTITY	OUTLAY	QUALITY	EMPLOYMENT	WEEKLY HOURS PER PERSON	HOURLY COMPENSATION	HOURS WORKED
				PRINTING AND PUBLISHING				
1948	0.365	7.656	2.793	0.900	812	37.2	1.78	1572
1949	0.376	7.615	2.860	0.908	809	36.8	1.85	1549
1950	0.407	7.560	3.079	0.934	820	35.1	2.06	1495
1951	0.417	7.997	3.331	0.914	843	36.9	2.06	1616
1952	0.429	8.217	3.524	0.927	855	36.8	2.15	1638
1953	0.449	8.533	3.832	0.939	876	36.9	2.28	1679
1954	0.468	8.603	4.029	0.944	886	36.5	2.39	1683
1955	0.487	8.786	4.279	0.943	905	36.6	2.49	1721
1956	0.519	8.924	4.629	0.930	929	36.7	2.61	1772
1957	0.542	9.014	4.890	0.936	940	36.4	2.75	1780
1958	0.560	8.889	4.982	0.943	930	36.0	2.86	1741
1959	0.573	9.234	5.287	0.950	945	36.6	2.94	1796
1960	0.561	10.048	5.632	1.003	973	36.6	3.04	1850
1961	0.600	9.760	5.851	0.966	983	36.5	3.14	1866
1962	0.622	9.853	6.125	0.972	994	36.2	3.27	1873
1963	0.640	9.919	6.344	0.971	999	36.3	3.36	1887
1964	0.660	10.224	6.745	0.983	1014	36.4	3.51	1922
1965	0.677	10.498	7.108	0.979	1043	36.5	3.59	1982
1966	0.708	10.919	7.730	0.985	1074	36.7	3.78	2047
1967	0.729	11.325	8.254	0.997	1108	36.4	3.93	2099
1968	0.773	11.505	8.891	0.997	1126	36.4	4.17	2132
1969	0.828	11.781	9.758	0.993	1155	36.5	4.45	2191
1970	0.876	11.673	10.224	1.010	1147	35.7	4.81	2127
1971	0.944	11.191	10.563	1.010	1107	35.6	5.16	2046
1972	1.000	11.380	11.380	1.000	1118	36.2	5.41	2102
1973	1.063	11.671	12.408	0.993	1153	36.2	5.72	2171
1974	1.150	11.555	13.288	0.995	1155	35.7	6.20	2144
1975	1.216	11.389	13.853	1.006	1136	35.4	6.63	2091
1976	1.313	11.570	15.197	1.013	1151	35.2	7.20	2110
1977	1.385	12.005	16.624	1.004	1201	35.4	7.53	2208
1978	1.472	12.583	18.525	1.009	1253	35.3	8.04	2303
				CHEMICALS AND ALLIED PRODUCTS				
1948	0.331	7.017	2.319	0.829	640	38.0	1.83	1265
1949	0.349	6.628	2.315	0.832	608	37.7	1.94	1191
1950	0.369	6.948	2.560	0.836	627	38.1	2.06	1243
1951	0.400	7.837	3.135	0.846	700	38.1	2.26	1385
1952	0.416	8.200	3.408	0.864	723	37.8	2.40	1420
1953	0.431	8.799	3.797	0.877	763	37.8	2.53	1501
1954	0.450	8.713	3.925	0.867	749	37.7	2.67	1468
1955	0.468	9.001	4.212	0.892	767	37.9	2.79	1510
1956	0.495	9.426	4.666	0.898	798	37.8	2.97	1570
1957	0.524	9.663	5.064	0.908	811	37.7	3.18	1591
1958	0.542	9.435	5.110	0.924	781	37.6	3.35	1528
1959	0.560	9.852	5.514	0.934	799	38.0	3.49	1578
1960	0.563	10.291	5.795	0.957	816	37.9	3.60	1609
1961	0.589	10.105	6.007	0.956	817	37.5	3.76	1595
1962	0.606	10.480	6.353	0.969	826	37.7	3.93	1618
1963	0.626	10.617	6.647	0.963	843	37.6	4.03	1649
1964	0.651	10.860	7.071	0.970	855	37.7	4.22	1674
1965	0.663	11.288	7.487	0.969	886	37.8	4.30	1743
1966	0.690	12.103	8.352	0.977	941	37.9	4.51	1853
1967	0.710	12.603	8.953	0.985	977	37.7	4.68	1913
1968	0.758	12.939	9.813	0.989	1007	37.4	5.02	1957
1969	0.809	13.350	10.803	0.989	1039	37.4	5.35	2019
1970	0.861	13.267	11.417	0.996	1028	37.3	5.73	1992
1971	0.914	12.891	11.787	1.006	989	37.2	6.15	1915
1972	1.000	12.579	12.579	1.000	980	36.9	6.69	1881
1973	1.070	12.981	13.889	1.000	1009	37.0	7.16	1941
1974	1.182	13.261	15.669	1.007	1028	36.8	7.95	1970
1975	1.302	13.266	17.274	1.019	1025	36.5	8.87	1947
1976	1.409	13.752	19.378	1.021	1051	36.8	9.62	2014
1977	1.529	14.113	21.583	1.016	1082	36.9	10.39	2077
1978	1.639	14.568	23.872	1.025	1105	37.0	11.23	2125
				PETROLEUM AND COAL PRODUCTS				
1948	0.366	2.955	1.082	0.827	222	36.5	2.57	421
1949	0.389	2.879	1.121	0.829	217	36.3	2.74	409
1950	0.391	2.942	1.149	0.834	219	36.6	2.76	416
1951	0.441	3.130	1.380	0.841	231	36.6	3.14	439
1952	0.469	3.232	1.515	0.855	235	36.4	3.40	446
1953	0.481	3.351	1.612	0.865	240	36.5	3.53	457
1954	0.505	3.334	1.682	0.873	237	36.5	3.73	450
1955	0.517	3.361	1.736	0.876	237	36.6	3.84	452
1956	0.543	3.369	1.828	0.883	236	36.6	4.06	450
1957	0.571	3.412	1.949	0.892	237	36.6	4.32	451
1958	0.584	3.296	1.924	0.906	225	36.6	4.49	429
1959	0.620	3.164	1.962	0.917	215	36.4	4.82	407
1960	0.620	3.113	1.931	0.936	208	36.3	4.93	392
1961	0.656	2.978	1.954	0.937	200	36.0	5.22	375
1962	0.658	2.929	1.927	0.947	194	36.1	5.29	364
1963	0.684	2.859	1.956	0.949	189	36.1	5.51	355
1964	0.689	2.813	1.938	0.959	184	36.2	5.60	346
1965	0.711	2.792	1.986	0.960	181	36.4	5.79	303
1966	0.724	2.826	2.047	0.969	181	36.5	5.95	344
1967	0.746	2.653	2.128	0.981	180	36.6	6.20	343
1968	0.793	2.915	2.311	0.988	185	36.2	6.64	348
1969	0.849	2.965	2.516	0.993	187	36.2	7.15	352
1970	0.869	3.050	2.649	0.992	190	36.7	7.31	362
1971	0.928	3.034	2.814	1.001	188	36.6	7.88	357
1972	1.000	2.994	2.994	1.000	184	36.9	8.48	353
1973	1.071	3.016	3.229	1.002	185	36.9	9.10	355
1974	1.206	3.222	3.887	1.005	190	38.3	10.28	378
1975	1.405	3.162	4.444	1.013	189	37.4	12.08	368
1976	1.531	3.280	5.022	1.018	194	37.7	13.22	380
1977	1.660	3.392	5.631	1.013	200	38.0	14.26	395
1978	1.776	3.554	6.311	1.022	205	38.5	15.39	410

	LABOR INPUT							
YEAR	PRICE	QUANTITY	OUTLAY	QUALITY	EMPLOYMENT	WEEKLY HOURS PER PERSON	HOURLY COMPENSATION	HOURS WORKED
				RUBBER AND MISCELLANEOUS PLASTIC PRODUCTS				
1948	0.380	2.938	1.116	0.923	323	37.4	1.78	628
1949	0.382	2.686	1.026	0.926	299	36.8	1.79	572
1950	0.406	3.067	1.247	0.925	324	38.8	1.91	654
1951	0.442	3.304	1.461	0.930	350	38.5	2.08	701
1952	0.460	3.380	1.554	0.940	353	38.6	2.19	709
1953	0.480	3.591	1.724	0.946	376	38.3	2.30	749
1954	0.493	3.325	1.640	0.960	347	37.8	2.40	683
1955	0.515	3.762	1.938	0.958	379	39.3	2.50	775
1956	0.544	3.757	2.044	0.959	388	38.3	2.64	773
1957	0.574	3.795	2.178	0.962	389	38.5	2.80	778
1958	0.597	3.495	2.086	0.971	365	37.4	2.94	710
1959	0.607	3.960	2.405	0.972	397	38.9	2.99	804
1960	0.626	3.936	2.464	0.986	399	37.9	3.13	787
1961	0.643	3.899	2.508	0.982	393	38.3	3.20	783
1962	0.644	4.439	2.858	0.992	438	38.7	3.24	882
1963	0.667	4.480	2.989	0.985	447	38.6	3.33	897
1964	0.691	4.687	3.240	0.985	463	39.0	3.45	938
1965	0.708	5.061	3.582	0.978	497	39.5	3.51	1021
1966	0.730	5.526	4.035	0.980	541	39.5	3.63	1112
1967	0.766	5.546	4.249	0.986	546	39.1	3.83	1109
1968	0.810	5.982	4.845	0.988	587	39.1	4.06	1194
1969	0.855	6.338	5.417	0.986	628	38.8	4.27	1268
1970	0.903	6.070	5.480	0.995	611	37.9	4.56	1203
1971	0.952	6.096	5.804	1.006	607	37.9	4.86	1195
1972	1.000	6.662	6.662	1.000	656	38.5	5.07	1314
1973	1.061	7.166	7.600	0.996	710	38.4	5.36	1419
1974	1.171	6.999	8.198	1.002	706	37.5	5.95	1377
1975	1.253	6.015	7.540	1.019	603	37.1	6.47	1165
1976	1.343	6.524	8.762	1.013	654	37.4	6.90	1271
1977	1.463	7.205	10.540	1.009	721	37.6	7.48	1409
1978	1.575	7.607	11.983	1.013	760	37.5	8.09	1480
				LEATHER AND LEATHER PRODUCTS				
1948	0.392	2.681	1.051	0.971	411	35.6	1.38	761
1949	0.390	2.558	0.997	0.976	396	35.2	1.38	724
1950	0.402	2.656	1.068	0.976	401	36.1	1.42	751
1951	0.433	2.503	1.085	0.973	386	35.4	1.53	710
1952	0.452	2.615	1.182	0.974	388	36.7	1.60	741
1953	0.469	2.589	1.214	0.974	391	36.0	1.66	733
1954	0.482	2.453	1.183	0.982	374	35.4	1.72	689
1955	0.496	2.574	1.276	0.976	386	36.2	1.75	728
1956	0.528	2.525	1.334	0.972	383	36.0	1.86	717
1957	0.545	2.474	1.349	0.972	377	35.8	1.92	703
1958	0.565	2.331	1.316	0.976	360	35.2	2.00	659
1959	0.583	2.479	1.445	0.971	375	36.1	2.05	704
1960	0.593	2.400	1.425	0.989	364	35.4	2.13	670
1961	0.609	2.361	1.439	0.972	360	35.8	2.15	670
1962	0.623	2.409	1.500	0.984	361	36.0	2.22	676
1963	0.649	2.328	1.510	0.979	351	35.9	2.30	656
1964	0.682	2.342	1.597	0.979	350	36.3	2.42	660
1965	0.692	2.393	1.655	0.973	357	36.5	2.44	678
1966	0.721	2.467	1.779	0.973	365	36.9	2.54	699
1967	0.761	2.382	1.813	0.975	355	36.5	2.69	674
1968	0.816	2.441	1.993	0.977	361	36.7	2.89	689
1969	0.880	2.269	1.996	0.975	345	35.8	3.11	642
1970	0.921	2.122	1.954	0.989	321	35.5	3.30	592
1971	0.951	2.041	1.942	1.000	302	35.8	3.45	563
1972	1.000	2.050	2.050	1.000	300	36.3	3.62	566
1973	1.047	2.002	2.096	0.994	297	36.0	3.77	556
1974	1.164	1.824	2.123	1.001	279	34.6	4.22	503
1975	1.244	1.634	2.031	1.017	247	34.5	4.58	443
1976	1.298	1.798	2.333	1.011	267	35.3	4.76	490
1977	1.413	1.730	2.443	1.004	262	34.9	5.14	475
1978	1.508	1.758	2.651	0.998	266	35.1	5.46	486
				LUMBER AND WOOD PRODUCTS EXCEPT FURNITURE				
1948	0.296	7.290	2.160	0.932	973	38.8	1.10	1961
1949	0.306	6.311	1.930	0.931	859	38.1	1.14	1699
1950	0.330	6.882	2.271	0.936	924	38.3	1.23	1843
1951	0.371	7.256	2.695	0.931	983	38.2	1.38	1954
1952	0.383	6.960	2.668	0.938	927	38.6	1.44	1858
1953	0.394	6.681	2.632	0.937	899	38.2	1.47	1786
1954	0.411	6.110	2.509	0.936	825	38.1	1.53	1636
1955	0.431	6.472	2.789	0.939	865	38.4	1.61	1727
1956	0.483	6.281	3.033	0.935	854	37.9	1.80	1683
1957	0.491	5.631	2.762	0.934	776	37.4	1.83	1510
1958	0.487	5.347	2.603	0.935	732	37.6	1.82	1433
1959	0.530	5.799	3.073	0.939	773	38.5	1.99	1547
1960	0.541	5.575	3.017	0.945	749	38.0	2.04	1479
1961	0.552	5.238	2.893	0.943	698	38.3	2.08	1392
1962	0.570	5.400	3.076	0.958	703	38.7	2.18	1413
1963	0.609	5.469	3.328	0.960	705	38.9	2.33	1428
1964	0.635	5.725	3.634	0.966	730	39.1	2.45	1485
1965	0.637	5.871	3.738	0.966	741	39.5	2.45	1523
1966	0.685	5.993	4.107	0.977	749	39.5	2.67	1537
1967	0.700	5.838	4.085	0.984	733	39.0	2.75	1487
1968	0.748	6.005	4.494	0.993	748	39.0	2.97	1515
1969	0.824	6.171	5.088	0.992	777	38.6	3.26	1559
1970	0.880	5.980	5.261	1.004	761	37.7	3.52	1493
1971	0.928	6.214	5.769	1.003	782	38.2	3.72	1552
1972	1.000	6.504	6.504	1.000	803	39.0	3.99	1630
1973	1.070	6.720	7.193	0.994	837	38.9	4.25	1693
1974	1.217	6.193	7.538	1.003	798	37.3	4.87	1547
1975	1.332	5.272	7.023	1.017	685	36.5	5.41	1299
1976	1.423	6.019	8.563	1.011	759	37.8	5.74	1492
1977	1.569	6.394	10.032	1.010	807	37.8	6.32	1587
1978	1.721	6.693	11.521	1.011	844	37.8	6.95	1658

YEAR	LABOR INPUT: PRICE	LABOR INPUT: QUANTITY	LABOR INPUT: OUTLAY	LABOR INPUT: QUALITY	EMPLOYMENT	WEEKLY HOURS PER PERSON	HOURLY COMPENSATION	HOURS WORKED
				FURNITURE AND FIXTURES				
1948	0.365	2.794	1.021	0.927	363	39.5	1.37	746
1949	0.373	2.552	0.952	0.930	338	38.7	1.40	679
1950	0.386	3.045	1.176	0.941	384	40.1	1.47	801
1951	0.429	2.943	1.264	0.939	378	39.5	1.63	776
1952	0.442	3.010	1.330	0.947	381	39.7	1.69	787
1953	0.461	3.053	1.407	0.950	389	39.4	1.77	795
1954	0.479	2.780	1.332	0.955	359	38.6	1.85	721
1955	0.503	3.046	1.532	0.956	383	39.6	1.94	789
1956	0.531	3.067	1.630	0.955	391	39.2	2.05	795
1957	0.547	3.005	1.643	0.957	389	38.5	2.11	777
1958	0.563	2.832	1.594	0.963	369	38.0	2.19	728
1959	0.591	3.036	1.794	0.964	387	38.7	2.30	779
1960	0.613	2.993	1.834	0.970	385	38.2	2.40	764
1961	0.626	2.848	1.783	0.969	366	38.2	2.45	728
1962	0.623	3.096	1.929	0.980	385	39.1	2.47	782
1963	0.645	3.117	2.009	0.977	387	39.3	2.54	790
1964	0.664	3.280	2.177	0.980	404	39.4	2.63	828
1965	0.671	3.476	2.334	0.978	426	39.7	2.65	880
1966	0.715	3.736	2.672	0.982	457	39.6	2.84	942
1967	0.738	3.615	2.667	0.981	452	38.8	2.92	912
1968	0.803	3.708	2.978	0.988	464	38.5	3.20	929
1969	0.863	3.753	3.241	0.985	473	38.3	3.44	943
1970	0.898	3.482	3.127	0.994	446	37.4	3.61	867
1971	0.939	3.528	3.311	1.002	443	37.8	3.80	872
1972	1.000	3.845	3.845	1.000	482	38.0	4.04	952
1973	1.078	4.037	4.351	0.998	514	37.5	4.34	1001
1974	1.184	3.803	4.504	0.999	497	36.5	4.78	942
1975	1.266	3.243	4.106	1.013	427	35.7	5.18	792
1976	1.349	3.556	4.795	1.015	454	36.7	5.53	867
1977	1.453	3.768	5.474	0.998	487	36.9	5.86	934
1978	1.563	4.002	6.257	1.006	510	37.1	6.36	985
				STONE, CLAY, AND GLASS PRODUCTS				
1948	0.327	5.500	1.798	0.874	579	38.4	1.56	1155
1949	0.336	5.033	1.692	0.877	540	37.6	1.61	1054
1950	0.356	5.495	1.957	0.878	571	38.7	1.70	1148
1951	0.391	5.941	2.322	0.883	610	38.9	1.88	1234
1952	0.397	5.806	2.305	0.896	591	38.7	1.94	1189
1953	0.426	5.911	2.515	0.904	601	38.4	2.09	1201
1954	0.443	5.647	2.499	0.911	573	38.2	2.20	1138
1955	0.462	6.070	2.801	0.913	604	38.8	2.30	1220
1956	0.491	6.109	3.046	0.915	619	38.6	2.45	1243
1957	0.517	6.044	3.127	0.921	609	38.0	2.60	1205
1958	0.531	5.753	3.055	0.930	579	37.7	2.69	1136
1959	0.548	6.360	3.485	0.936	615	39.0	2.79	1248
1960	0.558	6.403	3.572	0.948	619	38.5	2.88	1240
1961	0.571	6.177	3.524	0.949	595	38.6	2.95	1195
1962	0.595	6.313	3.757	0.963	603	38.4	3.12	1204
1963	0.610	6.452	3.938	0.961	612	38.7	3.20	1232
1964	0.635	6.698	4.251	0.968	627	38.9	3.35	1270
1965	0.650	6.877	4.471	0.966	642	39.1	3.42	1307
1966	0.677	7.118	4.815	0.975	658	39.2	3.59	1340
1967	0.700	6.980	4.887	0.980	647	38.8	3.74	1307
1968	0.758	7.010	5.311	0.986	650	38.6	4.07	1304
1969	0.804	7.294	5.865	0.986	674	38.7	4.32	1357
1970	0.854	7.120	6.084	0.994	657	38.5	4.63	1315
1971	0.915	7.056	6.457	1.005	646	38.4	5.01	1289
1972	1.000	7.219	7.219	1.000	667	38.2	5.45	1325
1973	1.059	7.693	8.140	1.000	707	38.4	5.77	1411
1974	1.158	7.557	8.754	1.006	701	37.8	6.35	1379
1975	1.261	6.875	8.667	1.020	641	37.1	7.00	1237
1976	1.376	7.086	9.754	1.018	660	37.2	7.64	1277
1977	1.496	7.321	10.949	1.015	682	37.3	8.27	1324
1978	1.621	7.760	12.575	1.021	714	37.6	9.02	1395
				PRIMARY METAL INDUSTRIES				
1948	0.303	14.558	4.405	0.905	1234	37.0	1.86	2373
1949	0.313	12.364	3.872	0.906	1088	35.6	1.92	2013
1950	0.336	14.317	4.806	0.909	1191	37.5	2.07	2324
1951	0.367	15.959	5.858	0.912	1304	38.1	2.27	2582
1952	0.390	15.059	5.872	0.923	1236	37.4	2.44	2407
1953	0.411	16.218	6.667	0.928	1319	37.6	2.59	2579
1954	0.428	13.656	5.935	0.932	1176	35.9	2.71	2194
1955	0.455	15.910	7.231	0.932	1281	37.8	2.87	2519
1956	0.484	16.296	7.880	0.935	1316	37.6	3.06	2572
1957	0.523	15.866	8.302	0.939	1313	36.5	3.33	2493
1958	0.547	13.167	7.208	0.947	1110	35.6	3.51	2052
1959	0.564	14.314	8.079	0.949	1138	37.6	3.63	2225
1960	0.585	14.463	8.462	0.959	1173	36.5	3.80	2225
1961	0.598	13.561	8.115	0.963	1094	36.5	3.91	2078
1962	0.614	14.159	8.687	0.973	1117	37.0	4.05	2147
1963	0.620	14.483	8.986	0.971	1127	37.6	4.08	2201
1964	0.642	15.519	9.971	0.977	1182	38.1	4.25	2345
1965	0.653	16.476	10.755	0.975	1249	38.4	4.31	2494
1966	0.681	17.148	11.685	0.980	1293	38.4	4.53	2581
1967	0.700	16.586	11.604	0.987	1267	37.6	4.68	2479
1968	0.753	16.629	12.526	0.991	1267	37.6	5.06	2475
1969	0.801	17.174	13.753	0.992	1303	37.7	5.38	2555
1970	0.851	16.148	13.736	0.995	1266	36.4	5.74	2394
1971	0.915	15.108	13.820	1.001	1180	36.3	6.21	2227
1972	1.000	15.479	15.479	1.000	1182	37.2	6.78	2284
1973	1.086	16.852	18.303	1.002	1266	37.7	7.37	2482
1974	1.214	17.188	20.858	1.007	1287	37.6	8.28	2519
1975	1.389	14.770	20.522	1.018	1145	36.0	9.59	2141
1976	1.513	15.033	22.745	1.019	1156	36.2	10.45	2177
1977	1.672	15.521	25.954	1.016	1189	36.5	11.51	2255
1978	1.808	16.219	29.322	1.018	1226	36.9	12.47	2351

	LABOR INPUT							
YEAR	PRICE	QUANTITY	OUTLAY	QUALITY	EMPLOYMENT	WEEKLY HOURS PER PERSON	HOURLY COMPENSATION	HOURS WORKED
				FABRICATED METAL INDUSTRIES				
1948	0.340	11.224	3.816	0.914	1106	38.2	1.74	2195
1949	0.352	10.011	3.522	0.917	1004	37.4	1.80	1952
1950	0.373	11.445	4.268	0.918	1105	38.8	1.91	2229
1951	0.408	12.778	5.219	0.927	1215	39.0	2.12	2466
1952	0.425	13.266	5.635	0.942	1244	38.9	2.24	2519
1953	0.441	14.555	6.420	0.950	1351	39.0	2.34	2740
1954	0.454	13.101	5.944	0.958	1229	38.2	2.43	2445
1955	0.470	14.042	6.605	0.959	1294	38.9	2.52	2618
1956	0.502	14.237	7.146	0.962	1318	38.6	2.70	2646
1957	0.524	14.365	7.520	0.968	1333	38.3	2.83	2654
1958	0.541	12.765	6.907	0.979	1194	37.6	2.96	2332
1959	0.563	13.653	7.690	0.983	1248	38.3	3.09	2485
1960	0.576	13.809	7.952	0.993	1258	38.0	3.20	2486
1961	0.589	13.323	7.841	0.992	1215	38.0	3.27	2401
1962	0.601	14.263	8.574	1.000	1276	38.4	3.36	2550
1963	0.618	14.434	8.926	0.993	1294	38.6	3.43	2600
1964	0.650	14.978	9.731	0.995	1333	38.9	3.61	2693
1965	0.663	15.865	10.523	0.988	1411	39.1	3.66	2872
1966	0.690	17.324	11.959	0.991	1527	39.4	3.82	3128
1967	0.720	17.654	12.716	0.993	1579	38.7	4.00	3179
1968	0.772	18.112	13.990	0.995	1629	38.4	4.30	3256
1969	0.822	18.689	15.363	0.991	1691	38.4	4.55	3374
1970	0.888	16.986	15.078	0.994	1575	37.3	4.94	3055
1971	0.947	16.065	15.219	1.005	1482	37.1	5.32	2859
1972	1.000	16.984	16.984	1.000	1535	38.1	5.59	3037
1973	1.061	18.401	19.519	0.999	1652	38.4	5.92	3295
1974	1.182	17.961	21.236	1.004	1646	37.4	6.64	3199
1975	1.304	16.085	20.982	1.017	1476	36.8	7.42	2828
1976	1.410	16.749	23.624	1.016	1532	37.0	8.01	2949
1977	1.530	17.388	26.606	1.013	1593	37.1	8.66	3071
1978	1.633	18.428	30.097	1.016	1681	37.1	9.28	3244
				MACHINERY EXCEPT ELECTRICAL				
1948	0.329	15.509	5.107	0.886	1437	38.7	1.77	2893
1949	0.340	12.956	4.411	0.885	1240	37.5	1.82	2418
1950	0.359	13.875	4.982	0.891	1266	39.1	1.94	2574
1951	0.395	17.342	6.856	0.898	1525	40.2	2.15	3191
1952	0.417	18.311	7.639	0.910	1605	39.9	2.30	3327
1953	0.441	18.511	8.159	0.916	1628	39.4	2.40	3338
1954	0.456	16.321	7.437	0.922	1471	38.2	2.54	2925
1955	0.467	16.995	7.940	0.923	1497	39.1	2.61	3044
1956	0.502	18.426	9.257	0.926	1609	39.3	2.81	3289
1957	0.524	18.182	9.534	0.931	1614	38.5	2.95	3227
1958	0.540	15.543	8.398	0.940	1398	37.6	3.07	2733
1959	0.565	17.064	9.649	0.945	1498	38.3	3.23	2983
1960	0.584	17.208	10.050	0.954	1509	38.0	3.37	2981
1961	0.598	16.677	9.976	0.960	1454	38.0	3.47	2871
1962	0.612	18.136	11.108	0.972	1528	38.8	3.60	3084
1963	0.626	18.563	11.626	0.969	1566	38.9	3.67	3166
1964	0.652	19.816	12.922	0.976	1644	39.2	3.85	3354
1965	0.667	21.418	14.295	0.974	1780	39.3	3.93	3635
1966	0.700	23.906	16.723	0.960	1952	39.7	4.15	4033
1967	0.722	24.306	17.537	0.989	2006	38.9	4.32	4061
1968	0.782	23.833	18.637	0.993	1998	38.2	4.70	3966
1969	0.837	24.865	20.806	0.994	2070	38.4	5.03	4134
1970	0.899	23.496	21.116	0.999	2014	37.1	5.44	3885
1971	0.951	21.442	20.391	1.006	1840	36.8	5.79	3521
1972	1.000	23.009	23.009	1.000	1922	38.0	6.05	3802
1973	1.059	25.631	27.153	1.000	2119	38.4	6.41	4236
1974	1.156	26.971	31.174	1.005	2255	37.8	7.03	4435
1975	1.283	24.750	31.754	1.016	2099	36.9	7.89	4026
1976	1.392	25.114	34.950	1.017	2112	37.2	8.56	4083
1977	1.516	26.227	39.750	1.014	2203	37.3	9.30	4274
1978	1.616	28.530	46.116	1.019	2363	37.6	9.97	4626
				ELECTRICAL MACHINERY, EQUIPMENT, AND SUPPLIES				
1948	0.353	9.353	3.299	0.857	978	37.2	1.74	1892
1949	0.368	8.010	2.945	0.860	843	36.8	1.82	1614
1950	0.369	9.535	3.515	0.865	968	37.9	1.84	1910
1951	0.403	10.931	4.410	0.876	1093	38.0	2.04	2162
1952	0.422	12.037	5.077	0.895	1180	38.0	2.18	2332
1953	0.438	13.454	5.895	0.906	1314	37.7	2.29	2573
1954	0.450	12.060	5.433	0.920	1183	36.9	2.39	2273
1955	0.465	12.800	5.947	0.921	1231	37.6	2.47	2410
1956	0.488	13.680	6.675	0.925	1306	37.7	2.60	2563
1957	0.514	13.860	7.119	0.933	1331	37.2	2.76	2576
1958	0.549	12.780	7.019	0.947	1220	36.9	3.00	2340
1959	0.576	14.683	8.463	0.948	1379	37.4	3.15	2685
1960	0.586	15.607	9.150	0.968	1451	37.0	3.28	2794
1961	0.611	15.524	9.488	0.964	1456	36.9	3.40	2792
1962	0.620	16.929	10.490	0.977	1557	37.1	3.49	3004
1963	0.640	16.469	10.543	0.972	1530	36.9	3.59	2938
1964	0.666	16.335	10.880	0.975	1511	37.0	3.74	2906
1965	0.680	17.473	11.884	0.968	1614	37.3	3.80	3128
1966	0.685	20.245	13.876	0.971	1857	37.4	3.84	3614
1967	0.721	20.750	14.952	0.983	1914	36.8	4.08	3661
1968	0.777	20.805	16.157	0.986	1933	36.4	4.42	3659
1969	0.840	21.121	17.732	0.986	1983	36.0	4.78	3712
1970	0.906	19.785	17.921	1.000	1871	35.3	5.23	3430
1971	0.961	18.457	17.740	1.008	1730	35.3	5.59	3176
1972	1.000	19.259	19.259	1.000	1782	36.0	5.77	3339
1973	1.051	21.251	22.341	0.994	1967	36.2	6.03	3706
1974	1.124	21.392	24.042	1.001	1985	35.9	6.49	3704
1975	1.263	18.630	23.535	1.019	1706	35.7	7.43	3169
1976	1.375	19.384	26.650	1.016	1783	35.7	8.06	3308
1977	1.490	20.381	30.373	1.008	1881	35.8	8.66	3506
1978	1.593	22.072	35.164	1.014	2029	35.8	9.32	3774

	LABOR INPUT							
YEAR	PRICE	QUANTITY	OUTLAY	QUALITY	EMPLOYMENT	WEEKLY HOURS PER PERSON	HOURLY COMPENSATION	HOURS WORKED
	TRANSPORTATION EQUIPMENT AND ORDNANCE EXCEPT MOTOR VEHICLES							
1948	0.318	5.641	1.795	0.870	473	37.0	1.97	911
1949	0.319	5.459	1.742	0.871	460	36.8	1.98	881
1950	0.327	5.506	1.800	0.875	456	37.3	2.04	884
1951	0.350	8.947	3.136	0.885	703	38.9	2.21	1422
1952	0.361	12.995	4.696	0.898	1009	38.8	2.31	2034
1953	0.386	14.752	5.698	0.906	1158	38.0	2.49	2288
1954	0.403	13.263	5.350	0.913	1050	37.4	2.62	2043
1955	0.425	12.838	5.461	0.913	1005	37.8	2.76	1976
1956	0.448	13.895	6.220	0.916	1072	38.3	2.92	2133
1957	0.472	14.727	6.946	0.922	1147	37.7	3.09	2247
1958	0.508	13.444	6.825	0.930	1044	37.4	3.36	2031
1959	0.534	13.521	7.225	0.932	1045	37.5	3.54	2040
1960	0.561	12.507	7.022	0.936	963	37.5	3.74	1879
1961	0.578	12.477	7.216	0.947	944	37.7	3.89	1853
1962	0.592	13.511	7.992	0.959	1004	37.9	4.04	1980
1963	0.630	13.620	8.578	0.959	1012	37.9	4.30	1997
1964	0.662	13.287	8.796	0.967	993	37.4	4.56	1931
1965	0.671	13.763	9.233	0.968	1021	37.7	4.62	1999
1966	0.691	16.421	11.349	0.974	1193	38.2	4.79	2370
1967	0.711	17.532	12.460	0.986	1268	37.9	4.98	2500
1968	0.764	17.438	13.322	0.992	1277	37.2	5.39	2472
1969	0.838	16.566	13.886	0.994	1228	36.7	5.92	2344
1970	0.912	13.783	12.567	0.998	1043	35.8	6.47	1941
1971	0.939	12.158	11.417	1.005	908	36.0	6.72	1700
1972	1.000	12.413	12.413	1.000	929	36.1	7.11	1745
1973	1.083	12.599	13.650	0.999	963	35.4	7.70	1773
1974	1.195	12.560	15.006	1.005	967	34.9	8.54	1757
1975	1.296	12.263	15.895	1.018	918	35.5	9.38	1694
1976	1.399	12.168	17.022	1.019	912	35.4	10.14	1679
1977	1.513	12.500	18.916	1.011	941	35.5	10.89	1737
1978	1.622	13.562	22.001	1.019	1011	35.6	11.76	1870
	MOTOR VEHICLES AND EQUIPMENT							
1948	0.265	10.107	2.679	0.899	758	36.6	1.86	1443
1949	0.279	9.929	2.773	0.901	736	37.0	1.96	1415
1950	0.308	11.406	3.519	0.904	802	38.8	2.17	1619
1951	0.339	11.647	3.948	0.909	843	37.5	2.40	1644
1952	0.360	11.233	4.043	0.921	787	38.2	2.58	1565
1953	0.379	13.243	5.021	0.927	911	38.7	2.74	1833
1954	0.392	11.264	4.420	0.934	777	38.3	2.86	1547
1955	0.413	13.444	5.548	0.935	890	39.9	3.00	1846
1956	0.448	11.591	5.192	0.939	800	38.1	3.28	1584
1957	0.472	11.196	5.283	0.945	772	37.9	3.47	1520
1958	0.512	8.841	4.526	0.956	617	37.0	3.81	1187
1959	0.504	10.142	5.110	0.960	686	38.0	3.77	1355
1960	0.514	10.712	5.510	0.969	719	37.9	3.88	1419
1961	0.525	9.450	4.962	0.973	643	37.3	3.98	1247
1962	0.539	10.916	5.881	0.982	701	39.2	4.12	1427
1963	0.565	11.574	6.538	0.978	745	39.2	4.30	1519
1964	0.594	11.884	7.056	0.980	769	38.9	4.53	1556
1965	0.617	13.342	8.236	0.977	846	39.6	4.70	1752
1966	0.651	13.559	8.825	0.961	879	38.8	4.97	1774
1967	0.677	12.493	8.451	0.987	835	37.4	5.21	1623
1968	0.743	13.784	10.242	0.989	891	38.6	5.73	1788
1969	0.790	13.738	10.849	0.991	922	37.1	6.09	1780
1970	0.837	11.811	9.882	0.997	816	35.8	6.50	1520
1971	0.955	12.537	11.971	1.002	848	36.4	7.45	1606
1972	1.000	13.688	13.688	1.000	887	38.1	7.79	1757
1973	1.078	15.083	16.252	0.998	970	38.4	8.38	1939
1974	1.230	13.014	16.005	1.004	911	35.1	9.62	1664
1975	1.348	11.446	15.424	1.015	787	35.4	10.66	1447
1976	1.436	13.465	19.341	1.015	878	37.3	11.36	1703
1977	1.595	14.792	23.592	1.010	954	37.9	12.55	1880
1978	1.704	15.515	26.444	1.015	1009	37.4	13.48	1962
	PROFESSIONAL PHOTOGRAPHIC EQUIPMENT AND WATCHES							
1948	0.343	2.655	0.912	0.855	274	37.3	1.71	533
1949	0.361	2.419	0.872	0.858	251	37.0	1.80	483
1950	0.383	2.743	1.051	0.863	275	38.1	1.93	545
1951	0.409	3.341	1.368	0.874	325	38.8	2.09	655
1952	0.431	3.708	1.597	0.892	355	38.6	2.24	712
1953	0.449	4.061	1.824	0.905	367	38.2	2.37	769
1954	0.471	3.795	1.789	0.919	366	37.2	2.53	708
1955	0.490	3.917	1.920	0.921	371	37.8	2.63	729
1956	0.514	4.210	2.165	0.925	396	37.9	2.77	780
1957	0.544	4.337	2.361	0.933	409	37.5	2.96	797
1958	0.569	4.118	2.344	0.946	387	37.1	3.14	746
1959	0.588	4.411	2.595	0.950	406	37.7	3.26	796
1960	0.597	4.538	2.711	0.970	412	37.5	3.38	802
1961	0.622	4.425	2.753	0.963	404	37.5	3.50	788
1962	0.632	4.629	2.924	0.975	414	37.8	3.59	814
1963	0.656	4.633	3.038	0.969	418	37.7	3.71	820
1964	0.676	4.655	3.145	0.971	419	37.7	3.83	822
1965	0.691	4.973	3.438	0.968	445	38.0	3.91	880
1966	0.708	5.645	3.995	0.971	498	38.5	4.01	997
1967	0.736	5.893	4.337	0.983	520	38.0	4.22	1027
1968	0.789	5.965	4.704	0.985	538	37.1	4.53	1038
1969	0.844	6.115	5.163	0.985	556	36.8	4.85	1064
1970	0.899	5.826	5.240	0.995	535	36.1	5.22	1004
1971	0.958	5.480	5.249	1.006	500	35.9	5.62	934
1972	1.000	5.826	5.826	1.000	523	36.7	5.83	999
1973	1.060	6.313	6.693	0.995	568	36.8	6.15	1088
1974	1.133	6.621	7.501	1.003	596	36.5	6.63	1132
1975	1.238	6.156	7.619	1.020	551	36.1	7.36	1035
1976	1.346	6.465	8.701	1.017	579	36.2	7.98	1090
1977	1.447	6.942	10.049	1.010	623	36.4	8.53	1178
1978	1.533	7.424	11.383	1.019	658	36.5	9.11	1249

YEAR	LABOR INPUT PRICE	QUANTITY	OUTLAY	QUALITY	EMPLOYMENT	WEEKLY HOURS PER PERSON	HOURLY COMPENSATION	HOURS WORKED
				MISCELLANEOUS MANUFACTURING INDUSTRIES				
1948	0.363	3.369	1.222	0.894	444	38.6	1.37	890
1949	0.386	3.050	1.179	0.896	410	37.7	1.47	804
1950	0.410	3.278	1.343	0.898	428	38.7	1.56	862
1951	0.446	3.283	1.464	0.898	432	38.5	1.70	864
1952	0.449	3.270	1.468	0.905	425	38.6	1.72	854
1953	0.464	3.503	1.627	0.909	455	38.5	1.79	911
1954	0.483	3.297	1.592	0.917	432	37.8	1.87	849
1955	0.509	3.347	1.705	0.916	434	38.2	1.97	863
1956	0.534	3.375	1.802	0.916	440	38.0	2.07	871
1957	0.566	3.218	1.823	0.919	421	37.8	2.20	828
1958	0.573	3.047	1.746	0.928	399	37.4	2.25	776
1959	0.610	3.196	1.951	0.930	412	37.9	2.40	812
1960	0.604	3.247	1.960	0.951	414	37.5	2.43	807
1961	0.617	3.153	1.945	0.944	403	37.6	2.46	789
1962	0.624	3.320	2.073	0.963	414	37.8	2.55	814
1963	0.642	3.293	2.114	0.960	413	37.7	2.61	811
1964	0.665	3.384	2.249	0.968	421	37.7	2.72	826
1965	0.688	3.562	2.449	0.967	441	38.0	2.81	870
1966	0.709	3.734	2.647	0.971	459	38.1	2.91	908
1967	0.750	3.674	2.753	0.975	455	37.6	3.09	890
1968	0.808	3.694	2.985	0.984	458	37.3	3.36	887
1969	0.859	3.723	3.200	0.985	465	37.0	3.58	894
1970	0.901	3.645	3.285	0.999	452	36.7	3.81	862
1971	0.943	3.584	3.380	1.006	444	36.5	4.02	842
1972	1.000	3.697	3.697	1.000	462	36.4	4.23	874
1973	1.066	3.794	4.044	1.001	477	36.1	4.51	896
1974	1.155	3.800	4.387	1.004	481	35.8	4.90	895
1975	1.230	3.516	4.322	1.010	442	35.8	5.25	823
1976	1.319	3.707	4.889	1.019	458	36.1	5.68	860
1977	1.416	3.779	5.351	0.998	476	36.1	5.98	894
1978	1.500	3.905	5.858	0.978	501	36.2	6.21	943
				RAILROADS AND RAIL EXPRESS SERVICE				
1948	0.302	19.276	5.817	0.880	1505	41.7	1.78	3262
1949	0.327	16.437	5.382	0.881	1351	39.6	1.94	2778
1950	0.359	15.572	5.587	0.875	1375	37.1	2.11	2651
1951	0.390	16.423	6.410	0.880	1435	37.3	2.31	2779
1952	0.407	15.845	6.452	0.888	1385	36.9	2.43	2658
1953	0.414	15.615	6.458	0.890	1361	36.9	2.47	2614
1954	0.424	13.927	5.907	0.891	1207	37.1	2.54	2328
1955	0.429	14.189	6.091	0.892	1198	38.0	2.57	2369
1956	0.469	14.005	6.567	0.894	1185	37.9	2.82	2333
1957	0.500	13.263	6.626	0.897	1118	37.9	3.01	2200
1958	0.534	11.408	6.094	0.904	957	37.8	3.24	1879
1959	0.555	11.177	6.199	0.910	925	38.0	3.39	1828
1960	0.572	10.707	6.120	0.915	886	37.8	3.51	1742
1961	0.575	10.083	5.796	0.927	812	38.3	3.58	1620
1962	0.584	10.038	5.864	0.938	793	38.6	3.68	1593
1963	0.594	9.837	5.847	0.939	771	38.9	3.75	1559
1964	0.605	9.872	5.970	0.948	756	39.4	3.85	1550
1965	0.640	9.625	6.156	0.950	735	39.5	4.08	1509
1966	0.651	9.645	6.280	0.961	724	39.7	4.20	1494
1967	0.687	9.248	6.358	0.973	696	39.1	4.49	1415
1968	0.722	9.095	6.571	0.983	667	39.7	4.77	1377
1969	0.768	8.897	6.836	0.991	643	40.0	5.12	1336
1970	0.847	8.592	7.273	0.984	626	39.9	5.59	1300
1971	0.941	8.217	7.731	1.008	597	39.1	6.37	1214
1972	1.000	7.885	7.885	1.000	575	39.3	6.72	1174
1973	1.141	7.977	9.105	1.005	572	39.7	7.70	1182
1974	1.266	7.843	9.929	1.008	579	38.5	8.57	1158
1975	1.342	7.373	9.893	1.017	548	37.9	9.17	1079
1976	1.520	7.268	11.049	1.020	528	38.6	10.41	1061
1977	1.651	7.310	12.066	1.018	534	38.5	11.29	1069
1978	1.794	7.304	13.102	1.021	530	38.6	12.30	1065
				STREET RAILWAYS, BUS LINES AND TAXICABS				
1948	0.407	3.333	1.358	0.970	426	41.1	1.49	911
1949	0.412	3.227	1.330	0.972	412	41.1	1.51	881
1950	0.431	3.074	1.324	0.969	393	41.2	1.57	842
1951	0.453	3.068	1.390	0.973	391	41.1	1.66	836
1952	0.469	3.062	1.435	0.979	388	41.1	1.73	829
1953	0.476	3.008	1.433	0.981	382	41.0	1.76	813
1954	0.494	2.855	1.409	0.984	362	40.9	1.83	770
1955	0.517	2.712	1.401	0.980	346	40.8	1.91	734
1956	0.525	2.651	1.393	0.981	338	40.8	1.94	717
1957	0.545	2.641	1.440	0.988	336	40.6	2.03	709
1958	0.541	2.537	1.372	0.993	322	40.4	2.02	677
1959	0.566	2.487	1.407	0.996	315	40.4	2.13	662
1960	0.564	2.500	1.411	1.000	316	40.3	2.13	663
1961	0.594	2.469	1.465	1.000	313	40.3	2.24	655
1962	0.605	2.440	1.477	1.005	307	40.4	2.29	644
1963	0.619	2.408	1.490	0.998	304	40.6	2.33	640
1964	0.645	2.357	1.519	1.001	301	39.9	2.43	624
1965	0.674	2.340	1.577	0.988	306	39.5	2.51	628
1966	0.731	2.332	1.703	0.996	308	38.8	2.74	621
1967	0.752	2.392	1.798	0.997	318	38.5	2.82	637
1968	0.821	2.363	1.940	0.998	319	37.9	3.09	628
1969	0.863	2.328	2.009	0.994	318	37.6	3.23	621
1970	0.885	2.397	2.121	1.008	322	37.7	3.36	631
1971	0.963	2.359	2.273	1.003	318	37.7	3.64	624
1972	1.000	2.292	2.292	1.000	310	37.7	3.77	608
1973	1.039	2.148	2.231	1.004	303	36.0	3.93	567
1974	1.152	2.108	2.428	1.011	306	34.8	4.39	553
1975	1.268	2.066	2.619	1.019	301	34.4	4.87	538
1976	1.371	1.999	2.741	1.018	298	33.6	5.26	521
1977	1.491	1.927	2.872	1.031	288	33.1	5.79	496
1978	1.592	1.933	3.077	1.022	292	33.1	6.13	502

	LABOR INPUT							
YEAR	PRICE	QUANTITY	OUTLAY	QUALITY	EMPLOYMENT	WEEKLY HOURS PER PERSON	HOURLY COMPENSATION	HOURS WORKED
				TRUCKING SERVICES AND WAREHOUSING				
1948	0.274	6.901	1.892	0.898	727	39.4	1.27	1488
1949	0.292	6.883	2.007	0.901	723	39.3	1.36	1479
1950	0.312	7.431	2.319	0.901	779	39.4	1.45	1596
1951	0.332	8.089	2.685	0.910	841	39.4	1.56	1722
1952	0.360	8.379	3.015	0.921	861	39.4	1.71	1762
1953	0.387	8.745	3.386	0.927	893	39.3	1.85	1826
1954	0.405	8.539	3.459	0.932	870	39.2	1.95	1775
1955	0.432	8.956	3.870	0.935	911	39.2	2.09	1855
1956	0.457	9.328	4.262	0.935	947	39.2	2.21	1931
1957	0.473	9.411	4.448	0.938	957	39.1	2.29	1944
1958	0.489	9.200	4.495	0.942	934	38.9	2.38	1891
1959	0.506	9.887	5.002	0.951	984	39.3	2.49	2012
1960	0.542	9.979	5.407	0.953	1002	38.9	2.67	2027
1961	0.553	9.938	5.493	0.959	989	39.0	2.74	2007
1962	0.566	10.402	5.890	0.972	1018	39.1	2.84	2072
1963	0.594	10.625	6.315	0.973	1030	39.5	2.99	2114
1964	0.610	10.995	6.703	0.980	1054	39.7	3.08	2174
1965	0.628	11.635	7.311	0.981	1097	40.3	3.18	2296
1966	0.651	12.228	7.960	0.992	1140	40.3	3.33	2388
1967	0.679	12.274	8.333	0.994	1154	39.8	3.49	2391
1968	0.731	12.763	9.324	1.001	1187	40.0	3.78	2469
1969	0.765	13.212	10.104	1.002	1227	40.0	3.96	2554
1970	0.821	12.949	10.625	1.010	1218	39.2	4.28	2483
1971	0.900	13.212	11.885	1.004	1237	39.6	4.66	2549
1972	1.000	13.608	13.608	1.000	1276	39.7	5.16	2635
1973	1.089	14.416	15.692	1.007	1342	39.7	5.66	2773
1974	1.176	14.333	16.852	1.000	1373	38.9	6.07	2777
1975	1.264	13.173	16.652	1.001	1287	38.1	6.53	2550
1976	1.385	13.522	18.735	1.005	1318	38.0	7.19	2605
1977	1.518	14.309	21.719	1.002	1397	38.1	7.85	2766
1978	1.652	15.260	25.211	0.999	1493	38.1	8.52	2959
				WATER TRANSPORTATION				
1948	0.293	3.165	0.928	0.953	274	33.9	1.92	483
1949	0.288	2.935	0.844	0.957	253	33.9	1.89	446
1950	0.320	2.756	0.883	0.939	242	34.0	2.07	427
1951	0.352	3.106	1.092	0.948	270	33.9	2.29	477
1952	0.382	3.059	1.168	0.959	263	34.0	2.51	465
1953	0.429	2.969	1.273	0.959	255	34.0	2.83	451
1954	0.427	2.731	1.168	0.955	236	33.9	2.80	416
1955	0.449	2.848	1.278	0.954	246	34.0	2.94	434
1956	0.463	2.947	1.365	0.952	255	34.0	3.03	450
1957	0.500	3.054	1.528	0.954	264	34.0	3.28	466
1958	0.492	2.694	1.327	0.959	232	33.9	3.24	409
1959	0.511	2.769	1.414	0.964	237	33.9	3.38	418
1960	0.556	2.746	1.526	0.954	237	34.0	3.64	419
1961	0.562	2.683	1.507	0.961	230	34.0	3.71	407
1962	0.588	2.688	1.581	0.974	227	34.0	3.94	402
1963	0.616	2.652	1.633	0.970	225	34.0	4.10	398
1964	0.624	2.768	1.728	0.978	233	34.0	4.19	412
1965	0.651	2.710	1.763	0.974	229	34.0	4.35	405
1966	0.690	2.910	2.008	0.988	244	33.8	4.68	429
1967	0.698	2.993	2.090	0.995	246	34.2	4.77	438
1968	0.773	2.933	2.267	1.003	245	33.4	5.33	426
1969	0.841	2.726	2.292	1.003	230	33.1	5.79	396
1970	0.911	2.627	2.393	0.993	223	33.2	6.21	385
1971	0.940	2.446	2.298	1.016	204	33.0	6.56	350
1972	1.000	2.390	2.390	1.000	208	32.2	6.87	346
1973	1.104	2.417	2.668	1.010	207	32.3	7.66	348
1974	1.191	2.421	2.885	1.017	208	32.0	8.32	347
1975	1.309	2.326	3.045	1.028	198	32.0	9.25	329
1976	1.446	2.315	3.348	1.028	198	31.8	10.22	326
1977	1.564	2.307	3.609	1.028	198	31.7	11.05	327
1978	1.653	2.547	4.210	1.037	211	32.6	11.77	358
				AIR TRANSPORTATION				
1948	0.243	1.414	0.344	0.958	92	36.3	1.99	173
1949	0.259	1.383	0.359	0.960	90	36.2	2.12	169
1950	0.278	1.388	0.386	0.963	90	36.3	2.28	169
1951	0.297	1.549	0.460	0.977	99	36.3	2.47	186
1952	0.310	1.801	0.559	0.986	114	36.2	2.61	214
1953	0.322	1.925	0.621	0.994	121	36.2	2.73	227
1954	0.335	1.963	0.657	0.996	123	36.2	2.84	231
1955	0.350	2.115	0.740	0.995	133	36.1	2.97	249
1956	0.361	2.434	0.878	0.993	153	36.2	3.06	287
1957	0.379	2.706	1.026	0.994	170	36.2	3.21	319
1958	0.391	2.705	1.058	0.993	170	36.2	3.31	319
1959	0.426	2.845	1.211	0.997	178	36.2	3.62	335
1960	0.441	3.088	1.362	0.987	195	36.2	3.71	367
1961	0.460	3.121	1.437	0.983	198	36.2	3.86	372
1962	0.485	3.183	1.544	0.992	200	36.2	4.10	376
1963	0.505	3.261	1.649	0.998	204	36.1	4.30	383
1964	0.537	3.410	1.833	1.005	215	35.6	4.61	398
1965	0.564	3.622	2.041	1.002	232	35.1	4.82	424
1966	0.585	4.072	2.384	1.010	258	35.2	5.04	473
1967	0.622	4.708	2.930	1.011	303	34.7	5.37	546
1968	0.665	5.215	3.467	1.014	335	34.6	5.75	603
1969	0.731	5.567	4.068	1.017	359	34.4	6.34	642
1970	0.831	5.493	4.564	1.025	357	33.8	7.27	628
1971	0.906	5.333	4.832	1.009	348	34.2	7.80	620
1972	1.000	5.343	5.343	1.000	352	34.2	8.53	626
1973	1.058	5.660	5.986	1.001	372	34.3	9.03	663
1974	1.133	5.727	6.488	0.995	375	34.6	9.61	675
1975	1.249	5.720	7.144	0.996	373	34.7	10.61	673
1976	1.377	5.760	7.934	0.997	377	34.6	11.71	678
1977	1.547	5.876	9.087	0.994	390	34.2	13.12	693
1978	1.707	6.100	10.414	0.997	412	33.5	14.52	717

LABOR INPUT

YEAR	PRICE	QUANTITY	OUTLAY	QUALITY	EMPLOYMENT	WEEKLY HOURS PER PERSON	HOURLY COMPENSATION	HOURS WORKED
PIPELINES EXCEPT NATURAL GAS								
1948	0.398	0.331	0.132	0.809	30	36.6	2.30	57
1949	0.405	0.321	0.130	0.812	29	36.5	2.35	55
1950	0.422	0.299	0.126	0.814	27	36.4	2.45	51
1951	0.454	0.315	0.143	0.827	28	36.4	2.68	53
1952	0.467	0.334	0.156	0.846	29	36.5	2.82	55
1953	0.486	0.327	0.159	0.860	28	36.4	2.98	53
1954	0.495	0.319	0.158	0.872	27	36.3	3.08	51
1955	0.511	0.309	0.158	0.880	26	36.2	3.21	49
1956	0.533	0.313	0.167	0.891	26	36.3	3.39	49
1957	0.548	0.318	0.174	0.904	26	36.3	3.53	49
1958	0.554	0.311	0.172	0.922	25	36.2	3.64	47
1959	0.583	0.302	0.176	0.936	24	36.1	3.89	45
1960	0.593	0.290	0.172	0.941	23	36.0	3.98	43
1961	0.621	0.279	0.173	0.948	22	35.9	4.20	41
1962	0.631	0.268	0.169	0.957	21	35.8	4.31	39
1963	0.646	0.260	0.168	0.953	20	36.6	4.40	38
1964	0.672	0.248	0.167	0.961	19	36.5	4.61	36
1965	0.663	0.249	0.165	0.963	19	36.5	4.56	36
1966	0.720	0.238	0.171	0.973	18	36.4	5.00	34
1967	0.731	0.241	0.176	0.984	18	36.4	5.14	34
1968	0.766	0.243	0.186	0.992	18	36.3	5.43	34
1969	0.788	0.245	0.193	1.000	18	36.3	5.63	34
1970	0.920	0.224	0.206	1.001	17	35.1	6.57	31
1971	0.934	0.234	0.218	1.011	17	36.2	6.74	32
1972	1.000	0.232	0.232	1.000	17	36.2	7.14	32
1973	1.080	0.218	0.235	1.005	16	36.1	7.74	30
1974	1.187	0.218	0.259	1.008	16	36.0	8.54	30
1975	1.401	0.227	0.318	1.010	17	35.0	10.10	31
1976	1.462	0.243	0.355	1.020	18	35.2	10.64	33
1977	1.608	0.242	0.389	1.015	18	35.2	11.65	33
1978	1.771	0.273	0.484	1.015	20	35.5	12.83	38
TRANSPORTATION SERVICES								
1948	0.321	0.751	0.241	0.880	83	36.9	1.52	159
1949	0.358	0.714	0.256	0.882	79	36.7	1.70	151
1950	0.355	0.690	0.245	0.875	77	36.7	1.67	147
1951	0.425	0.764	0.325	0.885	84	36.8	2.02	161
1952	0.420	0.796	0.335	0.895	87	36.6	2.02	165
1953	0.424	0.809	0.343	0.899	88	36.6	2.05	167
1954	0.474	0.766	0.363	0.900	83	36.7	2.29	158
1955	0.481	0.785	0.378	0.901	85	36.7	2.33	162
1956	0.507	0.783	0.397	0.898	85	36.7	2.44	162
1957	0.551	0.762	0.420	0.898	83	36.6	2.66	158
1958	0.558	0.725	0.404	0.900	79	36.5	2.70	150
1959	0.601	0.769	0.462	0.906	83	36.6	2.92	158
1960	0.620	0.795	0.493	0.901	86	36.7	3.00	164
1961	0.627	0.811	0.509	0.919	86	36.7	3.10	164
1962	0.641	0.837	0.537	0.941	87	36.6	3.25	165
1963	0.652	0.863	0.563	0.947	89	36.7	3.32	170
1964	0.656	0.915	0.601	0.959	93	36.7	3.38	178
1965	0.690	0.939	0.648	0.962	95	36.8	3.57	182
1966	0.702	1.054	0.740	0.984	105	36.5	3.71	199
1967	0.732	1.123	0.822	0.989	111	36.6	3.89	211
1968	0.781	1.124	0.878	0.995	111	36.5	4.18	210
1969	0.794	1.195	0.949	0.996	118	36.4	4.25	223
1970	0.869	1.213	1.055	0.991	122	35.9	4.63	228
1971	0.899	1.242	1.117	1.013	124	35.4	4.89	228
1972	1.000	1.236	1.236	1.000	127	34.9	5.38	230
1973	1.071	1.315	1.408	1.011	135	34.5	5.82	242
1974	1.167	1.396	1.629	1.017	141	34.9	6.38	255
1975	1.249	1.412	1.763	1.016	146	34.1	6.82	259
1976	1.387	1.471	2.041	1.025	152	33.8	7.64	267
1977	1.674	1.600	2.677	1.027	167	33.4	9.24	290
1978	1.668	1.879	3.134	1.036	192	33.9	9.29	337
TELEPHONE AND TELEGRAPH AND MISCELLANEOUS COMMUNICATION SERVICES								
1948	0.267	7.695	2.055	0.850	694	35.4	1.61	1278
1949	0.286	7.528	2.151	0.848	690	34.9	1.72	1252
1950	0.328	7.393	2.424	0.849	671	35.2	1.97	1228
1951	0.318	7.827	2.489	0.861	698	35.3	1.94	1283
1952	0.339	8.164	2.766	0.876	725	34.9	2.10	1315
1953	0.353	8.598	3.034	0.886	752	35.0	2.21	1370
1954	0.382	8.639	3.303	0.892	747	35.2	2.42	1367
1955	0.387	8.975	3.478	0.898	760	35.7	2.46	1411
1956	0.396	9.524	3.768	0.899	807	35.6	2.52	1495
1957	0.400	9.649	3.856	0.902	823	35.3	2.55	1509
1958	0.457	9.021	4.122	0.911	772	34.8	2.95	1397
1959	0.486	9.020	4.383	0.928	745	35.4	3.19	1372
1960	0.457	9.408	4.299	0.956	748	35.7	3.09	1389
1961	0.490	9.074	4.443	0.942	735	35.6	3.27	1359
1962	0.506	9.264	4.689	0.958	730	35.9	3.44	1364
1963	0.523	9.308	4.865	0.962	729	36.0	3.56	1365
1964	0.562	9.717	5.460	0.977	747	36.1	3.89	1404
1965	0.567	10.138	5.751	0.978	775	36.3	3.93	1463
1966	0.570	10.778	6.144	0.981	818	36.4	3.96	1550
1967	0.609	10.988	6.688	0.990	849	35.5	4.27	1567
1968	0.637	11.232	7.150	0.995	856	35.8	4.49	1593
1969	0.659	12.299	8.110	0.999	923	36.2	4.67	1738
1970	0.732	13.218	9.678	1.004	993	36.0	5.21	1857
1971	0.864	12.933	11.172	1.010	992	35.0	6.18	1807
1972	1.000	13.157	13.157	1.000	1005	35.5	7.09	1856
1973	1.061	13.613	14.445	1.002	1032	35.7	7.53	1917
1974	1.167	13.633	15.906	1.001	1046	35.3	8.27	1923
1975	1.331	13.201	17.566	1.002	1023	34.9	9.45	1858
1976	1.521	13.010	19.786	1.003	1009	34.9	10.81	1831
1977	1.610	13.363	21.520	0.999	1022	35.5	11.40	1887
1978	1.760	14.006	24.645	1.002	1061	35.8	12.49	1973

YEAR	LABOR INPUT PRICE	QUANTITY	OUTLAY	QUALITY	EMPLOYMENT	WEEKLY HOURS PER PERSON	HOURLY COMPENSATION	HOURS WORKED
				RADIO BROADCASTING AND TELEVISION				
1948	0.369	0.565	0.208	0.952	52	35.1	2.19	95
1949	0.380	0.604	0.229	0.957	55	35.3	2.27	101
1950	0.407	0.648	0.264	0.961	59	35.2	2.44	108
1951	0.429	0.707	0.303	0.968	64	35.1	2.59	117
1952	0.460	0.739	0.340	0.985	66	35.0	2.83	120
1953	0.478	0.802	0.383	0.996	71	34.9	2.97	129
1954	0.506	0.864	0.437	0.995	77	34.7	3.15	139
1955	0.529	0.894	0.473	0.988	80	34.8	3.27	145
1956	0.572	0.913	0.522	0.974	83	34.7	3.48	150
1957	0.588	0.945	0.556	0.976	86	34.6	3.59	155
1958	0.624	0.948	0.592	0.972	87	34.5	3.79	156
1959	0.629	0.991	0.624	0.980	90	34.6	3.85	162
1960	0.645	1.036	0.668	0.986	93	34.7	3.98	168
1961	0.663	1.056	0.700	0.988	95	34.6	4.10	171
1962	0.666	1.076	0.717	0.996	96	34.6	4.15	173
1963	0.686	1.123	0.771	0.999	99	35.0	4.28	180
1964	0.701	1.182	0.829	1.007	103	35.1	4.41	188
1965	0.732	1.221	0.894	0.994	108	35.0	4.55	197
1966	0.779	1.271	0.991	0.997	113	34.7	4.86	204
1967	0.784	1.359	1.066	1.001	121	34.5	4.91	217
1968	0.845	1.393	1.177	1.009	124	34.3	5.33	221
1969	0.864	1.481	1.279	1.005	131	34.6	5.43	236
1970	0.912	1.529	1.394	1.015	132	35.1	5.79	241
1971	0.930	1.565	1.456	1.012	136	35.0	5.88	248
1972	1.000	1.615	1.615	1.000	141	35.3	6.25	259
1973	1.056	1.668	1.761	0.998	146	35.2	6.58	266
1974	1.134	1.715	1.946	0.997	151	35.1	7.07	275
1975	1.230	1.737	2.138	1.002	156	34.2	7.70	278
1976	1.337	1.814	2.424	1.011	161	34.3	8.45	287
1977	1.464	1.889	2.765	0.998	170	34.3	9.12	303
1978	1.572	2.031	3.193	1.003	182	34.2	9.85	324
				ELECTRIC UTILITIES				
1948	0.289	4.172	1.205	0.890	309	37.7	1.99	606
1949	0.307	4.228	1.298	0.891	317	37.2	2.12	613
1950	0.329	4.282	1.407	0.894	321	37.1	2.27	619
1951	0.347	4.404	1.542	0.902	326	37.5	2.42	637
1952	0.371	4.492	1.668	0.915	329	37.1	2.63	635
1953	0.387	4.628	1.791	0.924	335	37.1	2.77	648
1954	0.402	4.680	1.883	0.931	336	37.2	2.90	650
1955	0.416	4.713	1.960	0.933	339	37.1	3.00	653
1956	0.436	4.805	2.093	0.936	342	37.3	3.15	664
1957	0.458	4.819	2.208	0.939	344	37.1	3.33	664
1958	0.483	4.910	2.373	0.947	352	36.7	3.54	671
1959	0.506	4.901	2.479	0.954	348	36.7	3.73	664
1960	0.517	4.982	2.578	0.965	349	36.8	3.86	667
1961	0.545	4.984	2.715	0.968	349	36.7	4.08	666
1962	0.562	5.005	2.815	0.977	347	36.7	4.25	663
1963	0.586	5.050	2.961	0.979	348	36.9	4.44	667
1964	0.615	5.131	3.155	0.989	349	36.9	4.70	671
1965	0.621	5.323	3.307	1.008	353	37.2	4.84	683
1966	0.662	5.316	3.517	0.995	357	37.3	5.09	691
1967	0.692	5.443	3.764	1.000	363	37.3	5.35	704
1968	0.739	5.527	4.083	0.999	369	37.2	5.71	715
1969	0.774	5.736	4.439	1.008	377	37.5	6.03	736
1970	0.847	5.849	4.955	0.995	387	37.8	6.52	760
1971	0.904	6.006	5.432	1.009	393	37.7	7.06	770
1972	1.000	6.010	6.010	1.000	401	37.3	7.73	777
1973	1.069	6.161	6.583	0.998	411	37.4	8.24	799
1974	1.147	6.199	7.112	1.000	416	37.1	8.87	802
1975	1.268	6.072	7.699	1.001	410	36.8	9.81	785
1976	1.433	6.016	8.620	0.999	411	36.4	11.07	779
1977	1.567	6.110	9.576	0.994	419	36.5	12.05	795
1978	1.677	6.455	10.826	1.001	435	36.8	12.98	834
				GAS UTILITIES				
1948	0.286	1.718	0.492	0.871	141	37.7	1.78	276
1949	0.305	1.743	0.532	0.872	144	37.2	1.90	280
1950	0.327	1.768	0.577	0.875	146	37.2	2.04	283
1951	0.350	1.850	0.647	0.883	150	37.6	2.21	293
1952	0.379	1.885	0.713	0.895	153	37.1	2.42	295
1953	0.399	1.958	0.782	0.904	157	37.2	2.58	303
1954	0.421	1.996	0.840	0.911	159	37.1	2.74	307
1955	0.440	2.025	0.892	0.913	161	37.0	2.87	310
1956	0.467	2.082	0.972	0.915	164	37.2	3.06	318
1957	0.498	2.103	1.047	0.918	167	37.0	3.27	320
1958	0.531	2.161	1.147	0.926	172	36.6	3.51	326
1959	0.563	2.177	1.225	0.933	171	36.6	3.75	326
1960	0.581	2.231	1.297	0.944	173	36.7	3.92	331
1961	0.605	2.233	1.352	0.946	173	36.6	4.09	330
1962	0.620	2.243	1.392	0.955	172	36.7	4.24	329
1963	0.642	2.263	1.453	0.957	173	36.8	4.40	331
1964	0.667	2.300	1.535	0.967	173	36.9	4.62	333
1965	0.649	2.444	1.585	1.006	176	37.0	4.67	340
1966	0.688	2.432	1.673	0.994	177	37.2	4.89	342
1967	0.714	2.491	1.778	0.999	181	37.1	5.10	349
1968	0.754	2.529	1.908	0.999	184	37.1	5.39	354
1969	0.783	2.623	2.055	1.008	188	37.3	5.64	364
1970	0.848	2.676	2.269	0.996	192	37.6	6.04	376
1971	0.904	2.747	2.484	1.009	195	37.5	6.52	381
1972	1.000	2.749	2.749	1.000	199	37.1	7.15	385
1973	1.066	2.819	3.006	0.998	204	37.3	7.61	395
1974	1.144	2.836	3.245	1.000	206	37.0	8.18	397
1975	1.271	2.779	3.531	1.001	203	36.7	9.10	398
1976	1.432	2.753	3.942	0.999	204	36.3	10.23	385
1977	1.568	2.796	4.384	0.995	208	36.4	11.15	393
1978	1.674	2.955	4.945	1.002	216	36.7	11.99	413

YEAR	LABOR INPUT PRICE	QUANTITY	OUTLAY	QUALITY	EMPLOYMENT	WEEKLY HOURS PER PERSON	HOURLY COMPENSATION	HOURS WORKED
WATER SUPPLY AND SANITARY SERVICES								
1948	0.198	0.648	0.129	0.935	88	35.5	0.79	162
1949	0.209	0.664	0.139	0.947	89	35.4	0.85	164
1950	0.225	0.670	0.150	0.945	90	35.5	0.91	166
1951	0.246	0.686	0.169	0.940	93	35.5	0.99	171
1952	0.269	0.695	0.187	0.953	93	35.4	1.09	171
1953	0.291	0.705	0.205	0.946	96	35.1	1.18	175
1954	0.317	0.696	0.221	0.928	98	34.5	1.26	176
1955	0.334	0.702	0.235	0.930	98	34.7	1.33	177
1956	0.360	0.714	0.257	0.928	99	34.9	1.43	180
1957	0.383	0.723	0.277	0.940	99	34.9	1.54	180
1958	0.415	0.733	0.304	0.941	102	34.6	1.67	182
1959	0.446	0.729	0.325	0.943	101	34.6	1.79	181
1960	0.471	0.733	0.345	0.942	101	34.6	1.89	182
1961	0.499	0.740	0.369	0.947	102	34.4	2.02	183
1962	0.516	0.756	0.390	0.967	102	34.6	2.13	183
1963	0.547	0.767	0.419	0.967	103	34.7	2.26	186
1964	0.583	0.781	0.455	0.980	103	34.7	2.44	187
1965	0.606	0.797	0.484	0.977	106	34.6	2.53	191
1966	0.639	0.821	0.524	0.988	108	34.6	2.69	195
1967	0.685	0.835	0.572	0.972	113	34.2	2.84	201
1968	0.730	0.864	0.630	0.986	115	34.3	3.07	205
1969	0.790	0.883	0.698	0.974	120	34.0	3.28	212
1970	0.838	0.945	0.792	0.988	125	34.5	3.53	224
1971	0.910	0.951	0.866	0.993	125	34.6	3.86	224
1972	1.000	0.957	0.957	1.000	125	34.5	4.27	224
1973	1.057	0.991	1.048	1.008	126	35.1	4.55	230
1974	1.139	0.996	1.135	1.003	130	34.5	4.88	233
1975	1.244	0.997	1.240	1.032	127	34.3	5.48	226
1976	1.375	1.000	1.375	1.043	125	34.7	6.12	225
1977	1.495	1.023	1.530	1.046	126	35.0	6.67	229
1978	1.612	1.069	1.723	1.041	132	35.1	7.16	240
WHOLESALE TRADE								
1948	0.363	31.213	11.340	0.913	3010	39.0	1.86	6111
1949	0.367	30.453	11.178	0.918	2934	38.9	1.88	5932
1950	0.392	30.462	11.936	0.914	2947	38.9	2.00	5954
1951	0.416	32.220	13.410	0.919	3100	38.9	2.14	6270
1952	0.415	33.129	13.758	0.929	3160	38.8	2.16	6375
1953	0.430	33.656	14.485	0.937	3190	38.7	2.26	6421
1954	0.445	33.397	14.860	0.941	3162	38.6	2.34	6347
1955	0.483	34.125	16.466	0.941	3220	38.7	2.54	6480
1956	0.517	35.268	18.229	0.940	3344	38.6	2.72	6705
1957	0.539	35.422	19.077	0.943	3370	38.3	2.84	6715
1958	0.538	35.440	19.061	0.950	3358	38.2	2.86	6665
1959	0.572	36.759	21.035	0.960	3424	38.4	3.07	6846
1960	0.570	38.400	21.903	0.981	3504	38.4	3.13	6999
1961	0.591	38.236	22.611	0.972	3519	38.4	3.22	7032
1962	0.605	39.303	23.768	0.983	3564	38.6	3.33	7148
1963	0.627	39.605	24.815	0.978	3610	36.6	3.43	7201
1964	0.661	40.713	26.900	0.984	3689	38.6	3.64	7397
1965	0.647	42.020	27.167	0.981	3801	38.7	3.55	7657
1966	0.695	44.152	30.704	0.992	3956	38.7	3.86	7954
1967	0.726	44.655	32.441	0.993	4031	38.4	4.03	8041
1968	0.784	45.483	35.666	0.997	4108	38.2	4.37	8158
1969	0.844	46.917	39.602	0.993	4246	38.2	4.69	8443
1970	0.865	47.747	41.318	0.998	4327	38.0	4.83	8550
1971	0.923	48.520	44.764	1.010	4360	37.9	5.21	8587
1972	1.000	49.111	49.111	1.000	4455	37.9	5.59	8778
1973	1.075	51.140	54.974	1.001	4673	37.6	6.02	9132
1974	1.207	51.500	62.138	1.005	4796	36.7	6.79	9157
1975	1.273	50.883	64.775	1.018	4706	36.5	7.25	8938
1976	1.374	52.679	72.392	1.017	4864	36.6	7.82	9257
1977	1.470	54.225	79.696	1.015	5017	36.6	8.34	9552
1978	1.576	57.323	90.337	1.022	5266	36.6	9.02	10021
RETAIL TRADE								
1948	0.340	61.848	21.000	0.981	8999	42.3	1.06	19777
1949	0.347	62.281	21.590	0.982	9009	42.5	1.09	19895
1950	0.366	63.074	23.110	0.988	9083	42.4	1.15	20025
1951	0.388	65.469	25.416	0.983	9511	42.3	1.22	20898
1952	0.392	65.876	25.812	0.987	9638	41.8	1.23	20943
1953	0.398	65.623	26.149	0.986	9738	41.2	1.25	20882
1954	0.433	64.813	28.066	0.983	9632	41.3	1.36	20685
1955	0.462	65.822	30.381	0.973	9898	41.2	1.43	21225
1956	0.476	66.332	31.606	0.958	10165	41.1	1.46	21708
1957	0.486	66.020	32.111	0.959	10260	40.5	1.49	21589
1958	0.472	65.149	30.753	0.956	10177	40.4	1.44	21377
1959	0.537	66.244	35.551	0.958	10369	40.2	1.64	21685
1960	0.519	68.911	35.739	0.990	10519	39.9	1.64	21844
1961	0.543	66.280	36.022	0.967	10465	39.5	1.68	21503
1962	0.564	67.476	38.027	0.984	10558	39.2	1.77	21502
1963	0.577	67.638	39.024	0.990	10621	38.8	1.82	21439
1964	0.663	69.246	45.898	0.992	10946	36.5	2.10	21902
1965	0.595	70.540	41.985	0.987	11332	38.0	1.87	22408
1966	0.700	72.057	50.408	1.001	11664	37.2	2.23	22577
1967	0.710	71.851	51.029	1.004	11823	36.5	2.27	22458
1968	0.799	73.251	58.561	1.010	12166	36.0	2.57	22746
1969	0.848	74.926	63.508	1.003	12672	35.6	2.71	23436
1970	0.806	77.284	62.274	1.025	12940	35.2	2.63	23657
1971	0.922	78.007	71.905	1.011	13236	35.2	2.97	24206
1972	1.000	78.409	78.409	1.000	13567	34.9	3.19	24595
1973	1.085	80.416	87.219	1.004	14050	34.4	3.47	25128
1974	1.189	80.024	95.135	1.004	14318	33.6	3.81	24995
1975	1.207	80.458	97.136	1.013	14412	33.2	3.90	24907
1976	1.344	82.823	111.333	1.019	14922	32.9	4.37	25500
1977	1.470	84.954	124.879	1.010	15628	32.5	4.73	26393
1978	1.569	87.960	138.029	1.012	16413	31.9	5.06	27252

YEAR	LABOR INPUT PRICE	QUANTITY	OUTLAY	QUALITY	EMPLOYMENT	WEEKLY HOURS PER PERSON	HOURLY COMPENSATION	HOURS WORKED
FINANCE, INSURANCE AND REAL ESTATE								
1948	0.354	25.605	9.056	0.878	1998	35.9	2.43	3732
1949	0.379	25.720	9.757	0.879	2012	35.8	2.61	3744
1950	0.409	26.334	10.783	0.871	2081	35.8	2.79	3870
1951	0.422	28.116	11.875	0.886	2188	35.7	2.92	4063
1952	0.410	29.829	12.238	0.902	2281	35.7	2.89	4232
1953	0.395	31.605	12.485	0.915	2383	35.7	2.82	4423
1954	0.393	33.250	13.080	0.924	2485	35.6	2.84	4604
1955	0.420	34.312	14.422	0.925	2569	35.6	3.04	4750
1956	0.402	35.368	14.228	0.922	2659	35.5	2.90	4912
1957	0.488	36.116	17.622	0.926	2710	35.4	3.53	4993
1958	0.482	36.816	17.753	0.932	2757	35.3	3.51	5058
1959	0.478	38.051	18.193	0.945	2813	35.2	3.53	5153
1960	0.479	40.627	19.443	0.981	2895	35.2	3.67	5300
1961	0.510	40.838	20.826	0.966	2954	35.2	3.85	5412
1962	0.569	42.356	24.102	0.981	3014	35.3	4.36	5528
1963	0.636	43.393	27.585	0.980	3087	35.3	4.87	5668
1964	0.668	44.983	30.071	0.990	3167	35.3	5.17	5815
1965	0.665	46.544	30.942	0.991	3270	35.4	5.15	6012
1966	0.690	48.395	33.409	1.001	3363	35.4	5.40	6186
1967	0.736	49.752	36.628	0.996	3488	35.3	5.73	6396
1968	0.817	52.307	42.746	0.999	3656	35.3	6.38	6702
1969	0.892	54.403	48.505	0.996	3813	35.3	6.94	6994
1970	0.904	55.753	50.402	0.998	3937	34.9	7.05	7152
1971	0.908	57.693	52.402	1.010	4028	34.9	7.16	7314
1972	1.000	58.626	58.626	1.000	4160	34.7	7.81	7504
1973	1.217	62.335	75.855	1.009	4399	34.6	9.59	7908
1974	1.310	63.712	83.444	1.009	4529	34.3	10.32	8082
1975	1.403	65.057	91.256	1.018	4600	34.2	11.16	8178
1976	1.515	66.631	100.934	1.024	4704	34.1	12.12	8331
1977	1.629	69.561	113.306	1.020	4915	34.2	12.98	8731
1978	1.601	74.912	119.953	1.028	5242	34.2	12.86	9326
SERVICES, EXCLUDING PRIVATE HOUSEHOLDS, INSTITUTIONS								
1948	0.238	42.414	10.101	1.009	5753	37.5	0.90	11233
1949	0.226	42.186	9.532	1.009	5730	37.5	0.85	11166
1950	0.242	43.219	10.470	1.021	5804	37.5	0.93	11304
1951	0.258	44.054	11.373	1.009	5997	37.4	0.98	11662
1952	0.278	45.471	12.648	1.017	6147	37.4	1.06	11940
1953	0.294	46.435	13.653	1.016	6289	37.3	1.12	12207
1954	0.312	46.968	14.636	1.019	6356	37.2	1.19	12310
1955	0.338	47.946	16.207	1.010	6554	37.2	1.28	12687
1956	0.377	49.987	18.843	1.004	6855	37.3	1.42	13304
1957	0.395	51.565	20.378	1.006	7105	37.1	1.49	13699
1958	0.413	52.176	21.566	1.005	7228	36.9	1.56	13864
1959	0.438	53.657	23.495	1.004	7470	36.8	1.65	14280
1960	0.436	57.024	24.877	1.033	7730	36.7	1.69	14752
1961	0.477	57.329	27.318	1.009	7978	36.6	1.80	15174
1962	0.493	59.733	29.467	1.020	8250	36.5	1.88	15645
1963	0.519	61.610	32.002	1.016	8558	36.4	1.98	16203
1964	0.561	64.202	36.023	1.017	8922	36.3	2.14	16863
1965	0.593	66.468	39.395	1.012	9324	36.2	2.25	17539
1966	0.642	69.435	44.593	1.012	9887	35.7	2.43	18337
1967	0.692	71.605	49.555	1.012	10306	35.3	2.62	18909
1968	0.746	73.621	54.950	1.012	10717	34.9	2.83	19429
1969	0.811	77.124	62.573	1.011	11339	34.6	3.07	20374
1970	0.879	78.935	69.406	1.023	11559	34.3	3.37	20617
1971	0.936	79.577	74.461	1.009	11871	34.1	3.53	21075
1972	1.000	83.012	83.012	1.000	12535	34.0	3.74	22177
1973	1.070	87.315	93.447	1.002	13242	33.8	4.01	23284
1974	1.164	89.397	104.016	1.000	13793	33.3	4.35	23890
1975	1.248	90.592	113.099	1.002	14057	33.0	4.68	24151
1976	1.335	94.059	125.530	1.009	14568	32.9	5.04	24909
1977	1.435	98.988	142.016	1.003	15393	32.9	5.38	26374
1978	1.569	103.879	162.935	1.014	16150	32.6	5.95	27369
PRIVATE HOUSEHOLDS								
1948	0.308	7.682	2.364	1.087	1936	36.1	0.65	3634
1949	0.312	7.547	2.357	1.084	1969	34.9	0.66	3578
1950	0.316	8.146	2.573	1.095	2179	33.7	0.67	3822
1951	0.340	7.833	2.662	1.089	2200	32.3	0.72	3696
1952	0.371	7.054	2.615	1.080	2088	30.9	0.78	3357
1953	0.398	6.757	2.691	1.071	2109	29.6	0.83	3241
1954	0.423	6.075	2.571	1.058	2021	28.1	0.87	2951
1955	0.444	6.875	3.053	1.046	2319	28.0	0.90	3377
1956	0.460	7.106	3.268	1.036	2479	27.3	0.93	3525
1957	0.479	6.942	3.323	1.032	2476	26.8	0.96	3456
1958	0.500	7.006	3.503	1.019	2578	26.4	0.99	3533
1959	0.527	6.737	3.553	1.005	2600	25.5	1.03	3444
1960	0.547	6.937	3.797	1.031	2577	25.8	1.10	3457
1961	0.573	6.516	3.734	0.999	2679	24.1	1.11	3354
1962	0.587	6.487	3.807	1.002	2716	23.6	1.14	3329
1963	0.598	6.407	3.831	1.004	2678	23.6	1.17	3281
1964	0.622	6.292	3.916	1.001	2704	23.0	1.21	3229
1965	0.654	6.066	3.968	0.998	2626	22.9	1.27	3123
1966	0.688	5.846	4.022	1.002	2578	22.4	1.34	2998
1967	0.729	5.739	4.182	1.002	2495	22.7	1.42	2944
1968	0.797	5.491	4.377	1.001	2464	22.0	1.55	2820
1969	0.856	5.183	4.439	0.992	2345	22.0	1.65	2686
1970	0.885	5.082	4.499	1.034	2293	21.2	1.78	2526
1971	0.963	4.723	4.550	0.998	2248	20.8	1.87	2432
1972	1.000	4.623	4.623	1.000	2207	20.7	1.95	2376
1973	1.072	4.478	4.799	0.998	2101	21.1	2.08	2306
1974	1.173	3.883	4.556	1.001	1916	20.0	2.29	1994
1975	1.262	3.625	4.575	1.003	1871	19.1	2.46	1857
1976	1.419	3.774	5.354	1.012	1874	19.7	2.79	1917
1977	1.530	3.832	5.864	1.014	1926	19.4	3.02	1941
1978	1.636	3.768	6.166	1.014	1886	19.5	3.23	1909

YEAR	PRICE	QUANTITY	OUTLAY	QUALITY	EMPLOYMENT	WEEKLY HOURS PER PERSON	HOURLY COMPENSATION	HOURS WORKED
		LABOR INPUT						
				INSTITUTIONS				
1948	0.387	3.909	1.514	0.931	727	31.2	1.28	1180
1949	0.415	4.158	1.725	0.931	774	31.2	1.37	1256
1950	0.426	4.375	1.862	0.947	799	31.2	1.43	1298
1951	0.451	4.554	2.054	0.945	833	31.2	1.52	1354
1952	0.464	4.738	2.198	0.957	856	31.3	1.58	1391
1953	0.492	4.945	2.432	0.955	895	31.3	1.67	1456
1954	0.513	5.123	2.628	0.958	925	31.3	1.75	1503
1955	0.526	5.397	2.838	0.951	979	31.3	1.78	1595
1956	0.544	5.624	3.059	0.942	1029	31.4	1.82	1677
1957	0.567	5.869	3.326	0.948	1066	31.4	1.91	1740
1958	0.587	6.159	3.616	0.953	1113	31.4	1.99	1817
1959	0.596	6.827	4.066	0.954	1234	31.4	2.02	2012
1960	0.591	7.638	4.517	0.972	1354	31.4	2.05	2208
1961	0.607	8.082	4.906	0.965	1443	31.4	2.08	2354
1962	0.614	8.717	5.351	0.980	1530	31.4	2.14	2499
1963	0.633	8.902	5.639	0.981	1562	31.4	2.21	2550
1964	0.646	9.213	5.955	0.989	1613	31.2	2.27	2619
1965	0.670	9.524	6.380	0.991	1664	31.2	2.36	2700
1966	0.703	10.052	7.068	0.992	1773	30.9	2.48	2849
1967	0.738	10.504	7.750	0.999	1859	30.6	2.62	2955
1968	0.761	10.978	8.358	1.005	1948	30.3	2.72	3071
1969	0.805	11.776	9.480	1.005	2024	31.3	2.88	3292
1970	0.879	11.307	9.940	1.004	2010	30.3	3.14	3166
1971	0.932	11.611	10.826	1.005	2047	30.5	3.33	3247
1972	1.000	11.712	11.712	1.000	2134	29.7	3.56	3292
1973	1.083	11.838	12.815	1.005	2162	29.4	3.87	3309
1974	1.157	12.028	13.917	1.009	2203	29.2	4.16	3349
1975	1.204	12.890	15.523	1.014	2343	29.3	4.34	3574
1976	1.294	12.948	16.752	1.021	2412	28.4	4.70	3566
1977	1.398	13.083	18.293	1.017	2462	28.2	5.06	3615
1978	1.484	13.780	20.450	1.027	2573	28.2	5.42	3772
				FEDERAL PUBLIC ADMINISTRATION				
1948	0.270	17.367	4.681	0.856	1428	34.7	1.82	2577
1949	0.288	17.619	5.078	0.856	1448	34.7	1.94	2613
1950	0.301	17.968	5.401	0.861	1468	34.7	2.04	2649
1951	0.318	22.518	7.161	0.872	1817	34.7	2.18	3279
1952	0.336	23.950	8.036	0.883	1910	34.7	2.33	3446
1953	0.348	22.737	7.905	0.895	1814	34.2	2.45	3226
1954	0.348	21.398	7.452	0.902	1693	34.2	2.47	3011
1955	0.374	21.625	8.080	0.908	1701	34.2	2.67	3025
1956	0.397	22.056	8.766	0.912	1727	34.2	2.85	3071
1957	0.415	22.198	9.206	0.919	1724	34.2	3.00	3066
1958	0.460	21.865	10.053	0.929	1703	33.7	3.36	2988
1959	0.465	22.190	10.314	0.931	1707	34.1	3.41	3027
1960	0.490	22.567	11.052	0.921	1755	34.1	3.55	3112
1961	0.508	23.226	11.807	0.947	1757	34.1	3.79	3116
1962	0.515	24.423	12.588	0.963	1818	34.1	3.91	3222
1963	0.542	24.750	13.408	0.966	1836	34.1	4.12	3254
1964	0.578	24.753	14.313	0.973	1823	34.1	4.43	3230
1965	0.600	25.114	15.076	0.977	1842	34.1	4.62	3265
1966	0.621	26.701	16.574	0.977	1964	34.0	4.78	3470
1967	0.625	28.737	17.975	0.987	2087	34.1	4.86	3699
1968	0.680	29.103	19.783	0.996	2098	34.0	5.33	3712
1969	0.732	28.897	21.139	0.994	2069	34.3	5.72	3693
1970	0.853	27.394	23.377	0.991	2029	33.3	6.66	3512
1971	0.915	27.724	25.366	1.008	1991	33.7	7.26	3493
1972	1.000	27.411	27.411	1.000	2005	33.4	7.87	3481
1973	1.075	27.006	29.025	1.006	1991	32.9	8.51	3409
1974	1.124	28.071	31.544	1.007	2039	33.4	8.91	3540
1975	1.234	28.357	34.992	1.010	2063	33.2	9.61	3566
1976	1.312	28.944	37.969	1.016	2074	33.5	10.49	3618
1977	1.413	29.042	41.036	1.016	2079	33.6	11.30	3630
1978	1.522	29.533	44.960	1.017	2105	33.7	12.19	3689
				FEDERAL GOVERNMENT ENTERPRISES				
1948	0.271	6.186	1.676	0.960	570	35.2	1.61	1042
1949	0.283	6.568	1.857	0.961	605	35.1	1.68	1105
1950	0.302	6.407	1.935	0.966	587	35.2	1.80	1073
1951	0.319	6.715	2.140	0.971	612	35.1	1.91	1118
1952	0.335	7.270	2.433	0.986	656	35.0	2.04	1193
1953	0.338	7.124	2.407	0.994	644	34.6	2.08	1159
1954	0.337	7.152	2.410	0.998	644	34.6	2.08	1159
1955	0.363	7.121	2.588	0.995	643	34.6	2.24	1157
1956	0.383	7.165	2.744	0.991	650	34.6	2.35	1170
1957	0.394	7.389	2.914	0.993	669	34.6	2.42	1204
1958	0.430	7.549	3.247	0.994	659	35.8	2.64	1228
1959	0.428	7.809	3.343	1.010	695	34.6	2.67	1251
1960	0.450	8.054	3.627	1.012	715	34.6	2.82	1287
1961	0.473	8.170	3.866	1.005	734	34.5	2.94	1315
1962	0.487	8.319	4.051	1.013	746	34.2	3.05	1328
1963	0.530	8.309	4.401	1.010	750	34.1	3.31	1331
1964	0.559	8.362	4.677	1.013	756	34.0	3.50	1335
1965	0.588	8.517	5.005	1.010	776	33.8	3.67	1364
1966	0.595	9.226	5.490	1.006	849	33.6	3.70	1484
1967	0.609	9.654	5.881	1.011	887	33.5	3.81	1544
1968	0.670	9.780	6.553	1.011	896	33.6	4.19	1565
1969	0.718	9.997	7.177	1.014	907	33.8	4.50	1595
1970	0.824	10.245	8.442	1.010	924	34.1	5.15	1640
1971	0.884	10.061	8.899	1.008	918	33.8	5.51	1615
1972	1.000	9.670	9.670	1.000	888	33.9	6.18	1564
1973	1.086	9.654	10.484	1.001	884	33.9	6.72	1560
1974	1.204	9.808	11.805	1.002	897	33.9	7.46	1583
1975	1.345	9.586	12.895	1.009	880	33.6	8.39	1537
1976	1.473	9.466	13.944	1.012	853	34.1	9.22	1513
1977	1.606	9.225	14.814	1.005	841	34.0	9.98	1485
1978	1.694	9.474	16.052	1.013	846	34.4	10.62	1512

	LABOR INPUT							
YEAR	PRICE	QUANTITY	OUTLAY	QUALITY	EMPLOYMENT	WEEKLY HOURS PER PERSON	HOURLY COMPENSATION	HOURS WORKED
				STATE AND LOCAL EDUCATIONAL SERVICES				
1948	0.259	13.883	3.599	0.909	1579	28.8	1.52	2367
1949	0.272	14.621	3.983	0.910	1660	28.8	1.60	2489
1950	0.279	15.392	4.292	0.930	1718	28.7	1.67	2564
1951	0.298	15.921	4.740	0.935	1768	28.7	1.80	2639
1952	0.326	17.115	5.574	0.960	1850	28.7	2.02	2763
1953	0.336	18.143	6.096	0.973	1944	28.6	2.11	2891
1954	0.354	19.211	6.797	0.984	2043	28.5	2.25	3025
1955	0.363	20.366	7.402	0.987	2180	28.2	2.32	3197
1956	0.388	21.467	8.320	0.989	2309	28.0	2.47	3363
1957	0.409	22.938	9.373	1.004	2426	28.1	2.65	3541
1958	0.430	24.355	10.470	1.014	2552	28.1	2.81	3724
1959	0.448	25.728	11.514	1.021	2687	27.9	2.95	3905
1960	0.469	27.703	12.979	1.036	2869	27.8	3.13	4143
1961	0.498	28.746	14.321	1.026	3006	27.8	3.30	4341
1962	0.527	29.945	15.784	1.033	3163	27.3	3.51	4493
1963	0.552	31.653	17.463	1.025	3375	27.3	3.65	4784
1964	0.573	33.788	19.345	1.026	3603	27.2	3.79	5102
1965	0.592	35.936	21.285	1.025	3890	26.9	3.92	5435
1966	0.635	38.189	24.255	1.018	4251	26.3	4.17	5816
1967	0.688	39.776	27.377	1.019	4537	25.6	4.52	6051
1968	0.745	41.772	31.126	1.017	4811	25.4	4.89	6366
1969	0.807	43.472	35.086	1.012	5069	25.3	5.27	6658
1970	0.882	45.206	39.856	1.009	5313	25.1	5.74	6944
1971	0.941	46.883	44.138	1.003	5563	25.0	6.09	7244
1972	1.000	48.570	48.570	1.000	5740	25.2	6.45	7528
1973	1.063	50.485	53.665	1.004	5923	25.3	6.89	7792
1974	1.124	51.998	58.426	1.007	6151	25.0	7.30	8006
1975	1.237	53.146	65.735	1.009	6355	24.7	8.05	8165
1976	1.341	53.945	72.352	1.014	6430	24.7	8.78	8242
1977	1.438	54.625	78.556	1.013	6562	24.5	9.40	8355
1978	1.512	56.311	85.124	1.021	6690	24.6	9.96	8547
				STATE AND LOCAL PUBLIC ADMINISTRATION				
1948	0.294	15.462	4.545	0.906	2153	32.4	1.25	3629
1949	0.298	16.828	5.022	0.905	2234	34.0	1.27	3954
1950	0.304	17.513	5.327	0.910	2311	34.0	1.30	4091
1951	0.321	17.959	5.764	0.922	2283	34.9	1.39	4139
1952	0.363	18.405	6.678	0.935	2305	34.9	1.59	4187
1953	0.377	19.211	7.238	0.943	2358	35.3	1.67	4331
1954	0.392	20.131	7.901	0.952	2469	35.0	1.76	4496
1955	0.407	20.746	8.435	0.957	2561	34.6	1.83	4611
1956	0.427	21.779	9.301	0.957	2701	34.4	1.92	4837
1957	0.446	22.813	10.185	0.965	2807	34.4	2.03	5024
1958	0.460	24.124	11.103	0.974	2945	34.4	2.11	5266
1959	0.476	24.386	11.619	0.974	2997	34.1	2.18	5321
1960	0.505	24.738	12.491	0.966	3073	34.1	2.29	5444
1961	0.513	26.539	13.613	0.986	3180	34.6	2.38	5724
1962	0.529	27.342	14.459	1.001	3229	34.6	2.49	5809
1963	0.552	27.882	15.394	0.999	3302	34.6	2.59	5935
1964	0.569	29.064	16.528	1.002	3426	34.6	2.68	6169
1965	0.597	30.156	18.009	1.001	3565	34.6	2.81	6408
1966	0.634	31.338	19.860	0.997	3765	34.1	2.97	6681
1967	0.684	32.379	22.153	1.002	3897	33.9	3.22	6873
1968	0.730	33.951	24.772	1.011	4054	33.9	3.47	7138
1969	0.794	34.643	27.515	1.004	4173	33.8	3.75	7339
1970	0.875	35.663	31.211	0.992	4349	33.8	4.08	7647
1971	0.935	37.557	35.117	1.007	4483	34.0	4.43	7929
1972	1.000	39.162	39.162	1.000	4714	34.0	4.70	8326
1973	1.079	40.802	44.032	1.006	4893	33.9	5.11	8623
1974	1.168	41.833	48.864	1.006	5020	33.9	5.53	8840
1975	1.259	43.613	54.889	1.008	5214	33.9	5.97	9196
1976	1.352	44.310	59.898	1.012	5263	34.0	6.44	9307
1977	1.443	45.376	65.486	1.012	5366	34.2	6.87	9531
1978	1.535	47.145	72.356	1.013	5610	33.9	7.31	9899
				STATE AND LOCAL GOVERNMENT ENTERPRISES				
1948	0.267	2.394	0.640	1.023	230	37.1	1.44	444
1949	0.283	2.495	0.707	1.020	239	37.3	1.52	464
1950	0.290	2.621	0.760	1.014	252	37.4	1.55	490
1951	0.309	2.784	0.859	1.027	260	38.0	1.67	514
1952	0.327	3.233	1.056	1.036	298	38.2	1.78	592
1953	0.340	3.308	1.138	1.033	303	38.5	1.87	607
1954	0.360	3.296	1.187	1.028	305	38.3	1.95	606
1955	0.382	3.337	1.274	1.019	311	38.4	2.05	621
1956	0.395	3.320	1.310	1.010	312	38.4	2.10	623
1957	0.410	3.338	1.368	1.008	315	38.3	2.18	628
1958	0.430	3.472	1.494	1.002	337	37.5	2.27	657
1959	0.453	3.863	1.750	1.016	354	39.2	2.43	721
1960	0.477	4.054	1.934	1.011	380	38.5	2.54	760
1961	0.496	3.959	1.962	1.001	389	37.1	2.62	750
1962	0.518	4.231	2.192	1.012	402	37.9	2.76	793
1963	0.539	4.312	2.325	1.008	429	36.4	2.87	811
1964	0.567	4.543	2.574	1.009	444	37.0	3.01	854
1965	0.601	4.618	2.777	1.009	458	36.4	3.20	868
1966	0.655	4.582	3.000	1.001	451	37.0	3.46	868
1967	0.697	4.631	3.227	1.012	454	36.8	3.72	868
1968	0.735	4.977	3.658	1.014	483	37.1	3.93	931
1969	0.791	5.179	4.094	1.018	502	37.0	4.24	965
1970	0.844	5.447	4.597	1.013	530	37.0	4.51	1020
1971	0.928	5.537	5.140	1.003	546	36.9	4.91	1047
1972	1.000	5.606	5.606	1.000	547	37.4	5.27	1063
1973	1.093	5.872	6.419	1.001	579	36.9	5.77	1112
1974	1.163	6.303	7.330	1.003	623	36.8	6.15	1192
1975	1.243	6.816	8.470	1.005	674	36.7	6.59	1286
1976	1.338	6.837	9.149	1.008	676	36.6	7.11	1286
1977	1.438	6.786	9.756	1.001	679	36.4	7.59	1286
1978	1.526	7.122	10.869	1.009	703	36.6	8.12	1338

Appendix C
Labor Cost Series, Manufacturing and Private Business, 1953–1980

Daniel S. Hamermesh

Table C.1 Manufacturing, 1953-80
(current dollars per hour)

Quarter	AHES	BLS Compensation	COSTWK	COSTTAX	ECNT	EC
1953I	1.651	2.036	2.223	1.151	2.808	1.433
II	1.671	2.058	2.249	1.166	2.852	1.456
III	1.701	2.079	2.274	1.180	2.757	1.412
IV	1.708	2.104	2.304	1.196	2.739	1.405
1954I	1.717	2.129	2.333	1.212	2.728	1.402
II	1.728	2.153	2.362	1.228	2.776	1.427
III	1.735	2.166	2.378	1.237	2.796	1.438
IV	1.741	2.200	2.418	1.259	2.819	1.452
1955I	1.753	2.211	2.433	1.268	2.832	1.460
II	1.774	2.223	2.449	1.277	2.860	1.475
III	1.808	2.259	2.491	1.300	2.898	1.496
IV	1.824	2.289	2.526	1.320	2.957	1.527
1956I	1.840	2.317	2.560	1.339	3.009	1.555
II	1.874	2.362	2.612	1.367	3.037	1.571
III	1.896	2.417	2.675	1.402	3.102	1.607
IV	1.934	2.462	2.727	1.431	3.156	1.637
1957I	1.956	2.491	2.763	1.451	3.181	1.652
II	1.974	2.515	2.791	1.467	3.171	1.650
III	1.996	2.547	2.830	1.489	3.216	1.675
IV	2.014	2.574	2.862	1.507	3.270	1.703
1958I	2.025	2.591	2.883	1.519	3.343	1.740
II	2.037	2.626	2.924	1.541	3.457	1.797
III	2.056	2.667	2.972	1.567	3.525	1.833
IV	2.074	2.699	3.010	1.589	3.510	1.829
1959I	2.102	2.712	3.027	1.599	3.518	1.834
II	2.127	2.739	3.060	1.617	3.512	1.834
III	2.117	2.756	3.081	1.629	3.554	1.856
IV	2.134	2.777	3.106	1.643	3.618	1.889
1960I	2.179	2.835	3.173	1.680	3.646	1.907
II	2.187	2.857	3.199	1.695	3.657	1.915
III	2.193	2.862	3.206	1.700	3.684	1.930
IV	2.214	2.899	3.248	1.724	3.745	1.962
1961I	2.222	2.920	3.274	1.739	3.792	1.988
II	2.244	2.938	3.296	1.752	3.831	2.009
III	2.250	2.956	3.318	1.765	3.842	2.016
IV	2.275	2.983	3.349	1.782	3.860	2.027

Quarter	AHES	BLS Compensation	COSTWK	COSTTAX	ECNT	EC
1962I	2.291	3.033	3.407	1.813	3.892	2.046
II	2.300	3.051	3.429	1.825	3.930	2.066
III	2.307	3.072	3.453	1.838	3.941	2.073
IV	2.329	3.105	3.491	1.859	3.938	2.074
1963I	2.344	3.127	3.518	1.874	3.996	2.104
II	2.367	3.141	3.535	1.883	3.997	2.105
III	2.374	3.169	3.567	1.901	4.012	2.115
IV	2.399	3.215	3.619	1.928	4.069	2.144
1964I	2.411	3.255	3.663	2.017	4.095	2.233
II	2.427	3.289	3.700	2.036	4.116	2.245
III	2.444	3.328	3.744	2.060	4.160	2.268
IV	2.449	3.337	3.754	2.064	4.202	2.289
1965I	2.471	3.352	3.770	2.141	4.251	2.391
II	2.496	3.368	3.788	2.150	4.281	2.407
III	2.508	3.389	3.811	2.162	4.321	2.428
IV	2.525	3.413	3.841	2.180	4.387	2.465
1966I	2.543	3.466	3.903	2.217	4.534	2.545
II	2.576	3.510	3.956	2.247	4.635	2.601
III	2.599	3.560	4.015	2.282	4.701	2.639
IV	2.635	3.603	4.066	2.312	4.775	2.681
1967I	2.667	3.644	4.116	2.341	4.773	2.683
II	2.696	3.685	4.165	2.370	4.796	2.698
III	2.725	3.740	4.230	2.408	4.804	2.707
IV	2.759	3.784	4.282	2.439	4.915	2.769
1968I	2.819	3.880	4.394	2.505	5.048	2.845
II	2.863	3.947	4.473	2.551	5.107	2.881
III	2.890	3.998	4.533	2.587	5.238	2.954
IV	2.945	4.074	4.622	2.640	5.330	3.008
1969I	2.979	4.129	4.688	2.679	5.462	3.082
II	3.023	4.189	4.759	2.722	5.546	3.131
III	3.081	4.269	4.853	2.777	5.660	3.197
IV	3.125	4.333	4.934	2.827	5.746	3.249
1970I	3.158	4.401	5.019	2.879	5.803	3.287
II	3.212	4.483	5.121	2.941	5.908	3.351
III	3.272	4.574	5.234	3.010	6.012	3.415
IV	3.292	4.620	5.295	3.049	6.077	3.456
1971I	3.377	4.728	5.428	3.130	6.171	3.516
II	3.425	4.784	5.502	3.176	6.265	3.573
III	3.469	4.840	5.576	3.223	6.402	3.653
IV	3.505	4.878	5.618	3.247	6.479	3.695
1972I	3.583	4.983	5.738	3.316	6.658	3.795
II	3.632	5.036	5.797	3.349	6.762	3.852
III	3.684	5.093	5.861	3.386	6.833	3.892
IV	3.750	5.170	5.948	3.436	7.002	3.984

Quarter	AHES	BLS Compensation	COSTWK	COSTTAX	ECNT	EC
1973I	3.806	5.299	6.094	3.520	7.347	4.172
II	3.861	5.385	6.190	3.575	7.403	4.206
III	3.938	5.479	6.296	3.636	7.446	4.234
IV	4.010	5.582	6.434	3.723	7.665	4.363
1974I	4.062	5.696	6.583	3.816	7.836	4.468
II	4.174	5.895	6.833	3.969	8.069	4.612
III	4.320	6.055	7.040	4.096	8.235	4.718
IV	4.463	6.292	7.336	4.277	8.470	4.866
1975I	4.556	6.497	7.596	4.436	8.737	5.030
II	4.623	6.644	7.790	4.558	9.102	5.240
III	4.711	6.752	7.940	4.654	9.314	5.369
IV	4.793	6.858	8.057	4.718	9.454	5.445
1976I	4.869	7.012	8.229	4.814	9.577	5.516
II	4.953	7.185	8.421	4.921	9.800	5.638
III	5.080	7.315	8.565	5.000	10.027	5.761
IV	5.176	7.479	8.747	5.102	10.193	5.853
1977I	5.267	7.664	8.954	5.217	10.497	6.019
II	5.372	7.788	9.089	5.289	10.545	6.047
III	5.505	7.947	9.265	5.386	10.688	6.127
IV	5.614	8.077	9.420	5.476	10.901	6.246
1978I	5.715	8.286	9.665	5.617	11.137	6.382
II	5.812	8.414	9.818	5.705	11.347	6.500
III	5.964	8.589	10.023	5.823	11.474	6.577
IV	6.111	8.781	10.252	5.954	11.917	6.821
1979I	6.260	9.001	10.523			
II	6.370	9.216	10.782			
III	6.470	9.394	10.999			
IV	6.617	9.590	11.237			
1980I	6.760	9.817	11.438			
II	6.920	10.177	11.870			
III	7.097	10.482	12.242			
IV	7.317	10.749	12.571			

Table C.2 Private Business, 1953-80
(current dollars per hour)

Quarter	AHES	BLS Compensation	COSTWK	COSTTAX	ECNT	EC
1953 I	1.786	1.849	2.050	1.070	2.632	1.350
II	1.809	1.870	2.074	1.083	2.676	1.372
III	1.836	1.896	2.103	1.099	2.578	1.327
IV	1.837	1.901	2.110	1.103	2.533	1.306
1954 I	1.847	1.918	2.129	1.113	2.517	1.299
II	1.868	1.937	2.151	1.125	2.564	1.323
III	1.878	1.948	2.164	1.132	2.588	1.336
IV	1.900	1.967	2.187	1.144	2.595	1.341
1955 I	1.900	1.973	2.194	1.149	2.596	1.342
II	1.923	1.998	2.223	1.164	2.642	1.366
III	1.936	2.009	2.236	1.172	2.642	1.367
IV	1.959	2.031	2.263	1.187	2.698	1.396
1956 I	1.998	2.079	2.318	1.217	2.774	1.536
II	2.034	2.117	2.363	1.241	2.790	1.447
III	2.058	2.142	2.393	1.258	2.823	1.465
IV	2.092	2.175	2.432	1.280	2.864	1.488
1957 I	2.127	2.219	2.484	1.308	2.909	1.513
II	2.148	2.241	2.511	1.324	2.896	1.509
III	2.168	2.262	2.537	1.338	2.927	1.526
IV	2.194	2.292	2.571	1.357	2.984	1.556
1958 I	2.213	2.310	2.593	1.370	3.061	1.595
II	2.233	2.324	2.610	1.379	3.158	1.642
III	2.260	2.357	2.648	1.400	3.228	1.678
IV	2.276	2.374	2.668	1.411	3.184	1.659
1959 I	2.295	2.407	2.706	1.432	3.216	1.677
II	2.306	2.420	2.722	1.441	3.188	1.665
III	2.329	2.443	2.749	1.456	3.244	1.695
IV	2.358	2.470	2.781	1.475	3.321	1.734
1960 I	2.397	2.520	2.840	1.506	3.337	1.745
II	2.408	2.528	2.851	1.513	3.327	1.742
III	2.407	2.530	2.855	1.517	3.346	1.753
IV	2.435	2.557	2.888	1.535	3.401	1.782
1961 I	2.460	2.586	2.922	1.555	3.469	1.817
II	2.490	2.620	2.963	1.578	3.535	1.852
III	2.503	2.635	2.982	1.589	3.541	1.858
IV	2.535	2.665	3.017	1.608	3.564	1.871

Quarter	AHES	BLS Compensation	COSTWK	COSTTAX	ECNT	EC
1962I	2.562	2.705	3.063	1.634	3.586	1.885
II	2.580	2.725	3.087	1.647	3.628	1.907
III	2.594	2.739	3.104	1.657	3.635	1.912
IV	2.625	2.774	3.145	1.679	3.630	
1963I	2.639	2.795	3.171	1.693	3.691	1.943
II	2.650	2.806	3.184	1.701	3.683	1.941
III	2.680	2.837	3.221	1.721	3.706	1.954
IV	2.707	2.870	3.258	1.741	3.749	1.977
1964I	2.761	2.922	3.316	1.831	3.795	2.070
II	2.782	2.944	3.341	1.843	3.801	2.074
III	2.817	2.985	3.386	1.868	3.848	2.099
IV	2.834	3.006	3.410	1.880	3.908	2.130
1965I	2.855	3.029	3.435	1.955	3.968	2.232
II	2.879	3.052	3.460	1.969	4.004	2.252
III	2.914	3.088	3.500	1.991	4.061	2.283
IV	2.949	3.124	3.545	2.017	4.151	2.333
1966I	2.983	3.187	3.618	2.060	4.329	2.430
II	3.037	3.245	3.687	2.100	4.458	2.501
III	3.089	3.293	3.744	2.133	4.531	2.543
IV	3.134	3.341	3.802	2.168	4.620	2.593
1967I	3.171	3.375	3.844	2.192	4.592	2.581
II	3.217	3.420	3.899	2.224	4.621	2.600
III	3.256	3.460	3.947	2.253	4.606	2.596
IV	3.289	3.499	3.994	2.281	4.721	2.660
1968I	3.379	3.601	4.113	2.351	4.870	2.745
II	3.433	3.659	4.183	2.392	4.916	2.773
III	3.485	3.722	4.258	2.436	5.076	2.863
IV	3.549	3.791	4.340	2.485	5.163	2.913
1969I	3.571	3.822	4.378	2.508	5.275	2.975
II	3.647	3.900	4.471	2.563	5.388	3.041
III	3.706	3.965	4.549	2.609	5.488	3.098
IV	3.772	4.035	4.637	2.664	5.587	3.158
1970I	3.820	4.097	4.718	2.715	5.639	3.194
II	3.873	4.162	4.801	2.768	5.719	3.244
III	3.949	4.248	4.909	2.833	5.820	3.306
IV	3.988	4.293	4.970	2.872	5.892	3.351
1971I	4.068	4.386	5.088	2.945	5.961	3.399
II	4.134	4.457	5.180	3.002	6.078	3.469
III	4.194	4.534	5.279	3.064	6.257	3.573
IV	4.224	4.561	5.311	3.083	6.334	3.615

Quarter	AHES	BLS Compensation	COSTWK	COSTTAX	ECNT	EC
1972I	4.305	4.678	5.449	3.164	6.535	3.728
II	4.352	4.736	5.518	3.204	6.658	3.797
III	4.398	4.795	4.881	3.244	6.730	3.839
IV	4.456	4.867	5.672	3.294	6.908	3.937
1973I	4.555	5.023	5.856	3.401	7.333	4.169
II	4.626	5.098	5.944	3.453	7.375	4.197
III	4.705	5.189	6.052	3.515	7.405	4.219
IV	4.772	5.272	6.157	3.580	7.604	4.333
1974I	4.844	5.364	6.276	3.653	7.758	4.424
II	4.986	5.521	6.469	3.769	7.919	4.524
III	5.123	5.680	6.665	3.887	8.069	4.618
IV	5.255	5.834	6.855	4.003	8.180	4.692
1975I	5.396	5.991	7.052	4.122	8.392	4.819
II	5.486	6.112	7.205	4.216	8.753	5.021
III	5.568	6.206	7.327	4.291	8.955	5.138
IV	5.675	6.333	7.473	4.375	9.133	5.238
1976I	5.775	6.473	7.635	4.469	9.242	5.304
II	5.893	6.612	7.794	4.559	9.432	5.411
III	6.005	6.742	7.943	4.645	9.679	5.548
IV	6.129	6.886	8.109	4.740	9.822	5.631
1977I	6.233	7.029	8.274	4.835	10.097	5.783
II	6.334	7.144	8.405	4.909	10.119	5.800
III	6.453	7.276	8.556	4.995	10.230	5.865
IV	6.565	7.390	8.695	5.076	10.439	5.984
1978I	6.734	7.591	8.934	5.216	10.658	6.112
II	6.863	7.724	9.096	5.311	10.878	6.237
III	7.013	7.894	9.299	5.429	11.008	6.318
IV	7.166	8.056	9.495	5.544	11.449	6.560
1979I	7.250	8.266	9.700			
II	7.429	8.455	9.904			
III	7.587	8.614	10.119			
IV	7.744	8.777	10.315			
1980I	7.935	9.022	10.609			
II	8.151	9.266	10.901			
III	8.331	9.474	11.152			
IV	8.529	9.696	11.419			

Contributors

Joseph R. Antos
Office of Economic Policy Analysis
Room S-2220
U.S. Department of Labor
200 Constitution Avenue, NW
Washington, D.C. 20210

B. K. Atrostic
Office of Research and Evaluation
Room 2021
U.S. Bureau of Labor Statistics
441 G Street, NW
Washington, D.C. 20212

Ernst R. Berndt
Massachusetts Institute of Technology
50 Memorial Drive
E52-252B
Cambridge, Massachusetts 02139

Charles Brown
Department of Economics
University of Maryland
College Park, Maryland 20742

James N. Brown
Economics Department
Princeton University
Princeton, New Jersey 08544

Richard V. Burkhauser
Department of Economics and Business Administration
Vanderbilt University
Nashville, Tennessee 37235

Martin David
Department of Economics
University of Wisconsin
1180 Observatory Drive
Madison, Wisconsin 53706

Ronald G. Ehrenberg
New York State School of Industrial and Labor Relations
Cornell University
Ithaca, New York 14853

Frank M. Gollop
Department of Economics
Boston College
Chestnut Hill, Massachusetts 02167

Daniel S. Hamermesh
Department of Economics
Michigan State University
East Lansing, Michigan 48824

George E. Johnson
Department of Economics
The University of Michigan
Ann Arbor, Michigan 48109

Dale W. Jorgenson
Department of Economics
Harvard University
1737 Cambridge Street
Cambridge, Massachusetts 02138

F. Thomas Juster
Institute for Social Research
The University of Michigan
P. O. Box 1248
Ann Arbor, Michigan 48106

Edward P. Lazear
Department of Economics
University of Chicago
Chicago, Illinois 60637

Arleen Leibowitz
The Rand Corporation
1700 Main Street
Santa Monica, California 90406

J. Stuart McMenamin
Criterion Incorporated
1110 Roselle Street
Suite A
San Diego, California 92121

Richard F. Muth
Department of Economics
Stanford University
Standford, California 94305

Donald A. Nichols
Department of Economics
University of Wisconsin
Madison, Wisconsin 53706

Walter Y. Oi
Department of Economics
University of Rochester
Rochester, New York 14623

Joseph F. Quinn
Department of Economics
Boston College
Chestnut Hill, Massachusetts 02167

Cordelia Reimers
Department of Economics
Hunter College
695 Park Avenue
New York, New York 10021

Donald B. Rubin
Department of Statistics
University of Chicago
5734 University Avenue
Chicago, Illinois 60637

R. Robert Russell
C. V. Starr Center
for Applied Economics
New York University
269 Mercer Street
New York, New York 10012

Timothy M. Smeeding
Department of Economics
University of Utah
Bu0-314
Salt Lake City, Utah 84112

Robert S. Smith
New York State School of
Industrial and Labor Relations
Cornell University
Ithaca, New York 14853

Jack E. Triplett
Office of Research and Evaluation
Room 2021
U.S. Bureau of Labor Statistics
441 G Street, NW
Washington, D.C. 20212

Author Index

Subject Index